GLOBAL INTELLIGENCE OVERSIGHT

Global Intelligence Oversight

GOVERNING SECURITY IN THE
TWENTY-FIRST CENTURY

Edited by Zachary K. Goldman
and Samuel J. Rascoff

<OXFORD
UNIVERSITY PRESS>

OXFORD
UNIVERSITY PRESS

Oxford University Press is a department of the University of Oxford. It furthers the University's objective of excellence in research, scholarship, and education by publishing worldwide. Oxford is a registered trademark of Oxford University Press in the UK and certain other countries.

Published in the United States of America by Oxford University Press
198 Madison Avenue, New York, NY 10016, United States of America.

Library of Congress Cataloging in Publication Data
Names: Goldman, Zachary K., editor. | Rascoff, Samuel James, editor.
Title: Global intelligence oversight : governing security in the twenty-first
    century / Edited by Zachary K. Goldman and Samuel J. Rascoff.
Description: New York : Oxford University Press, 2016. | Includes
    bibliographical references and index.
Identifiers: LCCN 2015051038 | ISBN 9780190458072 ((hardback) : alk. paper)
Subjects: LCSH: Intelligence service—Law and legislation. | National
    security—Law and legislation. | Internal security. | Legislative
    oversight.
Classification: LCC K3278 .G56 2016 | DDC 343/.01—dc23 LC record available at
http://lccn.loc.gov/2015051038

9 8 7 6 5 4 3 2
Printed by Edwards Brothers Malloy, United States of America

Note to Readers

This publication is designed to provide accurate and authoritative information in regard to the subject matter covered. It is based upon sources believed to be accurate and reliable and is intended to be current as of the time it was written. It is sold with the understanding that the publisher is not engaged in rendering legal, accounting, or other professional services. If legal advice or other expert assistance is required, the services of a competent professional person should be sought. Also, to confirm that the information has not been affected or changed by recent developments, traditional legal research techniques should be used, including checking primary sources where appropriate.

(Based on the Declaration of Principles jointly adopted by a Committee of the American Bar Association and a Committee of Publishers and Associations.)

For Stephanie
–ZKG

In memory of Julius L. Lassner, Captain, USMC-R-Retired: Patriot, Sage, Friend
–SJR

Contents

Contributors

Raphael Bitton, *Head of Legal Studies, Interdisciplinary Department, University of Haifa; Adjunct Lecturer, Sapir College School of Law*

Iain Cameron, *Faculty of Law, Uppsala University*

Ashley Deeks, *Associate Professor of Law; Senior Fellow, Center for National Security Law, University of Virginia School of Law*

Zachary K. Goldman, *Executive Director, Center on Law and Security; Adjunct Professor of Law, NYU School of Law*

Keiran Hardy, *Lecturer, School of Criminology and Criminal Justice, Griffith University*

The Honorable Jane Harman, *Director, President and CEO, Woodrow Wilson International Center for Scholars*

Christopher A. Kojm, *J.B. and Maurice C. Shapiro Professor of International Affairs, George Washington University*

Russell A. Miller, *Professor of Law, Washington and Lee University School of Law*

Dr. Jon Moran, *Reader in Security, University of Leicester*

Richard Morgan, *Senior Fellow (2014–2015), Center on Law and Security, NYU School of Law*

Daphna Renan, *Assistant Professor of Law, Harvard Law School*

Kent Roach, *Prichard-Wilson Chair in Law and Public Policy and Professor of Law, University of Toronto*

Samuel J. Rascoff, *Professor of Law; Faculty Director, Center on Law and Security, NYU School of Law*

Clive Walker, *Professor Emeritus, University of Leeds*

George Williams, *Anthony Mason Professor, Scientia Professor and Foundation Director, Gilbert + Tobin Centre of Public Law, Faculty of Law, University of New South Wales; Australian Research Council Laureate Fellow*

Acknowledgments

WE WOULD LIKE to extend our gratitude to the many people whose assistance and participation in this project enriched it in myriad ways. First and foremost we acknowledge Dean Trevor Morrison of NYU School of Law, who has championed the work of our Center, as have members of our Board of Advisors. Sarvenaz Bakhtiar, the Center's Director of Operations, and Richard Morgan, a Senior Fellow at the Center during the 2014–2015 academic year, contributed extensively to the volume. Blake Ratcliff of Oxford University Press also has been a steadfast source of guidance throughout the writing and editing process.

This project benefitted tremendously from a partnership with the Woodrow Wilson International Center for Scholars in Washington DC. Jane Harman, who has taken a significant national leadership role on questions of intelligence oversight, both in and out of government, lent her wisdom and experience to the volume. Meg King, Annie Manriquez, and Grayson Clary of the Wilson Center were close collaborators on the project, and the Wilson Center was a warm and hospitable host for a workshop in March 2015 where many early drafts of the volume's chapters were presented. Finally, the contributors themselves pushed our thinking about the past and future of intelligence oversight in ways beyond what is reflected in the volume, and for which we are very grateful.

Over the last several years, a number of NYU School of Law students have also made substantial contributions to the project. We are grateful for the work of Alexander Galanos, Megan Graham, Andrew Grubin, Meg Henry, Tim McKenzie, Emily Nix, James Ng, Eliana Pfeffer, Max Rodriguez, Clay Venetis, Amy Zajac, and Abby Zeith. Researchers at the Center on Law and Security, including Arrion Azimi, Desiree Baerlocher, Emily Cooper, Alba Sophia Hancock, Annika Heumann, David Hoffman, Holly Huxtable, Lydia Karagianni,

Zach Schwarzbaum, and Julia Solomon-Strauss also provided invaluable assistance at various stages of the project.

The idea for the volume was shaped by conversations with friends and colleagues in government, the academy, and global technology companies. It emerged from a realization that intelligence services will be at the forefront of the struggle against transnational threats such as cybercrime and terrorism, and that mechanisms of oversight accordingly deserve our utmost attention. Now, more than ever, these conversations are taking place in a transnational context.

We hope that this volume will help to shape the legal, policy, and public debates about intelligence oversight at an inflection point in the consideration about the role of intelligence in democratic governance, and that it will serve as a resource as the process of intelligence reform evolves around the world.

Preface

WHY INTELLIGENCE OVERSIGHT MATTERS

Jane Harman

DIRECTOR OF NATIONAL Intelligence James Clapper once said that "only one entity in the entire universe" is fully briefed on every American intelligence program: "That's God."[1]

But on our intelligence committees, 38 flesh and blood members of Congress work to oversee 17 spy agencies, a workforce of thousands, and a black budget that runs to tens of billions of dollars. I was one of them, Ranking Democrat on the House Permanent Select Committee on Intelligence from 2002 to 2006. With my Committee colleagues, I saw our Intelligence Community do big things right and big things wrong after the attacks of September 11, 2001. I saw heroism and I saw overreach. I pushed—we all pushed, in both parties—to represent the American people in our nation's most secret debates. It's one of the hardest jobs in politics or policy. Few notice, and virtually no one outside the community can learn, when you get it right. When it goes wrong, you cannot explain the context to those not cleared and "read in."

In or outside Washington, few people have nice things to say about Congress; Senator John McCain likes to joke that its approval ratings are down to paid staff and blood relatives.[2] Much of the criticism is fair. On too many occasions, toxic partisanship has undermined sound policymaking. Yet Congress remains the world's most important legislative body on intelligence questions, as well as an important check on the world's most successful Intelligence Community. We still mark key moments in the history of oversight with the names of committed members: the Pike Committee, the Church Committee, and in our era

---

[1] Doyle McManus, *Bloated Intelligence Apparatus Is Not Too Smart*, L.A. TIMES, July 22, 2010.

[2] Philip Bump, *The 113th Congress Reaches New Lows. In Everything.* WASH. POST. Dec. 15, 2014, *available at* http://www.washingtonpost.com/blogs/the-fix/wp/2014/12/15/the-113th-congress-reaches-new-lows-in-everything/.

the Feinstein Report.[3] Time after time, senators and representatives have proven uniquely qualified to ensure that our collection programs are legal, principled, and consistent with the highest expectations of the American public.

I've had a front-row seat at many of those efforts. I was a senior Senate staffer during the Watergate crisis, which eventually gave rise to the modern intelligence committees.[4] I was working in the Carter White House when the Foreign Intelligence Surveillance Act (FISA) passed Congress by large bipartisan margins. In the wake of the Iraq and 9/11 intelligence failures, I co-authored the Intelligence Reform and Terrorism Prevention Act (IRTPA), the largest reorganization of our intelligence community since 1947. To borrow a phrase from Dean Acheson, I've been "present at the creation" of most of our oversight infrastructure.[5] Some of the talented contributors in this volume will disagree with me about the role and impact of lawmakers. But in my experience, though it's rarely glamorous, congressional oversight works—and works better than most believe.

The House and Senate bring to the game key advantages that the executive and the judiciary branches don't have: full political independence, the power of the purse, and the attention of the American people. That's not to say there isn't good oversight work being done in the other branches. We need talented and committed individuals serving in a range of roles: as CIA inspectors general, as judges on the Foreign Intelligence Surveillance Court (FISC), or as members of the Privacy and Civil Liberties Oversight Board. All of these represent important bulwarks against the concentration of power by intelligence agencies.

But one key lesson of the Snowden disclosures was that Americans don't trust the executive branch to police itself; they insist on a second opinion. In other corners of our politics, we often appeal to judges and courts for that definitive answer. But citizens also find the judicial review process under FISA opaque and unsatisfying. Even when executive branch and judicial institutions function well—which I believe they often do—they face major obstacles to winning the public trust. Legally, most can't speak up for themselves. Most don't have the right platform to explain their work to the American people. Their silence leaves the public wondering: "Who's watching the watchmen?"

The world wants to know too. Given today's threats and today's data flows, intelligence is more and more an international effort—and the new oversight crosses borders. Multinational firms, especially the ones based in Silicon Valley, have become a key intelligence constituency. They answer to global user communities with their own opinions about espionage, privacy, and security. They depend on markets in Germany and Brazil, whose governments

---

[3] The Pike Committee was named for the chairman of the House Select Committee on Intelligence, Representative Otis Pike of New York. For the Pike Committee's final report, which was rejected by the Ninety-fourth Congress, see *CIA Report the President Doesn't Want You to Read*, The Village Voice, Feb. 11, 1976. For the final report of the Select Committee to Study Governmental Operations with Respect to Intelligence Activities, otherwise known as the Church Committee after its chairman Senator Frank Church of Idaho, see S. Rep. No. 94-755 (1976). For the Feinstein Report, *see*, Senate Select Committee on Intelligence, Committee Study of the Central Intelligence Agency's Detention and Interrogation Program, S. Rep. No. 113-288 (2014).

[4] The Senate Select Committee on Intelligence was created in 1976. S. Res. 400, 94th Cong. (1976). The House Permanent Select Committee on Intelligence was created in 1977. H.R. Res. 658, 95th Cong. (1977).

[5] Dean Acheson, Present at the Creation: My Years in the State Department (1969).

want visible and significant surveillance reform. And when they're disappointed by official oversight, they throw up their own barriers, such as encryption and litigation. Making the case that oversight works has always been key to the legitimacy of our collection, but the stakes of that argument are higher than ever.

Who can make the pitch that oversight works, and how can they make it effectively? For an inspiring example, I would point you to the Senate Intelligence Committee's report on CIA interrogation techniques.[6] Though some strongly dispute its methodology and conclusions, the report was a powerful, detailed reckoning with the compromises some individuals made in the pursuit of security after September 11. Fighting to declassify it, as Senator Dianne Feinstein did, was an act of incredible political courage. Senator John McCain said it best on the floor of the Senate: "The truth is sometimes a hard pill to swallow. It sometimes causes us difficulties at home and abroad. It is sometimes used by our enemies in attempts to hurt us. But the American people are entitled to it, nonetheless."[7] And he was right about the questions that oversight should ask of *all* our collection programs: "What were the policies? What was their purpose? Did they achieve it? Did they make us safer? . . . What did they gain us? What did they cost us?"[8]

We approach these questions in the context of a new security environment. Today, nonstate actors and unconventional warfare dominate the threat landscape: groups such as the Islamic State of Iraq and the Levant, al-Qaeda in the Arabian Peninsula, and Boko Haram. We battle hackers for hire, some bankrolled by rogue states such as Iran and North Korea. In cyberspace and on social media, we confront plots leveraging new tools: malware and zero days, Twitter and WhatsApp. We've been slow to adapt. The enemies we face today are not the enemies we knew in 2004 when we last reorganized the intelligence community. As I have argued elsewhere, twenty-first century oversight needs to ask new, disruptive questions.[9]

This book is part of an international conversation on the strengths and flaws of intelligence programs around the world. It's always been my firm conviction that liberty and security are *not* a zero-sum game. With good oversight, we get more of both; with poor oversight, we get neither. But making oversight work depends on developing strong public buy-in. Too much of the debate is shaped by unrealistic caricatures: of the CIA, of NSA, and of Congress. Dialogue is routinely undermined by misinformation and the requirements of secrecy. We urgently need more forums for informed debate.

Building this better conversation is thankless work. I had hoped the debate on the FISA Amendments Act of 2008 would build public understanding of what our privacy laws protect, and what our intelligence statutes authorize. Though I deeply regret that the Snowden leaks compromised key collection programs, the silver lining was a more robust discussion of the NSA. The debate around reauthorizing amendments to the USA PATRIOT Act in 2015 was yet another opportunity to engage with the American people.[10] But we haven't reached

---

[6] *Supra,* note 3.

[7] 113 Cong. Rec. 6411 (2014) (statement of Senator McCain).

[8] *Id.*

[9] Jane Harman, *Disrupting the Intelligence Community*, FOREIGN AFFAIRS, Mar./Apr. 2015.

[10] Some provisions of the USA FREEDOM Act of 2015 require declassification review of certain decisions, orders, or opinions of the Foreign Intelligence Surveillance Court, which will hopefully aid a greater public understanding of intelligence issues in the future.

consensus. Too often, I found myself agreeing with Mark Twain: misinformation gets half-way around the world before the truth can get its pants on.

Congress can do better. If there's one thing I wish were more widely understood, it's that members ask spies the tough questions every chance we get. We push back in briefings and we push back in hearings; in 2003, I wrote a classified letter to the CIA's general counsel warning that the interrogation program raised profound policy questions. We don't ask because we mistrust the people, committed public servants doing what they can to secure the country. We do it because no one else can give the public their say in classified conversations—can ask their questions and get the answers they deserve.

There's no such thing as perfect oversight, just as there's no such thing as perfect security. I know many are frustrated with the process, which seems to take two steps forward and one step back. Why didn't oversight prevent errors and overreach in the first place—during the Cold War, during the war with al-Qaeda, and during the Iraq War? Why are we constantly hearing about new mistakes, new and frightening surveillance programs, new and secret legal authorities we were never told about? Why haven't we already struck the perfect balance between privacy and security? Because there isn't one.

The only thing we know about our response to future threats is that there will be failures. It's the bad luck of the Intelligence Community that no one notices all the plots that never strike the homeland; overseers are in the same boat, earning no praise for the mistakes that were never made. General Stanley McChrystal jokes, "as an operator, you always learn that a successful mission is an operational stroke of genius. Anything that fails is an intelligence failure."[11] But if our Intelligence Community were to stand down, or if the oversight community were to step aside, we all know the results would be disastrous.

There's no single answer to the challenge; instead, this book offers a range of perspectives. You'll hear voices from Sweden, Australia, Israel, Canada, the U.K., and the United States. You'll read about the history of intelligence oversight, about strategic surprise, and about the impacts of new technologies. Of course, you'll find studies of a range of key actors in oversight: courts, legislators, inspectors general, outside commissions, international organizations, and multinational corporations.

The scholarship on display is impressive. I saw all of these scholars in action for a stellar workshop at the Wilson Center in March 2015; those conversations, and the proposals that came out of them, enrich this dialogue in actionable ways. No one gets the final word on intelligence—but the contributions in this book make for a much better public debate.

---

[11] General Stanley A. McChrystal, U.S. Army (Ret), The Evolution of Joint Special Operations Command and the Pursuit of Al Qaeda in Iraq, A Conversation with General Stanley A. McChrystal 12 (Jan. 28, 2013) (transcript *available at* http://www.brookings.edu/~/media/events/2013/1/28%20mcchrystal%20zarqawi/mcchrystal%20transcript.pdf).

Introduction

THE NEW INTELLIGENCE OVERSIGHT

Zachary K. Goldman and Samuel J. Rascoff

I. OVERVIEW

The oversight of intelligence agencies is undergoing a major transformation. Prior to the 1970s, when scandals in the United States led to the creation of oversight structures designed to guard against abuse, security services were largely unregulated, inhabiting a sphere of nearly plenary executive authority.[1] Institutions such as congressional intelligence committees, the Foreign Intelligence Surveillance Court (FISC), and inspectors general in various intelligence agencies are all products of this first wave of growth of intelligence oversight.

During that same period, intelligence services across the liberal democratic world followed this trajectory, moving from an opaque sphere of executive power to the realm of activities subject to some modicum of oversight. The U.K., for example, adopted a statutory framework governing the domestic security service, MI5, in 1989, and the foreign intelligence service, MI6, in 1994.[2] And the Shin Bet, Israel's domestic security service, received a

---

[1] A story is told that in 1973 CIA director James Schlesinger sought to brief Senator John Stennis, the chairman of the Senate Armed Services subcommittee dealing with intelligence, about certain Agency programs. On receiving the offer Senator Stennis reportedly replied, "No, no, my boy, don't tell me. Just go ahead and do it—but I don't want to know!" Loch K. Johnson, *The CIA and the Question of Accountability*, 12 INTELLIGENCE & NAT'L SEC. 178, 180 (1997). Now, by contrast, a former IC general counsel describes the National Security Agency (NSA) as "one of the most highly regulated entities in the world . . . subject to a spectrum of detailed scrutiny from across all three branches of government as a matter of law, policy, and practice." Rajesh De, *The NSA and Accountability in an Era of Big Data*, 7 J. NAT'L SEC. L. & POL'Y 301, 308 (2014).

[2] Clive Walker and Jon Moran's chapter contains an extensive discussion of the origins and oversight of the intelligence services in the U.K.

statutory foundation in 2000.[3] These statutes were significant because they paved the way for broader and more effective oversight systems.[4]

The story of these first-generation oversight institutions and their successes and failures at securing the goal of legally constrained intelligence practices has been extensively told.[5] This book carries the account forward. It focuses on an emerging set of institutions and processes involved in intelligence governance and a new set of questions about the purposes of intelligence oversight.[6] Institutionally speaking, two trends are especially noteworthy. The first concerns the role that transnational actors have begun to play in constraining intelligence services. Whether it is peer intelligence services exerting pressure on one another across national boundaries or global technology firms serving as vectors for constraining the practice of intelligence, intelligence oversight has taken a decidedly cosmopolitan turn. The second involves the outsized role that government actors relatively new to the intelligence oversight game have begun to play in this area. Some of these institutions are located within the executive branch or are quasi-independent agencies tasked with monitoring aspects of intelligence.[7] But perhaps no set of official institutions has evolved its approach to shaping the practice of intelligence as much as courts of general jurisdiction, both domestic and transnational.

The contributions to this volume focusing on courts (and other non-legislative oversight mechanisms) build on and complement a robust literature analyzing the role of the

---

[3] Raphael Bitton's contribution contains an extensive discussion of the origins and oversight of the intelligence services in Israel. Although the Mossad does not have an organic statute, there are several statutory provisions throughout the Israeli code that refer to aspects of Mossad operations.

[4] The contribution of Iain Cameron to this volume describes the jurisprudence of the European Court of Human Rights with respect to intelligence activities and the emerging requirement that intelligence authorities be established in statute.

[5] *See, e.g.*, Margo Schlanger, *Intelligence Legalism and the National Security Agency's Civil Liberties Gap*, 6 HARV. NAT'L SEC. J. 112 (2015); Samuel Rascoff, *Domesticating Intelligence*, 83 S. CAL. L. REV. 575 (2010); Emily Berman, *Regulating Domestic Intelligence Collection*, 71 WASH. & LEE L. REV. 3 (2014); Shirin Sinnar, *Protecting Rights from Within? Inspectors General and National Security Oversight*, 65 STAN. L. REV. 1027 (2013).

[6] In the context of this chapter (and more broadly throughout the volume), "oversight" refers to the process of supervising intelligence services before, during, or after specific activities, and dealing with both "matters of propriety and efficacy." Stuart Farson & Reg Whitaker, *Accounting for the Future or the Past?: Developing Accountability and Oversight Systems to Meet Future Intelligence Needs, in* THE OXFORD HANDBOOK OF NATIONAL SECURITY INTELLIGENCE 673, 678 (Loch K. Johnson ed., 2010). The process of oversight can embrace a range of considerations, including legality, efficacy and efficiency, financial supervision, consideration of human rights, and others. *See, e.g.*, Hans Born & Ian Leigh, MAKING INTELLIGENCE ACCOUNTABLE: LEGAL STANDARDS AND BEST PRACTICE FOR OVERSIGHT OF INTELLIGENCE AGENCIES 125 (2005) for a description of some of the factors that parliamentary oversight should take into account. In contrast, "accountability" is understood to have two components in the intelligence context: "answerability, the obligation of public officials to inform about and to explain what they are doing; and enforcement, the capacity of accounting agencies to impose sanctions on powerholders who have violated their public duties." Andreas Schedler, *Conceptualizing Accountability, in* THE SELF-RESTRAINING STATE: POWER AND ACCOUNTABILITY IN NEW DEMOCRACIES 13, 14 (Andreas Schedler, Larry Diamond & Marc F. Plattner eds., 1999).

[7] The U.K. and Australia, for example, each have adopted independent bodies whose task is to review the operation of counterterrorism laws. In the U.K., the body is the Independent Reviewer of Terrorism Legislation, and in Australia it is the Independent National Security Legislation Monitor. In the United States, the Privacy and Civil Liberties Oversight Board is similar, and is tasked with ensuring that civil liberties concerns are adequately accounted for in the development of counterterrorism law and policy. 42 U.S.C. 2000ee(c) (2015). Recent legislation has added a similar function to the office of the U.K.'s Independent Reviewer of Terrorism Legislation,

U.S. Congress and other national parliaments in governing intelligence agencies.[8] As Jane Harman points out in her preface, legislative bodies such as the U.S. Congress have notched some significant accomplishments in the post-9/11 era, including major reforms to the design of the U.S. Intelligence Community (IC) in 2004,[9] and, most recently, a comprehensive report on the CIA's Detention and Interrogation Program that issued from the Senate Select Committee on Intelligence.[10] Although parliamentary oversight across the liberal democratic world is not as robust,[11] it is inarguable that active and engaged legislatures are indispensable to effective intelligence governance. National legislatures enact the underlying statutory authorities that create intelligence services, adopt their budgets each year, and create the legal regimes that govern specific activities in which they are engaged, such as

---

though the office is not yet operational. And the German G10 Commission, whose role is analyzed by Russell Miller in this volume, serves a similar role in approving surveillance activities in that country.

[8] *See, e.g.,* AMY ZEGART, EYES ON SPIES (2011); MICHAEL ALLEN, BLINKING RED, CRISIS AND COMPROMISE IN AMERICAN INTELLIGENCE AFTER 9/11 (2013); L. ELAINE HALCHIN & FREDERICK M. KAISER, CONGRESSIONAL OVERSIGHT OF INTELLIGENCE: CURRENT STRUCTURE AND ALTERNATIVES 1–36 (2012); Hugh Bochel, Andrew Defty & Andrew Dunn, *Scrutinising the Secret State: Parliamentary Oversight of the Intelligence and Security Agencies,* 38 POL'Y & POL. 483–87 (2010); HANS BORN, PHILIPP FLURI & ANDERS JOHNSSON, PARLIAMENTARY OVERSIGHT OF THE SECURITY SECTOR (2003); Christopher M. Ford, *Intelligence Demands in a Democratic State: Congressional Intelligence Oversight,* 81 TULANE L. REV. 721–76 (2006); Roy Rempel, *Canada's Parliamentary Oversight of Security and Intelligence,* 17 INT'L J. INTELLIGENCE & COUNTERINTELLIGENCE 634–54 (2004); THE PARLIAMENTARY CONTROL OF EUROPEAN SECURITY POLICY (Dirk Peters, Wolfgang Wagner & Nicole Deitelhoff eds., 2008).

[9] Most prominently the Intelligence Reform and Terrorism Prevention Act of 2004, Pub. L. 108–458, 118 Stat. 3638 (2004), which resulted in the creation of the Office of the Director of National Intelligence to coordinate intelligence activities across the various components of the IC.

[10] STAFF OF S. COMM. ON INTELLIGENCE, 113TH CONG., REP. ON THE CENTRAL INTELLIGENCE AGENCY'S DETENTION AND INTERROGATION PROGRAM (Comm. Print 2014).

[11] As Kent Roach points out in his chapter, for example, Canadian legislators historically could not review classified materials. In the U.K., the Intelligence Services Act (ISA) of 1994, which established the U.K.'s Parliamentary Intelligence and Security Committee (ISC), originally conferred authority on the Committee to review the "expenditure, administration, and policy" of the intelligence services, but not their operations. The 1994 Act also contained limitations on the ability of the Committee to request specific documents (as opposed to requesting *information* more generally from the Services). Ian Leigh, *The UK's Intelligence and Security Committee, in* DEMOCRATIC CONTROL OF INTELLIGENCE SERVICES: CONTAINING ROGUE ELEPHANTS, 177, 182–83 (Hans Born & Marina Caparini eds., 2007). The Justice and Security Act of 2013 amended the jurisdiction of the ISC to include oversight over "the expenditure, administration, policy and operations" of MI5, MI6, and GCHQ, but included important limitations to the ISC's oversight of operational activities. Justice and Security Act 2013, c. 18 §§2(1), 3, 4 (UK). For discussions some of the incentives operating on congressional oversight in the United States, *see* Norman J. Ornstein & Thomas E. Mann, *When Congress Checks Out,* 85 FOREIGN AFF. 67, 80 (2006), (arguing that repeated intelligence oversight failures, and the general decline of oversight, are the result of "[i]deological polarization combined with near parity between the parties, [which] raised the stakes of majority control, weakening the institutional incentives that the founders had designed to ensure vigorous congressional oversight of the executive"); Marvin C. Ott, *Partisanship and the Decline of Intelligence Oversight,* 16 INT'L J. INTELLIGENCE & COUNTERINTELLIGENCE 81–88 (2003) (discussing party dynamics and difficulties with congressional oversight); Amy B. Zegart, *The Domestic Politics of Irrational Intelligence Oversight,* 126 POL. SCI. Q. 1, 2 (2011) (describing how "electoral incentives and internal congressional turf battles have led Congress to tie its own hands," resulting in "an intelligence oversight system that is rationally designed to serve the reelection interests of individual legislators and protect congressional committee prerogatives but poorly designed to serve the national interest.").

electronic surveillance or operations intended to influence political, economic, or military conditions abroad.[12] If the legal authorities for intelligence activities are vague, out of date, or inconsistent with social expectations, oversight institutions will commence their work at a considerable disadvantage. At the same time, as George Williams and Keiran Hardy note, if oversight institutions are weak, under-funded, and have narrow authorities with limited power to enforce change, they will not be effective.

In addition to its sustained consideration of the institutional landscape of the new intelligence oversight, this volume broadens our understanding of the purposes that a system of intelligence oversight ought to serve. Whereas in the first generation of intelligence oversight, the critical challenge was how to detect and deter official misconduct, the emerging oversight architecture addresses a variety of different concerns. One is how to reconcile a broad range of competing national interests—economic, diplomatic, and strategic—that now habitually arise in the intelligence domain. Another is how to secure the "consent of the governed" in a domain where public concerns are acute even as intelligence activities generally must remain (or aspire to remain) secret?[13]

This volume is intended as a contribution to the literature on comparative intelligence oversight.[14] It also adds to the literature on comparative administrative law,[15] as it is centrally concerned with an issue that figures prominently in that field—namely, reconciling the need for independence and expertise in government agencies on the one hand, with democratic accountability on the other.[16] By transcending customary boundaries between these and related intellectual disciplines, the volume generates meaningful insights for a wide range of scholars and practitioners.[17]

---

[12] In the United States, operations where it is "intended that the role of the United States Government will not be apparent or acknowledged publicly," are considered "covert action" and carry specific presidential approval and congressional notification procedures. 50 U.S.C. § 3093 (2014).

[13] *Intelligence Reform in a Post-Snowden World*, CENTER FOR STRATEGIC & INTERNATIONAL STUDIES (Oct. 9, 2015), http://csis.org/event/intelligence-reform-post-snowden-world-0.

[14] *See, e.g.*, NATIONAL INTELLIGENCE SYSTEMS: CURRENT RESEARCH AND FUTURE PROSPECTS (Gregory F. Treverton & Wilhelm Agrell eds., 2009); WHO'S WATCHING THE SPIES?: ESTABLISHING INTELLIGENCE SERVICE ACCOUNTABILITY (Hans Born, Loch K. Johnson & Ian Leigh eds., 2005); INTELLIGENCE ELSEWHERE: SPIES AND ESPIONAGE OUTSIDE THE ANGLOSPHERE (Philip H.J. Davies & Kristian C. Gustafson eds., 2013). Existing literature also focuses on oversight and control with respect to specific intelligence and national security concerns, such as surveillance and secrecy. *See, e.g.*, SURVEILLANCE, COUNTER-TERRORISM, AND COMPARATIVE CONSTITUTIONALISM (Fergal Davis, Nicola McGarrity & George Williams eds., 2014); SECRECY, NATIONAL SECURITY, AND THE VINDICATION OF CONSTITUTIONAL LAW (David Cole, Federico Fabbrini & Arianna Vedaschi eds., 2013).

[15] *See, e.g.*, COMPARATIVE ADMINISTRATIVE LAW (Susan Rose-Ackerman & Peter L. Lindseth eds., 2010); Kim Lane Scheppele, *The International Standardization of National Security Law*, 4 J. NAT'L SEC. L. & POL'Y 437 (2010).

[16] Francesca Bignami, *Comparative Administrative Law*, *in* THE CAMBRIDGE COMPANION TO COMPARATIVE LAW 145 (Mauro Bussani & Ugo Mattei eds., 2012).

[17] Specific country cases presented in the volume were selected from Western democracies that have both strong traditions of civil liberties and public accountability, and large well-resourced intelligence services with global mandates. We did not include chapters on every country that meets these criteria. But the chapters of this volume provide deep insights into the strengths and limitations of the systems designed to oversee many of the world's leading intelligence agencies.

II. INTELLIGENCE OVERSIGHT: NEW ACTORS, NEW INSTITUTIONS
A. An Emerging Transnational Oversight Ecosystem

From its emergence in the 1970s until recently, intelligence oversight has largely been defined by national boundaries.[18] As described briefly here and in more detail in the contributions of Ashley Deeks, Richard Morgan, and others, however, oversight is increasingly becoming transnational in nature as a set of cross-border influences shape intelligence activities in new ways.

Peer intelligence services are a particularly important source of constraint. Their influence derives from a number of factors, including the basic strategic reality that combating transnational threats such as terrorism, WMD proliferation, and cybercrime has intensified the degree of professional interdependence among intelligence agencies in the post-9/11 era. Furthermore, litigation in foreign courts,[19] official foreign government inquiries,[20] and the diplomatic interests of foreign governments[21] all contribute meaningfully to the evolving global intelligence oversight landscape.[22]

Perhaps no set of transnational actors has proved more important to the emergence of the new intelligence oversight than global technology companies such as Facebook, Google, and Microsoft. These firms have become a potent force in shaping the ability of law enforcement and intelligence agencies to collect information. Their influence has been wielded indirectly, through traditional interest group politics. But it can also show up through more direct interventions, for example by encrypting user data in a range of circumstances, frustrating the ability of government agencies to access it.[23] Beyond encryption, technology companies

---

[18] Some regard the mismatch between state-based oversight systems and expanding transnational cooperation among intelligence agencies as a weakness of the current arrangement. *See* Ian Leigh, *Accountability and Intelligence Cooperation: Framing the Issue, in* INTERNATIONAL INTELLIGENCE COOPERATION AND ACCOUNTABILITY 3–4 (Hans Born, Ian Leigh & Aidan Wills, eds., 2011). This volume demonstrates the ways in which the project of oversight is beginning to catch up to the transnationalization of intelligence itself.

[19] *See, e.g.*, Rachel Donadio, *Italy Convicts 23 Americans for C.I.A. Renditions*, N.Y. TIMES, Nov. 4, 2009, http://www.nytimes.com/2009/11/05/world/europe/05italy.html?_r=0?login=email (the 23 Americans, including CIA officers, were tried and convicted in absentia for the capture of Hassan Mustafa Osama Nasr, also known as Abu Omar, from Milan).

[20] *See, e.g.*, Marcel Furstenau, *German Parliament to Inquire into NSA*, DEUTSCHE WELLE, (Mar. 20, 2014) http://dw.com/p/1BTJg.

[21] Julian Borger, *Brazilian President: US Surveillance a "Breach of International Law,"* THE GUARDIAN (Sept. 24, 2013, 12:27 PM), http://www.theguardian.com/world/2013/sep/24/brazil-president-un-speech-nsa-surveillance. Indeed, the United States reportedly ceased certain intelligence collection activities in Western Europe in the aftermath of a series of intelligence controversies there. Ken Dilanian, *CIA Halts Spying in Europe*, ASSOCIATED PRESS (Sept. 20, 2014, 12:09 AM), http://news.yahoo.com/ap-exclusive-cia-halts-spying-europe-155821445--politics.html.

[22] In the last several years, global technology companies have argued that the perception that they cooperate closely with the U.S. IC has led to a decline in their business among foreign customers who wish to protect their privacy from the American government. This dynamic has caused those companies to become much more engaged in trying to shape the intelligence landscape. *See* Claire Cain Miller, *Revelations of N.S.A. Spying Cost U.S. Tech Companies*, N. Y. TIMES, Mar. 21, 2014, http://www.nytimes.com/2014/03/22/business/fallout-from-snowden-hurting-bottom-line-of-tech-companies.html.

[23] *Approach to Privacy*, APPLE, https://www.apple.com/privacy/privacy-built-in/ ("Your communications are protected by end-to-end encryption . . . we wouldn't be able to comply with a wiretap order even if we

also have sought to be more transparent with their customers about the amounts and types of government data requests they receive—information that historically has been protected as confidential by court orders.[24]

In the United States several changes have taken place in the oversight landscape in response to these transnational pressures. As Samuel Rascoff documents, the White House, uniquely suited to metabolize all of the competing interests at stake in intelligence matters, has become a more active participant in intelligence oversight. A new Presidential Policy Directive, PPD-28, mandates the consideration of a wider range of interests in the development of intelligence policy, including the economic interests of American companies and the privacy rights of non-U.S. persons.[25] And reflecting this new experience of intelligence interdependence, the CIA recently reestablished a senior position to manage intelligence liaison relationships, revealing the importance in the present threat environment of partnerships with peer intelligence services.[26]

These trends are still in their early stages, but they can be expected to play an increasingly important role in defining the emerging oversight architecture. As Western democracies continually evaluate their approaches to intelligence oversight, it is now imperative that transnational influences be considered. Some scholars, such as Kent Roach, suggest more formalized transnational structures such as an ombudsperson for the agencies that are part of the so-called Five Eyes intelligence alliance. Others recognize the imperative for transnational convergence of oversight in order to address problems that arise from the conflicting data access regimes to which global companies are subject.[27] Whether these mechanisms

---

wanted to.") (last visited Dec. 22, 2015); Craig Timberg, *Apple Will No Longer Unlock Most iPhones, iPads for Police, Even with Search Warrants,* WASH. POST (Sept. 18, 2014), http://www.washingtonpost.com/business/technology/2014/09/17/2612af58-3ed2-11e4-b03f-de718edeb92f_story.html.

[24] In order to resolve an impasse in the United States about what the companies could reveal and when, the Department of Justice and five major technology companies agreed on a protocol governing the information that companies can reveal about their receipt of national security process. Letter from James M. Cole, Deputy Attorney General, to Colin Stretch, Vice President and General Counsel, Facebook; Kent Walker, Senior Vice President and General Counsel, Google; Erika Rottenberg, Vice President, General Counsel/Secretary, LinkedIn; Brad Smith, Executive Vice President and General Counsel, Microsoft; and Ronald Bell, General Counsel, Yahoo (Jan. 27, 2014), *available at* http://www.justice.gov/iso/opa/resources/366201412716018407143.pdf.

[25] PRESIDENTIAL POLICY DIRECTIVE 28—SIGNALS INTELLIGENCE ACTIVITIES (Jan. 17, 2014). "Departments and agencies shall apply the term 'personal information' in a manner that is consistent for U.S. persons and non-U.S. persons" at ¶ 7. PPD-28 also mandated that the signals intelligence planning process should take into account U.S. "commercial, economic, and financial interests, including a potential loss of international trust in U.S. firms and the decreased willingness of other nations to participate in international data sharing, privacy, and regulatory regimes." *Id.*

[26] John Brennan, Director, Central Intelligence Agency, Remarks by Central Intelligence Agency Director John O. Brennan as prepared for delivery at the Council on Foreign Relations, Mar. 13, 2015, *available at* https://www.cia.gov/news-information/speeches-testimony/2015-speeches-testimony/director-brennan-speaks-at-the-council-on-foreign-relations.html.

[27] H. Christopher Boehning & Daniel J. Toal, *Microsoft Paves the Way for Data Privacy Battle,* N.Y. LAW J., Oct. 7, 2014, at 1–3 (2014); *In re* Warrant to Search a Certain E-Mail Account Controlled and Maintained by Microsoft Corp., 15 F. Supp. 3d 466 (S.D.N.Y. 2014).

develop organically, or instead are designed and constructed more deliberately, the transnational component of oversight will require sustained attention in the years to come.[28]

B. *The Growing Importance of Courts*

Judicial involvement in national security matters has tended to be relatively modest across the liberal democratic world. Even in countries such as Israel and the U.K., which have defied this trend, certain intelligence matters, especially those implicating the operations of foreign intelligence services, have eluded sustained scrutiny. But that, too, is changing in ways that carry significant implications for the project of intelligence oversight. Several of the book's chapters explore novel roles for the courts in the supervision of intelligence agencies and practices. Daphna Renan, for example, describes the operations of the FISC, which now superintends entire intelligence programs in addition to its more traditional role of approving surveillance warrants for specific targets. And Raphael Bitton underscores the role that judicial review of intelligence programs plays in reassuring the public of the legality and propriety of intelligence and national security activities.

The scope of recent judicial interventions in this area is striking. Intelligence liaison relationships, for example, have come under scrutiny in both Canada and the U.K. In Canada, the courts recently held that the Canadian Security Intelligence Service (CSIS) contravened its statutory mandate when it relied on assistance from Five Eyes intelligence partners in executing surveillance orders.[29] And early in 2015, the U.K.'s Investigatory Powers Tribunal (IPT), a judicial institution that reviews cases of alleged unlawful surveillance,[30] addressed a similar issue in a suit brought by a group of civil liberties organizations.[31] In that case, the IPT held that intelligence-sharing and collaboration arrangements between the U.K. and the United States contravened the European Convention on Human Rights (ECHR) because there was not enough public clarity about the legal framework governing such collaboration.[32] The Canadian Supreme Court has also ordered changes to the internal policies and procedures of CSIS designed to facilitate judicial review of decisions about counterterrorism measures. Specifically, the Court overturned a CSIS policy requiring its officers to destroy their operational notes after they write reports based on those notes,[33] holding that the retention of CSIS officers' original notes was necessary to enable the courts to assess the reasonableness of counterterrorism measures.[34]

---

[28] At the same time as the volume takes a transnational approach to questions of oversight, the substantive legal and policy standards governing intelligence activities, particularly in the context of electronic surveillance, are the subject of sustained transnational attention as well. *See* Ashley Deeks, *An International Legal Framework for Surveillance*, 55 VA. J. INT'L L. 291 (2015).

[29] *See* Kent Roach's contribution to this volume for an extended description and analysis of the decision and its implications.

[30] FUNCTIONS—KEY ROLE, INVESTIGATORY POWERS TRIBUNAL, http://www.ipt-uk.com/section.aspx?pageid=1 (last visited Aug. 24, 2015).

[31] *Liberty v. Secretary of State for Foreign and Commonwealth Affairs & Others*, [2015] UKIPTrib 13_77-H.

[32] Ironically, it was the revelation of that same partnership that rendered it lawful, as the leaks provided sufficient transparency for the public to be apprised of the ongoing activity. *Id.* ¶ 22.

[33] *Charkaoui v. Canada (Citizenship and Immigration)*, 2008 2 S.C.R. 326 (Canada).

[34] *Id.* ¶ 42. Of note, the D.C. Circuit Court of Appeals confronted a similar issue in *Latif v. Obama*, 677 F.3d 1175 (D.C. Cir. 2011) in the course of reviewing the propriety of Latif's detention at Guantanamo Bay, Cuba.

Courts have also begun to weigh in on the substantive scope of national security surveillance authority.[35] In the wake of the Snowden leaks, European data privacy activists sued Facebook, claiming that the circumstances under which U.S. government agencies can access the data of EU citizens exceeded the scope of what is permitted under EU data privacy rules.[36] The ECJ decision ruling that the current scheme for transferring data between the United States and EU violates those data privacy rules may carry significant implications for American companies. Of serious concern are potentially incompatible obligations on companies that are simultaneously subject to EU jurisdiction with respect to data privacy and U.S. jurisdiction for the purpose of complying with surveillance orders. Relieving this tension might, in turn, necessitate broader surveillance reform.[37]

The ECJ decision marks not only a quantitative change in the degree of judicial involvement in intelligence oversight, but also a qualitative shift in the discussion about whose rights should be protected by judicial processes. The United States has long maintained that noncitizens without a substantial connection to the United States do not enjoy constitutional protections against surveillance.[38] Other countries, including Germany, have taken a similar position, as Russell Miller documents in his chapter.[39]

But in recent years, scholars and privacy activists have argued that international human rights law provides a framework for limiting transnational intelligence activities regardless of the citizenship of the targets of surveillance.[40] Questions about the scope of legal protections

---

Latif argued that intelligence reports of interviews with him contained statements that were misunderstood. But the Court held that U.S. government intelligence reports are entitled to a "presumption of regularity" in part because "courts have no special expertise in evaluating the nature and reliability of the Executive branch's wartime records. For that, it is appropriate to defer to Executive branch expertise." *Id.* at 1177, 1182.

[35] The litigation described in this section of the Introduction, which predominantly focuses on the transnational impact of judicial determinations about intelligence, parallels domestic U.S. litigation that seeks to challenge intelligence programs. In *American Civil Liberties Union v. Clapper*, 785 F.3d 787 (2d Cir. 2015), the Second Circuit struck down the government's interpretation of Section 215 of the USA PATRIOT Act that permitted bulk telephony metadata collection. Cases such as *United States v. Muhtorov*, Case No. 12-cr-00033-JLK, 2013 U.S. Dist. LEXIS 61756 (D. Colo. 2013), are challenging the constitutionality of intelligence collected under different statutory authorities.

[36] Sam Schechner, *Max Schrems vs. Facebook: Activist Takes Aim at U.S.-EU Safe Harbor*, Wall St. J. Digits (Nov. 20, 2014, 12:40 PM), http://blogs.wsj.com/digits/2014/11/20/max-schrems-vs-facebook-activist-takes-aim-at-u-s-eu-safe-harbor/. The bilateral EU/U.S. agreement that governed the use of commercial data by companies that operate in both jurisdictions is called the "Safe Harbor," a voluntary arrangement allowing American companies to self-certify that they take precautions with respect to the personal data of users, thereby permitting those companies easily to transfer data between the United States and EU. The *Schrems* decision struck down the validity of this method of transferring data between the United States and Europe. *See Welcome to the U.S.-EU & U.S.-Swiss Safe Harbor Frameworks*, Export.gov, http://www.export.gov/safeharbor (last updated Oct. 9, 2015).

[37] Case C-362/14, Schrems v. Data Prot. Comm'r, 2015 E.C.R. ---.

[38] The contention is rooted in Fourth Amendment jurisprudence. *See* United States v. Verdugo-Urquidez, 494 U.S. 259 (1990).

[39] *See* Chapter 10 of this volume for Russell Miller's analysis of the German government's decision that the G10 Act does not apply to the "surveillance of telecommunications that take place outside Germany and do not involve Germans as one of the parties."

[40] *See, e.g.*, Marko Milanovic, *Human Rights Treaties and Foreign Surveillance: Privacy in the Digital Age*, 56 Harv. Int'l L. J. 81, 87 (2015) (arguing that "human rights treaties should apply to virtually all foreign

against surveillance have become relevant because the communications of intelligence targets—foreign spies and military leaders, terrorists, cyber criminals, and others—use the same devices and networks as the general population. (During the Cold War, by contrast, communications of interest to the IC often resided on dedicated networks.) This means that a broader category of persons may have their communications collected in the exercise of lawful foreign intelligence activities.

Although, in practice, no country appears to be embracing such a broad view of human rights protections, expansive understandings of human rights obligations could complicate the intelligence relationships between the United States and some of its allies whose courts may come to embrace a more capacious understanding of human rights requirements over time. Even in the United States, PPD-28 has gestured in the direction of enhanced privacy protections for non-U.S. persons, albeit as a matter of policy rather than law. The extent to which human rights law offers substantive protections to noncitizens will be an area of contestation, both in the courts and in the public arena, over the coming years.

Despite the general trend toward an expanded judicial role in the oversight of intelligence agencies, Iain Cameron and others identify structural obstacles to the role that courts can play in this area. The biggest such obstacle is the "accident of litigation," meaning that courts only review the cases and controversies referred to them, rather than taking a broad and proactive approach to the regulation of security services. Furthermore, in the intelligence domain, as in other areas of transnational law, there is often a mismatch between the authority of the agency responsible for carrying out a policy or activity and the jurisdiction of the court reviewing it. For example, although the European Court of Human Rights determined that Poland had violated the ECHR by cooperating with the CIA in the detention of Abd al Rahim al Nashiri, the mastermind of the 2000 USS *Cole* bombing,[41] that determination will not ultimately decide the fate of al Nashiri, who continues to be held by the United States, a country not subject to the jurisdiction of that court.

Additional obstacles to effective judicial review of intelligence activities include the complexity surrounding reliance on intelligence-derived evidence in criminal prosecutions and administrative processes, asymmetries in information between the government and private litigants with limited access to classified information, the lack of broadly accepted metrics for evaluating the efficacy of intelligence programs, and the foreign relations implications of judicial pronouncements in this area.

Although others have analyzed the performance of the judiciary in adjudicating national security matters generally,[42] this volume's reckoning with the role of the courts in intelligence

---

surveillance activities"); Ryan Goodman, *Should Foreign Nationals Get the Same Privacy Protections under NSA Surveillance—or Less (or More)?*, JUST SECURITY (Oct. 29, 2014, 10:33 AM), https://www.justsecurity.org/16797/foreign-nationals-privacy-protections-nsa-surveillance-or-or-more/. Additionally, in December 2013 the U.N. General Assembly adopted a Resolution on "The right to privacy in the digital age," expressing its deep concern "at the negative impact that surveillance and/or interception of communications, including extraterritorial surveillance and/or interception of communications . . . may have on the exercise and enjoyment of human rights." G.A. Res. 68/167, at 2, U.N. Doc. A/RES/68/167 (Dec. 18, 2013).

[41] Al Nashiri v. Poland, App. No. 28761/11, Eur. Ct. H.R., 1 (2014).

[42] *See, e.g.*, DAVID SCHARIA, JUDICIAL REVIEW OF NATIONAL SECURITY (2014) for a recent analysis of the ways in which the courts in Israel manage national security cases.

and surveillance is novel, as is its pervasively comparative focus. Over the coming years, both the possibilities and the limitations of judicial involvement in intelligence oversight will necessarily be debated.[43]

III. THE PURPOSES OF INTELLIGENCE OVERSIGHT

This volume's second major contribution, beyond its focus on the institutions and dynamics that are newly influential in shaping the intelligence oversight landscape, is to offer insights into the purposes that intelligence oversight may serve beyond legal compliance. These issues are highlighted by Zachary Goldman in his chapter devoted to the American IC, and by Jon Moran and Clive Walker in their contribution focusing on the U.K.[44]

There are two main goals that the new intelligence oversight aspires to promote (beyond ensuring legal compliance). The first is the establishment of processes to reconcile a broad range of national interests in the development and execution of intelligence policy and practices. These include the commercial interests of technology and telecommunications companies, the need for law enforcement to have authorized access to data, and the maintenance of basic Internet security. Intelligence officers are accustomed to considering the impacts that proposed activities may have on other intelligence interests, and perhaps also on military or diplomatic objectives, but not necessarily on these more far-reaching activities.

The second main objective of intelligence oversight should be to generate and maintain public trust in the activities of intelligence agencies. This goal is in some tension with the basic reality that, by their nature and institutional culture, intelligence services operate behind a veil of secrecy. But some degree of transparency (or at least translucency) at a programmatic level is necessary to foster accountability. In the 1970s, the U.S. Congress created the House and Senate Intelligence Committees in order to reconcile these competing pressures. The two committees were intended to serve as proxies for the American people in the governance of the IC.[45] But the core features of that bargain are in the process of being updated, with new institutions and processes being called on to complement the role that Congress has played and to serve as a bridge between the secretive IC and the public that it serves.

A. *Integrating Disparate Interests*

The reconciliation of competing national interests in intelligence has emerged as a core function of oversight in recent years as the size, complexity, and global scope of intelligence programs

---

[43] *See* David Anderson Q.C., A Question of Trust: Report of the Investigatory Powers Review 6 (2015), in which the U.K.'s Independent Reviewer of Terrorism Legislation recommends that surveillance warrants should be judicially authorized.

[44] For arguments that the expansion of the U.S. IC since 9/11 was potentially disproportionate and resulted in wasteful spending, *see, e.g.,* Dana Priest & Tom Arkin, Top Secret America: The Rise of the New American Security State (2011); John Mueller & Mark G. Stewart, *The Terrorism Delusion: America's Overwrought Response to September 11,* 37(1) Int'l Sec., Summer 2012, at 81. *See also* United States Senate Permanent Subcommittee on Investigations Majority and Minority Staff Report, Federal Support for and Involvement in State and Local Fusion Centers (Oct. 3, 2012).

[45] *See Surveillance, Security and Trust,* Wilson Ctr. (June 4, 2014), at 22:20, https://www.wilsoncenter.org/event/surveillance-security-and-trust.

has expanded. In practice, this means that oversight institutions and processes must incorporate a broad array of viewpoints in the formulation of intelligence policies and programs, beyond simply assessing the impact of intelligence activities on existing intelligence or defense equities. Three illustrative issues that should be weighed more systematically in the development of intelligence policy are economic interests (particularly those in the technology and telecommunications sector); the spillover effects that intelligence-driven data collection have for data collection in the law enforcement setting; and the impact of intelligence programs on Internet security.

Expanding the range of interests that should be considered in the intelligence process in the United States was a core recommendation of the Review Group on Intelligence and Communications Technologies, a group of former government officials and senior academics appointed by President Obama shortly after the surveillance leaks of 2013.[46] The Review Group embraced the view that "senior policymakers from the federal agencies with responsibility for US economic interests should participate in the [intelligence priorities] review process because disclosures of classified information can have detrimental effects on US economic interests."[47] A recent report of the U.K. Parliament's Intelligence and National Security Committee similarly acknowledged that intelligence activities with respect to decrypting communications may have "potentially serious" ramifications for the British economy, which must be considered the ministerial level.[48]

In recent years, controversy surrounding access to privately held data by intelligence agencies has spilled over into misgivings about access to data for law enforcement purposes, with potentially wide-ranging impacts on investigations focused on ordinary criminal activity. Microsoft, for example, is litigating the question of whether the U.S. government may obtain customer data with a search warrant when the data is stored on servers outside the United States.[49] Along similar lines, technology companies have sought to narrow the reach of

---

[46] Presidential Memorandum on Reviewing Our Global Intelligence Collection and Communications Technologies, 78 Fed. Reg. 49653 (Aug. 15, 2013), *available at* http://www.gpo.gov/fdsys/pkg/FR-2013-08-15/pdf/2013-19960.pdf.

[47] RICHARD A. CLARKE, MICHAEL J. MORELL, GEOFFREY R. STONE, CASS R. SUNSTEIN & PETER SWIRE, LIBERTY AND SECURITY IN A CHANGING WORLD: REPORT AND RECOMMENDATIONS OF THE PRESIDENT'S REVIEW GROUP ON INTELLIGENCE AND COMMUNICATIONS TECHNOLOGIES 31–32 (2013), *available at* https://www.whitehouse.gov/sites/default/files/docs/2013-12-12_rg_final_report.pdf [hereinafter "PRESIDENT'S REVIEW GROUP REPORT"].

[48] INTELLIGENCE AND SECURITY COMMITTEE OF PARLIAMENT, PRIVACY AND SECURITY: A MODERN AND TRANSPARENT LEGAL FRAMEWORK 68–69 (2015).

[49] *In re* Warrant to Search a Certain E-Mail Account Controlled and Maintained by Microsoft Corp., 15 F. Supp. 3d 466 (S.D.N.Y. 2014). That case arose when the government served a search warrant on Microsoft for data that was stored on a server in Ireland. The case produced a significant amount of controversy because of the general rule that search warrants do not have extraterritorial effect, even while subpoenas, issued with less legal process, compel recipients to produce documents in their possession, custody, or control, even if located outside the United States. Microsoft, keen to demonstrate its concern for its customers' privacy, challenged the warrant rather than comply with the Department of Justice request. For discussions about the issues presented in the case, *see, e.g.,* Jennifer Daskal, *The Un-territoriality of Data*, 125 YALE L. J. 326 (2015); Jennifer Daskal, *Magistrate's Compliance: Searching Electronic Data Overseas*, JUST SECURITY (May 9, 2014), https://www.justsecurity.org/10234/magistrates-compliance-searching-electronic-data-overseas/ (last visited Aug 31, 2015); Recent Case, In re *Warrant to Search a Certain Email Account Controlled & Maintained by Microsoft Corp.,* 128 HARV. LAW REV. 1019 (2015); Andrew K. Woods, GLOBAL NETWORK INITIATIVE, DATA BEYOND

government searches of electronic data, such that some but not all of a target's email and social media accounts would be accessible.[50] Taken together, these dynamics illustrate the concern that decisions made about intelligence law and policy necessarily carry substantial implications for law enforcement.

A final set of interests that the new intelligence oversight must account for pertains to Internet security. Although there are a number of specific areas in which this concern has arisen, the most concrete involves questions about what governments should do with software and other technical vulnerabilities that they discover or obtain.[51] These vulnerabilities, particularly if they are previously undisclosed flaws (known as "zero-day" exploits), may be useful in collecting intelligence because they enable penetration of a target's networks or systems. But because these vulnerabilities often exist in software programs or operating systems that are widely used, choosing to patch, rather than exploit, them would help prevent the kinds of data breaches that collectively cost companies billions of dollars each year.[52] Some security researchers have advocated a default rule that governments should disclose vulnerabilities, enabling companies to patch them and protect as many computer systems as possible.[53] Others recognize the importance of preserving previously unidentified flaws to conduct vital intelligence activities.[54] Regardless of how the balance is ultimately struck, the evolving oversight regime must account for this and similar tensions in the future.

Borders Mutual Legal Assistance in the Internet Age (2015), *available at* https://globalnetworkinitiative.org/sites/default/files/GNI%20MLAT%20Report.pdf; Orin Kerr, *A Different Take on the Second Circuit's Microsoft Warrant Case*, Wash. Post, Aug. 20, 2015, *available at* https://www.washingtonpost.com/news/volokh-conspiracy/wp/2015/08/20/a-different-take-on-the-second-circuits-microsoft-warrant-case/; Andrew Woods, *Lowering the Temperature on the Microsoft-Ireland Case*, Lawfare, Sept. 11, 2015, *available at* https://lawfareblog.com/lowering-temperature-microsoft-ireland-case.

[50] *See, e.g., In re* the Search of Information Associated with the Facebook Account Identified by the Username Aaron.Alexis That Is Stored at Premises Controlled by Facebook, Inc., No. 13-MJ-742, 2013 WL 7856600, at *4–5, 8-9 (D.D.C. Nov. 26, 2013) (Facciola, M.J.); *In re* the Search of Information Associated with [REDACTED]@MAC.COM That Is Stored at Premises Controlled by Apple, Inc., 14-228 (JMF), 2014 WL 945563 (D.D.C. Mar. 7, 2014) (Facciola, M.J.).

[51] *See* Michael Daniel, *Heartbleed: Understanding When We Disclose Cyber Vulnerabilities*, The White House (Apr. 28, 2014, 3:00 PM), https://www.whitehouse.gov/blog/2014/04/28/heartbleed-understanding-when-we-disclose-cyber-vulnerabilities.

[52] *See, e.g.,* Brian Krebs, The Target Breach, By the Numbers, Krebs on Security (May 14, 2014), http://krebsonsecurity.com/2014/05/the-target-breach-by-the-numbers; Ellen Nakashima, *Hacks of OPM Databases Compromised 22.1 Million People, Federal Authorities Say*, Wash. Post, July 9, 2015, http://www.washingtonpost.com/blogs/federal-eye/wp/2015/07/09/hack-of-security-clearance-system-affected-21-5-million-people-federal-authorities-say/; Paul Taylor, *Cybercrime Costs US $100bn a Year, Report Says*, Fin. Times, July 23, 2013.

[53] Bruce Schneier, Data and Goliath: The Hidden Battles to Collect Your Data and Control Your World 181 (2015) ("We have to err on the side of disclosure.").

[54] Stuxnet, the cyber tool that reportedly set back the Iranian nuclear program, apparently used four previously unknown "zero-day" exploits. Ryan Naraine, *Stuxnet Attackers Used 4 Windows Zero-Day Exploits*, ZDNet (Sept. 14, 2010), http://www.zdnet.com/article/stuxnet-attackers-used-4-windows-zero-day-exploits/; Steve Ranger, *Here's How the NSA Decides to Tell You about a Zero Day—Or Not*, ZDNet (2014), http://www.zdnet.com/article/heres-how-the-nsa-decides-to-tell-you-about-a-zero-day-or-not/.

B. *Fostering Public Trust in Intelligence Services*

The U.K.'s Independent Reviewer of Terrorism Legislation titled a recent report on that country's electronic surveillance system *A Question of Trust*,[55] with good reason. That is because trust is, perhaps, the single most important determinant of how intelligence agencies will fare in liberal democracies. Relationships mediated by trust include those between the government and telecommunications providers that generate and store relevant data, between technology companies and the consumers that use their products, and, perhaps most important, between intelligence agencies and the publics that they serve. Effective oversight is critical in fostering and maintaining trust in the institutions that carry out intelligence functions, all the more so because many of the tools that are habitually deployed to hold public institutions accountable in Western democracies are not available in the intelligence domain. For example, although the overall budget of the IC in the United States was first made public in 1997, reclassified the next year, and then declassified again for the 2007 budget,[56] detailed public scrutiny of the IC's finances is not possible. Similarly, the transparent "notice and comment" process by which many U.S. federal agencies make rules is not available when it comes to intelligence programs. And the U.S. Freedom of Information Act contains exemptions for classified and other intelligence material.

In this domain, too, change is afoot. The USA FREEDOM Act, signed into law in June 2015,[57] provides for the appointment of amici curiae to assist the FISC in the consideration of any application for an order that presents a novel or significant interpretation of the law.[58] The job of these "friends of the court" is to provide the FISC with "legal arguments that advance the protection of individual privacy and civil liberties."[59] Furthermore, the statute instructs the Director of National Intelligence to conduct a declassification review of any decision, order, or opinion of the FISC "that includes a significant construction or interpretation of any provision of law."[60] This change may go some way to addressing a situation in which legal opinions generated by government lawyers in secret are rooted in understandings of the law that are "not something that would . . . have occurred to an outside observer,"[61] as happened with interpretations of Section 215 of the USA PATRIOT Act permitting the IC to collect telephony metadata in bulk.

Public discussions about ways to enhance oversight and foster trust in the activities of intelligence agencies are not unique to the United States. France, which adopted legislation granting broad surveillance authorities in the wake of terrorist attacks in Paris in January 2015, accompanied the substantive provisions of the law with certain improvements to

---

[55] ANDERSON, *supra* note 43, at 6.

[56] Steven Aftergood, *FAS Wins Lawsuit against CIA on Intelligence Budget Disclosure*, FED'N AM. SCIENTISTS, (1997), http://www.fas.org/sgp/foia/victory.html; *DNI Releases Requested Budget Figure for FY 2016 Appropriations for the National Intelligence Program*, OFFICE DIR. NAT'L INTELLIGENCE: IC ON REC. (Feb. 2, 2015), http://icontherecord.tumblr.com/post/110169188318/dni-releases-requested-budget-figure-for-fy-2016.

[57] Pub. L. No. 114-23, 129 Stat 268 (2015).

[58] *Id.* § 401.

[59] *Id.* § 404(4)(A).

[60] *Id.* § 602(a).

[61] David Kris, *On the Bulk Collection of Tangible Things*, 7 J. NAT'L SECURITY L. & POL'Y 209, 273 (2014).

its oversight system.[62] The U.K. has also paid increased attention to the role of oversight as it modifies certain intelligence authorities. In a suit challenging the Data Retention and Investigatory Powers Act 2014, for example, the U.K. Divisional Court held that the statute violated EU data privacy rules, in large measure because of inadequacies in the oversight regime created by that statute.[63] As intelligence capabilities become more central to battling contemporary security threats, oversight will have to keep pace and discharge a critical role in fostering public trust and confidence in intelligence services.

IV. CONCLUSION

The world of intelligence is never static, and the challenges that the IC will face a generation from now are unlikely to resemble those that the IC faces today. Christopher Kojm's chapter highlights some of the problems and challenges that the U.S. IC is likely to confront in the coming years, and the implications of those challenges for the oversight of security services. The proliferation of "intelligence" units—whether in local police departments designed to map out gang territory, or in global banks designed to mitigate risk[64]—illustrates the imperative of collecting and processing information to inform decision-making processes.

As a result of a globally integrated world and logarithmic changes in the power of technology, even the most traditional of espionage activities—recruiting human agents—has undergone substantial shifts of late. The pervasive adoption of biometric identification technology at borders, for example, has made it harder for intelligence officers to travel under cover.[65] And we have only begun to consider what oversight should look like in the context of new capabilities, such as cyber operations. Offensive operations, such as those that reportedly damaged centrifuges in one of Iran's nuclear facilities;[66] government takedowns of networks of hijacked computers ("botnets") used to perpetrate all manner of cybercrime;[67] and the exploitation of

---

[62] Sam Schechner & Matthew Dalton, *French Constitutional Court Approves New Powers for Intelligence Services*, WALL ST. J., July 24, 2015, http://www.wsj.com/articles/french-constitutional-court-approves-new-powers-for-intelligence-services-1437730809.

[63] *Davis (on the application of) v. Secretary of State for the Home Department*, [2015] EWHC (Admin) 2092, [114] (Admin).

[64] *See, e.g.*, GOLDMAN SACHS, OUR DIVISIONS—LEGAL: BUSINESS INTELLIGENCE GROUP, *available at* http://www.goldmansachs.com/careers/why-goldman-sachs/our-divisions/legal/ (last visited Nov. 4, 2015).

[65] Kate Brannen, *To Catch a Spy*, FOREIGN POLICY, Apr. 6, 2015, *available at* http://foreignpolicy.com/2015/04/06/to-catch-a-spy-biometrics-cia-border-security/. In early 2010, the dangers of this new world for spies became clear. Over a period of several days, the activities and cover identities of a group of people who killed a Hamas arms trafficker in a Dubai hotel room, widely believed to be from Israel's Mossad, were unmasked in full view of the global public, even if they have not been publicly identified in true name, and have not been apprehended. *An Eye for an Eye: The Anatomy of Mossad's Dubai Operation*, Spiegel Online, Jan. 17, 2011, http://www.spiegel.de/international/world/an-eye-for-an-eye-the-anatomy-of-mossad-s-dubai-operation-a-739908.html.

[66] RALPH LANGNER, TO KILL A CENTRIFUGE: A TECHNICAL ANALYSIS OF WHAT STUXNET'S CREATORS TRIED TO ACHIEVE 1–36 (2013).

[67] *See, e.g.*, Complaint, *Microsoft Corp. v. John Does 1-8 Controlling a Computer Botnet Thereby Injuring Microsoft and its Customers*, No. A 13-CV-1014 (W.D. Tex. Nov. 25, 2013).

software or hardware vulnerabilities to effectuate search warrants are all examples of government employment of cyber capabilities that require appropriate oversight.[68]

Whether emphasizing traditional or emerging intelligence capabilities, this volume recasts the debate about intelligence oversight by highlighting the links between the purposes of oversight and the institutions established to conduct it. It promotes clear thinking about the inevitably linked questions of the "who" and the "why" of intelligence oversight. And in so doing, it enables the analysis of intelligence oversight, by scholars and policymakers, to become more dynamic, global, and multidimensional.[69] Taken together, the chapters in this volume will promote more nuanced scholarship about, and practice of, intelligence governance in a globalized world.

---

[68] *See* Steven M. Bellovin, Matt Blaze, Sandy Clark & Susan Landau, *Lawful Hacking: Using Existing Vulnerabilities for Wiretapping on the Internet*, 12 Nw. J. Tech. & Intell. Prop. 1 (2014).

[69] *See, e.g.*, David Cole, Terrorism and the Constitution: Sacrificing Civil Liberties in the Name of National Security (2006); Eric Posner & Adrian Vermeule, Terror in the Balance: Security, Liberty, and the Courts (2007); Laura K. Donohue, The Cost of Counterterrorism (2008); and Peter Margulies, Law's Detour: Justice Displaced in the Bush Administration, for conflicting views on the civil liberties impact (primarily within the United States) of early post-9/11 intelligence and counterterrorism policies.

PART ONE
Transnational Oversight

1

Intelligence Services, Peer Constraints, and the Law

*Ashley Deeks**

I. INTRODUCTION

Widespread disclosures about certain intelligence activities of several Western governments have prompted heated public debate about the legality, morality, and political wisdom of those activities. But the debate also has focused on the role and efficacy of intelligence oversight in constraining and modulating intelligence activities more generally. The best-known sources of intelligence community oversight tend to be entities prescribed in statute: parliamentary committees, inspectors general, and courts. The media and nongovernmental organizations have demonstrated that they, too, can play a watchdog role over intelligence activities, even if they lack formal authority to review, alter, or sanction those activities.[1]

This chapter identifies and analyzes for the first time another source of constraint on an intelligence community (IC): its peer ICs.[2] Peer ICs are the intelligence services of foreign

---

* Associate Professor, University of Virginia Law School. A longer version of this chapter first appeared in 7 HARV. NAT'L SEC. J. 1 (2016).

[1] *See generally* JACK GOLDSMITH, POWER AND CONSTRAINT: THE ACCOUNTABLE PRESIDENCY AFTER 9/11 (2012) (arguing that the executive branch faces a wide number of constraints on its actions, including because of widespread Internet access, leaks of classified information, and aggressive litigation by the ACLU). Other actors such as the International Committee of the Red Cross (ICRC) can play an oversight role when intelligence agencies conduct detentions during armed conflict.

[2] Peer ICs include the ICs of states that work together cooperatively on a long-term basis across political, military, and economic spheres and may be parties to collective self-defense treaties, such as NATO, as well as ICs that cooperate with each other on discrete issues. The partnership between the United States and U.K. is an example of the first type. The discrete cooperation between the United States and Iran to identify possible members of al-Qaida immediately after September 11, 2001, is an example of the second type. *See Iran Gave U.S. Help on Al Qaeda after 9/11*, CBS NEWS (Oct. 7, 2008), http://www.cbsnews.com/news/iran-gave-us-help-on-al-qaeda-after-9-11/.

states with which a state's IC works, whether on a one-off operation or in the context of a decades-long partnership. A peer IC can impose discipline or structural limits on the activities of its counterparts, including in ways that rely on or implicate the peer's domestic and international legal obligations.[3] Through various mechanisms (formal and informal, public and private), one state's IC can affect the way in which another IC conducts interrogation, detention, targeted killings, and surveillance; the amount and type of intelligence the other IC receives; and, less tangibly, how the other IC views its own legal obligations.[4] It is unsurprising that laws can constrain the IC to which they are directed. What is surprising, and what this chapter argues, is that the nature of IC relationships can lead to second-order effects that result in one state IC being constrained not only by its own domestic laws and rules, but also by the laws and legal interpretations of other states.

The idea of "peer constraints" intends to capture the limitations imposed on an IC in excess of those imposed by the IC's own laws. Measured against a baseline of an IC's domestic laws and regulations, peer constraints are those rules that increase the limits on the IC's operational flexibility. Another way to view the relationship between two ICs is as a series of transactions in which one IC "pays" for the other IC's cooperation. That "payment" sometimes takes the form of legal restrictions, which the first IC must accept if it wishes to complete the transaction. Even in the face of peer constraints, the first IC may be in a better overall position than if it were unable to obtain any peer cooperation. Nevertheless, the first IC is more fettered than it would be if operating alone, something that is increasingly rare.

These constraints complement the more public, transparent, and expected sources of oversight discussed elsewhere in this book, though they cannot replace them.[5] Indeed, peer constraints offer certain benefits that may be absent from other forms of oversight, including a granular understanding of operations, technologies, and techniques that outsiders lack, and an ability to minimize the politicization that frequently accompanies domestic critiques of ICs. Peer constraints are likely to become more prevalent as ICs face more law, more leaks,[6] and more litigation. As a result, it is important to understand when, where, and how these

---

[3] One scholar has argued that ICs may constrain each other based "almost exclusively" on shared professional ethos rather than law. Elizabeth Sepper, *Democracy, Human Rights, and Intelligence Sharing*, 46 TEX. INT'L L.J. 151 (2010). I argue that law itself can provide direct and indirect constraints in this context.

[4] We might think of these influences broadly as establishing "accountability": A is accountable to B when A is obliged to inform B about A's (past or future) actions and decisions, to justify them, and to suffer a penalty in the case of eventual misconduct. Andreas Schedler, *Conceptualizing Accountability*, in THE SELF-RESTRAINING STATE: POWER AND ACCOUNTABILITY IN NEW DEMOCRACIES 17 (Andreas Schedler et al. eds., 1999).

[5] This chapter assumes an inherent value in "oversight" in the broadest sense as a means to amplify legal compliance, minimize lawlessness, and foster a certain level of transparency, while recognizing that some forms of oversight can be ineffective or politicized. Ian Leigh, *More Closely Watching the Spies: Three Decades of Experiences*, in WHO'S WATCHING THE SPIES? 5–8 (Hans Born et al. eds., 2005).

[6] Thomas C. Bruneau & Kenneth R. Dombroski, *Reforming Intelligence: The Challenge of Control in New Democracies*, in WHO GUARDS THE GUARDIANS AND HOW: DEMOCRATIC CIVIL-MILITARY RELATIONS 163, 179 (Thomas C. Bruneau & Scott D. Tollefson eds., 2006) ("If the intelligence agencies know that in the future their files will be open for public scrutiny, they are logically more likely to keep a rein on the behavior of their members."). Declassification is one mechanism by which IC activities come to light, though many states set long time periods before they will declassify intelligence information. Leaks are another mechanism, and tend to reveal more recent information.

constraints can and do operate. Some have bemoaned the lack of oversight and account-ability surrounding liaison relationships.[7] This chapter tilts the prism to suggest that these relationships may in some cases impose peer constraints that result in increased individual rights protections and, at least among Western democracies, promote convergence around more restrictive substantive rules governing intelligence operations.

The idea that peer ICs can constrain each other undoubtedly will be met with some skep-ticism, especially in the wake of the U.S. Senate Select Committee on Intelligence (SSCI) report on the CIA's detention and interrogation program.[8] Some critics may acknowledge that peer ICs influence each other, but doubt that the influence pushes in a rights-protective direction. Others may argue that powerful states such as the United States need intelligence cooperation from their peers only on the margins, and easily can walk away from constraining peer pressure without incurring significant security costs. It is the goal of this chapter to iden-tify and explicate the ways in which peer mechanisms can and do impose real, though modest, constraints that produce more rights-protective behavior, notwithstanding those arguments.

II. COOPERATION AMONG INTELLIGENCE SERVICES

Before we explore how IC interactions can produce constraints, it is necessary to understand the contexts in which intelligence cooperation occurs. Although cooperation among ICs remains one of the most secret aspects of intelligence activity, it is possible to identify the basic reasons that state ICs cooperate and how they do so.[9] This section describes how and why ICs interact with each other, focusing on the increase in cooperation among ICs in the past decade.[10]

A. Why Intelligence Communities Interact

ICs interact because they must.[11] ICs inherently are secretive, driven to provide their own country with accurate information that allows their policymakers to make the best decisions for the country. If one IC had the capacity to obtain all of the intelligence it needed on its

---

[7] Sepper, *supra* note 3, at 169–72; Richard J. Aldrich, *International Intelligence Cooperation in Practice, in* INTERNATIONAL INTELLIGENCE COOPERATION AND ACCOUNTABILITY 252 (Hans Born et al. eds., 2011).

[8] For general critiques of intelligence liaison relationships, *see* Martin Scheinin & Mathias Vermeulen, *Human Rights Law and State Responsibility, in* INTERNATIONAL INTELLIGENCE COOPERATION AND ACCOUNTABILITY 18 (Born et al. eds., 2011); Sepper, *supra* note 3; Francesca Bignami, *Towards a Right to Privacy in Transnational Intelligence Networks*, 28 MICH. J. INT'L L. 663 (2007).

[9] Aldrich, *supra* note 7.

[10] *Id.* at 25 ("The most important change in the practice of intelligence since 1989 has been the exponential increase in complex intelligence cooperation.").

[11] For a basic discussion of the reasons that intelligence services collaborate, *see* Eric Rosenbach & Aki Peritz, *Confrontation or Collaboration?, in* INTELLIGENCE AND INTERNATIONAL COOPERATION (Belfer Center 2009), *available at* http://belfercenter.ksg.harvard.edu/files/international-cooperation.pdf. As evidence of the importance that the U.S. IC places on its foreign relationships, *see* Marc Ambinder, *The Real Intelligence Wars: Oversight and Access*, THE ATLANTIC, Nov. 18, 2009 (discussing fight between CIA and DNI for control over appointing senior intelligence representatives in foreign countries).

own, it would not need to turn to liaison services to obtain information. If one IC could conduct covert operations, unfettered, worldwide, that IC would not need to work with liaison services. But that is not the state of the world.

In practice, a single IC cannot obtain all the coverage it desires on its own, particularly as the sources of terrorism, transnational crime, and proliferation emanate from increasingly remote parts of the world.[12] Other services will have better linguists and more nuanced cultural understandings of geopolitics. Israel, for example, is skilled at monitoring situations in the Middle East.[13] The U.K. has history and expertise in South Asia, such that the intelligence it gathers in Afghanistan and Pakistan is in high demand.[14] Yet others have more nuanced understandings of local terror groups.[15] As Martin Rudner puts it, "All intelligence agencies enjoy certain comparative advantages. In some cases, these may derive from functional, tradecraft, or technical attribution . . . . In other instances the comparative advantage of intelligence agencies may derive from geography, where they enjoy a locational advantage, or from a socio-cultural affinity."[16]

Cooperating with foreign peers also allows ICs to share the cost and actual workload of processing information, and reduces physical risks to ICs that otherwise would be forced to operate in unfamiliar territory.[17] For example, the "Five Eyes" arrangement, first concluded between the United States and the U.K. in 1943 and later expanded to include Australia, New Zealand, and Canada, applies to communications intelligence. The arrangement provides for an exchange of intelligence personnel, joint regulations for handling the most sensitive material, and methods of and limits on distribution of shared intelligence.[18] It also allocates electronic surveillance collection among its members, recognizing that it is easier as a practical matter for some members to collect certain communications due to geographic proximity to the source.

---

[12] Aldrich, *supra* note 7, at 32.

[13] Marta Sparago, *The Global Intelligence Network: Issues in International Intelligence Cooperation*, 1 PERSPECTIVES ON GLOBAL ISSUES 1, 2 (2006), *available at* http://pgi.nyc/archive/vol-1-issue-1/The-Global-Intelligence-Network.pdf.

[14] Ravi Somaiya, *Drone Strike Lawsuit Raises Concerns on Intelligence Sharing*, N.Y. TIMES, Jan. 30, 2013.

[15] Dana Priest, *Foreign Network at Front of CIA's Terror Fight*, WASH. POST, Nov. 18, 2005 (describing "sometimes reluctant foreign intelligence services [that] had much more intimate knowledge of local terrorist groups and their supporters").

[16] Martin Rudner, *Hunters and Gatherers: The Intelligence Coalition against Islamic Terrorism*, 17 INT'L J. INTELLIGENCE & COUNTERINTELLIGENCE 193, 216 (2004).

[17] Charles Faddis, *Bin Ladin's Location Reveals Limits of Liaison Intelligence Relationships*, COMBATING TERRORISM CENTER AT WEST POINT 15, May 1, 2011 ("The attractions . . . are obvious: it is the officers of the foreign service who run the physical risk of meeting with often dangerous and unpredictable agents. There is no need to worry about language qualifications or other considerations involved with deploying American officers on the street. There are no dicey issues of national sovereignty to navigate and no danger of messy diplomatic flaps.").

[18] JAMES BAMFORD, THE PUZZLE PALACE: A REPORT ON AMERICA'S MOST SECRET AGENCY 391 (1982); JEFFREY RICHELSON & DESMOND BALL, THE TIES THAT BIND: INTELLIGENCE COOPERATION BETWEEN THE UNITED KINGDOM/UNITED STATES OF AMERICA COUNTRIES—UNITED KINGDOM, UNITED STATES OF AMERICA, CANADA, AUSTRALIA AND NEW ZEALAND 142–44 (1986).

This IC cooperation has increased with the rise of nonstate actors and globalization. Richard Aldrich has argued that states have increased cooperation among their ICs because of the need to address borderless problems such as financial instability, pandemics, and networked terrorist threats by nonstate actors.[19] As another scholar put it, "Detecting and assessing the so-called 'new threats' correctly requires increased intelligence cooperation between . . . agencies from different countries."[20] Threats to one state's security now can emanate from nonstate actors that are located in geographically remote locales, and small groups of such actors can inflict high levels of damage on state structures. As a result, states find themselves needing to cooperate with a wide group of states that may not be obvious partners.[21]

B. How Intelligence Communities Interact

Cooperation among ICs can take different forms, including exchanges of intelligence officials, intelligence information sharing, and intelligence operations sharing.[22] Within the category of intelligence information sharing, states may choose to allocate collection responsibilities among themselves, to share raw intelligence, or to share intelligence assessments.[23] The Five Eyes arrangement is a prime example of signals intelligence (SIGINT) information sharing. Many bilateral and multilateral intelligence exchanges occur, including between and among the Five Eyes member states and non-Five Eyes NATO countries, Japan, South Korea, and Israel.[24]

One example of intelligence operations sharing is Alliance Base, a joint center in Paris staffed by the CIA and intelligence services of France, the U.K., Germany, Canada, and Australia.[25] The ICs at Alliance Base plan and undertake joint counterterrorism operations in the field.[26] After September 11, the CIA reportedly also established joint operation centers in two dozen other countries, which serve to track and capture terrorists and disrupt al-Qaida's logistical and financial chains.[27] The goal of these "counterterrorist intelligence centers" is to empower foreign ICs to help the United States combat al-Qaida.[28] Another example is the reported rendition of Abu Omar from Italy to Egypt (which involved operational coordination between U.S. and Italian ICs). Stuxnet, a computer worm introduced into computers at an Iranian nuclear facility to damage its centrifuges, reportedly was a joint

---

[19] Aldrich, *supra* note 7, at 19; *see also id.* at 21 (describing cooperation among "improbable partners").

[20] Björn Müller-Wille, *For Our Eyes Only? Shaping an Intelligence Community within the EU* 5 (Eur. Union Inst. Sec. Studies, Occasional Paper No. 50, 2004).

[21] *See, e.g.*, John Davis, *Vital Cog: African Intelligence Efforts and the War on Terrorism, in* TERRORISM IN AFRICA: THE EVOLVING FRONT IN THE WAR ON TERROR 225 (John Davis ed., 2010) (describing U.S. intelligence relationships with Morocco, Algeria, and Kenya).

[22] Aldrich, *supra* note 7, at 22 n.13 (quoting H. Bradford Westerfield, *America and the World of Intelligence Liaison*, 11 INTELLIGENCE & NAT'L SEC. 523 (1996)).

[23] RICHELSON & BALL, *supra* note 18, at 135.

[24] *Id.* at 170.

[25] Aldrich, *supra* note 7, at 31.

[26] *Id.*; Dana Priest, *Help from France Key in Covert Operations*, WASH. POST, July 3, 2005.

[27] Priest, *supra* note 15.

[28] *Id.*

operation between the United States and Israel.[29] The United States and Israel also apparently cooperated in 2008 to kill Hezbollah operative Imad Mughniyeh.[30]

These are just some of the forms that informational and operational cooperation can take. What is important is that such interactions occur frequently among various sets of states, and often involve direct contacts between officials in peer ICs.

III. DRIVERS OF PEER CONSTRAINTS

Peer constraints are not new. As long as ICs have felt compelled to act consistent with the legal strictures that govern them (as most democratic services will), those ICs have had the need—and capacity—to impose constraints on the other ICs with which they cooperate. So why give more attention or credence to peer constraints today? Are there reasons to think that constraints operate more robustly today than they have in the past? This section identifies three phenomena that, both independently and interdependently, have conditioned the overall political and legal environment in which ICs now operate. A combination of leaks about IC programs, litigation challenging those programs, and a growing body of law to apply to IC programs has created a situation in which states and their ICs face increased pressures (for legal, political, or economic reasons) to constrain each other.

All of these developments are happening in the context of the changing nature of the security threats that many states face. The shifting focus of ICs to nonstate actors and the electronic collection of communications of many private citizens because of the changing structure of international telecommunications networks triggers—for many states—the potential relevance of more domestic and international laws in a way that increases the prevalence and power of peer constraints. In much of the discussion below, I focus on the United States, but many other states (particularly Western democracies) are subject to similar pressures.

A. Leaks and Other Disclosures

Edward Snowden's leaks of U.S. National Security Agency (NSA) information continue to reveal significant amounts of highly classified information about U.S. and foreign electronic surveillance programs. The leaks illustrated the extent to which the United States and other states spy on the communications of each other's leaders.[31] The leaks also contained information about NSA programs that collected massive amounts of telecommunications and internet information from average citizens, both U.S. and foreign.[32] Although revelations about the NSA have dominated the headlines, the United States is hardly the only state that engages in clandestine data collection on foreign citizens. Disclosures have come to light about bulk collection by France, Germany, Belgium, Sweden, and the U.K.[33]

---

[29] Ellen Nakashima & Joby Warrick, *Stuxnet Was Work of U.S. and Israeli Experts, Officials Say*, WASH. POST, June 2, 2012.

[30] Adam Goldman & Ellen Nakashima, *CIA and Mossad Killed Senior Hezbollah Figure in Car Bombing*, WASH. POST, Jan. 30, 2015.

[31] James Glanz & Andrew Lehren, *N.S.A. Spied on Allies, Aid Groups and Businesses*, N.Y. TIMES, Dec. 20, 2013.

[32] Barton Gellman & Ashkan Soltani, *NSA Surveillance Program Reaches "Into the Past" to Retrieve, Replay Phone Calls*, WASH. POST, Mar. 18, 2014.

[33] Adam Entous & Siobhan Gorman, *Europeans Shared Spy Data with U.S.*, WALL ST. J., Oct. 29, 2013; Steve Erlanger, *France, Too, Is Sweeping Up Data, Newspaper Reveals*, N.Y. TIMES, July 4, 2013; Gregor Peter Schmitz,

Though the Snowden leaks have occupied the spotlight for the past year, there have been many other disclosures in the past decade about secret or covert intelligence programs. For example, leaks from within the U.S. government revealed that President George W. Bush authorized the CIA to use lethal force against members of al-Qaida[34] and to undertake covert action against Iran to destabilize its government.[35] Some of the revelations appear to have been authorized by the U.S. executive branch itself, as when former CIA director Leon Panetta revealed shortly after the U.S. action in Pakistan that killed Osama bin Laden that the United States had undertaken the raid as a covert action.[36] Disclosures of this sort are relevant as state ICs consider whether and how to cooperate with each other, aware that their cooperation may come to light in the future.

Further, the media, human rights groups, and other private actors have uncovered on their own intelligence activities that have produced real-world effects on the ground—and, by virtue of ease of Internet communications, made these discoveries widely known. These intelligence operations include Stuxnet, a computer worm that destroyed about a thousand Iranian nuclear centrifuges. Computer scientists discovered the worm when it spread to computers outside of Iran.[37] Another example is the work of European parliamentarians and rights groups to track alleged CIA "'rendition' flights" throughout Europe.[38] Journalists and nongovernmental organizations have investigated targeted killings in Yemen and Somalia, something made easier by virtue of the fact that drone strikes—unlike, say, efforts to recruit foreign assets—produce visible physical effects.[39] These reports highlight previously unknown aspects of intelligence activities.

Sometimes the revealed activities are relatively uncontroversial, at least domestically. For instance, few U.S. citizens are likely to object if the United States puts pressure on the Iranian

---

Belgian Prime Minister Angry at Claims of British Spying, SPIEGEL ONLINE INT'L (Sept. 20, 2013), http://www. spiegel.de/international/europe/belgian-prime-minister-angry-at-claims-of-british-spying-a-923583.html; Benjamin Wittes, *Mark Klamberg on EU Metadata Collection*, LAWFARE (Sept. 29, 2013 1:03 PM), http://www. lawfareblog.com/2013/09/mark-klamberg-on-eu-metadata-collection/; Spencer Ackerman & James Ball, *Optic Nerve: Millions of Yahoo Webcam Images Intercepted by GCHQ*, GUARDIAN (U.K.), Feb. 28, 2014; Ewen MacAskill, *GCHQ Taps Fibre-Optic Cables for Secret Access to World's Communications*, GUARDIAN (U.K.), June 21, 2013. *See generally* IRA RUBINSTEIN, GREG NOJEIM & RONALD LEE, SYSTEMATIC GOVERNMENT ACCESS TO PERSONAL DATA: A COMPARATIVE ANALYSIS 14, 15 (CTR. FOR DEMOCRACY & TECH. 2013); Christopher Wolf, Prepared Testimony Before the Privacy and Civil Liberties Board: A Transnational Perspective on Section 702 of the Foreign Intelligence Surveillance Act (Mar. 19, 2014), https://www.pclob. gov/library/20140319-Testimony-Wolf.pdf.

[34] Tara McKelvey, *Inside the Killing Machine*, NEWSWEEK, Feb. 13, 2011 (describing interview with former CIA lawyer regarding targeted killing covert action).

[35] Brian Ross & Richard Esposito, *Bush Authorizes New Covert Action against Iran*, ABC NEWS (May 24, 2007), http://blogs.abcnews.com/theblotter/2007/05/bush_authorizes.html (describing covert action finding authorizing CIA to use propaganda, disinformation, and currency manipulation to pressure Iranian regime).

[36] *Panetta: Obama Made "Gutsy" Decision on Bin Laden Raid*, PBS NEWSHOUR (May 3, 2011), http://www.pbs. org/newshour/bb/terrorism-jan-june11-panetta_05-03/.

[37] David Sanger, *Obama Order Sped Up Wave of Cyberattacks against Iran*, N.Y. TIMES, June 1, 2013.

[38] Dick Marty, *Alleged Secret Detentions and Unlawful Inter-State Transfers involving Council of Europe Member States*, REPORT TO PARL. ASS., Doc. 10957 (2006), *available at* http://assembly.coe.int/committeedocs/ 2006/20060606_ejdoc162006partii-final.pdf.

[39] Part of this program may have come about as a result of information leaked or planted by U.S. government officials, whether in response to prior discoveries by journalists or proactively. *See* David Pozen, *The Leaky*

government using non-lethal tools. Other activities have prompted far more concern, because some of these IC activities directly implicate individual privacy and, occasionally, life and liberty.[40] In the face of these newly disclosed programs, members of the U.S. and foreign publics, foreign leaders, corporations, and civil liberties groups have pressured Congress and the executive branch to terminate or limit some of these activities. The U.K. and Australia face similar pressures.[41] Indeed, a relatively unusual alignment of interests has formed among corporations, elite opinion, and many "ordinary citizens"—all of whom are pressuring states to impose greater regulations on IC activities.[42]

B. Litigation

Relatedly, leaks and other disclosures about IC programs foster litigation. The more that is confirmed or alleged about intelligence programs, the greater the opportunity for those who oppose those programs to initiate litigation to halt or alter them.

In the past 10 years, many plaintiffs have challenged the legality in U.S. and European courts of different forms of IC activity. This contemporary role for courts stands in contrast to the highly cabined role they historically have played in overseeing ICs.[43] Recently in the United States, an individual who had been subject to rendition sued a CIA contractor, alleging that the company flew rendition flights on the CIA's behalf.[44] The father of a U.S. citizen placed on a secret, lethal targeting list sued the U.S. government, seeking to have a court declare that his son could be killed only in a limited set of circumstances.[45] And a U.S. criminal defendant argued that one of the NSA's programs, which provided the source of certain evidence against him, was unconstitutional.[46] In the U.K., a former Guantanamo detainee

---

Leviathan: Why the Government Condemns and Condones Unlawful Disclosures of Information, 127 Harv. L. Rev. 512, 560 (2013).

[40] *See* Aldrich, *supra* note 7, at 20 (describing intelligence operations today as "more kinetic and more controversial"); *id.* at 31 (describing ICs as moving beyond passive intelligence gathering to "fixing, enforcing and disruption"); The Report of the Detainee Inquiry 5.7 (2013), *available at* http://www.detaineeinquiry.org. uk/wp-content/uploads/2013/12/35100_Trafalgar-Text-accessible.pdf [hereinafter U.K. Detention Report] (reciting SIS assertion that before 2001, as a result of lack of prior operational need, U.K. SIS was not experienced in interviewing detainees in the field). Compare developments in the military field. In the 25 years after Vietnam, many U.S. military engagements involved "closer-than-usual contact with civilians and raised hard law-of-war issues—especially about detention, interrogation, and rules of engagement—that lawyers were vital in sorting out." Goldsmith, *supra* note 1, at 127. As IC activities involve (and are understood to involve) "closer-than-usual contact with civilians," it should not be surprising that IC lawyers assume an increasingly important role in helping operators navigate the laws. *Id.*

[41] Sam Ball, *UK Approves Mass Surveillance as Privacy Battle Continues*, France 24, Dec. 7, 2014, http://www. france24.com/en/20141207-uk-tribunal-approves-mass-surveillance-privacy-battle-continues-gchq-snowden; Ewen MacAskill & Lenore Taylor, *Australia's Spy Agencies Targeted Indonesian President's Mobile Phone*, Guardian (U.K.), Nov. 17, 2013.

[42] Ashley Deeks, *An International Legal Framework for Surveillance*, 55 Va. J. Int'l L. 291 (2015). The extent to which these pressures will result in meaningful changes to domestic or international laws remains to be seen.

[43] Goldsmith, *supra* note 1, at 84 ("The courts played no role in monitoring CIA activities" during Allen Dulles's time as CIA Director from 1953 to 1961.).

[44] Mohamed v. Jeppesen Dataplan, 614 F.3d 1070 (9th Cir. 2010) (en banc).

[45] Al-Aulaqi v. Obama, 727 F. Supp. 2d 1 (D.D.C. 2010).

[46] United States v. Muhtorov, Case No. 12-cr-00033-JLK-1 (D. Colo. 2014).

challenged the legality of U.K. intelligence activities, claiming the U.K. had provided information to the United States with which it questioned him using harsh interrogation techniques.[47] Another U.K. court recently allowed an individual to proceed with his claim that U.K. intelligence services, along with the CIA, rendered him to the Libyan government, which he alleges tortured him.[48]

Savvy plaintiffs have turned to foreign courts when they have failed to achieve victories in their own domestic courts. As Jack Goldsmith writes, "When the [Center for Constitutional Rights] failed to achieve what it viewed as adequate accountability for Bush administration officials in the United States in connection with detention and interrogation practices, it started pursuing, and continues to pursue, lawsuits and prosecutions against U.S. officials in Spain, Germany, and other European countries."[49] No doubt private plaintiffs (and possibly foreign states themselves) will attempt to use European courts to raise claims against individuals involved in the CIA's interrogation program.[50]

Plaintiffs also have turned to international courts. The European Court of Human Rights (ECtHR) held in *El Masri v. Macedonia* that Macedonia was responsible for the ill treatment of a German national allegedly detained by the CIA in Macedonia and rendered to Afghanistan.[51] The Court found that Macedonia violated Articles 3 (prohibition on torture and degrading treatment) and 5 (right to liberty and security) of the European Convention on Human Rights (ECHR) in cooperating with the United States. In a separate case, the ECtHR held that Poland violated the rights of two detainees who the CIA allegedly held and mistreated in secret detention facilities in Poland.[52]

Finally, several states have conducted criminal investigations or prosecutions surrounding intelligence activities, including prosecutions of a number of U.S. intelligence and military officials in Italy for allegedly rendering a radical sheikh from Milan to Egypt.[53] A German prosecutor investigated whether NSA tapped Angela Merkel's cell phone, but has not initiated a case.[54]

Although plaintiffs have hardly won all of their cases, they have won some. For example, as noted above, the ECtHR held that Macedonia violated the ECHR when it facilitated

---

[47] R v. Sec'y of State for Foreign & Commonwealth Affairs, [2010] EWCA (Civ) 65, [2010] 3 W.L.R. 554, [14] (Eng.). The U.K. settled the case. *Government to Compensate Ex-Guantanamo Bay Detainees*, BBC NEWS (Nov. 16, 2010), http://www.bbc.com/news/uk-11762636.

[48] Owen Bowcott, *Abdel Hakim Belhaj Wins Right to Sue UK Government over His Kidnap*, GUARDIAN (U.K.), Oct. 30, 2014.

[49] GOLDSMITH, *supra* note 1, at 199.

[50] Sophia Pearson, Christie Smythe & Joel Rosenblatt, *CIA Officials Linked to Torture Face Possible Prosecution, Future Stuck in U.S.*, BLOOMBERG (Dec. 11, 2014), http://www.bloomberg.com/news/articles/2014-12-11/torture-linked-cia-officials-face-future-stuck-on-u-s-; *UN Counterterrorism Expert Says U.S. Officials Must Be Prosecuted for CIA Torture*, CBC NEWS (Dec. 10, 2014), http://www.cbc.ca/news/world/un-counterterrorism-expert-says-u-s-officials-must-be-prosecuted-for-cia-torture-1.2866895.

[51] FACTSHEET: SECRET DETENTION SITES, EUR. CT. H.R., July 2014, *available at* http://www.echr.coe.int/Documents/FS_Secret_detention_ENG.PDF (describing case of El-Masri v. Macedonia).

[52] *Id.* (describing cases of Al Nashiri v. Poland and Abu Zubaydah v. Poland).

[53] Craig Whitlock, *Testimony Helps Detail CIA's Post-9/11 Reach*, WASH. POST, Dec. 16, 2006, at A1.

[54] Alexandra Hudson, *No Proof So Far That NSA Bugged Merkel's Phone: Prosecutor*, REUTERS (Dec. 11, 2014), http://www.reuters.com/article/2014/12/11/us-germany-usa-spying-idUSKBN0JP1QG20141211.

the transfer of Khaled el Masri to U.S. custody.[55] Binyam Mohamed's civil case in the U.K. prompted the House of Lords to order the U.K. government to publicly reveal evidence describing what the U.K. knew about Mohamed's treatment while in CIA custody.[56] When the results of litigation produce court decisions revealing and restricting IC activity, this alters the legal landscape within which those ICs are operating.[57] This means there is both new law to apply and a public focus on how the ICs are applying that law.

Disclosures of information about IC activities directly affect the availability of litigation as an option, because the disclosures may alter courts' assessments of jurisdictional issues such as standing, and privileges such as the State Secrets Privilege. Consider, for example, the changing analysis of standing in a series of cases challenging certain electronic surveillance allegedly conducted by the U.S. government under the Foreign Intelligence Surveillance Act.[58] In *Clapper v. Amnesty International*, decided before the Snowden leaks, the Supreme Court concluded that the plaintiffs, who claimed that NSA's surveillance was unconstitutional, lacked standing to challenge Section 702 of the FISA Amendments Act because their claims were too speculative.[59] After the Snowden leaks, in similar cases brought by plaintiffs against the NSA challenging its use of Section 215 of the PATRIOT Act, two federal courts found that comparable sets of plaintiffs had standing because the NSA's collection under Section 215 covered virtually all phone calls that passed through U.S. telecommunications providers.[60] Although the programs considered by the Supreme Court and the lower federal courts are distinct, it seems likely that the lower courts would have followed the Supreme Court's standing analysis in *Clapper* to dispose of the cases before them, but for the Snowden disclosures.[61] The Second Circuit ultimately held on the merits that Section 215 did not authorize the type of collection the U.S. government had undertaken.[62]

Finally, litigation is a way for plaintiffs to try to force the government *itself* directly to disclose certain classified information about its IC programs. Through statutes such as the U.S. Freedom of Information Act (FOIA),[63] plaintiffs seek information about intelligence

---

[55] El Masri v. the Former Yugoslav Republic of Macedonia, App. No. 39630/09 Eur. Ct. H.R. 65-66 (Dec. 13, 2012), http://hudoc.echr.coe.int/sites/eng/pages/search.aspx?i=001-115621#{"itemid":["001-115621"]}.

[56] Richard Norton-Taylor, *Binyam Torture Evidence Must Be Revealed, Judges Rule*, GUARDIAN (U.K.), Feb. 10, 2010.

[57] Cases such as this also shape the broader political and operational environment: in the wake of the *Mohamed* case, the United States reportedly slowed its sharing of sensitive information with the U.K. David Stringer, *Intelligence Ties between UK and US in Jeopardy*, ASSOCIATED PRESS, Feb. 11, 2010.

[58] Foreign Intelligence Surveillance Act, 50 U.S.C. §§ 1801–1885c (1978).

[59] Clapper v. Amnesty Int'l, 133 S. Ct. 1138 (2013).

[60] Klayman v. Obama, 957 F. Supp. 2d 1 (D.D.C. 2013) (holding that plaintiffs had standing to challenge NSA's bulk telephony metadata collection because their fear of being surveilled was not merely speculative); ACLU v. Clapper, 959 F. Supp. 2d 724, 738 (S.D.N.Y. 2013) ("Here, there is no dispute the Government collected telephony metadata related to the ACLU's telephone calls. Thus, the standing requirement is satisfied.").

[61] The plaintiffs in *ACLU v. Clapper* filed their case less than a week after Snowden leaked the Secondary Order of the FISA Court, which revealed the nature and scope of the NSA's Section 215 telephony metadata program (at least as it related to Verizon). See *Clapper*, 959 F. Supp. 2d at 735. The leaks therefore seem to be the direct cause of the litigation.

[62] ACLU v. Clapper, 785 F.3d 787 (2d Cir. 2015).

[63] 5 U.S.C. § 552 (2012).

activities, ranging from detention and interrogation to targeted killings.[64] In a number of U.S. cases, advocacy groups and journalists successfully have persuaded courts to order the government to release more than 150,000 pages of previously classified documents that revealed extensive information about intelligence programs.[65] Although plaintiffs have used FOIA for many years to seek information about intelligence, the recent leaks about activities undertaken by ICs mean there are more programs about which individuals can file FOIA requests.[66]

In short, litigation reflects an increasing interest in using the courts to cabin certain intelligence activities, and is altering the internal dynamics of ICs that are affected by the fact of litigation generally and by adverse court holdings in particular.

C. Legalization

The litigation just described leads to new case law that regulates ICs. But disclosures about intelligence activities also prompt nonjudicial actors to impose new rules on ICs directly, either through legislation or executive regulation. On the international plane, these same disclosures stimulate claims and counterclaims among states, which often use the substance and language of international law. This section argues that ICs have become increasingly legalized—that is, infused with law—in the past decade, predominately in terms of increased domestic regulation but also in terms of increasing international regulation.

1. Domestic Law

The number of legal officers within the CIA grew from 8 in the mid-1970s to approximately 150 in 2010.[67] Accompanying that rise in numbers came a shift in mindset: "the CIA legal staff . . . transformed itself from being indifferent to the law to being preoccupied by it."[68] Goldsmith further describes the "scores of legal restrictions on the executive branch" that are enforced by that "bevy of lawyers."[69] By way of example, "Presidential [covert action] findings in the early 1980s used to be very short, but now they are typically many pages long, full of . . . lawyerly caveats 'written for the front page of the New York Times' because of expected leaks."[70] This proposition illustrates the connection between the proliferation of leaks and the expanding legalization of ICs.

---

[64] ACLU v. Dep't of Defense, 351 F. Supp. 2d 265 (S.D.N.Y. 2005) (granting significant parts of plaintiff's request related to detention and interrogation); *N.Y. Times v. U.S. Dep't of Justice*, 756 F.3d 100 (2d Cir. 2014) (ordering government to release portion of OLC memorandum on targeted killings).

[65] GOLDSMITH, *supra* note 1, at 116 ("The rise of well-resourced advocacy groups that scrutinize government national security actions . . . is one of the great accountability innovations of the past decade.").

[66] U.S. DEP'T OF JUSTICE, SUMMARY OF AGENCY CHIEF FOIA OFFICER REPORTS FOR 2013 1 (2014), *available at* http://www.justice.gov/sites/default/files/oip/legacy/2014/07/23/2013-cfo-assessment.pdf (stating that the U.S. government faces ever-increasing numbers of FOIA requests).

[67] GOLDSMITH, *supra* note 1, at 87.

[68] *Id.*

[69] *Id.* at 107.

[70] *Id.* at 89.

Professor Margo Schlanger recently has written about a comparable phenomenon within the NSA, which she identifies as increased "intelligence legalism."[71] Three developments have produced this legalism: an increased number of substantive rules regulating NSA, some court enforcement of those rules, and empowerment of lawyers within the government.[72] Each of these developments reinforces the others: as the number of rules expands, the need for lawyers to help interpret and apply those rules grows; as the number of lawyers and their role grow, the lawyers become more powerful players within the IC; and as courts enforce the rules, both the lawyers and the operators will be increasingly attuned to law as a guiding principle for their actions.[73]

ICs outside the United States also have faced increased regulation in the past 15 years. In the U.K., the Regulation of Investigatory Powers Act 2000 structures the way in which public actors in the U.K. may conduct surveillance (including communications intercepts), investigations, and the use of covert intelligence sources.[74] Canada's 2001 Anti-Terrorism Act regulates the Communications Security Establishment of Canada (the NSA equivalent) and its collection operations. Australia's 2001 Intelligence Services Act provides a statutory basis for the Australian Secret Intelligence Service and Defence Signals Directorate, and imposes requirements of ministerial authorization and parliamentary oversight.[75] In short, since 2000 the intelligence-related statutes of these states have become increasingly detailed.[76]

The growing role for lawyers in U.K. intelligence operations becomes apparent in oversight reports related to rendition, interrogation, and detention. The U.K. Parliament's Intelligence

---

[71] Margo Schlanger, *Intelligence Legalism and the National Security Agency's Civil Liberties Gap*, 6 HARV. NAT'L SEC. J. 112 (2015).

[72] Schlanger bemoans this intelligence legalism on the grounds that it allows policymakers to avoid difficult decisions about whether a given policy is actually the most desirable one from a rights/security perspective. *Id.* at 185–86. I take no view on whether the domestic laws making their way into peer constraints strike the correct policy balance, though virtually all of the domestic laws discussed here reflect a shift toward a more rights-protective approach.

[73] *See, e.g.*, William Hague, Foreign Secretary, Statement to the House of Commons (June 10, 2013) (quoting U.K. Intelligence Services Commissioner's belief that "GCHQ staff conduct themselves with the highest levels of integrity and legal compliance"); President Obama, Remarks by the President on Review of Signals Intelligence (Jan. 17, 2014) [hereinafter Obama NSA Speech] ("[N]othing that I have learned since indicated that our intelligence community has sought to violate the law or is cavalier about the civil liberties of their fellow citizens."). *But see, e.g.*, Iain Cameron, *Beyond the Nation State: The Influence of the European Court of Human Rights on Intelligence Accountability, in* WHO'S WATCHING THE SPIES? 36 (Hans Born et al. eds., 2005) ("It is evident that in this area the law can serve, and has on occasion served, as a façade, concealing more or less serious divergences in practice.").

[74] Regulation of Investigatory Powers Act, 2000, c. 23 (U.K.) [hereinafter RIPA]. RIPA itself was a reaction to a 1997 decision of the European Court of Human Rights. *See* Halford v. United Kingdom, App. No. 20605/92, 24 Eur. H.R. Rep. 523 (1997). The 1989 Security Services Act apparently responded to the fact that the ECtHR had shown a "pronounced distaste for the British habit of relying on unregulated administrative discretion in matters affecting individual rights." Ian Leigh & Laurence Lustgarten, *The Security Service Act 1989*, 52 MODERN L. REV. 801, 803 (1989).

[75] *Intelligence Services Act* 2001 (Cth) (Austl.).

[76] *See* Aldrich, *supra* note 7, at 35 ("In the 1990s, the European intelligence services went through a regulatory revolution during which many services were given a legal identity and in some cases the European Convention on Human Rights was written into their core guidance.").

and Security Committee's (ISC's) Report on Rendition described how operators receive legal briefings on both domestic and international law to ensure that U.K. intelligence does not result in torture or mistreatment by other ICs.[77] The U.K. Detention Report revealed that in 2006 the U.K. Security Service (the FBI equivalent) and the Secret Intelligence Service (SIS) (the CIA equivalent) issued guidance about liaison relationships, recommending when to consult the Service's Legal Advisors.[78] The guidance also advised SIS officers involved in detainee operations to seek legal advice when sharing the location of a person of interest with peer services or receiving information from a peer service that is detaining someone of interest.[79]

In short, ICs have more domestic law to apply, and more lawyers to help the relevant agencies apply it. Just as militaries increasingly involve their lawyers in on-the-ground decision-making about targeting and detention, so too do ICs now rely more heavily on their lawyers to provide guidance that affects the nature, scope, and operation of intelligence programs.[80] This development makes particular sense in light of the fact that ICs increasingly are being asked to perform functions that have military aspects to them. Just as military judge advocates general now are fully incorporated into military operational decision-making, so too should we expect IC lawyers to begin to play a larger role in navigating comparable intelligence operations.

2. International Law

At the same time that ICs face extensive domestic regulatory regimes, they also are beginning to face persistent legal claims derived from a different source: international law. Particularly in the wake of the Snowden leaks, states and other actors claim that certain intelligence activities violate different aspects of international law. Some states and scholars now understand that the activities that some ICs are undertaking—bulk collection of telephonic and Internet communications, detention, interrogation, and targeted killings—affect private individuals (who are not associated with governments) in ways that earlier forms of intelligence activity did not. After all, ICs play a larger role than before in taking forcible actions against individual nonstate actors, including during armed conflicts.[81] Critics have argued that existing

---

[77] INTELLIGENCE AND SECURITY COMMITTEE, RENDITION 53 (2007) [hereinafter ISC Rendition Report].

[78] U.K. Detention Report, *supra* note 40, at 5.73.

[79] *Id.* at 5.83.

[80] GOLDSMITH, *supra* note 1, at 224 ("War has become hyper-legalized, and legality has become the global currency of legitimacy for military and intelligence action."); *id.* at 230 (noting that all significant military and intelligence actions have elaborate, law-heavy pre-clearance processes); Aldrich, *supra* note 7, at 35–36 (ICs spend extensive time arguing with their lawyers before conducting operations.).

[81] Aldrich, *supra* note 7, at 20 (describing intelligence operations today as "more kinetic and more controversial"); U.K. Detention Report, *supra* note 40, at 5.7 (reciting SIS assertion that as a result of lack of prior operational need, before 2001 U.K. SIS was not experienced in interviewing detainees in the field); *id.* at 5.49 (describing how U.K. provided guidance to their IC on Geneva Conventions, based on guidance for U.K. armed forces); INTELLIGENCE AND SECURITY COMMITTEE, REPORT ON THE HANDLING OF DETAINEES BY UK INTELLIGENCE PERSONNEL IN AFGHANISTAN, GUANTANAMO BAY AND IRAQ ¶ 89 (2005) [hereinafter ISC Detention Report] ("'For [the U.K.'s] civilian experts, this was not a new business; . . . I think it is true to say that on this occasion they were closer to the front line, they were more intimately involved with the interrogation process than was our experience in the past.'" (quoting the Chief of Defence Intelligence)).

international laws, many of which traditionally rarely had been read to regulate or prohibit spying or covert action, restrict those intelligence activities. Call this the "repurposing" of international law for ICs.

Claims that intelligence activities violate international law fall into four categories. First, various actors allege that bulk electronic surveillance violates the right to privacy contained in the International Covenant on Civil and Political Rights (and, for states parties to the Council of Europe, the ECHR).[82] Until recently, few had considered whether and how governmental electronic surveillance implicated those human rights protections.[83] Second, states have asserted that spying—particularly, electronic surveillance—from within embassies violates the Vienna Convention on Diplomatic Relations.[84] For example, Germany's Foreign Ministry summoned the U.K.'s ambassador to Germany to seek an explanation about reports that the U.K. was spying on Germany from within its embassy in Berlin. The Germany Ministry "indicated that tapping communications from a diplomatic mission would be a violation of international law."[85] Third, states argue that activities ranging from targeted killings to electronic surveillance violate customary international law norms of sovereignty and territorial integrity.[86] Fourth, ICs suddenly find themselves operating not only

---

[82] *Brazilian President Blasts U.S. for Spying*, XINHUA (Sept. 24, 2013), http://news.xinhuanet.com/english/world/2013-09/25/c_125440237.htm; *see also* Tom Risen, *Brazil's President Tells U.N. That NSA Spying Violates Human Rights*, U.S. NEWS (Sept. 24, 2013), http://www.usnews.com/news/articles/2013/09/24/brazils-president-tells-un-that-nsa-spying-violates-human-rights; Ryan Gallagher, *After Snowden Leaks, Countries Want Digital Privacy Enshrined in Human Rights Treaty*, SLATE.COM (Sept. 26, 2013 2:16 PM), http://www.slate.com/blogs/future_tense/2013/09/26/article_17_surveillance_update_countries_want_digital_privacy_in_the_iccpr.html (describing Germany's efforts to clarify that the ICCPR applied to electronic privacy); David Cole, *We Are All Foreigners: NSA Spying and the Rights of Others*, JUST SECURITY (Oct. 29, 2013 12:48 PM), http://justsecurity.org/2668/foreigners-nsa-spying-rights/; Martin Scheinin, *Letter to the Editor*, JUST SECURITY (Mar. 10, 2014 10:32 AM), http://justsecurity.org/8049/letter-editor-martin-scheinin/ (arguing that ICCPR Article 17 applies extraterritorially to regulate a state's surveillance of foreign nationals); Amnesty International, *Amnesty International Takes UK Government to European Court of Human Rights over Mass Surveillance*, Apr. 10, 2015, https://www.amnesty.org/en/latest/news/2015/04/amnesty-international-takes-uk-government-to-european-court-of-human-rights-over-mass-surveillance/.

[83] LAURA PITTER, COMMENTS OF HUMAN RIGHTS WATCH: PRIVACY AND CIVIL LIBERTIES OVERSIGHT BOARD HEARING 8 (2014) (implicitly recognizing lack of clarity in law when stating that "[c]oncepts of jurisdiction based on control over territory and persons . . . can and should adapt to the reality of mass digital surveillance . . . .").

[84] *Pakistan Lodges Protest against U.S. Surveillance*, KUWAIT NEWS AGENCY (July 4, 2014), http://www.kuna.net.kw/ArticleDetails.aspx?id=2385965&language=en (quoting Pakistan Foreign Office release as stating, "The US Embassy in Islamabad was conveyed today that [reported U.S. surveillance] against Pakistani government departments or other organizations, entities and individuals is not in accord with international law and recognized diplomatic conduct.").

[85] *Germany Calls in British Ambassador over Spying Reports*, DEUTSCHE WELLE BLOG (Nov. 5, 2013), http://www.dw.de/germany-calls-in-british-ambassador-over-spying-reports/a-17204342 (quoting British ambassador Simon McDonald); Barbara Miller, *Berlin Calls in British Ambassador over Spying Reports*, ABC (Nov. 5, 2013), http://www.abc.net.au/?WT.z_navMenu=abcNavLogo&WT.z_srcSite=news&WT.z_link=ABC%20Home.

[86] Qasim Nauman & Safdar Dawar, *U.S. Drone Strike in Pakistan Killed Senior Afghan Militant, Others*, WALL ST. J., June 12, 2014; Press Release, General Assembly, Third Committee Approves Text Titled "Right to Privacy in the Digital Age," U.N. Press Release GA/SHC/4094 (Nov. 26, 2013), *available at* http://www.un.org/News/

in peacetime (e.g., CIA operatives trying to acquire human intelligence on the Kremlin's plans for Russia's nuclear arsenal) but also in wartime (e.g., the CIA undertaking targeted killings or detentions of members of al-Qaida, with which the United States has concluded that it is in an armed conflict). In war, the laws of armed conflict apply.[87]

Although the underlying international rules have long existed, states historically have invoked those norms only occasionally to contest spying activities. Only recently can we see a systemic push to apply these existing norms more aggressively and with greater specificity to IC activities.[88] We thus can identify both domestic *and* international "intelligence legalism."[89]

Leaks, litigation, and the increasing applicability of legal rules are exposing the nature of IC activities that previously remained secret or were deniable, raising questions about the legitimacy of IC activities performed in the name of democratic states, and rendering more law directly applicable to IC activities. As a result, more ICs come to their liaison relationships with law on their mind, and more ICs are positioned, by choice or necessity, to constrain their peers.

IV. MECHANISMS OF PEER CONSTRAINTS

There are at least three types of mechanisms by which peer constraints can and do occur: formalized constraints, informal constraints, and public critiques. Although distinct mechanisms, in practice they bleed into and complement each other. Constraints among peer ICs stem from at least two sources. One source of constraints is endogenous to ICs themselves: the communities collectively establish professional rules and norms to guide their own interactions.[90] These norms may do significant work to constrain, but are not necessarily driven by or shaped around legal considerations. A second source of constraints—and the one on which this chapter focuses—is exogenous to ICs. The origins of exogenous constraints are found in law, policy, and oversight. The changing legal landscape in a particular state will affect the conduct of that state's IC. This process, in turn, may cause peer ICs to change their behavior.

Press/docs/2013/gashc4094.doc.htm (Indonesia claiming that extraterritorial surveillance violates the UN Charter, which contains the norms of territorial integrity and sovereignty).

[87] U.K. Detention Report, *supra* note 40, at 5.49 (describing how U.K. IC was briefed on Geneva Conventions); *id.* at 5.100–01 (describing how SIS staff dealing with detainees received training that included a strong emphasis on legal/human rights issues, and how SIS officers received, before deploying to Iraq, were briefed on Geneva Conventions, NATO agreements, and the law of armed conflict).

[88] The U.K. IC receives a comprehensive legal briefing that addresses the responsibilities of IC staff under U.K. law and U.K. responsibilities under international law. ISC Rendition Report, *supra* note 77, ¶ 174.

[89] Schlanger, *supra* note 71, at 117 (describing domestic "intelligence legalism").

[90] *See* Sepper, *supra* note 3, at 159; Peter Haas, *Introduction: Epistemic Communities and International Policy Coordination*, 46 INT'L ORG. 1, 3 (1992) (defining epistemic community as a group of professionals with shared normative and principled beliefs, shared causal beliefs, shared notions of validity, and a common policy enterprise).

A. Formal Arrangements

Section II described ways in which ICs cooperate. States have memorialized some of those cooperative arrangements in relatively formal agreements. One common form of agreement between peer ICs takes the form of "humane treatment assurances." Sometimes referred to as "diplomatic assurances," these arrangements arise when one state seeks to transfer an individual into another state's custody but fears that the state receiving him may mistreat him.[91] The receiving state may give assurances that it will not engage in certain actions against the transferred individual, and may also allow the sending state or another entity to have continued access to the person after transfer to monitor his treatment.[92]

This process of obtaining assurances, which often takes place in the context of extraditions and deportations, seems to occur in the context of intelligence activities as well. A Task Force set up by President Obama in January 2009[93] to examine U.S. policies related to detainee transfers, including those undertaken pursuant to intelligence authorities, recommended that "agencies obtaining assurances from foreign countries insist on a monitoring mechanism . . . to ensure consistent, private access to the individual who has been transferred, with minimal advance notice to the detaining government.[94] In addition, the Task Force made classified recommendations designed to ensure that "should the Intelligence Community participate in or otherwise support a transfer, any affected individuals are subjected to proper treatment."[95] Assuming the executive branch implemented the Task Force's recommendations, this suggests that the U.S. IC uses assurances to constrain the activities of some other ICs. Reports on Canadian IC activities reflect similar arrangements, which fall under the heading of "caveats" on the use of information.[96] The U.K. IC also seeks treatment assurances in various contexts, including when it is transferring detainees and when it is providing intelligence to a peer service that is likely to lead to human rights abuses by the peer service (which might, for example, use the intelligence to arrest and torture someone).[97] These treatment assurances constitute relatively formal constraints on the conduct of peer ICs.

---

[91] *See generally* Margaret L. Satterthwaite, *Rendered Meaningless: Extraordinary Rendition and the Rule of Law*, 75 Geo. Wash. L. Rev. 1333, 1379–94 (2007).

[92] *See* Ashley Deeks, *Avoiding Transfers to Torture*, Council on Foreign Relations Special Report No. 35, June 2008.

[93] Exec. Order No. 13,491, 3 C.F.R. 199 (2009–2010).

[94] Press Release, U.S. Department of Justice, Special Task Force on Interrogations and Transfer Policies Issues Its Recommendations to the President (Aug. 24, 2009), *available at* http://www.justice.gov/opa/pr/special-task-force-interrogations-and-transfer-policies-issues-its–recommendations–president.

[95] *Id.*

[96] Commission of Inquiry into the Actions of Canadian Officials in Relation to Maher Arar, Report of the Events Relating to Maher Arar 339 (2006) [hereinafter Arar Report] (describing Royal Canadian Mounted Police (RCMP) use of caveats to preclude peer services that receive intelligence information from using that information for unauthorized purposes); *id.* at 344 (recommending that the Canadian IC formally object to a foreign IC and foreign minister if it learns that the latter has made improper use of information provided by Canadian IC).

[97] ISC Rendition Report, *supra* note 77, ¶ 33 ("Where there are concerns [about detainee treatment], the Agencies seek credible assurances that any action taken on the basis of intelligence provided by UK Agencies would be humane and lawful."); U.K. Detention Report, *supra* note 40, at 5.73; HM Government, Consolidated Guidance to Intelligence Officers and Service Personnel on the Detention and Interviewing of Detainees Overseas, and on the Passing and Receipt of Intelligence Relating to Detainees (2010) (instructing personnel to consider obtaining assurances from liaison

Another way that states establish the fact of and rules for liaison cooperation is through bilateral intelligence cooperation agreements.[98] Several hundred treaties and agreements regulate cooperation in security and intelligence matters among the Five Eyes states alone.[99] That number grows to over a thousand when one includes exchanges of letters and memoranda and unwritten understandings concerning the transfer of intelligence information among those states.[100] Many other states presumably have comparable arrangements with their allies and partners.[101] As Richard Aldrich puts it, "Intelligence exchange between these organizations is a world within a world, governed by its own diplomacy and characterized by elaborate agreements, understandings and treaties."[102]

Although little is known about the contents of these arrangements, one recently came to light.[103] Edward Snowden leaked a memorandum of understanding (MOU) between the United States and Israel regarding the sharing of signals intelligence.[104] The MOU requires that the Israeli SIGINT National Unit (ISNU) handle the signals intelligence it receives in accordance with U.S. law; and prohibits Israel from deliberately targeting U.S. persons identified in the data.[105] Further, the MOU requires Israel to destroy upon identification any communication that is to or from a U.S. official.[106] It also appears that NSA trains Israeli personnel to protect U.S. person information.[107] If the United States-Israel MOU is representative of some of these agreements, it illustrates that states are—at least within certain limits—willing to agree at some level of formality to conform their behavior to peer requirements to accomplish shared goals.

The extent to which the constraints imposed by these formal arrangements are driven by legal concerns admittedly is difficult to determine. In view of the legalization phenomenon discussed in Section III, however, it seems likely that IC lawyers are involved in the drafting

---

partners as to the standards that have been or will be applied in relation to that detainee to minimize any risk of mistreatment) (cited in U.K. Detention Report, *supra* note 40, at 3.14).

[98] Section 105(f) of the National Security Act of 1947 authorizes the CIA director to "coordinate the relationships between elements of the intelligence community and the intelligence or security services of foreign governments . . . on all matters involving intelligence related to the national security or involving intelligence acquired through clandestine means." Exec. Order 12,333 gives the Director of National Intelligence the responsibility to "enter into intelligence and counterintelligence arrangements and agreements with foreign governments and international organizations." Exec. Order 12,333, 46 Fed. Reg. 59,941 at § 1.3(b)(4)(A) (Dec. 4, 1981).

[99] RICHELSON & BALL, *supra* note 18, at 141.

[100] *Id.* at 155.

[101] Aldrich, *supra* note 7 (describing various bilateral and multilateral relationships).

[102] Richard Aldrich, *Transatlantic Intelligence and Security Cooperation*, 80 INT'L AFF. 731, 739 (2004); *see also* ADAM SVENDSEN, INTELLIGENCE COOPERATION AND THE WAR ON TERROR: ANGLO-AMERICAN SECURITY RELATIONS AFTER 9/11 (2010) (identifying MOUs related to human and defense intelligence dating to the 1940s).

[103] Aldrich, *supra* note 7, at 22, n.16 (citing JEFFREY RICHELSON, THE U.S. INTELLIGENCE COMMUNITY 280–81 (2d ed. 1989)). More formal versions of these arrangements often specify that the parties cannot recruit each other's citizens as agents or operate on each other's territory without permission.

[104] Glenn Greenwald, Laura Poitras & Ewen MacAskill, *NSA Shares Raw Intelligence Including Americans' Data with Israel*, GUARDIAN (U.K.), Sept. 11, 2013.

[105] *Id.*

[106] *Id.*

[107] *Id.*

of these more formalized arrangements, and would ensure that their contents are consistent with their own states' legal obligations. If so, these formal arrangements may incorporate peer legal constraints.

B. Informal Mechanisms

Perhaps the most important constraining mechanisms are more informal, based on private peer influence and driven by the domestic and international legal constraints of peer states. The unifying idea among these informal mechanisms is that they emanate from one state but constrain ICs from other states, which are not *directly* subject to the first state's particular statutes, judicial decisions, or oversight bodies. Instead, they constrain peer ICs *transitively*: in order for the peer relationship between two ICs to function in a particular situation, one peer IC must alter its preferred behavior in order to allow the other IC to continue to cooperate. These informal mechanisms take four basic shapes: actual legal constraints on one peer IC that alter the behavior of other peer ICs, anticipated legal or regulatory changes that instill preemptive caution in one peer and then shift that caution to another peer, aggressive external oversight of one IC that alters the operational calculations in that IC's relationship with its peer ICs, and face-to-face influence among peer ICs as intelligence operations transpire on the ground.

What determines how strong this influence is? First, the capacity of an individual IC affects how much intelligence it can collect on its own and how much assistance it needs from partners. The willingness of one IC to be constrained by another is contingent on the value to that IC of what the other IC can offer: permission to use its airspace, intelligence about a suspected terrorist, access to information about a third state's military plans or acquisitions, etc. Second, the commitment by a particular IC to rule of law affects what actions the IC is willing to undertake and how far it is willing to push particular legal interpretations. Third, how quickly a state needs cooperation will affect the level of constraints it is willing to accept. Fourth, intelligence activities do not operate in a vacuum; in a case in which other equities (such as a trade or military relationship) are implicated, one IC might agree on balance to accept a peer's constraint even where the first IC would strongly prefer to conduct a particular activity without fetters. All four of these incentives affect how strong informal constraints can be. Recognizing that these informal constraints come in thicker or thinner forms, this section considers four possible manifestations in greater detail.

1. Peer Domestic Legal Constraints

The paradigmatic informal peer IC constraint arises when two ICs seek to cooperate and one state, by virtue of its international or domestic legal obligations, imposes a condition on the cooperation that alters how the other state behaves. This subsection offers two specific examples of peer domestic legal constraints to illustrate when and how ICs can constrain each other. It then identifies comparable forms of constraint that appear in the military and law enforcement contexts as further suggestive evidence that peer constraints exist in the IC arena.

a. Direct Evidence of Constraint

I. U.K. RESTRAINTS ON U.S. DETENTION, INTERROGATION, AND RENDITION

In the wake of revelations that the U.K.'s IC was involved—directly and indirectly—in U.S. "war on terror" activities such as detentions, rendition, and interrogation, the ISC investigated the U.K.'s participation in these activities.

The Intelligence and Security Committee (ISC) reports, taken as a whole, lead to the conclusion that the U.K. IC repeatedly has imposed informal legal constraints on U.S. IC activities. It has done so in particular through the use of caveats on information it shares with the United States, driven by U.K. legal obligations that often do not apply as a matter of black-letter law to the United States.[108] For example, where there are concerns about what a partner IC will do with an individual if the U.K. shares information about that individual, "the Agencies seek credible assurances that any action taken on the basis of intelligence provided by the UK Agencies would be humane and lawful."[109] Even before September 11, the U.K. sought assurances from the U.S. IC when the United States engaged in renditions to justice, to minimize the risk that the U.K. would provide intelligence that would allow the United States to target the subject of the rendition using lethal force or subject him to the death penalty.[110]

The U.K. not only imposed caveats about the purposes for which the United States could employ U.K. intelligence:[111] it also sought assurances, when transmitting questions to the U.S. IC to ask individuals in U.S. custody, that the detainees being interrogated would not be subject to torture or cruel, inhuman, or degrading treatment.[112] Although the ISC report

---

[108] *Id.*, ¶ U (describing 20-year use of caveats placed on intelligence and honored by the United States).

[109] *Id.*, ¶ 33. Although this chapter also discusses diplomatic assurances under the heading of "formal arrangements," it seems likely that ICs seek and receive at least some of these treatment assurances on a more informal basis, so they are discussed here as well. *See also* Arar Report, *supra* note 96, at 334, 338 (expressing view that RCMP must only provide information to liaison services in way that minimizes invasions of human rights); Keenan Mahoney et al., *NATO Intelligence Sharing in the 21st Century*, Columbia School of Int'l and Pub. Aff. Capstone Report, Spring 2013, at 27, https://sipa.columbia.edu/sites/default/files/AY13_USDI_FinalReport.pdf ("Another potential obstacle to intelligence cooperation with Germany is the concern over German intelligence being used for purposes that are not acceptable within the framework of German law. Examples of such activities include the death penalty, targeted killings, or interrogation methods that German law does not allow.").

[110] *ISC Rendition Report*, ¶ 38. The U.K. also appears to have sought assurances from other foreign ICs regarding the treatment of those rendered to justice. Those assurances were kept. *Id.* at 26.

[111] Compare Arar Report, *supra* note 96, at 339 (recommending that Canadian IC should impose caveats on the use of Canadian intelligence in every situation). The Canadian government has stated that it accepted 22 of the 23 recommendations contained in the Arar Report, http://www.parl.gc.ca/HousePublications/Publication.aspx?DocId=4144670&Language=E&Mode=1&Parl=40&Ses=2 (last visited Dec. 22, 2015). The government reports that "CSIS has pursued a number of important initiatives to improve its information handling practices, including: amending operational policy governing information-sharing and cooperation to restate the need to take the human rights record of a country into account before sending or using information from that country; conducting assessments of the human rights records of the countries and agencies with which it exchanges information; and introducing a new caveat to information it shares with foreign agencies that seeks assurances that any Canadian citizen detained by a foreign government will be treated in accordance with the norms of relevant international conventions." *Id.*

[112] *ISC Rendition Report*, ¶ 74. The U.K. IC also conveyed to Afghan interlocutors that detainees must not be mistreated and that SIS officers "must act according to UK laws on the matter, which were strict." U.K. Detainee Inquiry at 5.21.

does not describe what commitments the United States made in response, the report states that after September 11, "greater use was made of assurances with the Americans."[113] The U.K. sought similar assurances from states other than the United States.[114]

The U.K. also has refused to allow U.K. airbases or airspace to be used for U.S. renditions. In some cases, refusals such as these work as affirmative constraints—as where the use of U.K. airspace presents the only option for the United States to execute an operation. In other cases, this type of refusal simply increases the transaction costs for the United States, because the U.S. government must find alternative routes or methods by which to conduct an operation.[115] In some cases, this may mean that the United States attempted to work around U.K.-imposed constraints, perhaps by obtaining relevant intelligence from other, less-constrained sources or by seeking to use airports or facilities of less-constrained ICs. In other cases, however, in which the U.S. IC needed to continue to work with the U.K. IC, the U.S. IC would have had to modify its behavior.[116]

II. GERMAN CONSTRAINTS ON U.S. TARGETING   Peer constraints related to targeting, particularly of members of al-Qaida outside of the Afghan theater, also exist—and are likely to expand in the future. This is due in part to different perceptions between the United States and its allies about whether it is legally accurate to characterize the use of force against al-Qaida as part of an armed conflict.

In 2011, German intelligence officials informed their U.S. counterparts about a German citizen in Pakistan who had bragged about a suicide attack; the officials gave the U.S. IC his cell phone number and the address of a café in Mir Ali that he frequented. The United States reportedly used that information to target and kill the German citizen in a drone strike.[117] Germany's Interior Ministry subsequently instructed Germany's domestic intelligence service to stop providing U.S. intelligence officials with information that would enable them to locate German citizens and use force against them.[118] Assuming the United States continues to receive information from the Germans about German citizens in areas outside of the Afghan theater, the United States faces a peer constraint on how it uses that information—even though its own domestic and international legal rules might allow it to use lethal force to target the individual.

b. Parallel Constraints in Partner Military and Law Enforcement Operations

It should come as no surprise that peer constraints exist among ICs. After all, peer constraints—some overt, some made public through leaks—can be found in several other

---

[113] *Id.*

[114] *Id.* ¶ 171.

[115] *Id.* ¶ 157.

[116] *Id.* ¶ 158 (stating that renditions involving individuals who lived in the U.K. or who were believed to possess intelligence about terrorist activity in the U.K. "were dropped by the Americans after the [Security] Service had expressed concern at the proposal").

[117] Holger Stark, *Drone Killing Debate: Germany Limits Information Exchange with US Intelligence*, SPIEGEL ONLINE INT'L (May 17, 2011), http://www.spiegel.de/international/germany/drone-killing-debate-germany-limits-information-exchange-with-us-intelligence-a-762873.html.

[118] *Id.*

areas that directly implicate national security. Specifically, in any of a number of situations, one state's domestic law constrains how that state may cooperate with peer state agencies to pursue military or law enforcement operations or goals. A few examples should suffice.

In the context of military coalitions, peer constraints abound. During the NATO action in Kosovo, which involved air strikes against Yugoslav and Serbian forces, "the byzantine American procedures for approving targets needed to be replicated by every NATO government and its lawyers."[119] That means that each target that NATO bombed had to meet the highest common denominator of acceptability among the 28 NATO states. Thus, a state that interpreted law of war targeting rules particularly narrowly could "turn off" a proposed target that did not comply with that narrow interpretation. That is an example of a broad peer constraint.

We see similar constraints in the context of weapons bans and sales. For instance, in order for the United States to agree to sell cluster munitions to Israel, the United States constrained the Israeli government's use of those weapons.[120] The United States has insisted that Israel use cluster munitions only against organized Arab armies and, notably for legal purposes, only against clearly defined military targets and not in areas where civilians are known to be present or in areas normally inhabited by civilians.[121] These constraints, imposed by one military partner on another, are intended to tighten the rules of use beyond the rules that ordinarily would apply directly to the weapon's recipient.

Peer constraints pervade international law enforcement cooperation as well. One common example appears in extradition relationships: state parties to the ECHR cannot extradite an individual to a state that may impose the death penalty on her.[122] At one point, Mexico could not extradite individuals to the United States where those individuals faced life imprisonment without parole, even though life without parole is a lawful penalty in the United States.[123]

---

[119] GOLDSMITH, *supra* note 1, at 132. *See also* Spiegel Staff, *Obama's Lists: A Dubious History of Targeted Killings in Afghanistan*, SPIEGEL ONLINE INT'L (Dec. 28, 2014), http://www.spiegel.de/international/world/secret-docs-reveal-dubious-details-of-targeted-killings-in-afghanistan-a-1010358.html (noting that Germany repeatedly urged its allies in ISAF to remove suspects from the targeting list because it used a higher legal standard for who it could kill).

[120] JEREMY SHARP, CONG. RESEARCH SERV., RL33222, U.S. FOREIGN AID TO ISRAEL 10–11 (2009) (describing instances in which the United States restricted aid or rebuked Israel for possible improper use of U.S.-supplied cluster munitions).

[121] HUMAN RIGHTS WATCH, FLOODING SOUTH LEBANON: ISRAEL'S USE OF CLUSTER MUNITIONS IN LEBANON IN JULY AND AUGUST 2006 103 (2008), *available at* http://www.hrw.org/sites/default/files/reports/lebanon0208webwcover.pdf; David Cloud, *Inquiry Opened into Israeli Use of U.S. Bombs*, N.Y. TIMES, Aug. 25, 2006. *See also* U.S. Department of State, U.S. Export Policy for Military Unmanned Aerial Systems, Office of the Spokesperson (2015) (stating that the United States will require purchasers of U.S.-manufactured drones to "use these systems in accordance with international law, including international humanitarian law and international human rights law, as applicable," and use them "in operations involving the use of force only when there is a lawful basis for use of force under international law, such as national self-defense").

[122] Soering v. United Kingdom, 161 Eur. Ct. H.R. (ser. A) (1989) (holding that the U.K. could not extradite Soering to the United States because the very long time spent by those on death row in the United States exposes that individual to a real risk of inhuman or degrading treatment).

[123] *Mexico Alters Extradition Rules*, BBC NEWS (Nov. 30, 2005), http://news.bbc.co.uk/2/hi/4483746.stm (describing Mexican Supreme Court's reversal of four-year ban on extraditions to face life without parole).

Western militaries and law enforcement agencies today are infused with lawyers—certainly in a more public way than ICs, and in far higher numbers.[124] Goldsmith notes, "The U.S. military is filled from top to bottom with accomplished lawyers who work intimately with military commanders around the globe to ensure that they . . . comply with and are accountable to the maze of domestic, international, and foreign laws that govern every step of military activity, and to help them sort out political, diplomatic, strategic, and even tactical issues as well."[125] As the density of laws regulating the IC and the number of IC lawyers increase, it is predictable that IC peer constraints will flourish (though less publicly) in ways comparable to their cousins in the military and law enforcement contexts.

2. The Observer Effect

The behavior of states and their ICs is guided not only by the laws on the books: states also craft policies in anticipation of litigation, because the threat of having a court adjudicate and reject a national security policy gives the executive branch an important incentive to render those policies more rights-protective even before the court weighs in.[126] This phenomenon, which I have termed elsewhere the "observer effect," occurs particularly when three elements are in place. First, there must be a triggering event, which often means that a court has become seized with a national security case after an extended period of non-involvement in security issues.[127] Second, the executive branch must face robust jurisdictional and substantive uncertainty, leaving it unsure whether a court will take jurisdiction over a given national security-related case, and unsure how a court will rule on the merits if it does hear the case.[128] Third, a high likelihood of future litigation on related issues is more likely to sway the executive branch to alter a policy. As a rational actor that seeks to retain maximal control over policy-setting, the executive branch often responds to these three elements by shifting its policy to a position that gives it more confidence that courts would uphold the policy if hearing the case on the merits.[129]

Intelligence activities are prime candidates for the observer effect. As described above, many of these activities for decades have remained free from judicial regulation. This has changed in the past several years, with courts suddenly taking jurisdiction over cases related to surveillance, renditions, detainee treatment, and targeted killings, even if states tend to win on the merits. Executive branches now are aware that courts may step in to review their intelligence activities, and have far greater incentives to structure those activities with potential judicial oversight in mind.

When the observer effect operates on a single state and its IC, the state may craft its intelligence policies to be less aggressive than its domestic law might seem to allow. When a given IC crafts its policies more narrowly as a result of the observer effect, this can translate into

---

[124] GOLDSMITH, *supra* note 1, at 125 ("Until recently, however, lawyers did not play a large role in warfighting.").

[125] *Id.*

[126] Ashley Deeks, *The Observer Effect: National Security Litigation, Executive Policy Changes, and Judicial Deference*, 82 FORDHAM L. REV. 827, 830 (2013).

[127] *Id.* at 835.

[128] *Id.* at 838.

[129] *Id.* at 840–41.

increased constraints on peer ICs.[130] That is, the state operating under the observer effect will conclude that it has less leeway to conduct a particular intelligence activity, and may therefore conclude that it can only cooperate with a peer IC if they undertake a more modest joint operation. This is the opposite of the approach once proclaimed by Michael Hayden in his confirmation hearing to become CIA director—that he would play in fair territory, but there would be chalk dust on his cleats.[131]

How has this operated in the real world? U.K. courts surely have triggered the observer effect inside the U.K. government. Even though a court ultimately dismissed a lawsuit related to targeted killings in Pakistan, the U.K. IC remains nervous about future judicial ramifications of transmitting information to the United States. "[I]n light of [plaintiff] Mr. Khan's lawsuit and the potential for others, operatives across the British intelligence agencies are concerned that if they share information [with the United States], they could be 'punished by the judiciary for something the executive ordered them to do.' "[132] Further, the Noor Khan court stated, "I accept that it is certainly not clear that the defence of combatant immunity would be available to a UK national who was tried in England and Wales with the offense of murder by drone strike."[133] Statements such as this likely leave lingering concerns in the minds of officials whose tasks involve collecting or sharing intelligence that could be used to conduct drone strikes away from hot battlefields. The quantum of litigation in Europe more generally creates penumbral concerns about operating in gray areas, where the legal rules and precedents are not clear-cut. Knowing that these courts have evidenced sympathy for the idea of extending human rights rules to armed conflict and intelligence activities necessarily will prompt states to be cautious when developing policies that may be in some tension with human rights principles.[134]

In sum, the newfound role for courts in evaluating intelligence activities, coupled with untested legal principles and fear of further leaks[135] that may prompt additional litigation, have produced an atmosphere in which executive branches, including ICs, may self-constrain in ways that translate into additional peer constraints.

---

[130] It is not clear as a general matter whether there is an overall net gain or net loss when ICs operating in gray areas act less aggressively than the law allows. Excessive caution may impose costs, though those costs are nearly impossible to calculate. GOLDSMITH, *supra* note 1, at 231.

[131] SHANE HARRIS, THE WATCHERS (2011) (notes to 159); Paul Shinkman, *21st Century Spies: U.S. Tries to Make Rules for Those Who Play Out of Bounds*, U.S. NEWS (Aug. 23, 2013), http://www.usnews.com/news/articles/2013/08/23/21st-century-spies-us-tries-to-make-rules-for-those-who-play-out-of-bounds. Hayden made this statement in 2006, before the bulk of IC-related litigation and leaks took place.

[132] Somaiya, *supra* note 14.

[133] R (on the application of Khan) v. Sec'y of State for For. & Commonw. Aff., [2014] EWCA (Civ) 24 [19] (Eng.), *available at* http://justsecurity.org/wp-content/uploads/2014/01/Noor-Khan-v.-State-UK-Court-of-Appeal-2014.pdf.

[134] Ashley Deeks, *Litigating How We Fight*, 87 INT'L L. STUD. 427, 448 (2011).

[135] One of the CIA's own internal recommendations for future operations in response to the SSCI Report anticipates future leaks, stating that the CIA should "better plan covert actions by addressing at the outset the implications of leaks ...." CENTRAL INTELLIGENCE AGENCY, CIA COMMENTS ON THE SENATE

3. External Oversight of Peer ICs

Relatedly, if one partner state faces aggressive domestic oversight, or if its citizens have robust access to courts, that state may choose to avoid certain types of controversial cooperation with IC partners because it fears that the cooperation will be revealed in one of those fora. For instance, the proliferation and not infrequent success of U.K. litigation, much of which is connected to U.S.-U.K. cooperation, is likely to heighten U.K. caution when working with the United States on sensitive issues, because the political, financial, and resource-related costs to the U.K. have proven high, even when plaintiffs lose.[136] Conversely, the partners of a heavily overseen IC may fear that their cooperation will be revealed through the first state's oversight mechanisms, and be more hesitant to cooperate ex ante. These chilling effects serve as peer constraints because the circumstances surrounding the operations of one IC alter the behavior of a peer IC, including in ways that will be rights-protective.[137]

U.K. courts have proven quite willing to adjudicate the legality of U.K. detentions (in any location), treatment of detainees, and renditions.[138] These courts continue to involve themselves in intelligence issues notwithstanding the fact that the U.K. executive branch has made clear that it objects to having its courts pass judgment on U.S. conduct. For example, in the Noor Khan case, the U.K. government argued that the court should find the case non-justiciable because the "Court itself [] would necessarily have to make a series of determinations regarding the conduct of the Governments of third States (both the United States and Pakistan)."[139] Her Majesty's Government (HMG) went on to note, "There is a strong risk that any findings or assumptions by a UK court in this case would cause the US to revisit and perhaps substantially modify the historic intelligence sharing relationship and national security cooperation."[140] Notwithstanding these asserted concerns, in some cases the U.K. courts have forced disclosure. The ICs of the U.K. and United States now will act with the awareness that the information they exchange might be at risk of release

---

SELECT COMMITTEE ON INTELLIGENCE'S STUDY OF THE CENTRAL INTELLIGENCE AGENCY'S FORMER DETENTION AND INTERROGATION PROGRAM 17 (2013).

[136] Deeks, *supra* note 134, at 447.

[137] There surely will be cases in which State X simply declines to share intelligence with State Y, a peer IC that faces extensive external oversight. That would not be a constraint in the way this chapter means that term, though it would alter the behavior of State X and, as a result, the behavior of State Y (because the latter would lose an opportunity to act on a particular piece of intelligence).

[138] R (on the application of Al Skeini) v. Sec'y of State for Defence, [2007] UKHL 26, [2008] 1 A.C. 153 (H.L.) (appeal taken from Eng.); R (on the application of Al-Jedda) v. Sec'y of State for Defence, [2007] UKHL 58; R (on the application of Evans) v. Sec'y of State for Defence, [2010] EWHC (Admin) 1445; Serdar Mohammed v. Ministry of Defence, [2014] EWHC 1369 (QB).

[139] *Khan*, [2014] EWCA, *supra* note 133 (quoting witness statement of Mr. Morrison).

[140] *Id.* ¶ 23 (quoting witness statement of Mr. Morrison). The U.K. made similar submissions in the Binyam Mohamed case, where it asserted that revealing the intelligence information from the United States would be "profoundly damaging to the interests" of the U.K., particularly in light of the fact that the United States had asserted that the release of that information would adversely affect the U.S.-U.K. intelligence relationship. *See* Deeks, *supra* note 134, at 440, 447 (quoting then-State Department legal adviser John Bellinger as stating that the "public disclosure of these documents is likely to result in serious damage to US national security and could harm existing intelligence information-sharing arrangements between our two Governments").

to a court—and ultimately the public—especially when that information implicates legally contentious activities.[141]

Courts are not the only entities that oversee IC activities, as this book illustrates. Some non-judicial overseers have been particularly active in the wake of 9/11, producing reports that describe in detail the activities both of their domestic ICs and the actions of some liaison ICs. For example, the breadth and depth of ISC reporting on U.K. intelligence activities suggests that both the U.K. and its peer ICs are on notice that many of the U.K.'s activities (and the shortcomings of both the U.K. and its peers) may be revealed in ISC reports.[142] The U.S. Senate Select Committee on Intelligence's recent report on the CIA's detention and interrogation program likewise contains new, detailed discussions of U.S. interrogations and the use of secret sites in other countries, something that the U.S. IC worries will erode the trust of U.S. liaison services that agreed to cooperate with the United States based on an expectation of secrecy.[143]

4. Direct Operational Influence

There is an even more "street level" way in which one peer IC may constrain another. In addition to the higher-level constraints described in the prior sections, another level of constraint may occur when IC officials actually execute the activities originally negotiated among IC officials higher up the chain.

For example, during several months of 2004, several U.K. personnel were embedded at a U.S. detention facility in Iraq, a position that gave them direct exposure to U.S. operations.[144] The U.K. commanding officer had "full visibility of the US [standard operating] procedures" for the handling of detainees, which the U.K. determined fell within the requirements of the Geneva Conventions.[145] The U.K. ISC rendition and detention reports reflect various instances in which U.K. officers were authorized to try to stop interrogations and were required to express concerns to U.S. officials about any abuse they saw. In some cases, the U.K. officers intervened with their U.S. peers. As the ISC Detention report stated, "HMG's stated commitment to human rights makes it important that the Americans understand that we cannot be party to such ill treatment nor can we be seen to condone it. In no case should they be coerced during or in conjunction with an SIS interview of them. If circumstances allow, you should consider drawing this to the attention of a suitably senior

---

[141] Deeks, *supra* note 134, at 447. *See also* Belhaj filing (Her Majesty's Government invoked the act of state doctrine and informed the court of its concerns about litigation that would force it to release U.S. intelligence; court rejected that concern.).

[142] Germany faces strong parliamentary oversight of its intelligence services. Capstone Report, *supra* note 109, at 22 (discussing Parliamentary Control Committee and G10 Committee).

[143] SSCI report, Findings and Conclusions 2–3 (noting that report reveals "significant amount" of new information); *id.* at 15 (discussing foreign detention sites, though not by country name); GOLDSMITH, *supra* note 1, at 213; Radu-Sorin Marinas & Christian Lowe, *U.S. Torture Report Puts Romania's Role under Scrutiny*, REUTERS (Dec. 17, 2014), http://www.reuters.com/article/2014/12/16/us-usa-cia-torture-romania-idUSKBN0JU29H20141216 (noting that the SSCI report has shone an uncomfortable light on some European states that hosted secret detention facilities).

[144] ISC Detention Report, *supra* note 81, ¶ 95.

[145] *Id.*

US official locally."[146] If an SIS officer in the field witnessed the use of particular interrogation techniques in detainee interviews, that SIS officer was under instructions to ask the
state interviewing the detainee to stop the interview, state his concerns, withdraw from the
interview, and report the incident to his head office.[147] The U.K. subsequently reported that
it had followed up with the United States on most of the incidents of mistreatment described
in the ISC report, in theater or through intelligence and diplomatic channels.[148]

Some of these on-the-ground interactions altered—that is, constrained—how the United
States treated detainees. In June 2003, a U.K. officer who had been present while the United
States interviewed a detainee noted that the detainee expressed concern about lack of family contact.[149] The U.K. official raised the concern with the United States and was able to
arrange for the detainee to contact his family.

Having peer IC officials present during an operation can impose transaction costs. If those
peer officials observe a counterpart IC acting in a way that deviates from the agreed constraint, that peer has the opportunity (and sometimes the responsibility as a matter of law
or policy) to speak up. Even if the deviating counterpart continues to deviate, the actions of
the peer (and sometimes the peer's mere presence) have imposed transaction costs on him by
forcing him to explain and defend his action. Further, psychologists have shown that people
behave differently when they know they are being watched.[150]

In sum, the presence of peer IC officials during actual operations may affect—and
constrain—the behavior of a given IC, either directly (as when the peer IC official intervenes
in an interrogation) or indirectly (as when the mere presence of a peer official affects the way
the given IC chooses to behave).

C. Naming and Shaming

A third mechanism by which one state can constrain a partner IC is the use of overt political
pressure, as when State X publicly criticizes State Y for engaging in particular intelligence
activities that have come to light. The actors issuing these critiques invoke different principles of domestic and international law, based both on the factual scenario being criticized

---

[146] *Id.* ¶ 47.

[147] U.K. Detention Report, *supra* note 40, at 5.59; *id.* at 5.44 (noting that SIS officers were instructed to pass to
U.S. authorities any detainee complaints of mistreatment and, if SIS officers witnessed mistreatment, to regis-
ter their concern with U.S. authorities at the earliest opportunity).

[148] H.M. GOVERNMENT, GOVERNMENT RESPONSE TO THE INTELLIGENCE AND SECURITY COMMITTEE'S
REPORT ON THE HANDLING OF DETAINEES BY U.K. INTELLIGENCE PERSONNEL IN AFGHANISTAN,
GUANTANAMO BAY AND IRAQ 3 (2005), *available at* https://www.gov.uk/government/uploads/system/
uploads/attachment_data/file/224700/govt-response-isc-handling-detainees.pdf.

[149] ISC Detention Report, *supra* note 81, ¶ 87.

[150] Deeks, *supra* note 126, at 830 (citing psychological phenomenon in which people modify their behavior when
they know someone is studying them). It is clear that U.K. officials were "watching" U.S. detention operations,
though it is not clear whether the United States knew the U.K. officials were recording the terms under which
U.S. officials were conducting interviews and making other "pertinent observation[s] about the American
detention regime" that they would send back to the Foreign and Commonwealth Office and the Home Office.
U.K. Detention Report, *supra* note 40, at 5.35–36. The more that U.S. officials were aware of the U.K. reporting, the stronger the psychological effect would have been.

and on the particular critiquing state's understanding of the applicable law. When these criticisms produce changes to a peer IC's policies, they serve as peer constraints. Although naming and shaming has long been understood as a mechanism by which states can influence each other's behavior, it is only recently that states have undertaken extensive naming and shaming in the spying context.[151]

As a recent example, the Snowden leaks about U.S. and U.K. foreign electronic surveillance—including allegations that the NSA was spying on senior leadership of U.S. allies—produced high levels of criticism by peer states such as Germany and Mexico.[152] German chancellor Angela Merkel angrily chastised President Obama for allowing the United States to listen to her phone calls.[153] Brazilian President Dilma Rousseff cancelled her state visit with President Obama to send a clear signal of Brazil's displeasure that the NSA was tapping her calls.[154]

These critiques helped to compel a change in U.S. policy. In a January 2014 speech, President Obama announced, "[U]nless there is a compelling national security purpose, we will not monitor the communications of heads of state and government of our close friends and allies."[155] Also in January 2014, the Obama administration released Presidential Policy Directive 28 on Signals Intelligence Activities, which suggests that the United States will limit its existing surveillance of certain states' leadership.[156] The media subsequently reported that the CIA had stopped spying on friendly governments in Western Europe "in response to the furor over a German caught selling secrets to the United States and the Edward Snowden revelations of classified information held by the National Security Agency."[157] If true, the U.S. policy decision to suspend collection is an example of a peer constraint flowing from public naming and shaming.

Although naming and shaming is intended to constrain the behavior of other states, some of the naming and shaming has the unexpected effect of producing *self-constraints* on the states that are critiquing other ICs. Consider the critiques levied against the types of electronic surveillance conducted by the NSA and Government Communications Headquarters (GCHQ).

---

[151] *See generally* RYAN GOODMAN & DEREK JINKS, SOCIALIZING STATES: PROMOTING HUMAN RIGHTS THROUGH INTERNATIONAL LAW (2012); Emilie M. Hafner-Burton, *Sticks and Stones: Naming and Shaming the Human Rights Enforcement Problem*, 62 INT'L ORG. 689 (2008).

[152] Der Spiegel Staff, *Embassy Espionage: The NSA's Secret Spy Hub in Berlin*, SPIEGEL ONLINE INT'L (Oct. 27, 2013), http://www.spiegel.de/international/germany/cover-story-how-nsa-spied-on-merkel-cell-phone-from-berlin-embassy-a-930205.html (describing spying out of U.S. embassy in Berlin); Jens Glüsing et al., *NSA Accessed Mexican President's Email*, SPIEGEL INT'L ONLINE (Oct. 20, 2013), http://www.spiegel.de/international/world/nsa-hacked-email-account-of-mexican-president-a-928817.html (describing spying out of U.S. embassies in Mexico City and Brasilia).

[153] Geir Moulson & John-Thor Dahlburg, *Merkel Calls Obama to Complain about Surveillance*, YAHOO NEWS (Oct. 23, 2013), http://news.yahoo.com/merkel-calls-obama-complain-surveillance-184820910.html.

[154] Glüsing et al., *supra* note 152.

[155] Obama NSA Speech, *supra* note 73.

[156] Presidential Policy Directive 28, 2014 DAILY COMP. PRES. DOC 31, § 3 (Jan. 17, 2014) (stating that it is "essential that national security policymakers consider carefully the value of signals intelligence activities in light of the risks entailed in conducting these activities").

[157] Ken Dilanian, *CIA Halts Spying in Europe*, YAHOO NEWS (Sept. 20, 2014), http://news.yahoo.com/ap-exclusive-cia-halts-spying-europe-155821445--politics.html.

States ranging from Germany to Indonesia to the Bahamas have argued that the United States and U.K. are engaged in international law violations.[158] By taking these positions publicly, these states make it harder to claim that their own foreign surveillance activities are consistent with international law. It is possible to argue that particular types of surveillance (such as that which does not take place against diplomatic missions or assemble Internet content in bulk) will not implicate international legal principles. But the more states make affirmative statements about the illegality of particular kinds of espionage, the more they constrain their own ICs (or at least their own ability to claim that those actions are lawful).[159] Naming and shaming therefore can serve both as a form of peer constraint and a form of self-constraint on ICs.

* * * * *

These three manifestations of peer constraints—formal constraints, informal constraints, and naming and shaming—serve to influence the behaviors of ICs that partner with other ICs. Having identified how the mechanisms operate, it is important for us to try to assess how robust those mechanisms are and what advantages they may offer over other IC oversight mechanisms. It also is necessary to consider whether the mechanisms described herein more often function as tools to facilitate IC abuses of individual rights rather than limit such abuses. The next section undertakes these analyses.

V. EVALUATING PEER CONSTRAINTS
A. Conceptual Advantages of Peer Constraints

Peer constraints offer at least four advantages that are not found in oversight stemming from bodies such as parliamentary intelligence committees, inspectors general, or independent, executive-created bodies.[160]

First, peer ICs can understand the technologies and techniques of other ICs in ways that those other bodies cannot. No other actor is better suited to grasp the nuance of intelligence requirements, tools, and tradecraft than a peer IC. It is difficult for congressional committees, courts, and civil liberties groups to understand the complicated technology of ICs, which erects certain hurdles to true oversight. One reason that congressional oversight in the United States has proven weak is that "intelligence is a highly technical and cloistered business, requiring years of study or insider experience to understand."[161] To this extent, partner

---

[158] *Germany Calls in British Ambassador over Spying Reports*, supra note 85; Miller, *supra* note 85; Press Release, General Assembly, *supra* note 86; Rashad Rolle, *Lawyers to Act in N.S.A. Spy Row*, TRIBUNE 242 (June 5, 2014), http://www.tribune242.com/news/2014/jun/05/lawyers-act-ns-spy-row/.

[159] For example, Germany was condemned for hypocrisy when the media revealed that Germany had been cooperating with the NSA in spying on European (including German) companies. Henry Farrell, *The New Germany Spying Scandal Is a Big Deal*, WASH. POST, Apr. 23, 2015.

[160] I do not mean to suggest that peer constraints should serve as a replacement for any of these other bodies. Some forms of peer constraints work in part because of the existence and work of these other oversight bodies.

[161] Amy Zegart, *The Roots of Weak Congressional Intelligence Oversight*, HOOVER INSTIT. 6 (2011), http://media. hoover.org/sites/default/files/documents/FutureChallenges_Zegart.pdf. *See also id.* at 10 (noting that congressional oversight requires delving into highly technical issues without support from watchdog groups or other public sources that are available on unclassified issues).

ICs are in a better position to understand intelligence operations and to flag—at least in some cases—legal or compliance problems.[162]

Second, as discussed in Section IV, peer ICs engaged in joint operations with a given IC are in a better position than any other oversight body to directly observe the activity of that IC. Oversight bodies such as SSCI can evaluate intelligence programs, but in all cases they do so at a temporal and geographic remove. There is something distinct and particularly salient about a role for a "watcher" in a given operation. Knowledge by the executive branch that it ultimately will have to face hard questions from Congress affects the way in which the executive branch shapes a given operation.[163] But knowing that one or more peer ICs will be aware of the specifics of an operation and possibly will participate in it will affect how one IC thinks in advance about how to conduct that operation, and may cause it to tighten up the rules it sets for itself.

Third, liaison partners can offer particular kinds of carrots and sticks that other oversight bodies cannot. Although congressional overseers have the power of the purse, it is politically challenging to cut an intelligence service's budget.[164] Other actors such as executive branch prosecutors undoubtedly carry serious sticks in the form of the ability to conduct criminal investigations and file charges against IC officials who violate the law, but those prosecutions are uncommon. Entities such as PCLOB, civil liberties groups, and the media have the power of persuasion, but often have little to wield by way of sticks.[165] Partner ICs often have more direct carrots (in the form of intelligence to share or permission to give to operate on their territory or in their airspace) and sticks (in the form of intelligence to withhold or denial of such permission). This may make their influence as persuasive to their peers as other overseers with indirect or modest sticks. Peer ICs also can monitor and follow through on the on-the-ground commitments of another IC in a way that overseers further removed from operations cannot.[166]

Finally, peer constraints are relatively depoliticized because there usually will be no public audience for the constraining act. Peer constraints usually happen behind a veil of secrecy. Whereas overt oversight of ICs may be infused with politics, it is difficult to use peer constraints (other than naming and shaming) to achieve overt political goals because the public rarely will know that the liaison interaction even took place. Opacity of IC activity, therefore, has an upside: peer constraints avoid showboating.

---

[162] *See* Sepper, *supra* note 3, at 191 ("Intelligence professionals are those most likely to become aware of impropriety by partner agents and are therefore the best actors to conduct oversight and demand compliance with professional guidelines.").

[163] GOLDSMITH, *supra* note 1, at 92.

[164] Zegart, *supra* note 161, at 13, 15 (describing limited leverage of intelligence authorizers and ways in which IC circumvents authorizers to secure appropriations).

[165] *See* Aldrich, *supra* note 7, at 35 (describing lack of power of European Parliament and Commission to secure response from national governments on their rendition and secret detention sites reports).

[166] *See, e.g.*, Arar Report, *supra* note 96, at 347 (calling for Canadian IC to monitor the use of information by the liaison partner that received it from Canada). As previously mentioned, Canada implemented 22 of 23 of the Arar Report's recommendations, presumably including this one.

B. Strength of the Constraints

The earlier sections of this chapter argued that peer constraints exist among ICs and analyzed the different forms those constraints can take. In light of the fact that most intelligence activity remains classified and inaccessible to the public, however, can we know how strong the constraints actually are? Although it is very difficult to say with certainty how effectively constraints operate in any particular situation, it is possible to reach some tentative conclusions about when peer constraints will be stronger or weaker.

First, peer constraints will tend to be stronger among "rule of law" states (ROLSs), which generally are committed to diligent compliance with domestic legal requirements. ROLSs are more likely to impose peer constraints on others, and are more likely to respect the fact that other states may need to impose constraints on them. This means that the level of legalization of an IC in a ROLS and the quantum of oversight that IC faces will have a direct impact on the amount of constraint that state will need to impose on its liaison partners. This also suggests that the trend of increased legalization of intelligence issues means the possibility of peer constraints will only grow. And as it becomes harder and harder to keep secret IC activity secret, ICs and their senior executive branch decision-makers are more likely to impose rigorous policy constraints on themselves for fear of backlash if their activities are disclosed. That adds to the pile of constraints in play. In short, there are a limited number of states today that likely need to constrain their liaison partners (because there are a limited number of ROLSs with extensive intelligence capabilities), but the imperatives of constraint are on the rise as ICs face increased domestic legal regulation.

We also can predict with some confidence that constraints will be stronger when the state facing a peer's constraint firmly desires the intelligence or IC cooperation that the peer is offering. If the constraining peer stands as the best (or only) source of a particular piece of intelligence, or if the peer has the only airport that will allow the constrained state to conduct a particular operation, the latter is more likely to accede to the constraint. If an IC (whether a ROLS or not) has a variety of options to achieve a particular goal, it may use the less constraining alternative. In short, the size and uniqueness of the carrot being offered by the constraining state has a direct effect on whether the recipient state will accept the constraint.

Third, when constraints manifest themselves as critiques of a peer IC's actions (whether during an interrogation on the ground or in a name-and-shame context), those constraints will have more bite when the IC on the receiving end of the critique cares about its reputation in the eyes of the peer. A useful analog here is "acculturation," a theory that Ryan Goodman and Derek Jinks use to explain how states influence the behavior of other states.[167] Conformity with norms follows from the pressure of others who are within the same "group." As Goodman and Jinks put it, "The touchstone of this mechanism is that identification with a reference group generates varying degrees of cognitive and social pressures—real or imagined—to conform."[168] When President Obama remarked in January 2014, "For our

---

[167] Ryan Goodman & Derek Jinks, *How to Influence States: Socialization and Human Rights Law*, 54 DUKE L.J. 621 (2004).

[168] *Id.*

intelligence community to be effective over the long haul, we must maintain the trust of the American people, and people around the world,"[169] his statement reflected a certain amount of acculturation to the idea that states must restrain their surveillance of foreign nationals.

In sum, peer constraints can play an important and unique role in modulating the activities of other ICs, but are hardly a replacement for other forms of IC oversight. Instead, peer constraints supplement (and in many ways rely on) oversight from other sources, while bringing to the table certain unique advantages that other actors interfacing with ICs lack.

C. Critiques

The argument that peer constraints exist and can have a rights-protective influence on the operations of other ICs is open to several challenges. This section considers them.

1. Limited Number of Constraining ICs

Even if certain ICs can and do impose peer restraints on other ICs, one possible critique is that the number of constraining ICs is small. The bulk of the constraining ICs is likely to be Western democracies that have functional judicial and parliamentary systems, a tradition of legal compliance, a robust media, and a susceptibility to public pressure and critiques—that is, ROLSs.[170] This fact does not undercut the idea that peer constraints exist; it only means that a finite number of ICs are likely to act as constraining states in their relationships with liaisons. And, importantly, the bulk of those states that fall within the constraining state category are states with extensive intelligence capabilities. Thus, they have intelligence and capabilities from which other states would like to benefit. As a result, the constraints are more likely to have teeth.

2. Sacrifice of Principles for Security

Those who emphasize the insular and hidden nature of ICs will point to cases in which even ROLSs such as the United States have chosen to engage in activity that violates international law and norms. The recently released Senate Select Committee on Intelligence's report discloses both treatment of detainees that most would describe as torture and examples of liaison cooperation that facilitated—rather than constrained—that detention and treatment. States that fear terrorist attacks and are under pressure to take robust measures to defeat those threats often make decisions and take actions that prove harsh, foolhardy, or counterproductive in hindsight. These decisions can take at least three forms.

First, states may decide overtly to break the law.[171] A state that has made this decision will neither constrain other ICs nor respond to peer IC constraints. Second, one IC might seize

---

[169] Obama NSA Speech, *supra* note 73.

[170] It is hard to imagine, for instance, that China requires treatment assurances before sharing information with a partner IC that would allow the partner to locate and detain an individual.

[171] This seems to be the case with some CIA employees who used unapproved interrogation techniques. SSCI report, *supra* note 135, at 12 (noting that some detainees were subject to techniques that were not legally authorized). The U.K. Foreign Secretary gestured at the conundrum that occasionally may arise between legal compliance and security when he stated, "[M]y last point is a real area of moral hazard . . . . [If] you do get a bit of information which seems to be completely credible, but which may have been extracted through unacceptable

opportunities to circumvent its own laws by relying on other states to achieve for it what it cannot, or by taking advantage of situations created by liaison cooperation—more indirect forms of lawbreaking. For example, the *Washington Post* reported that Alliance Base allowed German intelligence officers to read German law enforcement information, something German intelligence cannot do directly within Germany.[172] Third, the fact that ICs generally operate in secret may create disincentives for any one IC to call to account its partners, particularly where those partners provide it with critical intelligence.[173] If the partners' actions are unlikely to come to light, the cost of criticizing or constraining the partners may appear higher than any benefit to be achieved by insisting on "secret" legal compliance. One can find examples in the post-9/11 years where the United States stopped criticizing partner states for their human rights records to encourage intelligence cooperation by those partners.[174]

Some of these critiques are more potent than others. With regard to the concern about relying on peer ICs to circumvent one's own domestic constraints, many of the ICs discussed here are bound by policies or laws that forbid them from asking other ICs to pursue actions they themselves could not undertake. In the United States, Executive Order 12333 states, "No element of the Intelligence Community shall participate in or request any person to undertake activities forbidden by this order."[175] Likewise, Canada has denied that it uses peer services to obtain information about Canadian citizens indirectly that it could not lawfully collect directly.[176] The U.K.'s ISC recently concluded that GCHQ did not circumvent U.K. law by using a NSA program to obtain the contents of private communications.[177]

The critique that ICs often have insufficient incentives to challenge each other's compliance with the law (or policy, or morality) is a fair one. For example, European states whose nationals have traveled to Syria to fight may be relying on U.S. intelligence even if they have

---

practices, do you ignore it? And my answer to that is . . . you have to make an assessment about its credibility. . . . [Y]ou cannot ignore it if the price of ignoring it is 3,000 people dead." ISC Detention Report, *supra* note 81, ¶ 33.

[172] Priest, *supra* note 15. *See also* SSCI Report, *supra* note 135, at 9 (noting that the CIA chose to detain Abu Zubaydah not at a U.S. military facility, where the CIA would have had to declare him to the International Committee of the Red Cross, but to a secret site in a different country).

[173] For instance, the U.K. Detainee Inquiry raised questions about whether the U.K. IC surfaced with sufficient vigor allegations of mistreatment of detainees with liaison partners, and about whether the assurances the U.K. sought were adequate. U.K. Detention Report, *supra* note 40, at 7.6.

[174] Priest, *supra* note 15 (describing CIA assistance to states with problematic human rights records, including Uzbekistan and Indonesia); Scott Shane, *CIA Role in Visit of Sudan Intelligence Chief Causes Dispute within Administration*, N.Y. Times, June 18, 2005 (noting controversy of inviting Sudan's intelligence chief to Washington in light of allegations that the Sudanese government was engaged in genocide and had terrorist ties).

[175] Exec. Order 12,333, § 2.12.

[176] CSIS officials indicated that it would be inappropriate for the CSIS in an effort to circumvent Canadian privacy laws to ask the U.S. government to intercept a particular Canadian communication as it passed through the United States. "Such behavior would draw the attention, and likely ire, of CSIS's review institutions: the inspector-general and the Security Intelligence Review Committee." Craig Forcese, *The Collateral Casualties of Collaboration: The Consequences for Civil and Human Rights of Transnational Intelligence Sharing*, in International Intelligence Cooperation, *supra* note 7, at 80, 82.

[177] Intelligence and Security Committee, Statement on GCHQ's Alleged Interception of Communications under the US PRISM Programme 2 (2013).

some misgivings about certain U.S. IC activities.[178] But the potency of this critique appears to be fading in view of the clear sense among ICs that it is very difficult to keep secret activities secret for any extended period of time. Thus, not only will troubling acts be made public, but the cooperation of peer ICs in those acts will be made public. This increases the incentives of at least some ICs to challenge and constrain.

There are clearly situations in which ICs do not constrain each other. The goal of this chapter is not to argue that peer ICs operate in all situations, or that they serve as a potent stand-alone tool for modulating IC behavior. Rather, the goal is to demonstrate that peer IC constraints exist and explore how and why they function. Further, there is reason to believe that peer constraints will become a more common and more robust phenomenon as leaks, litigation, and IC legalism continue to proliferate. Institutions make mistakes, and ICs are no exception. The fact that ICs have engaged in abuses and controversial activities does not undercut the fact that there are cases in which peer ICs pull in the opposite direction, toward a more cautious and rights-protective approach to liaison relationships.

3. Tying Superpowers Down?

Skeptics will argue that it is nearly impossible to constrain the IC of a superpower—in this case, the United States. On this theory, if one state has significantly greater intelligence capabilities than those of other states, the likelihood that that state will need assistance from any particular peer liaison service is quite small. The superpower IC may be able to obtain the desired assistance from another service that does not intend to impose constraints, or it may be able to undertake the desired action (arresting an individual, say) itself, even if it would be easier or more appealing to have another state arrest the person for the first state. As a result, the superpower rarely will find itself in a situation in which it needs to accept peer constraints in order to achieve its intelligence goals.

One answer to this critique is that even superpowers need assistance—at least sometimes—for reasons described in Section II.[179] This may be the case when the superpower has no choice but to work with a particular IC. Perhaps the person the superpower IC is seeking is located in State X and appears not to be leaving the state any time soon. Perhaps the electronic communications that the superpower requires can only be decrypted by State Y. One can imagine a number of situations in which liaison cooperation is not optional. It still may be the case that the less powerful IC chooses not to constrain the superpower IC in any meaningful way, perhaps because the less powerful IC views the costs of doing so as too high. But for peer ICs that have long-standing and durable relationships with the superpower and sufficiently valuable intelligence to offer over time, the superpower IC will realize that, as a repeat player, accepting certain constraints may be in its longer-term interest.

Recent developments show that even the U.S. "superpower" can be constrained by less powerful states.[180] The U.S. detention and interrogation program offers an example. As the

---

[178] Greg Miller, *Backlash in Berlin over NSA Spying Recedes as Threat from Islamic State Rises*, WASH. POST, Dec. 29, 2014.

[179] *See supra* Section II.A.

[180] Peer constraints against a superpower are likely to vary in their efficacy depending on what acts the constrainers seek to constrain. In view of the ever-expanding (and arguably legitimate) interest in gathering information and the powerful capacity of the United States to collect that information electronically, constraints are

SSCI report notes, "With the exception of [one country,] the CIA was forced to relocate detainees out of every country in which it established a detention facility because of pressure from the host government or public relations about the program."[181] By 2006, the CIA concluded that it was "stymied," and the "program [of secret detention and interrogation] could collapse of its own weight."[182] Shortly thereafter, the United States shut those secret facilities. If globalized trends related to national security threats continue to abound, there will continue to be many cases in which no single IC can manage those threats on its own.

VI. CONCLUSION

NSA's spokeswoman recently stated, "NSA works with a number of partners in meeting its foreign-intelligence mission goals, and those operations comply with U.S. law and with the applicable laws under which those partners operate."[183] In other words, NSA and its partners are peer-constrained. More broadly, the ICs of various states face peer constraints, forced to respond to domestic limitations imposed by their counterparts. Peer constraints offer an underexplored way in which ICs must modify their behavior based on legal rules. The direction in which leaks, litigation, and legalization are trending indicates that these constraints are only likely to grow in strength and complexity in the coming years.

---

unlikely to have a robust effect on that collection. Constraints are more likely to operate as a check on outright abuse or on certain uses of information or assistance (even if not clear abuses of authority).

[181] SSCI Report, *supra* note 135, at 15.

[182] *Id.*

[183] James Risen & Laura Poitras, *Spying by N.S.A. Ally Entangled U.S. Law Firm*, N.Y. Times, Feb. 15, 2014 (quoting Vanee M. Vines).

2

Oversight through Five Eyes

INSTITUTIONAL CONVERGENCE AND THE STRUCTURE
AND OVERSIGHT OF INTELLIGENCE ACTIVITIES

*Richard Morgan**

I. INTRODUCTION

In the early years of the Cold War, the United States and U.K. sought to formalize their procedures for cooperation in the field of signals intelligence (SIGINT) through the adoption of the BRUSA agreement,[1] later known as the UKUSA agreement.[2] Cooperation between the United States and the U.K. came to include cooperation with the former British dominions of Canada, Australia, and New Zealand. Nearly 70 years after its beginning, this cooperation, informally known as the "Five Eyes" partnership,[3] continues to function as a lasting and effective alliance. Such is an astonishing feat in the world of espionage, where (to paraphrase Henry Kissinger) states don't have friends . . . only interests.

---

* The author wishes to thank the New York University Center on Law and Security for its support during the drafting of this chapter, particularly Samuel Rascoff, Zachary Goldman, Sarvenaz Bakhtiar, Tim McKenzie, Annika Huemann, and Emily Cooper. This chapter is the sole work of the author and does not represent the views of the United States government. This chapter has been reviewed for classified information.

[1] Press Release, National Security Agency, UKUSA Agreement Release (June 24, 2010), *available at* https://www.nsa.gov/public_info/declass/ukusa.shtml.

[2] *See* UKUSA COMINT Agreement, June 1, 1951, *available at* https://www.nsa.gov/public_info/_files/ukusa/ukusa_comint_agree.pdf.

[3] John Ehrman & Jason Manosevitz, Book Review, *In Spies We Trust: The Story of Western Intelligence*, 58 STUD. INTELLIGENCE, 1 (2014), *available at* https://www.cia.gov/library/center-for-the-study-of-intelligence/csi-publications/csi-studies/studies/vol-58-no-2/pdfs/Ehrman-Manosevitz-Review-In%20Spies%20We%20Trust.pdf.

However, what is perhaps more impressive than the continued cooperation of these five separate governments is the remarkable degree to which their intelligence agencies have come to resemble each other over the years. Each of the five states has organized the duties and responsibilities of its various intelligence agencies along similar jurisdictional, functional, and intelligence discipline lines. Furthermore, the Five Eyes states have adopted similar methods of regulating (e.g., codification of intelligence agency authorities) and overseeing their intelligence agencies (e.g., parliamentary oversight committees, inspectors general).

In this chapter, I argue that the similarity of intelligence structures and oversight across the Five Eyes states is neither coincidental nor unintentional. Rather, it is the result of a phenomenon of isomorphic "institutional convergence" that results in the homogenization of state practices across a wide variety of contexts, be it environmental policies, healthcare, or the organization of armed forces. Understanding the process of isomorphic convergence is important not merely for descriptive purposes, but for prescriptive as well. Where emulated intelligence structures and oversight are effective, isomorphic convergence may promote diffusion of best practices; where such models are ineffective, isomorphic convergence may result in a "race to the bottom" in the conduct, regulation, and oversight of intelligence activities.

In Section II of this chapter, I provide a basic account of the theory of institutional convergence. In Section III, I demonstrate evidence of institutional convergence among both the intelligence "structures" (i.e., how intelligence agencies are organized) and oversight mechanisms of the Five Eyes states. Section IV provides examples of how each of the four main isomorphic processes (i.e., competition, coercion, normative persuasion, and acculturation) may have shaped parts of the Five Eyes alliance. Finally, Section V addresses the consequences of institutional convergence, and sets forth why understanding how convergence occurs is essential both for making international efforts at intelligence reform more effective and for ensuring that domestic intelligence structures and oversight are appropriately aligned with each other.

II. A COMPARATIVE APPROACH TO INTELLIGENCE STRUCTURES AND OVERSIGHT

This chapter examines what I term to be the structure of intelligence agencies together with the mechanisms designed for their oversight and regulation. By the "structure" of intelligence agencies, I am referring to how intelligence agencies are organized—for example, whether their responsibilities are divided along intelligence discipline lines (e.g., collection of intelligence through technical or human means), functional lines (e.g., military or civilian intelligence), or jurisdictional lines (e.g., foreign or domestic). By "oversight" and "regulation," I mean not only the legality of intelligence operations (i.e., whether agencies operate within the parameters established for them in law and policy), but also the "governance" of intelligence agencies, which considers whether intelligence agencies operate in an effective and efficient manner, consistent with societal expectations.

I should note at the outset that a comparative approach to intelligence that examines structure and oversight together is not without controversy. Some may argue that structure and oversight are separate government functions. For example, Michael Warner provides a realist account, which posits that intelligence organization (which he terms an intelligence "system") is the product of three broad independent variables: (1) strategy, which Warner defines to include inter alia a state's objectives, relative geopolitical power, and alliances; (2) technology, defined as how a state manages its resources, means of production, and social structures, which affects both the objects of intelligence and the means employed; and (3) regime, which includes the form and structure of the state's government, internal frictions, and—most important for present purposes—oversight.[4] Thus, for Warner, oversight is an independent variable that shapes the dependent variable of intelligence structure.

However, such an approach oversimplifies the separation of the roles of the overseer and overseen in intelligence activities. In parliamentary systems, ministers have roles of both executive directors and parliamentary regulators. In the United States, Congress both receives intelligence briefings to support legislative functions and exerts oversight through the House Permanent Select Committee on Intelligence (HPSCI) and Senate Select Committee on Intelligence (SSCI). Likewise, the attorney general, as the head of the Department of Justice, exercises supervision of certain intelligence agencies (e.g., the FBI and DEA), and plays a role in oversight as well (e.g., E.O. 12,333 reporting functions).[5]

Likewise, some may argue that structure and oversight are driven by different forces, and thus should be examined separately. For example, intelligence structure may be driven largely by functional explanations (e.g., states have separate SIGINT services because of natural efficiencies in grouping highly technical collection methodologies into one organization), whereas oversight may be driven by normative cultural concerns (e.g., traditions of limited government, civil liberties, etc.).

As I discuss below, I am not totally dismissive of the idea that influencing forces may have a disparate effect on oversight and structure, respectively. However, I would caution against any account that emphasizes specific and separate explanations for structure and oversight. Such an account would ignore, for example, that intelligence agencies may be structured in large part due to the same normative rationales (e.g., the CIA has no domestic authority, so as to avoid perception that it would be a Gestapo) as influence oversight, whereas oversight may also be driven by functional explanations (for example, many oversight mechanisms are specifically designed in order to maintain the secrecy of intelligence information).

More important, however, I contend that studying intelligence structure and oversight as separate frameworks increases the risk that we will view the influence of one upon the other as unidirectional, as Warner believes in labeling intelligence structures as a variable dependent on the independent variable of oversight. As I shall demonstrate below, there exists some evidence that influence moves both ways, in that changes in intelligence structures (in this case, convergence to an international standard) may precede and perhaps cause similar changes in oversight.

---

[4] Michael Warner, *Building a Theory of Intelligence Systems*, *in* NATIONAL INTELLIGENCE SYSTEMS, 26–34 (Gregory F. Treverton & Wilhelm Agrell eds., 2009).

[5] Exec. Order No. 12,333, §1.7(a), *reprinted as amended* 3 C.F.R. 13470 (2008).

III. INSTITUTIONAL CONVERGENCE

Prior to the mid-twentieth century, sociologists seeking to understand the structure of human organizations emphasized functionalist explanations, which is to say that organizations tend to be formed in order to address some collective problem. However, since that time, the field of sociology has emphasized a view of organizations as the product of "institutions," which in turn are defined as the "normative, cognitive, and regulative environments in which organizations ... operate."[6] According to this view, "institutionalization" is the "process by which ... rules and shared meanings move from abstractions to specific expectations, and in turn, to 'taken for granted' frames."[7] Thus, organizations are influenced and shaped by the institutional environments in which they exist, with the result tending to be homogenizing. Once institutional models for organizations develop, they become "diffused, which causes organizational structures to grow more and more alike."[8] Two of the leading proponents of such "Institutional Isomorphism," Paul DiMaggio and Walter Powell, noted studies demonstrating convergence of organizational forms in a variety of contexts, be it legal education, hospital management,[9] municipal administration,[10] or the structure of public television stations.[11]

Since the time of DiMaggio and Powell's groundbreaking article on the topic, Institutional Isomorphism has been applied to international politics through "world polity institutionalism," which "emphasizes the role of world-level cultural models that 'press all countries toward common objectives, forms, and practices.'"[12] Essentially, states increasingly adopt similar conceptions of the role of government, policy objectives, and organizational structures.[13] For example, national militaries tend to be organized in similar fashion, with a tripartite division of forces along the lines of armies, air forces, and navies; with commissioned officers and noncommissioned officers who "see themselves as military men first, a centralized command structure, high levels of internal differentiation, and promotion based on technical expertise and merit."[14] Such isomorphism may be driven by both cultural influences (e.g., the continuing legacy of colonial influence) and material factors (e.g., training and arms sales).[15] Likewise, isomorphism can also be observed in states' environmental laws,[16]

---

[6] Ryan Goodman & Derek Jinks, *Toward an Institutional Theory of Sovereignty*, 55 STAN. L. REV. 1749, 1756 (2003).

[7] *Id.*

[8] Jens Beckert, *Institutional Isomorphism Revisited: Convergence and Divergence in Institutional Change*, 28 SOCIOLOGICAL THEORY 150, 150 (2010).

[9] Paul J. DiMaggio & Walter W. Powell, *The Iron Cage Revisited: Institutional Isomorphism and Collective Rationality in Organizational Fields*, 48 AM. SOC. REV. 147, 148 (1983).

[10] *Id.* at 149.

[11] *Id.* at 152.

[12] Goodman & Jinks, *supra* note 6, at 1756.

[13] *Id.* at 1759.

[14] *Id.* at 1767 (quoting Alexander Wendt & Michael Barnett, *Dependent State Formation and Third World Militarization*, 19 REV. INT'L STUD. 321, 336–41 (1993)).

[15] *Id.* at 336–41 (quoting Alexander Wendt & Michael Barnett, *Dependent State Formation and Third World Militarization*, 19 REV. INT'L STUD. 321, 336–41 (1993)).

[16] *Id.* at 1762–63.

education policies,[17] arms procurement,[18] and adoption of principles associated with the laws of armed conflict (e.g., prohibitions on assassination and the use of chemical weapons).[19]

IV. INSTITUTIONAL CONVERGENCE IN THE FIVE EYES COUNTRIES

Before we examine the evidence of convergence among the Five Eyes intelligence services, three challenges should be noted. The first is the one associated with describing the structure of agencies whose work must often be obscured from public view. Although observers of state behavior may be able to readily identify instances of isomorphism in the public manifestations of states' power, such as the military organization and education policies listed above, when state action is conducted less openly, identifying whether and how isomorphism occurs becomes much more difficult. This problem is particularly acute in the field of espionage and other clandestine activity undertaken for national security purposes. To a degree, it is possible to determine whether isomorphic convergence is taking place across the organizational design of states' intelligence agencies, based upon the legislatively chartered functions and publicly stated missions of those agencies. However, because of the threat of exposing sources or methods, intelligence agencies must often keep their activities and functions secret. Therefore, we may not be able to determine at an operational level whether convergence is occurring in the manner in which those states conduct intelligence operations. Likewise, in terms of intelligence oversight, some measures of isomorphic convergence, such as the existence of parliamentary oversight committees, may be easily observed. However, other indications of convergence (or lack thereof) may not be visible, such as internal regulations, or the number and role of attorneys assigned to intelligence agencies.

A second challenge associated with assessing isomorphism in the intelligence realm is that, unlike human rights regimes or policy areas such as health and welfare, intelligence structure and oversight cannot be compared against an articulated international "standard."[20] States have proven unwilling to apply international law to the conduct of intelligence activities in the same manner as in many other areas (such as health and welfare) because, among other reasons, intelligence tends to be at the core of states' security interests and (almost by definition) is not intended to be public.[21] Although some have made claims that international agreements such as the Vienna Convention on Diplomatic Relations apply to intelligence activities,[22] there otherwise exists no international law directly governing the conduct of espionage.[23] In contrast, Katherine Linos has demonstrated in the areas of health and family

---

[17] *Id.* at 1763–64.

[18] *Id.* at 1768–69.

[19] *Id.* at 1769–78.

[20] However, some international organizations have made efforts to define intelligence accountability. *See, e.g.,* *Intelligence Governance*, DEMOCRATIC CONTROL OF THE ARMED FORCES, *available at* http://www.dcaf. ch/Programmes/Intelligence-Governance (last visited Dec. 22, 2015).

[21] Ashley Deeks, *An International Legal Framework for Surveillance*, 55 VA. J. INT'L L. 291, 313–14 (2015).

[22] *Id.* at 312–13.

[23] However, there have been some proposals for international standards that might apply to the conduct of intelligence activities. *See* VENICE COMMISSION, UPDATE OF THE 2007 REPORT ON THE DEMOCRATIC OVERSIGHT OF THE SECURITY SERVICES AND REPORT ON THE DEMOCRATIC OVERSIGHT OF SIGNALS INTELLIGENCE AGENCIES, Study No. 719/2013, CDL-AD(2015)006 (Apr. 7, 2015).

policy reforms that the presence of a single international policy model may exert strong influence on the diffusion policy across states, resulting in a high degree of homogenization.[24] Alternatively, where international models are weak, country-to-country diffusion has tended to dominate.[25]

If international standards (whether weak or strong) have the effects that Linos describes, then the complication in the realm of intelligence theoretically becomes twofold: not only may diffusion be impeded by a lack of an international standard, but state-to-state diffusion may also be impeded by the secrecy surrounding intelligence operations, which may preclude any one state's model from having sufficient transparency to serve as a model for others.[26] However, as will be demonstrated below, there exists some evidence that state-to-state diffusion of intelligence norms occurs. Likewise, the effect of international law on intelligence operations should not be wholly dismissed, as such operations are not conducted independent of states' other obligations, be they commitments to human rights principles, law of armed conflict, diplomatic relations, or domestic law enforcement. As Ryan Goodman and Derek Jinks have shown, these other commitments do constrain clandestine state activity, for example by creating prohibitions on the conduct of assassination.[27] Therefore, although it is certainly possible (if not probable) that secrecy and the lack of established international standards slow the diffusion of intelligence norms, they do not appear to completely prevent it. Rather, for present purposes, their main impact is to deny us a transparent standard of comparison against which to measure the extent of isomorphic convergence.

The third challenge associated with the account I provide below is that the data set is small: although the Five Eyes countries possess some of the most advanced intelligence capabilities in the world,[28] they nonetheless constitute only a fraction of states undertaking espionage activity. Furthermore, the five countries examined in this chapter are closely connected not merely in their aligned strategic interests, but also in their shared legal traditions, history, and language. Such cultural connections may serve as catalysts for convergence. For example, as will be discussed below, isomorphic convergence may be the result of normative persuasion facilitated by professional or social networks. If so, then a cultural affinity and generally shared language may help to foster the type of social networks that would lead to convergence.

I do not discount the potentially strong impact the close political and cultural alignment of Five Eyes states exerts on convergence in the intelligence realm. A necessary next step in the research agenda would be to examine whether isomorphic pressures influence states outside the Five Eyes alliance. In the meantime, however, examination of the Five Eyes states may nonetheless give us insight into a more basic, predicate question: Is any form of institutional convergence occurring in the intelligence realm? Although structural similarity among such a closely aligned set of countries is not dispositive as to whether the forces that lead to institutional convergence in other areas of states' behavior equally apply to intelligence activities,

---

[24] KATHERINE LINOS, THE DEMOCRATIC FOUNDATIONS OF POLICY DIFFUSION 33 (2013).

[25] Id. at 77.

[26] But see Ashley Deeks's chapter in this volume, arguing that peer intelligence services may have better insight into each others' actions than do their respective parliamentary overseers.

[27] Goodman & Jinks, supra note 6, at 1769–72.

[28] See, e.g., Nicole Perlroth, Researchers Find at Least 25 Countries Using Surveillance Software, N.Y. TIMES (Mar. 13, 2013), http://bits.blogs.nytimes.com/2013/03/13/researchers-find-25-countries-using-surveillance-software/.

a lack of evidence of similarity would strongly suggest the opposite, that is, that isomorphic pressures do not affect intelligence operations.

With those challenges in mind, I will now sketch out how the structure of intelligence agencies across the Five Eyes countries strongly suggests that a high degree of institutional convergence has taken place, and that the process of convergence may also be seen, albeit to a lesser extent, in the oversight mechanisms of those countries. Likewise, I will demonstrate that there is a temporal aspect to the convergence process as well, with each country proceeding through roughly similar processes of developing intelligence structures, and the regulatory and oversight mechanisms that govern them.

Looking across the intelligence communities of the Five Eyes countries, one notices a high degree of similarity in how those states divide agencies' responsibilities across intelligence disciplines and jurisdictional lines. Since the UKUSA alliance was created in the aftermath of the Second World War due to the need to share foreign communications intelligence,[29] it should come as no surprise that the Five Eyes countries would each possess stand-alone signals intelligence agencies. Beyond this, however, each state also possesses civilian, non-law enforcement agencies dedicated to the collection of national security intelligence within the state's domestic jurisdiction (the exception being the United States, where the Federal Bureau of Investigation exercises both law enforcement and intelligence authorities). Each state has also created a separate joint agency (i.e., consisting of all military services) dedicated to military intelligence issues. Likewise, each state has created an independent office or agency, responsible for conducting analysis, drawing on intelligence from across the whole of government. Finally, significant similarities exist in other domains, such as having separate offices or agencies for the analysis of geospatial intelligence, and (with the exception of Canada and New Zealand)[30] separate agencies for the collection of intelligence information abroad. See Table 2.1.

To fully appreciate how remarkable is the similarity of the Five Eyes states' intelligence structures, one must remember that there is nothing that dictates that intelligence agencies must be organized in this way. Although there may be efficiencies in specialization, there is nothing that requires (for example) that the agency conducting signals intelligence must be separate from the agency responsible for foreign intelligence collection. Indeed, as Russell Miller notes elsewhere in this volume, the German foreign intelligence service—the *Bundesnachrichtendienst* (BND)—combines both functions. Likewise, there is no reason that states might not combine foreign and military intelligence within one agency, as is the practice in Denmark.[31]

A review of the various mechanisms of intelligence oversight employed in the various Five Eyes states also reveals a high degree of similarity. Table 2.2 compares intelligence

---

[29] See UKUSA COMINT Agreement, *supra* note 2. *See also* Press Release, National Security Agency, *Declassified UKUSA Signals Intelligence Agreement Documents Available* (June 24, 2010), *available at* https://www.nsa.gov/public_info/press_room/2010/ukusa.shtml.

[30] In New Zealand and Canada, the domestic intelligence services (i.e., NZSIS and CSIS, respectively) are responsible for both domestic and foreign intelligence collection. *See Foreign Intelligence*, New Zealand Security Intelligence Service, *available at* http://www.nzsis.govt.nz/our-work/foreign-intelligence/; Anti-Terrorism Act, S.C. 2015 (Can.) (providing that "[i]f there are reasonable grounds to believe that a particular activity constitutes a threat to the security of Canada, [CSIS] may take measures, within or outside Canada, to reduce the threat").

[31] *About DDIS*, Danish Defence Intelligence Service, *available at* https://fe-ddis.dk/eng/About-DDIS/Pages/About-DDIS.aspx.

TABLE 2.1.

STRUCTURE OF FIVE EYES INTELLIGENCE COMMUNITIES

	United States	United Kingdom	Canada	Australia	New Zealand
Domestic Intelligence	Federal Bureau of Investigation (FBI)	Security Service (MI-5)	Canadian Security Intelligence Service (CSIS)	Australian Security Intelligence Organisation	New Zealand Security Intelligence Service (NZSIS)
Signals Intelligence	National Security Agency (NSA)	Government Communications Headquarters (GCHQ)	Communications Security Establishment (CSE)	Australian Signals Directorate (ASD)	Government Communications Security Bureau (GCSB)
Joint Military Intelligence	Defense Intelligence Agency (DIA)	Defence Intelligence	Canadian Intelligence Forces Command	Defence Intelligence Organisation (DIO)	Directorate of Defence Intelligence & Security
Foreign Intelligence	Central Intelligence Agency (CIA)	Secret Intelligence Service (MI-6)	(None: foreign intelligence activities conducted by CSIS)	Australian Secret Intelligence Service (ASIS)	(None: foreign intelligence activities conducted by NZSIS)
Geospatial Intelligence	National Geospatial-Intelligence Agency (NGA)	Defence Intelligence Fusion Centre	Canadian Forces Joint Imagery Centre	Australian Geospatial Intelligence Organisation	GEOINT New Zealand Team
Joint Analysis	National Intelligence Council	Joint Intelligence Council	Security and Intelligence Secretariat of the Privy Council Office	Office of National Assessments (ONA)	National Assessments Bureau

TABLE 2.2.

STRUCTURE OF FIVE EYES INTELLIGENCE OVERSIGHT.

	United States	United Kingdom	Canada	Australia	New Zealand
Legislative Charter	National Security Act (1947); Central Intelligence Agency Act (1949); (etc.)	Secret Service Act (1989); Intelligence Services Act (1994)	Canadian Security Intelligence Service Act of 1985	ASIO Act (1956); Intelligence Services Act (2001)	Security Intelligence Service Act (1969)
Parliamentary Oversight	SSCI & HPSCI (1976)	Intelligence and Security Committee (1994)	Standing Committee on Public Safety and National Security (2006)	Parliamentary Joint Committee on Intelligence and Security (1988, expanded 2001)	Intelligence and Security Committee Act (1996); Government Communications Security Bureau Act 2003
Inspector General	CIA (1989); DNI (2010)	Interception of Communications Commissioner (1986); Intelligence Services Commissioner (2000).	Office of Commissioner of CSE (1996);	Inspector-General of Intelligence and Security Act (1986).	Inspector-General of Intelligence and Security Act (1996).
Judicial Oversight of Domestic Communications Collection	Foreign Intelligence Surveillance Act of 1978	(None)[32]	Canadian Security Intelligence Service Act of 1985	(None)	Security Intelligence Service Act of 1969
Legislation Monitors	PCLOB (2004)	Independent Reviewer of Terrorism Legislation (1984);[33] Privacy & Civil Liberties Board (2015)[34]	(None)	Independent National Security Legislation Monitor (2010)	(None)

The roles of the Interception of Communications Commissioner and Intelligence Services Commissioner are roughly a hybrid of inspector general and judicial oversight. Ian Leigh, *Intelligence and Law in the United Kingdom*, in THE OXFORD HANDBOOK OF NATIONAL SECURITY INTELLIGENCE 640, 648 (Loch K. Johnson ed., 2010).

[32] The roles of the Interception of Communications Commissioner and Intelligence Services Commissioner are roughly a hybrid of inspector general and judicial oversight. Ian Leigh, *Intelligence and Law in the United Kingdom*, in THE OXFORD HANDBOOK OF NATIONAL SECURITY INTELLIGENCE 640, 648 (Loch K. Johnson ed., 2010).

[33] The role of the Independent Reviewer of Terrorism Legislation is spelled out in the Terrorism Act of 2006.

[34] Currently, the Privacy and Civil Liberties Board has yet to become operational.

oversight mechanisms across the Five Eyes countries. Indeed, sufficient similarity has arisen such that one could speak of a "Five Eyes model" of oversight, which would include, inter alia, the delineation of intelligence agencies' responsibilities in statutory law, oversight conducted by parliament and independent executive bodies such as inspectors general, judicial oversight of domestic signals intelligence collection, and (increasingly) independent offices designed to review legislation and regulations. Of course, this is not to say that the coordinate mechanisms of oversight are exactly the same from state to state. For example, there exist significant differences in the degree to which parliaments in the various states may have access to classified material. The distinct constitutional role that legislatures perform within each Five Eyes state may explain some of the difference; for example, one might expect a more formalized oversight role for Congress within the U.S. system of strict separation of powers. Likewise, I do not contend that the various mechanisms listed in Table 2.2 are without room for improvement. As the various chapters of this volume attest, there are many areas across the Five Eyes countries in which intelligence oversight could be improved.

Furthermore, there appears to be a temporal aspect to the convergence of intelligence oversight within the Five Eyes countries, with each state proceeding through similar stages of development. This process begins with intelligence activities being exclusively the domain of the executive, with the establishment and regulation of intelligence agencies conducted by executive fiat. At later stages, legislative oversight increases, through the codification of intelligence functions in statutory law, and the establishment of parliamentary oversight mechanisms. Finally (or rather later, if the evolution of oversight is a continuous process) independent executive oversight bodies are established, including inspectors general and legislation monitors.

For example, the Central Intelligence Agency—one of the oldest agencies within the U.S. Intelligence Community (IC)—traces its origins to the World War II-era Office of Strategic Services (OSS), created by executive order in 1942,[35] and the postwar Central Intelligence Group, created by executive order in 1946; these executive orders were supplanted by legislative authorization in the National Security Act of 1947,[36] and the Central Intelligence Agency Act of 1949.[37] The CIA and other members of the U.S. IC operated without formal congressional oversight until the establishment of the Senate Select Committee on Intelligence (SSCI) and House Permanent Select Committee on Intelligence (HPSCI) in 1976.[38] Such congressional oversight was supplemented by expanded "independent" executive oversight by way of, inter alia, inspectors general (the CIA in 1989,[39] and the Office of the Director of National Intelligence in 2010)[40] and the Privacy and Civil Liberties Oversight Board in 2004.[41]

Several of America's Five Eyes partners possess agencies with similar histories of evolving intelligence oversight. For example, the British Secret Intelligence Service and Security

---

[35] THOMAS F. TROY, *DONOVAN AND THE CIA* 150 (1981).

[36] 50 U.S.C. § 3035 *et seq.* (1947).

[37] 50 U.S.C. § 3501 *et seq.* (1949).

[38] RHODRI JEFFREYS-JONES, THE CIA AND AMERICAN DEMOCRACY 214 (3d ed. 2003).

[39] Pub. L. No. 101-193, § 801, 103 Stat. 1701, 1711–15 (1989).

[40] Pub. L. No. 111-259, § 405, 124 Stat. 2654, 2709–20 (2010).

[41] 42 U.S.C. § 2000ee (2004).

Service were established by the cabinet in 1909,[42] and then received legislative charters and respectively became subject to parliamentary oversight in 1989 (Security Service)[43] and 1994 (Secret Intelligence Service).[44] The two services became subject to the Intelligence Services Commissioner in 2000.[45] Likewise, the Australian Security Intelligence Organisation (ASIO) was established by a prime minister's directive in 1949,[46] placed on statutory footing in 1956,[47] became subject to parliamentary oversight in 1988,[48] Inspector General oversight in 1986, and the Independent Security Legislation monitor in 2010. In New Zealand, the Security Intelligence Service (NZSIS) was created by directive in 1956, and received a statutory charter in 1969.[49] NZSIS became subject to parliamentary and Inspector General oversight in 1996.[50] Finally, as the successor to various World War II signals intelligence units, Canada's Communications Security Establishment (CSE) was established as the Communications Branch of the National Research Council in 1946.[51] Legislation outlining CSE's responsibilities was passed in 2001.[52] Although the Canadian Parliament does not have a dedicated intelligence oversight committee analogous to those of other Five Eyes countries (the Security Intelligence Review Committee, an independent agency reporting to Parliament, oversees the work of Canada's domestic intelligence agency, the Canadian Security Intelligence Service), the CSE was made subject to oversight by the Commissioner of CSE in 1996.

V. PROCESSES OF CONVERGENCE

It is insufficient to simply show that there is a high degree of similarity in the structure of intelligence agencies and their oversight mechanisms; only by providing a theory as

---

[42] CHRISTOPHER ANDREW, DEFEND THE REALM 20 (2009).

[43] *Statutory Basis*, UNITED KINGDOM SECURITY SERVICE (MI5), *available at* https://www.mi5.gov.uk/home/about-us/how-we-operate/how-mi5-is-governed/statutory-basis.html (last visited Dec. 22, 2015).

[44] Intelligence Services Act, 1994, c. 13 (U.K.), *available at* http://www.legislation.gov.uk/ukpga/1994/13/pdfs/ukpga_19940013_en.pdf.

[45] *The Commissioner's Statutory Functions*, THE INTELLIGENCE SERVICES COMMISSIONER'S OFFICE, *available at* http://www.intelligencecommissioner.com/content.asp?id=4 (last visited Dec. 22, 2015).

[46] JEFFREY T. RICHELSON & DESMOND BALL, THE TIES THAT BIND 48 (1985).

[47] *Australian Security Intelligence Organisation Act 1956* (Cth), *repealed by* Australian Security Intelligence Organisation Act of 1979 (Cth), *available at* http://www.austlii.edu.au/au/legis/cth/num_act/asioa19561131956506/.

[48] David Martin Jones, *Intelligence and National Security: The Australian Experience, in* OXFORD HANDBOOK OF NATIONAL SECURITY INTELLIGENCE, 823, 832 (Loch K. Johnson ed., 2010).

[49] *NZSIS History*, NEW ZEALAND SECURITY INTELLIGENCE SERVICE, *available at* http://www.nzsis.govt.nz/about-us/nzsis-history/ (last visited Dec. 22, 2015).

[50] *Oversight*, NEW ZEALAND SECURITY INTELLIGENCE SERVICE, *available at* http://www.nzsis.govt.nz/about-us/oversight/ (last visited Dec. 22, 2015).

[51] *The Beginning: The Communications Branch of the National Research Council*, CANADIAN COMMUNICATIONS SECURITY ESTABLISHMENT, *available at* https://www.cse-cst.gc.ca/en/about-apropos/history-histoire/beginning-histoire (last visited Dec. 22, 2015).

[52] Bill C-36 (Can.), *available at* http://www.parl.gc.ca/HousePublications/Publication.aspx?Pub=Bill&Doc=C-36&Language=e&Mode=1&Parl=37&Ses=1 (last visited Dec. 22, 2015).

to what processes are driving the convergence processes can one argue that the story of convergence is one of correlation *and* causation. However, because of the secrecy associated with intelligence activities, empirical proof that institutional convergence is taking place may be difficult to achieve. Rather, in this section, I provide historical examples to illustrate how the four processes of isomorphic convergence (i.e., competition, coercion, normative pressures, and acculturation) call into question the alternative hypotheses, that is, that convergence is either coincidental, unintentional, or the natural result of states independently developing institutions as a natural reaction to shared experience. In other words, might not states bound by roughly the same budgetary, technical, and legal tools, simultaneously and independently arrive at similar methods of organizing and regulating their intelligence services?

Indeed, it is interesting to note many of the reforms of the ICs of the United States, Canada, New Zealand, and Australia occurred in the wake of political scandals in the 1970s, wherein intelligence services were perceived to have impermissibly meddled in domestic politics.[53] In the United States, the passage of the Foreign Intelligence Surveillance Act (FISA), promulgation of Executive Order 12,333, and establishment of congressional oversight committees were the result of, among other things, the Watergate scandal and the revelations of the Church and Pike Committees.[54] In New Zealand, the arrest (and subsequent acquittal) of a former New Zealand diplomat for passing information to the Soviet Union led to a report by Chief Ombudsman Sir Guy Powles[55] that resulted in significant reforms of the New Zealand Security Intelligence Service.[56] The Canadian Security Intelligence Service was established in response to the McDonald Commission's report on intelligence abuses by the RCMP Security Service, including actions taken during the Quebec separatist "October Crisis" of 1970.[57] In Australia, commissions led by Justice Robert Hope in 1977 and 1983 examined, respectively, ASIO surveillance of Labor Party members opposed to the Vietnam War, and the government's handling of a perceived improper relationship between a Labor party member and a Soviet diplomat (the "Combe-Ivanov Affair"). The Hope Commissions resulted in the passage of the ASIO Act of 1979, and the creation of a parliamentary oversight committee in 1988.[58]

Any attempt to dissect all of the causes of the various intelligence scandals of the past seven decades exceeds the scope of this chapter. Such causes may be both broad and varied.

---

[53] Stuart Farson & Reg Whitaker, *Accounting for the Future or Past?: Developing Accountability and Oversight to Meet Future Intelligence Needs, in* The Oxford Handbook of National Security Intelligence, 673, 679–81 (Loch K. Johnson ed., 2010).

[54] *Id.*

[55] *Id.*

[56] Richelson & Ball, *supra* note 46, at 68–80.

[57] Farson & Whitaker, *supra* note 53, at 685; Canadian Parliamentary Research Branch, The Canadian Security Intelligence Service 1–4 (2000).

[58] Frank Cain, *Australian Intelligence Organizations and the Law*, 27 U. New S. Wales L.J. 296, 307–09 (2004); John Faulkner, Surveillance, Intelligence and Accountability: An Australian Story 14–18, *available at* http://www.afr.com/rw/2009-2014/AFR/2014/10/23/Photos/cad23366-5a65-11e4-a5ea-c145dc509150_Surveillance,%20Intelligence%20and%20Accountability%20by%20senator%20John%20Faulkner.pdf (last visited Dec. 22, 2015).

Rather, my aim is to show that the organization and regulation of intelligence services may not have been the coincidental or autogenic response of governments responding to the same shared experience. In doing so, I remain agnostic as to which isomorphic process is primarily responsible for institutional convergence in the intelligence realm. For present purposes, what is important is that evidence of each process may be observed. Determining the relative weight to assign to each process is a central part of the research agenda I propose below.

A. Competition

To address the first point, evidence that competition drives isomorphism would suggest that similarity of design is, at the very least, not coincidental. In classic economic theory, market pressures reward specialization, and drive out of the market those firms that are less efficient than their competitors in producing goods and services. Yet at the same time, competitive pressures may also result in institutional convergence as "inefficient institutional solutions are eliminated."[59] Indeed, the homogenizing tendency of the market is perhaps intuitive to anyone who has found herself unable to tell the difference between the hamburgers of major fast food restaurant chains. Although DiMaggio and Powell did not directly address competition in their seminal paper on institutional isomorphism,[60] the hypotheses they set forth do suggest rationales as to why actors in a competitive market might converge onto homogenized structures. For example, organizational fields may experience isomorphic convergence when the means and ends of the organizations within the field are uncertain; under such circumstances, organizations will model themselves after organizations they perceive to be successful.[61] To return to the fast food example, a new entrant into the field would face a huge amount of cost and risk in trying to design a more efficient method of drive-through food service; therefore, one would be unsurprised to see a drive-through start-up adopt the same two-step system of ordering and delivery employed by the major fast food chains.

Jens Beckert speculates that internationally, "competition can cause isomorphic pressure if one assumes that countries compete with each other in providing favorable institutional conditions for globally mobile business."[62] It takes little imagination to extend Beckert's theory of international isomorphic pressure beyond global business to other goods over which states might compete, such as political power or military advantage. Indeed, as noted above, evidence exists that states do converge in areas of national security, such as the formation of armed forces.[63] Military history is replete with examples of states accruing temporary advantage through the deployment of an innovative tactic or weapon—be it chariots,[64]

---

[59] Beckert, *supra* note 8, at 160.

[60] DiMaggio and Powell intentionally avoided citing competition as an explanation of institutional homogenization, because they were seeking "an alternative to Max Weber's emphasis on the role of competitive market pressures in explaining processes of bureaucratization." *Id.*

[61] DiMaggio & Powell, *supra* note 9, at 154–55.

[62] Beckert, *supra* note 8, at 160.

[63] Goodman & Jinks, *supra* note 6, at 1765–78. It should be noted that Goodman and Jinks suggest that acculturation, rather than competition, drives convergence in the realm of national security.

[64] *See* WILLIAM H. MCNEILL, THE PURSUIT OF POWER 9–11 (1982).

gunpowder,[65] or tanks[66]—only to have the advantage diminish as the innovation is incorporated by the state's adversaries. Considering this, it should be unsurprising that states actively
attempt to gather information about adversaries' capabilities, in order to co-opt or mitigate
the advantages such capabilities present. Therefore, intelligence may be best understood as
the "collection, analysis, and dissemination of information for decision makers engaged in a
competitive enterprise. It is a process by which competitors improve their decision making
relative to their opponents."[67]

However, even if intelligence is part of a process of isomorphic convergence in the realm
of national security, do the forces of interstate competition drive convergence in the structure of intelligence agencies themselves? Evidence from the earliest days of modern espionage suggests that they do. In the latter half of the nineteenth century, advances in industrial
production began to revolutionize the field of military armaments (with the advent of
muzzle-loading rifles and steam-powered armored naval vessels),[68] transportation (with the
development of locomotives), and communication (through the development of telegra-
phy).[69] Combined, these innovations meant that a massive amount of firepower and manpower could be rapidly brought to bear on a state's adversary. It was precisely to avoid being
caught ill-prepared in light of these developments that both the U.K. and the United States
created their first, enduring modern intelligence agencies,[70] with the British War Office
establishing a military Intelligence Branch in 1873,[71] followed by both the United States and
the U.K. establishing naval intelligence offices in 1882,[72] and the United States creating a
Military Intelligence Division in 1885.[73]

The growing realization during the late Industrial era that superior intelligence could
give an adversary a considerable advantage in warfare also led, in the United States, to the
first law prohibiting espionage, the Defense Secrets Act of 1911. In introducing the Act,
Representative Reuben Moon noted that

[t]he issues of most modern wars have been settled quickly by reason of the preparation of the belligerents . . . In this contest of preparations, the question of knowledge
on the part of the enemy is of vital importance . . . Such knowledge may indeed settle
the contest. To prevent the acquisition of this information, nearly all of the nations

---

[65] *Id.* at 81 (describing Europe's rapid adoption of firearms in the fourteenth century, and the resulting military
advantage, which lasted until the twentieth century).

[66] *Id.* at 331–35 (describing the early successes of the U.K. and France in the use of tanks in World War I, followed
by widespread adoption of the tank during World War II).

[67] Jennifer E. Sims, *A Theory of Intelligence and International Politics, in* NATIONAL INTELLIGENCE SYSTEMS 58,
62 (Gregory F. Treverton & Wilhelm Agrell eds., 2009).

[68] MCNEILL, *supra* note 64, at 241.

[69] *Id.* at 249.

[70] TWIGGE ET AL., BRITISH INTELLIGENCE 92 (2008); JEFFREY T. RICHELSON, A CENTURY OF SPIES 5
(1995).

[71] RICHELSON, *supra* note 70, at 5.

[72] *Id.*

[73] MICHAEL E. BIGELOW, A SHORT HISTORY OF ARMY INTELLIGENCE, 10 (2012), *available at* http://fas.org/
irp/agency/army/short.pdf.

of the world with any developed system of national defense, except the United States, have on their statute books stringent laws under which they can restrain and to a degree prevent spying . . . [74]

In referring to the laws of other nations, Representative Moon may have had in mind the British Official Secrets Act of 1889, which being enacted prior to the Statute of Westminster of 1931 (removing the ability of the British Parliament to legislate on behalf of the dominions), applied equally in the U.K., Canada, Australia, and New Zealand. In form, the Official Secrets Act of 1889 and the Defense Act of 1911 are extremely similar, suggesting that the latter may have been based on the former.[75] Indeed, the Defense Secrets Act built on a bill passed in 1898, which penalized civilian violations of U.S. War Department Regulations. Among the regulations covered was an 1897 order restricting access to military facilities; the order was directly modeled on a British regulation dating from 1889.[76]

The arms race that spurred the development of army and naval intelligence organizations, as well as espionage laws and information classification systems, represented an era in which Anglo-American security cooperation was neither consistent nor formalized, and the two nations viewed each other as (at least theoretically) potential adversaries. Indeed, as late as 1930, the United States continued to maintain plans ("Plan Red") for a hypothetical war against the U.K. and its colonies and dominions.[77] In the nearly 70 years since the end of World War II, however, the interests of the United States, the U.K., Canada, Australia, and New Zealand have been sufficiently aligned so as to make the Five Eyes alliance an enduring and productive multilateral partnership. Bearing in mind that realist principle that "friendships between governments do not endure and coinciding interests at one moment easily diverge at the next,"[78] the Five Eyes alliance would nonetheless appear to be an instance in which competition (at least within the intelligence sphere) has been reduced to a minimum.

However, the direct competition between the nineteenth-century U.K. and United States that led the two countries to develop similar intelligence systems is but one type of competition that may generate isomorphic pressures. Another form—that is, where states not directly in competition with each other are nonetheless similarly subject to the competitive forces of the broader international environment—may also produce isomorphic pressures.

[74] H.R. Rep. No. 61-1942, at 2 (1911).

[75] For example, the first sections of both acts prohibit entering certain military facilities; documenting such facilities; communicating such documentation to an unauthorized individual, or, being authorized to have such documentation, communicating it to an unauthorized individual. *Compare* Official Secrets Act of 1889 (U.K.), *available at* https://en.wikisource.org/wiki/Official_Secrets_Act_1889; Defense Secrets Act of 1911 (U.S.), *available at* https://en.wikipedia.org/wiki/Defense_Secrets_Act_of_1911#/media/File:Defense_Secrets_Act_of_1911_page_1.png.

[76] Timothy L. Ericson, *Building Our Own "Iron Curtain": The Emergence of Secrecy in American Government*, THE AM. ARCHIVIST 18, 30 (2004).

[77] *See generally* Christopher M. Bell, *Thinking the Unthinkable: British and American Naval Strategies for an Anglo-American War, 1918–1931*, 19 INT'L HIST. REV. 789 (1997). A declassified copy of Plan Red may be found at http://strategytheory.org/military/us/joint_board/Estimate%20of%20the%20Situation%20-%20Red%20and%20Tentative%20Joint%20Basic%20Plan%20-%20Red.pdf.

[78] Jennifer E. Sims, *Foreign Intelligence Liaison: Devils, Deals, and Details*, 19 INT'L J. INTELLIGENCE & COUNTERINTELLIGENCE 195, 196 (2006).

Here, there is reason to believe that isomorphic convergence of intelligence structures within the Five Eyes may be driven by the Five Eyes intelligence competition with other states, terrorist groups, etc. The unstable global environment in which the Five Eyes partnership has developed is analogous to one of the scenarios under which DiMaggio and Powell predicted that an organizational field would experience isomorphic convergence, that is, when the goals of an organizational field are ambiguous. In such circumstances, isomorphic convergence may occur because, among other things, the uncertainty will lead organizations to adopt established models so as to appear legitimate in the eyes of key constituencies, because mimicry of established forms reduces the cost and conflict associated with independently assessing the organization's goals, or because organizations in the field may be dependent on the same resources.[79]

Applying this to the intelligence realm, consider the range of questions that the Five Eyes agencies have sought to address: Will the Soviet Union use force to prevent the dissolution of the Communist Bloc? Will the Arab coalition mount a surprise attack on Israel? Is Saddam Hussein pursuing nuclear weapons? Is al-Qaida planning a terrorist attack? In seeking to answer these questions, intelligence agencies have had to make difficult judgments regarding resource allocation, seeking to match their constrained capabilities against those threats to national security they perceive to be most urgent. Of course, history has shown that intelligence agencies do not always anticipate "strategic surprise" events, and when such failures occur, whatever cost to the intelligence agencies in terms of resources, political clout, or organizational independence may be dwarfed by the true cost of lives lost. Therefore, although we might say that in a sense the goal of the Five Eyes intelligence agencies may be clear—to prevent strategic surprise—the precise means by which that goal may be achieved are all too often uncertain. Under such circumstances, it is conceivable that policymakers wishing to assure their domestic constituencies (or perhaps their foreign allies) of their national security will, as a consequence, model their intelligence structures on those of states perceived to possess capable and effective ICs. At the operative level, this form of what I term "competitive alliance" convergence occurs due to mimicry of, or "acculturation" to foreign models perceived to be successful. I shall turn to the pure "acculturation" form of convergence in more detail later; for present purposes it is important to note that although mimicry or acculturation does the "legwork" of competitive alliance convergence, the process is driven by the international competitive enterprise of intelligence.

B. Coercion

If evidence of competition merely demonstrates that convergence is not necessarily the result of happenstance, then we must turn to another process to further rule out the possibility that convergence may be autogenic. To this end, evidence of interstate coercion would demonstrate that convergence is undertaken both consciously and not coincidentally. According to DiMaggio and Powell, homogenization "results from both formal and informal pressures exerted on organizations by other organizations on which they are dependent."[80] In the

---

[79] DiMaggio & Powell, *supra* note 9, at 155–56.
[80] *Id.* at 150.

context of international relations, "states and institutions influence the behavior of other states by escalating the benefits of conformity or the costs of nonconformity through material rewards and punishment."[81]

Elsewhere in this volume, Professor Ashley Deeks argues that peer intelligence communities can constrain each other, in part by denying logistical assistance or by withholding intelligence. Stated simply, if State A requires the assistance of State B in order to carry out some intelligence activity, and State B is unable or unwilling to assist due to State B's legal obligations, then the ultimate effect may be that State B's legal obligations constrain not only State B, but State A as well. The account provided by Professor Deeks is essentially one of coercion, that is, the modification of a state's behavior due to the withholding of material benefits by another. In Professor Deeks's accounts, such peer-to-peer coercion may limit intelligence activities. However, can the effects of coercion extend further, beyond the day-to-day conduct of intelligence activities, to the very structure of intelligence agencies and oversight mechanisms?

At least one incident from early in the Cold War demonstrates how inter-state coercion may result in convergence of intelligence structures. On September 5, 1945, Igor Gouzenko, a cypher clerk at the Soviet embassy in Ottawa, attempted to defect with a large cache of secret Soviet files. The initial Canadian response was almost comically inept, with the disbelieving Canadian press and Department of Justice turning away the would-be defector, and the Canadian government refusing his request for asylum. On the night of September 6, while hiding in his neighbor's apartment and contemplating suicide, Gouzenko watched through a keyhole as Soviet officials ransacked his apartment across the hall. The Soviet search team was scared off by the arrival of a Royal Canadian Mounted Police (RCMP) surveillance team, at which point—after having been on the run for over 30 hours—Gouzenko was finally offered asylum.[82] Upon examining the files provided by Gouzenko, Canadian and British officials were shocked to discover the degree to which Soviet intelligence agencies had infiltrated Allied governments, including nuclear weapons facilities. The Gouzenko affair was a public sensation, and led to a reorganization of "Special Branch," the RCMP's counterintelligence office.[83]

Yet the repercussions of the Gouzenko defection did not end there. Information obtained from Gouzenko contributed to attempts by the U.S. Army Security Agency (a forerunner of the NSA) to decipher Soviet diplomatic communications.[84] Code-named VENONA, this effort eventually led to the interception and decoding of over 3,000 classified Soviet telegrams sent between 1940 and 1948.[85] The VENONA program was among the most closely held secrets of its day, and revealed the identities of several prominent Soviet spies, including Klaus Fuchs, David Greenglass, and members of the "Cambridge Five" espionage ring.[86]

---

[81] Ryan Goodman & Derek Jinks, *How to Influence States: Socialization and International Human Rights Law*, 54 DUKE L.J. 621, 633 (2004).

[82] RICHARD J. ALDRICH, THE HIDDEN HAND: BRITAIN, AMERICA, AND COLD WAR SECRET INTELLIGENCE, 102–04 (2002); ANDREW, *supra* note 42, at 341–42 (2009).

[83] *Id.* at 108.

[84] RICHELSON, *supra* note 70, at 224–25.

[85] ANDREW, *supra* note 42, at 348.

[86] *Id.* at 376–79. ALDRICH, *supra* note 82, at 110.

Perhaps more important for present purposes, however, the VENONA program revealed that a leak within the Australian government was providing sensitive allied material to the Soviets.[87]

For the British, the timing of the discovery could not have been worse. British strategic policy in the aftermath of the Second World War was to continue its close cooperation with the United States. At the same time, Britain's relationships with its dominions abroad were invaluable assets, both in that the dominions provided Britain with important intelligence access,[88] and because the dominions offered the space and resources to facilitate the development of nuclear, biological, chemical, and missile technologies.[89] Thus, British interests required maintaining the United States' trust not only in the U.K., but in the dominions as well. The VENONA and Gouzenko revelations threatened the entire arrangement. Indeed, in 1948, the United States informed the British and Australian governments that it was placing an embargo on the transfer of any classified information to Australia.[90]

In response, the MI-5 director Sir Percy Sillitoe traveled to Australia and New Zealand, to convince the dominion governments of the need for improved counterintelligence capabilities. At first, both dominion governments proved skeptical. However, in September 1948, the Australian prime minister agreed to the founding of an agency "similar to MI-5."[91] The new agency, the ASIO, was founded on a charter based on that of MI-5, and MI-5 officers were dispatched to Australia to help set up the organization.[92] New Zealand likewise created a "Security Service" (later renamed the New Zealand Security Intelligence Service) modeled on MI-5 and ASIO.[93]

The Gouzenko and VENONA affairs thus demonstrate how coercion can contribute to the creation of intelligence structures of a design preferable to the state capable of providing or withholding material resources. The British rationale for demanding that the dominions create organizations similar to MI-5 was likely because such an organizational design gave the British greater confidence in the professionalism of the dominion services (and, perhaps more important, gave the United States greater confidence). However, it is conceivable that states may use coercion to shape other countries' intelligence services for a variety of reasons; for example, a state may use coercion in shaping a foreign state's intelligence service in order to develop even greater political leverage over the foreign intelligence service, perhaps by selecting the service's leadership, or by shaping the service's doctrine, or by orienting the foreign intelligence service to collect on specific intelligence targets. Alternatively a state may

---

[87] ALDRICH, *supra* note 82, at 110.

[88] ANDREW, *supra* note 42, at 371.

[89] ALDRICH, *supra* note 82, at 108–09.

[90] ANDREW, *supra* note 42, at 370; Jones, *supra* note 48, at 825–26. Ironically, both the Gouzenko and VENONA operations were ultimately compromised not by the Canadians or Australians, but by the Soviet spies William Weisband (a Russian linguist employed by the U.S. Army Security Agency) and Kim Philby (a British SIS official who also provided information on VENONA, and deflected suspicions of the Cambridge Five raised by the Gouzenko revelations). *See* ANDREW, *supra* note 42, at 347–49, 377–78.

[91] *Id.* at 370–71; Jones, *supra* note 48, at 826.

[92] *Id. See also* RICHELSON & BALL, *supra* note 46, at 48.

[93] *Id.* at 68. It should be noted that New Zealand did not create NZSIS until 1956, following the revelation of yet further Soviet espionage with ties to New Zealand and Australia, that is, the "Petrov" affair. *See id.*

simply find that international collaboration may be more efficient when its intelligence professionals are dealing with direct counterparts (e.g., a SIGINT intelligence agency may find it more efficient to work with another stand-alone SIGINT service, rather than a service that combines SIGINT and other disciplines). This suggests a "soft" form of coercion, wherein a state models its intelligence services on those of a dominant foreign country not because of the latter's explicit demands, but—although the conforming state may not necessarily be convinced of the merits of the dominant foreign state's model—the conforming state is nonetheless dependent on the dominant foreign state, and convergence ensures continued or more efficient cooperation.

Regarding intelligence oversight, the account of peer constraints offered by Professor Deeks suggests how material inducements may, at least indirectly, contribute to convergence of certain norms of intelligence oversight, if not formal mechanisms. It is easy to imagine scenarios under which State A's coercion of State B not only results in compliance with a legal standard, but also establishes a foothold for oversight mechanisms within State B. For example, upon receiving notice from State A that legal obligations preclude cooperation, intelligence officials in State B may turn to their own domestic legal advisors in order to better understand the nature of State A's concerns. If State B has not traditionally had a culture of legalism in its intelligence operations, then it is possible that State A's coercive denial of assistance has had the effect of planting the seed from which a norm of intelligence legalism might grow.

C. Normative Persuasion

The account thus far has demonstrated how evidence of interstate competition suggests that convergence in intelligence structures and oversight is not necessarily coincidental, and evidence of coercion suggests that convergence is likewise not autogenic. However, coercion is not the only process whereby states may consciously incorporate foreign models of state policy. States may freely elect to emulate global norms for a variety of reasons, including because states have genuinely internalized the norms, or out of a desire to be "seen" as compliant. In this section I address the former rationale. This method of isomorphic convergence has been variously termed attraction,[94] persuasion,[95] or normative pressures.[96] Common to all conceptions of this process of convergence is that "isomorphic institutional change occurs if institutional models exist that institutional entrepreneurs actively seek to imitate because they are interpreted as attractive institutional solutions to problems being faced."[97] Key to this approach is that "actors are consciously convinced of the truth, validity, or appropriateness of a norm, belief, or practice."[98] Whereas Goodman and Jinks emphasize the ultimate adoption of a set of beliefs by actors within an organization, DiMaggio and Powell focused on the process of belief inculcation, that is, the "professionalization" of organizational actors through education, legitimation, and personnel filtration.[99]

---

[94] Beckert, *supra* note 8, at 155.

[95] Goodman & Jinks, *supra* note 81, at 635.

[96] DiMaggio & Powell, *supra* note 9, at 152.

[97] Beckert, *supra* note 8, at 155.

[98] Goodman & Jinks, *supra* note 81, at 635.

[99] DiMaggio & Powell, *supra* note 9, at 152–53.

Demonstrating the normative persuasion process of convergence can be difficult, as it turns on the internal rationale of the group adopting the norm. States may openly profess to have adopted a norm, when in fact such statements may simply be a public face-saving measure in circumstances where the state has been coerced into adopting a norm, or where (as will be discussed below) a state does not truly embrace the norm, but feels social pressure to appear to do so. Therefore, what evidence may exist that a norm is actually held? First, absent some indication that a state is acting under coercion, normative persuasion may be evidenced by a state both formally adopting a norm, and actually implementing it in local practice. For example, if a state were a party to the Convention on the Elimination of All Forms of Discrimination against Women, evidence of normative persuasion might be found if the state's laws permitted women to vote, consistent with Article 7 of the Convention.[100] In that example, the state both formally adopts the international norm and demonstrates acceptance of the norm through its local practice. In contrast, if the state were a signatory yet permitted widespread disenfranchisement of women, then such would be evidence of what Goodman and Jinks refer to as "decoupling," that is, the state's adopting a norm, despite the norm being disconnected locally from social and functional demands.[101] Decoupling, where it occurs, is evidence of isomorphic convergence due not to normative persuasion, but to acculturation, as will be discussed below.

A second signal of normative persuasion is suggested by DiMaggio and Powell's emphasis on professionalization. Of course, the existence or nonexistence of professionalizing networks is not in and of itself determinative of whether normative persuasion is responsible for isomorphic convergence. Nonetheless, professionalizing networks are observable pathways by which normative persuasion may take place. Where they may be found, the case for normative persuasion may be plausible; where they are lacking, the case becomes much more difficult to make.

Do professionalizing networks exist with the Five Eyes countries? Elizabeth Sepper has argued that cooperation between the Five Eyes has resulted in the development of an "epistemic community," defined as "a network of professionals who share a specialized expertise and knowledge in a particular field," and derive a sense of shared identity through "shared practices, normative principles, and evaluative criteria within their domain."[102] Sepper notes the secrecy with which intelligence services operate, the necessity of security clearances for access to classified information, and the shared understanding of the role of intelligence in assisting national-level decision-making as common attributes of the Five Eyes intelligence services.[103]

A recent example demonstrates how a shared professional culture, at least as it related to the shared use of terminology, may have shaped the structure of intelligence agencies within the alliance. Until the 1990s, the U.S. IC divided responsibility for analysis of imagery

---

[100] Convention on the Elimination of All Forms of Discrimination against Women art.7, Dec. 18, 1979, 1249 U.N.T.S. 13.

[101] Ryan Goodman & Derek Jinks, Socializing States 42 (2013); Goodman & Jinks, *supra* note 81, at 649.

[102] Elizabeth Sepper, *Democracy, Human Rights, and Intelligence Sharing*, 46 Tex. Int'l. L. J. 151, 159 (2010).

[103] *Id.*

intelligence and geospatial information (e.g., maps and geodesy) among several distinct organizations. The inefficiency of this arrangement became apparent during the Gulf War, when many military commanders complained that they often found themselves unable to obtain imagery needed during battle. In response, Congress created the National Imagery and Mapping Agency (NIMA), which consolidated the responsibilities of six different agencies.[104] Following the September 11th attacks, then-NIMA director James R. Clapper coined the term "Geospatial Intelligence" to signify the synthesis of imagery and geospatial information.[105] In 2003, NIMA was formally renamed the National Geospatial-Intelligence Agency (NGA).[106] In the ensuing years, the GEOINT "discipline" has spurred the creation of professional groups,[107] conferences with international attendees,[108] professional publications,[109] and international academic courses of study.[110]

Although the term "geospatial information" appears to have been used in other Five Eyes countries prior to 2003, it was only subsequent to the designation of NGA that the term "geospatial intelligence" became formally embraced, with the U.K. renaming its Joint Air Reconnaissance Intelligence Centre the Defence Geospatial Intelligence Fusion Centre in 2012,[111] New Zealand's GCSB creating GEOINT New Zealand in 2012,[112] and Australia

---

[104] National Geospatial-Intelligence Agency, The Advent of NGA 15–24 (2011), *available at* https://www.nga.mil/About/Documents/04a_History.pdf.

[105] *See* National Geospatial-Intelligence Agency, *NGA in History: Lt. Gen. James R. Clapper, available at* https://www.nga.mil/About/History/NGAinHistory/Pages/JamesRClapper.aspx (last visited Dec. 22, 2015). *See also* Memorandum for the Principal Deputy Director of National Intelligence (Oct. 17, 2005), *available at* http://www.gwg.nga.mil/ntb/related/GEOINT_Definitions-Amplification_Memosigned.pdf.

[106] National Defense Authorization Act of 2004, Pub. L. No. 108-136, § 921, 117 Stat. 1392.

[107] *See, e.g.*, U.S. Geospatial-Intelligence Foundation, http://usgif.org/ (last visited Dec. 22, 2015).

[108] *See, e.g., Why Attend*, GEOINT 2013 Symposium, http://geoint2013.com/about/who-should-attend (last visited Dec. 22, 2015); Defence Geospatial Intelligence Conference, http://dgi.wbresearch.com/ (last visited Dec. 22, 2015); Geospatial Intelligence & Intelligence Asia Pacific, http://www.ginsasia.com/ (last visited Dec. 22, 2015).

[109] *See, e.g.*, Geospatial Intelligence Forum, http://www.kmimediagroup.com/gif.

[110] *See, e.g., Master of Professional Studies in Homeland Security—Geospatial Intelligence Option*, Pennsylvania State University Online, http://www.worldcampus.psu.edu/degrees-and-certificates/homeland-security-geospatial-intelligence/overview; *Bachelor of Science in Geography, Geospatial Intelligence Emphasis*, Brigham Young University, https://geography.byu.edu/Pages/Students/intel.aspx; *Center for Geospatial Intelligence*, George Mason University, http://cgeoint.gmu.edu/; *Master of Science in Geospatial Intelligence*, University of Nottingham, http://www.nottingham.ac.uk/pgstudy/courses/geography/geographical-information-science-msc.aspx; *New Degree in MSc Geospatial Intelligence Approved*, University of Leicester (Aug. 23, 2011, 8:42 AM), http://www2.le.ac.uk/departments/geography/newsevents/2010/mscgeospatialintelligence; *Imagery and Geospatial Intelligence syllabus*, Charles Sturt University, http://www.csu.edu.au/handbook/subjects/JST478.html. (last visited Dec. 22, 2015).

[111] *Guidance, Defence Intelligence: Roles*, U.K. Gov't, https://www.gov.uk/defence-intelligence-services#defence-geospatial-intelligence-fusion-centre (last visited Dec. 22, 2015).

[112] Prior to 2012, GEOINT New Zealand appears to have been named the Joint Geospatial Support Facility. *Compare* New Zealand Defence Force, Annual Report 12 (2011), *available at* http://www.nzdf.mil.nz/downloads/pdf/public-docs/2011/nzdf-annual-report-2011.pdf (listing Joint Geospatial Support Facility); New Zealand Defence Force, Annual Report 12 (2012), *available at* http://www.nzdf.mil.nz/downloads/pdf/public-docs/2012/nzdf-annual-report-2012.pdf (listing GEOINT New Zealand).

renaming the Defence Imagery and Geospatial Organisation the Australian Geospatial-Intelligence Organisation in 2013.[113]

What lies behind the diffusion of the "Geospatial Intelligence" concept? Of the isomorphic processes described above, pure competition seems an unsatisfactory explanation, considering the high degree of cooperation among the Five Eyes countries. Likewise, for whatever other benefit the United States may gain from the adoption of a specific intelligence term of art by its Five Eyes partners, the marginal benefit of those partners incorporating the term into the name of their intelligence agencies would seem rather insignificant. Under such circumstances, it seems unlikely that U.S. coercion was the rationale for the diffusion of the term. Admittedly, it is possible that acculturation may have been a primary cause for the adoption of the term, perhaps through the Five Eyes partners feeling "psychological pressure" to avoid "social sanctions" in not adopting intelligence methodologies employed by the United States, or as a result of a "competitive alliance" acculturation. However, even if that is true, the growth of international GEOINT professional organizations, academic programs, and professional literature at least suggests that normative persuasion played a role in the diffusion of the GEOINT "discipline." Thus, the more likely explanation for the diffusion of the GEOINT term is that intelligence professionals across the Five Eyes states became convinced (be it through education, professional contacts, etc.) that the term better captured the essence of their intelligence discipline. In contrast to the creation of ASIO and NZSIS, where British and American pressure "pushed" structural convergence, the adoption of GEOINT appears to be the result of a convergence "pull" on the part of the adopting states.

If professional communities may thus contribute to the diffusion of norms governing intelligence methodology (and the structure of intelligence agencies by extension), might they also contribute to the diffusion of norms of oversight? Margo Schlanger has made a credible argument that (at least within the United States), a professional community of intelligence lawyers exists. Schlanger criticizes what she terms "intelligence legalism" within the U.S. IC, that is, the growing prevalence of "substantive rules given the status of law rather than policy; some limited court enforcement of those rules; and empowerment of lawyers."[114] Such a compliance regime, to Schlanger's mind, focuses too much on the question of whether intelligence activities *can* be performed under the law, and not enough on the question of whether such activities *should* be performed. Yet regardless of whether "intelligence legalism" fails in Schlanger's opinion to optimize civil liberties, she nonetheless admits that such legalism has transformed the culture of U.S. intelligence. "Intelligence law professional networks exist," she notes, "there is a bar association group with conferences, newsletters, and continuing legal education sessions; there are journals, centers, and like markers of professional group-building."[115] Perhaps more important, Schlanger notes the growing number of attorneys within the U.S. IC, and the increasing comfort with which intelligence

---

[113] Press Release, Statement of the Prime Minister, Renaming the Defence Signals Directorate and the Defence Imagery and Geospatial Organisation (May 3, 2013), *available at* http://www.minister.defence.gov.au/2013/05/03/prime-minister-and-minister-for-defence-joint-media-release-2013-defence-white-paper-renaming-the-defence-signals-directorate-and-the-defence-imagery-and-geospatial-organisation/.

[114] Margo Schlanger, *Intelligence Legalism and the National Security Agency's Civil Liberties Gap*, 6 Harv. Nat'l. Sec. J. 112, 113 (2015).

[115] *Id.* at 197.

operators interact with those attorneys.[116] Furthermore, evidence exists that a community of intelligence law professionals exists internationally. For example, in discussing the implementation of Presidential Policy Directive 28, Office of the Director of National Intelligence General Counsel Robert Litt noted that the U.S. IC had "a robust ongoing dialogue with our European allies and partners about privacy and data protection."[117]

D. Acculturation

Evidence that states profess a conscious choice to mimic the design of other states' intelligence structures, although perhaps not dispositive, at least suggests that isomorphic convergence is not the unintentional result of states responding to similar circumstances. Acculturation is the "general process of adopting the beliefs and behavioral patterns of the surrounding culture . . . this mechanism induces behavioral changes through pressures to assimilate—some imposed by other actors, and some imposed by the self."[118] According to Goodman and Jinks, included within the concept of acculturation are several microprocesses, including mimicry, identification, and status maximization.[119]

Like in the case of normative persuasion, differentiating circumstances under which states adopt a global norm due to acculturation as opposed to other processes of isomorphic convergence is difficult. For example, both acculturation and coercion may include states assessing the social costs of non-adoption. However, what distinguishes the two processes is whether the social cost is perceived to likely translate into a material cost; in such cases, convergence may be attributed to coercion, rather than acculturation.[120] Likewise, differentiating acculturation from normative pressures is problematic, as it turns on whether the internal rationale for adoption stems from a genuine acceptance of the norm, or rather from a desire to be viewed as being in compliance. Goodman and Jinks have suggested that decoupling serves as a distinguishing indicator of acculturation.[121] Decoupling may be found where, for example, states adopt national science bureaucracies, even when scientists and engineers constitute less than 0.2 percent of the population,[122] or adopt educational curricula that are at odds with the state's vocational needs.[123]

In this section, I focus on the public statements of government officials regarding the adoption of parliamentary oversight of intelligence agencies, as an example of acculturation operating in the intelligence realm. Once again, the secrecy under which many intelligence policy decisions must be made precludes the complete exclusion of the possibility that other isomorphic pressures may be at play. Nonetheless, I believe that acculturation is one of, if not the dominant process in parliamentary oversight debate, for two reasons. First, there appear

---

[116] *Id.* at 151.

[117] Robert Litt, Remarks at the Brookings Institute (Feb. 4, 2015), *available at* http://icontherecord.tumblr.com/post/110099240063/video-odni-general-counsel-robert-litt-speaks-on.

[118] Goodman & Jinks, *supra* note 81, at 638.

[119] GOODMAN & JINKS, *supra* note 101, at 4.

[120] GOODMAN & JINKS, *supra* note 81, at 645.

[121] GOODMAN & JINKS, *supra* note 101, at 42; Goodman & Jinks, *supra* note 81, at 649.

[122] GOODMAN & JINKS, *supra* note 6, at 1764.

[123] *Id.*

to be no indications that any of the Five Eyes countries openly exerted material coercion in order to pressure another to adopt parliamentary oversight, and a realist account of rational state interest suggests that there would be little incentive for any Five Eyes state to do so. Second, although I do not doubt that the Five Eyes countries have internalized the general principle of the rule of law through parliamentary democracy, the fact that officials within the Five Eyes states explicitly refer to the mechanisms of partner states while weighing the issue of parliamentary oversight of intelligence services at least suggests a desire to be "seen" as being in accordance with the practices of the leading Western common law countries.

Perhaps the first trace of evidence of the "acculturation" of parliamentary oversight following the establishment of SSCI and HPSCI may be found in Australia. As a part of the First Royal Commission on Intelligence and Security (i.e., "Hope I"), Justice Robert Hope had undertaken several trips to—among other countries—the United States, Canada, and New Zealand, in order to investigate Australia's intelligence relationship with those countries, and to better understand intelligence oversight within those states.[124] At the time of Justice Hope's trips (June 1975–April 1976), the congressional oversight committees in the United States had just begun operation, with the Church and Pike Committees having been respectively established in January and February of 1975.[125] Considering the relative infancy of the of the U.S. congressional oversight example, it is perhaps unsurprising that in the Second Royal Commission (i.e., "Hope II," established in 1983) recommended against creating a parliamentary oversight committee in Australia.[126] Nonetheless, the Labor government led by Prime Minister Bob Hawke rejected Justice Hope's position, and proceeded to establish a Parliamentary Joint Committee on the Australian Security Intelligence Organisation.[127] In his ministerial statement concerning the Hope II Commission, Prime Minister Hawke—although not explicitly referencing the United States—noted the "relevant overseas experience of parliamentary scrutiny of intelligence and security agencies" as evidence that such committees could operate effectively.[128]

---

[124] Jim Stokes, *A Brief History of The Royal Commission on Intelligence and Security*, NAT'L ARCHIVES OF AUSTRALIA, *available at* http://www.naa.gov.au/collection/publications/papers-and-podcasts/intelligence-and-security/rcis-historyppaper.aspx (last visited Dec. 22, 2015). Interestingly, Justice Hope noted the similarity of the scope of his review with that of the review undertaken by Vice President Nelson Rockefeller of the activities of the Central Intelligence Agency. ROYAL COMMISSION ON INTELLIGENCE AND SECURITY, FIRST REPORT 3 (1977), *available at* http://recordsearch.naa.gov.au/SearchNRetrieve/Interface/ViewImage. aspx?B=4727802.

[125] JEFFREYS-JONES, *supra* note 38, at 200–01. The Senate Select Committee on Intelligence was created in May 1976, and the House Permanent Select Committee on Intelligence was created in July 1976. *Id.* at 214.

[126] Parliamentary Debates, House of Representatives, May 22, 1985 (Robert Hawke, Prime Minister) (Austl.) [hereinafter Parliamentary Debates], *available at* http://parlinfo.aph.gov.au/parlInfo/search/display/ display.w3p;query=%28Dataset%3Aweblastweek,hansardr,noticer,webthisweek,dailyp,votes,journals,o rderofbusiness,hansards,notices,websds%29%20ParliamentNumber%3A%2234%22%20Government_ Phrase%3A%22yes%22%20Context_Phrase%3A%22ministerial%20statement%22%20Speaker_ Phrase%3A%22mr%20hawke%22;rec=13.

[127] *Id.*

[128] *Id.* Although Prime Minister Hawke's ministerial statement did not explicitly reference the United States regarding parliamentary oversight of intelligence, it did reference the United States, Canada, and the U.K. specifically on the issue of establishing a warrant-based regime for domestic intelligence collection.

Although indications are thus perhaps somewhat scant that the U.S. experience directly influenced the creation of the Australian Parliamentary Joint Committee, evidence of the influence of the U.S. oversight model on Canadian intelligence reform debates is clearer. As mentioned above, a series of incidents connected to the RCMP Special Branch's surveillance of the Quebec separatist movement led to the establishment of a Commission of Inquiry concerning Certain Activities of the Royal Canadian Mounted Police (the "McDonald Commission").[129] The McDonald Commission recommended both the formation of a domestic intelligence service (i.e., the Canadian Security Intelligence Service) separate from the RCMP, as well as strengthened oversight procedures, including the creation of an Advisory Council on Security and Intelligence, and a Joint Parliamentary Committee on Security and Intelligence. The McDonald Commission drew inspiration from the United States for both of the proposed new oversight bodies: comparisons to the U.S. Intelligence Oversight Board were used in the case of the Advisory Council,[130] and comparisons to the congressional oversight committees were applied to the proposed Parliamentary Committee.[131] Ultimately, when the McDonald Commission's recommendations were enacted in the Canadian Security Intelligence Service Act of 1984, the proposed separate Advisory Committee and Joint Parliamentary Committee were not included, with portions of their responsibilities instead given to the Security Intelligence Review Committee, a body comprised of five Privy Councilors.[132] The failure to create a parliamentary oversight committee was objected to by the main opposition parties, who pointed to the U.S. congressional committees (as well as the system of oversight in Germany) as evidence that parliamentary oversight could be successful.[133]

In the U.K., Parliament passed the Intelligence Services Bill in 1994, which in addition to giving legislative footing to the Secret Intelligence Service also provided for parliamentary oversight of the U.K.'s intelligence services. As Jon Moran and Clive Walker note in their chapter, the impetus for codifying the roles and responsibilities of Britain's security services may have been to avoid adverse judgments before the European Court of Human Rights. Regardless what the catalyst for beginning the legislative process may have been, the experiences of other Five Eyes states loomed large in the ensuing parliamentary debate. During the debates in both the House of Commons and House of Lords, frequent reference was made—both positive and negative—to the merits of the parliamentary oversight mechanisms of the United States, Canada, and Australia.[134]

---

[129] COMMISSION OF INQUIRY CONCERNING CERTAIN ACTIVITIES OF THE ROYAL CANADIAN MOUNTED POLICE [hereinafter McDonald Commission], *available at* http://epe.lac-bac.gc.ca/100/200/301/pco-bcp/commissions-ef/mcdonald1979-81-eng/mcdonald1979-81-eng.htm (last visited Dec. 22, 2015).

[130] *Id.* at 885.

[131] *Id.* at 902–03. The McDonald Commission also noted the parliamentary oversight in Germany, as well as a lack of parliamentary oversight (at the time) in Australia and the U.K.

[132] *Origins of SIRC*, SECURITY INTELLIGENCE REVIEW COMMITTEE, http://www.sirc-csars.gc.ca/abtprp/ogsogc-eng.html (last visited Dec. 22, 2015).

[133] CANADIAN PARLIAMENTARY RESEARCH BRANCH, *supra* note 57, at 11.

[134] *See, e.g.*, Statements of the Hons. Dale Campbell-Savours, Tom King, Sir David Steel, Sir Peter Emery, Chris Mullin, Stuart Randall, Rupert Allason, Peter Mandelson, and William Waldegrave, House of Commons, 22 Feb. 1994 PARL. DEB., H.C., *available at* http://hansard.millbanksystems.com/commons/1994/feb/22/intelligence-services-bill-lords#S6CV0238P0_19940222_HOC_248; *see also* statements of Lords Richard, Hunt of Tanworth, Callaghan of Cardiff, Lester of Herne Hill, Chalfont, and Merlyn-Rees, 9 Dec 1993 PARL.

New Zealand also adopted parliamentary oversight in 1994. On December 19, during the parliamentary debate wherein the Intelligence and Security Agencies Bill was introduced, Prime Minister Bolger noted, "[w]hat is proposed is based on a review of practice and procedures that have been adopted in overseas countries, namely, Australia, Britain, and Canada. The changes contained in the Bills will bring New Zealand into conformity with this overseas practice."[135] Regarding the establishment of an inspector general, Prime Minister Bolger stated, "there are models overseas for this position, and, in developing the provisions relation to the New Zealand inspector-general, particular regard has been given to the role and functions of the similar Australian position." Likewise, in discussing the need for parliamentary oversight, Prime Minister Bolger emphasized that "[i]n developing the proposal for the establishment of the committee, close attention has been paid to the practice adopted by like Governments overseas. It is significant that in both Australia and Britain parliamentary oversight committees for intelligence and security agencies have been established by legislation."[136] The prime minister's positive reference to intelligence oversight was echoed by Helen Clark, then leader of the opposition, who noted that parliamentary oversight existed in Australia, Germany, and the United States. "[W]here others have gone," she concluded, "New Zealand should now follow."[137]

Finally, returning to Australia once again, although the U.S. oversight experience may have had little influence on the creation of the Parliamentary Joint Committee on ASIO, the same cannot be said when the question arose almost a decade later as to whether ASIS should be brought under the Parliamentary Joint Committee's purview. Following public disclosures of disaffected ASIS employees in 1994, a royal commission chaired by Justice Samuels and Michael Codd recommended that parliamentary oversight be extended to ASIS.[138] In the process, Samuels and Codd extensively reviewed the benefits of legislative oversight in the United States, Canada, and U.K.[139]

Thus, over the course of approximately 20 years, all of the Five Eyes states adopted some measure of legislative control over their intelligence agencies. That public officials in Australia, Canada, the U.K., and New Zealand felt compelled to publicly link their proposals for parliamentary oversight to the experiences of the other Five Eyes states (in particular congressional oversight in the United States) demonstrates that they either felt a social pressure to conform to a perceived norm, or, as Katherine Linos suggests, they believed that

DEB., H.L., *available at* http://hansard.millbanksystems.com/lords/1993/dec/09/intelligence-services-bill-hl#S5LV0550P0_19931209_HOL_113.

[135] Parliamentary Debate, Dec. 19, 1995 (N.Z.) (Statement of Rt.Hon. J.B. Bolger), *available at* http://www.vdig.net/hansard/archive.jsp?y=1995&m=12&d=19&o=46&p=50.

[136] *Id.*

[137] *Id.* (Statement of Rt.Hon. H. Clark), *available at* http://www.vdig.net/hansard/archive.jsp?y=1995&m=12&d=19&o=46&p=50.

[138] Jones, *supra* note 48, at 832.

[139] COMMISSION OF INQUIRY INTO THE AUSTRALIAN SECRET INTELLIGENCE SERVICE, REPORT ON THE AUSTRALIAN SECRET INTELLIGENCE SERVICE, PUBLIC EDITION 45–49 (1995), *available at* http://apo.org.au/files/Resource/policyhistory_reportonasis_mar_1995_ocrclearscan.pdf. The Commission also recommended that ASIS's functions be established in legislation, noting that the intelligence services of the United States, Britain, Canada, New Zealand, Germany, and South Africa all had legislative charters. *Id.* at 30–31, 34.

reference of foreign models would signal to voters that the policy had proven successful elsewhere.[140]

Of course, it would be incorrect to suggest that adoption of parliamentary oversight was not due, at least in part, to the legislators of the various states being normatively persuaded of the legitimate and effective role that they could play in regulating intelligence activities. However, proposals for parliamentary oversight were met with at least some controversy in all Five Eyes states (with the possible exception of New Zealand), suggesting that the norm of parliamentary oversight was not fully internalized at the time of adoption. Indeed, the extent and breadth of parliamentary oversight has been an evolving concept in many Five Eyes states. Although the United States had permanent congressional oversight committees since 1976, the Iran-Contra scandal of the 1980s led to Congress mandating in the Intelligence Authorization Act of 1991 that Congress be kept "fully and currently informed" of intelligence activities. Likewise, as noted above, the Australian Parliamentary Joint Committee was in operation for six years before its remit was expanded to cover the entire Australian IC, and not merely ASIO. These examples demonstrate, if not actual "decoupling" of Five Eyes states' early theory and practice regarding the principle of parliamentary oversight, then at least an initial incomplete incorporation of the norm.

VI. IMPACT OF CONVERGENCE

In this section, I outline some of the potential consequences of institutional convergence in intelligence structures and oversight. As noted above, due to the secrecy that shrouds most states' espionage activities, intelligence is a field that is unlikely to produce binding international treaties.[141] The same secrecy likely precludes the development of a customary international law of intelligence. Therefore, any diffusion of transnational norms may be the result of the kind of isomorphic pressures outlined above. For this reason, studying the processes of isomorphic convergence in the intelligence field is essential not merely to assist in developing an accurate account of how intelligence norms arise, but will also be beneficial to those who wish to actively influence the development of such norms.

In other domains, the effects of convergence have proven to be ambiguous, at times producing positive effects (e.g., the diffusion of various human rights principles),[142] while at other times leading to deleterious results (e.g., arms races),[143] or producing a "race to the middle."[144] However, there is some reason for optimism that on the whole, isomorphic convergence in the intelligence realm—both within the Five Eyes countries and in application to other states—will be in a rights-protective, rule-of-law direction. Within the Five Eyes

---

[140] LINOS, *supra* note 24, at 22–23. Linos also suggests a third option, which is that politicians reference foreign models to clarify that the proposal is mainstream, and not radical or inconsistent with voters' values. However, because this line of argument equates to politicians attempting to show voters that their values comport to the international norm (or vice versa), it is effectively the same as the pressure for social compliance as set forth by Goodman and Jinks. Thus, I do not address it separately.

[141] Deeks, *supra* note 21, at 47.

[142] GOODMAN & JINKS, *supra* note 101, at 60–74.

[143] *Id.* at 74.

[144] *Id.* at 76.

countries, a variety of new actors have entered the oversight debate, whose interests generally align with the promotion of transparency and privacy interests. Essentially, these groups
constitute international and domestic "elites" who through coordination and advocacy may
encourage a "ratcheting up" of ever-greater demands for more transparency and protection
of civil liberties.[145] Thus, even if "race to the middle" pressures exist, they may be counterbal-
anced by the rights-protective pressures from new actors in oversight. For countries without
or with weak intelligence oversight, a "race to the middle" might still be an improvement.[146]

If isomorphic convergence is likely to be the primary method of convergence of intelligence
oversight norms, then understanding the processes of convergence is essential for those wishing
to ensure that the convergence is in a rights-protective direction. The benefit of understanding
isomorphic pressures in advancing intelligence oversight norms may be observed in at least
two ways. The first is in identifying pathways of influence. For example, consider an example
where reform advocates in State A wish to further State B's compliance with a given intelligence
oversight norm. If coercion is the dominant form of isomorphic convergence, then the reform
advocates might be best served by encouraging their government to reduce or cut off State A's
assistance to State B until the latter adopts the oversight norm. In contrast, if persuasion is the
dominant isomorphic pressure, then advocates in State A might wish to focus on drawing elites
of State B into professional networks, wherein the intelligence oversight norm is advocated.

Second, understanding isomorphic pressures may help to inform debates about expanding cooperation, whether it be with respect to the Five Eyes alliance, NATO, or another
alliance. Goodman and Jinks have demonstrated how different isomorphic pressures may
have significant consequences for how state behavior may be altered through the structure
and enforcement of international agreements.[147] Although Goodman and Jinks's analysis is
based on a system of human rights agreements that are far more open and public than secret
governmental relationships, some of their conclusions nonetheless may apply. For example,
consider a hypothetical proposal to expand the Five Eyes alliance to include other countries,
dependent on those countries adopting certain norms related to intelligence collection and
distribution. Goodman and Jinks theorize that where acculturation is the dominant form
of norm diffusion, broadly expanding membership would increase the social pressures on
members of the alliance to conform, by increasing the degree to which the norm is "universal."[148] In contrast, where coercion is the dominant form of norm diffusion, a more restrictive
membership may be advisable, as conditioning membership in the alliance on adherence to
the norm would have the effect of forcing states to demonstrate compliance.

A. Sequential-Dual Convergence

In my account of isomorphic pressures, I have remained agnostic as to which method plays the
dominant role in the convergence of intelligence structures and oversight. Such a determination will likely occupy a central place in any future research in this area. However, the examples

---

[145] *Id.* at 147–48, 154–55.

[146] For some of the challenges of intelligence reform facing emerging democracies, *see* Thomas C. Bruneau &
Florina C. Matei, *Intelligence in Developing Democracies, in* OXFORD HANDBOOK OF NATIONAL SECURITY
INTELLIGENCE 757, 764–68 (Loch K. Johnson ed., 2010).

[147] Goodman & Jinks, *supra* note 81, at 656–703.

[148] *Id.* at 667.

of isomorphic pressures provided above appear to have operated at various points—and at times seemingly concurrently—in the histories of Five Eyes intelligence services. This suggests two important insights. First, as Goodman and Jinks suggest, it is possible that convergence processes operate through successive stages.[149] For example, although coercion may have played a role in the creation of the modern Australian Intelligence Community (AIC), subsequent reforms of the AIC may be more attributable to acculturation to prevailing ideals of intelligence regulation in Western democracies (e.g., the adoption of parliamentary oversight), or persuasion by interaction with Five Eyes governments (e.g., the adoption of GEOINT).

Second, in the account above, intelligence structures generally converged prior to the creation of intelligence oversight mechanisms. This suggests that it is not only important to understand the sequential effects of isomorphic pressures in general, but also the process by which specific related organizations sequentially converge. Intuitively, this "sequential-dual" convergence is not a surprising result. After all, convergence of intelligence structures permits comparison of "like to like," thus making it easier for proponents of convergence to argue that foreign oversight models are appropriate for local conditions. At a more basic level, however, a necessary precondition for the convergence of intelligence oversight mechanisms is that intelligence structures exist, or at least that some form of intelligence activity is taking place. In other words, oversight requires something to be overseen.

However, the question remains as to whether the sequential pattern of convergence of structures followed by convergence of oversight is inevitable, or whether it may in some circumstances be reversed, or not occur at all. Goodman and Jinks note that convergence of legal regimes may occur, despite an incongruity with local conditions. Therefore, it is certainly possible that a transnational norm for the design of an intelligence oversight regime might emerge, which through acculturation would be adopted by a state, despite being an inefficient or ineffective match to the state's security needs and intelligence structures.

For example, Goodman and Jinks identify three forms of "decoupling." The first form, that is, "public conformity vs. private acceptance," occurs when states formally adopt norms that are at odds with local traditions, leading to a lack of observance of the norm in practice. In the intelligence oversight realm, an example would be where parliamentary oversight is established, yet intelligence services are reluctant to share intelligence information with parliamentarians. A second form of decoupling, termed "demands vs. capacity," occurs when states simply do not have the means to comply with a global norm. Theoretically, such might occur in intelligence oversight when an independent oversight office is created, but budgetary constraints preclude it from being fully staffed. Finally, Goodman and Jinks identify "form vs. functional task demands" decoupling, wherein the global norm is at odds with the needs or circumstances of the adopting state. In the intelligence oversight realm, such could conceivably occur, for example, if extensive emphasis is placed on electronic surveillance oversight, yet the state has limited to nonexistent signals intelligence capabilities.

There is reason to believe that sequential-dual convergence of intelligence structures would affect oversight decoupling in each of the scenarios identified by Goodman and Jinks. When intelligence structures converge, they may help to create within each state constituencies that embrace a particular form of intelligence organization, which in turn may generate support for

---

[149] GOODMAN & JINKS, *supra* note 101, at 171.

(or at least not oppose) coordinating forms of oversight. For example, the segregation of signals intelligence into a separate intelligence agency may instill within intelligence practitioners a norm that signals intelligence should be separated from other law enforcement activities, or from other intelligence disciplines. If so, then this may facilitate convergence to a norm of separate oversight of domestic signals intelligence collection (e.g., FISA): on the one hand, separation of domestic signals intelligence collection emphasizes the unique threat to civil liberties that such may entail, and highlights the need for oversight distinct from that employed for traditional forms of surveillance; on the other hand, intelligence practitioners may be less likely to oppose separate domestic signals intelligence oversight, because assigning signals intelligence collection to a distinct agency may reduce the chance of "creep" by the oversight body into other areas of intelligence activity, such as HUMINT (human intelligence) collection or covert action.

Thus, sequential-dual convergence may reduce the chances of "public conformity vs. private acceptance" decoupling, by fostering a professional culture amenable to oversight compliance. Likewise, although the prior convergence of intelligence structures may not be able to prevent "demands vs. capacity" oversight decoupling caused by material resource limitations, it may reduce such decoupling resulting from a lack of technical expertise. The prior convergence of intelligence structures might result in the formation of a cadre of former practitioners, who may provide their subject matter expertise as advisors to newly converged intelligence oversight bodies.[150] In their review of intelligence reform in developing democracies, Thomas C. Bruneau and Florina C. Matei noted that institutions of intelligence and control and oversight often found themselves to lack "sufficient knowledge of security and intelligence matters to be able to have an informed opinion."[151] Likewise, intelligence agencies in developing democracies tended to be resistant to oversight, due to their perception of amateurism within oversight bodies.[152] The involvement of former practitioners in the oversight process might reduce both of these concerns. Of course, such a solution may be problematic in practice. Where reform is undertaken to correct for a history of corruption or human rights abuses, incorporation of former practitioners might have the effect of letting the "reformed" fox guard the henhouse.[153] Likewise, it is unlikely that states seeking to achieve greater intelligence accountability will wish to wait to create oversight bodies until converged intelligence structures produce individuals with sufficient expertise. Nonetheless,

---

[150] Many have argued that U.S. oversight mechanisms lack personnel with sufficient technical expertise. *See, e.g.*, Edward W. Felton, Responses to Questions for the Record, United States Senate Committee on the Judiciary (Oct. 2, 2013) (arguing for the need for a technical expert to assist the Foreign Intelligence Surveillance Court), *available at* http://www.judiciary.senate.gov/imo/media/doc/100213QFRs-Felten.pdf; HUGH BOCHEL ET AL., WATCHING THE WATCHERS: PARLIAMENT AND THE INTELLIGENCE SERVICES 5–6 (2014). However, many staff members of the congressional oversight committees have had significant experience as intelligence practitioners. *See* DAVID COLE, SECRECY, NATIONAL SECURITY AND THE VINDICATION OF CONSTITUTIONAL LAW 36 (2013); James S. Van Wagenen, *Critics and Defenders: A Review of Congressional Oversight*, STUD. INTELLIGENCE (1997), *available at* https://www.cia.gov/library/center-for-the-study-of-intelligence/csi-publications/csi-studies/studies/97unclass/wagenen.html.

[151] Bruneau & Matei, *supra* note 146, at 766.

[152] *Id.*

[153] For example, in Brazil, when Brazil created the *Agência Brasileira de Inteligência* (ABIN), several officials from the former *Serviço Nacional de Informações* (SNI) were retained. According to Bruneau and Matei, those officials and their heirs are alleged to have undertaken several illicit acts. *Id.* at 764.

dual convergence—even if simultaneous rather than sequential—may be essential in ensuring that oversight bodies may eventually draw on professionals with the requisite expertise necessary for the oversight bodies to be perceived as effective and legitimate.

Sequential-dual convergence may also impact "form vs. functional task demands" oversight decoupling, albeit perhaps indirectly. Under Goodman and Jinks's theory of acculturation, the stronger the links between two countries (such as through joint participation in international organizations), the greater the likelihood of convergence of state practices.[154] Furthermore, such "social network" effects may result in convergence of state policies not directly connected to the linkage between the two states; Xun Cao has demonstrated—controlling for causality—how states' membership in the World Trade Organization resulted in increased convergence of monetary and regulatory policies.[155] In sum, the more connected states are in one policy area, the more likely they may be to converge in other areas.[156]

Applying this theory to the sequential-dual convergence of intelligence structures and oversight suggests that the more states converge in how they organize their intelligence functions, the more likely they will be to converge in other areas, to potentially include how they conduct oversight. If this is true, then such may impact "form vs. functional task demands" decoupling, although the result would not necessarily be to decrease the mismatch between form and function. The story might go like this: imagine that State A has method "O" of conducting oversight, which is effective and efficient in overseeing the State A's method "S" of organizing its intelligence structures. Over time, State B adopts method "S" for organizing its intelligence structures. If the social network effect of convergence by State B to method "S" increases the chance of it likewise adopting method "O" of oversight, then the effect of sequential-dual convergence may be an avoidance of "form vs. functional" decoupling in State B. Alternatively, if the social network effect of State B adopting method "S" of intelligence structures results in State A adopting State B's method "O^1" of conducting oversight, then the result may be an increase of "form vs. functional task demands" decoupling in both State A and B, if method "O^1" of oversight is less effective and efficient than method "O" in overseeing method "S" of organizing intelligence structures.

B. Basic Elements of Convergence

The account provided above suggests that the prior convergence of intelligence institutions may heavily influence the latter convergence of intelligence oversight. Yet it is possible that the isomorphic process may begin at an even earlier stage, with the convergence of certain cultural, legal, and regulatory principles that provide the framework upon which latter institutional and oversight convergence is built. It is outside the scope of this chapter to definitively identify and chronicle the diffusion of all such elements of the primordial stew that fostered the emergence of the Five Eyes intelligence system. Nonetheless, if the Five Eyes model of intelligence oversight is to be advocated as a transnational norm, it would be beneficial to highlight at least a few common, predicate conceptions.

---

[154] GOODMAN & JINKS, *supra* note 101, at 48–49.

[155] *Id.* at 59.

[156] *Id.* at 48. The causal mechanisms for this correlation may vary; increased convergence may be due either to socialization, or through greater information exchange that such social linkages may create.

First, the Five Eyes states all share a general conception of what constitutes "intelligence." By this, I mean that the purpose of intelligence is the clandestine collection of information in order to inform policy.[157] Second, intelligence is generally separate from law enforcement,[158] or diplomatic or military activity.[159] Third, all of the Five Eyes states share a common understanding of the roles and responsibilities of different government branches in relation to intelligence activities. Specifically, all five states assign responsibility for the conduct of intelligence activities to the executive, and although the parliament may have a role in oversight, the intelligence services are prohibited from advancing the interests of any political party.[160] Fourth, all five states share generally similar conceptions of civil and human rights that intelligence oversight bodies would seek to enforce. Where states lack such predicate conceptions, the likelihood of decoupling between intelligence structures and oversight (especially of the "public conformity vs. private acceptance" variety) would likely be significantly increased.

---

[157] See, e.g., General FAQ: What Does ASIS Do?, AUSTRALIAN SECRET INTELLIGENCE SERVICE, https://www. asis.gov.au/About-Us/FAQ/General-FAQ.html (last visited Dec. 22, 2015)("Our primary function is to obtain and distribute foreign intelligence, not readily available by other means, to assist the Australian Government and policy-makers in making informed decisions on matters of national interest and security); Intelligence Collection and Analysis, CANADIAN SECURITY INTELLIGENCE SERVICE, https://www.csis-scrs.gc.ca/bts/ ntllgnc-en.php (last visited Dec 22, 2015)(CSIS collects "information in Canada and abroad and use it as the basis for providing advice to the Government of Canada in the form of intelligence reports about activities that may constitute a threat to the security of Canada"); New Zealand Security Service Act 1969, § 4 (N.Z.); Exec. Order No. 12,333, §1.1, reprinted as amended 3 C.F.R. 13470 (2008) ("The United States intelligence effort shall provide the President, the National Security Council, and the Homeland Security Council with the necessary information on which to base decisions concerning the development and conduct of foreign, defense, and economic policies....").

[158] See, e.g., Intelligence Services Act 2001 (Cth) §11(2) (Austl.) (Australian intelligence services shall not carry out law enforcement functions); New Zealand Security Intelligence Service Act 1969, § 4 ("It is not a function of the Security Intelligence Service to enforce measures for security."); 50 U.S.C. § 3036(d)(1) (1947) ("The Director of the Central Intelligence Agency shall have no police, subpoena, or law enforcement powers or internal security functions...."); Frequently Asked Questions: How Does CSIS Differ from RCMP?, CANADIAN SECURITY INTELLIGENCE SERVICE, https://www.csis-scrs.gc.ca/bts/fq-en.php (last visited Dec. 22, 2015)("While CSIS is strictly concerned with collecting information and security intelligence for the purpose of advising the government, the role of the RCMP and other law enforcement agencies is to investigate criminal activity and to collect evidence that can be used in criminal prosecutions."); FAQs, supra note 157 ("As an intelligence agency SIS has no powers of arrest. It works in support of law enforcement agencies but does not have law enforcement powers.").

[159] Evidence of the perception that intelligence is at least not synonymous with diplomatic or military functions may be seen in that in all five states, the main domestic and foreign intelligence agencies operate outside the foreign and defense ministries.

[160] See, e.g., Australian Security Intelligence Organisation Act 1979 (Cth) §§ 8, 20 (Austl.) (minister may not override Director-General "concerning the nature of the advice that should be given by the Organisation," and the Director-General is responsible that the "Organisation is kept free from any influences or considerations not relevant to its functions and nothing is done that might lend colour to any suggestion that it is concerned to further or protect the interests of any particular section of the community."); Security Service Act 1989, c.13, § 2(2)(b) (U.K.) (The U.K. Security Service "does not take any action to further the interests of any political party."); New Zealand Security Intelligence Service Act 1969 § 4AA(1)(c) (the NZSIS "does not take any action for the purpose of furthering or harming the interests of any political party"); 5 U.S.C. § 7323(b)(2)(A) (1993) (prohibiting members of the U.S. IC from participating in certain forms of political activity); GOVERNMENT OF CANADA

VII. CONCLUSION

This chapter has sought to demonstrate that the intelligence structures and oversight mechanisms of the Five Eyes states have undergone a process of isomorphic convergence, to the extent that a "Five Eyes Model" of intelligence may be observed. Such a model is characterized by codified agency task differentiation along jurisdictional and subject matter (i.e., domestic, foreign, and military) and intelligence discipline (i.e., SIGINT, GEOINT, all-source analysis) lines; oversight conducted by parliamentary committees, inspectors general, and independent executive offices; and judicial review of domestic signals intelligence collection. Furthermore, the process of oversight convergence has followed a similar pattern of the executive initially exercising exclusive responsibility for intelligence regulation, yet gradually sharing responsibility with the coordinate branches of government. Finally, I have demonstrated how each of the four processes of isomorphic convergence (i.e., competition, coercion, normative persuasion, and acculturation) may each have played a role in the convergence process.

Much work remains to be done in examining the effects of isomorphic pressures on intelligence systems. First, further research must be done to determine the exact microprocesses by which convergence occurs, which may in turn better inform our understanding of which of the four processes exerts the greatest influence on intelligence structures and oversight, respectively. Second, it is possible that the "story" of convergence within the Five Eyes states is not complete, and that the alliance members will continue to adopt or reject each other's innovations in structure and oversight, or perhaps draw on "norms" from outside of the alliance.[161] If so, then the relative weight of the various isomorphic processes may be dynamic, and may shift depending on future security threats, or potentially on the entrance of new actors in the intelligence oversight field. For example, Professor Sam Rascoff discusses how private actors such as transnational telecommunication firms, nongovernmental organizations, and the "blogosphere" have increasingly inserted themselves into the intelligence oversight debate. Future accounts of intelligence system convergence must consider the impact of such groups, potentially as epistemic communities that may foster normative persuasion, or global elites that may create social pressure on states, leading to acculturation. Third, further research should be conducted on the role of judicial actors in oversight convergence.[162] Fourth, the account

---

PRIVY COUNCIL OFFICE, CANADIAN SECURITY AND INTELLIGENCE COMMUNITY 2 (2001) (The Canadian intelligence services "provide the government with non-partisan advice on specific threats to Canadian safety and security."), *available at* http://bcp.gc.ca/docs/information/publications/aarchives/csis-scrs/pdf/si-eng.pdf.

[161] It is interesting to note the Scottish government's proposals for an intelligence service for an independent Scotland. The proposal includes many parts of the "Five Eyes model" of intelligence oversight, including a legislative charter for the proposed service, granting the Scottish Parliament specific oversight powers, legislative restrictions on domestic surveillance, and adoption of an office similar to the Intelligence Services Commissioner. However, the proposal also contemplates a single service, responsible for both domestic and foreign intelligence. *See* THE SCOTTISH GOVERNMENT, SCOTLAND'S FUTURE ch. 7, *available at* http://www.gov.scot/Publications/2013/11/9348/11 (last visited Dec. 22, 2015). This proposal, combined with the recent assignment of foreign intelligence collection responsibilities to CSIS, *see* Anti-Terrorism Act, *supra* note 30, suggests either an evolution or shift in the Five Eyes intelligence structure model away from a separation of foreign and domestic intelligence responsibilities.

[162] Zachary Goldman argues that courts impact intelligence oversight largely through "information forcing" by adjudicating litigation regarding the withholding or release of secret government information. If so, then it is interesting to note that all of the Five Eyes states have freedom of information laws, for example, the U.S.

above needs to be expanded to examine intelligence services outside of the Five Eyes states, so as to better understand the effect that factors such as language, culture, history, differing legal traditions, and divergent national security priorities exert on shaping intelligence systems.

Nonetheless, the account above does suggest some general prescriptive considerations for advocates of establishing the "Five Eyes" model as an international norm for intelligence oversight. First, simply mimicking the oversight mechanism of states perceived to be successful at regulating their intelligence agencies may lead to decoupling. Such may occur either because the oversight mechanisms are a poor fit for the importing state's intelligence structures (e.g., legislation monitors will likely be ineffective where parliaments have little leverage over the conduct of intelligence operations), or because states lack the technical expertise or resources for compliance (e.g., judicial oversight of signals intelligence may not be effective where judges lack secure facilities or the assistance of technical experts), or because actors within the intelligence system or the legislature may not have internalized the norms underpinning the mechanism of oversight (e.g., intelligence agencies may be reluctant to cooperate with parliamentary bodies, or the parliament may lack competence to protect classified information). Thus, either importing states must intentionally make their convergence to the Five Eyes oversight norm incomplete by adapting oversight mechanisms to local structural circumstances, or the importing state must import both the Five Eyes models of intelligence structure and oversight. At a minimum, importing states must adopt the basic elements identified in Section VI.B., above.

Second, sequential-dual convergence within the Five Eyes states took place over numerous decades, and was characterized by a gradual process of the executive sharing oversight with coordinate branches of government. Considering this, it is unlikely that states will seek to reform their intelligence oversight process through mimicking the Five Eyes model only once structural convergence has taken place. Nor should they; the Five Eyes experience has been, if anything, a process of evolutionary understanding that intelligence operations and oversight must go hand in hand. However, simultaneous structural and oversight reform may come at the cost of reformed oversight bodies not being able to immediately draw on a community of former practitioners with experience and expertise. As a result, the view of reformed oversight bodies' perceived efficacy and legitimacy may suffer during their initial stages of operation. As Bruneau and Matei suggest, this problem might be offset through efforts at professionalizing the intelligence services, educating the public on intelligence issues, and providing intelligence training to civilians who may become involved in the process of oversight.[163]

Freedom of Information Act (1966), Australian Freedom of Information Act (1982), New Zealand Official Information Act (1982), Canadian Access to Information Act (1983), and U.K. Freedom of Information Act. Likewise, four of the Five Eyes possess Privacy Acts: the United States (1974), Canada (1983), Australia (1988), and New Zealand (1993). Finally, many of the Five Eyes states have procedures for the exclusion of classified information at trial: in the United States, the Classified Information Procedures Act (1980); the common law Public Interest Immunity in the U.K.; the Canada Evidence Act (1985); and the Australian National Security Information Act (2004).

[163] Bruneau & Matei, *supra* note 146, at 766–67.

3

Oversight of Intelligence Agencies

THE EUROPEAN DIMENSION

Iain Cameron

I. INTRODUCTION

This chapter examines the European dimension to oversight of intelligence and security agencies. National security is—not surprisingly—a national responsibility. How this is organized, run, and overseen is a matter primarily for each European state. However, for states party to the intergovernmental organization the Council of Europe, or for member-states of the supranational organization the European Union (EU), there is a European dimension to oversight. A large part of this comes in the form of the case law of the European Court of Human Rights (ECtHR, part of the Council of Europe) dealing with the issue of intelligence accountability. Other parts of the Council of Europe also have an impact on intelligence oversight through different investigations, studies, and recommendations. For EU states, all of which are members of the Council of Europe, there are also certain EU institutions that can have an impact on intelligence oversight.

This chapter tries to give a picture of this complex European dimension to intelligence oversight. I begin by introducing how the EU affects security and intelligence. This short chapter cannot, and is not meant to, provide a description and analysis of every way in which this can happen, so complicated issues are summarized.[1] The main focus of this chapter is devoted to the ECtHR. The chapter concludes with a number of comments on the "added value" of the supervision that European institutions, particularly the ECtHR, exercise over states' laws and practices in this field.

---

[1] For more detail, *see* STEVE PEERS, EU JUSTICE AND HOME AFFAIRS LAW (3d ed. 2011).

II. EU MECHANISMS

EU institutions have only limited competence in issues of national security. Article 4 of the Treaty on European Union (TEU), provides that "the Union shall respect the . . . Member States essential State functions, including . . . safeguarding national security . . . national security remains the sole responsibility of each Member State."[2] This is further buttressed by Article 72 of the Treaty on the Functioning of the European Union (TFEU), which provides that the EU's competence in justice and security "shall not affect the exercise of the responsibilities incumbent upon Member States with regard to the maintenance of law and order and the safeguarding of internal security."[3]

Notwithstanding these exclusions, the EU has competence to agree on foreign policies to "safeguard its values, fundamental interests, security, independence and integrity" (Article 21 TEU).[4] This is natural enough bearing in mind the various security threats to the EU region (e.g., from North Africa, Ukraine, etc.), which would benefit from a unified EU approach. The EU Council has also adopted various general documents on security policy, but these primarily set out goals and duties of consultation and coordination between the member-states.[5]

Even though security as such remains a national competence, the creation of an internal market with freedom of movement of goods, persons, etc., generates a need for much better customs, immigration, and police cooperation. The EU has competence to adopt legislation in the area of police cooperation (Article 87 TFEU)[6] and, in relation to material criminal law, as regards organized crime and terrorism (Article 88 TFEU). This is shared, not exclusive, competence, meaning that the member-states can continue to legislate in these areas, as long as they do not violate existing EU rules. Although the EU can now adopt rules by qualified majority in what is Title V of the TFEU, which concerns the "area of freedom, justice and security," in most cases it seeks consensus among the member-states. An example of ongoing internal EU negotiations in a security-related area, which in turn affects the EU's ability to reach an agreement on the matter with the United States, is the proposal to create an EU obligation to retain Passenger Name Records (PNR).[7]

---

[2] Consolidated Version of the Treaty on European Union art. 4, Feb. 7, 1992, 2002 O.J. C 325/5 [hereinafter TEU].

[3] Consolidated Version of the Treaty on the Functioning of the European Union art. 72, Dec. 13, 2007, 2012 O.J. C326/01 [hereinafter TFEU].

[4] TEU, *supra* note 2, art. 21.

[5] *See A Secure Europe in a Better World—The European Security Strategy, in* European Union, External Security Strategy (2003), *available at* http://www.eeas.europa.eu/csdp/about-csdp/european-security-strategy/; and *Internal Security Strategy for the European Union—Towards a European Security Model, in* European Union, External Security Strategy (2010), *available at* http://www.eeas.europa.eu/csdp/about-csdp/european-security-strategy/.

[6] Anna J. Cornell, *EU Police Cooperation Post-Lisbon, in* European Police and Criminal Law Cooperation 149 (Maria Bergström & Anna J. Cornell eds., 1st ed. 2014).

[7] PNR involves a legal obligation on passengers or airlines to transfer to law enforcement authorities passenger names and identification (passport, etc.) numbers in advance of travel. This is problematic from a privacy perspective as it means that a databank can be built up of peoples' travel patterns (and also incidental information, such as requests for special meals, which in turn is a pointer regarding religion). *Passenger Name Record (PNR)*, European Commission—Migration and Home Affairs, http://ec.europa.eu/dgs/home-affairs/

EU legislation can either be directly effective in the member-states (i.e., a regulation) when a decision is made that virtually identical rules are desirable across the Union; or can be in the form of a directive, in cases when it is sufficient that the rules in member-states be harmonized. Directives require implementing national legislation that usually must be passed within two years from the adoption of the directive. EU law has precedence over national law.

The EU ordinary legislative process (Article 289 TFEU) is as follows: the European Commission has the right to initiate legislation, although laws also can be proposed by a quarter of the member-states, while the Council (the representatives of the governments), together with the European Parliament, formally adopt the legislation.

The result of this process is a patchwork of EU/national competence in many areas of the law. However, because of the national security exceptions (above), security and intelligence services, and their oversight, have been left largely untouched by EU law, with the exception of certain cooperation in the area of terrorism, in which law enforcement overlaps with security and intelligence.

The EU has legislated on data protection, both for ordinary and law enforcement purposes. EU data protection rules provide inter alia for independent oversight, meaning the creation of a national data protection authority with supervisory powers that has effective remedies available. An EU data protection supervisor has been created (for data within the EU institutions),[8] as has a consultative group linking the European Commission, national data protection authorities, and the EU data protection supervisor (the "Article 29 working group").[9] At the present time, security and intelligence agencies tend to be excluded from ordinary national procedural and substantive data protection rules, as well as from the supervision of national data protection authorities.[10] However, the EU is in the process of adopting improved legislation in the field. This includes a general data protection regulation[11] and a directive regarding processing of personal data by law enforcement.[12] These new rules place greater emphasis on independent control and remedies systems. Oversight of intelligence

what-we-do/policies/police-cooperation/passenger-name-record/index_en.htm (last visited July 7, 2015). Some EU states, such as the U.K., already have such an obligation under national law.

[8] European Data Protection Supervisor, https://secure.edps.europa.eu/EDPSWEB/edps/EDPS (last visited July 7, 2015).

[9] *Article 29 Working Party*, European Data Protection Supervisor, https://secure.edps.europa.eu/EDPSWEB/edps/site/mySite/Art29 (last visited July 7, 2015).

[10] This is the case for most, but not all, European states. For example, in Sweden, the databanks of the security police (the internal security agency) and the external, signals intelligence agency are subject to both the supervision of specialist bodies and the ordinary Data Inspectorate (using specialist security-screened staff). *See* Library of Congress, *Foreign Intelligence Gathering Laws: Sweden* (July 22, 2015), http://www.loc.gov/law/help/foreign-intelligence-gathering/sweden.php.

[11] Proposal for a Regulation of the European Parliament and of the Council on the protection of individuals with regard to the processing of personal data and on the free movement of such data (General Data Protection Regulation), Eur. Parl. Doc. COM (2012) 11 (2012).

[12] Proposal for a Directive of the European Parliament and of the Council on the protection of individuals with regard to the processing of personal data by competent authorities for the purposes of prevention, investigation, detection or prosecution of criminal offences or the execution of criminal penalties, and the free movement of such data, Eur. Parl. Doc. COM (2012) 10 (2012).

in a number of EU states is not strong (see below), and so the European Parliament and the European Commission are not happy with granting a blanket (nationally defined) security exemption to these data protection rules.

I should note that there is a European police body (EUROPOL). However, it has no operational capacity. Instead it receives data, including personal data, from member-states regarding terrorism and organized crime (but by no means all the data it wants or considers it needs) and produces crime assessments. It is overseen by a specialized data protection authority.

The decisions of the Council in internal security matters are usually prepared by government and security officials meeting in the Standing Committee on Internal Security (COSI) (Article 71 TFEU). The European Parliament works through various standing committees, especially the Committee on Civil Liberties, Justice and Home Affairs (LIBE). LIBE takes a keen interest in various issues connected to national security, commissioning reports and adopting (non-binding) resolutions. This is true even in issues within member-state competence (such as signals intelligence) on the grounds that these can affect matters within EU competence.[13]

The European Commission usually has the role of negotiating treaties on behalf of the EU with third states, while the Council approves treaties. Many of these treaties concern issues where competence is shared with the member-states, which are bound by their own constitutional rules on adoption of treaties. Thus, national parliaments are usually also involved in the ratification process. However, the European Parliament also must agree to most of the treaties that the EU ratifies. Consequentially, it has a lever with which to exert pressure on the Commission in its negotiations with third states. Even before the Snowden revelations, the European Parliament had been concerned about EU arrangements with the United States on data transfer and protection. The Commission has responded to these concerns,[14] and it has sought to reduce the scope of the present exceptions for national security in the ongoing "Umbrella Agreement" negotiations on data protection and on terrorist finance tracking.

The final institution that should be mentioned is the Court of Justice of the EU (CJEU). The CJEU can hear cases brought by EU institutions against each other, or by the Commission against a member-state. In the relatively rare cases where an EU norm or decision is directly issued to an individual, the individual can challenge this norm or decision before the CJEU. Security-related examples include the challenges to EU sanctions (and EU implementation of UN sanctions). Decisions made by the Council to "blacklist" suspected terrorist groups are supranational operative determinations that can only be challenged before the CJEU.[15] The CJEU case law in this area has attempted to reconcile fair trial concerns with demands

---

[13] *See* COMMITTEE ON CIVIL LIBERTIES, JUSTICE AND HOME AFFAIRS, REPORT ON THE US NSA SURVEILLANCE PROGRAMME, SURVEILLANCE BODIES IN VARIOUS MEMBER STATES AND THEIR IMPACT ON EU CITIZENS' FUNDAMENTAL RIGHTS AND ON TRANSATLANTIC COOPERATION IN JUSTICE AND HOME AFFAIRS, EUR. PARL. DOC. 2013/2188(INI) (2014).

[14] Communication from the Commission to the European Parliament and the Council—Rebuilding Trust in EU-US Data Flows, EUR. PARL. DOC. COM (2013) 846 (2013).

[15] *See generally* EU SANCTIONS: LAW AND POLICY ISSUES CONCERNING RESTRICTIVE MEASURES (Iain Cameron ed., 2013).

from states that the background material justifying targeting specific individuals be kept secret.[16]

Most of the cases that the CJEU deals with are not judgments validating or invalidating EU decisions but "preliminary rulings" on the validity, or interpretation, of EU laws when such a case is referred to the CJEU from a court in a member-state. These rulings are binding in regards to the interpretation of the law, but the national court that referred the case otherwise decides the outcome of the case by applying the law to the specific circumstances of the case. The CJEU follows a French judicial tradition (divergent from that of many other EU member-states, such as the common law states of the U.K. and Ireland) of not allowing dissenting opinions. This can mean that the ruling is, on occasion, Delphic. In other cases, the CJEU may choose to give only limited concrete guidance to the national court, deliberately leaving it room for maneuvering in how it adapts EU law to the national context.

Among the norms the CJEU applies is the European Convention on Human Rights (ECHR, see further below) and the EU's own rights catalog, the EU Charter of Fundamental Rights (EUCFR).[17] The EU is not a party to the ECHR, and is not likely to become a party in the near future. However, by virtue of Article 6(2) TEU, the ECHR is part of the "general principles" of EU law.[18] As such it is binding on the EU institutions, including the CJEU itself. The EUCFR contains a much longer list of rights than the ECHR. Where the rights in the two documents overlap, the EUCFR is interpreted in accordance with the ECHR, thus giving the ECtHR a certain interpretative influence even over the content of the EUCFR. The EUCFR applies to EU institutions when they legislate or adopt administrative acts. It also applies in the same way to member-states, but only to the extent that they are acting within the scope of EU law. Importantly, the European Commission cannot bring a case against a state for breaching the EUCFR in the way that it can if a state breaches the rules on the internal market. The lack of competence of the EU institutions in this respect is a deliberate feature of the system. EU states are assumed to protect human rights adequately at the national level, backed up, if necessary, by the possibility of individuals taking a case to the ECtHR.

An example where the EUCFR applies in an "EU as legislator" fashion was when the CJEU ruled that the Data Retention Directive was invalid.[19] In accordance with the directive, states had to legislatively require telecommunications companies to retain metadata for

---

[16] *See* Cian C. Murphy, *Secret Evidence in EU Security Law: Special Advocates before the Court of Justice?, in* SECRECY, NATIONAL SECURITY AND THE VINDICATION OF CONSTITUTIONAL LAW (David Cole, Federico Fabbrini & Arianna Vedaschi eds., 2014). The General Court (part of the CJEU) is in the process of revising its rules of procedure to deal with such cases. Draft Article 105(5) reads in part: "Where the General Court concludes that . . . certain information or material produced before it is relevant in order for it to rule in the case and is confidential vis-à-vis the other main party, it shall not communicate that information or material to that main party and shall weigh the requirements linked to the right to effective judicial protection, particularly observance of the adversarial principle, against the requirements flowing from the security of the Union or of one or more of its Member States or the conduct of their international relations." Council Doc. 15628/14, 2015 O.J. (L 105) 1.

[17] Charter of Fundamental Rights of the European Union, 2000 O.J. (C 364) 1.

[18] TEU, *supra* note 2, art. 6(2).

[19] Joined Cases C-293/12, C-594/12, Digital Rights Ir. v. Minister for Comm., 2014 E.C.R.

a period between six months and two years and to make it available for law enforcement/ internal security investigations. The CJEU, taking a number of different factors into account, found that the safeguards for data protection in the directive were not adequate. The ruling contained various Delphic passages, inter alia concerning whether it was possible at all to prescribe blanket metadata retention and whether existing "Safe Harbor" arrangements were valid.[20] As the directive has been implemented differently in different member-states, with different types of safeguards, it has not been easy for states to understand the exact implications the ruling has for their state.[21]

One other case should also be mentioned here, *Schrems v Data Protection Commissioner*.[22] This case is a consequence of the previous ruling invalidating the Data Retention Directive. Schrems, an Austrian citizen, objected to the transfers of his personal data to the United States by Facebook, on the grounds that his data (and all other Facebook data) would be accessible upon demand to the U.S. intelligence community. As Facebook Europe is based in Ireland, the legal challenge was brought against the Irish data protection commissioner, who had chosen not to stop such data transfers, on the basis that they were covered by the "Safe Harbor." The CJEU agreed with Schrems that, notwithstanding the Safe Harbor, the Irish data protection authority had the obligation to suspend data transfers if it considered that data protection standards in the United States were inadequate.

An example of the second type of situation in which the EUCFR applies is where a member-state invokes national security to justify making an exception to an EU right (such as freedom of movement—e.g., denying admission to a person based on national security grounds).[23] In such a situation, the CJEU can also rule on the proportionality of the exception.

III. THE ECtHR AND THE ECHR

The ECtHR can hear complaints from individuals alleging violations of the ECHR, after they have exhausted domestic remedies in the state against which they bring a case.[24] The 47 parties to the ECHR undertake to secure the listed rights for everyone subject to their jurisdiction.[25] This is the first thing to note about the ECHR: it is based on a cosmopolitan idea of rights, not a citizenship-based idea.[26] This is not surprising, bearing in mind the origins of

---

[20] Under Article 25(6) of Directive 95/46/EC the Commission may take a decision as to whether a third country ensures an adequate level of data protection (i.e., is a "Safe Harbor") by reason of its domestic law or of the international commitments it has entered into. For the decisions regarding the United States, *see* EUROPEAN COMMISSION, COMMISSION DECISIONS ON THE ADEQUACY OF THE PROTECTION OF PERSONAL DATA IN THIRD COUNTRIES, *available at* http://ec.europa.eu/justice/data-protection/international-transfers/ adequacy/index_en.htm.

[21] For the problems the judgment caused in Sweden, *see* Iain Cameron, *Law Enforcement Access to Metadata in Sweden, in* INFORMATION AND LAW IN TRANSITION (Anna-Sara Lind et al. eds., 2015).

[22] Case C-362/14, 13 November 2015.

[23] *See, e.g.,* Case C-300/11, ZZ v. Sec'y of State for Home Dep't (2013).

[24] European Convention for the Protection of Human Rights and Fundamental Freedoms art. 35, Nov. 4, 1950, E.T.S. 5 [hereinafter ECHR].

[25] *Id.* art.1

[26] *See generally* DAVID HELD, DEMOCRACY AND THE GLOBAL ORDER: FROM THE MODERN STATE TO COSMOPOLITAN GOVERNANCE (1995).

the ECHR: an entity created after World War II to address future issues similar to those that characterized the beginning of the Holocaust, that is, the legislative denial of full German citizenship to those of Jewish identity. The protection of the ECHR covers some 800 million people, and the ECtHR adopts around 1,500 judgments per year. It also takes about 90,000 "admissibility decisions" per year, that is, decisions to dismiss an application without an examination of the merits of the dispute (which occurs in approximately 90 percent of cases).[27]

The ECHR has also been incorporated in the national law of all member-states, through legislation requiring national courts and administrative agencies to apply it, and to take account of the case law of the ECtHR. This means that the court with the final authority on interpreting what is national law is not the national supreme or constitutional court, but the ECtHR. Thus, incorporation of the ECHR creates a "pluralist" legal order capable of affecting the distribution of power, not only between the national legislature and the courts but also between the national lower and higher courts.

The ECHR prescribes certain rights that contain an express clause permitting a state to limit the right in question on the basis of "national security." This type of clause can be found in the rights to a fair trial (Article 6);[28] to privacy, respect for family life and inviolability of correspondence (Article 8);[29] to freedom of expression (Article 10);[30] and to freedom of assembly and association (Article 11).[31] There are also national security limitations on the rights to liberty of movement, to freedom to choose a residence within a state (Article 2(3), Protocol 4),[32] and to review of a deportation decision (Article 1(2), Protocol 7).[33] Under certain circumstances, national security considerations can be taken into account in other articles where there is no such express limitation.[34]

Like domestic courts applying domestic human rights norms, the ECtHR must strike a balance between the competing interests of individuals and the state. The ECtHR nonetheless has less legitimacy compared to national constitutional courts when it comes to imposing

---

[27] *See* European Court of Human Rights, Analysis of Statistics 2013, at 4 (2014), *available at* http://www.echr.coe.int/Documents/Stats_analysis_2013_ENG.pdf. The main ground for rejection at the admissibility stage is the non-exhaustion of domestic remedies. Other significant grounds are set out in Article 35(3)(a), prescribing that the Court shall consider inadmissible any petition that is "incompatible with the provisions of the Convention," "manifestly ill-founded," or that constitutes "an abuse of the right of petition."

[28] ECHR, *supra* note 23, art. 6(1).

[29] *Id.* art. 8(2).

[30] *Id.* art. 10(2).

[31] *Id.* art. 11(2).

[32] Protocol 4 to the European Convention for the Protection of Human Rights and Fundamental Freedoms art. 2(3), Sept. 16, 1963, E.T.S. No. 46 [hereinafter ECHR Protocol 4].

[33] Protocol 7 to the European Convention for the Protection of Human Rights and Fundamental Freedoms art. 1(2), Nov. 22, 1984, E.T.S. No. 117 [hereinafter ECHR Protocol 7].

[34] The ECtHR has held that where there is an exceptional situation threatening public order, such as a wave of terrorist violence, then this background can be taken into account in determining the legitimacy of measures taken that allegedly infringe ECHR rights. *See, e.g.*, Brogan v. United Kingdom, 145-B Eur. Ct. H.R. (ser. A) ¶ 48 (1988).

its will on recalcitrant governments or legislatures. The ECtHR does not, and should not, function as a final court of appeal from domestic courts—as a form of European *cour de cassation*. Nor does it have an explicit function to harmonize the parties' national laws. All the ECtHR does is test the compatibility of national law and practice against the standards of the ECHR.

The ECHR was designed to be, and clearly is, *subsidiary* to the domestic systems dedicated to the protection of human rights.[35] This is particularly the case with regards to national security policymaking. In this and other sensitive areas, the ECtHR has adopted a stance of judicial restraint that permits states a degree of discretion, a "margin of appreciation," as to how they perform their obligations under the ECHR. The ECtHR justifies this partly on the basis of the subsidiary nature of the protection afforded by the ECHR[36] and the difficulty in identifying common European conceptions of the extent of the rights or restrictions in question.

As with any system of law built upon the development of norms by means of adjudication, the "accident of litigation," whereby courts make law according to the facts and circumstances of the cases that happen to come before them, is significant. The person complaining must show that he or she is a victim of an alleged violation of the ECHR. Satisfying the standing requirement is no easy task when security measures are involved, so the test has been modified in that context to allow a person to complain of a violation if that person can show there is a "reasonable likelihood" that he or she has been the victim of such practices.[37] Still, even with this relaxation of the requirements, some potential issues, for a variety of reasons (e.g., lack of awareness of one's legal rights, resignation on the part of the victim, the cost of litigation, poor legal advice, etc.) never make their way through the mill of domestic courts and the admissibility procedures to a judgment on the merits.[38]

The ECHR system is best described as a *semiautonomous* legal system. National law necessarily provides the framework within which ECHR concepts operate. The only material remedy the ECtHR can formally require for breach of the ECHR is the award of monetary compensation (Article 41), although the ECtHR has also, on rare occasions, made specific orders (usually to release a person unlawfully detained). However, a negative judgment can also indirectly involve other obligations, in particular, law reform and/or the reopening of domestic proceedings.[39] A judgment against the state thus returns to the national legal system for implementation.

---

[35] This is expressly recognized in European Convention on Human Rights art. 53, Sept. 3, 1953, C.E.T.S. No. 005 [hereinafter European Convention].

[36] *See, e.g.*, Jonas Christoffersen, Fair Balance: A Study of Proportionality, Subsidiarity and Primarity in the ECHR (2009).

[37] *See, e.g.*, Klass v. Germany, 28 Eur. Ct. H.R. (ser. A) (1978). This having been said, problems of proof can arise where it is, on the facts, equally likely that a private actor (e.g., a private security firm) has infringed an individual's rights. To ground state responsibility an applicant must show beyond a reasonable doubt that state agents are responsible for the alleged violation.

[38] Another important factor here is the requirement in European Convention Article 35 that a case be brought before the ECtHR within six months of the final domestic decision (in the case of secret measures, within six months of the decision becoming known to the applicant). This period will be reduced to four months for states party to the new amending Protocol 15.

[39] *See* Eur. Com. Min. *Recommendation No. R (2000) 2* 694th Meeting, (Jan. 19, 2000).

Under Article 46(2), the main function of supervising the execution of the ECtHR's judgment falls to the Committee of Ministers, that is, the Foreign Ministers of Council of Europe states (invariably represented by their ambassadors). Being a political body, the Committee of Ministers is inclined to accept the explanations given by a state that a problem has been remedied. But although one can usually rely on the good faith of a state to make the necessary reforms, one cannot always do so. Especially in the area of national security law and practice, there is the risk that a judgment is interpreted in a minimalist fashion so that any resulting law reform may be cosmetic only. Even if a reform is made bureaucratic resistance can weaken its impact. The more closed an area is to public scrutiny, the greater chance there is of such resistance succeeding. It is evident that in the area of national security, the law can serve, and has on occasion served, as a facade, concealing more or less serious divergences in practice.

The ECHR is an essential part of the system of constraints on national power, which European states voluntary accepted after the carnage of the Second World War.[40] But because the ECtHR has no mechanism for enforcing compliance with its judgments, this means that, in the area of national security, it is really only a system of "soft" persuasive power. This is a weakness that has become more serious as the number of authoritarian states in the Council of Europe (e.g., Russia, Turkey, Azerbaijan) has increased. This is not, however, a problem limited to the Council of Europe. There are several EU states that have major corruption problems of the state apparatus (Bulgaria, Romania), are bankrupt/dysfunctional (Greece), or are ruled by an increasingly authoritarian government (Hungary).

IV. THE ECtHR AND INTELLIGENCE ACCOUNTABILITY IN GENERAL

In what way, then, does the ECtHR affect intelligence accountability? The ECtHR is not about intelligence accountability in the way we normally understand the term: ensuring ministerial accountability to the legislature, exercising executive control over the security/intelligence apparatus, or employing judicial authorization where security/intelligence limits fundamental rights and continuous oversight of this apparatus by parliamentary and/or independent expert bodies. Instead, under the ECHR system, the "accountability" is at the state level: the contracting states are responsible in the realm of *international* law to the ECtHR, and each other, for how they comply with the ECHR. Therein lies part of the value of the system (something which is discussed further below). However, the constitutional aspect of accountability is also relevant, as a reason for finding, or not finding, a breach of the ECHR. In other words, the state will be responsible if it fails to construct and implement satisfactory accountability mechanisms and institutions at the national level, with the effect of allowing the exercise of unrestricted intelligence powers affecting rights under the ECHR.

In one sense, the ECtHR is yet another "fire brigade" system of intelligence accountability.[41] It only starts working when a problem seems to have emerged. Indeed, the requirement

---

[40] Jan-Werner Müller, Contesting Democracy: Political Ideas in Twentieth-Century Europe (2011).

[41] Matthew D. McCubbins & Thomas Schwartz, *Congressional Oversight Overlooked: Police Patrols vs. Fire Alarms*, 28 Am. J. Pol. Sci. 165 (1984); Loch K. Johnson, *Governing in the Absence of Angels: On the Practice*

of exhaustion of domestic remedies, and the relative slowness of Strasbourg procedures, means that the ECtHR often starts working years after the fire has started, and by the time a judgment is delivered, the fire may well have gone out. This, in itself, is not necessarily a disadvantage. Unlike a national legislature, which can give in to both moral and security panics, the ECtHR has a degree of detachment, born from its distance both in time and space from the case it is considering.

However, it cannot take a holistic approach to intelligence accountability in the way a legislature can—laying down general rules as to the mandate of an organization, its powers, the necessary internal and external controls over the exercise of those powers, and the available remedies against abuse of power. The particular facts of the case provide a strict procedural framework for the ECtHR, a crucial difference between judicial and legislative power. An allegedly unsatisfactory intelligence law or practice must be "fitted in" to an ECHR right. Thus, in such vitally important aspects of control as training of intelligence staff (designed to foster democratic sensibilities and "rights awareness"), allocating responsibility between different agencies and fiscal management effectively elude ECtHR scrutiny.

To put it another way, the procedural restraints on the ECtHR mean that it is limited to examining systems of accountability through the lens of the ECHR requirements, that a limitation on a given human right be for the "protection of national security," "in accordance with the law," "necessary in a democratic society," and accompanied by "effective remedies" at the national level. What do each of these concepts—which are the general requirements that must be met before a right under the Convention can be limited—mean?

The ECtHR has been reluctant to give abstract definitions of ECHR terms, and this also has been the case with national security.[42] The ECtHR naturally accepts the need to defend national security,[43] but it has become increasingly skeptical about the scope for abuse of the term. In *Iordachi and Others v. Moldova*,[44] "national security" was one of the bases for telecommunications surveillance. The ECtHR criticized the lack of concretization of "national security" and found a violation of Article 8 of the Convention.[45] But the ECtHR's emphasis on the need for adequate external controls on both the initiation of surveillance and what happens during and after surveillance operations showed that it had realized that the basic problem in Moldova could not be solved *only* by a fuller, or better, definition of national

---

of Intelligence Accountability in the United States, in HANS BORN, LOCH K. JOHNSON & IAN LEIGH, WHO'S WATCHING THE SPIES? ESTABLISHING INTELLIGENCE SERVICE ACCOUNTABILITY (2005).

[42] "By the nature of things, threats to national security may vary in character and may be unanticipated or difficult to define in advance." Al-Nashif v. Bulgaria, App. No. 50963/99, 36 Eur. H.R. Rep. 37, ¶ 121 (2002). *See also* Esbester v. United Kingdom, App. No. 18601/91, 18 Eur. H.R. Rep. CD72 (1993) (national security cannot be defined exhaustively); M. v. France, App. No. 10078/82, 41 D.R. 103, 117 (1985) it is for member states to decide whether it is necessary to criminalize particular conduct deemed to be damaging to national security.

[43] *See* Refah Partisi v. Turkey, App. Nos. 41340/98, 41342/98, 41343/98, and 41344/98, ¶ 96 (2003) (The ECtHR stated that ECHR freedoms "cannot deprive the authorities of a State in which an association, through its activities, jeopardises that State's institutions, of the right to protect those institutions . . . some compromise between the requirements of defending democratic society and individual rights [is] inherent in the Convention system.").

[44] Iordachi v. Moldova, App. No. 25198/02, [2009] ECHR 256.

[45] *Id.* ¶ 46.

security. The problem was that the judiciary was weak and the police, and the prosecutor's office (the *prokuratura*) were strong. This is a problem that continues to exist in other former Soviet states. One can link national security to a legal requirement that there be concrete indications of an ongoing or past serious security offense. With a security or intelligence service with a high degree of professionalism and tight internal routines, this can be an important safeguard against surveillance that is too speculative. One can also insist that a prosecutor obtain a court warrant before surveillance is initiated. But neither requirement is much of a safeguard if the court places the evidentiary threshold very low, accepts the prosecutor's view that any and every offences is "serious," and exercises no control over what the security agency subsequently does with the intelligence gathered as a result of the surveillance (especially when the security agency has a low degree of professionalism).

The ECtHR encountered a similar problem in *Association for European Integration and Human Rights and Ekimdzhiev v. Bulgaria.*[46] The applicable Bulgarian law allowed telecommunications surveillance for national security purposes. The ECtHR stated that this was acceptable if care was taken "not to stretch the concept of 'national security' beyond its natural meaning."[47] The Bulgarian law provided for judicial authorization of surveillance, but there were no external safeguards, judicial or otherwise, to check that the surveillance was actually being carried out in accordance with the law and the judicial authorization granted, and no subsequent control over the intelligence gathered. The ECtHR thus found a violation of Article 8.[48]

"Accordance with the law" means that the exercise of state power, in particular coercive power, must have support in statute law, subordinate legislation or case law.[49] This in itself is hardly onerous; however, the ECtHR has increasingly stressed the need for minimum standards of foreseeability and for discretionary powers to be drafted carefully, identifying the addressees, the objects of the exercise of power, and the limits, temporal and otherwise, on its exercise, among other factors.[50] It is with this requirement that the ECtHR has had greatest impact, particularly on law enforcement surveillance. However, the standards set out in the ECtHR's case law have to be adapted to fit the different context of national security surveillance, especially signals intelligence.[51]

The "necessity" requirement is essentially a test of the proportionality of an infringement, and involves looking at the control system for preventing abuse of discretionary powers.[52]

---

[46] Case of the Ass'n for Eur. Integration & H.R. v. Bulgaria, App. No. 62540/00 (2007).

[47] *Id.* ¶ 84. Another example of the ECtHR considering that a state has interpreted national security too extensively is *Soltysyak v. Russia*, App. No. 4663/05 (2011), (concerning a prohibition on the possibility of traveling abroad on the basis that the person had worked with secret defense projects).

[48] Ass'n for Eur. Integrration, *supra* note 46, ¶¶ 93–94.

[49] *See, e.g.,* Case of Kopp v. Switzerland, App. No. 23224/94 ¶ 55 (1998) (finding that the phrase "in accordance with the law" requires some basis in domestic law.)

[50] *Id.* ¶¶ 63–65 (explaining that the "in accordance with the law" standard requires that a measure be accessible and foreseeable, and that citizens must be given an adequate indication as to the circumstances and conditions of the measure's employment).

[51] The Venice Commission has attempted to do this. *See* VENICE COMMISSION, UPDATE OF THE 2007 REPORT ON THE DEMOCRATIC OVERSIGHT OF THE SECURITY SERVICES AND REPORT ON THE DEMOCRATIC OVERSIGHT OF SIGNALS INTELLIGENCE AGENCIES, CDL-AD(2015)006 ¶¶ 102–111 (2015), *available at* http://www.venice.coe.int/webforms/documents/default.aspx?pdffile=CDL-AD(2015)006-e.

[52] *See* Case of Malone v. United Kingdom, App. No. 8691/79 ¶ 81 (1984) (describing the necessity standard as requiring adequate guarantees against abuse).

Where the ECtHR finds that a measure complained of is not "in accordance with the law," then it does not proceed to examine whether the measure satisfies the requirements of "necessity in a democratic society."[53]

The right to "effective remedies" articulated in Article 13 of the ECHR is a variable requirement. The more serious the alleged violation of an ECHR right, and the more important the right is to the individual in question, the more remedies should be available. In national security issues, a body to which a person complains should have the competence and powers to carry out an effective investigation. The criteria for this are adequacy, thoroughness, impartiality and independence, promptness, and (a degree of) public scrutiny.[54] The ECtHR has increasingly stressed that remedies have to be effective not simply on paper, but in practice.

V. EXTRATERRITORIALITY

The primary impact of the ECHR as concerns national security will tend to be on internal security agencies: "jurisdiction" under Article 1 is usually synonymous with territory.[55] This having been said, the ECHR has a degree of extraterritorial effect. For example, intelligence activities carried out in another state can involve the commission of offenses (espionage, etc.) under the law of that other state, although rules of state and diplomatic immunity may mean that a prosecution cannot be brought. In contrast, the collection of intelligence on or over the high seas, or in the territory of another state with that state's permission, will not be in violation of the customary international law norm of nonintervention.

Under the ECHR, the issue is whether the European state engaged in intelligence activities need comply with the ECHR when it engages in such activities abroad. The case law of the ECtHR has dealt mainly with military forces abroad[56] such as naval vessels,[57] but even

---

[53] *See id.* ¶ 82 (declining to analyze whether a measure involved sufficient guarantees—thereby satisfying the necessity requirement—because the measures in question were not in accordance with the law).

[54] *See* Iain Cameron (2008), National Security and the European Convention on Human Rights—Trends and Patterns, Introductory Speech at the Stockholm International Symposium on National Security and the ECHR (Dec. 4–5, 2008) and COUNCIL OF EUROPE, DIRECTORATE GENERAL OF HUMAN RIGHTS AND RULE OF LAW, ERADICATING IMPUNITY FOR SERIOUS HUMAN RIGHTS VIOLATIONS (2011), *available at* http://www.coe.int/t/dghl/standardsetting/hrpolicy/Publications/Impunity_en.pdf.

[55] As already noted, because the ECHR applies to everyone within jurisdiction, there is no citizenship requirement. But this does not mean that any action within a state that has potential effects outside of the state grants a right to complain to the ECtHR. *See* Ben El Mahi v. Denmark, App. No. 5853/06 (2006), which concerned the controversy that arose when caricatures of the prophet Muhammad were published in a Danish newspaper. The ECtHR found no jurisdictional link between Denmark and Moroccan nationals complaining about their access to the publications in question: the case was accordingly ruled inadmissible.

[56] *See* Al-Jedda v. United Kingdom, App. No. 27021/08, 53 Eur. Ct. H.R. Rep. 23 (2011); Al-Saadoon v. United Kingdom, App. No. 61498/08 (2010); Ilaşcu v. Moldova, App. No. 48787/99 (2004). *See also* Venice Commission, Opinion on the International Legal Obligations of Council of Europe Member States in Respect of Secret Detention Facilities and Inter-state Transport of Prisoners, adopted by Venice Commission 66th Plenary Session, Opinion No. 363/2005 (Mar. 17–18, 2006) (regarding the host state's obligations under ECHR to control intelligence activities going on at foreign military bases in its territory).

[57] Hirsi Jamaa v. Italy, App. No. 27765/09 (2012); Medvedyev v. France, App. No. 3394/0351, Eur. H.R. Rep. 39 (2010).

extraterritorial security and intelligence activity fairly clearly fall within its jurisdiction.[58] In any event, the processing, analysis, and communication of intelligence material collected extraterritorially is clearly within national jurisdiction, and is governed both by national law and states' applicable human rights obligations.[59] To the extent that the ECHR applies extraterritorially, this means that states party to the ECHR are obliged to place intelligence activities occurring outside their borders that affect ECHR rights under independent controls, and to provide for effective remedies for complainants alleging rights violations.

To a foreign intelligence officer, this might seem a dramatic, indeed, unworkable requirement. The officer *has* to engage in activities potentially or actually violating foreigners' private lives. But this is not as unworkable as it might first appear. Under Article 1, a state is not held responsible for every act it commits: only those acts where it exercised *sufficient* control.[60] Thus, as regards military actions, the ECtHR has—controversially—stated that aerial bombing of a nonstate party is not "within jurisdiction."[61] Where the intelligence service of State A cooperates with the security service of the host state, State B, then disentangling their respective control over the activity in question may be difficult or even impossible.

The extension of jurisdiction also does not necessarily mean that the *same* controls must operate over foreign intelligence activities as operate over domestic intelligence activities. For surveillance operations it is Article 8 that is the main relevant article, and this does not require judicial controls. Under national constitutional law doctrines, judicial control over domestic intelligence activities may be the norm, whereas national doctrines on the separation of powers or judicial restraint in issues of foreign affairs or national security may operate to block judicial control over extraterritorial intelligence activities. In particular, the ECHR right of access to court in a civil suit (Article 6(1)) is an implicit right, and so may be made subject to implicit limits.

On the other hand, the principle is clear: where the activity is under the state's control, and it infringes an ECHR right, there must be adequate controls over it, and some organ must be created to which a person alleging a violation of his or her rights may turn to obtain an effective investigation of the allegation and, if the activity is not justified, an effective

---

[58] *See* Ocalan v. Turkey, App. No. 46221/99 (2005). *See also* the equivalent position taken by the U.N. Human Rights Committee regarding states' obligations under the International Covenant on Civil and Political Rights. In 2014, the U.N. Human Rights Committee stated: "The State party should (a) Take all necessary measures to ensure that its surveillance activities, both within and outside the United States, conform to its obligations under the Covenant, including article 17; in particular, measures should be taken to ensure that any interference with the right to privacy complies with the principles of legality, proportionality and necessity, regardless of the nationality or location of the individuals whose communications are under direct surveillance...." U.N. Human Rights Committee, Concluding observations on the fourth report of the United States of America, 3061st meeting (CCPR/C/SR/3061) ¶ 22 (Mar. 26, 2014). *See also* Special Rapporteur on the Promotion and Protection of Human Rights and Fundamental Freedoms while Countering Terrorism, 4th Ann. Rep., U.N. Doc. A/69/397 (Sept. 23, 2014) (by Ben Emmerson).

[59] In *Weber v. Germany*, App. No. 54934/00, ¶ 88 (2006), the ECtHR considered that "Signals emitted from foreign countries are monitored by interception sites situated on German soil and the data collected are used in Germany."

[60] *See* Case of Bankovic v. Belgium, App. No. 52207/99, [2001] Eur. Ct. H.R. 890, ¶ 39 ("the positive obligation to protect in Article 1 of the Convention applies proportionately to the control exercised").

[61] *Id.* ¶ 75.

remedy. The difficulties of proof in this area will usually be even greater than for alleged abuse of domestic power, so complaints are hardly likely to succeed.[62] But this does not alter the need to put adequate controls and remedies systems in place. Nor can one say that this is a waste of time and money. The whole point of controls systems (and much of the point of remedies systems) is to prevent violations of rights arising at all.

VI. AN OVERVIEW OF THE MAIN ECTHR SECURITY-RELATED CASE LAW

The most serious violations in "wars against terror" tend to be of the right to life and the prohibition against torture. There have been many judgments concerning abuses of these rights committed by security forces in Turkey and Russia.[63] The three cases to date concerning the former U.S. government's "rendition" policy also concern violations of Article 3 of the ECHR.[64]

The ECtHR has also delivered important judgments relating to the provision of remedies for deportations on security grounds (Articles 3 and 8, where the deportee risks torture or inhuman treatment, or the deportation interferes with family life, respectively)[65] and where the issue was the practical inability to know the content of, and thus challenge, a security assessment.[66] Other cases have concerned the (in)admissibility of secret torture evidence.[67]

---

[62] In *Weber v. Germany, supra* note 59, the applicants had argued that by intercepting private communications beginning and ending in another country the German authorities were violating international law. The ECtHR considered that the term "law" refers back to national law, including rules of public international law applicable in the state concerned. However, the ECtHR required proof in the form of "concordant inferences that the authorities of the respondent State have acted extraterritorially in a manner that is inconsistent with the sovereignty of the foreign State and therefore contrary to international law." *Id.* ¶ 87. The ECtHR in these circumstances found that the applicants failed to prove their allegations.

[63] For the earlier case law, *see generally* IAIN CAMERON, NATIONAL SECURITY AND THE EUROPEAN CONVENTION ON HUMAN RIGHTS (2000). For a selection of later case law, *see* European Court of Human Rights, *Factsheet—Terrorism and the ECHR*, http://www.echr.coe.int/Documents/FS_Terrorism_ENG.pdf, (November 2015).

[64] Al Nashiri v. Poland, App. No. 28761/11 (2014); Husayn v. Poland, App. No. 7511/13 (2014); El-Masri v. Macedonia, App. No. 39630/09 (2012) (Macedonian responsibility for handing over a person (wrongly) suspected of terrorism to U.S. agents, and the subsequent torture of the person in Afghanistan). At the time of this writing, several rendition applications are still pending. *See* Abu Zubaydah v. Lithuania, App. No. 46454/11; Al Nashiri v. Romania, App. No. 33234/12; Nasr v. Italy, App. No. 44883/09. In one sense, these U.S.-related cases are nowhere near as serious as the massive human rights abuses shown by the Turkish and, in particular, Russian Chechnya cases. On the other, they are as serious, as Western states do not look to Turkey or Russia for moral leadership.

[65] *See* Chahal v. United Kingdom, App. No. 22414/93, 23 Eur. H.R. Rep. 413 (1996), Al-Nashif v. Bulgaria, *supra* note 42. There has also been a series of cases dealing with a duty not to extradite to states where a person charged with security-related offenses could be subjected to the death penalty. *See* in particular Othman v. United Kingdom, App. No. 8139/09, [2012] Eur. Ct. H.R. 56.

[66] A v. United Kingdom, App. No. 3455/05, [2009] Eur. Ct. H.R. 301; Nolan v. Russia, App. No. 2512/04, [2009] Eur. Ct. H.R. 262 (exclusion of foreign Unification Church activist from country supposedly on national security grounds: violation of Article 9); Gulijev v. Lithuania, App. No. 10425/03 (2008) (expulsion on the basis of a "secret" report of the State Security Department, which was not disclosed to the applicant). The use of undisclosed intelligence material can naturally arise in other contexts, in particular as regards Article 5 (arrest and detention). *See* Cameron, *supra* note 63, at 267–86.

[67] *See* El Haski v. Belgium, App. No. 649/08 (2012).

Otherwise, the main ECHR article that has given rise to discussions regarding intelligence is Article 8, in relation to the specific issues of surveillance and records/screening. The leading case on security surveillance is *Klass v. Germany*,[68] now supplemented by two cases concerning signals intelligence, *Weber v. Germany*,[69] and *Liberty v. United Kingdom*.[70] In regards to security records/screening, the leading cases are *Leander v. Sweden*,[71] *Amann v. Switzerland*,[72] *Rotaru v. Romania*,[73] *Segerstedt-Wiberg v. Sweden*,[74] and *Shimovolos v. Russia*.[75]

The ECtHR has decided issues concerning fair trial in criminal cases (e.g., regarding the Turkish security courts),[76] and concerning the availability of judicial remedies for security decisions affecting "civil rights" (Article 6). In the latter cases, the ECtHR has required the creation of special mechanisms that reconcile the use of intelligence material with the right of fair proceedings in civil cases. These special mechanisms are relevant to intelligence

---

[68] Klass v. Germany App. No. 5029/71, 2 Eur. H.R. Rep 214 (1978) (upholding West German legislation allowing for secret surveillance of post and telecommunications because it was adequately supervised by five members of parliament and a Commission they appointed).

[69] *Weber v. Germany, supra* note 59 (finding that Germany's 1994 Fight against Crime Act, which authorized the recording and transmission of telephone calls, did not violate Article 8 because it contained adequate safeguards, including a three-month maximum period for recordings).

[70] Liberty v. United Kingdom, App. No. 58243/00, [2008] Eur. Ct. H.R. 568 (finding that the U.K.'s interception of all telecommunications traffic carried between two British Telecom radio stations violated Article 8, in part because the Interception of Communications Act of 1985 afforded the government overly broad discretion). As mentioned, the implications of all these cases are examined in detail in the 2015 Venice Commission Report on Signals Intelligence.

[71] Leander v. Sweden, App. No. 9248/81, 9 Eur. H.R. Rep. 433 (1987). The case is interesting inter alia because a government inquiry, long after the ECtHR judgment, revealed that the legal authority for the collection of security data, accepted by the ECtHR, was fatally flawed: the law stated one thing, but the practice was quite different. The result was law reform, establishing an independent monitoring body for the security police databanks.

[72] Amann v. Switzerland, App. No. 27798/95, 30 Eur. H.R. Rep. 843 (2000) (finding the interception of the applicant's phone call, and the recording of his information on a card, was not "in accordance of the law" because Swiss law did not indicate with sufficient clarity the scope and conditions of the government's wiretapping authority, and therefore the privacy interference was not foreseeable).

[73] Rotaru v. Romania, App. No. 28341/95 (2000). What was at issue was the then-existing law on filing of security information, which provided simply that the security service may collect, by any necessary means, information on threats to the national security of Romania. The ECtHR found this insufficiently clear as regards to the grounds for filing (and the methods that might be used—something that relates to security surveillance). Moreover, there were insufficient safeguards against abuse of discretion. Accordingly it was not "in accordance with law." The ECtHR also found a violation of Article 13 because there were no remedies available. The case led to law reform. Unfortunately, subsequent cases (below) indicate that the systems created for the monitoring of surveillance have not been working in practice.

[74] Segerstedt-Wiberg v. Sweden, App. No. 62332/00, 44 Eur. H.R. Rep. 2 (2006) (considering that continued storage of information collected on four of five applicants violated Article 8, but the government's refusal to advise applicants about the extent to which information was kept about them did not because such refusal furthered a legitimate interest in security).

[75] Shimovolos v. Russia, App. No. 30194/09 (2011) (security data files are not regulated by statute, but only a ministerial regulation, not in accordance with the law).

[76] *See* Cameron, *supra* note 63, at 297–302, Hulki Günes v. Turkey, App. No. 28490/95 (2003). *See also* Haas v. Germany, App. No. 73047/01, 40 Eur. H.R. Rep. 19 (2005).

accountability in the wide sense.[77] In several cases, the ECtHR ruled that safeguards that supposedly operated on paper did not function in practice. For example, in *Segerstedt-Wiberg v. Sweden*, the government argued that the Swedish Data Inspection Board had the power to award compensation for, or order the deletion of, inaccurate or out-of-date data. However, the ECtHR noted that the Data Inspection Board lacked the expertise to evaluate security databanks. There was an expert independent body tasked with overseeing these databanks, but it did not have the necessary powers to order deletion or compensation. The ECtHR accordingly found a violation of the ECHR.[78] In a number of other surveillance and databank cases, the ECtHR has considered that the regulation in subordinate legislation of a particular power was inadequate, or that a particular power had to be regulated.[79]

Controls and remedies existing only on paper have been a particular problem in Romania, where, unlike the majority of the other former Warsaw Pact states, important parts of the apparatus of the communist regime remained intact and continued to exercise control over the state. This section of the Romanian élite had no interest in either allowing access to the security databanks of the former regime or for improving independent controls on, and oversight of, the security sector.[80]

Finally, the ECtHR has looked at certain security issues relating to freedom of expression and information. It has examined the issue of protection of journalists' sources in security matters,[81] and it has considered that the failure of an intelligence agency to comply with

---

[77] For an early case, *see* Tinnelly v. United Kingdom, App. Nos. 20390/92 and 21322/93 (1998). *See also* A v. United Kingdom, *supra* note 66, where the ECtHR accepted that the British system of special advocates could compensate for deficiencies in the trial, but found that the essence of the right of fair trial was infringed in some of the applications, because the complainants did not even receive the gist of the allegations against them. The fairness of the British special advocate system is the subject of controversy. *See also* Joint Committee on Human Rights, Counter-Terrorism Policy and Human Rights (Sixteenth Report): Annual Renewal of Control Orders Legislation 2010, 2009-10, H.C. 395, at 21 (U.K.). *See also* Adam Tompkins, *National Security and the Due Process of Law*, 64 CURRENT LEGAL PROBS. 215 (2011); John Jackson, Justice, *Security and the Right to a Fair Trial: Is the Use of Secret Evidence Ever Fair?*, 4 PUB. L. 720 (2013). *See also* the pending case of *Gulamhussein v. United Kingdom*, App. Nos. 46538/11 and 3960/12, regarding the applicants' dismissal from their jobs at the Home Office for suspected involvement in terrorism. During their challenges to their dismissals, only limited disclosure took place, and a special advocate procedure was applied before the Employment Tribunal in the case of the second applicant. European states that place a greater emphasis on inquisitorial proceedings have not opted for security-screened advocates on the basis that the court can compensate for any inequalities in the position of the parties.

[78] *See* concluding section, *infra*.

[79] Shimovolos v. Russia, *supra* note 75; Uzun v. Germany, App. No. 35623/05 (2010) (use of GPS tracking devices); Bykov v. Russia, App. No. 4378/02 (2009) (Grand Chamber judgment finding a violation due to lack of judicial authorization of bugging device, i.e., "wearing a wire"). *See also* Roman Zakharov v. Russia, App. No. 47143/06, 4 December 2015 (Grand Chamber judgment finding a lack of effective judicial control over surveillance of mobile phones).

[80] Ass'n "21 December 1989" v. Romania, App. Nos. 3381/07, 18817/08 (2011) (mainly concerning access to databanks to establish responsibility for civilian deaths during the "revolution"—rather, a coup d'etat). The case also took up the continued Romanian failures to adequately regulate security surveillance and security databanks so as to comply with the earlier judgment in the Rotaru case. *See also* Bucur v. Romania, App. No. 40238/02 (2013); Popescu v. Romania (no. 2), App. No. 71525/01 (2007).

[81] *See, e.g.*, Telegraaf Media Nederland Landelijke Media B.V. v. the Netherlands, App. No. 39315/06 (2012).

the order of a data protection/freedom of information authority to reveal information can violate Articles 6 (fair trial) and 10 (freedom of expression).[82]

VII. OTHER COUNCIL OF EUROPE MECHANISMS

The Council of Europe was established after the Second World War and is an organization for regional cooperation concerning all matters except defense. It has adopted some 220 conventions on different matters. Apart from the already mentioned ECtHR and Committee of Ministers, the main components of the Council of Europe are the Secretariat, headed by the Secretary-General; various part-time expert bodies consisting of independent national experts; and the Parliamentary Assembly of the Council of Europe (PACE), which meets periodically, consisting of delegates from member-states' legislatures.

The Secretary-General has had only a very limited impact as regards intelligence accountability. The Secretary-General has a power under Article 52 of the ECHR to request information from member-states regarding their application of the ECHR, but this power has been used very sparingly. It was employed in connection with the CIA rendition flights, although no useful material was obtained from the European states that later turned out to have been operating detention facilities.[83]

PACE on the other hand has, like the European Parliament, taken a keen interest in issues related to national security. It has produced reports on different aspects of intelligence accountability, such as whistle-blowing,[84] the U.S. rendition program,[85] and "mass

---

[82] Youth Initiative for H.R. v. Serbia, App. No. 48135/06 (2013).

[83] COUNCIL OF EUROPE, SECRETARY GENERAL'S REPORT UNDER ARTICLE 52 ECHR ON THE QUESTION OF SECRET DETENTION AND TRANSPORT OF DETAINEES SUSPECTED OF TERRORIST ACTS, NOTABLY BY OR AT THE INSTIGATION OF FOREIGN AGENCIES (2006). States were asked to explain how their internal law ensured the effective implementation of the ECHR on four issues: (1) adequate controls over acts by foreign agents in their jurisdiction; (2) adequate safeguards to prevent, as regards any person in their jurisdiction, unacknowledged deprivation of liberty, including transport, with or without the involvement of foreign agents; (3) adequate responses (including effective investigations) to any alleged infringements of ECHR rights, notably in the context of deprivation of liberty, resulting from conduct of foreign agents; (4) whether since January 1, 2002, any public official has been involved, by action or omission, in such deprivation of liberty or transport of detainees; and whether any official investigation is underway or has been completed. *See* COUNCIL OF EUROPE, REPORT BY THE SECRETARY GENERAL ON THE USE OF HIS POWERS UNDER ARTICLE 52 OF THE EUROPEAN CONVENTION ON HUMAN RIGHTS, SG/Inf (2006) 5 (Feb. 28, 2006), *available at* https://wcd.coe.int/ViewDoc.jsp?id=976731&Site=COE.

[84] PARLIAMENTARY ASSEMBLY OF THE COUNCIL OF EUROPE, RECOMMENDATION 1916: PROTECTION OF WHISTLEBLOWERS (2010), http://assembly.coe.int/nw/xml/XRef/Xref-XML2HTML-en.asp?fileid=17852&lang=en. *See also* accompanying report Doc 12006 (2009), *available at* http://assembly.coe.int/nw/xml/XRef/Xref-XML2HTML-en.asp?fileid=12302&lang=en. This led to a Committee of Ministers Recommendation on the Protection of Whistleblowers, and an accompanying Explanatory Memorandum, CMRec (2014) 7E, *available at* http://www.coe.int/t/dghl/standardsetting/cdcj/CDCJ%20Recommendations/CMRec%282014%297E.pdf.

[85] There were a series of reports by the Swiss rapporteur Dick Marty, beginning with alleged secret detentions and unlawful inter-state transfers of detainees involving Council of Europe member-states (Doc. 10957). *See* PARLIAMENTARY ASSEMBLY OF THE COUNCIL OF EUROPE, ALLEGED SECRET DETENTIONS AND UNLAWFUL INTER-STATE TRANSFERS OF DETAINEES INVOLVING COUNCIL OF EUROPE MEMBER

surveillance."[86] The reports on the rendition program are a good illustration of the value, and limitations, of an international body investigating allegations of wrongdoing by security and intelligence agencies.[87] The chief investigator, the Swiss senator Dick Marty, received almost no cooperation from the United States, or from those European states that allegedly took part in the rendition program. Even if state representatives had been willing to give him information, the chief investigator was not in a position to hear evidence under oath or secret information in camera.[88] Marty's small investigative team was accordingly obliged to rely upon nongovernmental organization (NGO) material, investigative journalism (which in turn was to a significant extent based on whistle-blowing) and reconstruction of flights on the basis of information filed with the European air traffic control center, EUROCONTROL.

Marty's reports filled something of a vacuum of accountability, as at the time parliamentarians in national parliaments were unwilling or unable to initiate investigations into what their own states were doing in the "War against Terror." The reports are, in many ways, an impressive piece of investigation, even if the estimate of the number of suspected rendition flights turned out to be heavily exaggerated. Most of the conclusions in the report about cooperating European states have been borne out by subsequent revelations.

Nonetheless, PACE is not really in a position to make factual investigations of secret practices in the way a national oversight body, or commission of inquiry, can. It is a forum for discussion, adopting resolutions and recommendations. At best it can exert an influence on the Committee of Ministers, but in the area of intelligence and security generally, subsequent action by the Committee of Ministers is very unlikely. And even the Committee of Ministers cannot take binding action on states, only adopt resolutions or recommendations, or initiate a process of adopting a treaty (ratification of which is voluntary).

That said, PACE is able to commission reports and studies from the Venice Commission. Like PACE, the Venice Commission is not a fact-finding body, but instead an advisory body on constitutional matters, consisting of independent experts appointed by their governments. The Venice Commission has looked at the rendition program, but only the constitutional and international law aspects of it.[89] It also produced a detailed report on best practices in the field of accountability over domestic security services.[90] The impact of the latter report

---

STATES, Doc. 10957 (June 12, 2006), http://assembly.coe.int/nw/xml/XRef/Xref-XML2HTML-en.asp?fileid=11527&lang=en.

[86] PARLIAMENTARY ASSEMBLY OF THE COUNCIL OF EUROPE, MASS SURVEILLANCE, Doc. 13734 (Mar. 18, 2015).

[87] For a treatment of this issue in greater depth, *see* Aidan Wills, *European Parliament and Parliamentary Assembly of the Council of Europe Inquiries into Intelligence and Security Issues*, in ANTHONY S. FARSON & MARK PHYTHIAN, COMMISSIONS OF INQUIRY AND NATIONAL SECURITY: COMPARATIVE APPROACHES (2014).

[88] No such provisions exist in the statute of the Council of Europe setting out the powers of the Assembly and its subordinate bodies.

[89] Eur. Com. for Democracy through Law, *International Legal Obligations of Council of Europe Member States in Respect of Secret Detention Facilities and Inter-state Transport of Prisoners*, CDL-AD(2006)009 (Mar. 17, 2006), *available at* http://www.venice.coe.int/webforms/documents/default.aspx?pdffile=CDL-AD%282006%29009-e.

[90] Eur. Com. for Democracy through Law, *Democratic Oversight of the Security Services*, CDL-AD(2007)016 (June 11, 2007), *available at* http://www.europarl.europa.eu/meetdocs/2009_2014/documents/libe/dv/3_cdl-ad%282007%29016_/3_cdl-ad%282007%29016_en.pdf.

is primarily persuasive or educational: a number of different models are discussed, together with their strengths and weaknesses. An update of this report was adopted in 2015, which also deals with the special issues of accountability of signals intelligence agencies.[91]

These three reports from the Venice Commission, together with a recent report from the Council of Europe Commissioner on Human Rights,[92] all can be said to provide encouragement for law and administrative reform addressing security and intelligence activities in Europe. The intended audience then, is parliamentarians and NGOs, and those sections of public administration involved in oversight.

I will also note here that the Venice Commission can be asked not simply to produce a general opinion or study, but also to compile a specific report on a state's laws, either by the state itself[93] or by PACE. When the report is commissioned by the state itself and concerns draft legislation, then the likely influence of the Venice Commission is at its greatest; the state wants to improve its law in line with European best practices, and is thus willing to listen to the advice of the Venice Commission. This is usually not the case when PACE commissions a specific country report. In those cases, the intent is instead to focus a spotlight on unsatisfactory practices. PACE has, for example, requested the Venice Commission to produce reports in relation to particular powers of Russian security agencies.[94]

VIII. ANALYTIC CONCLUSIONS

What, then, is the "added value" of the European dimension of oversight, in particular, of the ECtHR's case law?

As mentioned above, the ECtHR is not a direct source of oversight. Instead, it is a mechanism for encouraging and pressuring states to achieve better-functioning national systems of oversight. The same can be said for all the other Council of Europe and EU organs' work in the area of intelligence and security.

The ECHR provides one of the few common standards applicable to all European states, and as such is invaluable as a platform upon which to elaborate more detailed European principles of accountability. Unlike under EU law, there is no exclusion of national security matters from the scope of the ECHR. The pan-European legal culture of the ECtHR can give a different perspective on the need to reform an unsatisfactory system, and the direction reform can take. Criticism from the ECtHR can provide the catalyst to break a national

---

[91] Eur. Com. for Democracy through Law, *Update of the 2007 Report on the Democratic Oversight of the Security Services and Report on the Democratic Oversight of Signals Intelligence Agencies*, CDL-AD(2015)006-e (Mar. 21, 2015), *available at* http://www.venice.coe.int/webforms/documents/?pdf=CDL-AD(2015)006-e.

[92] Council of Europe Commissioner for Human Rights, Democratic and Effective Oversight of National Security Services (2015).

[93] *See, e.g.,* Eur. Com. for Democracy through Law, *Opinion on the Law on the Information and Security Service of the Republic of Moldova*, CDL-AD(2006)011 (Mar. 17, 2006), *available at* http://www.venice.coe.int/webforms/documents/?pdf=CDL-AD%282006%29011-e; Eur. Com. for Democracy through Law, *Opinion on the Law on the Agency of Bosnia and Herzegovina for Information and Protection*, CDL(2002)006 & 005 (Jan. 28, 2001), *available at* http://www.venice.coe.int/webforms/documents/default.aspx?pdffile=CDL%282002%29005-e.

[94] *See* Eur. Com. for Democracy through Law, *Opinion on the Federal Law on the Federal Security Service (FSB) of the Russian Federation*, CDL-AD(2012)015 (June 20, 2012), *available at* http://www.venice.coe.int/WebForms/documents/default.aspx?pdffile=CDL-AD%282012%29015-e.

"log jam" and give the national legislature the opportunity to overhaul the whole field. The ECtHR case law shows that there can be situations when an international body places greater demands than those set by national courts and legislatures.

The rendition cases are a good illustration of this last point. As the ECtHR assesses *state* responsibility, its scrutiny cannot be blocked by national separation-of-powers doctrines. Nor is the ECtHR blocked by a refusal on the part of the executive branch to give evidence. The ECtHR is mainly content (indeed, has to be content) to let the national courts do the fact-finding in the case. Thus, the factual framework is settled, and the ECtHR can focus on structural and policy issues. This means that it will rarely *need* secret evidence to decide the case.[95] From the perspective of the respondent government, this can be both welcome and unwelcome. It can be welcome because it avoids the "graymail" problem of the applicant who tries to win his or her case on tactical grounds by forcing the government to choose between revealing intelligence that should almost invariably be kept secret (such as the identity of informants) and winning the case. It can be unwelcome because the ECtHR will rarely be impressed by a government refusal to submit requested evidence.[96] If the ECtHR considers that proof of a violation may follow from the coexistence of sufficiently strong, clear, and concordant inferences, or of similar unrebutted presumptions of fact, then it will find in favor of the applicant.

This is well illustrated by one of the recent rendition cases, *Husayn Abu Zubayda v. Poland*, in which the ECtHR stated,

> The level of persuasion necessary for reaching a particular conclusion and, in this connection, the distribution of the burden of proof, are intrinsically linked to the specificity of the facts, the nature of the allegation made and the ECHR right at stake. While it is for the applicant to make a *prima facie* case and adduce appropriate evidence, if the respondent Government in their response to his allegations fail to disclose crucial documents to enable the Court to establish the facts or otherwise provide a satisfactory and convincing explanation of how the events in question occurred, strong inferences can be drawn . . . the Convention proceedings do not in all cases lend themselves to a strict application of the principle *affirmanti incumbit probatio*. According to the Court's case-law under Articles 2 and 3 of the ECHR, where the events in issue lie wholly, or in large part, within the exclusive knowledge of the authorities, for instance as in the case of persons under their control in custody, strong presumptions of fact will arise in respect of injuries and death occurring during that detention. The burden of proof in such a case may be regarded as resting on the authorities to provide a satisfactory and convincing explanation.[97]

---

[95] Although it can receive secret evidence, it tends not to do so. A government can submit evidence that it requests be kept secret. Under Article 33(2) of its rules of procedure the ECtHR can choose not to make public evidence disclosed to it.

[96] If the government refuses to submit evidence that has been requested, then under Article 44C of the ECtHR Rules of Procedure "where a party fails to adduce evidence or provide information requested by the [ECtHR] . . . or to divulge relevant information of its own motion or otherwise fails to participate effectively in the proceedings, the Court may draw such inferences as it deems appropriate."

[97] Husayn v. Poland, *supra* note 64, ¶¶ 394–396.

Thus, a "state secrets" defense will not avail the respondent state either, if there is sufficient material already in the public domain.

Surprising though it might seem, there is a relatively high degree of compliance with judgments from the ECtHR. This is the case even though the primary "sanction" for not complying is only reputational—the state is embarrassed.[98] Having said this, for states with major structural problems in protection of rights the problem is that, although the state usually complies with the judgment by paying compensation, it does not correct the underlying structural problem that led to the violation in the first place.[99] With such states, the added value of the ECHR is naturally limited at the best of times. In areas of law and policy connected to national security, the chances of a negative ECtHR judgment actually leading to meaningful law reform in an authoritarian state are tiny.

There is nothing new here. Courts are gatekeepers of social change. They can facilitate it, but when powerful social forces resist change, the courts need the support of the executive branch to make it happen. The "least dangerous branch" of government steers by legitimacy, not force or money. If this is so for the U.S. Supreme Court, a well-established and powerful part of a federal system, then it is even more true for a (relatively) newly established international court. It is clear that, for powerful factions in the executive branch of several European states, it is still force or money that make the really strong arguments.[100]

By contrast, for a state that at least is attempting, in good faith, to behave as a *Rechtsstaat* (a state based on the rule of law), the value of the ECHR is not simply in terms of the actual case law of the ECtHR. The ECHR is part of the *public* law of the member-states. It thus influences the administrative bodies in administrative decision-making, the parliament in legislating, and the courts in judging. The decision to create intelligence oversight bodies, and the mandates these bodies received to monitor legality (including proportionality) in a number of states, including Belgium, Sweden, Denmark, Norway, and the Netherlands, has been strongly influenced by ECtHR case law. The ECHR standards are regularly referred to

---

[98] Article 3 of the Statute of the CoE states that every member "must accept the principles of the rule of law and of the enjoyment by all persons within its jurisdiction of human rights and fundamental freedoms." Thus, ultimately, a non-complying state can be expelled from the Council of Europe. This is not a likely scenario, although in 1969 Greece resigned from the organization, rather than be expelled, following the publication of a report from the Commission disclosing major Greek violations of the Convention.

[99] This may particularly be the case in EU states such as Romania and Bulgaria. The dismantling of safeguards for the rule of law that has occurred in recent years in Hungary means that it is also likely to be a problem in the future. *See* János Kornai, *Hungary's U-Turn*, 10 CAPITALISM & SOC. 2 (2015).

[100] The following point made by U.S. Supreme Court Justice Breyer on political maturity is instructive. Breyer noted President Eisenhower's decision in the 1950s to enforce the Supreme Court's desegregation decisions with the U.S. Army in the face of resistance by the state national guard, and stated that "Many people were upset with the Supreme Court's decision in Bush v. Gore, 531 U.S. 98 (2000). But while that decision has inspired a wide range of different responses and emotions, I have yet to read about the need for deploying paratroopers. Tracing the trajectory of the rule of law in this country reveals that we have arrived at the point where people will accept the fundamental legitimacy of judicial decisions even if they disagree with the outcomes of those decisions. This acceptance of the rule of law has come to exist only over time in this country. And it is an ideal that is not yet universal." Stephen G. Breyer, *Introduction of President Luzius Wildhaber*, 22 AM. U. INT'L L. REV. 517 (2007).

and applied by the oversight bodies in these states.[101] Even a state that tends to take a minimalist approach to ECtHR case law in national security issues, such as the U.K. has done,[102] has to show greater respect when the ECHR is applied by its own courts as public law.[103]

So far, the main ECtHR case law has dealt with setting minimum levels of foreseeability, particularly as regards legal authority to engage in secret surveillance and security filing/screening. The adequacy or otherwise of a legal mandate is an issue on which judges, national or international, are eminently suitable to pronounce. However, the real challenge for the future relates to the adequacy of the control and remedies mechanisms *in practice*. This is a more sensitive area for the ECtHR to take on, as it will involve it in a more policy-oriented exercise of assessing whether a particular blend of controls contains adequate safeguards for preventing abuse of power. The remedies and safeguards that should operate in the area of oversight can rarely be purely judicial in nature. The operation of the sort of quasi-judicial, political, or administrative remedies appropriate to this area can be assumed to be outside the experience of the majority of the judges on the ECtHR. Moreover, the requirements of Articles 8 and 13 of the ECHR in this respect are to ends (effective remedies and safeguards) rather than means. There is obviously room for different approaches in design of system. It is one thing for the ECtHR to say that a particular judicial proceeding satisfies or does not satisfy the procedural requirements of a "fair trial" in Article 6. It is quite another to lay down what type of remedies are necessary to comply with Article 13. As noted before, the ECtHR is not in the business of legislating for member-states, especially in areas that can be assumed to be politically controversial.

This having been said, it is not the ECtHR's job to balance the different factors and design the perfect system. The ECtHR only needs to indicate whether the system before it in a concrete case is *imperfect*. In reaching its conclusions in this regard, I would say that the ECtHR should have as its point of departure the fact that it is difficult for any court, acting alone, to effectively supervise surveillance—particularly in the realm of signals intelligence. Courts tend to assess state activity at the initiation of surveillance, under a "reasonable suspicion" standard. What is needed in addition is some sort of follow-up control on the intelligence gathered, an external monitor with an independent staff and sufficient power and authority to compel the production of *all* information, and sufficient expertise to evaluate it critically.

---

[101] One can note that there is a European dimension to oversight in the sense that the oversight bodies in these states also have a degree of cooperation with each other. Their mandates exclude them from exchanging secret information with one another, but there is considerable scope for cooperation on methodological and technical issues.

[102] In my view, the Security Services Act 1989 and the Intelligence Services Act 1994 were largely attempts to legally authorize "carrying on as before." I am not arguing that the U.K. intelligence and security services are actually engaged in massive wrongdoing, simply that the safeguards against this are internal, for example, the professionalism of these services. The external oversight safeguards are weak. For further discussion, *see* Ian Leigh, *Rebalancing Rights and National Security: Reforming UK Intelligence Oversight a Decade after 9/11*, 27 INTELLIGENCE & NAT'L SECURITY 722–38 (2012).

[103] *See* the British case of Liberty v. GCHQ, [2014] UKIPTrib 13_77-H, [2015] UKIPTrib 13_77-H. The court found that there was a (albeit small) deficiency in the British legal basis for signals intelligence. For the time period in question this surveillance was thus not "in accordance with the law."

Still, as the *Iordachi and Association for European Integration* cases show, these are of little significance if there is no desire on the part of the monitor to use these powers, or no political support for him or her to do so. In practice, the value of an external monitor will mainly depend on the political climate in which he or she works, the dedication of the officeholder, and the competence of his or her staff. These are fairly intangible things on which to form an opinion, far away in Strasbourg. The ECtHR is thus relatively ill-equipped to judge whether formal safeguards are real safeguards.

Still, it is not impossible for it to do so, as the *Segerstedt-Wiberg* case shows. Crucial to the ECtHR's ability to adjudicate the sufficiency of safeguards is the availability of reliable information from national sources other than the government, such as parliamentary commissions of inquiry. Comparative information generally on "better ways of doing things" is also helpful to counter a government argument that there is "no alternative." To some extent this comparative material is already available with the Venice Commission reports, and the Council of Europe Commissioner for Human Rights Report. Hopefully, even more material will become available as a result of academic projects and government and parliamentary commissions of inquiry. For example, the United States has made a lot of useful material available on signals intelligence.[104]

As noted in the first section, the EU will legislate, and adopt treaties on, areas indirectly touching intelligence accountability. However, the lack of formal EU competence in national security matters means that to a large extent it is forced to build upon the case law of the ECtHR. Many cases have already reached the ECtHR, and doubtless many more will. The ECtHR case law supplies an important part of the framework for discussion of oversight, but the actual discussion is, and should be, national. If there is no real interest at the national level in improved oversight, which is where such oversight must be implemented in any event, then it is asking a lot of the ECtHR to disprove of the oversight solution adopted by the state, even if most impartial observers would regard the system as gravely deficient.

---

[104] *See, e.g.,* Under Sec'y of Def. for Policy, U.S. Dep't of Def., Procedures Governing the Activities of DOD Intelligence Components That Affect United States Persons (1982), *available at* https://fas.org/irp/doddir/dod/d5240_1_r.pdf; Privacy and Civil Liberties Oversight Board (PCLOB), Report on the Surveillance Program Operated Pursuant to Section 702 of the Foreign Intelligence Surveillance Act (July 2, 2014); PCLOB, Report on the Telephone Records Program Conducted under Section 215 of the USA PATRIOT Act and on the Operations of the Foreign Intelligence Surveillance Court (Jan. 23, 2014); National Research Council of the National Academies, Bulk Collection of Signals Intelligence: Technical Options (2015).

4

Global Change and Megatrends

IMPLICATIONS FOR INTELLIGENCE AND ITS OVERSIGHT

Christopher A. Kojm*

I. INTRODUCTION

Change throughout the international system is profound and accelerating. The pace of political, economic, and technological change around the world is a major challenge for all institutions. In the private sector, executives understand that recognizing and adapting to a dynamic environment makes all the difference between financial success and failure.

In the public sector, the problem of understanding change is no different—and the stakes could not possibly be higher. Peace, prosperity, and security depend on the nature of our leaders' response. Across the U.S. government, key cabinet departments have policy-planning offices tasked with understanding the implications of change for their mission and adapting operations in response. At the National Security Council, a small office of strategic planning seeks to do the same across the government. It coordinates cabinet efforts on behalf of developing the President's National Security Strategy. And the imperative to adapt to a rapidly changing world, where foundational elements of the international environment appear to be changing as quickly as the politics of particular regions, is no different in the IC.

While the Intelligence Community (IC) seeks to inform policymakers about the nature of change and the challenges they are likely to confront, the IC also has to look inward. It needs to reflect on those same changes in the international environment and their implications for its own mission. Director of National Intelligence (DNI) James R. Clapper is cognizant of the challenge, and his plan for the next four years, the 2014 National Intelligence Strategy,

---

* Christopher A. Kojm is the J.B. and Maurice C. Shapiro Professor of International Affairs at the Elliott School of International Affairs, at George Washington University.

"sets forth the strategic environment, sets priorities and objectives, and focuses resources on current and future budgets, acquisitions and operations decisions."[1]

The purpose of this chapter is to elaborate on what that Strategy calls "the strategic environment." Director Clapper describes it as follows:

> I've often said publicly that the United States is facing the most diverse set of threats I've seen in my 50 years in the intelligence business. We face significant changes in the global and domestic environment and must be ready to meet the 21st century challenges and to recognize emerging opportunities.[2]

What are the key geopolitical trends and security threats that the IC will need to understand and analyze over the medium- to long-term, and, in turn, what challenges do they pose for its mission? Furthermore, what are the impacts of those trends and threats on the kinds of oversight that will be necessary to ensure the IC retains the trust and confidence of the American people? Although the majority of this chapter is focused on changes to the intelligence landscape, the nature of those changes will put pressure on the extant oversight architecture described throughout this volume.

First, gaining a greater understanding of the developments described in detail below—changes to demographic structures, to governance systems, and to the technological landscape—will depend more than ever before on unclassified information. This information might or might not be in the public domain, but it is less likely to be derived from clandestine collection. How might an oversight system designed to supervise the unique concerns attendant with an IC cloaked in secrecy need to adapt to manage one where a great deal of information comes from outside the IC? Will the institutions be the same? Will oversight over the two broad categories of information be able to coexist? The importance of clandestine collection will not recede with respect to specific intelligence problems—the intentions of the Russian leadership regarding Ukraine, or where al-Qaida is planning its next attack, for example. But the systems of oversight with respect to clandestine and open source collection might be different, and the ways in which they might differ demand sustained attention.

Second, the revolution in the use of "big data" techniques by the IC to analyze open source information, particularly social media materials, is only in its infancy. So too is the development of the oversight systems needed to ensure the legitimacy of the government's use of advanced data analytical techniques with respect to that open source data. The application of big data techniques to social media is aimed at generating insights into important trends based on the collection and analysis of large quantities of information generated by citizens of foreign countries. It is critical to understanding rapid political change in situations like that which preceded the Egyptian revolution in 2011. But it is information voluntarily placed in the public domain, and is collected openly, not clandestinely. Creating legal

---

[1] News Release, Office of the Director of National Intelligence, "DNI Unveils 2014 National Intelligence Strategy," Sept. 18, 2014, *available at* http://www.dni.gov/index.php/newsroom/reports-and-publications/ 204-reports-publications-2014/1114-dni-unveils-2014-national-intelligence-strategyDNI%202014.

[2] *Id.*

rules and ethical norms to govern the circumstances in which the IC can collect and use this material—both internal rules within the U.S. IC and international norms, at least among peer ICs—will be important in the years to come.

Third, the move to cloud computing (discussed below) will facilitate information-sharing both within and between IC agencies. But this trend will require the IC to develop (and, ideally, publicize) more detailed rules governing the use and dissemination of that data, and to hardwire those restrictions onto the data itself through sophisticated tagging technology. Such technology will facilitate compliance with use and dissemination rules, and potentially provide the public greater confidence in the IC. It will also, however, make it more important to consider use and dissemination in the initial stages of systems design, and to construct systems in such a way that they can easily be adapted as rules and technologies change. Questions of oversight will, therefore, begin to penetrate deeply into the most fundamental questions of technical management and IT systems design in the IC.

Fourth, changes in the security clearance system are likely to involve continuous monitoring of employee behavior, rather than background investigations of the kind that have served as a gateway into the IC for the past several decades. These techniques, however, raise questions about the privacy interests of IC employees. They will need to be accompanied, therefore, by parallel processes to ensure that employees are protected against inappropriate use of information gathered about them by IC agencies.

Finally, many of the trends shaping the intelligence landscape described below will require closer cooperation with the law enforcement and intelligence agencies of other countries. This, in turn, is likely to accelerate the parallel trends of institutional convergence and peer constraint that Richard Morgan and Ashley Deeks identify in their chapters.

The ways in which the IC handles these issues and answers these questions will make all the difference as to whether the IC can provide timely, accurate, and relevant intelligence for policymakers and retain the trust and confidence of the American people while doing so. The whole purpose of the intelligence enterprise, after all, is to assist policymakers in making better decisions—to enhance peace, prosperity, and security. So the task could not be more important.

II. MEGATRENDS

Several key priorities for the IC are country and issue specific. That list includes China, Iran, North Korea, and Russia, and support to deployed U.S. forces. It includes terrorism and proliferation. These priorities feature prominently in the Director's annual threat assessment testimony before Congress.[3] They consume a significant share of the time, attention, and resources of the IC. Intelligence requirements relating to them are of keen interest, year after year, across administrations. They represent a relatively stable portion of the intelligence portfolio; there is little doubt that language skills and technical expertise with respect to them will be necessary in the years ahead.

---

[3] James R. Clapper, Director of National Intelligence, Statement for the Record, Senate Select Committee on Intelligence: Worldwide Threat Assessment of the U.S. Intelligence Community (Jan. 29, 2014), http://www. dni.gov/files/documents/Intelligence%20Reports/2014%20WWTA%20%20SFR_SSCI_29_Jan.pdf.

For the balance of this chapter, I will focus my attention on a different set of challenges—powerful trends that in each case are profoundly shaping the international system, both for good and ill. They are in motion today, and are highly likely to continue. They are megatrends.

A. *The Diffusion of Power*

Perhaps the single most important fact about the international system today is the diffusion of power within it. The international order is becoming more chaotic. International agreement will become increasingly difficult, when it is possible at all. International institutions, already under great strain, will find it increasingly hard to meet the challenges for which they were established. The United Nations Security Council, following a brief period of comity at the end of the Cold War, is again blocked by disagreement and paralysis (e.g., with respect to the conflicts in Syria and Ukraine). Reform of the Security Council, although widely recognized as necessary, is paralyzed by a complete lack of agreement among permanent members as to what kind of reform should occur. New lending institutions sponsored by China challenge the World Bank's role. Both it and the International Monetary Fund face difficulties implementing institutional reforms and convincing governments and public opinion of their relevance.

The moorings of the post–World War II international order, underwritten by the United States, have long been slipping. The reasons are evident: the economic and financial power of the United States and its allies is in relative decline compared to the economies of China, India, and the G-20. The creation of the G-20 itself—rising in prominence at the time of the global financial crisis in 2009—reflects the fact that the advanced industrialized countries of the G-7 alone can no longer address the world's ills.

However, the G-20 has not done much better. Apart from the partial success of the 2009 Pittsburgh G-20 summit in resisting protectionism and stimulating growth in the global economy, the G-20 has had no better record in problem-solving. Why? Because the emerging economies have little interest in taking on responsibility for maintaining international order. They desire to benefit, and do benefit, from it. But they sidestep responsibility to support and uphold what they regard as an international system created of, by, and for the Western powers.

B. *Governance*

The diffusion of power is not only between states but also within states. Governance is the pressing question: Will governments adapt to change or be overwhelmed by it? States of all political stripes have difficulties governing.

The Arab Spring is the most pointed example. It led to the overthrow of regimes in Tunisia, Egypt, Libya, and Yemen. Stagnant regimes—hostile to reform, deeply corrupt, and repressive—could not survive popular protest and abandonment by the security forces. When the security forces did not step aside, as in Libya and Syria, ferocious war ensued.

Around the world, the growth of a middle class drives popular interest in more accountable government and greater political participation. Yet the path is full of pitfalls. The historical record shows that transitions from autocracy in the direction of democracy are marked by great instability. According to the Global Trends 2030 report, some 50 states in Africa,

Asia, and the Middle East somewhere on the path from autocracy to democracy are at major risk for instability between now and 2030.[4]

The advanced industrialized world has profound problems of governance as well. Elected leaders are unable to deliver on voter expectations of jobs and growth. In addition, the electorate is skeptical of the costs on behalf of promised benefits of long-term reform. As Jean-Claude Juncker, now president of the European Commission, said earlier, "We all know what to do, we just don't know how to get re-elected after we've done it."[5]

Since the 2008 financial crisis, confidence in government has dropped dramatically. Over 70 percent of Europeans polled by Pew Research in 2014 believe their voice does not count in the European Union, and 65 percent believe the EU does not understand the needs of its citizens.[6] The mood in Europe is downright bleak: "Just 5% of the public in Greece, 8% in Spain and 9% in Italy and only 22% in France and 27% in Poland say they are satisfied with the way things are going in their country."[7] In all of Europe, only Germans (59 percent) were positive about national conditions.[8] In France, President François Hollande's approval rating fell to 13 percent, a record low in the history of the Fifth Republic.[9] In Japan, economic problems weigh heavily as well: Japan has had five prime ministers in the past eight years.

C. *Individual Empowerment*

Governments everywhere are under stress because the governed are demanding so much more of them. Growing middle classes are wealthier, healthier, and better educated—and they want more say in their lives. Hundreds of millions in China, India, Brazil, Indonesia, Turkey, and other emerging economies have been lifted out of poverty in the past two decades; even conservative growth forecasts predict a doubling of the world's middle class between now and 2030, from 1 billion to 2 billion.[10] Average worldwide life expectancy has increased six years since 1990, to 73 years for girls and 68 for boys born in 2012. Over this same period of time, life expectancy in low-income countries has increased nine years, or an astounding 15 percent.[11] Worldwide educational attainment levels have increased 27 percent since 1990, to an average of 11 years in the developed world and seven in the developing world in 2010. The increase in educational attainment in East Asia was a

---

[4] NATIONAL INTELLIGENCE COUNCIL, GLOBAL TRENDS 2030: ALTERNATIVE WORLDS 50–51 (2012), *available at* http://www.dni.gov/files/documents/GlobalTrends_2030.pdf.

[5] *Profile: EU's Jean-Claude Junker*, BBC NEWS (July 15, 2014), http://www.bbc.co.uk/news/world-europe-27679170.

[6] Bruce Stokes, *Key Takeaways from the European Union Survey*, PEW RESEARCH CTR. (May 12, 2014), http://www.pewresearch.org/fact-tank/2014/05/12/5-key-takeaways-from-the-european-union-survey/.

[7] PEW RESEARCH CENTER, A FRAGILE REBOUND FOR EU IMAGE ON EVE OF EUROPEAN PARLIAMENT ELECTIONS 13 (2014), http://www.pewglobal.org/files/2014/05/2014-05-12_Pew-Global-Attitudes-European-Union.pdf.

[8] *Id.*

[9] *Hollande's Approval Ratings Climb Off Rock Bottom: French Poll*, REUTERS (Apr. 18, 2015), http://www.reuters.com/article/2015/04/18/us-france-hollande-poll-idUSKBN0N90EX20150418.

[10] NATIONAL INTELLIGENCE COUNCIL *supra* note 4, at 8–9.

[11] News Release, World Health Organization, World Health Statistics 2014: Large Gains in Life Expectancy (May 15, 2014), http://www.who.int/mediacentre/news/releases/2014/world-health-statistics-2014/en/.

remarkable 42 percent.[12] Worldwide, women are narrowing the gap with men in years of formal education—and in higher income countries have even moved ahead of men, though educational attainment has yet to be matched by closing the gap on earnings or political empowerment.[13]

D. Information Technology

The single greatest factor enhancing the power of these richer, healthier, and smarter individuals is information technology (IT). Through it, access to information is far more widespread—across national boundaries, within institutions, and outside institutions. IT has an inherent tendency to undermine the authority of institutions, especially governments, which have had comparative monopolies on access and control of information. More information enables more political participation. More information about the operation of markets means better and fairer prices. More information means that received wisdom on any topic is open to greater challenge. More information empowers individuals and is disruptive of the existing order.

In the Middle East and North Africa, the conditions for political upheaval had long been building, but it took the power of social media to ignite mass political rallies and revolt. Small groups of individuals used it to convene mass rallies and communicate across Egypt and around the world. Google's Middle East marketing head, Wael Ghonim, became both a protest leader in Egypt and a symbol for the power that social media could bring to the struggle.[14]

For many years, the security services in Egypt had success monitoring and containing the opposition, including its presence on the Internet. After the fall of Ben Ali in Tunisia on January 14, 2011, they were overwhelmed. Intermittent efforts to pull the plug on the Internet in Egypt only led to workarounds and more public anger. Mass rallies began in Cairo and cities across Egypt on January 25. By February 11 Mubarak was gone, swept from power.

The quick demise of Ben Ali and Mubarak pointed up the dangers for all autocrats of social media in the hands of technologically savvy and mostly young protestors. In September 2011, Vladimir Putin and President Dmitry Medvedev revealed their private agreement to trade places and return Putin to the Russian presidency, sparking a furious social media response and mass protests in the streets of Moscow in the winter of 2011–2012.[15]

The power of IT, both demonstrated and feared, led to increasingly pervasive monitoring and restriction by Russia and China. The West, on the one hand, celebrated the possibilities for human freedom and creativity of widely disseminated and ever-cheaper means of communication. State authorities in Russia and China fear exactly the implications of the same.

---

[12] Robert J. Barro & Jong-Wha Lee, *Educational Attainment from 1950 to 2010*, 32–35 (Nat'l Bureau of Econ. Research, Working Paper No. 15902), *available at* http://www.development.wne.uw.edu.pl/uploads/Courses/DW_barrolee_2010.pdf.

[13] NATIONAL INTELLIGENCE COUNCIL *supra* note 4, at 10–11.

[14] *Profile: Egypt's Wael Ghonim*, BBC NEWS (Feb. 8, 2011), http://www.bbc.com/news/world-middle-east-12400529.

[15] Charles Clover & Catherine Belton, "*I Will Transmit This to Vladimir*," FIN. TIMES (May 5, 2012 12:18 AM), http://www.ft.com/cms/s/0/4fc908b6-94ba-11e1-bb0d-00144feab49a.html.

Russia's narrative of the overthrow of President Viktor Yanukovich in Ukraine in February 2014 demonstrates autocratic states' wariness of social media; to the Russians, Yanukovich's downfall had nothing to do with his rejection of an Association Agreement with the European Union and popular revulsion at his use of force against demonstrators. Rather, it rests on Russian general Valery Gerasimov's interpretation of lessons of the Arab Spring: "The focus of applied methods of conflict has altered in the direction of the broad use of political, economic, informational, humanitarian, and other nonmilitary measures—applied in coordination with the protest potential of the population."[16] Seen through his lens, the potential of IT is as a consciously applied tool employed by foreign powers to overthrow what Gerasimov terms "perfectly thriving state[s]."[17]

IT not only changes the power balance between individuals and governments, it is causing upheaval of the business model for whole industries. To name a few: all of publishing (not just the well-known example of newspapers), the legal profession, university education, and the future of manufacturing. The challenge from IT is to cost structures, market share, and profitability. In every case, IT lowers barriers to entry, making it possible for individuals or small groups to take on tasks previously carried out only by large institutions.

The case of 3D printing is a prime example. Previously, manufacturing took place in vast factory complexes, costing hundreds of millions of dollars and employing thousands of people to forge, cut, drill, and machine metal or other material into an intended product. The manufacturing process was subtractive, analogous to the way a sculptor cuts a statue from a block of stone. Today and increasingly tomorrow, manufacturing will take place through a much simpler additive process. An individual will need a computer file, a 3D printer that fits easily inside a garage, and the right powder. The machine will read the file and use lasers or other power sources to fuse layer after layer of metal powder or other substrate to create the required object. Designs can be changed as quickly as one edits a computer file. Prototypes can be manufactured in hours or days versus weeks or months. The capital, land, and labor requirements of all production are vastly reduced.

What 3D printing will do is empower some, even as it has enormously disruptive results for many. What will become of the factory workers and the industries that used to employ them? Some will retire; most will need to seek new jobs. There has been, and always will be, a process of retraining and education, reinvestment in human capital. But will this time-consuming human process have a rapid enough turnaround time to provide sufficient employment opportunities for the next generation? The economic, societal, and ultimately political implications of the transformation of the workplace by IT need far more attention than they receive today.

E. Demographics

Any discussion of the future international environment must pay close attention to demographics. It is perhaps the only topic where we can speak about the future with near certainty.

---

[16] Valery Gerasimov, *Military-Industrial Kurier*, VPK News (Feb 27, 2013) (Robert Coalson trans., June 21, 2014), https://www.facebook.com/notes/robert-coalson/russian-military-doctrine-article-by-general-valery-gerasimov/10152184862563597.

[17] *Id.*

For example, we know the upper limit to the number of 18-year-olds that will enter the Chinese labor force in 2030 because they have all already been born.

Several demographic trends are noteworthy. First, 97 percent of the world's population growth between now and 2030 will be outside of the advanced industrial world.[18] Birth rates below replacement level mean that most of Europe and East Asia will have static or declining populations. The rich countries are aging rapidly. By the year 2030, most European countries as well as Japan, South Korea, and Taiwan will have populations with a median age above 45. One-quarter of Europeans will be above age 65.[19] There is no precedent in human history of societies with such an age profile. Societies with generous pensions and social welfare benefits simply cannot sustain an economic model in which the ratio of workers to pensioners moves in the direction of one to one. Germany and Japan will see the absolute number of young people decline by 25 percent: who will do tomorrow's work? Will societies in which political power rests with the elderly give priority to investment in young people and new technologies? The implications for economic growth, public finances, and future manpower for armed forces are troubling.

One perhaps obvious answer to future European labor needs would be immigration, or investment in existing and underutilized human capital. The vast majority of Muslims in Western Europe first came in the 1960s and 1970s to fill labor shortages in low-skilled jobs. They and their descendants are part of a Muslim population in Europe that has grown from 29 million in 1990 to 44 million in 2010 to an expected 58 million in 2030.[20] While its birth rate is falling, its annual growth rate of 1.6 percent is still far higher than that of the non-Muslim European population, which is in actual decline (−0.1 percent per annum).[21] However, terrorism attacks and the return of foreign fighters from Syria are fueling the growth of right-wing parties across Europe. There is growing ill will toward Muslims, strong resistance to further immigration from the Middle East and North Africa, and little prospect that European attitudes toward Muslims will change in the direction of social inclusion.

In Britain and the United States, birth rates have not fallen as dramatically as across most of the advanced industrial world. Both countries will experience population growth because of their openness to immigration. Population profiles between now and 2030 will change fairly modestly: the median age in Britain will rise from 40 to 42, and in the United States from 37 to 39.

China today is younger than the United States today (median age of 35) but by 2030 it will be older (median age of 43). One of the chief implications of the rapid aging of China's one-child generation is that the number of young people entering the work force is now peaking, and will be in steady decline between now and 2030. The number of senior citizens as a share of the population will double.[22] Although impacts on public finances will be more muted than in Europe because China provides fewer social services, the impacts on economic competitiveness will be profound. Labor rates in China will continue to rise,

---

[18] Roland Berger, Trend Compendium 2030 22–24 (2011), *available at* http://www.rolandberger.com/gallery/trend-compendium/tc2030/content/assets/trendcompendium2030.pdf.

[19] Arthur C. Brooks, *Europe's Decline*, N.Y. Times, Jan. 7, 2015, at A23.

[20] *The Future of the Global Muslim Population*, Pew Research Center (Jan. 27, 2011), http://www.pewforum.org/2011/01/27/future-of-the-global-muslim-population-regional-europe/.

[21] *Id.*

[22] Nicholas Eberstadt, *The Demographic Future*, Foreign Affairs, Nov./Dec. 2010, at 54–64.

and China must move up the value chain if it is going to continue to grow. The unskilled and semiskilled jobs are already flowing to Bangladesh, Vietnam, and Indonesia. China risks pricing itself out of the market unless it can develop an educated workforce to move into more sophisticated manufacturing and new export markets. China is at risk of becoming gray before it becomes rich.

In addition, the premium families place on boys and the pressures of the one-child policy have led to the widespread and underreported abortion of female fetuses.[23] Obstetric ultrasound technology, now widely available in South and East Asia, has been used not only as an instrument of prenatal care, but as a tool for identifying the sex of the fetus and terminating unwanted females.[24] In less than a generation, China will be facing a situation in which roughly 20 percent of the male population will have no prospect for marriage. Given that older and richer men will almost surely prevail in this competition for marriage, younger and poorer men will be at a great disadvantage. Young men in North Africa with grim prospects for employment and marriage fueled the Arab Spring. Will a future China fare any better?

Russia has one of the bleakest demographic profiles. Life expectancy for males (63 years) is shockingly low, some 15 years less than male life expectancy in the West.[25] Alcohol in the first instance plus smoking, poor diets, drug addiction, and AIDS are taking a toll. Although birth rates in Russia have recovered from their collapse in the 1990s, the small cohort now entering prime childbearing years points to likely further population decline between now and 2030.[26] Russia's workforce, in decline since 2007, will continue to decline in size for the next two decades. [27]

In the context of recent war and continuing unrest in Chechnya and the Caucasus, perhaps the greatest demographic issue facing Russia will be the integration of its large and expanding Muslim population. Russia's 20 million Muslims represent 14 percent of the country's population; by 2030 the Muslim share will reach 19 percent.[28] Given hostility toward Muslims in Russia, prospects for successful integration are not promising.

The demographic declines likely to occur in China and Russia stand in stark contrast to expanding populations elsewhere in the developing world. India, with an annual population growth of 1.1 percent a year, [29] will surpass China as the world's most populous country by 2025. India is entering what demographers call a window of opportunity, where the working-age population is at a maximum compared to the number of children (less than 30 percent) or

[23] Interview with Nicholas Eberstadt, Senior Advisor to the Nat'l Bureau of Asian Research, Scholar at the Am. Enter. Inst. (Dec. 2011), *available at* http://www.nbr.org/downloads/pdfs/outreach/NBR_IndiaCaucus_Dec2011.pdf.

[24] Chantal de Bakker, *Obstetric Ultrasound in the Developing World: An Advance in Prenatal and Maternal Health, or a Facilitator of Gender Selection?*, *in* 3 Boston U. J. Art & Sci. Writing Program 52, 55 (2011), http://www.bu.edu/writingprogram/files/2011/10/deBakker1011.pdf.

[25] *Country Health Profile:* Russia, WorldLifeExpectancy.com, http://www.worldlifeexpectancy.com/country-health-profile/russia (last visited May 28, 2015).

[26] Mark Adomanis, *"Dying" Russia's Birth Rate Is Now Higher than the United States'*, Forbes (July 25, 2013), http://www.forbes.com/sites/markadomanis/2013/07/25/dying-russias-birth-rate-is-now-higher-than-the-united-states/; *see also* Ankit Panda, *Actually, Russia's Population Isn't Shrinking*, The Diplomat (May 1, 2014), http://thediplomat.com/2014/05/actually-russias-population-isnt-shrinking/.

[27] National Intelligence Council *supra* note 4, at 80.

[28] *Id.*

[29] Interview with Nicholas Eberstadt, *supra* note 23, at 1.

senior citizens (less than 15 percent). Likewise, the world's highest birthrates are found in sub-Saharan Africa, where Nigeria will surpass the United States as the world's third most populous country around 2040.[30] Africa today contains 15 percent of the world's population; by 2050 one-quarter of humanity will live there.[31] The growing populations of India and Africa suggest significant potential for economic growth, the realization of which will be largely dependent on how well those regions manage their natural resources, and invest in human capital.

One striking correlation in demographic data is the correlation of youthful populations to armed conflict. Some 80 percent of the world's armed civil and ethnic conflicts since the 1970s have taken place in countries where the median age is below 25. Happily, the number of such countries—80 today—will decline to about 50 by 2030.[32] For Africa, this will still encompass some 35 countries. Outside of Africa, the list includes the Palestinian Territories, Yemen, Afghanistan, the tribal areas of Pakistan, and Chechnya in Russia.

Urbanization is a powerful trend that will surely continue. In 1900, only 15 percent of the world's population lived in cities.[33] Today, that share is 50 percent, and it will become 60 percent by 2030. The world's urban population will grow from 3.5 to 4.9 billion.[34] In other words, about 80 million people a year will move to urban areas—10 New York City equivalents each year. The opportunities are great: urban centers are the source of ideas, creativity, and 80 percent of economic growth.[35] But so are the challenges: housing, feeding, and providing the infrastructure for power, clean water, sanitation, transportation, and information services. The adaptation of new technologies can make cities leading examples of energy-efficient environmentally friendly living. Or a failure to plan and invest can lead to vast urban squalor, with millions living in shantytowns.

Migration. No discussion of demographics is complete without a discussion of migration. The United States accepts about 1 million legal immigrants each year (by far the largest number in the world) and the focus of domestic debate is on the status of the some 11 million undocumented immigrants within its borders.[36] As significant as these numbers seem, they pale in comparison to the human movements underway around the world. There are over 230 million international migrants in the world today, up from 154 million in 1990.[37] Of these, 136 million reside in the developed world.[38]

---

[30] Rakesh Kochhar, *Ten Projections for the Global Population in 2050*, PEW RESEARCH CENTER (Feb. 4, 2014), http://www.pewresearch.org/fact-tank/2014/02/03/10-projections-for-the-global-population-in-2050/.

[31] *Id.*

[32] NATIONAL INTELLIGENCE COUNCIL *supra* note 4, at 22.

[33] Patricia Clarke Annez & Robert M. Buckley, *Urbanization and Growth: Setting the Context, in* URBANIZATION AND GROWTH 2 (Michael Spence, Patricia Clarke Annez & Robert M. Buckley eds., 2009).

[34] NATIONAL INTELLIGENCE COUNCIL *supra* note 4, at 26.

[35] *Id.* at 28.

[36] Jie Zong & Jeanne Batalova, *Frequently Requested Statistics on Immigrants and Immigration in the United States*, MIGRATION POLICY INST. (Apr. 28, 2014), http://www.migrationpolicy.org/article/frequently-requested-statistics-immigrants-and-immigration-united-states#8 (noting that the foreign-born population in the United States today numbers over 40 million, or about 13 percent of the population).

[37] Press Release, United Nations, 232 Million International Migrants Living Abroad Worldwide—New UN Global Migration Statistics Reveal 1 (Sept. 11, 2013), http://www.un.org/en/ga/68/meetings/migration/pdf/UN%20press%20release_International%20Migration%20Figures.pdf.

[38] *Id.*

These numbers will surely rise because of the demographic trends already noted: people will move across borders in search of opportunity, from youthful to aging societies, and from countryside to cities.[39] The population movements are also internal. In China today, a staggering 250 million are internal immigrants—that is to say, residents of rural areas who seek employment in cities, but have no authorization for permanent residency. The number of internal immigrants worldwide is estimated at 740 million, or some 10 percent of the world's population.[40]

It is hard to generalize about the impact of these trends on the IC, but it is fair to say that every issue of concern (terrorism, proliferation, trafficking) will have a growing urban and transnational component—increasing the difficulty of the task, and underscoring the importance of international cooperation among intelligence and law enforcement services in addressing it. Such cooperation will be crucial, because the United States cannot possibly develop the expertise in language, dialects, and cultural norms to track every shantytown on the planet.

F. Pressure on Natural Resources

In coming decades, the population and environmental pressures on food, water, and energy resources will increase dramatically. Part of the growing food demand will come from population growth, from a global population of 7.1 to 8.3 billion by 2030. At least as great a share of the rising food demand will come from the growth of middle classes who can afford and will demand better diets. Overall, the worldwide demand for food is expected to increase by more than 35 percent by 2030. [41] Hundreds of millions of middle class consumers, especially in Asia, will demand protein-rich diets. The result will be more cropland devoted to support dairy, poultry, pork, and beef production.

Water. The leading use of freshwater resources today—some 70 percent—is for agricultural production. To meet projected worldwide demand for fresh water in 2030 will require a level 40 percent above current sustainable water supplies.[42] Over half of China's lakes and reservoirs are unfit for human consumption, according to the Chinese government's own standards.[43] China has only 7 percent of the world's surface water resources, even as it supports 20 percent of the world's population,[44] and there will be intense pressure on access to water resources in the years ahead. China's many dams on the Mekong are already a source of great concern for downstream Laos, Thailand, Cambodia, and Vietnam, and China has no agreements at all with any of its riparian neighbors on the use of water resources.[45] Turkey's dam

---

[39] Rainer Muenz, *Demography and Migration: An Outlook for the 21st Century*, MIGRATION POLICY INST. 5 (Sept. 2013), http://www.migrationpolicy.org/sites/default/files/publications/Demography-Migration-Outlook.pdf.

[40] *Id.* at 1.

[41] NATIONAL INTELLIGENCE COUNCIL *supra* note 4, at 30.

[42] *Id.* at 30–31.

[43] Damien Ma & William Adams, Op-Ed, *If You Think China's Air Is Bad...*, INT'L N.Y. TIMES, Nov. 8, 2013, at 10.

[44] *Id.*

[45] 1995 Mekong River Agreement, Apr. 5, 1995, 34 ILM 864; *see also* Brahma Chellaney, *China: Asia's Water Hegemon*, LIVE MINT (Sept. 16, 2014), http://www.livemint.com/Opinion/rMoWMFDmz8ADEeXGJj-kEMP/China-Asias-water-hegemon.html.

building on the Tigris and Euphrates is a source of tension with Iraq and Syria.[46] Ethiopia, Egypt, and Sudan recently reached preliminary agreement on water resources from the Blue Nile,[47] and the historical record to date has generally been one of peaceful agreement on water use across international boundaries. Still, there is no assurance that such a record will continue, especially in view of the intense demand for water resources. There are a total of 263 shared river basins that cross international boundaries,[48] and the use of water as a tool of political leverage is likely over the next decade, with upstream nations exerting control over downstream flow.[49] Those basins that support hundreds of millions of people—the Mekong, the Ganges-Brahmaputra, the Indus, the Nile, and the Tigris and Euphrates—will compel attention.

Energy. Just as in the case of food and water, the demand for energy resources will expand because of the growing global middle class. Estimates are a growth rate of some 50 percent by 2030, or about 1 percent per year. Few questions have a greater direct impact on the wealth of nations in such a short timeframe as the price and availability of energy. Fracking technology and shale oil and gas production in the United States have already upended energy markets. The Saudis' clear and stated intent not to lose market share to U.S. shale oil producers is having a dramatic impact on the international order. Russia, Iran, and Venezuela have been hit hard, as their budgets are based on oil prices in the $100-plus range; prices in the $50 to $60 range will blow holes in budgets, curtail social spending, and have unsettling effects on political stability. The benefits for overall energy importers—the United States, China, Europe, Japan—are large and in a positive direction.

The environmental consequences of the shale oil and gas revolution are mixed. On the plus side, the falling cost of natural gas has prompted a major shift from coal to natural gas in United States power plants. The desire to cut costs and at the same time meet EPA regulations via cleaner burning gas than coal has led to a drop in United States greenhouse gas emissions, leading to levels not seen since the early 1990s.[50] On the other hand, fracking uses large amounts of water and produces large amounts of wastewater; there has also been pollution of groundwater in many communities. The proffered answer from industry is two-fold: as the technology matures, and as large companies committed to safety become bigger players, the environmental record will improve, and the technology's use of water resources will become more efficient. However, some states are not convinced.[51]

---

[46] Ilektra Tsakalidou, *The Great Anatolian Project: Is Water Management a Panacea or Crisis Multiplier for Turkey's Kurds?*, New Security Beat (Aug. 5, 2013), http://www.newsecuritybeat.org/2013/08/great-anatolian-project-water-management-panacea-crisis-multiplier-turkeys-kurds/.

[47] "Egypt, Ethiopia, and Sudan Sign Accord on Nile Dam," Al-Jazeera, Mar. 24, 2015. http://www.aljazeera.com/news/2015/03/egypt-ethiopia-sudan-sign-accord-nile-dam-150323193458534.html.

[48] National Intelligence Council, Global Water Security 10 (2012), *available at* http://www.dni.gov/files/documents/Special%20Report_ICA%20Global%20Water%20Security.pdf.

[49] *Id.* at 4.

[50] Total Carbon Dioxide Emissions from the Consumption of Energy, U.S. Energy Information Administration, http://www.eia.gov/cfapps/ipdbproject/iedindex3.cfm?tid=90&pid=44&aid=8&cid=regions&syid=1990&eyid=2012&unit=MMTCD (last visited May 31, 2015).

[51] Clare Foran, *New York State Moves to Ban Fracking*, Nat'l J. (Dec. 17, 2014), http://www.nationaljournal.com/energy/new-york-state-moves-to-ban-fracking-20141217.

Climate Change. For the development of green technologies, falling oil prices are a worry, because they jeopardize the financial calculus for existing green projects, discourage investors, and put off the day when the marginal cost of solar and other green technologies becomes broadly competitive with conventional energy producers. Not so, say clean energy proponents. Dramatic improvements and falling costs for solar power and energy storage point the way to its rapid adaptation even if hydrocarbon prices remain low.[52]

Finally, the overall greenhouse gas and climate change implications of the food, water, and energy story are not good ones. Although the United States-China climate change accord in November 2014 is a positive step in advanced and developing economies working together, it remains to be seen how much India and other key developing countries will follow China's example. Moreover, even United States' and Chinese actions applied across the board and adapted by others would still not be enough to meet the goal of limiting global warming to just 2° centigrade. The world economy and its current level of emissions puts us on a glide slope that points to a 3° to 6° centigrade rise in temperature by the end of the twenty-first century.[53]

G. *Technologies*

The next two decades will bring disruptive technological change that will shape our lives for both good and ill. IT is the foremost area, but there are several other fields where the changes will be dramatic and profound. I note just a few technology trends of greatest concern and interest.

The Internet of things. Information technologies already control and regulate nearly all systems—power generation and distribution, water, transportation, financial transactions, and manufacturing. Seemingly all activities are becoming "informatized" through the presence of sensors that record, analyze, and transmit data. Increasingly, information technologies will report out data on the vehicles we drive, the appliances we own, and even our exercise habits and vital signs. Internet nodes will reside in such everyday things as food packages and furniture.[54] The number of Internet-connected devices has outnumbered the human population since 2008, and by 2020 could number anywhere between 26 to 50 billion.[55] The possibilities for economic advantage—more efficient supply chains and logistics, greater productivity—are great. But so are the threats, as an open market for aggregated sensor data helps criminals and spies.[56] Indeed, as a National Intelligence Council study notes, "[f]oreign manufacturers could become both the single-source and single-point-of-failure for mission-critical Internet-enabled things. Manufacturers could also become vectors for delivering everyday objects containing malicious software that causes havoc in everyday life.

---

[52] *See generally* Edward Lucas, *Let There Be Light*, THE ECONOMIST, Jan. 17, 2015, at Special Report Section 1-7.

[53] NATIONAL INTELLIGENCE COUNCIL *supra* note 4, at 31.

[54] NATIONAL INTELLIGENCE COUNCIL, CONFERENCE REPORT ON DISRUPTIVE CIVIL TECHNOLOGIES: SIX TECHNOLOGIES WITH POTENTIAL IMPACTS ON US INTERESTS OUT TO 2025, at 27 (2008), *available at* http://www.dni.gov/files/documents/2008%20Conference%20Report_Disruptive%20Civil%20 Technologies.pdf.

[55] Jack Moore, *Report: Government Has Only 5 Years to Secure the Internet of Things*, NEXTGOV (Nov. 19, 2014), http://www.nextgov.com/cybersecurity/2014/11/report-government-has-only-5-years-secure-internet-things/99446/.

[56] NATIONAL INTELLIGENCE COUNCIL *supra* note 54, at 27.

An open market for aggregated sensor data could serve the interests of commerce and security no less than it helps criminals and spies identify vulnerable targets."[57]

The long list of state-sponsored and politically motivated cyber attacks to date—by Russia on Estonia, Georgia, and Ukraine; by North Korea on South Korea and Sony Entertainment; by Iran on Saudi ARAMCO and New York financial institutions; by China on U.S. corporations, think tanks, and government agencies—and the long list of harmful data hacks (Target, Home Depot, JP Morgan, etc.) are just a prelude to profound future threats to data security with respect to privacy, the economy, and national security.

Synthetic biology. Huge strides have been made in understanding DNA sequencing, the "computer code" of all living things. Whereas the cost of sequencing the first human genome was $3 billion, that cost today is about $1,000.[58] Researchers can sequence 45 human genomes in one day, in comparison with sequencing the first, which took 15 years.[59] The possibilities are endless—for understanding diseases and treating them, for improving health at dramatically reduced costs, for the development of new crops to feed humanity and biofuels to reduce reliance on fossil fuels. The scientific modification of crops—made possible by our rapidly evolving genetic knowledge of plant cells—will be critically important in coming decades both to feed an expanding and wealthier population and to meet changing agricultural patterns brought about by climate change.[60]

Unfortunately, the possibility for the crafting of dangerous pathogens, or mutations with unforeseeable consequences if they ever were released outside the lab, are great as well. The analog to a 3D printer in the world of biology is a polymerase chain reaction (PCR) machine, which can both identify DNA sequences and make multiple copies of them—and costs $600.[61] The barriers to entry for human betterment through the life sciences are disappearing—and so are the barriers to the proliferation of deadly or unknown and possibly dangerous life forms.

Robotics have already transformed the way we live, and will continue to do so. In 1990 the U.S. auto industry employed 1 million individuals, who manufactured 9.8 million automobiles. In 2013, 16 percent fewer workers produced 12 percent more automobiles.[62] Improvements in productivity are attributable to automation: the U.S. auto industry today utilizes 1,111 robots for every 10,000 autoworkers.[63] Over 1.3 million robots were in operation around the world in 2013.[64] A new generation is emerging for service sector applications,

---

[57] *Id.*

[58] *See generally* Erika Check Hayden, *Is the $1,000 Genome for Real?*, NATURE (Jan. 15, 2014), http://www.nature.com/news/is-the-1-000-genome-for-real-1.14530.

[59] *An Introduction to Next-Generation Sequencing Technology*, ILLUMINA (April 21, 2015), p. 3. http://www.illumina.com/content/dam/illumina-marketing/documents/products/illumina_sequencing_introduction.pdf

[60] NATIONAL INTELLIGENCE COUNCIL, *supra* note 4, at 92–93.

[61] *Biohackers of the World, Unite*, THE ECONOMIST: TECHNOLOGY Q., Sept. 6, 2014 Q3, http://www.economist.com/news/technology-quarterly/21615064-following-example-maker-communities-worldwide-hobbyists-keen-biology-have

[62] *Employment, Hours, and Earnings from the Current Employment Statistics Survey*, UNITED STATES DEPARTMENT OF LABOR: BUREAU OF LABOR STATISTICS, http://data.bls.gov/timeseries/CES3133600101?data_tool=XGtable (last visited June 1, 2015).

[63] *Industrial Robot Statistics*, INTERNATIONAL FEDERATION OF ROBOTICS, http://www.ifr.org/industrial-robots/statistics/ (last visited June 1, 2015).

[64] *Id.*

including cleaning and maintenance.[65] Their capabilities to repeat given tasks tirelessly and efficiently will make them cost-effective as the price per unit drops. Remote and autonomous vehicles are already in use in defense (unmanned aerial vehicles), in mining (drilling robots, autonomous trucks, automated trains),[66] and in exploration (deep sea exploration,[67] and the Mars rover, as the most famous example). Unmanned aerial vehicles will surely be utilized by more of the world's armed forces, and we will see expanding civil applications for survey work, crop and livestock monitoring, and commercial delivery services. Self-driving vehicles will soon be coming to major highways near us.[68]

H. Technology Futures

While I have highlighted IT, the Internet of things, 3D printing, synthetic biology and robotics, technological advances "are bewildering in their complexity, uncertain in their path to deployment, and difficult to assess in terms of individual and collective impact."[69] Some modesty is in order, as most technological forecasting has failed miserably throughout history.[70] The "next big thing" usually eludes experts.

However, that does not diminish the political and social importance of technological change, even if forecasters are wrong about particular technologies. As Michael Nacht and Zachary Davis note, today's technology environment differs markedly from what existed at the dawn of the nuclear age in the 1940s:

> [T]hese advances are not solely in the hands of the great powers, but are accessible to medium powers, failed states, nongovernmental organizations that may or may not be in the service of governments, terrorist groups seeking to overthrow established governments, criminal cartels motivated to utilize these technologies for financial gain, and individuals and small groups who are developing advanced technologies in part to further their definition of preferred societal goals.[71]

III. IMPLICATIONS FOR THE IC

Taken together, the diffusion of power, challenges of governance, and the empowerment of individuals point to a decrease in state capacity and an increase in the multiplicity of

---

[65] NATIONAL INTELLIGENCE COUNCIL *supra* note 4, at 87.

[66] Len Calderone, *Mining with Autonomous Vehicles*, ROBOTICS TOMORROW (Feb. 1, 2013 8:38 AM), http://www.roboticstomorrow.com/content.php?post_type=1824.

[67] Bill Chadwick, *Remotely Operated Vehicles (ROVs) and Autonomous Underwater Vehicles (AUV)*, NATIONAL OCEANIC AND ATMOSPHERIC ADMINISTRATION. http://oceanexplorer.noaa.gov/explorations/02fire/background/rovs_auvs/rov_auv.html (last visited Dec. 23, 2015).

[68] Paul Lienert & Joe White, *Google Wants to Bring Self-Driving Cars to Market By 2020*, BUS. INSIDER (Jan. 14, 2015), http://www.businessinsider.com/r-google-partners-with-auto-suppliers-on-self-driving-car-2015-1.

[69] Michael Nacht & Zachary Davis, *Exploring Latency and Power, in* STRATEGIC LATENCY AND WORLD POWER: HOW TECHNOLOGY IS CHANGING OUR CONCEPTS OF SECURITY 1 (Zachary Davis, Ronald Lehman & Michael Nacht eds., 2014).

[70] *See, e.g., Top 30 Failed Technology Predictions*, LISTVERSE.COM (Oct. 28, 2007), http://listverse.com/2007/10/28/top-30-failed-technology-predictions/.

[71] Nacht & Davis, *supra* note 69.

new actors and new threats. The ability of governments to protect their citizenry against the multitude of threat vectors will continue to erode. For the IC, the implications are profound. There will be fewer resources arrayed against a bigger collection of potential adversaries, of which nonstate actors will represent the fastest growing component. What should the IC do?

A. Partnerships

A large part of the answer must be partnerships. The IC will need stronger ties with international counterparts, with domestic law enforcement, with the private sector, and, above all, with the IT industry. Because the differential in United States' power compared to the rest of the world will continue to diminish, the U.S. government as a whole—including the IC—will need allies and partners to accomplish foreign policy and security goals. This must include ever-closer ties with sister security services, especially Five Eyes partners, because of the shared threats that we and our allies face. Relationships with other partners will come to approach the Five Eyes relationship in terms of both intensity and importance to us.

Because threats are more amorphous and multidirectional, partnership with law enforcement—and tapping the deep knowledge law enforcement brings of local communities—will also grow in importance. Because every threat vector at some point transits cyberspace, partnerships with the creators, purveyors, and system operators of IT also will need to grow.

B. Cybersecurity

Although this chapter is hardly the first or last to mention cybersecurity's importance for the U.S. government and the IC, the theme cannot possibly be overemphasized in current discussion. The creation of Cyber Command and its dual-hatting with the Director of the National Security Agency underscore the importance of a close alignment of the offensive, defensive, and intelligence-gathering missions.[72] CIA director John O. Brennan's announcement of the creation of a Cyber Directorate at the CIA is the public manifestation of the importance of cyber to the entire enterprise of human intelligence, and he has made clear why and how the agency must be reformed.[73] Cyber will become as important to the IC as overhead systems became half a century ago.

C. Ties to Silicon Valley

The transformation of all industries, services, and every human activity by IT means that the IC cannot do its job if it is not in the forefront of IT. Moreover, it cannot provide the

---

[72] *See generally* Michael S. Rogers, Admiral, U.S. Navy, Commander, U.S. Cyber Command, Director, N.S.A., Chief, C.S.S., Discussion at State of the Cybersecurity Union at The Center for Cyber & Homeland Security at George Washington University (May 11, 2015) (video *available at* http://cchs.gwu.edu/state-cybersecurity-union-discussion-admiral-michael-rogers).

[73] Andy Greenberg, *Cyberespionage Is a Top Priority for CIA's New Directorate*, WIRED (Mar. 9, 2015 12:00 PM), http://www.wired.com/2015/03/cias-new-directorate-makes-cyberespionage-top-priority/.

expertise essential for protecting the nation's information networks if it is not a leader. In his 2015 State of the Union Address, President Obama underscored the IC's role:

> No foreign nation, no hacker, should be able to shut down our networks, steal our trade secrets, or invade the privacy of American families, especially our kids. We are making sure our government integrates intelligence to combat cyber threats, just as we have done to combat terrorism . . . . If we don't act, we'll leave our nation and our economy vulnerable. If we do, we can continue to protect the technologies that have unleashed untold opportunities for people around the globe.[74]

The IC's mission requires a continuing and close relationship with Silicon Valley and the nation's leading IT firms. Such a relationship is absolutely vital—and of course is troubled right now in the aftermath of the Snowden revelations. IT firms are losing international customers because of perceived links to the U.S. IC; in turn, the IC and law enforcement worry about increased encryption and a cool if not outright hostile reception from former close IT partners.

It will take time and lots of dialogue to mend those broken ties. The basis for reconciliation is a deeper understanding of mutual interest: IT firms cannot prosper in a world without security—the kind only government can provide—and the U.S. government in turn must accept a more law- and rule-based process for access to data and expertise that changes perceptions of corporate complicity in surveillance. Rebuilding constructive relations will not be easy or swift, but farsighted leaders in both worlds can and will get us there.

D. Outreach

The international order is changing before us. The IC cannot possibly grasp these changes, or analyze and find meaning in them for policymakers, without full-time engagement in what it refers to as the "open source" world. There is a time and place for the collection of secrets—on terrorism, on hard target countries, on leadership plans and intentions. By no means do I want to diminish their importance and necessity. Yet the IC cannot fulfill its mission of providing insight to policymakers without a deep, open, and direct engagement with every field of endeavor described in this chapter. This dialogue must include United States' academics, think tanks and corporations, and their international counterparts. Globalization means that no organization—including the U.S. IC—can stay at the top of its game without strong external relationships and continuous engagement.

Concomitant with engaging experts, the IC will need vigorous efforts to bring into its own ranks demographers, hydrologists, agronomists, and geologists, and solar energy, battery storage, synthetic biology, and robotics experts, among others. The IC historically has had very strong scientific and technical expertise related to military applications. As a recent blue-ribbon Commission points out, the IC needs a much broader understanding of

---

[74] Barack Obama, President, United States, State of the Union Address (Jan. 20, 2015) (transcript *available at* http://www.whitehouse.gov/the-press-office/2015/01/20/remarks-president-barack-obama-prepared-delivery-state-union-address).

scientific and technical intelligence,[75] including with respect to civil and commercial applications. Keeping strong relationships with the National Laboratories will also be essential here.

In order to effectuate proper outreach, the IC must overhaul how it conducts security clearances and carries out the counterintelligence (CI) mission. How is it that major financial firms bring on new employees—who handle multibillion dollar transactions—with just a credit check and law enforcement check? The answer is not long background investigations, but continuous monitoring of their activities. The IC should be liberal and encouraging of outreach—and the hiring of new talent—with the clear stipulation that all communication with professional contacts must take place on government systems, and that those communications are subject to monitoring. When necessary, a contact might need to be curtailed for CI reasons. But that approach is far more beneficial to the mission than suffocating restrictions on contacts, and the delay and denial of bringing on board talent the IC needs.

E. Intelligence Integration

Not only does the IC need broad and deep engagement with expertise outside its ranks, it also needs to knit this expertise together internally in order to make sense of it for the policymaker. There is only one way to achieve this goal, and Director Clapper is pursuing it—intelligence integration.

Creativity and innovation result from individuals of diverse backgrounds and perspectives interacting in ways that press them, stress them, and ultimately test the validity of their ideas. The model in the sciences, and now in the IC, is cross-domain collaboration. Building on the examples of Centers for Counterterrorism and Non-Proliferation, in 2010 DNI Clapper directed the creation of National Intelligence Managers responsible for the totality of intelligence activity on a given region or topic. In part, DNI Clapper was building on the historical example of the National Intelligence Council, which since 1979 has worked on community-coordinated analytic assessments incorporating the views of all agencies. He wanted to establish this same model of integration across collection and the totality of intelligence activities. It was also, in his judgment, what the spirit and letter of the 2004 law creating the DNI required him to do. This approach is sound. Though its implementation is a work in progress, Director Brennan's recently announced reform to create Mission Centers at the CIA is animated by the same principle of integration.[76]

Cross-domain collaboration within and across issue areas is absolutely critical to the success of the intelligence enterprise going forward. Peer review by the diverse membership of the National Intelligence Council has been standard practice in the drafting of National Intelligence Estimates since 2003. This process of wide review and collaboration makes analysis better and less prone to serious error of the kind seen in the 2002 Iraqi Weapons of Mass

---

[75] National Commission for the Review of the Research and Development Programs of the United States Intelligence Community, Report: Unclassified Version 6 (2013), *available at* http://www.fas.org/irp/eprint/ncrdic.pdf.

[76] Press Release, John Brennan, CIA Director, Unclassified Version of March 6, 2015 Message to the Workforce from CIA Director John Brennan: Our Agency's Blueprint for the Future (Mar. 6, 2015), https://www.cia.gov/news-information/press-releases-statements/2015-press-releases-statements/message-to-workforce-agencys-blueprint-for-the-future.html.

Destruction Estimate. The IC's own sponsored research shows that teams consistently make better forecasts than individuals.[77]

Central to intelligence integration is a single IT platform through which all agencies can collaborate. The IC is on track to adopt a single IT backbone; all data will move to the cloud. This transition to the cloud will enhance collaboration and information-sharing, as well as security through the tagging of all information and individual profiles to access that information. The cloud will also save money, necessary to overall mission success at a time of diminishing resources.[78] But from the perspective of oversight, this common architecture will put a premium on clear rules about data use and dissemination, data features that encode those restrictions to the greatest extent feasible, and audit functions that enable both real-time and post hoc review of data use where appropriate.

F. Big Data Analytics

The IC, like every successful commercial enterprise, will need to incorporate big data analytics into its work. Companies get a jump on market trends through monitoring and shaping social media. For the IC, what data sets and analysis can help provide insight on political change? Could the IC have provided better warning of the emergence of the Arab Spring? Journalist and scholar Robin Wright writes that social ferment, particular among Arab youth, pointed to the political upheaval that followed.[79] For the IC, the question is how to move from individual reports to trend analysis.

What are the tools, models, social media sources, and other data sets that can help the IC track change and give warning about discontinuity? These data sets are global in nature, and it is not obvious how traditional oversight models of foreign rules and domestic rules will apply. Many forces—foreign government partners, high technology firms, and just the sheer difficulty of separating out data from U.S. persons—will push the IC in the direction of a single set of rules for the handling of such data. Privacy protections that previously applied only to U.S. persons are likely, over time, to be extended to others.

G. Crowdsourcing

The IC will also need to embrace crowdsourcing, a technique whose forecasting value has been demonstrated over time by those individuals who make money using it.[80] IC -sponsored projects, open to wide public participation, demonstrate its value, with predictions on international events often more accurate than those of career analysts with access

---

[77] *Teams Better than Individuals at Intelligence Analysis, Research Finds*, Am. Psychological Ass'n (Jan. 13, 2015), http://www.apa.org/news/press/releases/2015/01/intelligence-analysis.aspx.

[78] *IC IT Enterprise Fact Sheet*, Office of the Director of National Intelligence, http://www.dni.gov/files/documents/IC%20ITE%20Fact%20Sheet.pdf (last visited June 8, 2015).

[79] *See generally* Robin Wright, Rock the Casbah: Rage and Rebellion across the Islamic World (2011).

[80] Larry Cao, *Crowdsourcing Investment Insights: How and Why It Works*, Chartered Fin. Analyst Inst. (May 9, 2014), http://annual.cfainstitute.org/2014/05/09/crowdsourcing-investment-insights-how-and-why-it-works/.

to classified information.[81] In my view, results from crowdsourcing should be routinely presented along with the IC's own analytic judgments. When those results are similar, it can give analysts greater confidence in their judgments, because a tested alternative analytic methodology has provided a similar answer. When those results are at significant variance, it provides an opportunity for analysts to review anew their assumptions, the quality of the data, and their chain of reasoning. In both cases, the policy customer will be better served.

IV. LOOKING OUTWARD
A. Congress

As former Ranking Member on the House Intelligence Committee Jane Harman noted in her preface to this volume, congressional oversight of the IC remains critical. At a fundamental level, Congress legislates the underlying legal authorities that govern the IC, and must ensure that those laws are updated as necessary so that they are consistent with the evolving needs of our national security interests, and the evolving expectations of the American people. It also sets the budget of the IC each year, and in the process of so doing exercises vital oversight of the programs, priorities, and operations of the IC. These functions are indispensable, but must be supplemented by more specific oversight as needed. Several specific ways in which the congressional role in intelligence oversight might be reformed are described below.

B. Congressional Oversight—Committee Membership

The domain of human knowledge necessary for the IC to understand and analyze is ever-expanding. The requirements for successful oversight are equally daunting. Under House Rules, the 22 men and women on the House Permanent Select Committee on Intelligence (HPSCI) include at least one member from the Appropriations, Armed Services, Foreign Affairs, and Judiciary Committees.[82] By resolution, the 15 members of the Senate Select Committee also include two members (one from each side of the aisle) from the Appropriations, Armed Services, Foreign Relations, and Judiciary Committees.[83]

Because of the growing importance of science and technology issues, I believe it should also become standard practice for the Intelligence Committees to require members from the House Science, Space and Technology Committee and the Senate Commerce, Science and Transportation Committee, especially its Science and Space subcommittee. The leadership in both Chambers should also assign members and senators knowledgeable about IT to the Intelligence committees (irrespective of other Committee assignments), and give the Committees more ability to hire high-tech staff expertise.

---

[81] *See generally* Alix Spiegel, *So You Think You're Smarter than a CIA Agent*, NPR, (Apr. 2, 2014 3:55 PM), http://www.npr.org/blogs/parallels/2014/04/02/297839429/-so-you-think-youre-smarter-than-a-cia-agent.

[82] Rules of the House of Representatives, 113th Cong., Rule X, cl. 11(a)(1).

[83] *About the Committee*, U.S. SENATE SELECT COMMITTEE ON INTELLIGENCE, http://www.intelligence.senate.gov/about.html (last visited June 8, 2015).

C. Congressional Oversight—Committee Jurisdiction

Intelligence. The most glaring oversight problem for intelligence is that all appropriations for the National Intelligence Program come through the House and Senate Defense Appropriations subcommittees. Those Committees are responsible and hard-working, but they cannot possibly provide the quality of oversight the National Intelligence Program deserves when its annual appropriation ($50.5 billion in Fiscal Year 2014)[84] is dwarfed by annual Department of Defense funding ($581.2 billion in Fiscal Year 2014).[85]

A single oversight subcommittee for intelligence in the House and Senate, reporting out a single appropriations bill for the National Intelligence Program, is a far better approach. An often-repeated and crucial change to the law advocated by former 9/11 Commission members, among others, is a single appropriations bill for intelligence, providing the DNI the funds to execute the program.[86] Such a change would streamline budget development and execution, and enable a far more flexible, responsive, and effective allocation of resources to meet changing intelligence priorities—and better serve intelligence consumers.

Homeland Security. The second glaring oversight problem relates to the Department of Homeland Security. It reports to 92 Committees and subcommittees—an oversight structure that not only burdens and wastes the time of senior officials but provides no effective oversight.[87] Perhaps the most telling evidence of poor oversight is that since its inception in 2003, the Department of Homeland Security has yet to have an authorization bill become law.

The most effective structural arrangement for oversight of a Department is one authorizing Committee and one appropriations subcommittee in both the House and Senate. Senior officials can reasonably be expected to testify and respond to four committees, whose oversight provides effective checks and balances on the work of the executive branch and on each other. The 9/11 Commission recommended this institutional arrangement for the Department of Homeland Security in 2004. No progress toward this goal has been made.[88] The 9/11 Commissioners summarized their views in their tenth anniversary report:

> Many experts have told us that Congress' refusal to reform its antiquated oversight weakens the country's security by diminishing Congress' effectiveness as a partner in the overall security endeavor. Ultimately, streamlining Congress' oversight of DHS

---

[84] Press Release, Office of the Director of National Intelligence, DNI Releases Budget Figure for Fiscal Year 2014 National Intelligence Program (Oct. 30, 2014), http://www.dni.gov/index.php/newsroom/press-releases/198-press-releases-2014/1134-dni-releases-budget-figure-for-fy-2014-national-intelligence-program.

[85] Office of the Undersecretary of Defense (Comptroller)/Chief Financial Officer, United States Department of Defense, Fiscal Year 2015 Budget Request, Overview, March 2014, 1–4 (2014).

[86] Former 9/11 Comm'rs, Today's Rising Terrorist Threat and the Danger to the United States: Reflections on the Tenth Anniversary of the 9/11 Commission Report 21, 24 (2014), *available at* http://bipartisanpolicy.org/wp-content/uploads/sites/default/files/files/%20BPC%209-11%20Commission.pdf.

[87] *Id.* at 7.

[88] *Id.* at 21.

and intelligence is not a question of preserving committee chairs' power or prerogatives. It is an imperative of national security.[89]

D. Public Understanding and Trust

Reforms to the IC's relationship with its oversight committees will certainly improve both
the IC's effectiveness and accountability. The most important reform, however, relates to the
IC's good name and reputation. Over the long term, no institution of government can carry
out its mission without the support of the American people. In our democratic and open
system of government, that support rests on public understanding and trust.

There is ample evidence that trust in the IC, especially the National Security Agency, has
taken a body blow in the aftermath of the 2013 Snowden revelations. It can be seen in polls,[90]
commentary,[91] and votes in the House of Representatives.[92] Further, the summary of the
Senate Select Committee on Intelligence "Committee Study of the CIA's Detention and
Interrogation Program" (declassified in December 2014), documents a dark chapter in the
CIA's history.[93]

To win and build public support, the IC must close these chapters and look to the future.
It will be a slow road; reputations take decades to build, even as they can be lost in a day. At
least some of the steps are clear.

First, the IC should pursue, as the president outlined in his 2015 State of the Union
Address, efforts to increase transparency and build more safeguards against the abuse of surveillance programs:

> So while some have moved on from the debates over our surveillance programs,
> I haven't. As promised, our intelligence agencies have worked hard, with the recom-
> mendations of privacy advocates, to increase transparency and build more safeguards
> against potential abuse.[94]

---

[89] *Id.* at 24.

[90] *Obama's NSA Speech Has Little Impact on Skeptical Public*, Pew Research Ctr. (Jan. 20, 2014), http://
www.people-press.org/2014/01/20/obamas-nsa-speech-has-little-impact-on-skeptical-public/.

[91] *See generally* Ron Wyden, Senator, Remarks as Prepared for Delivery for the Center for American Progress
Event on NSA Surveillance (July 23, 2012) (transcript *available at* http://www.scribd.com/doc/155530126/
Wyden-Speech-on-NSA-Domestic-Surveillance-at-Center-for-American-Progress); Rand Paul, *NSA's
Verizon Surveillance: How the White House Tramples Our Constitution*, The Guardian (June 7, 2013 6:45
PM), http://www.theguardian.com/commentisfree/2013/jun/07/nsa-verizon-surveillance-constitution.

[92] Adam Serwer, *House Votes Overwhelmingly to Roll Back NSA Spying*, MSNBC (June 25, 2014 5:07 PM),
http://www.msnbc.com/msnbc/house-votes-overwhelmingly-roll-back-nsa-spying.

[93] *See generally* Senate Select Committee on Intelligence, Committee Study of the CIA's
Detention and Interrogation Program (2012), *available at* https://www.aclu.org/files/assets/
SSCIStudyCIAsDetentionInterrogationProgramES.pdf.

[94] Obama *supra* note 74; *see also* Robert Litt & Alexander W. Joel, *Interim Progress Report on Implementing PDD-
28*, Office of the Director of National Intelligence (Oct. 17, 2014), http://www.dni.gov/index.
php/newsroom/reports-and-publications.

In this respect, the president and the IC should give consideration to a new Executive Order spelling out constraints on surveillance and safeguards against abuse. President Ford's 1976 Executive Order banning political assassination not only established policy, it shaped public opinion for decades to follow. So too could a new Executive Order imposing constraints and safeguards on surveillance activities that are consistent with the evolving expectations of the American people, and that expose them only to a degree of risk they find acceptable.

Second, the Privacy and Civil Liberties Oversight Board (PCLOB) needs to enhance its profile and influence. Its 2014 report and recommendations on Section 215 and Section 702 of the FISA Amendments Act of 2008 were exceptionally thoughtful public documents.[95] Through its hearings and reports, the Board can and should become a leading voice in the public discussion on privacy and civil liberties.

A good model for the PCLOB is the National Safety and Transportation Board, viewed by all as authoritative on the subject of transportation accidents. If the PCLOB comes to be viewed over time as a similar authoritative voice on privacy and civil liberty matters, its imprimatur will mean a lot to the IC. A PCLOB report, if it is seen as a careful review and opines favorably on an IC practice, will have a positive impact with Congress and the public. A strong PCLOB can help rebuild public trust.

Third, shutting the door forever to the practice of torture is necessary to rebuild public trust. President Obama's Executive Order of January 22, 2009, banning torture[96] became the law of the land in the Defense Authorization Act he signed into law in November, 2015. By law, all interrogations by all U.S. agencies will now take place according to the rules in the United States Army Field Manual—a very important step forward.

Fourth, IC leaders must engage in a forthright and sustained dialogue with the American public. They are really no different from senior officials in any other agency of the American government, or the elected officials who represent us. They have an obligation to explain to the American people what they do and why they do it. Consistent with protection of sources and methods, they also need to speak to their priorities, and their problems, and what needs to be done to fix them. Making the effort to educate the American people about the intelligence enterprise is central to winning their support and willingness to fund it in the future.

Now, there are many obstacles. Every incentive internal to the IC points in the opposite direction. Every press contact and every public comment by every intelligence officer will now be required to have explicit prior approval. Intelligence culture recoils from public contact or discussion. Yet it is precisely the lack of public discussion and understanding that harms the IC. In the absence of a factual record and public debate, Edward Snowden's narrative prevailed—and the IC played and is still playing catch-up. Director Clapper himself has acknowledged the problem. In a September 2014 speech, he observed: "One of my big

---

[95] Privacy and Civil Liberties Oversight Board, Report on the Surveillance Program Operated Pursuant to 702 of the Foreign Intelligence Surveillance Act (2014), *available at* http://www.pclob.gov/events/2014/july02.html; Privacy and Civil Liberties Oversight Board, Report on the Telephone Records Program Conducted under Section 215 of the USA Patriot Act and on the Operations of the Foreign Intelligence Surveillance Court (2014), *available at* https://www.pclob.gov/library/215-Report_on_the_Telephone_Records_Program.pdf.
[96] Exec. Order No. 13491, 3 C.F.R. 199 (2009–2010).

takeaways from the past 16 months is that we need to be more transparent. And, if we're going to profess transparency, we need to practice transparency, whenever we can."[97]

There is no better way to renew our institutions of government—and enhance their ability to serve us well for years to come—than through public discussion, debate, and review. For the IC's leaders, the process is time-consuming and often frustrating. Yet the success of the IC depends upon it. Out of this public struggle of ideas, a better, stronger IC will emerge—and our nation will be better for it.

[97] James R. Clapper, Director of National Intelligence, Remarks as Delivered at the AFCEA/INSA National Security and Intelligence Summit (Sept. 18, 2014) (transcript *available at* http://www.dni.gov/files/documents/AFCEA%20INSA%20NS%20%20Intell%20Summit_2014-09-18.pdf).

PART TWO
Judicial Oversight

5

The FISC's Stealth Administrative Law

*Daphna Renan**

I. INTRODUCTION

This chapter explores the relationship between Fourth Amendment law and administrative procedure in the governance of intelligence programs. It brings to the surface and analyzes an emergent dynamic lurking in the recent case law from the Foreign Intelligence Surveillance Court (FISC): the role of administrative procedure *inside* Fourth Amendment law. Administrative rules today put meat on the bones of Fourth Amendment reasonableness at the FISC.[1] This development is in many respects salutary. Administrative rules enable a more systemic, dynamic, and grounded approach to intelligence oversight than traditional Fourth Amendment review would permit.

But the type of administrative law that the FISC has created in the intelligence space is anemic at best. Elsewhere in the administrative state, we have long worried about runaway agencies pushing on the legal bounds of their authorities or adopting policies out of step

* Assistant Professor of Law, Harvard Law School; formerly Attorney Advisor, Office of Legal Counsel, 2010–2012, and Counsel, Office of the Deputy Attorney General, 2009–2010. The views expressed are my own and the discussion is based only on publicly available documents. For helpful comments, I am grateful to Alex Abdo, Kate Andrias, Nicholas Bagley, Rachel Barkow, Gabby Blum, Adam Cox, Andrew Crespo, Barry Friedman, Rebecca Ingber, John Manning, Jon Michaels, David Pozen, Margo Schlanger, Larry Schwartztol, the editors of this volume, and participants at the March 2015 workshop on Intelligence Oversight held at the Woodrow Wilson International Center for Scholars in Washington, DC. I also thank Pat Gavin and Asaf Lubin for excellent research assistance.
[1] By administrative rules, I mean general and prospective legal rules created in the first instance by agencies, as opposed to Congress or courts. As elaborated in the text, administrative rules today govern whether and under what circumstances agencies can acquire, use, share, and retain the information that they collect through intelligence programs and activities.

with their political overseers and the public. Administrative law has developed a set of structural and procedural safeguards in response to those threats. Lawmaking by agencies requires transparency, participatory opportunity, and adversarial judicial review. The administrative law of intelligence is different: it is devoid of these safeguards. We are relying on administrative rules to do crucial work to give content to Fourth Amendment reasonableness, but without the conditions that have come to legitimate administrative rule-making elsewhere in the regulatory state.

This chapter illuminates the FISC's emergent "administrative Fourth Amendment law" and begins to explore avenues for reform. Fourth Amendment law and administrative law are interconnected in the project of intelligence governance. Because we have not adequately explored their interaction, we have not developed the legal and institutional tools to protect and improve it. The chapter uses a close study of a significant foreign intelligence program to develop this claim. But programmatic surveillance is in no sense limited to this program—or to the foreign intelligence space. A deeper understanding of the interaction between Fourth Amendment law and administrative procedure thus has far-reaching implications.

Administrative procedure can come into the Fourth Amendment framework in a few different ways. Administrative process can improve judicial decision-making by putting better information before the courts. On this view, administrative process helps courts, on their own, to sort through difficult legal and factual questions. Administrative law also can provide a different focal point for legal analysis. Rather than a focus on the level of individualized suspicion necessary for acquiring information, for example, administrative law can shift some attention to the rules that govern program administration—such as the rules that address how information can be used and shared by the myriad agencies involved in a complex surveillance program. Agencies might also engage in a type of rule-setting that is different—more holistic and more granular—than the rules a court would design in the first instance. Finally, administrative process can provide an additional space for the interest-balancing that Fourth Amendment reasonableness requires. In particular, it can enable a type of efficacy review that courts in the United States have not shown a willingness to undertake on their own.[2]

The chapter begins with a brief overview of the Section 702 program. It then uses this program to demonstrate a changing institutional role for the FISC. Designed in the 1970s around the model of criminal-law warrants, the FISC today also makes administrative law. It reviews agency rule-making for compliance with statutory mandates, and it uses those administrative rules to elaborate Fourth Amendment protections. I argue that although there are benefits to this approach, it is in tension with the structural framework under which the FISC continues to operate. One solution would be to integrate ideas of structural reasonableness from administrative law—such as visibility and participatory opportunity, in addition to adversarial judicial review—with substantive Fourth Amendment reasonableness review. After exploring this important and, today, absent interplay between structural and substantive reasonableness review, I point to a third dimension of reasonableness. I argue

---

[2] This chapter builds on a theoretical framework developed in Daphna Renan, *The Fourth Amendment as Administrative Governance*, 68 STAN. L. REV. __ (forthcoming, 2016). Where appropriate, please cite to that work.

that evaluating efficacy is an important, but today unrealized dimension of constitutional reasonableness review—one that calls for extrajudicial governance tools to help address it. The chapter concludes by briefly suggesting two potential directions for intelligence reform.

Before turning to the Section 702 case study, a brief note on the scope of the Fourth Amendment: The current conception of Fourth Amendment rights is territorially based.[3] As relevant to foreign intelligence law, this means that the Fourth Amendment applies to domestic communications as well as to U.S. persons' communications overseas, but not to non-U.S. persons abroad.[4] As we will see below, surveillance technologies "directed at" non-U.S. persons overseas can (and do) sweep up many domestic communications and communications of overseas U.S. persons. For this reason, even under a territorially conscribed Fourth Amendment, a surveillance program such as Section 702 that collects the content of email and other communications implicates significant Fourth Amendment interests. I take the territorially based conception of the Fourth Amendment as fixed in my analysis.

II. ADMINISTERING INTELLIGENCE: THE SECTION 702 CASE STUDY

Section 702 of the Foreign Intelligence Surveillance Act authorizes warrantless surveillance directed at non-U.S. persons overseas to acquire foreign intelligence, when specific conditions are satisfied.[5] Enacted as a part of the 2008 FISA Amendments Act, Section 702 permits the attorney general and the Director of National Intelligence jointly to authorize surveillance conducted inside the United States, but targeting only non-U.S. persons reasonably believed to be located outside the United States, to collect foreign intelligence information.[6] As a recent report by the Privacy and Civil Liberties Oversight Board (PCLOB), an administrative review board, explained, Section 702 forms the legal basis for a "complex surveillance program . . . that entails many separate decisions to monitor large numbers of individuals, resulting in the annual collection of hundreds of millions of communications of different types, obtained through a variety of methods, . . . and involving four [different federal] agencies that each have their own rules governing how they may handle and use the communications that are acquired."[7]

The statutory authority requires the targets of Section 702 collection to be non-U.S. persons reasonably believed to be overseas,[8] and it requires the federal government to conduct

---

[3] *See* United States v. Verdugo-Urquidez, 494 U.S. 259, 274–75 (1990) (holding that the Fourth Amendment has no application to a physical search in a foreign country of the residence of a citizen of that country who has no voluntary attachment to the United States).

[4] *See generally* Jennifer Daskal, *The Un-Territoriality of Data*, 125 YALE L.J. 326, 336–43 (2015).

[5] Foreign Intelligence Surveillance Act of 1978 Amendments Act of 2008, Pub. L. No. 110-261, 122 Stat. 2436 (codified as amended at 50 U.S.C. § 1881a (2012)). FISA defines "person" to include not just an individual, but also "any group, entity, association, corporation, or foreign power." *See* 50 U.S.C. § 1801(m) (2012).

[6] *See* 50 U.S.C. § 1881a(a) (2012). Section 702 originated in a presidential surveillance program that evolved in several iterations into the program that exists today. For a brief history of the program, see PRIVACY AND CIVIL LIBERTIES OVERSIGHT BOARD, REPORT ON THE SURVEILLANCE PROGRAM OPERATED PURSUANT TO SECTION 702 OF THE FOREIGN INTELLIGENCE SURVEILLANCE ACT 16-20 (2014) [hereinafter PCLOB, SECTION 702 REPORT], *available at* www.pclob.gov/library/702-Report.pdf.

[7] *See* PCLOB, SECTION 702 REPORT, *supra* note 6, at 86.

[8] *See* 50 U.S.C. § 1881a(a) (2012).

Section 702 collection pursuant to "targeting" and "minimization" procedures drafted by the agencies and approved by the FISC.[9] Targeting procedures are designed to ensure that the Section 702 authority is only used to target persons reasonably believed to be outside the United States, and that targeting occurs in such a manner as to prevent the collection of entirely domestic communications—that is, communications where the sender "and all intended recipients" are known to be inside the United States at the time of acquisition.[10] Every agency that receives Section 702 data has its own minimization procedures, which govern the agency's use, retention, and dissemination of that data.[11] Those minimization procedures set forth, for example, how an agency may search or "query" the Section 702 data sets, including the conditions under which an agency may search the Section 702 data for information about a specific U.S. person.[12]

Until recently, the agencies' targeting and minimization procedures, along with the FISC's decisions approving them, were classified.[13] A flurry of declassification activity in the aftermath of Edward Snowden's revelations about aspects of the Section 702 program, combined with the first public review and report on the program by the PCLOB, have made facets of the program considerably more accessible to the public, though a number of the agency procedures remain classified.[14]

The NSA conducts two types of collection under Section 702. Under "PRISM collection," the government provides a "selector," such as an email address, to a U.S.-based communications provider such as an Internet Service Provider (ISP), and the ISP gives communications to or from that selector to the government.[15] "Upstream collection" under Section 702, by contrast, requires providers who control the telecommunications "backbone" to intercept communications involving the selector (again, for example, the email address) while those communications are still in transit.[16]

The NSA has adopted, and the FISC has approved, upstream collection procedures that allow the acquisition of "to," "from," and "about" communications.[17] "To" or "from" communications are directed to or from a particular email address or other selector.[18] "About" communications are those in which the selector of a targeted person (such as that person's email address) is included or referenced somewhere in the communication, such as in the body of another individual's email, "but the targeted person is not necessarily a participant in the communication."[19]

---

[9] § 1881a(d)–(e) (2012).

[10] § 1881a(d)(1)(B) (2012).

[11] § 1881a(e) (2012); PCLOB, SECTION 702 REPORT, supra note 6, at 7–8.

[12] PCLOB, SECTION 702 REPORT, supra note 6, at 8.

[13] See id. at 3, 42.

[14] The discussion of the Section 702 program in this chapter is taken from the PCLOB Report and the declassified FISC opinions.

[15] See PCLOB, SECTION 702 REPORT, supra note 6, at 7.

[16] Id.; see also [Caption Redacted], [Docket No. Redacted], 2011 U.S. Dist. LEXIS 157706, at *5 (FISA Ct. Oct. 3, 2011).

[17] See PCLOB, SECTION 702 REPORT, supra note 6, at 37.

[18] See id.

[19] See id.

While Section 702 is a warrantless surveillance authority directed at non-U.S. persons overseas, many domestic and U.S. person communications are also acquired as a result of the program.[20] We can think about this as a problem of "spillovers": surveillance directed at one group sweeps up the communications of a different group entirely.[21] In some ways, this type of collection has always been a concern of surveillance law. If the police have a warrant to tap my phone, they may also collect your communications when you call me. But the spillovers problem in a program such as Section 702 is different both in scale and in the types of communications that will be acquired. With "about" communications, for example, the communications themselves will be exclusively between individuals of whom none is a target of the surveillance.

Technology further compounds this problem, as recent developments in the upstream collection program under Section 702 illustrate. In 2011, officials in the Intelligence Community (IC) reportedly discovered and revealed to the FISC for the first time that any single transaction acquired as part of NSA's upstream collection might actually include many different discrete communications, some of which are wholly unrelated to the purpose of collection.[22] This is because it was not technologically feasible for the NSA to exclude those other (irrelevant) communications in the course of its upstream collection.[23] Put differently, the NSA might collect a transaction that includes many discrete communications, some of which will be "to," "from," or "about" a target, and some of which will not be "to," "from," or "about" a target at all.

This revelation upended prior understandings about the actual scope of upstream collection.[24] Indeed, prior to this discovery in 2011, there was not even a term for the type of collection that was actually happening—what the government now labeled "Multi-Communication Transactions" or MCTs.[25]

The revelation that upstream collection contained MCTs eroded two "fundamental underpinnings" of the FISC's prior Fourth Amendment and statutory analysis.[26] First, whereas the court had previously understood that the NSA would not acquire communications where the sender and recipients were located inside the United States, the court now understood that separating out and preventing certain kinds of this acquisition was not technologically feasible.[27] Instead, the NSA was acquiring tens of thousands of these "wholly domestic communications."[28]

---

[20] *Id.* at 38.

[21] Renan, *supra* note 2, manuscript (dated Jan. 15, 2016) at 22–25.

[22] [Caption Redacted], [Docket No. Redacted], 2011 U.S. Dist. LEXIS 157706, at *5 (FISA Ct. Oct. 3, 2011).

[23] *Id.* at *37–38 ("[T]he government explained that NSA's upstream collection devices have technological limitations that significantly affect the scope of collection. . . . Moreover, at the time of acquisition, NSA's upstream Internet collection devices are generally incapable of distinguishing between transactions containing only a single discrete communication to, from, or about a tasked selector and transactions containing multiple discrete communications, not all of which may be to, from, or about a tasked selector . . . .").

[24] *Id.* at *18–36.

[25] *Id.* at *33–34.

[26] *Id.* at *39–40.

[27] *Id.* at *40.

[28] [Caption Redacted], [Docket No. Redacted], 2011 U.S. Dist. LEXIS 157706, at *40 (FISA Ct. Oct. 3, 2011).

Second, the court had previously understood that the NSA's upstream collection would acquire communications with U.S. persons or persons inside the United States only under specific circumstances—that is, when a communication was to, from, or "about" the target.[29] With the MCTs discovery, however, the FISC now understood that wholly unrelated communications involving U.S. persons or persons inside the United States were getting swept up in these multiple communications transactions as well.[30]

The MCTs discovery prompted a series of exchanges between the FISC and the NSA on the question of whether MCTs rendered the upstream collection program unlawful. The FISC initially held that the NSA had failed to craft administrative rules sufficiently protective of Fourth Amendment interests to comply with Fourth Amendment reasonableness.[31] The court also found the minimization procedures lacking on statutory grounds.[32] The rules "proposed by NSA for handling MCTs," the court concluded, "tend to maximize, rather than minimize, the retention of non-target information, including information of or concerning United States persons."[33] The court identified a range of considerations, emphasizing that although the court did "not intend[] to provide a checklist of [necessarily sufficient] changes" to the agency's rules, it also was not satisfied that the agency's efforts at minimization were adequate.[34] In response, the NSA revised its procedures, and the FISC ultimately approved MCT collection under the revised protocols.[35]

The Section 702 program is an important surveillance program for the IC,[36] and it appears to be one of the rare instances where the FISC pushed back through written opinions on the executive's programmatic design of intelligence gathering. The FISC pushed back, moreover,

---

[29] *Id.* at *45–46.

[30] *Id.* The court was unable to quantify the precise effects on Fourth Amendment interests. *See id.* at *46–47 ("On the current record, it is difficult to assess how many MCTs acquired by NSA actually contain a communication of or concerning a United States person, or a communication to or from a person in the United States."). But the FISC noted that "NSA is likely acquiring tens of thousands of discrete communications of non-target United States persons and [*sic*] persons in the United States, by virtue of the fact that their communications are included in MCTs selected for acquisition by NSA's upstream collection devices." *Id.* at *47.

[31] *See id.* at *97–111.

[32] *See id.* at *65–92. Although the court initially rejected the government's minimization procedures, it approved the targeting procedures. *See id.* at *55–65. The FISC's approval of the government's targeting procedures, as a matter of statutory analysis, nevertheless raised concerns about compliance with the purpose of the Section 702 statute. *See id.* at *64–65 ("By expanding its Section 702 acquisitions to include the acquisition of Internet transactions through its upstream collection, NSA has, as a practical matter, circumvented the spirit of [Section 702] with regard to that collection. . . . But the meaning of the relevant statutory provision is clear and application to the facts before the Court does not lead to an impossible or absurd result.").

[33] *Id.* at *108.

[34] [Caption Redacted], [Docket No. Redacted], 2011 U.S. Dist. LEXIS 157706, at *86–87 (FISA Ct. Oct. 3, 2011).

[35] *See* [Caption Redacted], [Docket No. Redacted], 2011 U.S. Dist. LEXIS 157705, at *25 (FISA Ct. Nov. 30, 2011).

[36] *See, e.g.*, Public Hearing Regarding the Surveillance Program Operated Pursuant to Section 702 of the Foreign Intelligence Surveillance Act Before the Privacy and Civil Liberties Oversight Board, Transcript at 13 (statement of Robert Litt, General Counsel, Office of the Director of National Intelligence), *available at* https://www.pclob.gov/library/20140319-Transcript.pdf (last visited Mar. 19, 2014)(stating that the Section 702 program has been an important source of information "not only about terrorism but about a wide variety of other threats to our nation").

through administrative procedure—that is, through the FISC's review of the adequacy of the governing administrative rules.

A focus on the FISC's review of the Section 702 program, however, risks obscuring a crucial divide in the emergent administrative law of intelligence. Section 702 creates an intelligence program that by statutory design is closely supervised by the FISC. Other intelligence programs are not. Collection under Executive Order 12333, for example, occurs entirely outside of the province of FISC review.[37] And the administrative rules that govern the uses of information involving domestic or U.S. persons acquired under Executive Order 12333 do not receive any judicial review. Until recently very little was known about these procedures, and information on some agencies' procedures remains classified.[38]

That distinction can make a focus on the Section 702 program useful, however, because it is in some respects the administrative law of intelligence "at its best." It is administrative procedure developed through ongoing and routinized FISC review. And yet, even in this form, the emergent legal and institutional framework has considerable limitations. For that reason, the Section 702 program provides an opportunity to take stock of current legal and institutional developments, as well as to identify potential directions for more widespread reform.

III. THE FISC'S "ADMINISTRATIVE FOURTH AMENDMENT LAW"

The Section 702 program highlights a change in the institutional role of the FISC itself. The FISC was built on the warrant model—a framework that no longer describes much of the work that the FISC actually performs.[39] When FISA was first enacted in 1978, it created a warrant-like process for foreign intelligence collection inside the United States.[40] The original FISA authorized a judge on the newly established FISC to grant an application for an order approving electronic surveillance to collect foreign intelligence if the court determined there was "probable cause" to believe that the target of surveillance is "a foreign power or an agent of a foreign power," and that "each of the facilities or places at which the electronic surveillance is directed is being used, or is about to be used, by a foreign power or an agent of a foreign power."[41] The requirements for a FISA order are different, and in some

---

[37] *See, e.g.,* John Napier Tye, *Meet Executive Order 12333: The Reagan Rule That Lets the NSA Spy on Americans,* WASH. POST (July 18, 2014), http://www.washingtonpost.com/opinions/meet-executive-order-12333-the-reagan-rule-that-lets-the-nsa-spy-on-americans/2014/07/18/93d2ac22-0b93-11e4-b8e5-d0de80767fc2_story.html.

[38] The Privacy and Civil Liberties Oversight Board is currently reviewing intelligence activities conducted under Executive Order 12333 and, in February 2015, published a chart on the status of Executive Order 12333 procedures at each of the agencies and elements within the intelligence community. *See* PRIVACY AND CIVIL LIBERTIES OVERSIGHT BOARD, STATUS OF ATTORNEY GENERAL APPROVED U.S. PERSON PROCEDURES UNDER E.O. 12333 (Feb. 10, 2015) [hereinafter STATUS CHART ON E.O. 12333 PROCEDURES], *available at* www.pclob.gov/library/EO12333-AG-Guidelines-February-10-2015.pdf.

[39] *See, e.g.,* William C. Banks, *Programmatic Surveillance and FISA: Of Needles in Haystacks,* 88 TEX. L. REV. 1633, 1641–49, 1653 (2010); ELIZABETH GOITEIN & FAIZA PATEL, BRENNAN CENTER FOR JUSTICE, WHAT WENT WRONG WITH THE FISA COURT 3, 30 (2015) [hereinafter BRENNAN CENTER REPORT].

[40] The FISA Amendments Act of 2008 extended application of FISA for the first time to both U.S. persons and non-U.S. persons abroad. *See* 1 DAVID S. KRIS & J. DOUGLAS WILSON, NATIONAL SECURITY INVESTIGATIONS & PROSECUTIONS § 4:2 (2d ed. 2012).

[41] 50 U.S.C. § 1805(a)(2) (2012).

respects less stringent than the traditional warrant process for criminal law surveillance, but they track core indicia of the warrant framework.[42] The FISC is charged with making a judicial determination of probable cause and particularity, as defined by FISA and crafted to suit the intelligence space.[43] Though the question whether FISA orders would qualify as "warrants" for purposes of the Fourth Amendment's Warrant Clause is unsettled,[44] the warrant framework is what shaped the FISC's original design.[45]

A second feature of FISA's original design was its requirement for "minimization procedures." These are rules, adopted or approved by the attorney general, that are "designed to protect, as far as reasonable, against the acquisition, retention, and dissemination of nonpublic information [that] is not foreign intelligence information" and that concerns U.S. persons.[46] Whereas the warrant-like requirements grew out of the law of criminal procedure, the minimization-procedures requirement supplemented traditional Fourth Amendment law. Fourth Amendment law ordinarily applies to the initial collection or acquisition of information, but not to the uses of information once it is in the government's hands.[47] Minimization procedures in the original FISA complemented the more traditional warrant-like role for the FISC in reviewing probable cause determinations and authorizing surveillance.[48]

In an age of programmatic intelligence, however, the FISC's role has changed. To be sure, the FISC continues to review and authorize individual FISA applications based on a showing of probable cause that the target is an agent of a foreign power. But administrative rules today take center stage. The FISC reviews administrative interpretations of statutory authority and statutory constraints for fidelity to congressional intent. And it reviews administrative policymaking, in the form of targeting and minimization procedures, articulated and implemented through agency rules. In the absence of judicially approved probable cause

---

[42] See 1 KRIS & DOUGLAS, *supra* note 40, §§ 11:5–7.

[43] 50 U.S.C. § 1805(a)–(c) (2012).

[44] See In re Sealed Case, 310 F.3d 717, 744 (FISA Ct. Rev. 2002). The Supreme Court has never decided the question whether a foreign-intelligence exception to the Fourth Amendment's warrant requirement exists. See United States v. U.S. Dist. Court (Keith), 407 U.S. 297, 308–309 (1972) (reserving the question). The courts of appeals that have reached this question have found a foreign-intelligence exception under certain circumstances. For a nuanced discussion of the relevant Supreme Court precedent and the decisions of the lower courts, see PCLOB, SECTION 702 REPORT, *supra* note 6, at 89–91.

[45] See, e.g., S. REP. NO. 95-701, at 53 (1978), *as reprinted in* 1978 U.S.C.C.A.N. 3973, 4022 ("In determining whether probable cause exists under [FISA], the court must consider the same requisite elements which govern such determinations in the traditional criminal context."); see generally BRENNAN CENTER REPORT, *supra* note 39, at 29–30.

[46] Sealed Case, 310 F.3d at 731; *see* 50 U.S.C. § 1801(h) (2012) (defining "minimization procedures").

[47] See Margo Schlanger, *Intelligence Legalism and the National Security Agency's Civil Liberties Gap*, 6 HARV. NAT'L SEC. J. 112, 124–27 (2015) (discussing FISA's minimization-procedures requirement and explaining how "it deviates foundationally from non-intelligence Fourth Amendment doctrine").

[48] The courts to consider the constitutionality of traditional FISA orders emphasized FISA's "expanded conception of minimization that differs from that which governs law-enforcement surveillance." United States v. Belfield, 692 F.2d 141, 148 (D.C. Cir. 1982) (citation omitted) (rejecting Fifth and Sixth Amendment challenges to traditional FISA process); see generally PCLOB, SECTION 702 REPORT, *supra* note 6, at 94 (collecting citations).

determinations, this administrative lawmaking function is what gives content to Fourth Amendment reasonableness in programmatic intelligence such as Section 702.[49]

The FISC's MCTs review reflects this dynamic. Whether the NSA can conduct upstream collection that acquires MCTs raises very difficult legal questions under the Fourth Amendment and under the Section 702 statute itself. As detailed above, Section 702 authorizes a warrantless surveillance program directed at non-U.S. persons overseas. But the court now understood that, as a result of MCTs, the government was sweeping up tens of thousands of wholly domestic communications, as well as the communications of U.S. persons "that are not to, from, or about a tasked selector."[50] As the FISC observed, "NSA's acquisition of MCTs substantially broadens the circumstances in which Fourth Amendment-protected interests are intruded upon by NSA's Section 702 collection," raising serious concerns about the reasonableness of the program under the Fourth Amendment.[51]

To decide these questions, the FISC reviewed a statutory interpretation adopted by the intelligence agencies and implemented through administrative rules. And the FISC scrutinized those administrative rules for compliance with Fourth Amendment reasonableness. That interaction between underspecified congressional mandates, administrative rules, and FISC review is what determined the content of the Fourth Amendment protections.

Yet as an institutional design, the warrant framework that drove the FISC's original design and continues to structure its work is the antithesis of administrative law. Administrative law in the United States is built on the principles of transparency, participatory process, and adversarial judicial review.[52] The warrant framework, by contrast, is built around an idea of a magistrate judge reviewing facts to determine whether a preexisting legal standard has been satisfied.[53] Warrant procedures are secret and ex parte. And they presume that the hard work of lawmaking has already happened elsewhere. The legal requirements are generally in place by the time the magistrate judge receives the warrant application.[54] So although the role that the FISC is actually performing has changed dramatically in the context of programmatic intelligence, we have not yet reconciled the legal framework of intelligence governance with the new administrative law function that the FISC today performs. The FISC is relying on administrative rules to do crucial work to give content to Fourth Amendment

---

[49] In reviewing a predecessor program to Section 702 called the Protect America Act, the FISA Court of Review identified a "matrix of safeguards" relevant to Fourth Amendment reasonableness, emphasizing that minimization procedures provide an important "backstop against identification errors as well as a means of reducing the impact of incidental intrusions into the privacy of non-targeted United States persons." *In re* Directives Pursuant to Section 105B of Foreign Intelligence Surveillance Act, 551 F.3d 1004, 1015 (FISA Ct. Rev. 2008).

[50] [Caption Redacted], [Docket No. Redacted], 2011 U.S. Dist. LEXIS 157706, at *40, *46 (FISA Ct. Oct. 3, 2011).

[51] *Id.* at *101.

[52] These principles and their practical implications are contested, however, even in the context of traditional administrative law. *See, e.g.*, Nicholas Bagley, *The Puzzling Presumption of Reviewability*, 127 Harv. L. Rev. 1285 (2014) (arguing against the presumption in favor of judicial review of agency action, while recognizing that this presumption is currently a "cornerstone" of administrative law).

[53] *See* Orin S. Kerr, *A Rule of Lenity for National Security Surveillance Law*, 100 Va. L. Rev. 1513, 1518 (2014) ("The magistrate serves an essentially ministerial role of making sure that no orders will issue unless the rule maker's standards have been satisfied.").

[54] *See id.* at 1516–18.

reasonableness, but without the structural conditions that have come to legitimate administrative governance elsewhere in the administrative state.[55]

This section argues that the role of administrative rules in elaborating Fourth Amendment
protections can be salutary, but that the structural principles that accompany administrative
lawmaking elsewhere should be extended to the intelligence space.

A. Administrative Procedure Enables a More Systemic, Dynamic, and Grounded Approach to Fourth Amendment Reasonableness Review

The FISC opinions addressing MCTs reveal an intelligence court in some ways deeply
attuned to the role of administrative procedure in giving content to Fourth Amendment
reasonableness. The legal question at issue was whether the Fourth Amendment tolerated
the collection of many thousands of wholly domestic and U.S. person communications unrelated to foreign intelligence as a result of a program that authorizes warrantless foreign intelligence collection directed at non-U.S. persons overseas. The action played out at the level of
administrative rules. The FISC initially rejected the NSA's rules as inadequately protective of
Fourth Amendment interests. And the court ultimately upheld the program's legality, notwithstanding MCTs, because of changes to the NSA's minimization procedures.

By focusing on the administrative rules that shape the program of collection as a whole,
the FISC is able to overcome considerable limitations of the traditional Fourth Amendment
framework. Administrative procedure, first, enables a more systemic approach to Fourth
Amendment reasonableness review. The conventional Fourth Amendment test is transactional.[56] It focuses on the one-off interaction, quintessentially at a particular moment in
time.[57] Traditional Fourth Amendment law proceeds search by search. This transactional

---

[55] This development in the FISC is in some ways of a piece with other pockets of Fourth Amendment law,
where the Supreme Court occasionally has looked to administrative rules to constrain executive discretion
in the absence of a warrant. *See, e.g.*, Mich. State Police v. Sitz, 496 U.S. 444 (1990); *see also* Eve Brensike
Primus, *Disentangling Administrative Searches*, 111 COLUM. L. REV. 254 (2011) (describing incoherence in
administrative search doctrine and attributing it to the Supreme Court's entanglement of two distinct types
of searches: dragnets and special subpopulation searches). As Primus explains, both dragnets and special subpopulation searches initially were circumscribed under Fourth Amendment law, in part because they were
cabined either to circumstances involving only minimally intrusive government conduct or to those involving
only diminished privacy expectations. *See id.* at 262–301 (tracing gradual doctrinal entanglement). The FISC,
though, is using administrative rules to shape Fourth Amendment protections for surveillance implicating the
content of domestic communications (intrusions that are not minimal) and individuals who do not have a
diminished privacy interest under the traditional Fourth Amendment tests. Moreover, the FISC is unique in
its close and ongoing scrutiny of evolving administrative rules that undertake to establish—ex ante, generally,
and programmatically—the protections for different types of individuals, subject to different types of privacy
protections, given their different relationships to the Fourth Amendment, and the varied types of collection
and use enabled by emergent surveillance tools.

[56] For an analysis of the transactional structure of traditional Fourth Amendment law and its limitations, see
Renan, *supra* note 2, manuscript at 10–25.

[57] The difficulties of this approach were on display in *United States v. Jones*, 132 S. Ct. 945 (2012), a recent Supreme
Court opinion addressing the question of whether ongoing GPS tracking of a suspect's car over 28 days,
which resulted in a 2000-page dossier about the individual, constituted a "search" for purposes of the Fourth
Amendment. The majority opinion, authored by Justice Scalia, held that the installation of the GPS device
constituted a trespass and, as a result, a "search" under the Fourth Amendment. Justice Alito, concurring in the

approach is reflected in the warrant framework. The warrant authorizes a particular search in a particular place. And the warrant inquiry focuses attention on the moment of acquisition. What the government does with the information it has lawfully collected traditionally was not considered a Fourth Amendment question.[58]

The privacy implications of surveillance programs, however, are cumulative. And they are meaningfully determined not solely by acquisition, but also by use.[59] How can the information collected under these programs be accessed, used, shared, and retained? Which agencies may do so, and pursuant to what checks and constraints? These use-based questions are especially significant because the Fourth Amendment interests implicated by an intelligence program can be different at different stages of the program. For example, when the government collects information pursuant to Section 702, can it then use the resulting data sets to search for specific U.S. persons? When can it run this type of individuated search, and pursuant to what limitations or protections? Does it matter which agency is running the search—should the legal rules be different for the CIA or the FBI? Should the rules be different depending on the purpose of the search (for example, whether it is part of an intelligence report, or a counterterrorism investigation, or a child pornography investigation)? All of these questions arise only after the government has already collected the information at issue—that is, they fall outside of the traditional Fourth Amendment focus on acquisition.

Focusing on the administrative rules that shape the contours of a particular intelligence program enables a more systemic and ongoing approach to Fourth Amendment reasonableness. Rather than the one-off interaction, administrative rules reveal the broader implications and cumulative effects of a particular exercise of the government's search-and-seizure power. Administrative rules also enable a court to see how the front-end and back-end restrictions fit together. A more permissive collection authority might call for more restrictive use and sharing rules, for example, and the governing administrative rules form the connective tissue. In the Section 702 program, the front-end search (that is, the initial collection) is warrantless. We might be especially concerned, then, with the back-end restrictions on searches in the resulting data sets, at least when those searches involve individuals protected by the Fourth Amendment.

---

judgment (and joined by three justices), rejected the majority's reasoning, emphasizing that the use of GPS for long-term tracking is what was really at stake in the case. *See id.* at 961; *see also id.* at 954 (Sotomayor, J., concurring). For a more detailed discussion of the Court's approach in *Jones*, see generally Orin S. Kerr, *The Mosaic Theory of the Fourth Amendment*, 111 MICH. L. REV. 311 (2012).

[58] *See, e.g.,* Erin Murphy, *Databases, Doctrine and Constitutional Criminal Procedure*, 37 FORDHAM URB. L.J. 803, 810–21 (2010); Erin Murphy, *Paradigms of Restraint*, 57 DUKE L.J. 1321, 1358–62 (2008) (discussing the limited role that Fourth Amendment constraints have played in the government's use of data after it has been collected).

[59] *See, e.g.,* SIMON CHESTERMAN, ONE NATION UNDER SURVEILLANCE: A NEW CONTRACT TO DEFEND FREEDOM WITHOUT SACRIFICING LIBERTY 238 (2011) ("[M]any of the debates over intelligence are likely to move from whether a wiretap should be authorized to how information so gathered might be used."); CHRISTOPHER SLOBOGIN, PRIVACY AT RISK: THE NEW GOVERNMENT SURVEILLANCE AND THE FOURTH AMENDMENT 5 (2007) ("[G]overnment use of communications, physical, and transaction surveillance should be closely watched and subject to meaningful regulation.").

Second, administrative procedure enables a dynamic approach to Fourth Amendment reasonableness. The MCTs discovery illustrates the iterative and interactive nature of the FISC's contemporary Fourth Amendment review. The executive branch designed, and the FISC initially approved, a set of administrative rules governing Section 702 collection. But the technological facts turned out to be very different from what the legal rule-makers initially understood them to be. Indeed, executive branch officials had to come up with a new term ("MCTs") to describe the technical discovery—the existing terminology could not capture it.[60] The revised understanding of technical feasibility required reforms to the underlying administrative rules, which, in turn, led to novel Fourth Amendment interpretations by the FISC.

Third, Fourth Amendment reasonableness review often collapses into an amorphous and somewhat abstract balancing test between government need and individual privacy interests. The government interest at issue will get framed as a national security interest, and this almost always tips the balance. Administrative procedure can help to ground this inquiry—it can make the assessment of government need and privacy intrusion more granular. The question becomes not whether a government interest exists, but how that interest is being advanced—pursuant to what constraints and institutional safeguards. We can see this in the FISC's review of MCTs. The FISC pored over the rules governing access, retention, and sharing of information collected as a result of the MCTs, and the court rejected those rules that were insufficiently tailored to address the underlying Fourth Amendment concerns.[61]

In this way, administrative procedure also enables Fourth Amendment reasonableness review to address spillovers. The traditional tools of Fourth Amendment law (such as the warrant requirement) ask whether the exercise of the executive's search power is justified as directed at a particular individual. Those doctrinal rules are limited, however, in their ability to protect the Fourth Amendment interests of those *not* targeted by the collection authority, but whose communications are nevertheless swept up in the collection itself. Administrative rules can tailor Fourth Amendment protections to address spillovers through, for example, the development of minimization requirements.

B. *The Missing Structural Safeguards*

The FISC's turn to administrative procedure to give content to Fourth Amendment reasonableness thus has considerable benefits. Fourth Amendment reasonableness elaborated through administrative rules can be more systemic, dynamic, and grounded than Fourth Amendment reasonableness review without it. And administrative procedure enables Fourth Amendment law to be more responsive to the Fourth Amendment interests of those individuals who are not themselves the "targets" of collection.

But the use of administrative procedure to give meaning to the Fourth Amendment also carries distinct risks. An enduring concern is agencies distorting their legal authorities

---

[60] NSA's former Director of Compliance, John DeLong, has described how executive officials had to "invent[] terminology in 2011 to describe what was occurring" in the acquisition of the newly labeled MCTs. *See Inside NSA Part II*, THE LAWFARE PODCAST 19:24–19:38 (Dec. 17, 2013, 11:30 AM), http://lawfare.libsyn.com/episode-53-inside-nsa-part-ii-wherein-we-interview-the-agency-s-chief-of-compliance-john-de-long.

[61] [Caption Redacted], [Docket No. Redacted], 2011 U.S. Dist. LEXIS 157706, at *76–111 (FISA Ct. Oct. 3, 2011).

and circumventing the democratic process. A Fourth Amendment doctrine dependent on administrative rules should be especially attentive to those risks, for search-and-seizure law constructs crucial safeguards in a world of ever-increasing surveillance capacity.[62]

American administrative law has developed a set of structural and procedural safeguards to make administrative lawmaking more legally and politically accountable. The legal framework of modern American administrative law has looked to transparency, reason-giving, participatory process, and adversarial judicial review to legitimate it.[63] These doctrinal and institutional developments are grounded in several overlapping ideas. Agencies (and other government actors) are understood to act differently when their policymaking occurs in the light. Participatory opportunities for those affected by agency lawmaking are understood to enhance both political accountability—by creating opportunities for involvement in agency lawmaking—and deliberative process.[64] And judicial review provides an external check on the boundaries of administrative discretion.[65]

Administrative procedure inside the Fourth Amendment is different. The FISC is relying on administrative rules to give content to Fourth Amendment reasonableness, but without creating the conditions that legitimate administrative lawmaking elsewhere in the regulatory state. The FISC's MCTs opinions reveal the development of very novel legal rules for the governance of programmatic intelligence under Section 702 and the Fourth Amendment, but without any consideration of the process by which those underlying legal rules were developed. Indeed, prior to the Snowden leaks, even the fact of MCTs collection was classified. By contrast, in administrative law, the deference courts give administrative rules—and the interpretations of statutory authorities that are embedded in those rules—is intertwined with procedural safeguards such as notice and the opportunity for public comment.[66] Yet

---

[62] Renan, *supra* note 2, manuscript at 32–33. Some scholars have suggested that distrust of executive power is a Fourth Amendment "first principle." *See* Raymond Shih Ray Ku, *The Founders' Privacy: The Fourth Amendment and the Power of Technological Surveillance*, 86 MINN. L. REV. 1325, 1326 (2002); Carol S. Steiker, *"First Principles" of Constitutional Criminal Procedure: A Mistake?*, 112 HARV. L. REV. 680, 686 (1999) (reviewing AKHIL REED AMAR, THE CONSTITUTION AND CRIMINAL PROCEDURE: FIRST PRINCIPLES (1997)) (discussing earlier works of Telford Taylor and Tracey Maclin).

[63] These principles are in some respects transnational, as an emergent field of global administrative law has argued. *See generally* Benedict Kingsbury et al., *The Emergence of Global Administrative Law*, 68 L. & CONTEMP. PROBS. 15, 17 (2005) ("[G]lobal administrative law [is defined] as comprising the mechanisms, principles, practices, and supporting social understandings that promote or otherwise affect the accountability of global administrative bodies, in particular by ensuring they meet adequate standards of transparency, participation, reasoned decision, and legality, and by providing effective review of the rules and decisions they make.").

[64] *See, e.g., id.* at 38 ("Decisional transparency and access to information are important foundations for the effective exercise of participation rights and rights of review. They also promote accountability directly by exposing administrative decisions and relevant documents to public and peer scrutiny.").

[65] *See* ADMINISTRATIVE LAW: THE AMERICAN PUBLIC LAW SYSTEM 970 (Jerry Mashaw et al. eds., 7th ed. 2014) ("Judicial review of administrative action exposes the tensions between two insistent demands: that the government respect the law and that courts not run the government.").

[66] *See generally* Renan, *supra* note 2, manuscript at 34–35 (describing administrative-law framework). It is important to note that administrative-law deference is bounded and still tethered to statutory constraints. Under the familiar *Chevron* framework of U.S. administrative law, a court asks whether Congress has answered the legal question at issue and, if the statute is ambiguous, whether the agency's interpretation is reasonable. *See* Chevron U.S.A., Inc. v. Nat. Resources Defense Council, Inc., 467 U.S. 837, 842–43 (1984). A softer form

the FISC today applies what is in effect a highly deferential approach to the government's interpretation of its underlying legal authorities, without looking for any of those structural and process-oriented protections.

IV. THE LAYERS OF FOURTH AMENDMENT REASONABLENESS
A. Substantive and Structural Reasonableness

One way to think about the foregoing concerns is as a different dimension of Fourth Amendment reasonableness—what we might think of as *reasonableness as structural safeguards*.[67] This idea of reasonableness is familiar to students of American administrative law. Reasonableness in administrative law is in part about a set of structural and process-oriented expectations for how agencies make law. This approach to reasonableness is largely absent from Fourth Amendment law.[68]

Reasonableness in traditional Fourth Amendment law is instead a substantive determination about the reasonableness of the intrusion at issue—it is about *reasonableness as intrusion protection*. As the FISC explained in the MCTs opinion, " 'a court assessing reasonableness [under the Fourth Amendment] must consider 'the nature of the government intrusion and how the government intrusion is implemented. The more important the government's interest, the greater the intrusion that may be constitutionally tolerated.' "[69]

If administrative procedure gives content to Fourth Amendment protections, however, then Fourth Amendment reasonableness is a layered construct. We need both reasonableness-as-intrusion-protection and reasonableness-as-structure to play into the court's review. Put differently, if administrative rules today shape the substance of the FISC's Fourth Amendment reasonableness review, then the FISC also should take into account the structure and process by which those administrative rules are developed. This layered approach to reasonableness would help to reconcile the work of administrative procedure "inside" the Fourth Amendment.

One likely response is that administrative law's structural reasonableness is incompatible with the foreign intelligence function. Administrative law's structural safeguards are rooted in ideas of transparency and participation, whereas foreign intelligence work depends on secrecy. That view has shaped the current approach to intelligence governance, creating secret

---

of administrative-law deference, called *Skidmore* deference, accords judicial deference to the agency on the basis of "the thoroughness evident in its consideration, the validity of its reasoning, its consistency with earlier and later pronouncements, and all those factors which give it power to persuade, if lacking power to control." Skidmore v. Swift & Co., 323 U.S. 134, 140 (1944). Under either *Chevron* or *Skidmore*, statutory interpretations that exceed reasonable bounds cannot be sustained.

[67] This theory of Fourth Amendment reasonableness is introduced and elaborated in Renan, *supra* note 2, manuscript at 36–38.

[68] Of course, the warrant clause provides a set of structural safeguards by interposing a neutral magistrate and imposing a measurement of just cause. Outside the warrant clause, however, Fourth Amendment doctrine's treatment of structural considerations has been fleeting and ad hoc. *See generally* Renan, *supra* note 2, manuscript at 36–38 (discussing case law).

[69] [Caption Redacted], [Docket No. Redacted], 2011 U.S. Dist. LEXIS 157706, at *97 (FISA Ct. Oct. 3, 2011) (quoting *In re* Directives, 551 F.3d 1004, 1012 (FISA Ct. Rev. 2008)).

administrative rules, secret court proceedings, and secret judicial opinions to govern foreign intelligence.[70] Secrecy protects the government's foreign intelligence capabilities from its adversaries and prevents targets from switching to communication channels less susceptible to governmental surveillance.[71]

This objection fails, however, to appreciate the institutional and legal shift described above. When the FISC reviews warrant-like questions—for example, the question whether there is just cause to direct surveillance against a particular foreign intelligence target—there is a sound basis for secret decision-making. But the FISC today is also reviewing federal *law-making* by agencies—administrative rules that determine the legal architecture of surveillance programs.[72] And those surveillance programs sweep up the communications of many domestic and U.S. persons. Questions such as whether Section 702 authorizes "about" collection, or whether and under what conditions the FBI may search for specific U.S. persons in the PRISM data sets—these types of questions determine the domestic law of intelligence. When those legal rules form the basis of the FISC's Fourth Amendment reasonableness analysis, moreover, they make the constitutional law of intelligence.

The benefits of secrecy in the intelligence context also need to be traded off against the costs of disclosure (through leaks and other means) that the government cannot control or predict. As others have written, important sociological, technological, and practice-oriented developments are diminishing "the half-life of secrets."[73] The choice today may be less about secrecy versus transparency than about transparency when and how. Making the overarching legal framework of surveillance programs more visible and participatory may make those programs more resilient.[74] There surely will need to be operational details that remain classified, and the appropriate boundaries of secrecy will continue to raise complex questions. I do not mean to minimize the difficulty of those questions or of the task of paving a more transparent approach to intelligence lawmaking. But the fundamental legal framework of intelligence programs belongs in the light.[75]

---

[70] *See, e.g.,* Eric Lichtblau, *In Secret, Court Vastly Broadens Powers of N.S.A.,* N.Y. Times, July 7, 2013, at A1 (describing emergent body of secret law by the FISC).

[71] *Accord* David S. Kris, *On the Bulk Collection of Tangible Things,* 7 J. Nat'l Sec. L. & Pol'y 209, 275 (2014) (writing in connection to secret legal analysis that sustained the bulk metadata collection program under Section 215 of FISA, "[u]ntil the June 2013 unauthorized disclosures, none of the three branches of government had found a safe way to disclose to the public the 'secret law' underlying [the Section 215] program").

[72] *See, e.g.,* Kerr, *supra* note 53, at 1525–31; *see generally* Sudha Setty, *Surveillance, Secrecy, and the Search for Meaningful Accountability,* 51 Stan. J. Int'l L. 69 (2015); Lichtblau, *supra* note 70.

[73] *See* Peter Swire, *The Declining Half-Life of Secrets and the Future of Signals Intelligence,* New America Cybersecurity Fellows Paper Series (July 2015).

[74] *See, e.g., id.* at 1 ("[T]he declining half-life of secrets is an important factual reason to bring greater transparency and more perspectives into the governance of sensitive signals intelligence activities."); *see generally* The President's Review Group on Intelligence and Communications Technologies, Liberty and Security in a Changing World 125 (2013), *available at* https://www.whitehouse.gov/sites/default/files/docs/2013-12-12_rg_final_report.pdf ("There is a compelling need today for a serious and comprehensive reexamination of the balance between secrecy and transparency.").

[75] The argument for more transparent lawmaking in the intelligence space has been advanced by scholars, advocates, and actors in every branch of government. *See, e.g.,* Am. Civil Liberties Union v. Clapper, 785 F.3d 787 (2d Cir. 2015); Stephen Braun, *Former FISA Judge Says Secret Court Is Flawed,* Seattle Times (July 9, 2013 3:16 PM), www.seattletimes.com/seattle-news/politics/former-fisa-judge-says-secret-court-is-flawed/;

A different type of objection would accept the need for greater transparency and political accountability over surveillance programs, but would seek to foreclose the development of legal rules governing intelligence by any institutional actor other than Congress. Orin Kerr has advanced this view, arguing that courts should adopt an interpretive rule—the rule of lenity—in order to prevent elaboration of the foreign intelligence statutes through judicial review.[76] Kerr would require courts to construe ambiguous or silent statutory text as prohibitive of the activity that the government seeks to undertake, in an effort to force Congress to engage the legal question itself and to set the relevant legal rules through legislation.[77]

My concern with Kerr's approach, however, is that the legal rules governing surveillance evolve too rapidly for Congress to draft (and redraft) them alone.[78] If the question is whether to adopt a particular surveillance authority, such as the Section 702 authority, we surely want Congress engaged. But Kerr's approach fails to grapple with the role that administrative rules today play in implementing and shaping the parameters of any particular surveillance program. Questions such as whether Section 702 permits MCTs acquisition and under what circumstances reflect the quickly evolving technological realities of surveillance. We cannot expect Congress through legislation to micromanage the myriad, dynamic, and yet exceptionally significant legal dimensions of these programs. Administrative procedure enables a more nimble interplay among congressional design, administrative elaboration, and judicial review.[79]

There is a third type of objection, however—a concern that the legitimating tools of administrative procedure might make more palatable an expanding surveillance state that should instead be resisted. Perhaps suggestive of this type of argument, Margo Schlanger argues in a recent article that a "compliance focus, and the prevalence of rights and law talk[] actually dampens the prospects of civil liberties policymaking, both by crowding it out and by rendering surveillance more politically acceptable and therefore making political or policy-based claims for reform less likely to succeed."[80] Schlanger traces a burgeoning compliance "ecosystem," of which the FISC is today an important part. And she argues that a focus on compliance, rights, and law has shifted attention away from policy questions about what types of surveillance *should* be conducted, channeling legal and policy debate instead to questions about what types of surveillance *can* lawfully be achieved.[81]

Barack Obama, President of the United States, Remarks by the President on Review of Signals Intelligence (Jan. 17, 2014 11:15 AM) (transcript available at www.whitehouse.gov/the-press-office/2014/01/17/remarks-president-review-signals-intelligence); Press Release, Ron Wyden Senator for Oregon Website, Senators: End Secret Law—Bipartisan Group of Senators Introduce Bill to Declassify FISA Court Opinions (June 11, 2013), *available at* www.wyden.senate.gov/news/press-releases/senators-end-secret-law; *see also* sources cited *supra* notes 72–74.

[76] *See* Kerr, *supra* note 53, at 1535 ("The principle of the rule of lenity should be adapted to apply in the context of national security surveillance law. . . . Under this approach, courts would be unable to engage in common-law decision making designed to make policy or resolve difficult legislative questions.").

[77] *Id.*

[78] This is an argument that I develop in Renan, *supra* note 2, manuscript at 27–30.

[79] *See* Jody Freeman & David B. Spence, *Old Statutes, New Problems*, 163 U. PA. L. REV. 1, 2–5, 10–11 (2014).

[80] *See* Schlanger, *supra* note 47, at 173.

[81] *See id.* at 174.

It is important, however, to distinguish compliance oversight from other types of legal oversight. A decades-long focus on institutionalizing compliance might have contributed to the failure to adequately institutionalize rights and strive for a more democracy-protecting law. But the answer lies at least in part in disentangling compliance oversight from other types of law and rights review. Compliance oversight is about the processes through which an agency, as a complex organization, ensures its conformance with the legal rules that govern it.[82] In a time of technological complexity, compliance institutions play a significant role translating legal rules to operational realities;[83] and they help foster greater conformity with the legal framework. Yet compliance institutions are only as effective as the legal framework that they implement. Compliance institutions might be the conductor, but they do not write the musical score.

Administrative law can help to shift some attention back to that score—to the way that the governing legal framework is itself developed. By making administrative lawmaking more visible and participatory, administrative law helps to infuse that lawmaking process with voices (and value judgments) external to the operational agencies, and it requires the agencies to defend their legal decisions in public. Agencies preparing for a public accounting of their legal rules may act differently than agencies preparing for a secret assessment.[84] A more visible and participatory process of intelligence lawmaking might ultimately be more acceptable to the public, then, in part because it might lead to a different type of surveillance.[85]

There is a related concern, however, that I share with Schlanger: the "should" set of questions for intelligence governance has been inadequately institutionalized inside the administrative state.[86] While Schlanger situates this realm of policy trade-offs and balancing in contrast to and maybe even in tension with rights, I want to suggest that it is an important dimension of Fourth Amendment reasonableness—albeit not one that the courts can realize on their own.

---

[82] *See, e.g.*, Law of Governance, Risk Management, and Compliance (Geoffrey P. Miller ed., 2014) (defining compliance as "the processes by which an organization polices its own behavior to ensure that it conforms with applicable rules and regulations").

[83] John DeLong, NSA's first Director of Compliance, has described compliance as "the bringing-rules-to-life business" in a technologically complex environment. Gregory J. Millman, *Compliance in Government: Q&A with John DeLong of the NSA*, Wall St. J., Risk & Compliance Report (Jan. 23, 2014, 12:26 PM), http://blogs.wsj.com/riskandcompliance/2014/01/23/compliance-in-government-qa-with-john-delong-of-the-nsa/.

[84] Indeed, this has led some scholars and policy analysts to urge the intelligence agencies to adopt the "front-page rule" in making surveillance decision-making, "at least in the specific context of communications intelligence that takes place in the homeland or that affects US persons abroad." Jack Goldsmith, *A Partial Defense of the Front-Page Rule*, The Hoover Institution (Jan. 29, 2014) (emphasis omitted); *see* Swire, *supra* note 73, at 5–7; President's Review Group, *supra* note 74, at 170. *But see* Walter Pincus, *"Front-Page Rule" Is Unprecedented in U.S. Intelligence Community*, Wash. Post, Dec. 25, 2013.

[85] This is an empirical question beyond the scope of this short chapter. But the changes to surveillance law and policy that followed the Snowden leaks and the declassification efforts that those leaks have triggered are suggestive. *See, e.g., infra* text accompanying notes 95–97 (discussing the USA FREEDOM Act of 2015).

[86] *See* Schlanger, *supra* note 47, at 174; Margo Schlanger, *Offices of Goodness: Influence without Authority in Federal Agencies*, 36 Cardozo L. Rev. 53, 55–56 (2014).

B. Reasonableness-as-Efficacy[87]

As a substantive matter, Fourth Amendment reasonableness requires an evaluation of liberty-security policy trade-offs. It seems to call for an evaluation of the efficacy or appropriateness of surveillance.[88] The MCTs disclosure revealed that thousands of domestic communications were getting swept up as part of the upstream collection program. Given this revelation, was the upstream collection program still justified? The FISC, in effect, punted. It noted potentially relevant considerations such as the very small amount of data that the government acquires under upstream collection given the parallel, simultaneous, and vast downstream collection program,[89] and the significant spillovers problem presented by the MCTs.[90] But the court did not look behind the government's assertions of a significant security need.[91]

Although the FISC exercised a careful oversight function in connection to the administrative constraints on intrusion—finding the initial protocols insufficiently responsive to the spillovers problem, and approving the revised procedures—the court did not meaningfully examine the "should" set of questions. Put differently, although the FISC engaged in a rigorous reasonableness-as-intrusion review, it largely threw up its hands when it came to reasonableness-as-efficacy.

The FISC's reluctance to address efficacy is reflective of a broader judicial approach to this set of questions.[92] The Supreme Court has observed that Fourth Amendment reasonableness is in part about efficacy,[93] but the Court has largely resisted establishing a meaningful doctrinal test. This doctrinal approach might reflect a set of institutional competence concerns about the judiciary's ability to review the efficacy of surveillance programs.[94] To develop a legal and institutional framework responsive to reasonableness-as-efficacy, then, we may need to supplement judicial review with a different kind of administrative oversight—with administrative review focused on the making of legal policy rather than compliance.

---

[87] The following is taken from Renan, *supra* note 2, where the argument is more fully developed.

[88] *See* Tracey L. Meares, *Programming Errors: Understanding the Constitutionality of Stop-and-Frisk as a Program, Not an Incident*, 82 U. CHI. L. REV. 159 (2015); Tracey L. Meares & Bernard E. Harcourt, *Foreword: Transparent Adjudication and Social Science Research in Constitutional Criminal Procedure*, 90 J. CRIM. L. & CRIMINOLOGY 733 (2000).

[89] [Caption Redacted], [Docket No. Redacted], 2011 U.S. Dist. LEXIS 157706, at *36–37 (FISA Ct. Oct. 3, 2011).

[90] *Id.* at *54 ("[T]he record before this Court establishes that NSA's acquisition of Internet transactions likely results in NSA acquiring annually tens of thousands of wholly domestic communications, and tens of thousands of non-target communications of persons who have little or no relationship to the target but who are protected under the Fourth Amendment.").

[91] *Id.* at *98–99 (concluding that government's interest "is of the highest order of magnitude," and accepting government's representations that NSA's upstream collection is "uniquely capable of acquiring certain types of targeted communications containing valuable foreign intelligence information").

[92] Schlanger has posited that the FISC is even less inclined to review the "should" set of questions than other courts because of structural features of the FISC judges' relationship to the government. Schlanger describes the "advice-giving, iterative drafting, [informal] briefings" and other interactions that define a "collaborati[ve]" relationship among the FISC judges, their permanent staff, and the government agencies involved in litigation before them. *See* Schlanger, *supra* note 47, at 164–66.

[93] *See, e.g.*, Vernonia Sch. Dist. 47J v. Acton, 515 U.S. 646, 663 (1995).

[94] For a more detailed discussion of these considerations, see Renan, *supra* note 2, manuscript at 64–67.

V. CONCLUSION: TWO POTENTIAL DIRECTIONS FOR REFORM

The just-enacted USA FREEDOM Act of 2015 has taken some steps to make FISC decision-making more visible and to create limited opportunities for contested adjudication.[95] The statute provides for the appointment of amicus curiae under certain conditions at the discretion of a judge of the FISC.[96] And it mandates declassification review for the FISC's significant legal interpretations.[97] These are valuable first steps. But the very architecture of administrative lawmaking in the intelligence space requires rethinking. In concluding, this chapter suggests two potential avenues for reform. The suggestions are preliminary and underdeveloped, but they point to directions for future analytic refinement and policy analysis.

The structural architecture of modern administrative law in the United States is grounded in the Administrative Procedure Act (APA). The APA creates statutory obligations for a more public and participatory process when agencies effectively "make law." An APA for intelligence programs could do the same.[98] I do not suggest a mechanical extension of the APA's notice-and-comment rules. The structural and procedural obligations on agencies will need to be tailored to the activity of intelligence gathering and the realities of technological flux. It might be, for example, that focusing these regulatory mechanisms on the use-based dimensions of surveillance programs—that is, on the questions when and pursuant to what safeguards information involving domestic and U.S. communications may be shared, used, or retained—will be more viable than bringing acquisition methods into the light. But we need to more deeply grapple with how to extend the underlying structural principles of transparency, some form of public input, and adversarial judicial review to the intelligence space. FISA could be amended to impose new structural safeguards, or a separate framework statute for intelligence programs could be enacted.

---

[95] *See* Uniting and Strengthening America by Fulfilling Rights and Ensuring Effective Discipline Over Monitoring Act of 2015 ("USA FREEDOM Act of 2015"), Pub. L. No. 114-23, §§ 401–402.

[96] The judge's discretion is somewhat constrained. The statute provides that the FISC "shall appoint" amicus curiae "to assist [the court] in the consideration of any application for an order or review that, in the opinion of the court, presents a novel or significant interpretation of the law, unless the court issues a finding that such appointment is not appropriate;" and it provides that the FISC "may appoint" amicus curiae "in any instance as such court deems appropriate or, upon motion, permit an individual or organization leave to file an amicus curiae brief." *See id.* § 401.

[97] *See id.* § 402.

[98] The existing APA largely excludes the intelligence agencies and the foreign intelligence function from its requirements. *See* Adrian Vermeule, *Our Schmittian Administrative Law*, 122 HARV. L. REV. 1095, 1112–13 (2009). Adrian Vermeule has argued that in the context of emergencies, these "grey" and "black" holes are inevitable. *Id.* at 1131–42. As the argument in the text has sought to establish, however, intelligence rule-making is not emergency administrative law; it is today routinized governance of ongoing collection and use of domestic communications. *See* Samuel J. Rascoff, *Domesticating Intelligence*, 83 S. CAL. L. REV. 575 (2010) (conceptualizing domestic intelligence as risk assessment and proposing a regulatory approach to its governance). For a broader discussion of the APA in connection to surveillance and to types of policing outside of the intelligence space, see Renan, *supra* note 2; Barry Friedman & Maria Ponomarenko, *Democratic Policing*, 90 N.Y.U. L. REV. 1001 (2015); Christopher Slobogin, *Panvasive Surveillance, Political Process Theory, and the Nondelegation Doctrine*, 102 GEO. L.J. 1721 (2014).

This type of reform would address reasonableness-as-structural-safeguards. Yet we also need to create a space for reasonableness-as-efficacy review. And for this sort of reasonableness review, we likely will need to look beyond the courts. One possibility would be to create or utilize an existing administrative structure to supplement the role of the FISC in reviewing surveillance programs.[99]

The PCLOB is an agency, fairly new on the scene, but perhaps well suited to take on this function. The Board's mandate is to ensure that privacy and civil liberties are "appropriately considered" in the executive branch's counterterrorism activities.[100] The PCLOB's oversight role, however, is limited to a reporting function, and its mission is limited to counterterrorism activities.[101]

A more muscular PCLOB could be required to review the efficacy of intelligence programs.[102] Such a role could be institutionalized by statute or implemented in some respects through an executive order, and it could take the form either of a recommendation to the president or a certification to the FISC. In either form, the PCLOB's finding of efficacy could also have bearing on the FISC's Fourth Amendment reasonableness review.

In assuming such a role, the PCLOB would provide an important interface between the intelligence agencies and the domestic public. We are already seeing the PCLOB begin to play this role. In a recent report on the Section 702 program, for instance, the PCLOB convened a public comment period through the website www.regulations.gov, and held a series of public hearings with participants from the privacy advocacy community, trade associations, technology companies, and academia.[103] The Board also met with members of the IC, the Justice Department, the White House, and congressional committee staff.[104] As a result of the PCLOB's report, moreover, the complex surveillance program is today more transparent.

Building out reasonableness-as-efficacy review, then, might also help us to address some of the structural concerns of transparency and participatory opportunity. A FISC more attuned to those structural considerations might even link its relatively deferential approach to efficacy to the availability of this more robust and transparent administrative check.

These suggestions are preliminary. But they gesture at the possibility of a more integrated, more resilient administrative Fourth Amendment law.

---

[99] This proposal to institutionalize efficacy review is taken from Renan, *supra* note 2, where it is more fully developed.

[100] 42 U.S.C. § 2000ee(c) (2012).

[101] *See id.* § 2000ee(e) (2012).

[102] Indeed, the PCLOB itself identified the need for efficacy metrics and analysis for counterterrorism programs, *see* PCLOB, Section 702 Report, *supra* note 6, at 148 ("The government should develop a comprehensive methodology for assessing the efficacy and relative value of counterterrorism programs."), and the PCLOB's first two major reports on surveillance programs have considered the efficacy of those programs, *see id.* at 107–110 (concluding that "the Section 702 program has proven valuable in a number of ways to the government's efforts to combat terrorism"); PCLOB, Report on the Telephone Records Program Conducted under Section 215 of the USA Patriot Act and on the Operations of the Foreign Intelligence Surveillance Court 146 (2014) ("[finding] little evidence that the unique capabilities provided by the NSA's bulk collection of telephone records actually have yielded material counterterrorism results that could not have been achieved without the NSA's Section 215 program") (emphasis omitted), *available at* https://www.pclob.gov/library/215-Report_on_the_Telephone_Records_Program.pdf.

[103] *See* PCLOB, Section 702 Report, *supra* note 6, at 3–4, 179–90.

[104] *See id.* at 2–3.

6

In Law We Trust

THE ISRAELI CASE OF OVERSEEING INTELLIGENCE

*Raphael Bitton**

I. INTRODUCTION

This chapter introduces the Israeli Intelligence Community (IC) and its oversight mechanisms. The exceptional challenges facing the Israeli national security community alongside the strong liberal political framework of the Israeli government create an exceptional comparative case study. This chapter consists of eight sections: Section II presents the importance of the Israeli example of intelligence oversight; Section III introduces the components of the Israeli IC; Section IV outlines the purposes of overseeing intelligence in general; Section V presents the existing oversight mechanisms in Israel.

Section VI demonstrates the clear preference for legal and judicial oversight of intelligence in Israel. Since the 1970s, in a process that overlapped with the general expansion of judicial activism in Israel, the Israeli Supreme Court has expanded its involvement in particular in intelligence and security-related matters.[1] The Court has amended its threshold and procedural rules in a manner that has incentivized nongovernmental organizations (NGOs) to file petitions concerning the activity of the Israel Defense Forces (IDF), the Israeli General Security Service (SHABAK), and the Israeli Directorate of Military Intelligence (AMAN) in the West Bank, Gaza, and Lebanon. Accordingly, the Supreme Court has issued rulings

---

* Head of Legal Studies, Interdisciplinary Department, University of Haifa; Adjunct Lecturer, Sapir College School of Law. All translations from, and citations to, Hebrew language sources are the author's own. I would like to thank Alon Cohen, Asa Kasher, Gadi Ezra, Menny Mautner, and the participants of the Comparative Intelligence Oversight Workshop (at the Woodrow Wilson Center in Washington, DC) for valuable discussions and comments on various related issues. For superb editorial contribution and comments I deeply thank Richard Morgan, Samuel Rascoff, and Zachary Goldman. Special thanks are owed to Gadi Ezra for excellent research work and comments.
[1] For several theories and explanation on the origins of the rising judicial activism in Israel, see *infra* Section VII.1.

in cases of targeted killing, torture, and claims of former intelligence agents in a manner unprecedented in the Western world.

In addition, Section VI presents the methods through which the supremacy of judicial and legal oversight is enabled. Intuitively, the Court is not the optimal institution for overseeing intelligence. It is slow, reactive, and lacks intelligence expertise. It typically offers its remedy ex post and is hardly willing to discuss general policies. Section F analyzes the amended procedures that the Supreme Court has adopted in intelligence-related cases. These adaptations include relaxing standing requirements and justiciability limitations, recognizing public petitioners, stalling the resolution of cases, and holding frequent ex parte hearings with the intelligence experts. I argue that these amendments are aimed at addressing the Court's deficiencies in supervising the IC. They transformed Israeli judicial oversight into an active, ongoing, and knowledgeable process overseeing specific acts and general policies alike.

Section VII offers an explanation of this counterintuitive preference for judicial supervision. Current literature on judicial independence and activism is generally insufficient in explaining this unique Israeli phenomenon. Section VII therefore offers two alternative explanations for judicial supremacy, both related to local factors. The first anchors the extreme degree of legal involvement in a far broader shift of powers within Israel's basic political structure. The second explanation argues that the legal and judicial involvement reflects a broader strategy to cope with the emerging problem of international delegitimization. The Israeli judicial system enjoys a remarkable reputation for being both active and independent. It is considered to be liberal in terms of its sensitivity to human rights and willingness to limit the executive branch. I argue that rather than discouraging judicial intervention, the executive branch actually invites such intervention in the realms of intelligence-related and national security matters, as it allows executive branch policies to be legitimated by a well-respected judicial system. This invited intervention bears a cost for the executive branch by limiting its discretion. And yet, such limitation is certainly preferable to scrutiny by international tribunals. In addition, as most international tribunals act based on a residual concept of jurisdiction, once the Israeli judicial system deals with a certain matter, it offers by its very resolution some level of protection to the security officers involved. Finally, for the executive branch, an additional perceived benefit of this method of supervising intelligence activities is that, by definition, it leaves most sensitive foreign intelligence issues out of any practical supervision. This is because in most cases, foreign intelligence activities are legally victimless in the sense that their target is rarely aware of the activity and hence cannot initiate proceedings. In other cases, the victim will most likely avoid any legal proceedings in Israel.[2]

II. THE IMPORTANCE OF THE ISRAELI COMMUNITY AS A CASE STUDY

Ever since its first day of independence, Israel has been in a continuous conflict on several fronts. Particularly in the cases of terrorism or preventing the proliferation of weapons of

---

[2] The rare lawsuit of Hezbollah operative Mustafa Dirani against the foreign intelligence 504 Unit only arose from an alleged interrogation in a secret facility in Israel. Civil Further Appeal 5698/11 State of Israel v. Dirani (Heb.); Civil Application of Appeal 993/06 State of Israel v. Dirani (Heb.); Civil Appeal Request (HCJ) 993/06, The State of Israel v. Dirani (Heb.)

mass destruction, Israel's IC is the key player. Israel's proximity to hostile nations and limited territorial depth magnifies the threats that it faces from surprise attacks, terrorism, and unconventional weapons. Accordingly, one would expect to find Israel adopting a very conservative legal approach on issues of national security and law. Surprisingly, concerning issues of law and security, Israel's judicial and legal system is exceptionally active and independent.

Due to this anomaly, Israel's intelligence organizations are, in many cases, among the first to ignite legal debates about national security measures such as targeted killings and torture in "ticking time bomb" situations.[3] Israel's early "exposure" to threats combined with an active legal system makes Israeli discourse on law and intelligence relatively mature, and hence an attractive case study.

III. THE ISRAELI IC

Three organizations stand at the heart of the Israeli IC: SHABAK, MOSSAD (Israel's foreign intelligence organization), and AMAN.[4] Israeli military intelligence includes the signals intelligence (SIGINT) service, Unit 8200 (similar to America's National Security Agency and the U.K.'s Government Communications Headquarters), imagery intelligence (IMINT), and other technology-based collection units. Also considered to be members of the IC are the Intelligence Department of the Police (part of the Directorate of Interrogations and Intelligence of the national police) and the Center for Policy Research (part of the Ministry of Foreign Affairs).

SHABAK serves as Israel's domestic intelligence organization. It exercises some foreign intelligence functions, being responsible for intelligence collection and analysis in the Gaza Strip, the West Bank, Southern Lebanon, and the Sinai Peninsula.[5] SHABAK is also responsible for preventing domestic terrorism and political subversion.[6] SHABAK's tasks also include counterintelligence, and ensuring the security of official VIPs, aviation, and other strategic assets, as well as being the primary arm for verifying the security clearances of members of the intelligence and defense communities as well as other officials.

The 1967 War transformed the SHABAK dramatically.[7] Its main focus ever since has been the prevention of terrorist activity against Israeli and Jewish targets originating from Gaza

---

[3] *See* HCJ 769/02 Pub. Comm. against Torture in Israel v. Gov't of Israel 62(1) PD [2006] (concerning targeted killing); HCJ 5100/94 Pub. Comm. against Torture v. Gov't of Israel 53(4) PD [1999] (concerning torture).

[4] ISRAEL'S SILENT DEFENDER: AN INSIDE LOOK AT SIXTY YEARS OF ISRAELI INTELLIGENCE 3 (Amos Gilboa & Ephraim Lapid eds., 2012).

[5] *Id.* at 4–5.

[6] On SHABAK's effectiveness in carrying out its missions *See* Yitzhak Ben Israel, *Coping with Suicide Terrorism— The Israeli Case, in* TICKING BOMB: CONFRONTING SUICIDE ATTACKS 9–46 (Golan Hagai & Shay Shaul eds., 2006) (Isr.); Isaac Ben-Israel et al., *R&D and the War on Terrorism: Generalising the Israeli Experience, in* SCIENCE AND TECHNOLOGY POLICIES FOR THE ANTI-TERRORISM ERA 55–56 (Andrew D. James ed., 2006); Asaf Zussman & Noam Zussman, *Assassinations: Evaluating the Effectiveness of an Israeli Counterterrorism Policy Using Stock Market Data*, 20 J. ECON. PERSPECTIVES 193 (2006).

[7] Prior to the 1967 War, the SHABAK was mainly focused on counterintelligence and domestic espionage. *See ISA History during the Second Decade (1957–1967)*, SHABAK.GOV, http://www.shabak.gov.il/English/ History/Pages/ISA-History_57-67.aspx (last visited June 6, 2015).

and the West Bank. These activities led the SHABAK to be at the heart of some of Israel's more painful public scandals.[8] In retrospect, these scandals were probably the catalysts for a dramatic normative change in both the legal approach to the SHABAK and, vice versa, in SHABAK's approach to law. Since 2000, SHABAK has operated under a statutory mandate, and its activity has been the subject of hearings in court frequently.[9]

The MOSSAD is Israel's foreign intelligence organization.[10] The Director of the MOSSAD reports directly to the Israeli prime minister (PM). The MOSSAD's main tasks include collection of intelligence against enemy states, and preventing terror against Israeli and Jewish targets.[11]

AMAN is Israel's largest intelligence arm. Some of its tasks overlap substantially with the other organizations. Accordingly, it collects human intelligence (through Unit 504) and has under its command Israel's top operational unit: Sayeret Matkal. AMAN is unique in comparison to its foreign equivalents in two main respects: its leadership position in advanced technology-based intelligence and in intelligence analysis. Through AMAN, Israel belongs to a very small "club" of states that design, build, launch, and operate espionage satellites. Moreover, Israel's military intelligence is specifically unique in comparison to other Western military intelligence organizations because of its leading role as the "national analyst."[12]

IV. THE PURPOSES OF OVERSIGHT

Literature on intelligence oversight typically sets the goals of oversight as "legality, propriety, effectiveness and efficiency."[13] The obscure sphere in which intelligence organizations

---

[8] *See, e.g.,* the "Bus 300 Scandal" and the "Nafsu Scandal" that are further dealt with *infra* notes 47–48.

[9] The range of cases that involve SHABAK includes claims about interrogations, targeted killing, and ethnic profiling. *See* HCJ 1265/11 Public Comm. Against Torture in Israel v. Attorney General [2012] (concerning the procedure for handling complaints of suspects who were interrogated by SHABAK); CrimA 645/05 Zeliger v. The State of Israel (concerning interrogation methods of SHABAK) (Heb.); HCJ 5682/02 Plony v. The Prime Minister (a case involving a group of SHABAK employees who argued against the designated internal supervisor for fear of conflict of interests) (Heb.); LaborA 48783-05012 Plonit v. Comm'r of the Civil Service (an appeal of an acting commander of a unit that her appointment in SHABAK has been reviewed and terminated); HCJ 9416/10 Adallah—the Legal Ctr. for Arab Minority Rights in Israel, et al. v. Ministry of Homeland Sec. and Gen. Sec. Serv. [2013] (concerning an appeal against legislation that exempts SHABAK from audio and video recording of interrogations); HCJ 4797/07 Ass'n for Citizen's Rights in Israel v. Airports Authority, et al [2012] (Heb.) (concerning SHABAK's aviation security procedures that were allegedly based on ethnic profiling). An account has been written by a former legal advisor concerning SHABAK's perspective of its involvement in legal matters. Eli Bahar, *The Role of the Legal Counsel in Security Agencies*, Policy Paper 101 (Israel Democracy Institute, 2013) (Heb.).

[10] The name MOSSAD is an acronym that stands for "The Institution for Intelligence and Special Tasks."

[11] MOSSAD has two additional tasks. First, MOSSAD handles covert diplomatic relations with foreign groups and nations. Second, MOSSAD also provides for the security of Jewish communities around the world. For a general account of MOSSAD's activities and its less well-known tasks such as covert diplomacy, *see* EFRAIM HALEVY, MAN IN THE SHADOWS: INSIDE THE MIDDLE EAST CRISIS WITH A MAN WHO LED THE MOSSAD (2008).

[12] Shmuel Even & Amos Granit, *The Israeli Intelligence Community: Where To?*, 97 INSS MEMORANDA (2009) (Isr.). AMAN's function (among others) as the main intelligence analysis organization is unique in the sense that peer organizations, such as the CIA's Directorate of Intelligence, are typically civilian agencies.

[13] Hans Born & Gabriel Geisler Mesevage, *Tool 1: Introducing Intelligence Oversight, in* OVERSEEING INTELLIGENCE SERVICES: A TOOL KIT 7 (Hans Born & Gabriel Geisler Mesevage eds., 2012). *See*

operate, combined with their immense powers, raises both legal and ethical concerns. Accordingly, intelligence oversight should also verify that the IC is successful and effective in achieving its goals, lest the state become exposed to the risks of surprise attack, terrorism, and threats to national interests.[14]

One can only appreciate the real need for intelligence oversight if the less generalized harms of espionage are listed. Indeed, intelligence collection is a "dirty hands" business. It involves the use of deception, manipulation, surveillance, privacy intrusions, and harsh methods of interrogation. The collection of human intelligence reflects an extreme instance of an instrumental treatment of humans and the commoditization of loyalty to a community or a nation.[15]

The harms resulting from espionage might affect a far broader group than the recruited intelligence agents. The members of the IC who employ problematic means might be affected themselves. Moral lines may become blurred. The selective use of harmful means might become a nonselective habit. When successful officers are promoted, there is a risk that the management level and organizational culture will become morally affected as well. Considering the fact that heads of intelligence organizations may develop political careers, the risk of blurred lines may be exported into the political sphere. The harms of intelligence might affect even wider circles. When targeted effectively, a community that is the target of intelligence efforts might suffer collective harms such as the breakdown of social solidarity.[16]

also Thomas C. Bruneau, *Controlling Intelligence in New Democracies*, 14 INT'L J. INTELLIGENCE & COUNTERINTELLIGENCE 323 (2001); Ian Leigh, *More Closely Watching the Spies: Three Decades of Experience*, *in* WHO'S WATCHING THE SPIES?: ESTABLISHING INTELLIGENCE SERVICE ACCOUNTABILITY 5–6 (Hans Born et al. eds., 2005); Heidi Kitrosser, *Congressional Oversight of National Security Activities: Improving Information Funnels*, 29 CARDOZO L. REV. 1049 (2008); FRANK JOHN SMIST, JR., CONGRESS OVERSEES THE UNITED STATES INTELLIGENCE COMMUNITY (1947–1989) 274–79 (1990); AIDAN WILLS, GUIDEBOOK: UNDERSTANDING INTELLIGENCE OVERSIGHT (2010); Aidan Wills, *Financial Oversight of Intelligence Services*, *in* OVERSEEING INTELLIGENCE SERVICES: A TOOL KIT (Hans Born & Gabriel Geisler Mesevage eds., 2012).

[14] *See, e.g.,* Zachary Goldman's contribution to this volume, which discusses some of the differences between goals of intelligence oversight. There are practical and ethical concerns regarding intelligence failures in alerting surprise attacks. *See* Raphael Bitton, *The Legitimacy of Spying among Nations*, 29 AM. U. INT'L L. REV. 1009 (2014); EPHRAIM KAM, SURPRISE ATTACK: THE VICTIM'S PERSPECTIVE 228–29 (1988).

[15] Raphael Bitton, *Intelligence Agents, Autonomous Slaves and the U.S. Supreme Court's Wrong (and Right) Concept of Personal Autonomy*, 7 EUR. J. LEGAL STUD. 5 (2014); Ross Bellaby, *What's the Harm? The Ethics of Intelligence*, 27(1) INTELLIGENCE & NAT'L SEC. 93 (2012); JOHN P. LANGAN, *Moral Damages and the Justification of Intelligence Collection from Human Sources*, *in* ETHICS OF SPYING: A READER FOR THE INTELLIGENCE PROFESSIONAL 104 (Jan Goldman ed., 2006).

[16] There are social ramifications to espionage by SHABAK and AMAN. *See* YOSIF MAHMOUD HAJ-YAHIA ET AL., ALLEGED PALESTINIAN COLLABORATORS WITH ISRAEL AND THEIR FAMILIES: A STUDY OF VICTIMS OF INTERNAL POLITICAL VIOLENCE 63–66 (1999); HILLEL COHEN, ARMY OF SHADOWS: PALESTINIAN COLLABORATION WITH ZIONISM (1917–1948) 233–36 (2008). For a historical account of American social paranoia due to fear of clandestine communist penetration, *see* RICHARD M. FRIED, NIGHTMARE IN RED: THE McCARTHY ERA IN PERSPECTIVE 3 (1990); ROBERT GRIFFITH, THE POLITICS OF FEAR: JOSEPH R. McCARTHY AND THE SENATE 116 (1987); RICHARD GID POWERS, NOT WITHOUT HONOR: THE HISTORY OF AMERICAN ANTICOMMUNISM 273–74 (1995).

An IC might even harm its own nation and community. Failing to raise the alert on a surprise attack or terrorist act might lead to fatal results. In contrast, a false alert might lead a nation into an unnecessary war or international tension. In a manner similar to an autoimmune disease, which may harm the body by aggressively trying to protect it, intelligence activities might be harmful by disproportionally undermining privacy and basic rights. ICs also can be harmful because they operate in a manner that is inherently opposite to democratic basic principles of transparency, decency, and accountability.

An examination of the existing oversight mechanisms over the Israeli IC reveals that although the circles of potential harm and costs are wide, the means of supervision to ensure cost-effectiveness are limited. I now move to examining the existing oversight mechanisms of the Israeli IC.

V. EXISTING OVERSIGHT MECHANISMS IN ISRAEL
A. Ministerial Supervision

Ministerial supervision of the Israeli IC is divided between the Defense Office and PM's Office. By overseeing the army in general, the Minister of Defense supervises AMAN. Considering that Israeli military intelligence includes Israel's main research and analysis department, SIGINT units, IMINT wing, and most technology-oriented intelligence collection, the Minister of Defense oversees a substantial portion of the IC. The Director of AMAN is also under the command of the IDF Chief of Staff, the commander of the Israeli military.

SHABAK and MOSSAD, Israel's two main human intelligence organizations, are both supervised directly by the PM's Office. Typically, in most democracies, these types of organizations are under the supervision of a minister-level political figure rather than the head of government. Naturally, the very limited availability of the PM raises doubts as to the effectiveness of prime ministerial supervision over the Israeli intelligence services.[17]

In 2009, the role of the Minister for Intelligence and Strategic Affairs was created. Although this position is considered to be the ministerial supervisor of the IC, the heads of the various organizations are subordinated to other ministers, namely the PM (SHABAK and MOSSAD) and the Minister of Defense (AMAN). It is still unclear if this is a meaningful attempt to revolutionize ministerial supervision of intelligence in Israel, or if it is (what many suspect) to be merely a new position with an attractive title nearly empty of meaning.[18] It is safe, however, to summarize this particular type of ministerial supervision in Israel as relatively weak in comparison to similar positions in other Western democracies (such as the Director of National Intelligence in the United States).

Unlike other members of the Israeli IC, SHABAK is statutorily supervised by a Ministerial Committee for the Service's Affairs.[19] The Committee consists of five members, including

---

[17] Some of Israel's leaders such as Ariel Sharon, Yitzhak Rabin, and Menachem Begin have elected at certain periods to keep the Ministry of Defense under their ministerial responsibility. Such periods of an exclusive ministerial control over the IC may reflect a substantial vacuum of supervision.

[18] Even & Granit, *supra* note 12, at 41; Ofer Shelah, *What Does the Minister of Intelligence Affairs Do?*, NRG (Feb. 6, 2009), http://www.nrg.co.il/online/1/ART1/898/191.html (Heb.).

[19] General Security Service Law, 5762-2002, SH No. 1832 § 5 (Isr.).

the PM, the Minister of Defense, the Minister of Justice, and the Minister of Homeland Security.[20] It serves as the government's designated oversight body to which SHABAK submits mandatory reports on its activities not less than once every three months.[21] This Ministerial Committee also approves regulations issued by the PM to govern SHABAK's activity. There is no publicly available information on a parallel ministerial body overseeing MOSSAD or AMAN. However, the Israeli Ministerial Committee for Security and Foreign Policy (the "Cabinet") is the government's supreme executive forum on issues of defense and intelligence. Consequently, even if its oversight is limited in scope, the Cabinet fulfills some role of ministerial supervision over the entire IC.

B. Parliamentary Supervision

Parliamentary supervision of the Israeli IC is conducted mainly by the Sub-Committee for Intelligence and Secret Services of the Committee for Security and Foreign Affairs (the "Sub-Committee"). The Sub-Committee also serves as the statutory parliamentary oversight committee for the implementation of the General Security Service Law (SHABAK Law). It performs its oversight functions in two main formats: routine oversight and special inquiries.

In its routine oversight capacity, the Sub-Committee conducts closed-door hearings with senior intelligence officers and receives regular reports from the various intelligence services.[22] The Sub-Committee may also function as a parliamentary inquiry committee. In the past, it has investigated the Jonathan Pollard Scandal (1985), the frustrated attempt to kill Hamas leader Khaled Mashaal in Jordan (1997), the intelligence collection and analysis concerning Iraq's weapons of mass destruction (2004), and the suicide of a former Mossad employee who was arrested and held in total secrecy in an Israeli prison (2013).[23]

C. The Committee of Heads of Services

Although not formally an oversight mechanism, the Committee of Heads of Services (VARASH) addresses some of the purposes of intelligence oversight. The VARASH is essentially a coordination body of four members: Director of the MOSSAD, Director of the SHABAK, Director of AMAN, and the Prime Minister's Military Secretary. Among all the purposes of overseeing intelligence, the VARASH can be most effective in increasing efficacy (by sharing information, targets, expertise, and human resources) and by avoiding

---

[20] *Id.* at § 5(b). The four appointments described in the statute are mandatory. The fifth appointment is discretionary.

[21] *Id.* at § 12 (Isr.).

[22] SHABAK submits mandatory reports to the Sub-Committee on its activity and the use of special intrusive means.

[23] *See* Sub-Committee for Intelligence Services, KNESSET.GOV, http://www.knesset.gov.il/committees/heb/docs/defense_17_6.pdf (Heb.) (last visited Jan. 9, 2016); REPORT OF THE SUB-COMMITTEE FOR INTELLIGENCE SERVICES OF THE KNESSET, JONATHAN POLLARD (1987), *available at* http://www.knesset.gov.il/committees/heb/docs/bitachon11.pdf (Heb.); KNESSET FOREIGN AFFAIRS AND DEFENCE COMM., THE COMMITTEE OF ENQUIRY INTO THE INTELLIGENCE SYSTEM IN LIGHT OF THE WAR IN IRAQ (2004), *available at* http://www.knesset.gov.il/committees/eng/docs/intelligence_complete.pdf.

unnecessary redundancy in allocating resources. The VARASH has no statutory capacity. Its resolutions are legally non-binding, and history has demonstrated that its effectiveness is very much dependent upon the personal relations among the directors of the services at any given time.[24]

D. Legal Counsel

Some of the most powerful elements in supervising and overseeing the Israeli IC are the various legal advisors. All three main intelligence organizations in Israel operate under the scrutiny of the attorney general (legal advisor to the Israeli government). In addition, all three intelligence services have their own internal legal advisors.[25] These legal advisors address all aspects of intelligence oversight. They are focused, however, on verifying the propriety and legality of the particular organization's activity rather than on improving efficiency.

This chapter argues that Israel's concept of intelligence oversight leans heavily toward legal and judicial mechanisms. Two supposedly independent bodies, the legal advisors and the judiciary, perform the legal scrutiny. As elaborated in Section VI, the phenomenon of strong legal departments within the intelligence agencies has evolved over the last 30 years. It affects mainly the SHABAK.[26] It also affects AMAN given the strong position of military counsels. The MOSSAD, as a foreign intelligence organization, is the least affected by this phenomenon. The MOSSAD is less affected by the internal authority of its legal advisors because the MOSSAD is less exposed to judicial intervention in its foreign intelligence mission, which is the factor that most empowers the legal advisors within the SHABAK and AMAN.

E. State Comptroller and Internal Supervisor

Normally a former judge, the State Comptroller manages a relatively large team of investigators that examine all aspects of governmental activity. The Comptroller enjoys a high level of independence. Historically, reports from the State Comptroller have not focused on the IC. In recent years, however, the IC seems less immune to the Comptroller's inquiries.[27]

---

[24] During the early 1960s, close relations between the directors of MOSSAD and AMAN led to unprecedented successful cooperation between the agencies. *See* Granit & Even, *supra* note 12, at 22. AMAN and SHABAK similarly managed to reach a successful understanding between the agencies' directors concerning intelligence collection and analysis in the occupied territories. *Id.* at 39. In contrast, during years 2000–2007, members of the VARASH did not manage to overcome old disagreements. *Id.* at 40, 42–44.

[25] For two recent accounts of the role of SHABAK legal advisors, *see* Eli Bahar, *The Role of the Legal Counsel in Security Agencies*, Policy Paper 101 (Israel Democracy Institute, 2013) (Isr.); ARIE ROTTER, ISR. NAT'L DEF. COLL. RESEARCH CTR., ON THE MISSION AND CONCEPT OF ROLES OF GATEKEEPERS IN INTELLIGENCE ORGANIZATIONS: THE CASE OF THE ISRAELI SECURITY AGENCY (2009).

[26] The SHABAK website's description of the work of the legal directorate best illustrates the strong position and deep involvement of the legal advisors in the operational and strategic aspects of SHABAK activities. *General Security Service Legal Department.* SHABAK.GOV, http://www.shabak.gov.il/about/yoamash/Pages/yoamash-page.aspx (last visited June 6, 2015) (Heb.).

[27] Intelligence-related issues have been a focus of the Comptroller's investigations. For example, the Comptroller investigated the deadly accident that occurred during the training of Israel's top elite unit, Sayeret Matkal (supervised directly by the Chief of AMAN). Allegedly, the accident happened while the team was preparing for an operation targeting the killing of the then-Iraqi president, Saddam Hussein. THE STATE COMPTROLLER, A REPORT ON THE FINDINGS OF THE INQUIRY CONCERNING THE "ZEELIM B" DISASTER (1999) (Isr.).

Recently, even the MOSSAD's sensitive units have become a subject of its reports and harsh criticism.[28] Nevertheless, the Comptroller seems to be focused mainly on the procedural issues of proper management rather than on reviewing the way discretion is applied and operational decisions are taken.

The State Comptroller inspects the intelligence services in tandem with their respective internal supervisors. The Supervisor of the Defense System, in addition to the national Inspector General, supervises AMAN.[29] Each of the two other civil organizations, SHABAK and MOSSAD, has its own internal supervisor that serves as an inspector general-like official within the respective organizations.[30] Between the two organizations, only the internal supervisor of the SHABAK acts according to a statutory mandate.[31] All three supervisors also act as ombudsmen and examine employee complaints.[32] The positions of all three supervisors are characterized by the inherent tension between their organizational affiliation and the need to constitute an objective and "external" supervising arm.[33]

F. Internal Investigations

The ability to effectively investigate apparent criminal offenses conducted in relation to intelligence activities is an additional oversight mechanism. When criminal offenses reflect a security risk, such as espionage, then SHABAK is the authorized investigating agency. In other cases, the authority changes according to the organization and the relevant circumstances.[34]

Under the radar of public awareness, the State Comptroller also looked into the interrelatedness of the different research components of the community. THE STATE COMPTROLLER, REPORT NO. 50A: ASPECTS OF INTERRELATIONS AMONG RESEARCH ELEMENTS WITHIN THE INTELLIGENCE COMMUNITY (1999) (Isr.).

[28] Yuval Azulay, *Comptroller Slams Mossad for Wasting Money*, GLOBES (Mar. 29, 2011, 16:32), http://www.globes.co.il/en/article-1000634291.

[29] AVIEZER YAARI, CIVIL CONTROL OF THE IDF (2004) (Isr.), *available at* http://www.inss.org.il/uploadImages/systemFiles/Memo%2072.pdf (Heb.).

[30] ROTTER, *supra* note 25.

[31] There are different academic approaches to internal supervision generally as well as the role of the SHABAK supervisor in particular. *See id.* Although it lacks a statutory mandate, it is believed that the MOSSAD has its own internal supervisor.

[32] General Security Service Law, 5762-2002, SH No. 1832 § 13(d) (Isr.).

[33] Consider the tension between the *embedded* and the *external* approach to internal supervision. *See* ROTTER, *supra* note 25. Due to its statutory position, the structural aspects of SHABAK's internal supervision can be examined more closely. Its supervision work is characterized by a marginal public footprint. The internal supervisor of the SHABAK reports directly to the PM and not to the Director of SHABAK. General Security Service Law, 5762-2002, SH No. 1832 § 13 (Isr.). However, the internal supervisor's independence seems limited because he or she is also expected to perform tasks assigned to the supervisor by the Director of SHABAK. *Id.* at § 13(d). The Internal Supervisor of SHABAK is also required to submit mandatory reports to the Ministerial Oversight Committee and to the Parliamentary Sub-Committee. *Id.* § 13(e)(5).

[34] Offenses committed by AMAN officers are investigated by the Interrogations Branch of the Military Police. Suspects who are MOSSAD employees, unless suspected of a security-related offense, are supposed to be treated like ordinary citizens. SHABAK employees, due to their continuous close relations with the police, are subject to investigations by the Department for Police Investigations within the Ministry of Justice. Police Ordinance § 49(j).

Internal investigations concerning interrogations by SHABAK are performed by the MAVTAN (Supervisor of Complaints of the Interrogated).

Interrogations represent the element of intelligence work that is most prone to ethical and legal misconduct such as torture. Interrogators operating behind closed doors to secretly search for potentially lifesaving information offers fertile ground for misconduct. For instance, during the 1980s, a series of scandals revealed an organizational culture in the SHABAK in which force was used in interrogations and SHABAK officers submitted false testimonies in court.

The Landau Report and the "Torture Case" of the Supreme Court probably rooted out this organizational culture of misconduct. The Landau Report asserted the Court's authority over SHABAK.[35] The Supreme Court, by equating SHABAK's interrogation authority to that of the police, put an end to the ex-ante regulated use of force during interrogations of suspected terrorists.[36] Still, the investigation of complaints from interrogated suspects is a credible and effective mechanism for preventing a relapse to a culture of misconduct.

Fulfilling that role, the MAVTAN investigates complaints against interrogators in a balanced manner. On the one hand, the MAVTAN offers an accessible, credible, safe, and effective mechanism for handling complaints. On the other hand, the MAVTAN prevents the abuse of the complaint procedure by screening out frivolous complaints made as a means to expose interrogation methods, or meant to increase political pressure on the SHABAK and its interrogators.

All complaints of interrogated suspects are submitted to the MAVTAN.[37] Following extensive pressure by NGOs and a series of appeals to the Supreme Court, SHABAK eventually agreed that the MAVTAN would no longer be an employee of the SHABAK. Accordingly, the office currently resides within the Ministry of Justice, and serves as a preliminary mechanism for reviewing complaints against interrogators. If a criminal investigation is recommended by the MAVTAN, the Department for Police Investigations in the Ministry of Justice is responsible for conducting it.[38]

---

[35] COMMISSION OF INQUIRY INTO THE METHODS OF INVESTIGATION OF THE GENERAL SECURITY SERVICE REGARDING HOSTILE TERRORIST ACTIVITIES, LANDAU COMMISSION REPORT (1987) [hereinafter "LANDAU COMMISSION REPORT"]. The Landau Report was issued by the Inquiry Committee concerning the Methods of Interrogation of the General Security Service on Terrorist Activity. The Committee, headed by former Supreme Court justice Moshe Landau, concluded that SHABAK interrogators routinely used physical pressure. In October 1987, the Israeli cabinet approved its final report, which laid down guidelines for the use of a "moderate measure of physical pressure."

[36] The Supreme Court did not, however, rule out the application of the doctrine of necessity during interrogations. This defense may immunize an interrogator from criminal responsibility for torture. The Court determined, however, that the defense of necessity could only be granted ex post and never serve as a regulated defense ex ante. See HCJ 5100/94 Pub. Comm. against Torture v. Gov't of Israel 53(4) PD [1999].

[37] Complaints could possibly be submitted through a lawyer, a family relative, or an NGO. It should be noted that the function of MAVTAN is solely devoted to reviewing SHABAK's interrogations.

[38] The Supreme Court is deeply involved in this process, practically guiding the SHABAK, as well as the attorney general and even the Parliament, about the right process for internal investigations of interrogation-related complaints. See, e.g., HCJ 1265/11 The Public Committee against Torture in Israel v. The Attorney General [2012]. It was argued that during the years 2001–2008, the MAVTAN decided that 598 out of 598 complaints did not justify the opening of a criminal investigation. Only in a few cases was a disciplinary process against SHABAK employees opened, and in several cases internal regulations were amended. The Supreme Court

G. *Judicial Scrutiny*

This chapter argues that there is a strong tendency toward "legalistic" methods of overseeing the IC in Israel.[39] Among the forms of legal oversight, judicial scrutiny is exceptionally powerful. Section VI will present evidence of the power of judicial scrutiny in Israel. Section VII offers potential explanations for this unique preference. This section is therefore limited to outlining the various methods through which courts in Israel scrutinize intelligence-related activity.

The Israeli IC is exposed to judicial scrutiny in every main legal field: constitutional law, administrative law, criminal law, and civil law. No agency enjoys any type of a priori immunity. The fact that no writ of certiorari is required in order for a petition to be heard by the Israeli Supreme Court reflects the high degree of exposure to judicial scrutiny that Israeli agencies receive. Since the Supreme Court has essentially narrowed the standing doctrine to a marginal threshold requirement and allowed NGOs and third parties to act as "public petitioners," there are few barriers to legal scrutiny of the IC.[40]

Intelligence affairs are normally subject to judicial scrutiny on issues relating to public law and international law. Another significant basis for legal scrutiny is criminal law. Criminal judges oversee intelligence during various phases of criminal procedure: when approving arrest requests for suspects in security offenses, when overseeing the extension of preventive detentions,[41] and when hearing criminal cases against suspected terrorists and spies.[42] Furthermore, intelligence matters can sometimes be at the center of civil cases. Claims for

---

reaffirmed the legality of the process, but sent a clear message to the MAVTAN that it will look into specific complaints as a means to prevent inappropriate results in the long-term. *See also* HCJ 1447/04 The Center for Protecting the Individual v. The General Attorney (unpublished); HCJ 3533/08 Sweti v. The Minister of Defense (unpublished) (Heb.); HCJ 6138/10 The Center for Protecting the Individual v. The General Attorney (unpublished) (Heb.).

[39] Although this section focuses on judicial scrutiny as an overseeing mechanism in Israel, the view of the judicial arm as an oversight system is not unique to Israel. Frederic F. Manget, *Intelligence and the Rise of Judicial Intervention, in* HANDBOOK OF INTELLIGENCE STUDIES 43 (Loch K. Johnson ed., 2009).

[40] The reduced threshold requirements also applies to Palestinians from the West Bank and the Gaza Strip. DAVID KRETZMER, THE OCCUPATION OF JUSTICE: THE SUPREME COURT OF ISRAEL AND THE OCCUPIED TERRITORIES 24–25 (2002).

[41] The Supreme Court has ruled on preventative detentions by SHABAK. HCJ 3267/12 Halala & Diab v. Military Commander of Judea and Samaria [2012] (unpublished). The Supreme Court has considered cases involving various aspects of the administrative arrests made by SHABAK in the West Bank and Gaza. HCJ 317/13 Mamduh Abra v. Military Commander [2013] (in which the Supreme Court ruled that the Court must be the detainee's solicitor in these proceedings and hence must carefully review on his behalf the confidential intelligence material). Accordingly, in HCJ 2320/98 El- Amla v. The Military Commander of Judea and Samaria, 52(3) PD [1998] (Heb.), the Supreme Court insisted on releasing a suspect from detention against SHABAK's recommendation. In HCJ 3239/02 Marab v. Military Commander of Judea and Samaria 57(2) PD [2002], the Supreme Court nullified ad hoc legislation that permitted longer administrative arrests during a massive military conflict. Even the shortage of SHABAK interrogators did not serve to justify the ad hoc legislation.

[42] The Yehuda Gil case is an exemplary criminal one that dealt with intelligence. SCC 3166/99 Yehuda Ben-Moshe Gil v. The State of Israel, PD 54(4) 193. In that case, the Court seems to have neglected its oversight role and approved of designating Gil as a spy. In fact, Gil spied for Israel. By making fraudulent reports of meetings where his agent never arrived, he committed a criminal offense. Although he was technically spying, his actions did not qualify as criminal espionage.

damages by former intelligence agents of the SHABAK are just one example. Whereas American intelligence agencies are generally immune from claims by former agents,[43] Israeli courts are open to hearing such claims.[44]

In addition, it should be noted that alongside traditional forms of judicial scrutiny there exist judicial-like methods of scrutiny. For instance, SHABAK serves as the security clearance authority. All employees of the Israeli intelligence and defense communities are required to go through SHABAK's security clearance check. The negative implications of a clearance denial are clear: such a resolution undermines the employee's freedom of occupation, which is otherwise protected under the Basic Law: Freedom of Occupation. Denial of a security clearance also affects the designated employee's income and even her reputation and dignity. Therefore, while acting in its capacity as the supreme authority for security clearance, SHABAK is subjected to a judicial-like scrutiny.[45]

H. Nongovernmental Organizations (NGOs)

Review of the milestones of intelligence-related litigation leaves very little in doubt about the important role of NGOs in overseeing intelligence in Israel. Having information and resources, NGOs are the catalysts of many petitions and legal proceedings, maintain a high profile in parliamentary hearings (mainly concerning security-related legislation), and are effective in raising public awareness.[46]

I. Media Coverage

Many intelligence scandals would have been buried forever unless brought into daylight thanks to investigative reporting. In Israel, this form of oversight has proven to be both

---

[43] See Tenet v. Doe, 544 U.S. 1 (2005).

[44] See, e.g., lawsuits from family members that sought a claim for recognition and compensation following the loss of their relatives who allegedly operated as agents for SHABAK. CC (Jer) 1260/98 Halwa Abu-Labda v. State of Israel; CC 467/95 (Jer.) Raida Bat-Omar Muhammad Armush v. State of Israel, Dinim 32(2) 156. The Court heard a case where the SHABAK officers showed cooperation by sharing information from their records. In fact, SHABAK did not even argue for non-justiciability. A petition to the Supreme Court by Jonathan Pollard led the Israeli government to issue an official release in which it recognized his role as an intelligence agent and assumed responsibility for his activity. HCJ 2633/97 Pollard v. The Prime Minister. In contrast, the U.S. Supreme Court ruled that a contract between an agent and a case officer is unenforceable in court. Totten v. United States, 92 U.S. 105 (1875). It seems the U.S. Supreme Court even bans the filing of such a lawsuit. Tenet, 544 U.S. 1. See also Webster v. Doe, 486 U.S. 592 (1988); CIA v. Sims, 471 U.S. 159 (1985); Goung v. United States, 860 F.2d 1063 (Fed. Cir. 1988). These examples emphasize the need to seek an explanation of the unique legal approach of both the Israeli IC and the Israeli Supreme Court. The conclusion from these cases is that SHABAK is a willing, rather than an involuntary, player.

[45] Any person affected by SHABAK's decision on security clearance can lodge a complaint with a special statutory committee. The committee consists of three members and is chaired by a former judge of the Court of Appeals. The fact that all its members are appointed by the prime minister seems to diminish its apparent independence. General Security Service Law, 5762-2002, SH No. 1832 § 15(b)(1) (Isr.).

[46] Infra note 69. For a critique of NGOs' "Lawfare" activity concerning Israeli activity in Gaza, see NGO Monitor, The NGO Front in the Gaza War: The Durban Strategy Continues, in NGO MONITOR MONOGRAPH SERIES (Gerald M. Steinberg ed., 2009).

effective and valuable, as the Bus 300 Scandal clearly demonstrated.[47] During this episode, hijackers of a bus were reported by SHABAK to have been killed during the hostage rescue by the authorities, but eventually the public learned from a photo taken by a journalist that they were in fact killed in custody after the takeover. The power of investigative reporting was further underscored by the disclosure of photos of SHABAK leaders, which ignited the "Nafsu Scandal."[48] In this case, an Israeli army officer was unjustifiably sentenced to long years in prison for espionage when in fact his interrogation involved the use of force, threats, and lying in court.

Media scrutiny, along with the legal scrutiny of the attorney general and state attorney, initiated the inquiry that led to the Landau Commission's revelation that the SHABAK had applied force in interrogating suspects and developed an organizational culture of systematic lying in court.[49] The change in SHABAK's culture was immediate and radical.[50] The SHABAK's remarkable record in terms of preventing terror, unharmed by the reforms that followed the affair, makes one wonder if the organizations in the world that have not gone through a "Bus 300-like scandal" are not those that one needs to fear most.

Nevertheless, in some cases, the media can itself create an intelligence event. For instance, the attempt by Mordechai Va'anunu, a former Israeli nuclear technician, to disclose the secret details of Israel's alleged nuclear weapon to a foreign newspaper has been labeled by the Israeli Court as an instance of espionage.[51]

---

[47] In fact, in one case it took only a single photo in one newspaper to change Israeli intelligence forever. The photo showed two SHABAK agents holding and leading a captured, *living* terrorist who had been part of a group that had hijacked a bus. The photo was taken minutes after an elite unit took over the bus and successfully rescued the hostages. Soon after the attack, an IDF spokesman announced that all terrorists were killed during the takeover. The photo shocked the public because it revealed that SHABAK had acted in a normative vacuum, and terrorists were intentionally killed after being arrested alive. Top leaders of SHABAK had manipulated an inquiry committee and obstructed justice. In the end, the photo ignited one of Israel's biggest scandals, known as the "Bus 300 Scandal." *See* Eyal Pascovich, *Not above the Law: Shin Bet's (Israel Security Agency) Democratization and Legalization Process*, 1 J. INTELLIGENCE HIST. 54 (2015).

[48] Nafsu, an Israeli officer, was forced to confess to charges of espionage he did not commit. Only after Nafsu spent seven years in prison was it revealed that his confession was the result of a brutal interrogation, including threats he could not resist. *Nafsu Affair 1987*, SHABAK.GOV, http://www.shabak.gov.il/ShowListItem. aspx?listid=List14&itemid=20 (last visited June 6, 2015) (Heb.).

[49] *See* LANDAU COMMISSION REPORT, *supra* note 35.

[50] Arie Rotter, *A Decade since the Supreme Court Decision on Interrogations (H.C.J. 5100/94)—A Successful Gamble*, INTERNATIONAL INSTITUTE FOR COUNTER-TERRORISM (Feb. 21, 2010), http://www.ict. org.il/Article/408/A%20Decade%20Since%20the%20Supreme%20Court%20Decision%20%20on%20 Interrogations%20%28%20HCJ%205100094%29%20-%20A%20Successful%20Gamble.

[51] According to the Court: "The fact that these news are published to all of our enemy countries and their agents, at the same time, with no exceptions, and to all the terrorist groups out there, doubles and triples the severity of the action. The assemblage of our enemies is keeping a close watch on every secret information that might arrive from Israel in order to deepen its knowledge; and here, each and every one of them is being served with secret information, on a silver plate, without any effort." CrimA 172/88 Mordechai Vaanunu v. The State of Israel, 44(3) PD 265, 299 (Heb.). CrimA 8445/11 Anat Kam v. The State of Israel [2012] (Heb.) involved a similar case where a young soldier leaked thousands of top secret documents to a journalist (Uri Blau of Haaretz). Both SHABAK and Supreme Court Justice Meltzer seem to have made a clear distinction between the right of the journalist to gather information and the duty of the soldier to refrain from communicating secrets, deeming a breach of the latter duty to be an act of espionage.

VI. THE UNIQUE PREFERENCE FOR LEGALIST OVERSIGHT

This chapter argues that judicial and legal scrutiny is the most prominent means of intelligence oversight in Israel. In this section I outline the elements of the Israeli preference for judicial oversight. In other words, I show how judicial and legal scrutiny have proven to be both powerful and preferable in Israel. In Section VII, I offer two potential explanations for this exceptional preference.

A. Proven Legal Supremacy

One of the most important signs of the influence of the legal community in overseeing intelligence in Israel is the central and decisive role that legal personas played in the main intelligence-related scandals of the past. The "Bus 300" Scandal seems to represent the point in time in which the legal system asserted its supremacy. In the rare frontal clash between the leaders of the SHABAK and the leaders of the legal community, the attorney general, the state attorney, and the Supreme Court prevailed. Ever since the "Bus 300" Scandal, the supremacy of the rule of law over intelligence (at least in the domestic realm) has only expanded.[52]

The Landau Committee, chaired by the chief justice, marked another instance of legal supremacy over the IC by eliminating a legal double standard between citizens and agencies on the one hand, and the intelligence services on the other hand. In response, SHABAK submitted to the new condition of only one rule, namely the rule of law. The process continued in the "Torture Case," in which the Supreme Court invalidated SHABAK's special permits for applying "moderate physical pressure" in the interrogations of terrorists. SHABAK submitted to the new reality and did not seek new legislative authority from Parliament.

B. All Aspects of Intelligence Are Scrutinized

The most important indication of the high measure of judicial scrutiny of intelligence in Israel is the wide and unprecedented spectrum of intelligence-related matters subjected to judicial scrutiny. The Supreme Court has heard and issued verdicts or preliminary orders on the legitimacy of Israel's policy of targeted killing in the West Bank and Gaza Strip,[53] the legitimacy of applying physical pressure in interrogations of suspected terrorists,[54] and the legitimacy of the preventive detention of Hezbollah members and others who were held as "bargaining chips" in exchange for missing Israeli soldiers.[55] The extent of judicial scrutiny was demonstrated when the Supreme Court decided to hear the lawsuit of an enemy combatant that was filed against intelligence officers. A Lebanese Hezbollah leader who was

---

[52] Consider Eyal Pascovich's historical account of this process. *See* Pascovich, *supra* note 47. *See also* Rotter, *supra* note 25.

[53] HCJ 769/02 Pub. Comm. Against Torture in Israel v. Gov't of Israel 62(1) PD [2006].

[54] HCJ 5100/94 Pub. Comm. Against Torture in Israel v. Gov't of Israel 53(4) PD [1999].

[55] Originally, the Court approved the preventive detention. Prev. Det. A. 10/94 Plonim v. The Minister of Defense (1997). However, Chief Justice Barak reconvened the Supreme Court for an additional hearing in which he personally, and in a rare manner, amended his opinion from the first hearing (Further Crim. A. 7048/97 Plonim v. The Minister of Defense, PD 54(1) 721 (2000)).

captured and released later filed a civil lawsuit against the state for damages allegedly suffered at the hands of Unit 504 interrogators in a secret facility.[56] Only when the claimant returned to Lebanon and to his senior role in Hezbollah did the Supreme Court order the suspension of the lawsuit for so long as the conflict is active.[57]

The Israeli Court also heard a lawsuit by members of the SHABAK's VIP Security Division against the intelligence service,[58] a petition against ethnic-based profiling guided by SHABAK in Israel's airports,[59] the petitions of families of former recruited human sources of SHABAK,[60] and petitions against censorship concerning details of MOSSAD senior officials.[61] The Israeli Court also scrutinized the authority and the process of conducting internal screening of complaints against SHABAK by interrogated persons.[62]

This wide spectrum of intervention is part of a larger process of growing judicial involvement in matters of law and national security. Accordingly, the Israeli Court heard cases involving the legality of employing phosphorous-based bombs in Gaza, humanitarian needs in times of warfare, the use of preventative detentions, and the order permitting the IDF to use the voluntary assistance of local Palestinians to offer safe surrender to wanted terrorists.[63] The Court similarly heard cases on the legitimacy of demolishing the houses of terrorists, deporting terrorists, and the legitimacy of the route of the separation barrier with the Palestinians.[64]

---

[56] As previously mentioned, "Unit 504" is AMAN's HUMINT collection unit.

[57] Civil Further Appeal 5698/11 State of Israel v. Dirani (Heb.); Civil Application of Appeal 993/06 State of Israel v. Dirani (Heb.).

[58] Labor Case 8420/05 (TA) Ploni v. SHABAK (Heb.).

[59] HCJ 4797/07 Ass'n for Citizen's Rights in Israel (Heb.).

[60] *See Abu-Labda* and *Armush* cases, *supra* note 44.

[61] HCJ 680/88 Meir Snitzer et al. v. Military Censor and Minister of Defense, 42(4) PD 617 [1989]. In an earlier case, the former mythological head of MOSSAD, Harel, filed a petition against the government's resolution not to approve the publication of his book's manuscript. HCJ 130/68 Isser Harel v. The Government of Israel, 59(1) PD 241 [2005]. The verdict itself was only released in 2005.

[62] HCJ 1265/11 Pub. Comm. Against Torture in Israel [2012]; HCJ 1266/11 Mahmoud Sweiti v. The Attorney General (Heb.).

[63] HCJ 4764/04 Physicians for Human Rights v. IDF Commander in Gaza, 58(5) PD 385 [2004] (on the supply of basic resources [food, water, electricity, medical], during combat in Gaza); HCJ 3799/02 Adalah—Legal Ctr. for Arab Minority Rights in Israel v. Commander of Cent. Command [2005] (on the use of voluntary assistance by local Palestinians during arrest operations); HCJ 4146/11 Yoav Hess & 116 Petitioners v. Chief of Staff [2013] (Isr.) (on adjudicating on the IDF's use of white phosphorous bombs in populated areas).

[64] The Court has heard a long list of security-related cases. For example, the Court heard cases on preventive detentions. *See, e.g.,* HCJ 317/13 Mamduh Abra v. The Commander of IDF Forces in the West Bank Military Court of Appeals; HCJ 2320/98, El-Amla v. The Military Commander of Judea and Samaria (Heb.); HCJ 3239/02 Marab v. IDF Commander in the West Bank, and Judea and Samaria Brigade Headquarters. Cases have also been heard involving the demolition of the houses of terrorists and the deportation of suspected terrorists. *See, e.g.,* HCJ 358/88 Ass'n for Civil Rights in Israel v. Cent. District Commander [1989]. The Court has also considered the legality of the separation barrier. *See* HCJ 2056/04 Beit Sourik Village Council v. Israel & Commander of the IDF Forces in the West Bank 58(5) PD 807 [2004]; HCJ 7957/04 Mara`abe v. Prime Minister of Israel [2005]; HCJ 2056/04 Manzur v. The State of Israel [2006].

C. Lack of Independent Alternatives

The preference for the judicial method of intelligence oversight is also demonstrated by the relative weakness of other potential alternatives. A comparative view of the Israeli IC indicates that two typical components are missing. First, the system lacks a professional linking point between the political leader and the elements of the community. The community has no "Director of National Intelligence" equivalent because the heads of SHABAK and MOSSAD report directly to the PM. Both the Minister for Intelligence Affairs and the Head of the Security Council are far from functioning as a serious hub for intelligence coordination.[65]

The other missing elements in the Israeli structure are public authorities devoted to independently overseeing intelligence organizations. The structural equivalents to the German G-10 Commission (G-10), the Canadian Security Intelligence Review Committee (SIRC), or the American Privacy and Civil Liberties Oversight Board (PCLOB) do not exist in Israel. Ongoing supervision is mostly in the hands of the legal advisors and the Court. Claims against violations of constitutional rights by the intelligence organizations seem to have one main route: the judicial one.

Prior to explaining the preference for legal and judicial oversight, one needs to offer an explanation for the very ability of the judicial system to serve as a substitute oversight body. Indeed, courts generally are expected to be limited in overseeing intelligence. They are designed to verify lawfulness and resolve specific disputes. Courts are also reactive in nature. They cannot look into an intelligence-related matter on their own initiative. Because prevention of future harm is not the modus operandi of courts, in most cases, they can only offer an ex post resolution to the issues they address. Courts typically limit their resolution to resolving the specific case in front of them, and hence are limited in their review of a *policy* in general.

Effective intelligence oversight, however, requires totally different institutional competencies. Beyond ensuring legality, it requires that other aspects of intelligence activities be monitored, such as ethics and efficacy. Intelligence oversight must be *ongoing* rather than limited to passively responding to a filed claim. Compared to special oversight bodies, courts also suffer from limited resources, including time and expertise. If we realize that courts are very limited in overseeing intelligence, a preliminary question arises as to how Israeli courts managed to become (and remain) the primary vehicle of supervision.

D. Overcoming the Judicial Shortcomings in Oversight

In this section I argue that the judicial supremacy in intelligence oversight in Israel has been maintained by, inter alia, applying various adaptations to the judicial process that are unique to the Israeli context. These adaptations address the deficiencies of the judicial system described above, such as being responsive, acting ex post, and lacking professional expertise in matters of intelligence.

The Supreme Court addressed these deficiencies by practically abolishing the standing doctrine; by reducing to nearly zero the limitations on justiciability of security-related issues;

---

[65] As previously noted, recent governments have established the Office of the Minister of Intelligence Affairs.

by hearing espionage-related cases that are not heard in the U.S. and the U.K. courts; by hearing appeals against policies rather than acts; by adapting a flexible judicial process concerning intelligence matters (which literally enables the court to "manage," rather than rule on a case); and by applying proportionality tests that allow the Court to overcome its lack of expertise.[66]

From the Supreme Court's perspective, preventing the rise of alternative routes of scrutiny required that all potential claims be diverted to the judiciary. One way of closing the doors of potential competitors is to open the Court's doors wide open. This could be achieved, in theory, by increasing the pool of potential petitioners, or by extending the scope of justiciable matters. In Israel, the Court's doors were opened to the widest extent by allowing both.

The first step toward reducing threshold limitations was the abolishment of the doctrine of standing. Originally, the standing doctrine served as a filter for the Court to refrain from dealing with theoretical petitions that concern policy issues rather than specific disputes. Petitioners had to show a direct interest in resolving the dispute rather than a general interest in the larger policy debate. In a gradual process, the Supreme Court narrowed the standing doctrine to reflect a nearly nonexistent limitation on filing petitions.[67] Moreover, the status of public petitioners has been recognized, and they may officially argue for the public's interest rather than their own.[68]

Abolishing the standing doctrine and recognizing the status of public petitioners directly influenced the number and nature of the petitions on matters of law and national security. NGOs that are the typical public petitioners normally attack *policies* rather than a *specific act*. They are repeat players with a high degree of expertise. Indeed, due to its quick and decisive resolution of matters, the Court constitutes an attractive route for NGOs on issues of intelligence and security. The Israeli Supreme Court can also offer a "consensus bypass." Issues of intelligence and national security generally are characterized by a great deal of public support of the government. The Supreme Court, by both not necessarily reflecting consensus popular public opinion and by enjoying a high degree of independence, offers an escape route from

---

[66] *See, e.g.,* HCJ 2056/04 Beit Sourik Village Council v. Israel & Commander of the IDF Forces in the West Bank 58(5) PD 807 [2004].

[67] Former Chief Justice Aharon Barak points at the *Aloni* case as the turning point in the Court's drastic narrowing of the doctrine of standing. HCJ 852/86 Aloni v. The Minister of Justice, 41(2) PD 1, 22–25 (1987); AHARON BARAK, THE JUDGE IN A DEMOCRACY 191 (2008).

[68] HCJ 910/86 Ressler v. Minister of Defense 42(2) PD 441, 472 [1988]. The consideration of the legality of targeted killings is a powerful example of the unique Israeli approach. The Israeli Supreme Court has heard and issued a verdict on the matter. HCJ 769/02 Pub. Comm. Against Torture in Israel v. Gov't of Israel 62(1) PD [2006]. The case was heard in response to a petition filed by an NGO. The petition attacked the legality of the policy in general. The U.S. case of *Al-Aulaqi v. Obama* stands in contradistinction. *Al-Aulaqi v. Obama,* 727 F. Supp. 2d 1 (D.D.C. 2010). The father of al-Aulaqi, a senior al-Qaida operative targeted by the United States who also happened to be an American citizen, filed a petition to attack the legality of the then-expected targeted killing of his son. On December 7, 2010, in what seems unbelievable in the eyes of Israeli jurists, the U.S. District Court dismissed the case on the basis of lack of standing and non-justiciability. LISA HAJJAR, LAWFARE AND ARMED CONFLICT: COMPARING ISRAELI AND US TARGETED KILLING POLICIES AND CHALLENGES AGAINST THEM (2013), *available at* http://www.aub.edu.lb/ifi/international_affairs/documents/20130129ifi_pc_ia_research_report_lawfare.pdf.

mainstream political pressures and security positions. Accordingly, many of the important petitions are initiated by NGOs on general policy issues concerning law and intelligence.[69]

Israeli courts further extended their scrutiny to issues that are not justiciable in other liberal countries. For instance, as part of limiting the standing doctrine and in compliance with its newly developed notion of justiciability, Israeli courts have heard the petitions of a very large number of former agents and former human sources.[70] Typically, the agents or their families will seek protection or compensation.[71] In contrast, in a series of rulings, the U.S. Supreme Court determined claims of intelligence agents to be non-justiciable.[72] A similar gap in the judicial approach to justiciability is demonstrated in targeted killing cases. While similar cases were dismissed in the United States and the U.K., the Israeli Supreme Court heard an intelligence-related, targeted killing case.[73]

Generally speaking, judicial scrutiny only cures harms ex post and lacks the ability to oversee an activity in an *ongoing* manner. The rational judicial preference for the avoidance of competition in intelligence oversight therefore may have led to the adaption of a more flexible format of judicial review. In intelligence-related cases, the Supreme Court frequently elects to "manage" the case rather than simply move to an immediate resolution. One technique for achieving that goal is to stall the proceedings. Rather than issuing a verdict, the Court simply holds the case pending. In some cases, it has held a case pending after bringing the state and the appellant to mutually agreed terms for this "interim" period.[74] During the stalled interim period, the Court becomes a de facto supervisor of an *ongoing* process. It participates in shaping reality in "real time," rather than deciding on the legality of an act ex post. In so doing, it has abandoned its traditional adversarial role of ex-post analysis of the legal acceptability of such reality once formed.

Another adaptation that allows for a more flexible judicial oversight process is the use of ex parte hearings. For instance, in the case concerning profiling, the Supreme Court stalled the verdict in order to allow a supervised process of curing the harms of discrimination by SHABAK in an agreed-upon manner that balanced SHABAK's needs. Throughout the

---

[69] NGOs have filed the petitions against, inter alia, SHABAK's and IDF's policies of targeted killings in the West Bank and Gaza, SHABAK's methods of interrogating suspected terrorists, SHABAK's regulations of profiling in aviation security, AMAN's detention of Hezbollah operatives, and SHABAK's policy of handling complaints involving torture.

[70] Hillel Cohen & Ron Dudai, *Human Rights Dilemmas in Using Informers to Combat Terrorism: The Israeli-Palestinian Case*, 17 TERRORISM AND POLITICAL VIOLENCE 229 (2005); HAJ-YAHIA ET AL., *supra* note 16.

[71] CC (Jer) 1260/98 Halwa Abu-Labda v. State of Israel; CC 467/95 (Jer) Raida Bat-Omar Muhammad Armush v. State of Israel, Dinim 32(2) 156.

[72] Totten v. United States, 92 U.S. 105 (1875); Tenet v. Doe, 544 U.S. 1 (2005). *See also* Goung v. United States, 860 F.2d 1063 (Fed. Cir. 1988); Webster v. Doe, 486 U.S. 592 (1988); CIA v. Sims, 471 U.S. 159 (1985). For a theoretical analysis of the U.S. Supreme Court's holding on this issue, *see* Bitton, *supra* note 15.

[73] It is interesting to compare the Israeli targeted killing case, HCJ 769/02 Pub. Comm. against Torture in Israel, to the American case, *Al-Aulaqi v. Obama*, 727 F. Supp. 2d 1 (D.D.C. 2010). A U.K. court has followed an approach similar to the *Al-Aulaqi* holding. Khan v. Secretary of State for Foreign and Commonwealth Affairs, [2012] EWHC 3728 (Admin) (Eng.).

[74] For instance, in the appeal against SHABAK's and IDF's policies of targeted killings, the appeal was filed on 2002 and the verdict was issued in 2006. HCJ 769/02 Pub. Comm. against Torture in Israel v. Gov't of Israel 62(1) PD [2006].

process, the Chief Justice held several ex parte hearings with SHABAK's representatives. The justices were presented with classified material on SHABAK's methods of securing aviation. Such meetings mitigate the judges' lack of expertise and information on intelligence-related matters.[75] Practically, the Chief Justice transformed the judicial process to resemble an ongoing flexible kind of supervision. It ignored the passive, adversarial approach and took an active and ongoing managerial approach. When acting in accordance with its traditional role, a judge hears the appellant and the representative of the state and issues his or her ruling thereafter. In the new format, stalling the procedures and the use of frequent ex-parte meetings allows the judge to bring the state's position into the "right" spectrum of legality over time, through discussions and repeated "amendments" to the state's position. By employing this process, the judges mitigate the lack of expertise, and relative shortage of time and speed that characterize the traditional role of courts.

This pattern of judicial "management" of national security cases may have another effect of closing some of the "civil liberties gap" in intelligence, as described by Margo Schlanger.[76] Schlanger suggests that the format of legal advice on intelligence matters in the United States (alongside low level of judicial scrutiny) lead to "intelligence legalism." It is basically a legality-based decision-making process rather than a wider process of decision-making. The legalism-driven process is based on simply asking "*is X legal*" rather than applying a broader process of "*Should we do X.*" It seems that in Israel, the deep judicial managerial-type involvement leads to the latter, namely to a broader process. Taking for example the aviation security case, it seems that judges, as opposed to legal advisors, use their floating threat of coercive intervention as a means to force broader considerations into the final results.

Another mechanism for overcoming the deficiencies of the judicial oversight process is the use of the "third proportionality test." This test also helps the Court to overcome its lack of professional intelligence expertise. Proportionality is a universal legal concept. It is applied in international law, constitutional law, and administrative law.[77] The Supreme Court's test of proportionality is divided into three consecutive tests. The first determines whether the act or statute can rationally achieve its goals, while the second test evaluates whether the act employs the least harmful means.

---

[75] HCJ 4797/07 The Association for Citizen's Rights in Israel v. Airports Authority and the General Security Service (the appeal was filed in 2007 and a verdict was issued only on Mar. 10, 2015. The verdict itself seems as merely one more milestone in the process that the court manages. The Supreme Court has marked the susbstantial improvements in the screening process that SHABAK adapted throughout the nearly eight years of a "managed" judicial process. These improvements, according to the Supreme Court, made the original petition irrelevant. The Court clearly pointed out that the petition's original legal thesis has not been decided upon, for now. The appellants are invited to file a new petition should the improved process applied by SHABAK prove to be unconstitutional).

[76] Margo Schlanger, *Intelligence Legalism and the National Security Agency's Civil Liberties Gap*, 6 HARV. NAT. SEC. J. 112 (2015).

[77] Amichai Cohen & Yuval Shany, *A Development of Modest Proportions: The Application of the Principle of Proportionality in the Targeted Killings Case*, 5 J. INT'L CRIM. JUST. 310 (2007); Daphne Barak-Erez, *Israel: The Security Barrier—Between International Law, Constitutional Law, and Domestic Judicial Review*, 4 J. CONSTIT. L. 549 (2006).

The third test, which requires that the government maintain a reasonable ratio between the expected public good and the expected harm to the individuals involved, provides discretion for the Court to reach its result. The third test lacks clear borders and leaves the judge with substantial freedom. It addresses the Court's lack of expertise in intelligence matters through a balancing equation, with on the one side, the public benefit (calculated by the intelligence and security professional in a manner that the Court can hardly dispute), and on the other side, the harm to human rights of the involved individuals ("calculated" in human rights "cost" in a manner that effectively puts the Supreme Court in a role of human rights expert). As there is no defined formula for balancing security against human rights, the third proportionality test allows the Court to resolve the case on the basis of proportionality by giving weight to the human rights side of the equation.[78]

The application of a wide test, such as the third test of proportionality, allows the justices of the Israeli Supreme Court to apply non-legal considerations within a legal framework, using legal terminology. When weighting costs and benefits from the constitutional or the administrative perspective, policy considerations are dragged into the legal test. In a sense, this may close in Israel some of the "civil liberties gap" that may exist in the United States as suggested by Schlanger and that are arguably caused by the application of strictly legalistic narrow considerations.[79]

Judicial adaptation is further reflected in the personal background of many of the judges. A review of the backgrounds of Supreme Court judges serving between 1990 and 2012 shows that 34 percent previously served in high-ranking legal positions in the executive branch, which often entailed, inter alia, intelligence oversight functions. In addition, 14 percent previously served either as military judges or as prosecutors. The prior experiences of Supreme Court judges reduce a potential sense of professional inferiority when dealing with intelligence-related cases.[80]

VII. EXPLAINING THE STRENGTH OF JUDICIAL OVERSIGHT—GENERAL EXPLANATIONS

In previous sections, I argued that intelligence oversight in Israel leans strongly toward the judicial and legal mechanisms of supervision. I have further indicated various techniques through which this judicial supremacy is maintained in spite of the Court's deficiencies in overseeing intelligence. In this section, I tackle the question of why this supremacy is tolerated by Israeli politicians. As will be further illustrated, this phenomenon is typically

---

[78] Accordingly, in the "Separation Wall" case, the judges concentrated on what seemed to them as the "maximal" price in terms of harm to human rights, and required that the level of security be lowered, if needed, in order to maintain this "reasonable" level of human rights. HCJ 2056/04 Beit Sourik Village Council v. Israel & Commander of the IDF Forces in the West Bank PD 58(5) 807 [2004].

[79] See Schlanger, supra note 76.

[80] This observation is owed to Gadi Ezra. One could argue that a higher group of judges who held former positions with the state could lead into a bias toward the position of the state. This chapter does not deal with this question. However, it seems clear to me that at least in the Israeli case, this phenomenon of judges who are former counsels for the state reduces expertise inferiority when judging cases involving the state.

explained by the impact of judicial independence on public support, the importance of judicial independence from transitions of power within a democracy, and an active judiciary as a mechanism for shifting blame and credit with regard to politicians.

The ascendency of judicial oversight of the IC requires explanation because it is, in fact, a kind of self-imposed scrutiny from the perspective of Israeli politicians. In Israel, the fact that the executive branch enjoys—by definition—the majority position in Parliament[81] underscores this puzzling phenomenon. Why should the Israeli government accept a wide range of judicial scrutiny over its intelligence agencies when it can limit it by new legislation? Given the parliamentary majority enjoyed by the government, what stops the Israeli government from limiting the scope of judicial review by legislation, or from establishing new public agencies that are tasked with intelligence oversight? In light of the general structural deficiencies of judicial scrutiny of the IC outlined above, such a move would seem to make sense and align with the practice of other Western democracies.

I begin by reviewing typical theoretical explanations for judicial independence in general, focusing on three alternative theories. The first views judicial independence as the outcome of higher public support for the judicial branch compared to the executive and parliamentary branches.[82] The second explanation rationalizes judicial independence as a kind of insurance for politicians calculated to minimize the foreseeable risks of losing power through elections.[83] The third explanation argues that judicial independence serves the politician in enabling a shift in responsibility and credit.[84]

Although these three general explanations support the special Israeli phenomenon of judicial oversight of intelligence, they fail to explain its unique magnitude. I therefore present these arguments in the Israeli context, and offer two alternative explanations that are unique to Israel: the general tectonic shift of powers in the Israeli model of separation of powers and the problem of international legitimacy.[85]

---

[81] Basic Law: The Government, 3.

[82] Matthew C. Stephenson, *Court of Public Opinion: Government Accountability and Judicial Independence*, 20 J. L. ECON. & ORG. (2004); Georg Vanberg, *Legislative-Judicial Relations: A Game-Theoretic Approach to Constitutional Review*, 45 AM. J. POL. SCI. 346 (2001).

[83] J. Mark Ramseyer, *The Puzzling (In)dependence of Courts: A Comparative Approach*, 23 J. LEGAL STUD. 721 (1994); Matthew C. Stephenson, *"When the Devil Turns. . .": The Political Foundations of Independent Judicial Review*, 32 J. L. STUD. 59 (2003). In contrast, Cohen's work counterintuitively views judicial independence as a means that increases re-election probability for the politician. Alon Cohen, *Independent Judicial Review: A Blessing in Disguise*, 37 INT'L R. L. & ECON. 209 (2013).

[84] Eli M. Salzberger, *A Positive Analysis of the Doctrine of Separation of Powers, or: Why Do We Have an Independent Judiciary?*, 13 INT'L REV. L. & ECON. 349 (1993); Ran Hirschl, *The Political Origins of the New Constitutionalism*, 11 IND. J. GLOBAL L. STUD. 71 (2004).

[85] Offering a thorough definition of judicial independence is far beyond the scope of this section. "Judicial independence" refers to the intuitive idea of the scope of practical ability of the judicial branch, especially the Supreme Court, to rule against the will or position of the political leadership whether ex ante or ex post. I refer to the court's practical ability, whether assigned to the court according to the constitutional structure or practically enabled by the politician irrespective of the court's formal authority (as in cases where the court proclaims that it is authorized to review a matter without any formal authorization). See Salzberger, *supra* note 84.

A. Judicial Independence as Reflection of Public Support

According to this argument, the politicians allow judicial independence as a result of relatively high public support for the judicial branch.[86] The idea of public support of the judicial branch as the source of its independence is well founded. As the judicial branch has only very limited institutional resources of its own, implementation of its decisions is totally dependent upon the willingness of the executive branch to adhere to and enforce its verdicts. Taking the Court's public support into account rationalizes the willingness of politicians to allow judicial independence at the politicians' expense. An attempt to limit such independence might lead into an angry adverse reaction of the public toward the politicians.

An Israeli account of the "public support" argument may even identify the historical turning point that led to the accelerated process of judicial activism. Daniel Friedman anchors the process in the strategic surprise of the 1973 War that caused the Israeli people to suffer "a complete loss of trust in its leadership."[87] During the latter half of the 1980s, according to Friedman, the Court took advantage of the growing weakness of the political sphere and the fragile security conditions and adopted a more activist approach toward issues that it previously considered to be non-justiciable.[88]

In the late 1970s, Israel's political polarization, which started with the first political transition in the country's history, also contributed to the system's inability to effectively perform, and eventually led to a major crisis in the public's trust.[89] The 1990s saw a deepening ethnic and religious divide, as well as growing inflation, which deepened the mistrust toward the political sphere and increased its perception as corrupt and inefficient. This unfortunate reality convinced many to rely on other apolitical institutions such as the judicial branch.[90]

In contrast, Menachem Mautner views the Court as a passive player, used by former elites in order to maintain power. The Court's public support was used to compensate for this group's decline in electoral power. The turning point was the 1977 transition of power from the political "left" to political "right" rather than the 1973 War. The elite "group of Liberal Former Hegemons," as Mautner calls them, responded to the political loss of power during the 1977 elections, and therefore had to relocate its political activity from the Knesset into the Supreme Court as well as to other apolitical entities in the administrative branch.[91] As a result, the Court experienced a conceptual transformation within its rulings, from an institution that was supposed to resolve disputes, to a political institution that ruled on moral and distributive issues alike.[92]

---

[86] James L. Gibson et al., *On the Legitimacy of National High Courts*, 92 AM. POL. SCI. REV. 343 (1998); Vanberg, *supra* note 82, at 347.

[87] *See* DANIEL FRIEDMAN, THE PURSE AND THE SWORD: THE TRIALS OF THE ISRAELI LEGAL REVOLUTION 41–42, 77 (2013) (Heb.).

[88] *Id.* at 67.

[89] Gad Barzilai, *Judicial Hegemony and Social Change*, 3 POLITICS 31 (Dec. 1998).

[90] Nir Keidar, *The Interpretive Revolution: The Rise of the Purposive Interpretation in Israel*, INYUNEY MISHPAT L. R. 26, 737, 767 (2002).

[91] MENACHEM MAUTNER, LAW AND THE CULTURE OF ISRAEL 156–57 (2011).

[92] *Id.* at ch. 6 (for additional discussion of the Court's increasingly activist role).

It is unlikely that this explanation of "public support" can explain judicial independence in general, let alone in the extreme Israeli case. Ostensibly, there should be a rational, direct correlation between the popular support rate of the judiciary and its independence. Surprisingly, the data on popular support of the Israeli Supreme Court during the last two decades indicates that the opposite is true. During this period, the Supreme Court's popular support dropped dramatically, yet during the same time frame, the Supreme Court has been more independent and activist on issues of intelligence and security.[93]

When it comes to the Israeli intelligence and security community, one should not assume that public support leans necessarily toward the Court. In fact, available data shows that the defense community enjoys a comparatively higher support rate.[94] On matters of law and intelligence, public opinion will likely not be tolerant of legal limitations imposed by the Court on the defense community. When it comes to issues of torturing suspected terrorists, targeted killings of terrorists, special arrest techniques that increase soldiers' safety, aviation security, and profiling, the public may not side with the Supreme Court. It might, in fact, gather that it is more exposed to terror due to the Court's intervention.

Moreover, for the "public support" argument to work, the public must monitor the Court's orders and the response of the other branches. As mentioned, when it comes to well-known cases, the public might not be in favor of the Court's intervention. As the majority of cases before the Supreme Court generally receive little public attention, it is doubtful the public can monitor the relations between the branches in order to punish the executive and parliamentary branches for reducing the Court's independence.[95]

B. *The Court's Independence as an Insurance against Democratic Transitions*

Another approach views judicial independence as a strategic move on the part of elected politicians.[96] Judicial independence is explained as a kind of cost that politicians willingly assume in a competitive political environment. An independent court balances the risk of expected transitions of power.[97] According to this theory, Party A agrees to increase the court's power at Party A's expense only because Party B, which is expected one day to take power, will face the same limitations.

---

[93] *See* Yael Hadar, *Israeli Public's Trust in Government's Institutions in the Recent Decade*, 63 PARLIAMENT, THE ISRAELI INSTITUTE FOR DEMOCRACY (2009) (http://www.idi.org.il/) (Heb.). It is possible, however, that the drop in support does not simply follow from the activism of the Court, but actually reflects the response of the public to the consequences of its activism. If this is true, then the argument of public support as the basis for a court's independence is problematic unless it is the kind of intentional support to the court's activism that disappears as the court becomes activist in a specific manner.

[94] *Id.* at p. 7/13 Table 6. According to this survey, the Israeli Army enjoys the highest support rate among all institutions.

[95] In this regard, the late Chief Justice Landau had argued that: "There is the fear that the Court will be perceived as if it has abandoned its proper position and went down to the public debate's arena, where its decisions will be accepted with great applause by some and by a complete rejection by others . . . as I well know that the public will not pay attention to our legal reasoning but rather to our final conclusion only, and that the Court's reputation, as an institution might be harmed." HCJ 390/79 Duweikat v. Israel [1979].

[96] There are several current theories on the issue of judicial independence. *See* Cohen, *supra* note 83.

[97] *Id.*

This argument is appealing. However, the assumptions that underlie this argument are not necessarily valid in the Israeli case. In order for this argument to work, both ends of the political sphere must view the courts as apolitical and unbiased. This may not necessarily be the case in Israel, considering that the "right wing" continuously criticizes the Supreme Court for having a clear "left wing" tendency.[98]

Intuitively, the IC constitutes a potential threat to orderly political transitions if its capabilities are abused for political gains. In this respect, the argument of "judicial independence as political insurance" seems especially relevant in the intelligence oversight context. However, although this argument may explain judicial independence in general (and even more specifically in the intelligence context), it fails to explain why specifically the Israeli Supreme Court should necessarily be the supervising authority that offers this "insurance" against political transitions. The argument fails to explain why politicians should consider the Court to be preferable over other, similarly apolitical authorities, such as the State Comptroller. More importantly, it fails to explain the magnitude of the local factor, namely the comparatively significant role judicial scrutiny plays in overseeing intelligence in Israel.

If we view Israeli practice over the last 20 years, which saw an expansion in judicial oversight of intelligence, there seems to be hardly any difference in the approach of political leaders toward the IC, whether they come from the "right" or from the "left" wing of the political spectrum. The relevance of the "insurance" view is diminished by the reality that the IC enjoys a very high level of popular support and seems to be located outside the political debate.

C. The Court's Independence as a Mechanism for Shifting Blame and Credit

According to the "Blame and Credit" argument set forth by scholars such as Eli Salzberger, judicial independence is nothing more than a rational limitation that the political branches assume for their own sake. Delegating decision powers to the Israeli courts is beneficial because it allows politicians to shift blame for politically costly policies to the judiciary. Politicians therefore tolerate judicial independence because it optimizes their own political balance of credit and blame.[99]

Although attractive, the "blame and credit" explanation of judicial independence depicts an unrealistic public consciousness. On the one hand, this argument views the public as very naïve, to the point of not understanding the politicians' repeated and disingenuous blame for the Court. On the other hand, the public is assumed to be very sophisticated, in that it is perceived to be capable of identifying those cases in which the Court purportedly made a difficult decision, and those in which the politician made the decision. In contrast, one would expect the public to simply view the politician as responsible either way, that is, for the troubling resolution by the Court, or for not amending it ex post.

Nevertheless, it may be that this argument is not necessarily weak when applied to the Israeli case of judicial scrutiny of the IC. In many intelligence-related cases, the Court has

---

[98] Consider, for instance, Judge Zamir's response to the perception that the Supreme Court is "a branch of Meretz" (a left-wing political party in Israel). Isaac Zamir, *Nine of the Supreme: Reflections after Judgement Interview*, 7 ALEI MISHPAT L. R. 31 (2009) (Isr.).

[99] Salzberger, *supra* note 84.

intervened by applying customary international law.[100] If the Court and the politicians have managed to convince the public that these resolutions cannot be altered (being based on a norm that is superior to domestic law), then Salzberger's argument may offer some support of the extreme degree of judicial oversight of intelligence in Israel. And yet, as in the typical intelligence-related case the public is frequently expected to side with the government, why would the political leadership delegate power to the Court, and waive the perceived credit?

D. Explaining the Counterintuitive Judicial Oversight—Local Arguments

Consequently, a review of the literature on judicial independence reveals that general arguments cannot sufficiently explain the supremacy of the judiciary in overseeing intelligence in Israel. I therefore offer two alternative explanations, both of which are based on particular Israeli circumstances. However, when analyzed later, both may be relevant for thinking about the future of intelligence oversight in other democracies.

The first explanation anchors the extreme judicial role in intelligence oversight in the wider phenomenon of a tectonic transition of powers among Israel's branches of government. The second explanation ties this exceptional judicial involvement to an international relations problem from which Israel uniquely suffers, namely that of international legitimacy.

1. The Rise of the Judicial Branch and Legal Advisors in Israel

I argue that the extreme involvement of judges and legal advisors in intelligence oversight is part of the far larger phenomenon of rising judicial activism and empowerment of legal advisors across Israeli government. Although one (judicial and legal oversight of intelligence) is argued to be merely an instance of the other (judicial independence in general), both seem to have reached an unprecedented degree.

During the 1980s and 1990s, the judicial and legal system of Israel underwent a revolution. The Supreme Court roundly amended legal doctrines as well as its own precedents. Threshold requirements for filing petitions against the government or Parliament, such as the standing doctrine, were practically abolished.[101] Justiciability limitations on scrutiny of general policies were essentially removed.[102] The Supreme Court permitted new and open-ended causes of action, such as lack of reasonability, which were joined by additional open-ended proportionality tests.[103]

These new developments in the legal doctrine of Israeli public law allowed for a shift in judicial scrutiny to being value-oriented.[104] The reasoning of the Supreme Court has transformed. Rather than being formalistic and anchored in the wording of legislation, judges

---

[100] This may be tied to empirical research that indicates that one of the signs of judicial activism is a growing tendency to apply international law in domestic cases. Osnat Grady Schwartz, *International Law in Domestic Judges' Decisions: The Relationship between Broad Role Perception and a Strong Internationalist Inclination*, 34 TEL AVIV U. L. REV. 475 (2011).

[101] KRETZMER, *supra* note 40, at 24–25.

[102] *Id.* at 23–24.

[103] *See* Cohen & Shany, *supra* note 77.

[104] MAUTNER, *supra* note 91.

now independently sketch the purposes of the legislation and the values it is supposed to promote. These revolutionary developments continued when the Supreme Court proclaimed its
authority to nullify unconstitutional laws of Parliament.[105] These advances were followed by
the judicial development of the constitutional right of human dignity into a whole category
of constitutional rights.[106]

This legal revolution was also enabled by strengthening the position of the attorney general. The attorney general's advice was transformed from a shield against external scrutiny
into an ongoing mechanism of internal examination. The Supreme Court has practically
forced the government to accept the advice of the legal advisor. Due to the new open-ended
legal doctrine, value-based reasoning, and tests of reasonability and proportionality, legal
advisors have become the ultimate legal and policy authorities in the executive branch.[107]

One could argue that the legal advisors in Israel are, in fact, in a weaker position in comparison to their U.S. counterparts. Taking, for instance, Ingber's account of legal advising on
national security matters in the United States, it seems that the judicial reluctance to adjudicate national security cases puts the American legal advisor, in practice, in a nearly lawmaking
position.[108] In contrast, the Israeli legal advisor's opinion in many cases may be understood
as "just" a preliminary opinion until the (well-expected) hearing in Court. I believe such a
conclusion will miss the real nature of the relations between legal advisors and the judiciary
in Israel. The strong judicial support to the advisors' role when in controversy with the ministerial executive level puts the advisors in an exceptionally powerful position while advising
the executive branch. As Friedman's account shows, the active role of the Supreme Court
does not come on the expense of the advisors because both institutions reciprocally reinforce
one another.

In addition, a relatively high number of legal advisors have been appointed to the Supreme
Court (in a process that practically requires the support of the Supreme Court judges). The
high number of legal advisors serving on the Supreme Court fortifies the position of the legal
advisors, and creates close relations between the Supreme Court and the legal advisors.[109]
The fact that the attorney general is also the head of the prosecution further multiplies its

---

[105] CA 6821/93 United Mizrahi Bank, Ltd. v. Migdal Cooperative Village [1995].

[106] Izhak Englard, *Human Dignity: From Antiquity to Modern Israel's Constitutional Framework*, 21 CARDOZO
L. REV. 1903, 1926 (1999); FRIEDMAN, *supra* note 87, at 587; Gideon Sapir, *Constitutional Revolutions: Israel
as a Case Study*, 5 INT'L J.L. IN CONTEXT 355 (2009).

[107] MAUTNER, *supra* note 91; FRIEDMAN, *supra* note 87, at 584 n.3.

[108] Rebecca Ingber, *Interpretation Catalysts and Executive Branch Legal Decisionmaking*, 38 YALE J. INT'L L. 359
(2013).

[109] FRIEDMAN, *supra* note 87, at 590. Friedman points to the fact that many former advisors were elevated to
seats on the Supreme Court, including Judges Shamgar, Zamir, and Barak. Some former general counsels
included Judges Bach, Beinisch, and Arbel. Accordingly, Friedman argues that a comparative review shows
that in Israel, when there is a legal dispute between the attorney general and the government, the first opinion
prevails. As a sign of the alleged symbiotic relationship, Friedman points out that the Supreme Court has
extended its support for the primacy of the legal opinions of the attorney general. HCJ 4267/93 Citizens
for Administration in Good Order v. The Prime Minister of Israel; AMITAI—Citizens for Administration
in Good Order v. The Prime Minister of Israel, 47(5) PD 441 [1993]. In this case, the Supreme Court ruled
that if the government rejects the opinion of the attorney general, a private lawyer cannot stand as alternative
representation. FRIEDMAN, *supra* note 87, at 166–74.

significance. The legal advisors advise ministers who are subject to the advisors' discretion in criminal cases. In considering a legal advisor's counsel, the ministers are aware that if a complaint against them arises, the advisor has the discretion to initiate a serious investigation and legal proceedings.[110]

Understanding the greater dynamics of the local Israeli experience puts the exceptional involvement of the Court and legal advisors in overseeing intelligence in Israel into context.[111] If judicial activism and legal advising in Israel have exceeded that of other Western democracies, Israeli judges and legal advisors should demonstrate a comparatively atypical involvement with overseeing intelligence.

However, when it comes to the involvement of jurists with intelligence, the political branches adopted a new approach. The government in Israel, by definition, enjoys the trust of the majority in Parliament. And yet, as opposed to other constitutional legal matters, the government seems to be a participant in the process of judicial scrutiny of intelligence rather than an unwilling bystander. A serious alternate agency for supervising intelligence was not considered by the government. Most of the intelligence and security-related cases of the Supreme Court were left unanswered by an adhering government. Although the government controls the Parliament, it generally does not initiate contra-court legislation, not even limited or narrow legislation intended to restore the previous and more conservative interpretation of the law. There must be something beyond the large revolutionary process of greater court jurisdiction and involvement of legal advisors that the branches of government are going through.[112] I argue that the source of the tacit division among the government, the Supreme Court, and the legal advisors is the emerging problem of international legitimacy.

2. The Problem of International Legitimacy

Israel has managed to build an efficient defense and intelligence force. However, it has lately faced the new and emerging "battlefield" of international legitimacy. Among all Western democracies that are engaged in antiterrorism campaigns, Israel's problem of international legitimacy is unique.[113] Israel's challenge explains the unique role of the judiciary and of legal advisors in overseeing intelligence.

---

[110] Friedman argues that an unprecedented number of ministers and even prime ministers were removed from office due to criminal charges. FRIEDMAN, *supra* note 87, at 285, 584.

[111] For a totally different account of the government-legal advisor relation on national security matters in the United States, see: James E. Baker, *The National Security Process and a Lawyer's Duty: Remarks to the Senior Judge Advocate Symposium*, 173 MILITARY L. REV. 124 (2002).

[112] This does not suggest that in fields other than intelligence and national security, the government by definition responds to the Court's intervention by counter-legislation. However, taking account of the supposedly high public support for the government's position, such governmental passivity is special and thought-provoking.

[113] For example, there have been an unprecedented amount of condemnations of Israel by the U.N. Human Rights Council. In 2014, there were 50 such condemnations, which is almost more than the total number of all other condemnations worldwide. Richard Goldstone has written on the council's bias against Israel. Richard Goldstone, Op-Ed., *Reconsidering the Goldstone Report on Israel and War Crimes*, WASH. POST (Apr. 1, 2011), http://www.washingtonpost.com/opinions/reconsidering-the-goldstone-report-on-israel-and-war-crimes/2011/04/01/AFg111JC_story.html.

According to this argument, judicial activism in matters of intelligence and defense is not a legal offensive on the executive branch. To the contrary, judicial activism is used as a shield. The remarkable reputation of the Israeli Supreme Court creates a legitimacy basis for Israel's security agencies. Although the legitimacy threat is indeed a unique threat to Israel, I will conclude with a few thoughts on its potential relevancy to other democracies.

Israel faces the threat of political and legal illegitimacy. The new legal threat is the main source for the exceptional legal involvement in overseeing intelligence in Israel. The political delegitimization campaign is not new. It carries various forms and various degrees. Israel is probably the only member of the United Nations that witnessed calls from other states against its very right of existence.[114] Other, less extreme voices, frequently criticize and delegitimize Israel for its part in the Israeli-Palestinian conflict.[115]

Although these critical initiatives have been occurring for years, several factors have increased their effect since the 1990s. The end of the Cold War opened a window of opportunity for effective international initiatives.[116] International agents ceased to have a priori immunity for the simple status of being a protégé of a superpower. Globalization and networking technology enables more effective and rapid initiatives. Economic sanctions, even when not adopted by the Security Council, pose a real strategic hazard.

I contend that the pressure that led to jointly accepted judicial and legal oversight is the consequence of the fear of growing legal illegitimacy. Since the 1990s, Israel has faced a growing legal delegitimization challenge that carries three different, though related forms: jurisdiction by international tribunals (mainly international criminal enforcement), universal criminal jurisdiction of domestic systems, and ad hoc fact-finding and inquiry commissions.

Like the United States and Russia, Israel is not a member of the Rome Statute. However, Israel still faces a growing threat to individuals in its intelligence and defense community resulting from complaints to the International Criminal Court (ICC), primarily concerning its activity in Lebanon, Gaza, and the West Bank.[117] Israel is even exposed, as a state, to undesired rulings of the International Court of Justice (ICJ) irrespective of whether the basis of that court's jurisdiction is voluntary.[118]

Another source of legal concern is the case of domestic legal systems that apply universal criminal jurisdiction. Israeli leaders of the intelligence and defense community face repeated

---

[114] Josh Levs, *Iran Leader's Call to "Annihilate" Israel Sparks Fury as Nuclear Deadline Looms*, CNN (Nov. 10, 2014), http://edition.cnn.com/2014/11/10/world/meast/iran-annihilate-israel.

[115] MARTIN A. WEISS, ARAB LEAGUE BOYCOTT OF ISRAEL (2013); David Storey, *Academic Boycotts, Activism and the Academy*, 24 POL. GEOGRAPHY 992 (2005).

[116] Counterintuitively, it may be that the return to a Cold War-like condition, as is frequently feared, carries a potential positive from the Israeli perspective of addressing the legitimacy threat. A Cold War-like condition may entail a frozen international community, including a stop to anti-Israeli delegitimizing initiatives.

[117] For example, the recognition of the Palestinian Authority as a member of the Rome Statute may lead to the ICC's jurisdiction over issues concerning the Israeli activity in the Palestinian territories regardless of whether Israel is a party to the Rome Statute.

[118] *See, e.g.,* the advisory opinion of the ICJ. *Legal Consequences of the Construction of a Wall in the Occupied Palestinian Territory, Advisory Opinion*, Advisory Opinion, 2004 I.C.J. 136 (June 9); David Kretzmer, *The Advisory Opinion: The Light Treatment of International Humanitarian Law*, 99 AM. J. INT'L L. 88 (2005). Although an advisory opinion as opposed to a case (which would require voluntary jurisdiction), the legal threat is nonetheless quite similar.

criminal complaints and sometimes arrest warrants in various countries such as the U.K., Spain, Turkey, and Belgium.[119] For example, the former Director of SHABAK, Avi Dichter, had to cancel a visit to Spain for fear of arrest.[120] Former Chief of AMAN and Chief of Staff, Moshe Yaalon, faced an arrest warrant in New Zealand and a lawsuit in the United States.[121] From some perspectives, this threat is even more complicated than the threat of international tribunals. The sporadic complaints reflect a threat that Israel cannot centrally deal with through, among other things, diplomacy.[122] Even reaching an understanding with the local executive branch cannot guarantee the desired resolution.[123]

Another legal threat of illegitimacy results from ad hoc fact-finding and inquiry committees that are established to review the legality of Israel's activities. The 2008–2009 hostilities against Hamas in Gaza led to the Goldstone Report.[124] The capture of the merchant vessel

---

[119] For a thorough and critical account of the use of universal criminal jurisdiction by NGOs, *see* Anne Herzberg, *NGO "Lawfare": Exploitation of Courts in the Arab-Israeli Conflict, in* NGO MONOGRAPH SERIES, (Gerald M. Steinberg ed., 2010).

[120] Gill Hoffman, *Dichter Turns Down Speech in Spain for Fear of Arrest*, JERUSALEM POST (Oct. 25, 2010), http://www.jpost.com/Breaking-News/Dichter-turns-down-speech-in-Spain-for-fear-of-arrest. Dichter also had to deal with a civil lawsuit in the United States. Matar v. Dichter, 563 F.3d 9 (2d Cir. 2009).

[121] Belhas v. Ya'alon, 515 F.3d 1279 (D.C. Cir. 2008). Considering the New Zealand incident, *see Ex-Israeli Army Chief Praises NZ for Wiping Arrest Warrant*, NEW ZEALAND HERALD (Dec. 3, 2007), http://www.nzherald. co.nz/nz/news/article.cfm?c_id=1&objectid=10413558. A similar case in the U.K. involved General Almog, former Israeli Commander of Southern Command, for his part in a targeted killing operation. Dominic Casciani, *Police Feared "Airport Stand-Off,"* BBC News (Feb. 19, 2008), http://news.bbc.co.uk/2/hi/uk/7251954.stm; Anshel Pfeffer, *Fear of Arrest Still Prevents Israeli Officials from Visiting Britain*, HA'ARETZ (May 30, 2012), http://www.haaretz.com/news/diplomacy-defense/fear-of-arrest-still-prevents-israeli-officials-from-visiting-britain.premium-1.433452; Attila Somfalvi, *Meridor Cancels UK Visit for Fear of Arrest*, YNET NEWS (Jan. 11 2010), http://www.ynetnews.com/articles/0,7340,L-3978224,00.html; *Israeli Military Delegation Call Off Official Visit to Britain over Fears They Could Be Arrested for War Crimes*, DAILY MAIL (Jan. 5 2010), *available at*; http://www.dailymail.co.uk/news/article-1240797/Israeli-military-delegation-official-visit-Britain-fears-arrested-war-crimes.html. Ian Black & Ian Cobin, *British Court Issued Gaza Arrest Warrant for Former Israeli Minister Tzipi Livni*, THE GUARDIAN (Dec. 14 2009), *available at* http://www.theguardian.com/world/2009/dec/14/tzipi-livni-israel-gaza-arrest.

[122] Barak Ravid, *Britan Grants Livni Temporary Immunity from Arrest Warrant during Visit*, HA'ARETZ (May 13, 2014), http://www.haaretz.com/news/diplomacy-defense/.premium-1.590453.

[123] Ian Black, *Gordon Brown Reassures Israel over Tzipi Livni's Arrest Warrant*, THE GUARDIAN (Dec. 16 2009), *available at* http://www.theguardian.com/world/2009/dec/16/tzipi-livni-israel-arrest-warrant; Barak Ravid, *Britain Apologizes to Livni over Arrest Warrant*, HA'ARETZ, (Dec. 16, 2009), *available at* http://www.haaretz. com/print-edition/news/britain-apologizes-to-livni-over-arrest-warrant-1.2042. Even when the doctrine of universal jurisdiction was narrowed in the U.K. (although not necessarily removed), the decentralization of the legal threat remains a major issue, as demonstrated in the case of Military Intelligence Chief Yadlin, who was delayed in London for an arrest warrant issued in Turkey. Itamar Eichner, *Former MI Chief Yadlin Delayed at Heathrow Airport*, YNET NEWS (Oct. 11 2013), http://www.ynetnews.com/articles/0,7340,L-4451523,00. html.

[124] Hum. Rights Council, *Human Rights in Palestine and Other Occupied Arab Territories: Report of the United Nations Fact Finding Mission on the Gaza Conflict*, U.N. Doc. A/HRC/12/48 (Sep. 15, 2009). The Goldstone Committee was followed by another committee that was tasked with the need to verify whether Israeli authorities complied with international law standards in their manner of investigating complaints of violations of international law by its security forces. Human Rights Council, *Report of the Committee of Independent Experts in International Humanitarian and Human Rights Laws to Monitor and Assess Any Domestic, Legal or*

Mavi Marmara by Israeli Navy commandos led to the formation of a consensual international inquiry committee, in addition to a complaint to the ICC.[125] The Schabas Committee was given the task of reviewing the legality of the 2014 conflict in Gaza.[126] These legal challenges lead to an acute need for the creation of a legal shield that can deflect such emerging legal threats. To this end, the Supreme Court serves a major role in bolstering legitimacy through its oversight of the intelligence and defense communities. The Court enhances legitimacy in three different ways.

First, the very understanding that Israel is characterized by an independent and active judicial system serves to remove Israel from the image of a state that engages in intentional war crimes. Second, due to the remarkable reputation of the Israeli Supreme Court as an active institution that is sensitive to human rights, matters that have been resolved by the Supreme Court are widely believed to be firmly established as a rule to be followed by the executive branch.[127] Indeed, it seems that once the Supreme Court resolves an issue, the legal debate over this issue diminishes.[128]

Both the executive and judicial branches are aware of the role of the Supreme Court and of its legitimizing function.[129] The executive branch, however, pays the inevitable price of

---

Other Proceedings Undertaken by Both the Government of Israel and the Palestinian Side, in the Light of General Assembly Resolution 254/64 including the Independence, Effectiveness, Genuineness of These Investigations and Their Conformity with International Standards, U.N. Doc. A/HRC/15/50 (Sept. 23, 2010).

[125] Secretary-General's Panel of Inquiry, *Report on the 31 May 2010 Flotilla Incident* (Sept. 2011), *available at* http://www.un.org/News/dh/infocus/middle_east/Gaza_Flotilla_Panel_Report.pdf. The Report, alongside other reports concerning the same incident, was followed by a complaint against Israel to the ICC. The incident nearly led to a formal investigation. *See* International Criminal Court, Situation on Registered Vessels of Comoros, Greece and Cambodia: Article 53(1) Report (Nov. 6, 2014), http://www.icc-cpi.int/iccdocs/otp/OTP-COM-Article_53(1)-Report-06Nov2014Eng.pdf. There has been commentary on this decision and on considerations of legitimacy from an Israeli perspective. *See* Pnina Sharvit Baruch & Keren Aviram, *The Decision on the Gaza Flotilla by the ICC Prosecutor: A Warning for the Future,* INSTITUTE FOR NATIONAL SECURITY STUDIES (Nov. 7, 2014), http://www.inss.org.il/index.aspx?id=4538&articleid=8173.

[126] Human Rights Council Res. S-21/1, U.N. Doc. A/HRC/RES/S-21/1(July 23, 2014).

[127] Ronen Shamir, *"Landmark Cases" and the Reproduction of Legitimacy: The Case of Israel's High Court of Justice,* 34 LAW & SOC'Y REV. 781, 795–96, 798, 801 (1990). Shamir even suggests that from the Court's wording it is clear that the judges themselves take into account the legitimizing effect and seek to "sell" it to the government as a cost-effective duty. *Id.* at 798.

[128] For instance, the debate over the legality of targeted killings or SHABAK's interrogation methods weakened dramatically once the Supreme Court issued its opinion on the matter.

[129] For example, the Foreign Office has referred to the Supreme Court's verdicts in its press releases. *See* Jabareen, *The Rise of Transnational Lawyering for Human Rights, infra* note 131, at 145. Similarly, the Foreign Office issued a press release to increase the legitimacy of the entire legal process. Israeli Ministry of Foreign Affairs, *New Investigation Policy regarding Palestinian Casualties from IDF Fire in Judea and Samaria* (Apr. 6, 2011), http://mfa.gov.il/MFA/AboutIsrael/State/Law/Pages/New_investigation_policy_Palestinian_casualties_ID F_fire_Judea_Samaria_6-Apr-2011.aspx. In another case, the Foreign Office even took the trouble to mention in its press release that an inquiry commission has been appointed by the Israeli government as the result of intervention by the Supreme Court. The Court's unofficial opinion was communicated during the deliberation concerning a petition to enforce the opening of a criminal investigation in relation to the Salah Shehada targeted killing case. *See* Israeli Ministry of Foreign Affairs, *Salah Shehadeh-Special Investigatory Commission* (Feb. 27, 2011), http://mfa.gov.il/MFA/AboutIsrael/State/Law/Pages/Salah_Shehadeh-Special_Investigatory_Commission_27-Feb-2011.aspx.

substantial delegation of oversight powers to the judicial branch. This limits its independence due to the corresponding intensive judicial intervention.

Second, the concern with legitimacy also explains the lack of special oversight agencies in Israel. Israeli equivalents to the SIRC or G-10 may have better know-how to perform ongoing ex ante and ex post supervision over the Israeli IC. However, such agencies cannot provide the executive branch with the extremely valuable asset of international legal legitimacy. If they are ever established, agencies of this type will not enjoy the exceptional reputation that the Supreme Court enjoys. Rather, they will be viewed by international public opinion as dependent organizations that serve the Israeli government.[130] It seems that NGOs are becoming aware of the use of the Supreme Court as an anchor of legal legitimacy. Accordingly, some NGOs have recently raised arguments against the very legitimacy of the Court, painting the Supreme Court as an Israeli agent rather than as an objective, legitimizing agent.[131]

Third, the use of judicial reputation as a legitimacy shield is intended to protect individuals, in addition to policies. It seems that legal advisors within the defense community initiate immediate investigations with the intention of bringing every relevant case of apparent misconduct to an Israeli court.[132] This seeming strategy is probably based on the preference of international tribunals such as the ICC to act subject to the residual jurisdictional principle of "complementarity," which defers in most instances to the legal processes of domestic systems.[133] Given the reputation of the Israeli judicial system, it is believed that tribunals such as the ICC will not impose their jurisdiction over cases that have already been resolved by Israeli courts. This is a broader version of legal supervision, and as a consequence, the executive branch actively invites judicial intervention rather than acting merely as a passive respondent.[134] In addition, the higher degree of legal involvement may be an indication of a growing concern over legitimacy considerations in Israel.

---

[130] For example, the MAVTAN, namely the commissioner for verifying the complaints of interrogated persons, is portrayed by NGOs as being a biased body. In contrast, the Supreme Court is viewed differently, even on issues when it repeatedly sides with the government.

[131] *See* Hassan Jabareen, *The Rise of Transnational Lawyering for Human rights*, 1 J.L. & Soc. Ref. 137, 147 (2008) (Isr.). For a similar version in English, *see* Hassan Jabareen, *Transnational Lawyering and Legal Resistance in National Courts: Palestinian Cases before the Israeli Supreme Court*, 13 Yale Hum. Rts. & Dev. L.J. 239 (2010).

[132] Israeli Ministry of Foreign Affairs, *IDF Investigating Exceptional Incidents from Operation Protective Edge* (Sept. 10, 2014), http://mfa.gov.il/MFA/ForeignPolicy/IsraelGaza2014/Pages/IDF-investigating-exceptional-incidents-from-Operation-Protective-Edge-10-Sep-2014.aspx.

[133] Following a complaint arising from the takeover of the Marmara flotilla to Gaza, the ICC Prosecutor decided to close the case without ICC involvement. Israel's Foreign Office made a direct link between the reputation of the Israeli legal system and the decision, stating: "The Prosecutor also decided to close this file without addressing the issue of complementarity, according to which the ICC will not investigate incidents which are subject to appropriate investigation by the relevant state. In this context, it should be stressed that Israel is recognized by leading experts in the international community as a state governed by the rule of law with effective and independent investigative mechanisms which meet high international standards." Israeli Ministry of Foreign Affairs, *ICC Prosecutor Closes Comoros Flotilla Preliminary Investigation* (Nov. 6, 2014), http://mfa.gov.il/MFA/PressRoom/2014/Pages/Reaction-to-ICC-decision-to-close-the-preliminary-inquiry-on-the-Mavi-Marmara-incident-6-November-2014.aspx.

[134] The government even extended the mandate of the Turkel Inquiry Committee beyond the Marmara incident to include a review of compliance with international law requirements, and Israeli procedures for investigating claims involving alleged violations of humanitarian law by Israeli forces. The Committee included

This apparent Israeli executive branch call for judicial intervention sketches a different pattern than the one argued by Deeks in relation to the United States.[135] Deeks argues that the judiciary in the United States is continuously present although in a passive manner. By merely "observing" the executive branch, even without involvement in actual litigation, its potential intervention is taken into account by an executive branch that alters its decisions accordingly with the intention of avoiding litigation. In contrast, my argument shows that the Israeli security community operates quite differently. Rather than seeking to avoid litigation, it actually invites the Court's scrutiny. Apparently, whereas the American executive branch avoids litigation, the Israeli executive branch seeks the legitimacy that is the byproduct of litigation. The differences in the legitimacy problems that the two intelligence and defense communities face (namely, the Israeli and the U.S. communities) may well reflect differences in their approaches to national security litigation.

A practical question remains, however, whether the Court on issues of intelligence and defense is creating a new, "better" human rights norm or is merely supplying a "legitimacy certificate" to the defense community. According to Ronen Shamir's argument, the Supreme Court strategically builds its reputation as independent and pro–human rights vis-à-vis the government in cases concerning the West Bank. Shamir argues that high-profile cases are apparently decided against the Israeli government. Yet, when examined closely, these cases do not in fact impose strict legal limits on the government, and even may contradict many other low-profile cases that reflect the "real" judicial approach. Shamir's argument is not convincing, as it assumes a naïve audience for the Court's judgments that does not seem to suit the international focus on Israel's activity.

The Supreme Court, instead, does in fact dramatically limit the range of freedom and discretion of the intelligence agencies. It grants legitimacy in return for real compliance with international law and standards. From the Israeli government's perspective, it is still a cost-effective bargain. The government's bargain for legitimacy by handing over some of its autonomy to the Israeli Supreme Court is worthwhile. The alternative might be disastrous. The norm that the Supreme Court may impose is expected to be less restrictive than the judgment of an international tribunal on the same matter.[136]

The Supreme Court's ruling concerning the security barrier in the West Bank, for example, illustrates this analysis. The Supreme Court, in its list of verdicts on this issue, forced the government to amend the route of the barrier. The Israeli Supreme Court looked into every single mile that was challenged in a long process, and even made a request to be supplied with a topographic model and aerial photos of the relevant areas.[137] And yet, from the government's

---

international observers and officially enjoyed the advice of foreign scholars. In this way, the government sought a basis of legitimacy for its investigation procedures. *See* THE PUBLIC COMMISSION TO EXAMINE THE MARITIME INCIDENT OF 31 MAY 2010, SECOND REPORT, ISRAEL'S MECHANISMS FOR EXAMINING AND INVESTIGATING COMPLAINTS AND CLAIMS OF VIOLATIONS OF THE LAWS OF ARMED CONFLICT ACCORDING TO INTERNATIONAL LAW (2013).

[135] Ashley S. Deeks, *The Observer Effect: National Security Litigation, Executive Policy Changes, and Judicial Deference*, 82 FORDHAM L. REV. 827 (2013).

[136] A common Israeli perception views the very exposure of SHABAK, MOSSAD, or IDF combatants to an international tribunal as a reflection of a national trauma.

[137] *See* HCJ 2056/04 Beit Sourik Village Council v. Israel & Commander of the IDF Forces in the West Bank 58(5) PD 807, 30–44. [2004].

perspective, making these concessions to the Court made sense considering a more problematic alternative clearly contemplated in the ICJ's advisory opinion on the matter.[138]

The same pattern is seen in classic intelligence cases. In the "Torture Case" SHABAK asked the Court to accept the legality of the use of moderate physical pressure in "ticking time bomb" situations.[139] An international tribunal might otherwise have ruled that the ban on physical pressure in interrogations is absolute.[140] Once again, the Supreme Court took a hybrid approach. It nullified the legality of moderate pressure, but did not nullify the potential ex post application of the defense of necessity. Similarly, in the targeted killings cases, the state wanted the Court to recognize the status of terrorist organization members as "unlawful combatants."[141] An alternative international tribunal may have denied such status and ruled that the ban on targeted killing is absolute.[142] Although the Supreme Court denied the status of unlawful combatants, it left a narrow legal justification for targeted killing by deeming terror operatives to be civilians who take part in hostilities.[143]

Intelligence oversight by the Court is therefore ideal for the executive branch. It mainly affects domestic intelligence and leaves the more sensitive foreign clandestine activity beyond the scope of effective overseeing. Even better from the Court's and the state's perspective is the fact that this filtering out of foreign intelligence issues is inherent to the nature of foreign intelligence and hence requires no special procedure or active resolution. Foreign intelligence is practically "victimless" in the sense that the victim is hardly aware of the undermining of his or her basic rights. Under such circumstances there is no party that is in a position to initiate legal proceedings. Take for instance the targeted killings by Israeli forces in Israeli-controlled territories. When similarly conducted abroad, these activities are typically not ascribable to Israel. Even when they are, the typical target, such as an enemy state or terrorist organization, is unlikely to file a lawsuit in an Israeli tribunal. As mentioned, because the Court's intervention is responsive, it does not involve supervising "victimless activity."

VIII. CONCLUSION

This chapter offers a practical observation on intelligence oversight in Israel. It points to the exceptional role that the judicial and governmental legal advisors play in the intelligence oversight process. It offers a link between the major role of the judiciary in overseeing intelligence and the uniqueness of the legitimacy threat to Israel. If the argument of "legitimacy-seeking" is correct, than it may contribute to the debate over new appointments to the Supreme Court and their effect on the Court's rulings. Some critics may believe that new

---

[138] *See* ICJ Advisory Opinion, *supra* note 118.

[139] HCJ 5100/94 Pub. Comm. against Torture in Israel.

[140] Jamie Mayerfeld, *In Defense of the Absolute Prohibition of Torture*, 22 PUB. AFFAIRS Q. 109 (2008).

[141] HCJ 769/02 Pub. Comm. against Torture in Israel v. Gov't of Israel 62(1) PD [2006]. The status of unlawful combatants would have allowed SHABAK and IDF to kill terrorists as if combatants in war, but such terrorists would be denied POW status if arrested.

[142] *See, e.g.*, Hajjar, *supra* note 68.

[143] Protocol Additional to the Geneva Convention of 12 August 1949, and Relating to the Protection of Victims of International Armed Conflicts (Protocol I), art. 51(3).

conservative appointments to the Supreme Court may reverse the Court's course into lower activism. However, if the "legitimacy-seeking" argument is sound, then what drives Israeli activism on national security and intelligence matters is not necessarily the composure of the judges and their approaches to activism but rather (mainly) the level of legitimacy concerns that the government faces. If this is the case, so long as the legitimacy threat remains lurking, the post-Barak Supreme Court is expected to be just as activist on issues of security and intelligence.[144]

Although this analysis seems confined to the Israeli case of intelligence oversight, it may also be relevant to other democracies in two different ways. First, as in the case of targeted killing, Israel may be the first, but is not likely to be the last, to cope with legal legitimacy challenges to the practice. As asymmetric conflicts continue, the major global role of countries such as the United States and the U.K. might eventually transform targeted killings into an issue of legitimacy.[145] If such legitimacy challenges cannot be dealt with politically, the Israeli pattern of overseeing the intelligence and defense communities may be duplicated. If the argument that this chapter offers is correct, a growing involvement of local courts in these countries may be a sign of unsuccessful attempts to deal with the legitimacy threat politically.

Second, the international community may need to draw a line beyond which the legitimacy threat to Israel will be counterproductive in terms of judicial promotion of human rights. If the legal illegitimacy threat reaches a boiling point, the judicial branch will no longer be able to serve as a shielding buffer, and its independence might be diminished by Israeli politicians (as its legitimizing effect is the reason for its exceptional independence to begin with). For the present, the Israeli Supreme Court is destined to seek the elusive balance between its own international reputation and domestic expectations. The art of this balance is what makes the Supreme Court the only body in Israel that can both oversee covert activity and offer overt legitimacy.

---

[144] Obviously, I do not argue that the Supreme Court will be similarly activist in a totally unrelated manner to new appointments. However, so long as new appointments are on the Barak-Gruins spectrum (when Barak is an example of *most activist* and Gruins is an example of *least activist*) the legitimacy concern is expected to remain as a main catalyst of activism on matters of intelligence and national security.

[145] JOSEPH FELTER & JARRET BRACHMAN, A RESPONSE TO THE SETON HALL STUDY: AN ASSESSMENT OF 516 COMBATANT STATUS REVIEW TRIBUNAL (CSRT) UNCLASSIFIED SUMMARIES (2007); David Scheffer, *Whose Lawfare Is It, Anyway*, 43 CASE W. RES. J. INT'L L. 215 (2010); Geert-Jan Alexander Knoops, *Drones at Trial. State and Individual (Criminal) Liabilities for Drone Attacks*, 14 INT'L CRIM. L. REV. 42 (2014); Hajjar, *supra* note 68; *William Hague Facing Legal Action over Drone Strikes*, BBC (Mar. 11, 2012), http://www.bbc.com/news/uk-17335368; Jack Serle, *First UK Legal Challenge to CIA Drones Reaches Court of Appeal*, BUREAU OF INVESTIGATIVE JOURNALISM (Dec. 4 2013), http://www.thebureauinvestigates.com/2013/12/04/first-uk-legal-challenge-to-cia-drones-reaches-court-of-appeal/; Jack Serle, *UN Expert Labels CIA Tactic Exposed by Bureau "a War Crime,"* BUREAU OF INVESTIGATIVE JOURNALISM (June 21, 2012), https://www.thebureauinvestigates.com/2012/06/21/un-expert-labels-cia-tactic-exposed-by-bureau-a-war-crime/.

7

Review and Oversight of Intelligence in Canada

EXPANDING ACCOUNTABILITY GAPS

*Kent Roach**

I. INTRODUCTION

Canada, like most developed countries, is taking a whole-of-government approach to security with particular emphasis on the prevention of terrorism. Unfortunately, review and oversight lags well behind the increased intensity and integration of its national security activities. Accountability gaps are growing as security agencies are receiving more legal powers and funds to work together, while review and oversight is still conducted in departmental and agency-based silos. In short, Canada has an inadequate twentieth-century review and oversight structure that is not appropriate for its twenty-first-century whole-of-government approach to security matters. Such an inadequate review and oversight structure places both rights and security at risk, and in doing so has the potential to undermine public and international confidence in Canada's security performance.

A central argument of this chapter is that all three branches of government have an important role to play in bridging accountability gaps.[1] This chapter will also suggest that the extraordinary Canadian inquiry into Maher Arar's 2002 rendition to Syria and the 2013 decision by Judge Mosley on the subcontracting of CSIS surveillance to Five Eyes partners suggest that review should be extended to transnational security investigations. As with

---

* Prichard-Wilson Chair in Law and Public Policy and Professor of Law, University of Toronto. I thank the Pierre E. Trudeau Foundation for its generous financial support of my work.
[1] The President's Advisory Committee in the United States has likewise advanced proposals that called for enhanced review of NSA activities by all three branches of government. PRESIDENT'S REVIEW GROUP ON INTELLIGENCE AND COMMUNICATIONS TECHNOLOGIES, LIBERTY AND SECURITY IN A CHANGING WORLD (2013).

domestic matters, review and oversight of transnational intelligence networks such as the Five Eyes has the potential to pay large dividends for security, rights, and public confidence. Nevertheless, it is dogged by exaggerated concerns that enhanced review will result in the leaking of secret information.

A. Dynamic Intelligence Capabilities, Static Review and Oversight Structures

The mismatch between expanding intelligence capabilities and static review and oversight arrangements has become more pronounced in the last several years. These oversight lacunae exist both with respect to review aimed at compliance with law, and with respect to oversight of the efficacy of security activities.

Most recently, the Canadian government has failed to improve its outdated review structure even while giving its civilian intelligence service, the Canadian Security Intelligence Service (CSIS), many more powers in the wake of two lone wolf terrorist attacks in October 2014 inspired by the Islamic State terrorist group. In the course of considering the new powers, the then Conservative government maintained that the review and oversight status quo was adequate despite an unprecedented public debate on the subject that saw four former prime ministers (from both the Liberal and Conservative political parties), former judges, and review body officials call for enhanced legislative and executive watchdog review of national security activities.[2] As a result, Canada remains the only country in the Five Eyes intelligence alliance that does not give any legislators access to information classified as secret.[3] A new Liberal government elected in October 2015 has promised to introduce legislation giving a parliamentary security committee access to secret information. As of the end of 2015, it has yet to introduce legislation to such effect.[4]

The previous Canadian government defended its refusal to give parliamentarians access to secret information on the basis that they may leak secret information, even though current reform proposals would subject parliamentarians who received secret information to the stringent provisions of Canada's version of an Official Secrets Act. This fear of leaks is exaggerated. Nevertheless, it reflects Canada's heavy reliance on foreign—especially U.S.—intelligence, and long-standing suspicions that parliamentarians (including those committed

---

[2] Jean Chretien, Joe Clark, Paul Martin & John Turner, *A Close Eye on Security Makes Canadians Safer*, GLOBE & MAIL, Feb. 19, 2015.

[3] Senator Hugh Segal, Chair, *Interim Report of Special Senate Committee on Anti-terrorism*, Mar. 2011, at 45; Hugh Segal, *Freedom and Security: The Gordian Knot for Democracies, in* AFTER THE PARIS ATTACKS 177–80 (Edward Iacobucci & Stephen Toope eds., 2015).

[4] The Liberal Party's 2015 election party platform recognized that Canada was the "sole nation among our Five Eyes allies whose elected officials cannot scrutinize security operations" and promised to "create an all-party committee to monitor and oversee the operations of every government department and agency with national security responsibilities". Liberal Party of Canada, *Real Change: A New Plan for the Middle Class* (2015) 31–32. The first task assigned to the Minister of Public Safety in a November 2015 mandate letter from Prime Minister Justin Trudeau is to "assist the Leader of the Government in the House of Commons in the creation of a statutory committee of Parliamentarians with special access to classified information to review government departments and agencies with national security responsibilities." Mandate Letter to Hon. Ralph Goodale at http://pm.gc.ca/eng/minister-public-safety-and-emergency-preparedness-mandate-letter (last visited Dec. 28, 2015).

to the separation of Quebec from the rest of Canada) cannot be trusted with access to secret information.

The previous Conservative government rejected as "needless red tape"[5] recommendations for expanded executive watchdog review that originated in a commission of inquiry into Maher Arar's post 9/11 rendition.[6] Many agencies, most notably the Canadian Border Services Agency, foreign affairs, and military officials, are not subject to dedicated independent national security review. The accountability gap identified by the Arar Commission in 2006 has been widened by 2013 legislation that fails to ensure that the RCMP complaints body has access to secret information necessary to review the RCMP's national security activities and permissive 2015 legislation facilitating the sharing of security information to 17 designated federal agencies.[7] This runs the risk, recognized in the Arar case, of harming human rights and privacy by allowing possibly unreliable intelligence to be shared and used against terrorist suspects.

Canada's accountability gaps are not limited to matters associated with human rights and legality: they also extend to issues of the effectiveness or efficacy of counterterrorism measures. The latter deficiency was revealed by another inquiry: this time a review of deficiencies in the prevention and investigation of the 1985 bombing of Air India Flight 182. This inquiry into Canada's largest mass murder and the world's most deadly act of aviation terrorism before 9/11 (331 deaths in total) was not started until 2006, in part because of delays in the investigation that saw only one person convicted of manslaughter and two others acquitted of murder in 2005. In 2010, this inquiry recommended an enhanced oversight role for the prime minister's National Security Advisor (henceforth PMNS Advisor) including new powers to resolve disputes between CSIS and the Royal Canadian Mounted Police (RCMP) over whether to risk the disclosure of secret intelligence in criminal proceedings by involving the RCMP. It also recommended that CSIS be required to share information about possible terrorism offenses with the PMNS Advisor.[8] Despite having appointed the inquiry and having its recommendations echoed by a unanimous and bipartisan Senate Committee in 2011,[9] the government refused to implement these recommendations.

Even under the new information-sharing legislation, CSIS retains its discretion not to share information about terrorism with the police or the PMNS Advisor because of CSIS's

---

[5] David Pugliese, *Government Knows Best: No Need for More Oversight on Spy and Security Agencies*, OTTAWA CITIZEN, Feb. 1, 2015 at http://ottawacitizen.com/news/national/defence-watch/government-knows-best-says-conservative-mpno-need-for-more-spy-and-security-agency-oversight.

[6] COMMISSION OF INQUIRY INTO THE ACTIONS OF CANADIAN OFFICIALS IN RELATION TO MAHER ARAR A NEW REVIEW MECHANISM FOR THE RCMP'S NATIONAL SECURITY ACTIVITIES (Ottawa: Government Services, 2006) [hereinafter "THE ARAR COMMISSION"]. The author served on this Inquiry's research advisory committee.

[7] ENHANCING RCMP ACCOUNTABILITY ACT, S.C. 2013, c 18, PART VI; SECURITY OF CANADA INFORMATION SHARING ACT, S.C. 2015, c 20 (Can.).

[8] COMMISSION OF INQUIRY INTO THE INVESTIGATION OF THE BOMBING OF AIR INDIA FLIGHT 182, PUBLIC WORKS, VOL. 3 AIR INDIA FLIGHT 182: A CANADIAN TRAGEDY (2010) [hereinafter AIR INDIA COMMISSION VOL 3]. The author served as director of research (legal studies) of this inquiry.

[9] Senator Hugh Segal, chair, *Interim Report of Special Senate Committee on Anti-Terrorism*, Mar. 2011 Recommendations 8–15.

fear of broad constitutional disclosure obligations for criminal trials, which might result in disclosing sources, methods, and confidence from foreign agencies.[10] New legislation enacted in 2015 may aggravate tensions between the RCMP and CSIS by granting CSIS's human sources the same broad privilege against being identified in court proceedings as police informers enjoy.[11] Continued inadequacies in both ministerial/executive and legislative oversight of security powers may make it more difficult to conduct terrorism prosecutions because it will allow CSIS to continue to ignore its evidentiary responsibilities when it collects intelligence in terrorism investigations. In other words, Canada's growing accountability gaps can have harmful effects on both rights and security.

And Canada's accountability gaps are, indeed, growing. Since the two terrorist attacks in Quebec and Ottawa in October 2014, Canada has enacted security laws that provide CSIS new powers and privileges.[12] These include the authority for CSIS to conduct surveillance outside of Canada. Additionally, CSIS may violate Canadian laws, including the Canadian Charter of Rights and Freedom (henceforth "the Charter"), in taking measures within and outside of Canada to reduce or disrupt security threats. The previous Conservative government defended these new powers on the basis that they require judicial warrants issued by specialized national security judges. This starkly raises the issue of the strengths and weaknesses of judicial oversight.

The new emphasis in Canada on judicial oversight, as well as the important role that ad hoc inquiries—appointed at the discretion of the cabinet and run by sitting or retired judges—have had with respect to intelligence matters, reflects the weaknesses of legislative and executive watchdog oversight in Canada. CSIS already has to obtain warrants for surveillance, and such applications are heard by specially designated judges of the Federal Court, headquartered in Ottawa.[13] CSIS's new powers raise the issue of the abilities of these judges, who often spend up to half their time on national security matters, effectively to oversee ongoing and integrated security activities. In a fascinating case released in 2013, one of the specially designated judges took CSIS to task when he learned from executive watchdog reviewers

---

[10] Canadian prosecutors must disclose all relevant and non-privileged material in their possession to the accused even if the material is not used in the criminal trial or is not exculpatory. R. v. Stinchcombe [1991] 3 S.C.R. 326.

[11] PROTECTION OF CANADA FROM TERRORISTS ACT, S.C. 2015, c 9 (Can.). See Kent Roach, *The Problems with the New CSIS Human Source Privilege in Bill C-44*, 61 CRIM. L.Q. 451 (2014). For a decision holding that the creation of the new statutory privilege that prevents the disclosure of identifying information about CSIS's human sources affects substantive rights and should not be applied retrospectively to limit pre-existing disclosure in civil litigation *see Canada (Attorney General) v. Almalki* 2015 FC 1278.

[12] PROTECTION OF CANADA FROM TERRORISTS ACT, S.C. 2015, c 9 (Can.), ANTI-TERRORISM ACT, R.S.C. 2015, c. C-20 (Can.). These new powers include the new privilege to protect CSIS's confidential sources from disclosure discussed in above note 11. It also includes new information sharing powers and new powers for CSIS to take steps short of inflicting bodily harm or obstructing justice to reduce threats to the security of Canada. The new powers contemplate that CSIS can engage in such threat reduction actions even in violation of laws and Charter rights if the disruption activities are authorized by a warrant granted by a specially designated Federal Court judge. As of the end of 2015, it is not clear whether the Liberal government will repeal this new power for CSIS to engage in disruption. For arguments that the new government should repeal this measure see Craig Forcese and Kent Roach *False Security: The Radicalization of Canadian Anti-Terrorism* (2015) chs.8, 14.

[13] CANADIAN SECURITY INTELLIGENCE SERVICE ACT, R.S.C. 1985, c. C-23 § 21 (Can.).

that CSIS has subcontracted surveillance of a target outside of Canada to Canada's "Five Eyes" signals intelligence partners.[14] This case (henceforth called the Mosley judgment after the judge in the first instance) and the new prominence of judicial oversight make Canada a good context in which to examine the strengths and weaknesses of judicial intelligence review and oversight relative to executive and legislative oversight.[15]

In short, the central argument of this chapter is that oversight and review structures have failed to keep pace with Canada's whole-of-government and transnational security activities. Failure to close this gap may harm both the effectiveness and propriety of Canadian national security efforts.

B. Outline

The first part of the chapter will define and distinguish review and oversight, even though common discussion and even expert commentary often conflate the two. It will also examine the nature and dangers of accountability gaps and relate them to the goals of protecting rights and ensuring effective security responses.

The second part will examine legislative review of national security activities. Canada lags behind other democracies with respect to legislative review, and the Liberal government elected in October 2015 has promised enhanced parliamentary review. Nevertheless, previous proposals before Parliament and the record in other democracies do not provide grounds for optimism that legislative committees alone will be effective in promoting either propriety- or efficacy-based accountability.

The third part will examine the strengths and weaknesses of judicial review and oversight of national security activities in Canada. The Mosley judgment[16] suggests that the judiciary may be a more effective mechanism for propriety-based review than many have imagined. At the same time, it suggests that judges may depend on other review mechanisms to learn how an intelligence agency actually conducts warranted activity. Moreover, even at its heroic best, judicial oversight will focus on issues of legality and propriety, not efficacy and effectiveness. Intelligence agencies will also have incentives—and often the ability—to take measures that avoid or limit any inconvenient judicial oversight.

The fourth part will suggest that national security activities dominated by the executive must be closely tracked and monitored by the watchdog arm of the executive. Review bodies should be creatively staffed, and can be seen as hybrids that mimic the independent judiciary and the representative legislature. There is a need for effective whole-of-government review that can follow the trail of intelligence throughout government. There is also a need for whole-of-government oversight in the public interest that counteracts the limited and bureaucratic interests of particular security agencies.

Even if it were possible for Canada to get its accountability house in order, transnational accountability gaps would still be a problem. This is especially true for smaller powers such as

---

[14] In the matter of an application by X for a warrant pursuant to Sections 12 and 21 of the Canadian Security Intelligence Service Act, [2013] F.C. 1275, *aff'd* [2014] F.C.A. 249. Leave to appeal to the Supreme Court granted Feb. 6, 2015, but the appeal was abandoned by the government.

[15] *See also* Raphael Bitton's chapter in this volume.

[16] [2013] F.C. 1275, *aff'd* [2014] F.C.A. 249.

Canada that heavily rely on intelligence and security cooperation from more powerful allies. The last part of this chapter will argue that transnational accountability reform is necessary, and perhaps not utterly impossible.

II. THE DANGER OF ACCOUNTABILITY GAPS FOR BOTH RIGHTS AND SECURITY

Following the approach of Canada's Arar Commission, this chapter will distinguish review from oversight even though public discourse often conflates the two terms.[17] "Review" refers to the ability of an independent reviewer outside the chain of command to evaluate security activities after the fact. In contrast, "oversight" refers to a real-time process where those who practice oversight are able to influence the conduct they are examining.[18] This distinction breaks down in some contexts, especially in relation to the judiciary that approves activities in advance but can also review them after the fact.

A. The Role of Independent Reviewers: SIRC and the CSE Commissioner

The Arar Commission stressed the importance of reviewer independence from the activities that they review, so that reviewers are not co-opted by having given prior approval to national security activities that have failed or had unintended effects.[19] The Security Intelligence Review Committee (SIRC) that reviews the activities of CSIS does so after the fact and issues annual reports based on audits of CSIS activities. [20] SIRC has three to five members who are appointed by the prime minister and serve renewable five-year terms. Another independent reviewer is the CSE Commissioner, who is a sitting or retired judge who reviews the activities of CSE, Canada's signal intelligence agency.[21] Both of these review bodies only have powers to make findings and recommendations. They are generally not briefed about and certainly do not have a veto over ongoing operations. The detachment of these organizations means that they cannot stop ongoing abuse or illegality: they are supposed to bring fresh eyes to security activities after the fact.

B. Executive Oversight by Responsible Ministers and the Prime Minister's National Security Advisor

In a traditional parliamentary system, responsible ministers oversee the conduct of agencies. The RCMP has lead responsibilities for national security policing and, along with CSIS, reports to the Minister of Public Safety. CSE, the signals intelligence agency, reports to the

---

[17] For additional elaboration of the distinction between efficacy- and propriety-based review, *see* Reg Whitaker & Stuart Farson, *Accountability in and for National Security*, 15(9) IRPP CHOICES 1 (2009).

[18] ARAR COMMISSION, *supra* note 6, at 456–58.

[19] *See id.* at 457–58.

[20] On the work of SIRC, see its website. SECURITY INTELLIGENCE REVIEW COMMITTEE, http://www.sirc-csars.gc.ca/index-eng.html (last visited Dec. 28, 2015).

[21] On the Commissioner's work, see its website. OFFICE OF THE COMMUNICATIONS SECURITY ESTABLISHMENT COMMISSIONER, http://www.ocsec-bccst.gc.ca/index_e.php (last visited Dec. 28, 2015).

Minister of Defence. The Minister of Public Safety issues a series of ministerial directives to CSIS and the RCMP, but with respect to the latter, oversight is limited by the quasi-constitutional doctrine of police independence in determining the targets of investigation and charges.

Canada has seen a centralization of powers in the prime minister's office throughout government. This is particularly true with respect to national security activities. The office of the Prime Minister's National Security Advisor (PMNS Advisor) was created in 2003 to play a coordinating role with respect to the government's intelligence. This role spans not only CSIS and CSE but also includes intelligence capabilities within defense, foreign relations, and border services agencies.[22] The PMNS Advisor is a civil service position located in the Privy Council Office, which provides nonpartisan civil service support for the prime minister. The PMNS Advisor is responsible for effective coordination of intelligence and is assisted by a security and intelligence secretariat and a foreign assessments secretariat. The PMNS Advisor is also responsible for an Integrated Threat Assessment Centre and chairs meetings of deputy ministers on national security.[23] The Air India Commission recommended enhancement of the PMNS Advisor's powers as a way of improving executive oversight. These enhancements would include giving the Advisor powers to resolve disputes between the RCMP and CSIS over the disclosure of secret intelligence through police investigations and possible terrorism prosecutions.[24] The government has not acted on this recommendation.

C. Accountability and Accountability Gaps

Accountability refers to the process in which officials and organizations provide explanations and justifications for their conduct. It is possible for accountability to occur even if the body demanding an account does not have the power to control or change the behavior that it examines. Accountability is usually associated with the need to reveal and prevent improprieties such as possible complicity in torture or invasions of privacy. Propriety includes concerns with the legality of security powers, but also with their proportionality and their effects on privacy and civil liberties. The Arar Commission focused on review for propriety because of concerns that various Canadian officials—including police, intelligence, customs, and foreign affairs officials—were complicit in Maher Arar's detention and rendition in 2002 from the United States and his subsequent torture in Syria.

There are also demands for accountability for efficacy or effectiveness generally in the wake of real or perceived intelligence failures. Efficacy-based review focuses on whether security activities are efficient and effective in preventing terrorism and countering other threats to national security, such as espionage. The Air India Commission evaluated "how effectively the government uses the resources available to it to deal with the terrorist threat,"[25] with particular attention to the distribution of intelligence. Like the Arar Commission, the Air India Commission had to examine a range of security actors, including CSIS, CSE, the

---

[22] Note that Australia has had a similar position since 2008, and the U.K. does as well. *See* Hardy and Williams chapter in this volume.

[23] ARAR COMMISSION, *supra* note 6, at 196–98.

[24] AIR INDIA COMMISSION VOL 3, *supra* note 8, at ch. 2.

[25] AIR INDIA COMMISSION VOL 3, *supra* note 8, at 1.

RCMP, and various air safety officials who failed to stop two bombs from being placed by Sikh terrorists on two Air India planes departing from Canada.

The key role played by the Arar and Air India inquiries, as well as the 1981 McDonald Commission, which made recommendations that led to the creation of CSIS in 1984 as a civilian intelligence agency, are themselves a testament to the relative shortcomings of the ordinary processes of legislative, executive, and judicial review and oversight of national security activities. All three inquiries were hybrid ad hoc institutions headed by sitting or former judges, but technically part of the executive. All three inquiries were given powers to examine secret information that had been denied to legislative committees. In addition, the Arar and Air India commissions were given wide-ranging "whole of government" mandates that are denied to both Ministers and executive watchdog agencies such as SIRC and the CSE Commissioner.

Accountability gaps are caused by a number of factors. One is a mismatch between whole-of-government security activities and siloed or stovepiped accountability structures. The stovepiped nature of accountability adversely affects review bodies such as SIRC who do not have jurisdiction to examine the conduct of other agencies. It also affects oversight mechanisms because the Minister of Public Safety provides direction to CSIS but the Minister of Defence provides direction to CSE—despite the fact that both intelligence agencies frequently work together. Terrorism financing initiatives span even more ministries, including Finance, Revenue, Public Safety, and Justice.

The second cause of accountability gaps is a lack of access to secret information. This can compound the problem of siloed and limited jurisdiction. It can prevent a reviewer such as SIRC from examining both ends of an information-sharing relationship even within the federal government. A combination of jurisdictional limits and secrecy issues can frustrate review. The Arar Commission recommended the creation of statutory gateways that would allow the three review bodies for CSIS, CSE, and the RCMP to share secret information with each other and to conduct joint reviews. Statutory gateways that explicitly authorize the sharing of secret information are necessary because unauthorized sharing of classified information is a crime under the Security of Information Act—Canada's version of the Official Secrets Act.[26]

The Arar Commission also recommended that a number of agencies with important security responsibilities, such as those responsible for border security, foreign affairs, and financial intelligence, be subject to independent review dedicated to matters of security.[27] The Canadian government rejected this 2006 recommendation even while allowing security information to be more readily given to 17 different agencies designated under the 2015 Security of Canada Information Sharing Act.

The previous Conservative government's position was that existing review by the Privacy Commissioner and the Auditor General is adequate. However, the Privacy Commissioner raised concerns in a 2014 report that it has inadequate powers to review security information-sharing and does not have full access to information that is classified as secret.[28] The Auditor

---

[26] Security of Information Act, R.C.S. 1985, c. O-5 (Can.).

[27] Arar Commission, *supra* note 6, at 580ff.

[28] Office of the Privacy Commissioner of Canada, Checks and Controls: Reinforcing Privacy Protection and Oversight for the Canadian Intelligence Community in an Era of Cyber-Surveillance (2014).

General, for its part, focuses on matters of economy, but has issued some helpful reports on national security and the inadequacy of the review structure in that field.[29]

A lack of effective resources can also contribute to accountability gaps. The Commissioner for the CSE has an annual budget of around $2 million and authorization for 10 full-time staff to review CSE, which in turn has a reported budget of $350–422 million and almost 2,000 full-time staff.[30] SIRC, with an annual budget under $3 million and 17 full-time staff, reviews CSIS, which has over 3,200 employees and a budget of over $500 million.[31] To its credit, the previous Conservative government in its April 2015 budget almost doubled SIRC's budget with a $12.5 million commitment spread over five years.[32] Nevertheless, SIRC, unlike the Australian Inspector General of Intelligence and Security,[33] still does not have the power to examine other intelligence matters in government, including the work of CSE. It cannot even follow the trail of CSIS intelligence to other parts of the Canadian government that may be informed and act on it. It also cannot examine the activities of other federal agencies that may assist CSIS in its investigations.

D. Summary

It is important to distinguish between after-the-fact review, such as that conducted by SIRC and the CSE Commissioner, and real-time oversight conducted by ministers and the PMNS Advisor. The former focuses on questions of propriety including legality and human rights while the latter focuses on effectiveness and efficiency. Unfortunately, two recent commissions of inquiry in Canada have concluded that the structures of both review and oversight are inadequate and outdated. Both review and oversight suffer from being focused on particular agencies while the Canadian government, like many other governments, increasingly takes a whole-of-government approach to security.

The accountability gaps that have emerged between whole-of-government security activities and their reviewers can harm rights, including privacy. This in turn affects public confidence and social acceptance of intelligence and other security activities. Accountability gaps can hurt security if they prevent overseers from being properly and timely informed, or if they undermine coordination and dispute resolution between security agencies.

III. LIMITED LEGISLATIVE ACCOUNTABILITY

Canada, unlike most democracies, does not give any parliamentarians routine access to secret information.[34] To be sure, committees in the House of Commons and in Canada's unelected Senate examine matters related to terrorism and national security, but they do so without the

---

[29] Whitaker & Farson, *supra* note 17, at 29–30.

[30] COMMUNICATIONS SECURITY ESTABLISHMENT COMMISSIONER, ANNUAL REPORT 2012–2013 (2012).

[31] Chris Hall, *CSIS Watchdog Agency Starved of Staff, Resources*, CBC NEWS (Feb. 20, 2015), http://www.cbc.ca/news/politics/csis-watchdog-agency-starved-of-staff-resources-1.2965276.

[32] Ian MacLeod, *Spy Watchdog May Become Super-Sized: Experts*, OTTAWA CITIZEN, Apr. 21, 2015.

[33] *See* Hardy and Williams chapter in this volume.

[34] Nicholas MacDonald, *Parliamentarians and National Security in Canada*, 35(4) CAN. PARLIAMENTARY REV. 33, 33–41 (2011).

benefit of classified information. This is in contrast to executive watchdog committees such as SIRC or ad hoc public inquiries that have access to secret information but are subject to governmental controls on publicizing such information.

A. The Failure to Implement the McDonald Commission's Recommendations for a Democratic Approach to National Security

In 1981, the McDonald Commission recommended that a parliamentary committee be created with an ability to hear classified information in camera. It recognized the risk of leaks, but concluded that Canadian legislators were no less trustworthy than those in other democracies—including Australia and the United States—that had access to classified information.[35] It recognized that Parliament had traditionally shied away from discussing security matters, but argued that parliamentarians had a democratic responsibility for the actions of security services. It recommended a small Joint Committee of experienced parliamentarians from the House of Commons and the Senate, including leaders of the opposition parties or those appointed by them. The Committee would have jurisdiction over all intelligence matters except criminal intelligence ones involving the RCMP. The committee would hear in camera briefings from the minister responsible for CSIS as well as from SIRC. Although SIRC produces public annual reports, it also writes many more classified reports to the Minister of Public Safety. The McDonald Commission predicted that the new parliamentary committee "should be as much concerned with the effectiveness of the security intelligence organization as with the legality or propriety of its operations."[36]

The McDonald Commission's recommendations were a response to widespread illegal activity by the RCMP in the aftermath of domestic terrorism in October 1970 that resulted in the declaration of martial law. Although the government accepted many of the Commission's recommendations, including the creation of CSIS and the SIRC, it rejected the creation of a parliamentary committee. In 1983, a Senate Committee concluded that a parliamentary committee might duplicate the review work of SIRC. It also noted the "vagaries of time, changes in membership and overwork" that beset all legislative committees. The Committee and likely the government's main objection to a parliamentary committee, however, was "the problem of maintaining the security of information." Although the Committee cited the "partisan motivations"[37] of legislators as a concern in this regard, an unstated concern was that some members might then or in the future be committed to the separation of Quebec. This was a delicate subject as some of the RCMP illegalities that led to the creation of SIRC were aimed at the Parti Quebecois, which was elected as a provincial government of Quebec in 1976 and that as a government held two subsequent referenda asking for a mandate for Quebec to separate from Canada. Another concern was that, given Canada's reliance on foreign intelligence, future leaks might reveal not only Canada's secrets but those of its allies, especially the United States, U.K., and France.

---

[35] COMMISSION OF INQUIRY CONCERNING CERTAIN ACTIVITIES OF THE ROYAL CAN. MOUNTED POLICE, SECOND REPORT: FREEDOM AND SECURITY UNDER THE LAW 902 (1981).

[36] Id. at 899.

[37] SPECIAL SENATE COMMITTEE ON THE CANADIAN INTELLIGENCE SERVICE, REPORT OF THE SPECIAL SENATE COMMITTEE ON THE CANADIAN INTELLIGENCE SERVICE, NOVEMBER 1983, at 32 (1983).

B. Current Controversies and Proposals

Not much in the way of legislative accountability has changed since the rejection of the McDonald Commission's recommendations. To be sure, some parliamentary committees—especially in the unelected Senate—have issued some valuable reports, including some that revealed deficiencies in Canada's security operations. At the same time, however, major security scandals have been handled outside of Parliament. For example, the government in 2004 appointed a public inquiry to examine the actions of Canadian officials in relation to Maher Arar. SIRC and the RCMP review body were not able to get to the bottom of the matter in part because they could not share secret information. Although a parliamentary committee would not similarly be limited by jurisdictional silos, it would not be able to gain access to secret information.

In 2004 and 2005, a parliamentary committee report and a subsequent bill were introduced that would have created a statutory committee modeled on the U.K.'s statutory Intelligence and Security Committee.[38] The Committee would have access to secret information, but the quid pro quo was that the parliamentarians on the committee would be persons permanently bound to secrecy and subject to prosecution for leaks under the strict terms of Canada's Security of Information Act. Parliamentarians and the committee itself would not be able to rely on parliamentary privilege.[39] The bill was not passed before the 2006 election. The Conservative government did not reintroduce it, but a number of private member bills were introduced. One such bill was particularly weak because it would give the responsible minister final and non-reviewable power to decide how much, if any, secret information to provide the Committee.[40] Another bill was more robust in giving the Committee the traditional right enjoyed by parliamentary committees to compel witnesses and the production of material, but it too proposed a statutory committee subject to secrecy legislation and without inherent parliamentary privileges.[41]

Parliament took a more aggressive approach that relied on parliamentary privileges with respect to examining whether the Canadian military was complicit in torture when they transferred their detainees to Afghan officials in Afghanistan in the late 2000s. A parliamentary committee examined this issue,[42] but was repeatedly rebuffed by military, foreign affairs, and other officials who claimed they could not reveal information because it was classified as secret. The government insisted that disclosure of the requested documents would violate the law, place the lives of Canadian Forces members at risk, and make it more difficult for Canada to work with its allies.[43] The speaker of the House of Commons made an unprecedented ruling in April 2010 that the government of Canada was prima facie in contempt of Parliament.[44] Given that the government at the time did not have a majority of seats in the

---

[38] National Security Committee of Parliamentarians Bill, c. C-81 (Can.).

[39] R.S.C. 1985, c. O-5.

[40] National Security Committee of Parliamentarians Bill c. C-551 § 14 (Can.).

[41] Intelligence and Security Committee of Parliament Act, 2014, Bill. S-220 § 16 (Can.).

[42] About, the Special Committee on the Canadian Mission in Afghanistan, http://www.parl. gc.ca/CommitteeBusiness/AboutCommittees.aspx?Cmte=AFGH&Language=E&Mode=1&Parl=40& Ses=3 (last visited May 31, 2015).

[43] Reg Whitaker, *Prime Minister vs. Parliament*, The Toronto Star, Dec. 18, 2009.

[44] CBC News, *Afghan Records Denial Is Privilege Breach: Speaker*, CBC News, Apr. 27, 2010.

Commons, a vote in support of the contempt motion could have defeated the government. The government entered into negotiations with opposition parties, resulting in the adoption of an ad hoc process that allowed a few members of Parliament—assisted by retired judges— limited access to secret documents. This process resulted in the release in redacted form of a minority of the requested documents,[45] but the matter eventually lost political momentum and the work of the ad hoc committee did not continue.[46] No permanent reforms emerged from a controversy that commanded the headlines for months. The threat of contempt is not likely to be a viable threat to force a government to reveal secret information to parliamentary committees, especially when the government has a clear majority in parliament.

Demands for parliamentary access to secret information resurfaced in early 2015 when the government introduced legislation to increase CSIS's powers. Four former prime ministers joined by former officials wrote an open letter calling for enhanced review, including parliamentary review. They stated:

> The four of us most certainly know the enormity of the responsibility of keeping Canada safe, something always front of mind for a prime minister. We have come together with 18 other Canadians who have served as Supreme Court of Canada justices, ministers of justice and of public safety, solicitors-general, members of the Security and Intelligence Review Committee and commissioners responsible for overseeing the RCMP and upholding privacy laws . . . . We all agree that protecting public safety is one of government's most important functions and that Canada's national security agencies play a vital role in meeting that responsibility. Yet we all also share the view that the lack of a robust and integrated accountability regime for Canada's national security agencies makes it difficult to meaningfully assess the efficacy and legality of Canada's national security activities. This poses serious problems for public safety and for human rights. . . efforts to enhance parliamentary oversight of national security agencies have also been unsuccessful. For example, in October 2004, a report calling for parliamentary oversight over national security activities was presented to the minister of public safety; this report contained an oversight structure that was agreed upon by representatives of all parties in both the House of Commons and the Senate. Legislation was introduced at the time, but not adopted before the next election.[47]

Despite the above extraordinary intervention, the government continued to resist calls for enhanced parliamentary oversight of national security. The Conservative government's rationale for its refusal is consistent with the Liberal government's refusal in 1984 to implement the McDonald's Commission recommendation for a parliamentary committee. The rationale is the fear that Canadian parliamentarians will leak secret information.[48] Even opposition parties who propose reform no longer support the McDonald Commission's

---

[45] CBC News, *Afghan Detainee Files Perused by MPs*, CBC News, July 10, 2010.

[46] Laura Payton, *Afghan Detainee Records Still Hold Questions, MPs Say*, CBC News, June 22, 2011.

[47] Chretien et al., *supra* note 2.

[48] Tonda MacCharles, *Government Plans Four Amendments to Soften Anti-terror Bill C-51*, Toronto Star, Mar. 30, 2015.

recommendation and contemplate that parliamentarians, like civil servants, would be subject to the strict terms and possible prosecutions under Canada's version of the Official Secrets Act if they leak information.

C. Is Increased Legislative Involvement a Good Idea?

With the October 2015 election of a new Liberal government, enhanced parliamentary review will remain on the Canadian political agenda. Nevertheless the high turnover rate among Canadian parliamentarians and the haphazard nature of their knowledge and interest in security matters suggest that the benefits of enhanced legislative review can be overstated. The unelected Senate has much more continuity and more expertise on security matters than the elected House of Commons. Although the Senate played a key role in the creation of the CSIS Act in 1984, its influence and democratic legitimacy has declined significantly since that time.

Comparative experience supports the idea that legislative review of security activities is at best likely to make modest contributions. The Intelligence and Security Committee in the U.K. is the model for current reform proposals in Canada, but Canadian accounts of the ISC often discount U.K. criticisms of its performance on sensitive issues, including possible complicity in torture.[49] Prime Minister Cameron was forced to appoint a public inquiry to examine such matters[50] despite ISC reports on that matter, and some still think a public inquiry should have been appointed to examine the failure to prevent the 2005 London bombings.[51] Legislative committees are also vulnerable to the conduct of all of their members.[52]

The performance of legislative review in the United States has been, if anything, even less inspiring than in the U.K. Various members of Congress were briefed on the activities of the NSA after 9/11, but it took the *New York Times* to reveal President Bush's illegal orders for NSA domestic spying in 2005, and then the Snowden leaks, to focus public attention on the NSA's collection of bulk data.

There are concerns that legislators in Congress often lack the expertise or the incentive to conduct effective oversight.[53] Giving legislators access to secret information but no mechanism for revealing their concerns may only allow the government to claim legitimacy for illegal and improper conduct. Some commentators have made interesting recommendations that would give opposition parties with access to secret information powers to push for the declassification of documents,[54] but there has been little uptake on such proposals. Drawing

---

[49] *See* Moran and Walker chapter in this volume.

[50] Rowena Mason, *UK Torture Inquiry Could Summon Blair and Straw*, The Guardian, Dec. 14, 2014.

[51] Esther Addley, *7/7 Survivors End Battle for Public Inquiry into Bombings*, The Guardian, Aug. 1, 2011.

[52] Stephen Castle, *British Lawmaker Accused of Influence Peddling, Steps Down as Intelligence Panel Chairman*, N.Y. Times, Feb. 24, 2015.

[53] Amy B. Zegart, Eyes on Spies: Congress and the United States Intelligence Community 85 (2011).

[54] Bruce Ackerman, Before the Next Attack: Preserving Civil Liberties in an Age of Terrorism 85 (2006); Stephen Schulhofer, *Oversight of National Security Activities in the United States, in* Secrecy, National Security and the Vindication of Constitutional Law 42 (David Cole et al. eds., 2013).

on his long career in intelligence, David Omand has warned that a committee with powers to release secret information may actually see less such information.[55]

Although the need to maintain public confidence is often posited as the goal for increased accountability measures, it is not clear that a legislative committee with limited access to secret information will promote confidence in the general public. Confidence in legislators seems at an all-time low. Rather than relying on its members, much of the legitimacy of a legislative committee might come from constructive engagement with civil society.

It is especially important that a committee be prepared to hear from well-informed critics of the security establishment. To this end, thought should be given to allowing counsel or other support staff for committees to have a greater role in deciding what witnesses will appear before a legislative committee. There was public controversy over what witnesses were called to comment in committee over recent Canadian security bills introduced and enacted in 2015. The Common committees for example did not hear from the Privacy Commissioner despite the impact that the bill would have on the work of that parliamentary office. Opposition parties were able to call some witnesses, but the government was able to use its majority status to call more witnesses.[56] The debate was more partisan than previous security debates.

One way to counteract the danger of making national security a partisan issue would be to depart from the model used in Canada of allowing the government to appoint the chair. As David Omand has suggested, a new mechanism could require the appointment of an opposition member as chair.[57] Another alternative would be the German practice of allowing majority and minorities take turns electing the chair of a review committee, with the chair frequently rotating.[58] The new Liberal government has promised that the Chairs of all Committees will be elected by the members of the committees by secret ballot, but has not yet proposed legislation governing a new security committee.[59]

Canadian legislative committees are notoriously under-resourced. A national security committee's effectiveness could be improved by having security experts advise the committee members. Canadian committees do not have their own counsel, but a national security committee would benefit from such assistance due to the complex legal issues inherent in security matters especially when secret information in involved. Counsel should also be able to challenge first in committee, and then if necessary in court, the government's practice of over-claiming secrecy. One of the advantages of Canadian commissions of inquiry is that they have been staffed with lawyers who have challenged with some success governmental claims of secrecy.[60]

---

[55] DAVID OMAND, SECURING THE STATE 265 (2010) (arguing that changing parliamentary oversight in the U.K. from its current form to a Select Committee would result in government witnesses having less freedom to testify).

[56] Kady O'Malley, *Bill C-51: Privacy Watchdog Daniel Therrien Blocked from Committee Witness List*, CBC NEWS, Mar. 12, 2015.

[57] Omand, *supra*, note 55.

[58] ARAR COMMISSION, *supra* note 6, at 344.

[59] "House of Commons committees off to scrappy, skeptical start" December 12, 2015 at http://www.cbc.ca/news/politics/commons-committees-delays-1.3362114.

[60] Canada (Attorney General) v. Canada (Commission of Inquiry into the Actions of Canadian Officials in Relation to Maher Arar) 2007 F.C. 766.

D. Summary

Canada lags well behind other democracies in legislative review and oversight of national security. Given how much information is classified (and over-classified) as secret, it is difficult for parliamentarians to engage in credible review without access to secret information. Even basic data such as the numbers of those on no-fly lists and hundreds of review reports prepared by SIRC and the CSE Commissioner are classified as secret. As such, no Canadian legislator has access to such information. This severely diminishes the ability of Parliament to hold security officials accountable.

That said, the experience of other countries suggests that legislative access to secret material is no panacea that will eliminate accountability gaps. Moreover, access to secret information with no mechanism for disclosure causes its own dilemmas. Although increased legislative review may increase parliamentary and public knowledge of national security matters, it is a mistake to place too much faith in legislative review of national security activities or to ignore the possibility that such review may give the government legislative cover for questionable activities.

IV. THE INCREASING EMPHASIS ON JUDICIAL OVERSIGHT
A. The Least Dangerous Branch?

In theory, the judiciary is the least able of all three branches to hold government to account for its national security activities. The Arar Commission explained that "the judiciary is a reactive institution" that can only respond to misconduct when it becomes the subject of litigation. It warned that, because of secrecy, "affected individuals may never know that they have been subject to a national security investigation."[61] Even if individuals do have such knowledge, they may not have the resources to bring a court challenge. Even if they do, they may face great secrecy barriers in their litigation.

Even without considering the judiciary's traditional deference on national security matters, the institutional constraints of the judiciary suggest that it is poorly suited to hold government to account for secret national security activities. The judiciary will only be concerned about one component of propriety: legality, including constitutionality. Nevertheless, there are increasing signs in Canada that more reliance is being placed on judicial oversight of intelligence and national security activities.

B. The Role of Specially Designated Judges of Canada's
Federal Court

Since its creation as a civilian intelligence agency in 1984, CSIS has had to obtain warrants from specially designated judges to conduct electronic and other forms of surveillance. The judges are members of the Federal Court, which reviews the administrative activities of the federal government. The judges review not only CSIS's warrant applications but also the use of its intelligence to justify immigration decisions. In several of those cases, they have found

---

[61] ARAR COMMISSION, *supra* note 6. at 491.

CSIS to have breached its duty of candor to the court, a duty that is especially high when the government is allowed to make ex parte representations to the Court in closed hearings.[62]

Judges as independent and impartial persons generally command more public confidence and attention than legislators or even executive watchdogs. Specialized security courts such as the Foreign Intelligence Surveillance Court in the United States or specially designated members of the Federal Court in Canada raise some delicate issues. On the one hand, there is a danger that such specialized courts may degrade the judicial "brand" if they are seen as too close to the government, too secretive, or even captured by their close working relationship with intelligence agencies.[63] On the other hand, specialized judges may have greater confidence and greater abilities in supervising intelligence agencies. They may also feel particularly aggrieved and responsible if they have discovered that the government and the intelligence agencies have been less than candid with them or done more than they authorized.

C. New CSIS Powers

Legislation enacted in Canada in the wake of the October 2014 terrorist attacks gives CSIS unprecedented new powers that go beyond its traditional mandate as a pure intelligence agency. These new powers include ones to conduct surveillance outside of Canada and to violate Canadian laws including the Charter to reduce security threats within Canada.[64]

The previous Conservative government that enacted these measures defended the sufficiency of existing review and oversight mechanisms over these new powers on the basis that they require warrants to be granted by specially designated judges of the Federal Court. For example, former Minister of Defence Jason Kenny argued that the new legislation "doesn't give new powers to police or intelligence agencies but rather to judges, to courts…".[65] The government argued that these powers are consistent with the Charter because they must be authorized on a case-by-case basis by a specially designated Federal Court judge who must find that the requested powers are proportionate to the security threat, and because they cannot include powers to cause death or bodily harm, invade sexual integrity, or obstruct justice.[66]

Critics of the new powers, including myself and Craig Forcese,[67] argue that the new warrant regime is overbroad because it allows judges to authorize violations of any Charter right including some that are not easily subject to limitation. The new warrant proceeding is, in our view, very different from traditional CSIS warrants or other search warrants because it contemplates judges pre-authorizing Charter violations rather than granting warrants to

---

[62] In the matter of an application by X for a warrant pursuant to Sections 12 and 21 of the Canadian Security Intelligence Service Act, [2013] F.C. 1275 at ¶ 118.

[63] For my prior expression of some of these concerns, see Kent Roach, *The Law Working Itself Pure?*, in GUANTANAMO AND BEYOND: EXCEPTIONAL COURTS AND MILITARY COURTS IN COMPARATIVE PERSPECTIVE (Oren Gross & Fionnuala Ni Aoláin eds., 2013).

[64] Protecting Canada from Terrorist Act S.C. 2015 c.9; Anti-terrorism Act, 2015 S.C. 2015 c. 20. For an analysis of these laws in relation to broader Canadian antiterrorism strategy, see CRAIG FORCESE & KENT ROACH, FALSE SECURITY: THE RADICALIZATION OF CANADA'S TERROR LAWS (2015).

[65] Laura Payton, *C-51 Confusion Abounds as Tories Rush Bill C-51 to Committee*, CBC NEWS (Feb. 20, 2015), http://www.cbc.ca/news/politics/c-51-confusion-abounds-as-tories-rush-anti-terrorism-bill-to-committee-1.2963569.

[66] CANADIAN SERVICE INTELLIGENCE SERVICE ACT, R.S.C. 1985, c. C-23 §§ 12.1(2)–(3).

[67] FORCESE & ROACH, *supra* note 64, ch.7.

prevent unreasonable searches and seizures.[68] We have also argued that warrant procedures are not robust protections for Charter rights because they are conducted in secret without the affected party or perhaps even a special advocate being present to play an adversarial role. In part based on the American experience with the Foreign Intelligence Surveillance Court,[69] we predict that many of these new warrant decisions will remain secret for operational reasons and may never be appealed or challenged in criminal proceedings. The new Canadian provisions do not provide for the appointment of amicus curiae to challenge applications for warrants that raise general issues, and there are no provisions requiring the release of redacted warrant judgments, as there are in the USA Freedom Act.[70]

D. *The Mosley Judgment*

A case of particular relevance to the enhanced emphasis on judicial oversight of new intelligence powers given to CSIS started in 2009, when Justice Mosley, one of the judges of the Federal Court of Canada specially designated to deal with security matters and a former civil servant expert in security issues, issued warrants to allow CSIS to intercept communications of Canadian citizens outside of Canada. The issue of whether the CSIS Act authorized such foreign activities had been a matter of controversy, but has subsequently been confirmed in 2015 legislation that provides that specially designated judges can authorize investigative activities outside of Canada without regard to any other law.[71]

In August 2013, upon reading the annual public report of the CSE Commissioner, which suggested that CSIS should provide the Federal Court with additional information about assistance that had been received in carrying out the warrant, Justice Mosley convened a new hearing on his own initiative.

He was assisted in this hearing by security-cleared amicus who had access to relevant classified information. Such amicus are appointed at the discretion of the court, and the Chief Justice of the Federal Court has indicated that they will be appointed to assist with the new warrants created by Parliament in 2015.[72] Such lawyers can be helpful to the extent that they can serve an adversarial challenge function.

Justice Mosley and the amicus also had access to the CSE Commissioner's classified report to the Minister of Defence. Justice Mosley drew on a SIRC report to note that the subcontracting of surveillance to Five Eyes partners was not an isolated incident, but had occurred with as many as 35 warrants issued since 2009. This underlines how judges in the national security context may benefit from other review structures.

---

[68] ANTI-TERRORISM ACT, R.S.C. 2015, c. C-51 (adding § 21.1 to the CSIS Act).

[69] The Privacy and Civil Liberties Oversight Board in the United States has been critical of some FISC decisions, and has recommended use of special advocates to provide adversarial challenge and steps to encourage more appeals and declassification of judgments. PRIVACY AND CIVIL LIBERTIES OVERSIGHT BOARD, REPORT ON THE TELEPHONE RECORDS PROGRAM CONDUCTED UNDER SECTION 215 OF THE USA PATRIOT ACT AND ON THE OPERATIONS OF THE FOREIGN INTELLIGENCE SURVEILLANCE COURT (2014), *available at* https://www.pclob.gov/library/215-Report_on_the_Telephone_Records_Program.pdf.

[70] HR 2048-14 §§ 401–402.

[71] CANADIAN SECURITY INTELLIGENCE ACT R.S.C. 1985, c. C-23 § 21(3.1).

[72] Cristin Schmitz, *The Chief Justice Shows Where Line Is Drawn*, LAWYERS WEEKLY (July 3, 2015), *available at* http://www.lawyersweekly.ca/articles/2417.

In a declassified but redacted judgment released in December 2013, Justice Mosley concluded that CSIS had misled him by not revealing its plans to draw on the assistance of CSE's Five Eyes signal intelligence partners in carrying out the surveillance. He called this a "deliberate decision to keep the Court in the dark about the scope and extent of the foreign collection efforts that would flow from the Court's issuance of a warrant."[73] He did not reveal which foreign agency within the Five Eyes had assisted CSIS, or what precise assistance they provided. He did, however, conclude that the tasking of foreign agencies by Canadian officials to conduct surveillance was unlawful. Although the warrants he granted had been used as "protective cover,"[74] they did not and could not authorize the use of foreign agencies to conduct surveillance. He concluded that the enabling legislation of CSIS and CSE should not be interpreted as authorizing requests that would invade human rights and Canadian sovereignty.

Justice Mosley expressed concerns that Canada could lose control of intelligence it asked its foreign partners to collect. Indeed, he emphasized that past experience in the Arar and other cases of Canadians tortured in part because of Canadian information-sharing underlined the grave risks when Canada loses control over its own intelligence.[75] He ruled that no reference should be made by CSIS, CSE, or its legal advisors to the erroneous idea that CSIS warrants authorized the tasking of foreign agencies.

In a final gesture indicating potential synergies and reinforcement between judicial and independent watchdog executive review, he required that a copy of his decision be provided to both SIRC and the CSE Commissioner. His order indicated that henceforth judges should be informed whether requests had been made to foreign agencies to obtain information about Canadian targets outside of Canada. If so, this might affect a judge's determination of whether a Canadian warrant was necessary.[76]

This judgment demonstrates how judges can both supplement and fill some of the gaps left in the review of the work of intelligence agencies. Justice Mosley interpreted the CSIS Act so as to prevent a transnational accountability gap that would occur if Canada tasked foreign agencies to conduct surveillance of Canadian targets, leaving Canada without control of the intelligence produced by its own targeting and tasking. Judicial attempts to plug accountability gaps are to be welcomed. Nevertheless such judicial creativity will generally only occur when agencies engage in illegal misconduct. Indeed, much of Justice Mosley's bold judgment was premised on the assumption that Canadian tasking of surveillance to its Five Eye partners would violate both domestic and international law.

Although Justice Mosley's trigger was a particular warrant, his judgment, assisted by the reports of executive watchdog reviewers, also sought to establish general rules to govern the collection of intelligence going forward. As Professor Renan points out in her chapter, this has the virtue of bringing some rules to intelligence gathering, albeit not always in the most transparent, robust, or expert manner.[77] That said, although parts of the Mosley judgment were redacted, they appear not to affect those parts that set forth rules to govern similar

---

[73] In the matter of an application by X for a warrant pursuant to Sections 12 and 21 of the Canadian Security Intelligence Service Act, [2013] F.C. 1275 at ¶ 117.

[74] *Id.* ¶ 110.

[75] *Id.* ¶ 115.

[76] *Id.* ¶ 124.

[77] On the similar phenomena of the American FISC *see* Dapha Renan's chapter in this volume.

warrant requests in the future. As in other areas, judicial policy-making may compensate for legislative and executive failures to address the relevant issues.

E. *Short-Circuiting Warrant Requirements?*

Justice Mosley's judgment contemplates that Canadian agencies can avoid the Canadian warrant process by obtaining information about Canadian targets from foreign agencies. There are no specific rules that prevent Canadian intelligence agencies from asking foreign agencies to perform tasks for them.

In the national security context we must be aware that rights-friendly interventions such as the Mosley judgment may produce substitution effects in which intelligence agencies find less constrained ways to achieve similar results.[78] In this context, CSIS could simply ask foreign agencies to obtain information without any suggestion that such a process was authorized by Canadian law or under a Canadian warrant. Intelligence agencies may have an incentive to avoid the warrant process by employing other means. Judges will never know about cases where warrants could have been sought, but were not. This underlines the continued importance of legislative and executive review of the secret activities of intelligence agencies.

It remains to be seen how often CSIS will seek warrants for surveillance or other activities outside of Canada to reduce threats to the security of Canada. At the same time, warrants will be required if CSIS wishes to violate Canadian laws or Charter rights within Canada. The new legislation is silent on what, if any, accountability measures judges will provide to ensure that security agencies do not go beyond the terms of new warrants. Justice Mosley's judgment suggests that judges may not tolerate activity beyond what they have authorized *if they find out about it*. It is not comforting, however, that it appears to have been Justice Mosley's extracurricular reading of external reports that led to the discovery that CSIS had subcontracted surveillance to foreign allies.

Even more troubling is that the new CSIS warrants allow either the judge or CSIS itself to ask "another person"[79] to assist in the execution of the warrants. In the Mosley decision the "other person" was CSE, which was subject to its own independent review. It will be recalled that it was the public report of the CSE Commissioner that prompted Justice Mosley to call a hearing to explore how CSIS was executing the warrant he had originally granted in 2009. In other contexts, however, the "other person" may be domestic or foreign agencies not subject to review. Although the Mosley judgment reveals strengths of judicial oversight, it also reveals that judicial oversight may be dependent on the initiative and expertise of both the judge who issues the warrant and of executive watchdog reviewers.

F. *Summary*

Even if judges strictly and expertly enforce the limits that they have placed on warrants, the nature of CSIS warrants means that the appropriateness of the limits that they set may not

---

[78] On the phenomena of substitution effects between different counterterrorism instruments, *see* Kent Roach, *Comparative Counter-Terrorism Law Comes of Age, in* Comparative Counter-Terrorism Law 11–12 (Kent Roach ed., 2015).

[79] Canadian Security Intelligence Service Act, R.S.C. 1983, c. C-23 §§ 22.3(1), 24.1(1), *amended by* R.S.C. 2015, c. C-51.

generally be tested on appeal. Because there is no requirement that a target for the warrant be notified, and because CSIS warrants will not generally obtain evidence to be used in criminal proceedings, it is unlikely that targets of the new warrants will be able to have the warrant reviewed once it has been granted.

The Mosley judgment reveals some of the potential of judicial oversight and the ability of judges to enforce the limits and requirements that warrants place on intelligence agencies. Nevertheless, it also reveals how judicial oversight may be dependent on the findings of executive watchdog reviewers. These reviewers are also the only ones in Canada in a possible position to see if CSIS avoids applying for warrants for intelligence activities that should be conducted subject to judicial oversight. A substitution effect of the Mosley judgment may be that CSIS and other intelligence agencies will rely even more on foreign agencies to provide intelligence that Canadian agencies could have obtained themselves, albeit subject to a warrant issued by a Canadian judge and executive watchdog review.

V. STOVEPIPED AND PARTIAL EXECUTIVE WATCHDOG REVIEW

As discussed in the first part of this chapter, executive watchdog review in Canada is conducted both by a sitting or retired judge acting as Commissioner of the CSE and by the members and staff of SIRC who have access to all secret information held by CSIS (except Cabinet confidences). These executive review mechanisms are hybrids between the executive and other branches of government. Like other parts of the executive branch, they can be tasked by and report to responsible ministers. In the case of the CSE commissioner, the review body borrows from the brand of the judiciary with respect to independence and impartiality of judges. SIRC borrows from the brand of the legislature in ensuring representation from all major political parties. SIRC, like the CSE Commissioner, is also presently headed by a retired judge.

A. The Need for a Government-Wide National Security Review Body or "Super SIRC"

In 2006, the Arar Commission recommended a significant expansion of SIRC's mandate to include the national security activities of Citizenship and Immigration Canada, Transport Canada, the Financial Transactions and Report Analysis Centre, and the Department of Foreign Affairs. It also recommended a revitalized RCMP complaints agency being given jurisdiction to review the national security work of the Canada Border Services Agency. Further, it suggested that statutory gateways be created between review agencies so that they could share secret information and conduct joint reviews of joint operations among CSIS, RCMP, and CSE. It also recommended a coordinating committee with an independent chair, composed of the chairs of the three main review bodies.

All of these recommendations recognized and were united by the need for whole-of-government review to match whole-of-government security responses.[80] At the same time, the Commission ultimately opted for maintaining expertise by recommending that an expanded SIRC, CSE Commissioner, and RCMP review body all remain in place instead of

---

[80] Kent Roach, *Review and Oversight of National Security Activities with Some Reflections on Canada's Arar Commission*, 29 CARDOZO L. REV. 53 (2007).

proposals made to the Commission for the creation of one big review committee or "super SIRC" that could review all national security activities.

Much water has passed under the bridge since the Arar Commission's recommendations. As a member of the Arar Commission's research advisory committee, I supported its 2006 recommendations. A decade later, however, my view is that nothing less than a super SIRC is now necessary to renovate Canada's antiquated review structure. In 2006, it was realistic to expect that the new Conservative government, with its commitment to strengthening parliamentary review, might adopt some version of a bill introduced by the Martin government for a national security committee of parliamentarians. Although the subsequent Afghan detainee affair strengthened the case for a parliamentary committee with access to secret information, no permanent parliamentary reform emerged from that crisis. The government has subsequently abolished the Office of the Inspector General for CSIS, which acted as the minister's eyes in ensuring the legality of CSIS conduct. It also rejected the Arar Commission's recommendations that the RCMP review body receive unrestricted access to secret information or statutory gateways with SIRC when it reformed the Civilian Review and Complaints Commission for the RCMP. In addition, the government, contrary to the Arar Commission's recommendations that audit-based reviews are essential for effective review of secret national security activities, decided that the RCMP review body cannot conduct reviews if it would compromise its ability to hear external complaints arising from the policing activities of almost 20,000 RCMP officers.[81]

Perhaps most important, nothing less than a super SIRC could review information-sharing under the 2015 Security of Canada Information Sharing Act,[82] which allows 17 different departments (many subject to no independent review) to receive broadly defined security information. The Conservative government that enacted the law argued that the existing review structures including the Privacy Commissioner and the Auditor General were up to the task.[83] Nevertheless, this ignored the stovepiped nature of existing reviews and the limited expertise and capacity that the Privacy Commissioner (concerned only with privacy) and the Auditor General (concerned with government economy) bring to the task of reviewing information sharing and other integrated national security activities.

A super SIRC could eventually take on the work of the CSE commissioner and the minimal national security review work done by the Civilian Review and Complaints Commission for the RCMP. The goal would be to expand SIRC's mandate so that it has jurisdiction to examine all national security matters within the federal government. This would allow SIRC to follow the trail of intelligence, information-sharing, and other national security activities throughout government without the need for statutory gateways. The Conservative government demonstrated some willingness to give SIRC more resources, but legislative reform is required to give SIRC a wider mandate and access to secret information held by agencies other than CSIS.

---

[81] Enhancing RCMP Accountability Act S.C. 2013 c.18 Part VI.

[82] S.C. 2015 c.20.

[83] GOVERNMENT OF CANADA, BACKGROUNDER TO THE SECURITY OF CANADA INFORMATION SHARING ACT (2015), *available at* http://news.gc.ca/web/article-en.do?nid=926879.

A super SIRC might include a sitting or retired judge to benefit from association with the judiciary. It should also include better representation from civil society in partial recognition that the existing political parties represented on SIRC do not command the same type of support from the public—and especially the young—as they once did. Those who serve on a super SIRC either permanently or part-time should be prepared to cut ties that may lead to reasonable perceptions of conflict of interest. Such a diverse committee should ideally have more resources and a mandate to contribute to public education and public hearings than the existing review bodies.

SIRC's renewed mandate should continue not to be limited to questions of legality. One weakness of the CSE Commissioner is that it is restricted to questions of legality. This has meant that the Commissioner's conclusions about legality of CSE programs revealed by the Snowden leaks have understandably been couched in terms that mirror the language of the CSE's enabling statute quickly enacted after 9/11. In other words, the Commissioner has often stressed that CSE activities are not "directed" at Canadians or persons in Canada, and that the information it collects is used for the "purpose of foreign intelligence." These phrases mirror CSE's statutory mandate in s.273.64 of the National Defence Act,[84] but are at odds with fundamental Charter principles that stress that government's conduct may be unconstitutional because of its effects on persons even if the purposes animating the state are entirely proper. CSE's mandate is presently being challenged under the Charter, and the tension between the purpose-based statutory framework and the effects-based Charter framework has only been increased by the Supreme Court's recent decision recognizing privacy and anonymity interests in even basic metadata.[85] Conclusions of legality are only as good as the underlying law.

A super SIRC, like the Arar Commission, should be able to challenge government refusals to allow it to publish part of its reports because of secrecy concerns. Such challenges should be rare, but they would help prevent governments over-claiming secrecy. A less transparent alternative that would still be better than the status quo would be to allow SIRC to submit its secret reports to a parliamentary committee that could then question in camera the head of the relevant agency and the responsible minister(s) about their responses to SIRC's classified findings and recommendations. The parliamentary committee might even be given powers, perhaps subject to a supra-majority requirement, to order that parts of the classified SIRC reports be made public.

B. *The Need for Government-Wide Oversight of Efficacy: An Enhanced Role for the Prime Minister's National Security Advisor?*

Even if whole-of-government propriety review could be achieved, the issue of oversight for efficacy would still remain. As suggested above, oversight in a parliamentary system traditionally comes from the executive branch, including the minister who is responsible for the intelligence agency. At the same time, there is also a trend toward centralizing powers within

---

[84] R.S.C. 1985 c.N-5.
[85] R. v. Spencer, [2014] 2 S.C.R. 212.

the prime minister's office, and the prime minister traditionally has significant national security responsibilities.

The Air India Commission recommended that the Prime Minister's National Security (PMNS) Advisor play an enhanced oversight role for all national security activities. The previous Conservative government rejected this recommendation for enhanced oversight even though it had been echoed in 2011 by a unanimous and bipartisan report of a special Senate Committee.[86]

The Air India Commission's recommendations could be criticized as a further trend toward presidential-style powers in the prime minister's office and for short-circuiting ministerial accountability. There are also concerns that requiring a PMNS Advisor to make critical operational decisions about the disclosure of secret intelligence or other operational decisions might slow down a national security system that some fear is already too lethargic. At the same time, the need for central coordination of multiple antiterrorism tools is great. The Minister of Public Safety plays a key role, but intelligence (including foreign, military, and financial intelligence) crosses many ministerial boundaries. There is a need for central coordination.

The new Liberal government has not shown interest in giving the PMNS increased powers. It has, however, committed itself to enhanced Ministerial accountability. It has also appointed its most senior cabinet minister to serve as the Minister of Public Safety.[87]

C. A Canadian Joint Intelligence Committee?

One alternative for improving oversight directed toward efficacy would be a Canadian version of the Joint Intelligence Committee (JIC) in the U.K. Cabinet Office. The JIC includes the heads of all three intelligence agencies as well military intelligence. It directs intelligence collection and analysis and advises the prime minister. David Omand, who served on the JIC, has stressed how the JIC's practice of formulating collective decisions led all the members to better appreciate the other's perspective and "may be one reason why the UK has been able to work across domestic/overseas and policy/intelligence organizational boundaries on counter-terrorism [. . .] in ways that other nations with their more compartmentalized intelligence and police structures have not yet achieved."[88] If the agency heads have to cooperate and answer questions in such a committee, this should also influence all those who report to them.

Australia has recently proposed the creation of a new executive counterterrorism committee to be chaired by a national counterterrorism coordinator. The new committee is intended "to ensure that all agencies are working in the closest possible harmony."[89] The policy review stressed

---

[86] Senator Hugh Segal, chair, *Interim Report of Special Senate Committee on Anti-terrorism*, Mar. 2011, Recommendations 8–15.

[87] The Minister of Public Safety is the Honourable Ralph Goodale. See "The Canadian Ministry (by order of precedence" at http://www.pco-bcp.gc.ca/index.asp?lang=eng&page=prec (last visited Dec. 28, 2015). For arguments that a senior Minister should be appointed Minister of Public Safety "if national security is to be a priority and if there is to be a chance for effective co-ordination of increased security powers. . ." see Forcese and Roach *False Security, supra* note 64, at 370.

[88] OMAND, *supra* note 55, at 40.

[89] GOVERNMENT OF AUSTRALIA, REVIEW OF AUSTRALIA'S COUNTER-TERRORISM MACHINERY 22 (2015).

that counterterrorism "needs to be more consistently whole-of-government in outlook. We must ensure all relevant government departments and agencies bring their expertise to bear."[90]

In Canada, there would be a case for including the highest-ranking RCMP officer with national security responsibilities in any central coordinating committee. As the Air India Commission recommended, there would be a need for someone independent of the RCMP and CSIS such as the PMNS Advisor to resolve disputes arising from the conflict between intelligence and evidential priorities in terrorism investigations. Whether through some combination of a Canadian version of a JIC and/or an enhanced role for the PMNS Advisor, it is important that there be oversight of the effectiveness of how different agencies work together to achieve positive national security outcomes.

D. Summary

In the absence of something such as a super SIRC and enhanced oversight by the PMNS Advisor, perhaps assisted by a Canadian version of the JIC, fundamental accountability gaps will remain both with respect to the propriety and efficacy of enhanced and integrated security powers, including increased sharing of intelligence. Indeed, CSIS's new powers and its increased ability to "go it alone" by taking measures to reduce threats to the security of Canada make it even more important to renew Canada's inadequate review and oversight of the national security executive.

Legislative and judicial review can contribute at the margins, but executive review and oversight of the national security executive is absolutely fundamental. The Arar and Air India Commissions may have been overambitious in their reform recommendations, but it is unfortunate that alternative reforms have yet to be implemented.

VI. LOOMING ACCOUNTABILITY GAPS FOR TRANSNATIONAL COUNTERTERRORISM

Even if Canada was somehow able to get its domestic accountability house in order, there would still be problems with accountability for transnational national security activities. Perhaps because Canada is a relatively small country that relies heavily on intelligence and other forms of security cooperation, its experience demonstrates how its security efforts depend in no small part on the actions of other nations.

A. The Failure of the Arar Commission to Hold the United States and Syria Responsible for Rendition and Torture

The Arar Commission was appointed by the Canadian government in 2004 to examine the actions of a range of Canadian intelligence, policing, customs, and consular access officials who were all involved in Maher Arar's case. In this way, the Commission plugged whole-of-government accountability gaps. At the same time, it faced transnational accountability gaps because Arar was rendered by the United States and held and tortured by Syrian intelligence.

---

[90] Id. at 26.

The Commission invited the governments of both the United States and Syria to participate, but they exercised their sovereign right to refuse. The result was gaps in our knowledge about why Arar was rendered and discrepancies in the official American and Canadian responses to the case. In Canada, Arar received a C$10.5 million settlement. In the United States, he remained on terrorist watch lists.[91]

The Arar Commission was able only indirectly to hold the United States and Syria responsible for their more direct role in Arar's torture. After an examination of trans-European inquiries into rendition, Hans Born and Aidan Wills have concluded that transnational institutions will always be less important than domestic institutions in achieving accountability because of difficulties they will encounter accessing secret information.[92] This may be true, but there is no reason why there should not be attempts to close transnational accountability gaps.

B. *The UN 1267 Ombudsperson*

The idea of transnational accountability mechanisms may be dismissed by many as not feasible because of the unwillingness of countries to share secret information.

The refusal of the U.S. government to participate in Canada's Arar inquiry was likely related to the unwillingness of the United States to reveal secret information about its rendition program and the intelligence that it used to render Arar to Syria. Some recent reports suggest that there were disputes within the CIA at the time about whether Arar was a threat, and there were also likely disputes between the Department of State and intelligence agencies about whether assurances that Arar would not be tortured in Syria were credible.[93] As always, secrecy claims can serve legitimate interests in protecting sources, methods, and ongoing investigations, but they can also protect governments from embarrassment.

The risk of disclosure of secret intelligence was routinely cited as a barrier to review of the UN Security Council's terrorist listing process, but recent improvements in the delisting process, including the creation of an Ombudsperson to supervise that process, suggest that secrecy is not always an insurmountable obstacle to transnational accountability measures.

The Ombudsperson was created by Security Council Resolution 1904 at the end of 2009. From that time to July, 2015, the Ombudsperson considered 64 delisting requests, and of 52 completed cases has had 39 individuals and 28 entities delisted with 7 requests being refused. The Ombudsperson has also entered into arrangements with 15 countries about access to classified information.[94]

---

[91] *See generally* Kent Roach, *Uneasy Neighbors: Comparative American and Canadian Counter-Terrorism*, 38 WILLIAM MITCHELL L. REV. 1701, 1729–49 (2011).

[92] Hans Born & Aidan Wills, *International Responses to the Accountability Gap*, *in* INTERNATIONAL INTELLIGENCE COOPERATION AND ACCOUNTABILITY 199 (Hans Born, Ian Leigh & Aidan Wills eds., 2011).

[93] Alex Panetta, *Maher Arar's Arrest, Torture Almost Stopped by the CIA, Ex-spy Says*, CBC NEWS (Apr. 5, 2015), http://www.cbc.ca/news/canada/maher-arar-s-arrest-torture-almost-stopped-by-cia-ex-spy-says-1.3021759.

[94] Ombudsperson, *Report of the Ombudsperson Pursuant to Security Council Resolution 2161* (2014), U.N. Doc. S/2015/533 (July 14, 2015) at paras 6 and 13. On the work of the 1267 Ombudsperson, *see* http://www.un.org/en/sc/ombudsperson.

The Ombudsperson can be seen as a form of transnational accountability that has had some of the benefits of domestic accountability. The Office was created in response to a growing number of court judgments that raised concerns about the secretive backlisting process.[95] The Security Council retains ultimate authority over listing and delisting, but now has to veto the Ombudsperson's delisting request. Delisting has protected the rights of some who were placed on the terrorist list on the basis of inadequate or unreliable intelligence. The Ombudsperson's actions also have some marginal security benefits by removing entities that should not be listed and persons who are deceased and no longer a threat that should command limited security resources. The process has increased confidence in the listing process so that, for better or worse,[96] it was featured in Security Council Resolutions 2178 and 2253 in response to the foreign terrorist fighter problem.

C. A Review Function for the Five Eyes?

The Five Eyes relationship among the signals intelligence agencies of the United States, the U.K., Australia, Canada, and New Zealand is one of the oldest and best-known intelligence networks. It has frequently been described as a "gentleman's agreement."[97] Like the UN listing process, the Five Eyes has suffered some recent public relations blows, in this case from the Snowden leaks. This raises the issue of whether the Five Eyes partnership should consider creating its own type of Ombudsperson or Inspector General to review intelligence collection, sharing, and other forms of cooperation between its members.

Given that the five partners have personnel exchanges and the NSA provides funding to some of the other partners, it should not be impossible for the close partners to agree on some common oversight measure. In all review measures, it is important to distinguish between what information a security-cleared reviewer is able to see (ideally all relevant information) and what information the reviewer can release publicly. In the case of the latter, each member-state could be given a veto on what information can be made public. This would mean that the government would only have to trust the Ombudsperson and his or her staff not to leak information.

If the Five Eyes move in the direction of formal review, it could be agreed that persons from all the member-states would hold the Inspector General position on a rotating basis and that each state could have a veto over nominations. The member-states might find it in their interest to appoint not simply "safe hands," but people with public credibility and who can work with the various domestic oversight and review mechanisms, including civil society and telecommunications and Internet companies who are playing an increasingly important with respect to signals intelligence.

---

[95] Craig Forcese & Kent Roach, *Limping into the Future: The 1267 Sanctions Committee at the Cross-Roads*, 42 GEO. WASH. INT'L L. REV. 217 (2011).

[96] For my criticisms of listing as a technique that always be behind recruitment to foreign terrorist groups such as those operating in Iraq and Syria, *see* Kent Roach, "Thematic Conclusions and Future Challenges," *in* COMPARATIVE COUNTER-TERRORISM LAW 726 (2015).

[97] James Cox, *Canada and the Five Eyes Intelligence Community*, OPEN CANADA (Dec. 8, 2012), http://open-canada.org/features/the-think-tank/essays/canada-and-the-five-eyes-intelligence-community/.

To be sure, the ability of a transnational Ombudsperson for the Five Eyes to gain trust and access to secret information could be its Achilles heel. The UN 1267 Ombudsperson has struggled with this issue, and has only concluded a formal agreement with one country and less formal "arrangements" with others. The UN Ombudsperson does not have an arrangement with the United States which is commonly perceived to be the dominant player in the listing process. That said, the 1267 Ombudsperson has reached an arrangement with the other Five Eyes countries except Canada. Secrecy issues should less be insurmountable with respect to review that is limited to members of a close intelligence alliance as opposed to the entire United Nations.

The real issue for the Five Eyes agencies will be whether the benefits of increased review would be worth the costs, including the possibility of leaks. Depending on the full fallout from the Snowden and other leaks, the agencies may well find such a mechanism useful in reassuring their own reviewers, courts, Internet companies, and the public that the seemingly boundless world of signals intelligence actually respects the rule of law. The existence of such a mechanism might make judges such as Justice Mosley more trusting of interaction between the member-states. It might also lead to greater confidence that member agencies were not circumventing domestic restrictions by tasking other members to do what they may be prohibited from doing at home. It could also lay the basis for the adoption of best or highest standards among the five member-states. It is also possible that an accountability mechanism for the Five Eyes could address the efficacy as well as the propriety of signals intelligence and thus address wide-spread skepticism about the efficacy of mass collection of various forms of data. To be sure, transnational accountability will be difficult to achieve, but that is not an excuse for not trying.

VII. CONCLUSION

This chapter has critically examined intelligence review and oversight structures in Canada. It has defined review as an after-the-fact process conducted by independent bodies such as SIRC and the Commissioner who reviews the work of the CSE. Such review focuses on the propriety of conduct and results in findings and recommendations that the agencies and their responsible minister—and ultimately the prime minister—are free to reject. Such a process of review should be distinguished from oversight that can intrude into the chain of command. Oversight is primarily concerned about the efficacy of security measures, though such issues cannot be completely distinguished from propriety issues. In a parliamentary democracy, the responsible minister and ultimately the prime minister is responsible for the oversight of national security activities.

This chapter has drawn a generally bleak picture of the state of review and oversight in Canada that is beset by worsening accountability gaps. One aspect of a Canadian accountability gap is that SIRC, which reviews CSIS, and the Commissioner, who reviews CSE, remain tethered to the jurisdictions of their respective agencies even when the agencies understandably conduct joint operations. In other words, Canada has a siloed twentieth-century review structure that does not match twenty-first century whole- of-government security practices.

Canada's lead review agency, SIRC, has recently received increased funding but it, unlike the Inspector General of Intelligence in Australia or a number of Commissioners in the U.K., lacks jurisdiction to see national security information held by other agencies even when those agencies work with CSIS. Review and oversight structures need to be updated to match the increased intensity and integration of national security activities. A "super SIRC" with whole-of-government national security jurisdiction is necessary.

Another aspect of Canada's distinctly large accountability gap is that legislative committees in Canada are denied access to classified or secret information. The former Conservative government resisted calls to provide any committee with such classified information largely on the basis that Canadian parliamentarians cannot be trusted with secret information. This rationale will strike many as shocking and misguided. It is. Nevertheless it echoed the rationale that was given more than 30 years ago in rejecting the McDonald Commission's recommendation that a Joint Parliamentary Committee with access to classified information was necessary to ensure that CSIS was subject to appropriate democratic accountability. The new Liberal government elected in October 2015 is committed to giving a parliamentary committee access to secret information and the ability to review all security agencies. That said, the details that will govern such a committee are not known as of the end of 2015. Moreover, the value of increased legislative review should not be oversold, especially given the limited capacities of parliamentarians, the limited nature of retrospective review and the inability of parliamentarians to publicize the secret information they may receive.

A final form of accountability gap relates to oversight which is distinct from review because it involves command and control capabilities. Although CSIS and the RCMP both report to the Minister of Public Safety, the 2010 Air India Commission found that the status quo was not adequate to ensure that the conflicting mandates of the two agencies were reconciled in the public interest. It proposed an enhanced role for the PMNS Advisor to resolve inevitable disputes between the two agencies as well as to co-ordinate the multiple agencies in many different ministries that have national security responsibilties. These recommendations were echoed by a unanimous and bipartisan Senate committee report in 2011. The former Conservative government has not acted on any of these recommendations even while it gave CSIS new powers and a human source privilege that may unintentionally impede terrorism prosecutions. The new Liberal government has also not shown interest in the Air India recommendations and has instead affirmed the importance of Ministerial responsibility by appointing its most senior Cabinet minister as the Minister of Public Safety.

Canada's review and oversight status quo is inadequate. This is especially so in light of new security powers and a permissive information-sharing regime that Canada created in response to two October 2014 terrorist attacks. SIRC has been given an increased budget, but is still confined to the CSIS silo and lacks powers to review whole of government security efforts. The new government has affirmed the importance of Ministerial responsibility but this is an awkward fit with whole of government security responses.

Canada's failure so far to modernize its review and oversight structures is unfortunate. Security agencies may resist new review and oversight structures, but there is no reason to conclude that enhanced review and oversight will harm security. Effective review and oversight can improve practices of security agencies and increase public confidence in them.

The only form of review and oversight that has recently intensified in Canada is judicial review and oversight. The previous Conservative government defended the increased powers it granted to CSIS in 2015 on the basis that many of these powers will require a warrant and thus be subject to judicial oversight. The focus on the judiciary is an attempt to ensure that the new powers are consistent with the Charter. It also reflects the credibility of the judiciary, especially compared to the well-known inadequacies of legislative and executive review.

Indeed, the Canadian state has consistently turned to the judiciary when inadequate review and oversight have produced large scale security crises and failures. Examples include inquiries headed by sitting or retired judges into RCMP illegalities in the wake of the October 1970 Crisis, the catastrophic intelligence failures that led to the 1985 Air India bombing and the subsequent botched investigations, and the involvement of Canadian officials in Maher Arar's rendition and torture in the wake of 9/11.

Under new legislation enacted in 2015, judges have an additional and regularized oversight role with respect to authorizing new powers that allow CSIS to conduct investigations outside of Canada, and to disrupt or reduce security threats inside and outside of Canada, if need be by violating laws and constitutional rights.[98]

Alas, it is not clear how effectively judges will be able to discharge their new oversight functions given that warrant requests will be heard in secret in warrant hearings where the target is not represented and where appeals are not likely to occur. At the same time, Justice Mosley's 2013 judgment that criticizes CSIS for subcontracting surveillance to foreign Five Eyes partners indicates how judges may rise to the new challenge of administering these new warrants, if they discover that CSIS has gone beyond what was authorized by the warrant. In this and other cases, effective judicial oversight may require correspondingly effective executive and legislative review. This review, however, has fallen behind increased whole of government security efforts and high levels of secrecy that surround efforts to respond to international terrorism. A final concern is that CSIS may be able to circumvent warrant requirements, especially if they are perceived as too demanding and onerous. There will also be no judicial oversight of increasing information-sharing under the 2015 legislation.

In the end, the Canadian experience suggests that all three branches of government need to be engaged in the difficult but necessary task of review and oversight of the high-risk world of intelligence. Even then, events such as Maher Arar's rendition underline the need for some form of transnational review in order to satisfy the fundamental principle that reviewers need powers, resources, and access to information that are commensurate to those of the security officials they review. In short, without transnational accountability there will be another accountability gap that misses the way that nations frequently interact in the collection and sharing of intelligence. The project of developing transnational review mechanisms is in its infancy. The greatest obstacle appears to be fears about disclosing secret information to transnational reviewers. As with domestic matters, however, the project is important because inadequate review and oversight threatens both our rights and our security.

---

[98] Anti-terrorism Act, 2015 c. 20; Canadian Security Intelligence Service Act, R.S.C., 1985, c. C-23; *see* Craig Forcese & Kent Roach, *Stumbling toward Total Information Awareness: The Security of Canada Information Sharing Act*, 17 Can. Privacy L. Rev. 66 (2015) for a discussion of the bill.

PART THREE

Executive Branch and Independent
Oversight

8

The Emergence of Intelligence Governance

*Zachary K. Goldman**

I. INTRODUCTION

The post-9/11 expansion of intelligence activities and the 2013 leak of documents describing surveillance programs of the U.S. National Security Agency (NSA) have produced the most robust public discussion about intelligence oversight in decades. The debate has taken place throughout the community of Western democracies, and, at least with respect to structural issues, is about far more than just surveillance. The questions that have been asked about the oversight of signals intelligence—about how best to guard against abuses, about limitations of the institutions currently involved in oversight, and about the entities that may be best-suited to balance all of the national interests at stake in the consideration of intelligence programs—apply with equal force to a wide range of intelligence activities. This dialogue, moreover, transcends the United States. Questions about the purposes, structure, and limitations of institutions involved in intelligence oversight are widespread in rights-respecting democracies.

In the context of these deliberations, this chapter suggests a new way to frame questions about intelligence oversight. The most fruitful area of inquiry, in light of the discussions over the last several years, is not to ask whether the current architecture of oversight is (unidimensionally) "sufficient" for the job. Rather, more analytically profitable questions would ask whether the purposes for which institutions of oversight were designed remain consistent with

---

* Executive Director, Center on Law and Security and Adjunct Professor of Law, NYU School of Law. I wish to thank David Anderson, Ashley Deeks, Beth George, Richard Morgan, and Sam Rascoff for helpful comments and critiques. Megan Graham, Eliana Pfeffer, Annika Heumann, and Emily Cooper provided excellent research assistance.

the roles the public expects those government agencies to play. In the United States, the main institutions currently engaged in oversight—agency general counsels and inspectors general, the Department of Justice, the Foreign Intelligence Surveillance Court (FISC); and the congressional intelligence committees—are primarily concerned with ensuring legal compliance, and most of them emerged from the first great period of intelligence reform in the 1970s. As the volume as a whole demonstrates, many Western democracies have similar institutions, and all those with mature, effective, and well-resourced intelligence agencies have similar concerns.

Institutions designed to ensure compliance with the law are, however, necessary but not sufficient to address the kinds of criticisms that emerged from the leak of documents describing surveillance activities by the NSA in 2013, and that characterize the debate about issues such as the use of drones in counterterrorism strikes in addition to national security surveillance. Institutions of oversight closely supervise these programs, and their legality has been evaluated by rigorous government processes (including, at least with respect to some surveillance programs, by all three branches of government). But some important segments of the American population still perceive them as illegitimate. What is the role of intelligence oversight in this context—when activities have been deemed lawful but are nonetheless profoundly contested? How can institutions of oversight build trust in the Intelligence Community (IC) with respect to activities that, by their nature, will remain largely secret?

This chapter argues that a broader conception of oversight—one focused on governance rather than narrowly on legal compliance—is needed to rebuild trust in the U.S. IC. In this respect, two types of institutions must coexist. Institutions focused on ensuring legal compliance—such as the FISC and agency general counsels—must work in parallel with institutions engaged in governance, such as the Privacy and Civil Liberties Oversight Board (PCLOB), the President's Intelligence Advisory Board (PIAB), and congressional intelligence committees, which should see their roles as serving as proxies for the American people in the oversight of intelligence activities.

The bodies intended to ensure that the U.S. IC follows the law are incredibly effective. Indeed, there have been no revelations of systematic unlawful behavior in the thousands of documents leaked about signals intelligence activities over the last several years. But compliance with the law alone is not enough to generate trust for inherently secret activities that carry the potential for abuse in an era in which radical transparency is the norm. At the same time as Americans' expectations about intelligence oversight are changing, the range of national interests implicated by the governance of intelligence has expanded. New actors, such as American technology companies with global business interests and foreign allies, have a significant role to play in shaping and constraining intelligence activities.[1] In an era of unprecedented threat and unprecedented transparency, institutions of governance must be able to mediate between the IC and the people in order to ensure that intelligence activities in this, and in all Western democracies, remain effective, legitimate, and sustainable.

This chapter will first offer a brief history of the period in which most of the institutions currently engaged in intelligence oversight in the United States emerged. After describing those institutions, it will draw a distinction between institutions whose goal is to ensure compliance

---

[1] Samuel Rascoff's contribution to this volume describes some of the ways in which global technology companies are encouraging the executive branch to become more involved in intelligence oversight.

with the law, and those designed to embrace a broader view of governance for the IC, illustrating the applicability of this framework to a broader range of intelligence activities than just surveillance. Finally, the chapter will describe some of the specific institutions (and institutional changes) involved in bringing about a broader framework of intelligence governance.

II. THE HISTORY: COMPLIANCE AS A RESPONSE TO CRISIS
A. *The Origins of the American Intelligence Oversight System*

In December 1974, revelations of abuses committed by the U.S. IC hit the front pages of *The New York Times*. In a series of articles that stretched until February 1975, Seymour Hersh revealed wide-ranging unlawful activities conducted by American intelligence agencies. The Central Intelligence Agency (CIA), Hersh alleged in the articles, surveilled student groups and a member of Congress, and infiltrated domestic antiwar groups;[2] maintained files on American citizens, participated in break-ins, mail inspections, and electronic surveillance inside the United States;[3] and sought to overthrow the government of Chilean president Salvador Allende and then misled Congress about having done so, among many other allegations.[4] The Hersh exposés of 1974 followed earlier revelations of wrongdoing by the IC related to the Watergate break-in and surveillance activity related to the Vietnam War.[5]

The disclosures led to the establishment of several congressional and executive commissions of inquiry and substantial changes to the underlying legal authorities governing the U.S. IC. The work of the Church, Pike, and Rockefeller investigations initiated the most comprehensive reforms of the IC since the National Security Act of 1947, which created the CIA and the National Security Council.[6] The inquiries focused primarily on whether the IC violated the law, and if so, what circumstances facilitated the activities in question.[7] The reforms that emerged were aimed at creating an architecture of compliance that would

---

[2] Seymour Hersh, *Huge C.I.A. Operation Reported in U.S. against Antiwar Forces, Other Dissidents in Nixon Years,* N.Y. TIMES, Dec. 22, 1974, at A1.

[3] Seymour Hersh, *Colby Said to Confirm C.I.A. Role in U.S.,* N.Y. TIMES, Jan. 1, 1975, at A1.

[4] Seymour Hersh, *Helms Said Nixon Sought Chile Coup,* N.Y. TIMES, Feb. 9, 1975, at A1.

[5] *See, e.g.,* Betty Medsger & Ken W. Clawson, *Stolen Documents Describe FBI Surveillance Activities,* WASH. POST, Mar. 24, 1971; Alfred E. Lewis, *5 Held in Plot to Bug Democrats' Office Here,* WASH. POST, June 18, 1972; Bob Woodward & Carl Bernstein, *Break-In Memo Sent to Ehrlichman,* WASH. POST, June 13, 1973.

[6] In January 1975, the Senate established the Select Committee to Study Government Operations with Respect to Intelligence Activities (later known as the Church Committee after its chairman, Senator Frank Church of Idaho); in February 1975, the House also established its own Committee (the Pike Committee, in honor of its chairman, Representative Otis Pike) to investigate issues relating to the CIA's budget and effectiveness; and in January 1975, President Gerald Ford created the Commission on CIA Activities within the United States (later known as the "Rockefeller Commission," led by Vice President Nelson Rockefeller), whose mandate focused on whether the CIA complied with existing law, and what safeguards might be necessary to prevent future lack of compliance. Exec. Order. No. 11,828, 40 Fed. Reg. 1219 (Jan. 4, 1975).

[7] S. 21, 94th Cong. (1975) ("*Resolved,* To establish a select committee of the Senate to conduct an investigation and study of governmental operations with respect to intelligence activities and of the extent, if any, to which illegal, improper, or unethical activities were engaged in by any agency of the Federal Government[.]"); Gerald Hines, "Looking for a Rogue Elephant: The Pike Committee Investigations and the CIA," *Studies in Intelligence,* Winter 1998/1999, 81.

prevent the intelligence agencies from engaging in such wrongdoing again.[8] The institutions forming the backbone of today's oversight system, such as the congressional intelligence committees, the Foreign Intelligence Surveillance Court, and agency inspectors general, emerged from this process (during the 1970s, and, with the Iran/Contra scandal, the 1980s) in which abuse led to reforms focused on ensuring legal compliance.

The crises of the 1970s and 1980s that generated the current oversight landscape occurred against a backdrop in which there was minimal formal oversight of the IC. These crises were characterized primarily by unlawful behavior and failures of oversight,[9] and the primary objective of the reforms that emerged was to prevent similar conduct in the future. The first series of crises, which took place during the 1970s and culminated in the Church Committee investigations, primarily concerned unlawful surveillance and other forms of investigative activity,[10] whereas the second crisis, the Iran/Contra Affair of the 1980s, related to lack of compliance with covert action requirements.[11]

By illustrating the ways in which the system of oversight was designed to promote compliance, the chapter will demonstrate limitations in the ability of extant oversight institutions to perform a broader governance function.

B. Laying a Foundation: Intelligence Reforms of the 1970s

The fact that the institutions that emerged from reforms of the 1970s were designed to ensure compliance is no surprise given the legal and institutional background against which they were created. The evolution and purposes of these institutions came about in large measure because, before the investigations conducted by Senator Church, Representative Pike, and Vice President Rockefeller, there were very few institutions involved in intelligence oversight. The United States did not have an independent peacetime intelligence agency until 1947, when the United States created the CIA. Even after the establishment of the CIA, there were few formal congressional institutions dedicated specifically to oversight of its activities. Indeed, from the adoption of the National Security Act in 1947 "until the domestic spy scandal of 1974, the Congress passed no laws related to intelligence accountability."[12] Before

---

[8] Select Committee to Study Governmental Operations with Respect to Intelligence Activities, Intelligence Activities and Rights of Americans, S. Rep. No. 94-755, pt. 2, at 296 (1976) [hereinafter Church Committee Report] ("Establishing a legal framework for agencies engaged in domestic security investigation is the most fundamental reform needed to end the long history of violating and ignoring the law[.]").

[9] Id. at 138 ("The internal inspection mechanisms of the CIA and the FBI did not keep—and, in the case of the FBI, were not designed to keep—the activities of those agencies within legal bounds. Their primary concern was efficiency, not legality or propriety.").

[10] Covert action also occupied the attention of the Church Committee, which devoted an entire set of hearings to the issue. But the legal architecture governing covert action that emerged from that reform process was skeletal until the Iran/Contra affair of the 1980s substantially thickened the regulation of covert action.

[11] The Iran/Contra scandal also focused significant attention on the constitutional allocation of foreign affairs powers between the executive branch and Congress, an issue that is beyond the scope of this chapter. See Harold Koh, The National Security Constitution: Sharing Power after the Iran-Contra Affair (1990).

[12] Loch K. Johnson, The Church Committee Investigation of 1975 and the Evolution of Modern Intelligence Accountability, 23 Intelligence & Nat'l Security 206 (2008).

the Church and Pike investigations, congressional jurisdiction over the CIA was fragmented among four different subcommittees in the House and Senate (the armed services and appropriations committees in each chamber), and the Agency was "subjected to roughly twenty-four hours of legislative 'probing' in both chambers over an entire year."[13] Permanent Senate and House Intelligence Committees were not created until 1976 and 1977 respectively.[14]

Even though the oversight mechanisms predating the Church Committee investigations were not robust, there were laws that did govern the conduct of the IC—laws that the agencies were accused of violating during the "Era of Skepticism" that began in 1974.[15] Indeed, the Church Committee found that "legal questions involved in intelligence programs were often not considered. [And on] . . . other occasions, they were intentionally disregarded in the belief that because the programs served the 'national security' the law did not apply."[16] The Committee found that senior intelligence officials "generally failed to assure compliance with the law."[17] In this situation, where there was no effective background framework of oversight institutions, and there was insufficient attention to legal compliance in the design of intelligence programs, Senator Frank Church of Idaho, chairman of the eponymous Committee, thought it necessary to document the activities of the IC in order "to achieve fundamental, statutory improvements."[18]

The Church Committee therefore proceeded to catalog in painstaking detail harms committed by members of the IC in order to make the case for reform, which, in several instances, formed the basis for specific legislative changes that followed the investigations. Two subjects of investigation in particular, surveillance and covert action, led to laws that created statutory frameworks and institutions designed to prevent the incidents revealed in the 1970s from recurring.

Surveillance: The first issue that led to specific legislative changes during the investigations of the 1970s focused on warrantless surveillance that intercepted the communications of American citizens. Like many of the other controversial subjects revealed during the 1970s, Operation Shamrock, in which the NSA collected international telegrams of U.S. persons, was revealed in an article in *The New York Times*.[19] In the operation described by the *Times*, which began shortly after World War II, the NSA requested international cables of RCA Global, ITT World Communications, and Western Union International, with the goal of obtaining "telegrams sent by foreign establishments in the United States or telegrams that appeared to be encrypted."[20] In the course of doing so, communications of U.S. citizens were monitored.[21] Beyond Shamrock, the NSA also added to its " 'watch lists,' at the request of

[13] Loch K. Johnson, A Season of Inquiry 7 (1985).
[14] S. 400, 94th Cong. (1976); H.R. Res. 658 (1977)
[15] Johnson, *supra* note 13, at 278.
[16] Church Committee Report, *supra* note 8, pt. 2, at 137.
[17] *Id.*
[18] Johnson, *supra* note 13, at 34.
[19] Nicholas M. Horrock, *National Security Agency Reported Eavesdropping on Most Private Cables*, N.Y. Times, Aug. 31, 1975, at A1.
[20] L. Britt Snider, *Recollections from the Church Committee's Investigation of NSA*, Stud. Intelligence, Winter 1999–2000, at 45.
[21] *Id.*

various intelligence agencies, the names of Americans suspected of involvement in civil dis-obedience or drug activity which had some foreign aspects."[22]

Warrantless surveillance, however, had a long history in the United States,[23] and the pro-cess that ultimately led to the adoption of the Foreign Intelligence Surveillance Act (FISA) in 1978 emerged because of the confluence of the abuses documented by Senator Church and a case, *United States v. United States District Court (Keith)*, that the Supreme Court decided in 1972.[24] The *Keith* case famously held that a warrant is required for the conduct of domes-tic security surveillance notwithstanding the constitutional basis of the president's power in that realm.[25] The Court, however, carefully limited its holding to the domestic security surveillance context and went out of its way to express "no opinion as to, the issues which may be involved with respect to activities of foreign powers or their agents."[26]

The Court thereby invited Congress to fill the foreign intelligence surveillance void, and in 1973 bills were introduced in the House and Senate that would establish a judicial proce-dure for granting a warrant for foreign intelligence surveillance. The Nixon administration was not supportive of such legislation.[27] Indeed, in a 1974 hearing on an early version of the bill, Assistant Attorney General Henry Petersen said "Let me be very brief. We oppose these bills. That is it."[28] But in 1976 the Ford administration reversed the executive branch's previ-ous views, and transmitted to Congress a draft bill that would provide for judicial orders approving electronic surveillance for foreign intelligence purposes. In his letter transmitting the legislation, President Ford noted that the law "will provide major assurance to the public that electronic surveillance for foreign intelligence purposes can and will occur only when reasonably justified in circumstances demonstrating an overriding national interest, and that they will be conducted according to standards and procedures that protect against possibili-ties of abuse."[29]

Ford's legislation and the substantive provisions of FISA itself followed the searing revela-tions of the Church and Pike Committees. And indeed, those revelations shaped specific provisions in the law designed to guard against the abuses that had occurred in the absence of any statutory regulation of foreign intelligence surveillance.

---

[22] CHURCH COMMITTEE REPORT, *supra* note 8, pt. 2, at 104.

[23] Wiretapping for domestic security purposes—that is, surveillance for purposes other than pure criminal law enforcement—dates to the 1930s. Trevor Morrison, *The Story of* United States v. U.S. District Court (Keith): *The Surveillance Power, in* PRESIDENTIAL POWER STORIES (Christopher Schroeder & Curtis Bradley eds., 2008). In 1934, President Roosevelt ordered an investigation into the Nazi movement in the United States, and in 1936, the president ordered the investigation broadened to "subversive movements," including fascism and communism. CHURCH COMMITTEE REPORT, *supra* note 8, pt. 2, at 24–25.

[24] 407 U.S. 297 (1972).

[25] *Id.* at 320.

[26] *Id.* at 321–22.

[27] H.R. REP. No. 95-1283, pt. 1, at 13 (1978).

[28] *Foreign Intelligence Surveillance Act: Hearing on H.R. 7308 Before the Subcomm. On Courts, Civil Liberties and the Admin. of Justice of the H. Comm. on the Judiciary*, 95th Cong. 1 (1978) (internal quotation marks omitted).

[29] Letter from Gerald R. Ford, President, to the Speaker of the House and the President of the Senate Transmitting Legislation concerning the Use of Electronic Surveillance in Obtaining Foreign Intelligence Information (Mar. 23, 1976), available at http://www.presidency.ucsb.edu/ws/?pid=5747.

Thus, FISA included in the definition of "electronic surveillance" the acquisition of the contents of any wire or radio communication "sent by or intended to be received by a particular, known United States person who is in the United States, if the contents are acquired by intentionally targeting that United States person."[30] This definition of "electronic surveillance" was designed specifically with the abuses of the Church era in mind, and thus the Senate Committee Report on the draft legislation noted that "the watchlisting activities of the National Security Agency, if directed against the international communications of particular U.S. persons who are in the United States, would require a court order under this provision."[31] It was designed to prevent "U.S. persons who are located in the United States from being targeted in their domestic or *international* communications without a court order no matter where the surveillance is being carried out," and represented a departure from language in earlier drafts of the bill.[32]

Similarly, the definition of the "United States," which shaped the scope of the statute's coverage, reflected abuses documented in the Church Reports. The statutory definition that was ultimately adopted encompassed "all areas under the territorial sovereignty of the United States and the Trust Territory of the Pacific Islands,"[33] in response to evidence publicized about "CIA activities in Micronesia."[34]

In combination with the legal gap identified in the *Keith* case, the surveillance excesses described by the Church Committee had "prompted Congress to consider regulating electronic surveillance conducted for national security purposes,"[35] initiating a process that resulted in the adoption of the law. FISA is perhaps the clearest example of legislative and institutional change that emerged from the period of the 1970s. The Act established not only a legal framework for obtaining surveillance warrants for foreign intelligence information, but also a brand new institution (the FISC) staffed by federal judges to review and approve those warrants. The FISC began with a narrow purpose: to adjudicate applications for foreign intelligence surveillance warrants.[36]

In the post-9/11 era, however, the FISC shifted to superintending entire surveillance programs, which represented a fundamentally new role for the institution. This shift in the role of the court, however, took place without any fundamental changes in the structure of the FISC as originally conceived in 1978. These changes in the court's role, which took place without corresponding adjustments to the court's structure, led to significant unease about whether the FISC is optimally designed, particularly after the extent of the changes in the court's role became known to the public.[37]

---

[30] Foreign Intelligence Surveillance Act, Pub. L. No. 95-511, § 101(f)(1), 92 Stat. 1783, 1785 (1978).
[31] S. REP. NO. 95-701, at 34 (1978).
[32] *Id.* at 33–34.
[33] Foreign Intelligence Surveillance Act, Pub. L. No. 95-511, § 101(j), 92 Stat. 1783, 1786 (1978).
[34] S. REP. NO. 95-701, at 47 (1978).
[35] 1 DAVID S. KRIS & J. DOUGLAS WILSON, NATIONAL SECURITY INVESTIGATIONS & PROSECUTIONS 107 (2d ed. 2012).
[36] 50 U.S.C.A. § 1804 (2010).
[37] Daphna Renan's contribution to this volume addresses some of the significant legal and policy questions that have emerged from the FISC's role in superintending intelligence programs rather than simply approving the issuance of individual warrants. The USA FREEDOM Act, Pub. L. No. 114-23, 129 Stat. 268 (2015), signed into law in June 2015, enacted several reforms to the FISC, including providing for the appointment of amici

Covert Action: The second significant area of controversy that led to concrete legislative change was in the realm of covert action, the regulation of which evolved over a period spanning not only the controversies of the 1970s, but also the Iran/Contra affair of the 1980s. The period of covert action reform began in 1974 with the Hughes-Ryan Amendment to the Foreign Assistance Act of 1961,[38] culminated in the Intelligence Authorization Act of 1991, and was characterized by a progressive tightening of covert action requirements and the development of robust processes to ensure compliance with those legislative mandates.

This progressive evolution was an explicit reaction to the perceived excesses of the U.S. government's covert action program revealed during the 1970s and 1980s. Specifically, the Hughes-Ryan Amendment came about "following a series of revelations about CIA activities in Vietnam and its involvement in the Watergate scandal," after which "Congress took its first meaningful steps to control covert action."[39] The solution embodied in the Hughes-Ryan amendment required the president to make a "finding" that a proposed covert action is important to the national security of the United States, and to report that finding to Congress. The legislation marked the first "successful effort by legislators to place controls over the CIA since its creation."[40] Prior to the enactment of Hughes-Ryan, there had been "no *external* accountability regarding covert action to Congress."[41] By requiring the president to make a finding about the proposed action and to report that finding to Congress, the Amendment "forced the President to be accountable for covert action."[42] This requirement had its origins in the Church Committee's difficulty in identifying with confidence who had ordered various assassination plots against foreign leaders such as Fidel Castro amidst an institutional culture that prized plausible deniability for the president,[43] and is nearly unique among Western democracies.[44]

Once Congress established a framework for presidential accountability regarding covert action during the 1970s, the next episode in which substantial changes to that framework emerged came in the aftermath of the Iran/Contra affair in the 1980s. The Iran/Contra affair arose in the context of support the United States provided to anti-communist guerrillas, the

---

curiae and mandating declassification review with respect to certain FISC opinions. It did not, however, fundamentally change the structure of the court to account for the shift to programmatic supervision of the IC.

[38] Pub L. 93-559 § 32, 88 Stat. 1795, 1804 (1974). The Hughes-Ryan Amendment instituted for the first time a requirement that the president issue a finding that a proposed action is "important to the national security of the United States" and that the proposed operation be reported to relevant committees of the House and Senate.

[39] Elizabeth Rindskopf Parker & Bryan Pate, *Rethinking Judicial Oversight of Intelligence, in* REFORMING INTELLIGENCE: OBSTACLES TO DEMOCRATIC CONTROL AND EFFECTIVENESS 51, 55 (Thomas C. Bruneau & Steven C. Boraz, eds., 2007).

[40] JOHNSON, *supra* note 13, at 10.

[41] Genevieve Lester, External Accountability: Congress, Opposition, and Oversight Development (May 2012) (unpublished Ph.D. dissertation, U.C. Berkeley) (on file with author).

[42] *Id.*

[43] JOHNSON, *supra* note 13, at 57–62.

[44] Hans Born, *Parliamentary and External Oversight of Intelligence Services, in* DEMOCRATIC CONTROL OF INTELLIGENCE SERVICES: CONTAINING ROGUE ELEPHANTS 171 (Hans Born & Marina Caparini eds., 2007).

Contras, who emerged in opposition to the Sandinista regime in Nicaragua during the early 1980s. Such support had been prohibited by the Boland Amendment, signed into law by President Reagan in 1984, and so was funded by clandestine arms sales to Iran orchestrated by members of the National Security Council working in concert with private actors. The arms sales were also intended to help secure Iranian assistance in obtaining the return of American hostages held in Lebanon.[45]

A significant number of important legal issues were raised by the affair, including questions about the appropriate allocation of authority between Congress and the executive to regulate foreign affairs.[46] More important for the purposes of this chapter, however, were weaknesses that the affair revealed in the mechanisms of compliance with covert action requirements. Indeed, the congressional committee that investigated the affair concluded that "the Iran-Contra Affair resulted from the failure of individuals to observe the law, not from deficiencies in existing law or in our system of governance."[47] The most significant problems identified during the Iran/Contra investigations revolved around the process of issuing presidential findings about covert action, and specifically focused on the timing of congressional notification,[48] and the promulgation of retroactive findings, among other issues.[49]

After the core features of the Iran arms sales and support for the Contras became public, investigations took place and reform proposals emerged whose goal was to tighten the architecture of compliance and to prevent the abuses that took place during the 1980s from recurring. The changes to the legal instruments regulating covert action that emerged from the Iran/Contra investigations were embodied in the Fiscal Year 1991 Intelligence Authorization Act.[50] Some of the main changes included the imposition of a statutory requirement that covert action findings be reduced to writing;[51] a prohibition on sanctioning "a covert action, or any aspect of any such action, which already has occurred,"[52] and a mandate that the covert action be reported to the congressional intelligence committees "as soon as possible" after it is approved and before the initiation of the activity.[53] These were just several of the many changes designed to correct specific deficiencies identified in the Iran/Contra affair.

---

[45] *See, e.g.,* William C. Banks, *While Congress Slept: The Iran-Contra Affair and Institutional Responsibility for Covert Operations,* 14 SYRACUSE J. INT'L L. & COM. 291, 295–308 (1988) for a description of the affair.

[46] *See* HAROLD KOH, THE NATIONAL SECURITY CONSTITUTION: SHARING POWER AFTER THE IRAN-CONTRA AFFAIR (1990) for an authoritative discussion of these issues.

[47] REPORT OF THE CONGRESSIONAL COMMITTEES INVESTIGATING THE IRAN CONTRA AFFAIR WITH SUPPLEMENTAL, MINORITY, AND ADDITIONAL VIEWS, S. REP. NO. 100-216, H.R. REP. NO. 100-433, at 423 (1st Sess. 1987) [hereinafter IRAN CONTRA REPORT].

[48] *Id.* at 423 ("Congress was never notified of the Iranian arms sales, in spite of the existence of a statute requiring prior notice to Congress of all covert actions, or, in rare situations, notice 'in a timely fashion.'").

[49] JOHN RIZZO, COMPANY MAN: THIRTY YEARS OF CONTROVERSY AND CRISIS IN THE CIA 107 (2014) (describing issues related to the promulgation of retroactive findings).

[50] Rindskopf Parker & Pate, *supra* note 39, at 57.

[51] Intelligence Authorization Act for Fiscal Year 1991, Pub. L. No. 102-88, § 503(a)(1), 105 Stat. 429, 442 [hereinafter Intelligence Authorization Act of 1991].

[52] *Id.* at § 503(a)(2), 105 Stat. at 442.

[53] *Id.* at § 503(c)(1), 105 Stat. at 443.

III. THE CONTEXT: THE CURRENT LANDSCAPE
OF INTELLIGENCE OVERSIGHT

Oversight of the U.S. IC exists as a latticework of offices and agencies with different roles, functions, and origins. Some of those entities are internal to the IC; others, such as the Department of Justice, are members of the executive branch with oversight functions. Both of the other coordinate branches of government—Congress and the courts—are involved in oversight, and external bodies such as the PCLOB, the PIAB, and the Intelligence Oversight Board (IOB) also play a role in the oversight structure.

- *Internal Intelligence Community Oversight Bodies:* There are a wide range of bodies internal to the 16 members of the U.S. IC that oversee their activities. Many of the IC agencies have their own general counsels and offices of compliance. Agency general counsels are charged with ensuring that employees of each IC member organization comply with the law.[54] Many of the IC agencies also have inspectors general. In 1989, for example, both the CIA and the Department of Justice (of which the FBI is a component), created statutory inspectors general. NSA has an inspector general, but that office is not Senate-confirmed. Several of the IC agencies also have statutorily mandated civil liberties officers.[55]

- *Executive Branch Oversight Bodies:* Beyond the oversight mechanisms internal to the 16 members of the IC, other executive branch agencies also have significant oversight responsibilities. These include, in different circumstances, the Department of Defense, the Office of the Director of National Intelligence, and Department of Justice, among others. The White House also provides oversight, particularly with respect to covert action.[56] Of the existing executive branch oversight agencies, the Department of Justice is most actively involved in superintending the IC. In the context of the FISA Section 702 surveillance, for example, the Department of Justice's National Security Division (NSD) reviews in depth the NSA's tasking procedures and orders at regular on-site meetings at the National Security Agency.[57]

- *Congressional Oversight:* Congressional oversight of the IC is deep and multifaceted. Two of the most direct and important ways in which Congress, particularly through the intelligence committees, oversees the IC are the appropriations process and

---

[54] *See, e.g., What We Do, Office of General Counsel,* OFFICE OF THE DIRECTOR OF NATIONAL INTELLIGENCE, http://www.dni.gov/index.php/about/organization/office-of-general-counsel-what-we-do (last visited Aug. 23, 2015) ("OGC's mission is to provide accurate and timely legal guidance and counsel to the DNI and to the ODNI to ensure all employees and contractors assigned to the ODNI comply with U.S. law and any applicable regulations and directives.").

[55] 42 U.S.C. § 2000ee-1 (2014).

[56] 50 U.S.C.A. § 3093(a) (West 2014).

[57] *See* discussion of DOJ oversight of Section 702 surveillance program in PRIVACY AND CIVIL LIBERTIES OVERSIGHT BOARD, REPORT ON THE SURVEILLANCE PROGRAM OPERATED PURSUANT TO SECTION 702 OF THE FOREIGN INTELLIGENCE SURVEILLANCE ACT, 70-75 (2014) [hereinafter PCLOB 702 REPORT].

congressional notification requirements. During the appropriations process, Congress reviews intelligence programs and can defund those with which it is dissatisfied.[58] Reporting or notification processes are codified in specific statutes, and provide an important vehicle through which Congress can exercise control over specific activities in which the IC is engaged.[59] Congress has also adopted statutes, such as the covert action statute, which impose reporting obligations on the executive branch. It also can establish independent commissions such as the 9/11 Commission, and conducts oversight through the adoption of authorization acts and confirmations of senior officials.

- *Independent External Oversight Institutions:* Independent external oversight bodies also play an important role in overseeing the IC. In the United States, this category includes independent bodies such as the PCLOB, the PIAB, and the IOB (the PCLOB and PIAB are independent bodies even though located within the executive branch, and the IOB is part of the PIAB).

- *The Courts*: The courts are also an important part of the oversight system in the United States and elsewhere. The main judicial institution involved in intelligence oversight is the FISC. The FISC's jurisdiction is limited, however, to the review of foreign intelligence surveillance warrants, as well as other foreign intelligence surveillance matters involving U.S. persons or collection taking place inside the United States. General Article III courts also have had occasion to review intelligence matters, but a narrow conception of standing, the state secrets privilege,[60] and other doctrinal concerns have limited their role.[61] Indeed, the Director of the Administrative Office of the United States Courts recently urged, in the context of proposals to expand the role of the FISC, that "[c]are should be taken not to place the Courts in an 'oversight' role that exceeds their constitutional responsibility to decide cases and controversies."[62] Within these limitations, however, courts will play an important role in any more comprehensive conception of oversight, and later sections will illustrate why it is important that they do so.

Each type of institution serves as an important component of an overall oversight program for the IC. As the chapter shifts to a broader conception of governance for the IC, it will

---

[58] *See, e.g.*, SHANE HARRIS, THE WATCHERS: THE RISE OF AMERICA'S SURVEILLANCE STATE 247–48 (2010) (describing the termination by Congress of Total Information Awareness, an early post-9/11 surveillance program).

[59] *See, e.g.*, the reporting requirements embodied in 50 U.S.C.A. § 3091(a)(1) (West 2014) ("The President shall ensure that the congressional intelligence committees are kept fully and currently informed of the intelligence activities of the United States, including any significant anticipated intelligence activity . . . ."); and 50 U.S.C.A. § 1881f(b)(1)(D) (West 2014) (requiring the Attorney General to provide to the congressional intelligence oversight committees "a copy of an order or pleading . . . that contains a significant legal interpretation of the provisions of section 1881a" of the Foreign Intelligence Surveillance Act).

[60] Mohamed v. Jeppesen Dataplan Inc., 614 F.3d 1070 (9th Cir. 2010).

[61] Stephen I. Vladeck, *National Security and* Bivens *after* Iqbal, 14 LEWIS & CLARK L. REV. 255 (2010) (discussing limitations to the availability of *Bivens* remedies in national security cases).

[62] Letter from the Honorable John D. Bates, Director, Administrative Office of the United States Courts, to Senator Dianne Feinstein, Chairman, Select Committee on Intelligence, United States Senate, at 2 (Jan. 13, 2014), *available at* http://www.feinstein.senate.gov/public/index.cfm/files/serve/?File_id=3bcc8fbc-d13c-4f95-8aa9-09887d6e90ed.

pay particular attention to independent oversight institutions because of their unique ability to cultivate and maintain trust between the American people and their IC. This is so both because of the specific advantages that can be conferred by external oversight bodies, and because of some of the limitations attendant with competing alternatives.

IV. MODERN INTELLIGENCE GOVERNANCE
A. The Purpose of Oversight: Compliance versus Governance

When former NSA contractor Edward Snowden began in June 2013 leaking documents describing surveillance programs, the public and political reaction had a very different focus than during the first period of reform to the intelligence oversight system described above. Rather than widespread allegations that the intelligence agencies willfully violated the law, the general thrust of the more contemporary critiques was of a wholly different sort. This was because, unlike the controversies of a previous era, there was "no evidence that the NSA had knowingly or intentionally engaged in unlawful or unauthorized activity."[63]

Instead, "Snowden's revelations demonstrated how the implicit bargain that has governed the U.S. intelligence community since the 1970s has broken down"[64] because of a lack of public trust that the oversight agencies embodying that bargain effectively serve as a proxy for the American people.[65] Indeed, a recent White House survey demonstrated that 67 percent of respondents "do not trust . . . at all" our nation's intelligence agencies when it comes to information collection and data privacy. The same survey showed that 85 percent of respondents were "very much" concerned about the legal standards and oversight governing data collection, the highest level of extreme concern about any category of data practices.[66]

Controversy over the last several years, therefore, swirled around a different set of concerns than during the 1970s—specifically, disquiet about whether the laws governing the IC, or interpretations of those laws by the executive branch and the courts, were appropriate.[67] The

---

[63] Geoffrey R. Stone, *What I Told the NSA*, HUFFINGTON POST (Mar. 31, 2014), http://www.huffingtonpost.com/ geoffrey-r-stone/what-i-told-the-nsa_b_5065447.html ("The Review Group found no evidence that the NSA had knowingly or intentionally engaged in unlawful or unauthorized activity. To the contrary, it has put in place carefully-crafted internal procedures to [*sic*] ensure that it operates within the bounds of its lawful authority.").

[64] Daniel Byman & Benjamin Wittes, *Reforming the NSA: How to Spy after Snowden*, FOREIGN AFF., May–June 2014, at 129.

[65] Robert Litt, General Counsel, Office of Dir. of Nat'l Intelligence, Speech, Brookings Institute: U.S. Intelligence Community Surveillance One Year after President Obama's Address (Feb. 4, 2015) (transcript and video *available at* http://icontherecord.tumblr.com/post/110099240063).

[66] EXECUTIVE OFFICE OF THE PRESIDENT, BIG DATA: SEIZING OPPORTUNITIES, PRESERVING VALUES 79 (2014). *See also* Mary Madden & Lee Rainie, *Americans' Attitudes about Privacy, Security and Surveillance*, PEW RESEARCH CENTER, May 20, 2015, *available at* http://www.pewinternet.org/2015/05/20/americans-attitudes-about-privacy-security-and-surveillance/ ("65% of American adults believe there are not adequate limits on the telephone and internet data that the government collects"). *See also* Editorial, *The U.S. Intelligence Chief's Gag Order Does Not Stir Trust*, WASH. POST, Apr. 23, 2014; Ken Dilanian, *U.S. Must Win Back Trust on Intelligence Gathering, Obama Says*, L.A. TIMES, Mar. 25, 2014; Jon Cohen & Dan Balz, *Poll: Privacy Concerns Rise after NSA Leaks*, WASH. POST, July 24, 2013.

[67] This criticism applies most to the interpretation of Section 215 of the USA PATRIOT ACT permitting bulk collection of telephony metadata. *See* PRIVACY AND CIVIL LIBERTIES OVERSIGHT BOARD, REPORT ON

leaks really, then, revealed "a lack of social agreement about the proper contours of the rules,"[68] including about whether current interpretations of key constitutional provisions are consistent with society's expectations,[69] rather than about significant illegal behavior. Debates also revolved around policy choices made by the IC in areas where there is no direct legal authority, such as whether the NSA should stockpile zero-day exploits,[70] or whether it should monitor communications of lawful foreign intelligence targets such as a foreign leader.[71]

This form of criticism, which acknowledges that the intelligence agencies largely followed the law, but nevertheless engaged in activities that do not have the support of an important portion of the American people, is significantly different from the type of criticism that animated the Church, Pike, and Rockefeller investigations of an earlier era. And although it highlights important questions about the process of reviewing and approving of certain intelligence collection activities,[72] it is not a wholesale indictment of all institutions that superintend the IC.

What emerged from the controversies in 2013 is, more than anything, the realization that there are at least two different ways of understanding the purpose of intelligence oversight. The first is aimed at ensuring compliance—making sure that the IC follows the law.[73]

THE TELEPHONE RECORDS PROGRAM CONDUCTED UNDER SECTION 215 OF THE USA PATRIOT ACT AND ON THE OPERATIONS OF THE FOREIGN INTELLIGENCE SURVEILLANCE COURT 57–103 (2014) [hereinafter PCLOB 215 REPORT]; RICHARD A. CLARKE, MICHAEL J. MORELL, GEOFFREY R. STONE, CASS R. SUNSTEIN & PETER SWIRE, LIBERTY AND SECURITY IN A CHANGING WORLD: REPORT AND RECOMMENDATIONS OF THE PRESIDENT'S REVIEW GROUP ON INTELLIGENCE AND COMMUNICATIONS TECHNOLOGIES 167–73 (2013) [hereinafter NSA REVIEW GROUP REPORT]; David S. Kris, *On the Bulk Collection of Tangible Things*, 7 J. NAT'L SECURITY L. & POL'Y 209 (2014); Casey J. McGowan, Note, *The Relevance of Relevance: Section 215 of the USA PATRIOT ACT and the NSA Metadata Collection Program*, 82 FORDHAM L. REV. 2399 (2014). But it also applies to other collection programs that were revealed by Snowden. *See, e.g.*, Laura Donohue, *Section 702 and the Collection of International Telephone and Internet Content*, 38 HARV. J.L. & PUB. POL'Y 117 (2015); Alan Butler, *Standing Up to Clapper: How to Increase Transparency and Oversight of FISA Surveillance*, 48 NEW ENG. L. REV. 55, 56 (2013).

68 Benjamin Wittes, *Legal Safeguards, Not Disarmament*, CATO UNBOUND: A JOURNAL OF DEBATE (June 11, 2014), http://www.cato-unbound.org/2014/06/11/benjamin-wittes/legal-safeguards-not-disarmament.

69 *See, e.g.*, Ron Wyden, Mark Udall, & Martin Heinrich, Op-Ed., *End the N.S.A. Dragnet, Now*, N.Y. TIMES, Nov. 26, 2013, at A25 (describing efforts to repeal "constitutionally questionable surveillance activities"); Josh Gerstein, *Judge: NSA Phone Program Likely Unconstitutional*, POLITICO, Dec. 16, 2013 (describing District Judge Richard Leon's ruling that the 215 program likely violates the Fourth Amendment). The D.C. Circuit Court of Appeals later vacated Judge Leon's opinion and remanded to the District Court for further proceedings. Obama v. Klayman, 800 F.3d 559 (D.C.Cir., Aug. 28, 2015).

70 Zero-day exploits are exploits of which those responsible for software creation and deployment were unaware before their use. *See* Michele Golabek-Goldman & Paul Stockton, *Curbing the Market for Cyber Weapons*, 32 YALE L. & POL'Y REV. 101 (2013).

71 NSA REVIEW GROUP REPORT, *supra* note 67, at 167–73.

72 Criticisms of the oversight process were many and varied, including before the 2013 leaks. Julian Sanchez, *Where's the Oversight on NSA Spying?*, POLITICO, Aug. 16, 2013; Adam Schiff, *Let the Sun Shine on Surveillance Court*, 35 NAT'L L. J. 38 (2013); Andrea Peterson, *Patriot Act Author: "There Has Been a Failure of Oversight"*, WASH. POST, Oct. 11, 2013; David Ignatius, Op-Ed., *Intelligence Oversight in Free Fall*, WASH. POST, Dec. 13, 2007.

73 "Compliance" at the level of large organizations is generally understood to mean programs that are "reasonably designed, implemented, and enforced so that the program is generally effective in preventing and detecting

The second type of oversight is oriented toward providing a broader form of governance to the IC. The objectives of institutions that effectuate broader governance concerns should be to ensure that the strategic priorities of the IC are appropriate, that its legal authorities are consistent with those priorities, and that resources and institutional mandates exist to facilitate the priority activities of the IC. These institutions should also help ensure that the right kinds of procedures for reviewing and approving significant intelligence activities are in place so that the actions of the IC are consistent with public expectations.

In short, the institutions of intelligence oversight must serve as a proxy for the American people, reflecting their views and their values in an arena in which secrecy poses an obstacle to utilizing the normal mechanisms of obtaining popular assent. And although Congress has a critical role to play in providing such political governance, structural factors have limited the ability of congressional intelligence oversight mechanisms to perform this type of role.[74]

The criticism describing intelligence activities as lawful but nonetheless illegitimate[75] illustrates architectural limits on the ability of oversight institutions designed to guarantee compliance simultaneously to ensure that the activities of the IC are appropriately governed. It demonstrates that although the institutions designed to ensure compliance work well, those same institutions have difficulty with a broader role.

The "lawful but illegitimate" criticism also questions whether the extant oversight structure can adequately deal with questions about strategic constitutional interpretation in an era of rapid technological change. This might come up, for example, when the IC must interpret the scope of the Third Party Doctrine, which generally holds that records voluntarily turned over to a third party do not enjoy constitutional protection, in response to the development of novel technologies.[76]

Complaints that intelligence agencies such as the NSA "continue[] to evade oversight" therefore miss the mark.[77] It is not that the oversight system in this country has failed; rather the failure is in the disjunction between what the American oversight system is designed to do, and what "we the people" may expect of it.

[unlawful] conduct." U.S. SENTENCING GUIDELINES MANUAL § 8B2.1(a) (2014). Other important components of effective compliance programs include institutions to superintend the program, standards and procedures to prevent and detect unlawful conduct, identifiable responsibility for its implementation, monitoring and auditing, and mechanisms for employees to seek guidance on permissible conduct, among other things. *Id.*

[74] *See infra* text accompanying notes 85–100.

[75] Laura K. Donohue, *NSA Surveillance May Be Legal—But It's Unconstitutional*, WASH. POST, June 21, 2013 ("The government defends the programs' legality, saying they comply with FISA and its amendments. It may be right, but only because FISA has ceased to provide a meaningful constraint."); Paul Rosenzweig, Op-Ed., *The NSA's Phone Collection Order—It May Be Legal, But Is It Wise?*, FOX NEWS (June 6, 2013), http://www.foxnews.com/opinion/2013/06/06/nsas-phone-collection-order-it-may-be-legal-but-is-it-wise/.

[76] Two recent Supreme Court cases, *United States v. Jones*, 132 S. Ct. 945 (2012) and *Riley v. California,* 134 S. Ct. 2473 (2014), have caused some to question the long-term viability of current interpretations of the Third Party Doctrine, though neither case overturned the doctrine. Legal advisors inside the executive branch, however, continually confront novel applications of the Third Party Doctrine.

[77] *See, e.g.*, Yochai Benkler, Op-Ed., *How the NSA and FBI Foil Weak Oversight*, THE GUARDIAN, Oct. 16, 2013.

B. Broader Applicability of a Governance Framework

An institutional framework for intelligence oversight framed around the need for improved governance applies not only to the context of surveillance, but also to a wide range of other intelligence activities. Indeed, many of the debates about controversial intelligence programs in the post-9/11 era—debates that have previously been framed in the language of the legality of those programs—would be more beneficially analyzed through a broad governance framework.

Debates about the legality of drone strikes abroad, for example, have tended to dominate the public discourse about their use. Thus, during the Senate confirmation hearings for CIA director John Brennan, the conversation focused on the legal issues involved in the drone campaign. The hearings began with a discussion of legal memos authored by the Department of Justice's Office of Legal Counsel (OLC). Then, during his opening statement, Brennan noted that he would promote "public discussions" about quintessentially legal issues such as the "basis . . . thresholds, criteria, processes, procedures, approvals, and reviews of" counterterrorism strikes by Unmanned Aerial Vehicles (UAVs).[78] And the confirmation process concluded only after a 13-hour filibuster by Senator Rand Paul to determine whether the administration claimed the legal authority to "use a weaponized drone to kill an American not engaged in combat on American soil."[79]

But what has received a lot less attention than the very important debate over the legality of drone strikes, and the procedural questions involved in their use, are discussions that institutions of intelligence governance would be well-suited to address. These include the profound strategic dilemmas related not only to the effectiveness of such strikes, but also to the opportunity costs to traditional intelligence collection and analysis involved in having the IC perform this role. These include questions about what the priorities of the CIA, as the lead foreign human intelligence agency, should be; debates that have surfaced fleetingly in several specific contexts in the post-9/11 era, but that would benefit from more sustained institutional consideration.

One specific area in which these questions have arisen revolves around which agency—the military or the CIA—should retain control of the major part of the nation's drone fleet. In response, at least in part, to the perception that the lack of transparency surrounding the program is a product of its home in the IC, the Obama administration announced a process "of phasing the C.I.A. out of the drone war and shifting operations to the Pentagon."[80] But besides the transparency rationale for such a shift, the government might do so because it has concluded that there "is no reason for the CIA to maintain a redundant fleet of armed drones, or to conduct military operations that are inherently better suited to" the military's Special Operations Command.[81] This is an example of the kinds of reasoning that might

---

[78] Transcript of Open Hearing on the Nomination of John O. Brennan to be Director of the Central Intelligence Agency Before the United States Senate Select Committee on Intelligence, February 7, 2013, at 5–7, 23, *available at* http://www.intelligence.senate.gov/sites/default/files/hearings/transcript.pdf.

[79] Letter from Eric H. Holder, Jr., Attorney General, to Senator Rand Paul, United States Senate (Mar. 7, 2013) (*available at* http://abcnews.go.com/images/Politics/Senator%20Rand%20Paul%20Second%20Letter.pdf).

[80] Peter Baker, *Pivoting from War Footing, Obama Acts to Curtail Drones*, N.Y. TIMES, May 24, 2013, at A1.

[81] Micah Zenko, *Transferring CIA Drone Strikes to the Pentagon: Policy Innovation Memorandum No. 31*, COUNCIL ON FOREIGN RELATIONS (Apr. 2013), http://www.cfr.org/drones/transferring-cia-drone-strikes-pentagon/p30434.

animate discussions about the governance and efficient functioning of the IC, rather than the legality of the program.

Second, and more generally, questions have periodically surfaced about whether the top priority the IC has placed on counterterrorism has come at too high a price for other intelligence mandates. This critique surfaced most acutely during the revolutions in the Arab world in the spring of 2011. During that time, debate swirled around whether the IC's focus on counterterrorism, which necessitates close relationships with partner governments in the Arab world and which demands substantial resources, limited the ability of the United States to foresee impending instability in the Middle East.[82]

A final example that illustrates the kinds of issues implicated by a broader conception of governance than the main oversight bodies are currently engaged in revolves around which intelligence agency should control human intelligence collection in war zones. Specifically, in the last several years, the Defense Intelligence Agency (DIA) proposed the creation of a "Defense Clandestine Service" (DCS) to parallel the CIA's National Clandestine Service, and which would be tasked with collecting military intelligence overseas.[83] Congressional opposition ultimately pared back the proposal because of concerns about cost and the relationship between operations of the proposed DCS and those of the CIA.[84] But the discussion itself, about whether the DIA should set up a parallel spying operation to relieve the CIA of some activities that directly support military operations, is an example of the salience and strategic importance of broad questions of intelligence governance.

A more sustained focus on intelligence governance would embrace questions such as the three just described, alongside questions of the legality of such activities. For these and other questions, legal and compliance issues are a part—but only a part—of the suite of issues with which an effective and holistic oversight structure must grapple.

This is because such mixed questions of law and policy about the range of activities in which the IC should be engaged reflect core questions for which there should be some proxy for public involvement. Oversight bodies engaged more holistically in evaluating intelligence governance are capable of serving this task in ways that institutions of compliance are not. This is so for two main reasons.

First, independent external oversight mechanisms are uniquely positioned to ensure that the priorities and authorities of the IC are consistent with the expectations of democratic populations. They do so in two ways. Their mandate is explicitly tied to the public, representing their interests through their missions, which are to work with the executive concerning the impact of intelligence programs on privacy and civil liberties, and on the efficacy of such programs. In doing so, they stand in for the public in an otherwise secret world, as they study issues in depth and issue reports to the public, the president, and Congress.

---

[82] Joshua Foust, *Myopia: How Counter-Terrorism Has Blinded Our Intelligence Community*, THE ATLANTIC, Nov. 13, 2012; Robert Johnson, *U.S. Intelligence Agencies Are Losing Ground in the Arab Spring*, BUS. INSIDER, (June 13, 2011, 4:22 PM), http://www.businessinsider.com/robert-johnson-us-intelligence-agencies-are-losing-major-ground-in-the-arab-spring-2011-6.

[83] Greg Miller, *DIA to Send Hundreds More Spies Overseas*, WASH. POST, Dec. 1, 2012.

[84] Greg Miller, *Pentagon's Plans for a Spy Service to Rival the CIA Have Been Pared Back*, WASH. POST, Nov. 1, 2014.

Second, the staffing of independent external oversight institutions keeps them connected to the broader populace, as they are often comprised of individuals who do not work full-time in the IC. This provides them with a unique perspective, and may enable them to better discern the limits of intelligence activities that will be publicly acceptable. While the individuals who serve on independent oversight boards have other employment, they also have security clearances sufficient to allow them to review the most sensitive intelligence programs, enabling them to stand in the shoes of the public as they review these programs. Independent oversight bodies also are not responsible for the operation/execution of intelligence programs, and so, unlike executive branch agencies (and IC agencies themselves), they are able to assess the utility and impact of particular programs in a more holistic and dispassionate manner.

C. *Congress and Intelligence Governance*

As has been demonstrated above, the primary objective of the Church Committee investigation was to determine "whether this Government's intelligence activities were governed and controlled consistently with the fundamental principles of American constitutional government" and "to propose effective measures to prevent intelligence excesses, and . . . sound guidelines and oversight procedures with which to govern and control legitimate activities."[85] What resulted were institutions of compliance—a group of internal and external offices and institutions such as agency general counsels and the FISC[86]—that were designed to ensure that the IC follows the law. It has become clear, though, that ensuring compliance is only one part of a holistic conception of oversight, and that what is needed in addition to the institutions of compliance are institutions able to provide a broader form of governance to the IC.

There is a great deal of potential for Congress to effectuate the broader vision of governance with which this chapter is centrally concerned—namely a form of governance able to establish and enforce priorities for the IC, to supervise the legal authorities effectuating those priorities to ensure they are consistent with the expectations of the American people, and to provide adequate resources to ensure that the IC's priorities can be fulfilled. And Congress has enacted remarkable and far-reaching intelligence reforms in the post-9/11 era.[87]

Structural factors, however, have sometimes limited Congress's role in intelligence oversight. Specifically, research has demonstrated that intelligence matters are generally not salient to individual voters. Given that "legislators will engage in greater oversight the more they are rewarded for it by constituents and organized interest groups," the lack of robust constituent interest means that intelligence oversight may not take top priority.[88]

---

[85] CHURCH COMMITTEE REPORT, *supra* note 8, pt. 2, at v.

[86] RIZZO, *supra* note 49, at 44 (describing how the CIA's Office of the General Counsel doubled in size from 9 members to 18 in the immediate aftermath of the Church Committee report).

[87] Since 9/11, Congress has comprehensively reformed the architecture of homeland security, counterterrorism, and intelligence in the United States. Landmark pieces of legislation include the Homeland Security Act of 2002, Pub. L. No. 107-296, 116 Stat. 2135; The Intelligence Reform and Terrorism Prevention Act of 2004, Pub. L. No. 108-458, 118 Stat. 3638; The FISA Amendments Act of 2008, Pub. L. No. 110-261, 122 Stat. 2436; and the USA FREEDOM Act of 2015, Pub. L. No. 114-23, 129 Stat. 268.

[88] *See* AMY ZEGART, EYES ON SPIES: CONGRESS AND THE UNITED STATES INTELLIGENCE COMMUNITY 36–38 (2011) for a recent comprehensive analysis of the role of Congress in intelligence oversight.

In addition to the general point about the political incentives that influence intelligence oversight, there are two other categories of reasons that Congress has not played as active a role intelligence oversight as it might.

- *Fragmentation of Responsibility:* Fragmentation of responsibility for intelligence oversight among several congressional committees has been identified as an obstacle to effective oversight both before and after the Church Committee investigations,[89] including by the 9/11 Commission.[90] This is especially true with respect to the IC budget, because "budgetary authority [is] fragmented between the intelligence committees and the appropriations committees," which can mean that Congress has only "weak budgetary power over executive branch intelligence agencies."[91] On substantive issues too, congressional intelligence committees continue to "share jurisdiction [over] certain activities with other congressional committees."[92] The fragmentation of congressional oversight responsibility means that, too often, a holistic approach to oversight is difficult.

- *Information Asymmetry:* Information asymmetries between Congress and the executive can also challenge effective congressional oversight. The intelligence agencies are housed within the executive branch, classification decisions are made by the executive branch, and decisions about the flow of documents ultimately are made by executive officials, even in circumstances where there are congressional reporting requirements.[93] Also, the information that does go to Congress is "provided

---

[89] *See* CHURCH COMMITTEE REPORT, *supra* note 8, pt. 1, at 11. ("The legislative branch has been remiss in exercising its control over intelligence agencies. . . . The closeted and fragmentary accounting which the Intelligence Community has given to a designated small group of legislators was accepted by the Congress as adequate[.].").

[90] NATIONAL COMMISSION ON TERRORIST ATTACKS UPON THE UNITED STATES, THE 9/11 COMMISSION REPORT 103 (2004) [hereinafter 9/11 COMM'N REPORT] (discussing fragmented nature of congressional appropriations and oversight of intelligence organizations; *see also id.* at 419–23 (recommending each house of Congress create a single committee responsible for intelligence oversight to prevent attacks in the future).

[91] ZEGART, *supra* note 88, at 28–29.

[92] ERIC ROSENBACH & AKI J. PERITZ, BELFER CTR. FOR SCI. & INT'L AFFAIRS, HARV. KENNEDY SCH. OF GOV'T, CONFRONTATION OR COLLABORATION?: CONGRESS AND THE INTELLIGENCE COMMUNITY 24–27 (2009), *available at* http://belfercenter.ksg.harvard.edu/files/IC-book-finalasof12JUNE.pdf "Because of overlapping jurisdiction and shared responsibilities among congressional committees, the [authorization] process can be long and complex." *Id.* at 24. After the budget has been authorized, it must then be appropriated. "The majority of the intelligence budget appears as a secret lump-sum amount in the Defense Appropriations Bill." *Id.* at 26. *See also* Anne Joseph O'Connell, *The Architecture of Smart Intelligence: Structuring and Overseeing Agencies in the Post-9/11 World*, 94 CAL. L. REV. 1655, 1662 (2006) ("The House Appropriations, Armed Services, Budget, Energy and Commerce, Government Reform, Homeland Security, International Relations, and Judiciary Standing Committees and the House Permanent Select Committee on Intelligence . . . all oversee at least some part of the Intelligence Community. . . . The Senate Appropriations, Armed Services, Budget, Energy and Natural Resources, Foreign Relations, Homeland Security and Governmental Affairs, and Judiciary Standing Committees and the Senate Select Committee on Intelligence . . . all exercise intelligence-related jurisdiction.").

[93] ROSENBACH & PERITZ, *supra* note 92, at 20.

only to the committees that have responsibilities in the national security area."[94] And, moreover, when members of the congressional intelligence committees receive briefings, their ability to take notes or discuss intelligence matters with their staff or other experts is often limited. Lawmakers have noted that the value of these sessions is sometimes reduced because "intelligence officials would not volunteer details if questions were not asked with absolute precision."[95] And in any event, lawmakers generally cannot discuss publicly any concerns they may have about intelligence programs. Witness, for example, statements by Senator Ron Wyden in 2011 that "there are two PATRIOT Acts in America. The first is the text of the law itself, and the second is the government's secret interpretation of what they believe the law means."[96] Wyden went further, arguing that when "the American people find out how their government has secretly interpreted the PATRIOT Act, they are going to be stunned and they are going to be angry."[97] Wyden could say no more, however, because the interpretation of Section 215 to which he was referring was, at the time, classified.

Indeed, the substantial disagreement about the basic facts regarding what the congressional leadership knew about controversial interpretations of Section 215 of the USA PATRIOT Act before they became public illustrate the challenges involved with congressional oversight. Representative Jim Sensenbrenner, one of the authors of the PATRIOT Act, claims that "most" members of Congress were not briefed on the programs revealed in leaks in June 2013.[98] The administration, by contrast, declassified letters to Congress in which the bodies were notified that the IC was conducting bulk telephony metadata collection under the authority of Section 215.[99] And when Congress does devote legislative energy to questions of intelligence oversight, it is often in response to "fire alarm" rather than more consistent "police patrol" models of supervision.[100]

Congress plays a very important role in the oversight of intelligence agencies, particularly as members of Congress are briefed—and provide feedback—on intelligence programs and operations on an ongoing basis. But for the reasons identified above, structural changes would further improve the role of Congress in intelligence oversight.

---

[94] L. Britt Snyder, CIA Ctr. for the Study of Intelligence, *How Intelligence Sharing Works in Present*, SHARING SECRETS WITH LAWMAKERS, https://www.cia.gov/library/center-for-the-study-of-intelligence/csi-publications/books-and-monographs/sharing-secrets-with-lawmakers-congress-as-a-user-of-intelligence/3.htm (last visited Aug. 28, 2015). "Members of these committees receive preference from the Intelligence Community in satisfying their requests on an individual basis."

[95] Peter Wallsten, *Lawmakers Say Obstacles Limited Oversight of NSA's Telephone Surveillance Program*, WASH. POST, Aug. 10, 2013.

[96] 157 Cong. Rec. S3369 (daily ed. May 26, 2011) (statement of Sen. Ron Wyden).

[97] 157 Cong. Rec. S3386 (daily ed. May 26, 2011) (statement of Sen. Ron Wyden).

[98] Jim Sensenbrenner, Op-Ed., *This Abuse of the Patriot Act Must End*, THE GUARDIAN, June 9, 2013.

[99] *See, e.g.*, Letter from Ronald Welch, Assistant Attorney General for Legislative Affairs, to Representative Silvestre Reyes, Chairman, House Permanent Select Committee on Intelligence 1 (Dec. 14, 2009), *available at* http://www.dni.gov/files/documents/2009_CoverLetter_Report_Collection.pdf.

[100] Mathew D. McCubbins & Thomas Schwartz, *Congressional Oversight Overlooked: Police Patrols versus Fire Alarms*, 28 AM. J. POL. SCI. 165–79 (1984).

V. THE OUTLINES OF A GOVERNANCE FRAMEWORK

In this context, with limitations to the effectiveness of congressional oversight, and most extant oversight bodies focused on compliance,[101] it is important to focus on other external institutions that are able to provide effective governance to the IC. The objective of such organizations is not primarily to ensure that intelligence programs comply with the law on an ongoing basis—other institutions have that goal as their primary mission.[102] Rather they exist in parallel with the institutions of compliance such as the FISC and agency general counsels. And their objective should be to help shape formulation of intelligence laws, regulations, and policies in the first instance in a way that is consistent with the expectations of the American people.[103] Most important, external oversight bodies can serve as a proxy for the American people, informing and engaging with the public about intelligence matters.

The most senior leaders of the IC recognize that they will have to operate in an environment of increased transparency.[104] As they do so, external oversight bodies can help mediate a balanced public conversation that protects operational secrecy while generating public trust in the activities of the IC.[105]

A. Independent Bodies

In the United States, the main external governance bodies are the PCLOB, which arose for the third time and received a full-time chairman in May 2013, and the PIAB. The PCLOB was first set up in 2004 in response to 9/11 Commission Report advice to provide a board to protect civil liberties in the counterterrorism struggle.[106] The PIAB's predecessor was created in 1956. The PCLOB and the PIAB, as external institutions, have several advantages in conducting oversight.

PCLOB: The PCLOB is able to provide unique value in intelligence governance because it both has access to the broad range of intelligence programs and is "committed to making information available to the public . . . and, to the greatest extent possible, making its reports

---

[101] Ben Wittes, *The NSA, Oversight, the Law, and Why Compliance Is the Ball Game,* LAWFARE (Sept. 27, 2013 9:22 AM), https://www.lawfareblog.com/nsa-oversight-law-and-why-compliance-ball-game.

[102] Certain issues, particularly those of constitutional interpretation, can be categorized both as questions of compliance and as questions of governance.

[103] *See* 42 U.S.C.A. § 2000ee(c)(2) (West 2015) (the purpose of the Privacy and Civil Liberties Oversight Board is to "ensure that liberty concerns are appropriately considered in the development and implementation of laws, regulations, and policies related to efforts to protect the Nation against terrorism.")

[104] James R. Clapper, Director of National Intelligence, Remarks as Delivered by The Honorable James R. Clapper Director of National Intelligence AFCEA/INSA National Security and Intelligence Summit (Sept. 18, 2014), *available at* http://www.dni.gov/index.php/newsroom/speeches-and-interviews/202-speeches-interviews-2014/1115-remarks-as-delivered-by-the-honorable-james-r-clapper-director-of-national-intelligence-afcea-insa-national-security-and-intelligence-summit. "One of my big takeaways from the past 16 months is that we need to be more transparent. And, if we're going to profess transparency, we need to practice transparency, whenever we can."

[105] Josh Gerstein, *Intelligence Agencies Tout Transparency,* POLITICO, Feb. 3, 2015.

[106] 9/11 COMM'N REPORT, *supra* note 90, at 395.

and recommendations available to the American people."[107] The PCLOB effectuates this purpose by collecting information about IC activities, advising the president on matters of privacy and civil liberties in intelligence programs, and disseminating information in an unclassified format to the public. In its information-gathering role, it has the ability to obtain agency records from a wide range of executive branch sources, to hold public hearings with respect to matters under study, to coordinate the activities of federal agency privacy and civil liberties officers, and to request "that the Attorney General subpoena on the Board's behalf parties outside of the executive branch to produce relevant information."[108] Its reports include not only those that are publicly available (e.g., on the Section 215 and 702 surveillance programs), but also semiannual reports to Congress and to the president about its activities, which "shall be in unclassified form to the greatest extent possible, with a classified annex where necessary."[109]

By gathering information from the IC and seeking the input of the public and outside experts through hearings, the PCLOB is able to inform the American people about intelligence matters, and to incorporate the interests of the public in civil liberties protection into its recommendations and reports. In the future, the role of the PCLOB could be expanded to include the receipt of complaints or concerns from those inside the IC about the design or implementation of intelligence programs. It could also be expanded to focus on a broader range of intelligence programs than those associated with counterterrorism, to which its statutory mandate restricts it. The composition of the Board might also be adjusted to include technologists and members with academic and operational experience in intelligence.

PIAB: The PIAB has a limited role in overseeing compliance by the IC, but its unique value lies in providing advice to the president "on the effectiveness with which the Intelligence Community is meeting the nation's intelligence needs, and the vigor and insight with which the community plans for the future."[110] Like the PCLOB, the PIAB issues reports to the president at least two times per year on issues such as the quality, effectiveness, and performance of the IC (unlike those of the PCLOB, these reports are not made public). And although the PIAB has "full access to the complete range of intelligence-related information," it does not interface with the public as much as the PCLOB does.[111]

Though the PCLOB and the PIAB are structured differently, together, they share a focus on questions of oversight that are much broader than just whether the IC is following the laws as they are written. They both also employ a similar staffing model, using outside experts who are "not employed by the Federal Government," and who are "independent of the Intelligence Community, [and] free from day-to-day management or operational responsibilities."[112] By ensuring that members of the PCLOB and PIAB are not employed in any

---

[107] *About the Board*, Privacy and Civil Liberties Oversight Board, http://www.pclob.gov/about-us (last visited Aug. 27, 2015).

[108] *Id.*

[109] 42 U.S.C.A. § 2000ee(e)(1)(B)(ii) (West 2015).

[110] *Introduction*, President's Intelligence Advisory Board and Intelligence Oversight Board, http://www.whitehouse.gov/administration/eop/piab (last visited Aug. 27, 2015).

[111] *About the PIAB*, President's Intelligence Advisory Board and Intelligence Oversight Board, http://www.whitehouse.gov/administration/eop/piab/about (last visited Aug. 27, 2015).

[112] *Id. See also* 42 U.S.C.A. § 2000ee(h)(3) (2007)("An individual appointed to the [Privacy and Civil Liberties Oversight] Board may not, while serving on the Board, be an elected official, officer, or employee of the Federal Government, other than in the capacity as a member of the Board.")

other capacity by the IC, the two bodies ensure a degree of independence that makes them effective surrogates for the American people as the Boards advise the president and Congress on intelligence activities.

Empowering bodies such as the PCLOB and PIAB would help ensure that a governance perspective is represented and adopted in the oversight of the American IC. The role of the PIAB can also be altered to include more public-facing functions.

B. A View from across the Pond

The PCLOB and the PIAB have close counterparts in the U.K. and Australia, from whom they can draw analogies as they consider an expanded role that they might play in intelligence oversight. Specifically, the U.K. and Australia have Independent Reviewers of Terrorism Legislation (the Australian office is called the Independent National Security Legislation Monitor). The U.K. also has independent Commissioners—the Interception of Communications Commissioner, and the Intelligence Services Commissioner—who play a role in mediating between the public and the intelligence community. They have high-level security clearances, so they have access to the most sensitive national security programs, but also are independent of the government and have a mandate to review and issue reports on intelligence community activities.

This structure has two effects: First, insofar as the reports are made public, they help shape the public discourse and dialogue about intelligence issues so that the public is informed—in general terms—about what is being done in its name; and second, the knowledge that programs pushing the boundaries of legal or political acceptability might come under review and become public might temper the willingness of the intelligence agencies to embrace programs that push the boundaries too far. The important functions such an agency can play, however, are tempered by the inherent weaknesses of an office that can only make recommendations and does not have any legislative or enforcement powers.[113]

As of this writing, legislation has been proposed in the U.K. that would reform the structure and organization of the intelligence oversight system there. While the allocation of authorities among various oversight bodies might change (and new institutions might be created), most of the core features of the oversight system described in this section will likely be retained.

1. External Review Bodies

The role of the Independent Reviewer of Terrorism Legislation in the U.K. "is to inform the public and political debate on anti-terrorism law in the United Kingdom, in particular through regular reports which are prepared for the Home Secretary or Treasury and then laid before Parliament."[114] The Reviewer writes annual reports of the main counterterrorism legislation in the U.K. (the "Terrorism Acts"), and also ad hoc reports that focus on specific statutory authorities or terrorism issues as requested.

---

[113] See, e.g., the contribution of George Williams and Keiran Hardy to this volume, which identifies the particular weaknesses of an office that is dependent on the government to make any changes it might wish to see.

[114] The Reviewer's Role, INDEPENDENT REVIEWER OF COUNTERTERRORISM LEGISLATION, https://terrorismlegislationreviewer.independent.gov.uk/about-me/ (last visited Aug. 27, 2015).

Rather than engage in legal analysis to determine whether intelligence programs are consistent with the law, the Independent Reviewer's main role is "to look at the use made of the statutory powers relating to terrorism, and consider whether, for example, any change in the pattern of their use need[s] to be drawn to the attention of Parliament. For more than 35 years, successive Independent Reviewers have used their reports to ask whether special powers continue to be necessary for fighting terrorism, and to make recommendations for reform."[115]

This kind of independent assessment—informed by access to sensitive intelligence programs, and asking questions about how and whether legal authorities are appropriate—could be a useful complement to institutions of compliance in the United States. Of note, the U.K. has recently proposed legislation that would create a Privacy and Civil Liberties Board, which would be subordinate to the Independent Reviewer, and which would focus on counterterrorism (this office is not yet operational).[116]

2. Intelligence Commissioners

An additional complement to the Independent Reviewer is the Interception of Communications Commissioner (ICC), whose role is to carry out inspections of each of the interception agencies twice each year, and to keep "under review the interception of communications and the acquisition and disclosure of communications data by intelligence agencies, police forces and other public authorities."[117] The Intelligence Services Commissioner has a similar role, but more broadly superintends the rest of the intelligence agencies.

In a similar way to the Independent Reviewer, the two intelligence Commissioners issue reports that help ensure the operations of the intelligence agencies remain linked to public expectations about their roles. The knowledge within the intelligence agencies that they will be inspected at regular intervals also likely exerts an ex ante effect on the programmatic choices that they make.

And although the Commissioners' role is only in part linked to an evaluation of the legality of intelligence programs, the existence of the Commissioners and their periodic inspections are critical to a holistic evaluation of the adequacy of the oversight system in the U.K. In this context the Investigatory Powers Tribunal, a judicial body charged with investigating complaints against intelligence agencies, noted with approval the ICC's report, which put "considerable information into the public domain so far as compatible with the needs of national security."[118]

---

[115] David Anderson, Q.C., Independent Reviewer of Terrorism Legislation, The Terrorism Acts in 2013 3 (July 2014) (internal citations and quotation marks omitted).

[116] David Anderson, Q.C., *Independent Review and the PCLB*, Independent Reviewer of Terrorism Legislation (Jan. 31, 2015), https://terrorismlegislationreviewer.independent.gov.uk/independent-review-and-the-pclb/.

[117] *Interception of Communications Commissioner's Office*, *available at* http://www.iocco-uk.info/default.asp (last visited, Jan. 3, 2016).

[118] Liberty v. Privacy International, [2014] UKIPTrib 13_77H, ¶ 92, *available at* http://www.ipt-uk.com/docs/IPT_13_168-173_H.pdf.

C. The Courts—The Least Dangerous Branch?

A more expansive conception of governance in the United States could also include a broader role for Article III courts[119] and judicial review in the oversight architecture.[120] Such involvement would entail greater receptivity by the courts to the adjudication of legal challenges to intelligence programs. There are, however, currently a range of obstacles to an expanded judicial role in the governance of intelligence in the United States.[121] Nevertheless, Article III courts have begun tentatively to embrace a broader role in adjudicating disputes about the permissible scope of intelligence programs. In this context, the Second Circuit Court of Appeals recently rejected the government's argument that the FISC is the sole forum that can hear cases challenging controversial interpretations of intelligence collection statutes (in that case, Section 215 of the USA PATRIOT Act).[122]

Some strictures, such as justiciability limits to the role of courts in national security, have been construed as structural, and thus more difficult to change through incremental interpretive practices or legislation.[123] Others, such as the State Secrets Privilege (SSP), are more susceptible to amendment to facilitate a greater judicial role in oversight. Indeed, in the last several years, a number of changes have been proposed to the SSP that would make it easier to bring cases about intelligence or national security programs. The president of the American Bar Association (ABA), for example, criticized the ability of the government, under the SSP as construed, to "terminate a court case simply by declaring that it would compromise national security without having the court scrutinize that claim."[124] The ABA went on to propose the adoption of legislation that would involve the courts more directly in evaluating the merits of government SSP claims and in rectifying the perceived imbalance between plaintiffs and the government in the current operation of the privilege. Other proposals would create a greater administrative architecture for review of the government's claims under the SSP, arguing that "Administrative law mechanisms used in other areas of national security law but wholly lacking in the state secrets context will more appropriately deter abuse by addressing the incentives problems that judicial review alone cannot."[125] Reforms such as those would help break down some of the barriers to greater judicial involvement in intelligence matters.

---

[119] *See* Alexander Bickel, The Least Dangerous Branch: The Supreme Court at the Bar of Politics (1962) for a classic discussion of the role of the Supreme Court in American political life.

[120] The question of what reforms should be made to the FISC is not a subject taken up in this chapter.

[121] Contributions to this volume by Raphael Bitton, Daphna Renan, and Kent Roach in particular focus on alternative views of the role of the courts in intelligence and national security.

[122] Am. Civil Liberties Union v. Clapper, 785 F.3d 787, 803–10 (2d Cir. 2015).

[123] *See, e.g.,* Al-Aulaqi v. Obama, 727 F. Supp. 2d 1, 35 (D.D.C. 2010) (dismissing on standing grounds a suit brought by the father of al-Qaida leader Anwar al-Aulaqi); *Clapper v. Amnesty Int'l,* 133 S. Ct. 1138 (2013) (dismissing on standing grounds a suit challenging surveillance purportedly conducted under Section 702 of FISA). *See also* Stephen I. Vladeck, *Standing and Secret Surveillance,* 10 I/S: J. L. & Pub. Pol'y Info. Soc'y 551, 554 (2014) for a discussion of justiciability limitations on the role of the courts in adjudicating surveillance cases, including whether Congress can define injuries and confer standing for violation of surveillance statutes.

[124] *Oversight Hearing on Reform of the State Secrets Privilege Before the H. Comm. on the Judiciary,* 110th Cong. 2 (2008) (written statement of H. Thomas Wells Jr., President-Elect of the American Bar Association).

[125] Beth George, Note, *An Administrative Law Approach to Reforming the State Secrets Privilege,* 84 N.Y.U. L. Rev. 1691, 1693 (2009).

Even without these reforms, courts may play an increasing role in the oversight of intelligence agencies. This chapter, though, focuses on two likely effects of greater judicial involvement in matters of national security: first, the ability of diminished barriers to litigating national security cases to shape ex ante decision-making processes and program design within the executive, and second, the ability of courts and litigation to serve an information-forcing role.

1. Ex ante Effects on Executive Decisions

The first impact of greater judicial involvement in intelligence and national security is what Ashley Deeks has called the "Observer Effect"—a phenomenon whereby a "high degree of confidence [in the executive branch] that a court will review its policy" gives it "strong incentives to select a policy option it is confident a court would uphold."[126] The possibility of judicial review of executive intelligence actions thus "leads to non-mandatory policy changes by the executive—even before a court reaches the merits of a case challenging that policy (or a related one)—as a result of newfound uncertainty about whether and how courts may evaluate those policies."[127]

There is strong evidence from the recent report on the CIA's Detention and Interrogation Program, written by the Senate Select Committee on Intelligence, that the "Observer Effect" had an impact on the conduct of that program.[128] In June 2006, the Supreme Court handed down its landmark opinion in *Hamdan v. Rumsfeld*, 548 U.S. 557 (2006), in which it held that the Military Commission convened to prosecute the petitioner, Salim Hamdan, was not consistent with Common Article 3 of the Geneva Conventions. Attorneys at the CIA analyzed the decision, and noted it that it could have a "significant impact on current CIA interrogation practices[,]"[129] despite the fact that the interrogation program itself had not yet come under review. The decision also caused the Department of Justice's OLC to withdraw a draft memorandum it had prepared on the impact of the Detainee Treatment Act on the permissible use of Enhanced Interrogation Techniques (EITs). The CIA did not make use of the EITs again until July 2007, over a year after the *Hamdan* opinion was issued.[130]

The structural force of the *Hamdan* opinion can be seen in the fact that Supreme Court review of national security practices in one area of the law (military commissions) shaped the design and execution of the detention and interrogation program. A greater judicial willingness to entertain the merits of sensitive intelligence and national security programs in civil litigation against the government would represent a fairly substantial departure from past practice.[131] But it would be a departure that would likely have an important impact on the

---

[126] Ashley Deeks, *The Observer Effect: National Security Litigation, Executive Policy Changes, and Judicial Deference*, 82 Fordham L. Rev. 827, 834 (2013).

[127] *Id.*

[128] Staff of S. Comm. on Intelligence, 113th Cong., Committee Study of the Central Intelligence Agency's Detention and Interrogation Program (Comm. Print 2014) [hereinafter SSCI RDI Study].

[129] *Id.* at 159 (internal quotation marks omitted).

[130] *Id.*

[131] Stephen I. Vladeck, *The New National Security Canon*, 61 Am. U. L. Rev. 1295 (2012).

development of intelligence policies and programs. Indeed, one scholar and former executive branch national security lawyer has noted that litigation has an "inordinate influence" on the "process and results of executive decisionmaking[,]"[132] and "tends to take precedence over other catalysts" for changes in executive branch legal positions on national security.[133] Even the *possibility* of judicial review of a broader range of intelligence programs would be likely to have an important effect on their formulation.

2. Information Forcing

Litigation also has an information-forcing function, both while it is in process and in response to judicial decisions, as the government must stake out clear legal positions during the course of a case and respond to court orders at its conclusion. A recent case in the Freedom of Information Act (FOIA) context demonstrates the possibilities. In 2010, *New York Times* reporters Scott Shane and Charlie Savage filed a FOIA request for legal opinions relating to the legal regime governing targeted killings abroad (the ACLU filed a similar request the next year, and the cases were consolidated). Their initial requests were denied, and they brought suit to force disclosure.

An argument that the plaintiffs raised was that the government had waived its ability to deny the FOIA requests on grounds of classification (among others) because executive branch officials had spoken publicly about the issues analyzed in documents that were the subject of the request. Despite the extensive public discussion of the matters at issue in the litigation, Judge Colleen McMahon of the Southern District of New York felt compelled by the extant legal framework to deny the FOIA requests, noting that the "Alice-in-Wonderland nature of this pronouncement is not lost on me."[134] The Second Circuit Court of Appeals reversed the Southern District, and the government disclosed redacted versions of the memos at issue.[135]

The ability of the courts to force disclosure is most clear in the FOIA context, as the subject matter of the lawsuit is itself the release of documents. But there are a large number of other scenarios in which litigation can force the government to disclose information important to the public debate about intelligence programs or policies, including by compelling the government to take a legal position on an issue in the course of preparing briefs during litigation.[136] This process has an important role in teaching about the limits and theories underlying government action. But that said, there will always be a limit to how much information can and should be disclosed about such programs—limits that courts will almost certainly be cautious to avoid transgressing.

---

[132] Rebecca Ingber, *Interpretation Catalysts and Executive Branch Legal Decisionmaking*, 38 YALE J. INT'L L. 359, 366 (2013).

[133] *Id.* at 368.

[134] New York Times Co. v. U.S. Dep't of Justice, 915 F. Supp. 2d 508, 515 (S.D.N.Y. 2013).

[135] New York Times Co. v. U.S. Dep't of Justice, 752 F.3d 123 (2d Cir. 2014).

[136] *See* Ingber, *supra* note 132, at 375. *See also*, CHARLIE SAVAGE, POWER WARS: INSIDE OBAMA'S POST-9/11 PRESIDENCY 117, 118-121 (2015), for a discussion of the role that litigation played in catalyzing the Obama administration's position on the scope of its non-criminal detention authority ("the legal process drove the policy process.")

VI. CONCLUSION

At the same time as changes are being debated to the oversight architecture, the national security environment, and in particular the counterterrorism environment, is changing rapidly. The changes to the counterterrorism strategy of Western democracies will, in turn, put pressure on existing oversight frameworks, and enhance the imperative to create oversight structures capable of dealing with a more proactive and preventative approach to counterterrorism law and policy.

Specifically, in the wake of a series of terrorist attacks in Paris and the increased number of Westerners traveling to places such as Iraq, Syria, and Yemen, there will be increased attention to what one scholar has termed "targeted pre-crime prevention"—the imposition of constraints on suspected terrorists that are less restrictive than criminal prosecution.[137] In the United States, these constraints have primarily taken the form of financial sanctions and the no-fly list.

But outside the United States, countries have more extensive experience with a broader range of such constraints, the most prominent examples of which are the Control Orders and Terrorism Prevention and Investigation Measures (TPIMs) in the U.K. Control orders included measures such as house arrest, curfews, and electronic tagging, and have been modified over time by judicial orders and legislation.[138] More recently, proposed legislation in the U.K. would have enabled the government to confiscate the passports of suspected terrorists, to ban British citizens suspected of terrorism from returning home, and to bar the payment of ransoms by insurance companies, and would impose obligations on universities to develop policies to prevent the propagation of extremism on campus.[139] French authorities, too, have recently revoked the passports of suspected ISIS recruits who were believed to be planning to travel to Syria,[140] and have dramatically expanded their surveillance authorities.[141]

If the counterterrorism challenge in the United States becomes more pressing because of a successful attack, there will be increased pressure to adopt similar measures, and it is thus important to begin systematic work on the regime that might be necessary to govern this activity, and preventative counterterrorism measures more broadly.

Operating historically in an environment of near-total secrecy, the IC has not had to think much about its relationship to the public. As long as it effectively managed its relationship with Congress and did not violate the law, it was unlikely that lawful intelligence collection programs would be subject to further scrutiny. That has changed, likely forever.[142] But so too has the range of threats that the IC must analyze and mitigate, from traditional nation-state rivals, to terrorist groups (some of which control territory), to cyber threats, which originate with both criminal gangs and state actors, and many others.

---

[137] Jennifer C. Daskal, *Pre-crime Restraints: The Explosion of Targeted, Noncustodial Prevention*, 99 CORNELL L. REV. 327, 358 (2014).

[138] KENT ROACH, THE 9/11 EFFECT: COMPARATIVE COUNTERTERRORISM 280 (2011).

[139] Matthew Holehouse, *Counter-terrorism Bill: What It Contains*, THE TELEGRAPH, Nov. 26, 2014.

[140] Polly Mosendz, *France Confiscates Passports of Six Suspected ISIS Recruits*, NEWSWEEK, Feb. 23, 2015.

[141] Alissa J. Rubin, *Lawmakers in France Move to Vastly Expand Surveillance*, N.Y. TIMES, May 5, 2015.

[142] *See, e.g.*, PETER SWIRE, THE DECLINING HALF-LIFE OF SECRETS AND THE FUTURE OF SIGNALS INTELLIGENCE, NEW AMERICA FOUNDATION (July 2015).

Governing the IC—setting its priorities, shaping its legal authorities, and allocating its resources in a way that is consistent with the legitimate expectations of the American people—has become a substantially more difficult task. As the IC has changed, so too have the kinds of institutions needed to govern it. The institutions of compliance will always remain vitally important. But institutions of governance that can serve as a proxy for the American people, providing the public with information about intelligence activities and protecting the interests of the public under conditions of secrecy, are more important than ever.

9

The President as Intelligence Overseer

*Samuel J. Rascoff**

I. INTRODUCTION

For the president to serve as an intelligence overseer, sounds, at first blush, like a contradiction in terms. In the aftermath of Watergate and the intelligence scandals exposed by the Church[1] and Pike[2] Committees, the framers of the new oversight architecture took presidential control of the IC as a given, and saw in the White House-intelligence complex the capacity for tyranny and abuse. They therefore chose to empower the other branches of government and to interpose a range of traditional as well as "internal" separation-of-powers checks to resist executive dominance. In their view, and in the view of scholars of national security law,[3] the White House is and ought to be an object, not a source, of intelligence oversight.[4]

---

* Professor of Law, Faculty Director, Center on Law and Security, New York University School of Law. This Chapter is based on a longer Article that was published in the *Harvard Law Review*. Samuel J. Rascoff, *Presidential Intelligence*, 129 HARV. L. REV. 633 (2016).

[1] S. Res. 21, 94th Cong. (1975) (establishing a "select committee of the Senate to conduct an investigation and study with respect to intelligence activities carried out by or on behalf of the Federal Government," later called the "Church Committee" after its chairman, Senator Frank Church). For the report issued by the Church Committee, see Final Report of the Select Committee to Study Governmental Operations with Respect to Intelligence Activities, S. Rep. No. 94-755 (1976).

[2] H.R. Res. 138, 94th Cong. (1975), *replaced and expanded by* H.R. Res. 591, 94th Cong. (1975) (establishing a parallel committee in the House, later known as the "Pike Committee" after its chairman, Representative Otis Pike). For the report issued by the Pike Committee, see Recommendations of the Final Report of the House Select Committee on Intelligence, H.R. Rep. No. 94-833 (1976).

[3] JACK GOLDSMITH, POWER AND CONSTRAINT: THE ACCOUNTABLE PRESIDENCY AFTER 9/11 (2012).

[4] In a short essay in the *Harvard Journal on Legislation*, James Baker (who has served as a senior intelligence lawyer in government and is currently General Counsel of the FBI) expressed the view that "it is first and foremost

But championing what I refer to as presidential intelligence—the sustained, routinized, and process-driven governance by the White House of American spying—seems odd only because of a basic misconception that the IC marches in lockstep with the White House. In fact, a decentralized IC that has proved adept at empire-building, and has been largely unconstrained by the political executive, has revealed itself to be profoundly vulnerable to a range of questionable intelligence-gathering practices, carrying out activities that, while conferring uncertain benefits, have led to significant diplomatic blowback, jeopardized the bottom lines of American industry, and pushed the envelope (at the very least) on questions of privacy and civil liberties.[5]

Presidential intelligence takes as its starting point these misalignments between the political executive and the IC, and seeks to address them by harnessing the White House's unique capacity systematically and in ongoing fashion to shape the metes and bounds of intelligence collection.[6] Presidential intelligence is not merely a good idea: it is an emerging reality on the ground. In this chapter I set out to describe and defend its recent arrival on the scene, and to encourage its future growth through sound institutional design.

I first show that, as a descriptive matter, the norms of presidential control that have characterized the majority of the regulatory state for decades have recently begun to take hold in the domain of intelligence collection.[7] Transposing the concepts and architectures of presidential administration to national security, and in particular to the world of intelligence, may seem odd, but is essentially plausible.[8] In fact, although they clearly rest on different constitutional foundations, there is a lot to recommend the analogy between the intelligence apparatus and the administrative state, beginning with a shared pedigree: Both are mid-twentieth-century transplants to Washington and are uneasy fits with the preexisting traditions and institutional life of American constitutionalism. Both grounded their legitimacy

---

the President's responsibility to conduct oversight of intelligence activities." James A. Baker, *Symposium Introduction: Intelligence Oversight*, 45 HARV. J. LEGIS. 199, 201 (2008).

[5] *See* Loch K. Johnson, *The CIA and the Question of Accountability, in* ETERNAL VIGILANCE? 50 YEARS OF THE CIA 178, 180 (Rhodri Jeffreys-Jones & Christopher Andrew eds., 1997) ("Nor did the Executive Office of the Presidency (EOP) offer reliable accountability over the intelligence establishment that sprawled beneath the White House in the organizational chart of the federal government."). For an assessment of the power wielded by the national security bureaucracy, *see* Michael Glennon, *National Security and Double Government*, 5 HARV. NAT'L. SEC. J. 1 (2014).

[6] Some of these misalignments can be thought of as ex ante, in the sense that they represented deviations from presidential preferences from the beginning. But most are better thought of as ex post misalignments, in that it was only after the Snowden leaks fundamentally altered the operative incentives that the president saw a need to act. *See* David Cole, *Must Counterterrorism Counter Democracy*, N.Y. REV. BOOKS, Jan. 8, 2015 (noting that "all three branches of government changed their tune once Snowden disclosed the program," at which point President Obama "appointed an expert review panel, and endorsed several of the reforms it suggested.").

[7] See Elena Kagan, *Presidential Administration*, 114 HARV. L. REV. 2245 (2001). My claims are not limited to any particular intelligence agency or collection platform. Whereas many of the post-Snowden developments that I document are particularly focused on electronic surveillance, the conceptual issues they implicate generalize to other intelligence disciplines.

[8] In thinking about the ways that intelligence has previously defied the norms of the administrative state, and in contemplating the path by which that exceptionality is now under pressure, I am indebted to the scholarship of Rachel Barkow, who has questioned the non-applicability of administrative law norms to the world of criminal

early on in claims of politically neutral technocracy before broadening their foundations to rely heavily on legal institutions and processes. But over the last generation, their trajectories have diverged considerably, with the intelligence apparatus having in large measure retained its strong ideals of bureaucratic independence from politics, even as the balance of the regulatory state has been transformed by ever-increasing presidentialization.[9] The reabsorption of the intelligence state into the mainstream of administrative law and regulation through its own belated process of presidentialization is powerful proof not of the exceptionality of national security but of its banality.[10]

My second main contribution, also descriptive, is to offer an account of how and why the current moment has proved especially propitious for the ascendancy of presidential intelligence. In particular, I call attention to the role that technology and telecommunications firms on the one hand, and allied governments on the other, all themselves intelligence collectors and connoisseurs, have played in catalyzing and shaping the emerging dynamics in this area, making common cause with more traditional civil society groups in pushing back against a range of intelligence collection practices. Presidential intelligence is emerging in a climate in which separation-of-powers type checks are supplied by businesses and foreign governments that are increasingly critical (especially when it comes to public perceptions) of American intelligence gathering. This state of affairs is itself underwritten by heightened levels of transparency and what one scholar has dubbed "the declining half-life of secrets,"[11] which has altered the incentives that used to operate in this area.[12]

My third contribution is to tally some potential costs and benefits of the turn to the institutional presidency as a source of political direction and accountability for the post-9/11 intelligence bureaucracy. On the one hand, presidential control has the capacity to make

---

law. *See, e.g.,* Rachel E. Barkow, *Institutional Design and the Policing of Prosecutors: Lessons from Administrative Law*, 61 Stan. L. Rev 869 (2009).

[9] There is a sense in which the emergence of presidential intelligence is better thought of as a re-emergence in that previous administrations attempted, but ultimately failed, to get the project off the ground. It is suggestive that Executive Order 12,333, 3 C.F.R. 200 (1982) (governing the IC), never served as a font of centralized control on par with Executive Order 12,291, 3 C.F.R. 127 (1982) (requiring agencies to employ cost-benefit analysis), perhaps because the Iran-Contra scandal impaired the Reagan White House's ability to centralize control of intelligence. *See* Griffin B. Bell with Ronald J. Ostrow, Taking Care of the Law 139–41 (1982) (noting that in "the first months of the Reagan Administration . . . [t]he Heritage Foundation . . . proposed undoing virtually all intelligence reform measures," including "doing away with the" Foreign Intelligence Surveillance Court (FISC), but concluding that the Reagan administration was ultimately unable to realize these ambitions).

[10] *Cf.* Roy Godson, Dirty Tricks or Trump Cards: U.S. Covert Action and Counterintelligence 246 (1995) ("In terms of separation of powers, the world of U.S. intelligence has been 'normalized.'"); Gregory F. Treverton, *Intelligence: Welcome to the American Government, in* Intelligence and National Security: The Secret World of Spies, An Anthology 347 (Loch K. Johnson & James J. Wirtz eds., 3d ed. 2011) (noting that, as judged by the way in which congressional oversight of intelligence functions, the IC belongs to the mainstream of American government).

[11] Peter Swire, New Am. Cybersecurity Initiative, The Declining Half Life of Secrets and the Future of Signals Intelligence (2015).

[12] *See* David E. Pozen, *Deep Secrecy*, 62 Stan. L. Rev. 257, 318–19 (2010). The relationship between visibility and secrecy is complex. *See* Samuel J. Rascoff, *Counterterrorism and New Deterrence*, 89 N.Y.U. L. Rev. 830, 844–56 (2014).

intelligence sounder on policy and economic grounds,[13] to enhance the ways in which the intelligence apparatus is made democratically accountable, and even potentially to enhance certain rights-protections—in some cases more effectively than other oversight tools. At the same time, presidentialization runs the risk of politicizing intelligence, heightening partisan gridlock, and even, under certain specifications, recreating the conditions for abusive practices of the sort that prompted the significant intelligence reforms of the 1970s, or that doomed elements of the President's Surveillance Program (PSP) a decade ago.

Presidential intelligence is intended as a complement to existing oversight mechanisms, not a substitute for them. It is certainly not a panacea, any more than presidential administration has proved to be one.[14] I offer no predictions as to where intelligence policy will come to rest in the United States in the coming years, or as to how presidential intelligence will fare in practice if (as I expect) it develops into a defining feature of intelligence governance.[15] But designed smartly, presidential intelligence represents a meaningful opportunity to enhance the effectiveness, accountability, and attentiveness to civil liberties of a crucially important and inevitably delicate instrument of American power.

II. PRESIDENTIAL INTELLIGENCE: A BASELINE

The president has always had extensive contact with the IC across a range of intelligence functions. First and most basically, he has always been the consumer-in-chief of intelligence, and the IC has always stood prepared to advise him (and his senior staff) on issues of concern. Each day, the IC prepares an intelligence digest for the president that is then briefed to him, the vice president, and a handful of other officials, in person, by the head of American intelligence (or his designate), who doubles as the president's personal intelligence advisor.[16]

---

[13] *See, e.g.,* Kent Roach, *Review and Oversight of National Security Activities and Some Reflections on Canada's Arar Inquiry,* 29 CARDOZO L. REV. 53, 55 (2007) (arguing that there is good reason for "separating the processes of oversight and review . . . [for the] efficacy of national security activities and . . . [for their] propriety."). *Cf.* James A. Baker, *supra* note 4 at 200-01 ("When it comes to conducting oversight of the United States intelligence community . . . it seems that our goals should include ensuring that taxpayers' funds are spent appropriately and efficiently on programs and activities that produce useable intelligence information; that intelligence activities are effective in protecting the United States and its interests from foreign threats; and that intelligence activities are conducted in a lawful manner at all times.").

[14] Thomas O. Sargentich, *The Emphasis on the Presidency in U.S. Public Law: An Essay Critiquing Presidential Administration,* 59 ADMIN. L. REV. 1, 35–36 (2007) (criticizing the tendency of the presidential administration literature to mythologize the capacity of the White House, noting that its "accountability and effectiveness claims present a picture of the President as a white knight uniquely able to vindicate the public interest.").

[15] *Cf.* JACK GOLDSMITH, POWER AND CONSTRAINT: THE ACCOUNTABLE PRESIDENCY AFTER 9/11 at 210 (2012) ("To say that the presidential [accountability system] helped generate a consensus about the counterterrorism policies the President can legitimately use does not, unfortunately, mean that it generated the right policies—the ones best designed to prevent terrorist attacks while . . . preserving other values as much as possible.").

[16] For details on the president's daily brief, see *The Evolution of the President's Daily Brief,* CIA, https://www.cia.gov/news-information/featured-story-archive/2014-featured-story-archive/the-evolution-of-the-presidents-daily-brief.html (last visited Jan. 15, 2015). Different directors have adopted different postures toward the president. Writing in *Time Magazine* about the close personal tie between President Obama and CIA director John Brennan, former spy Robert Baer observed that "[t]he last CIA director with a close personal relationship with his President was Reagan's CIA director Bill Casey," who, Baer goes on to say, "played an important role in

Another critical node of intense presidential involvement in intelligence involves covert action. Intelligence reformers in 1974 imposed the requirement that "no appropriated funds could be expended by the CIA for covert actions unless and until the President found that each such operation was important to national security, and provided the appropriate committees of Congress with a description and scope of each operation in a timely fashion."[17] The president also enjoys considerable authority to shape the IC from the standpoint of its structure, budget, and organizational priorities. As set out in Executive Order 12,333, the charter order that has governed the intelligence state for over 30 years,[18] the president is empowered to specify the roles and responsibilities of various components of the IC. The White House's capacity to shape the agenda of the intelligence bureaucracy in terms of what "requirements" they collect against is also considerable. For example, President Clinton issued PDD-35 to establish intelligence priorities in a post–Cold War landscape.[19] And although the intelligence budgeting process remains opaque and involves bureaucratic sleights-of-hand such as "reprogramming," it is clear that the White House, with the assistance of a small, dedicated intelligence staff at Office of Management and Budget, plays a key role here.

All of the aforementioned points of contact between the White House and the intelligence agencies are, of course, hugely important. But when it comes to the sustained oversight of how intelligence is collected—what has rightly been called "the bedrock of intelligence"[20]—the president's role has been relatively limited. Certain highly sensitive collection programs do garner White House attention.[21] But it remains the case that the core "business" of the

---

shaping Reagan's foreign policy." Robert B. Baer, *What Awaits John Brennan at the CIA*, Time (Jan. 9, 2013), http://swampland.time.com/2013/01/09/what-awaits-john-brennan-at-the-cia/. Notably, Casey was the first (and perhaps also the last) CIA director to "take a place at the White House table as a fully participating Cabinet member." *See* Eric Pace, *William Casey, Ex-C.I.A. Head, Is Dead at 74*, N.Y. Times (May 7, 1987), http://www.nytimes.com/1987/05/07/obituaries/william-casey-ex-cia-head-is-dead-at-74.html.

[17] *See, e.g.*, Marshall Curtis Erwin, Cong. Research Serv., RL 33715, Covert Action: Legislative Background and Possible Policy Questions 1 (Apr. 10, 2013), *available at* https://www.fas.org/sgp/crs/intel/RL33715.pdf.

[18] Executive Order 12,333 is perhaps best known for its prohibition of assassination. *See* Exec. Order No. 12,333, 3 C.F.R. 200, § 2.11. But it also serves as something like a basic charter for the IC and as the "principal governing authority for United States intelligence activities [overseas]." Richard A. Clarke Et Al., President's Review Grp. On Intelligence And Commc'ns Techs, Liberty And Security In A Changing World 70 (2013) [hereinafter PRG]. Reform of the order in 2008, designed in large measure to bring it into conformity with the intelligence reform statute of 2004, *see* Stephen B. Slick, The 2008 Amendments to *Executive Order 12333, United States Intelligence Activities* (2014) http://www.cia.gov/library/center-for-the-study-of-intelligence/csi-publications/csi-studies/studies/vol-58-no-2/pdfs/Slick-Modernizing%20the%20IC%20Charter-June2014.pdf , generated bipartisan pushback on Capitol Hill, *see* Eli Lake, *Bush's Order on Intelligence Sparks a Furor in Congress*, N.Y. Sun (Aug. 1, 2008), http://www.nysun.com/national/bushs-order-on-intelligence-sparks-a-furor/83046/.

[19] Press Briefing, Mike McCurry, Office of the Press Sec'y (Mar. 10, 1995), *available at* http://fas.org/irp/offdocs/pdd35.htm.

[20] *See* Mark M. Lowenthal, Intelligence: From Secrets to Policy 87 (2015).

[21] The president and his senior staff are involved in approving highly sensitive technical collection decisions. *See, e.g.*, Bob Woodward, Veil: The Secret Wars of the CIA, 1981–1987, 30 (2005) (tapping undersea cables required presidential sign off). *See also* Ryan Lizza, *State of Deception: Why Won't the President Rein in the Intelligence Community?*, New Yorker (Dec. 16, 2013), http://www.newyorker.com/magazine/2013/12/16/state-of-deception (describing a briefing President Obama received in early February 2009 setting

spy agencies (running the gamut from CIA to NSA to FBI to NGA, and so on) is largely ungoverned by the White House. Intelligence scholars have long called for tighter political control of intelligence collection, such as when Harry Howe Ransom recommended that "[n]o foreign secret action should be undertaken until after the most careful weighing of risks against possible gains, and particularly a careful and realistic analysis of the prospects for secrecy and the consequences of public exposure."[22] But unlike the case of covert action regulation, there has been (at least until Snowden) no watershed culminating in a formal demand that presidents pay systematic attention to intelligence gathering. To understand why, it is useful to consider why the sorts of centripetal forces that operate across the broad sweep of American public life have tended to be weaker in this area.

III. THE EMERGENCE OF PRESIDENTIAL INTELLIGENCE

Although the emergence of presidential intelligence does not lend itself to precise periodization, it is my contention that the revelation of surveillance practices by Edward Snowden can be thought of as the fulcrum for marking the transition. Jack Goldsmith captures the moment and its upshot with precision:

> Pre-Snowden, the US government faced few constraints in its collection and analysis other than what the law imposed, what its technology could achieve, and what its large budget permitted. Within these constraints, it could focus solely on the national security benefit side of communications surveillance, for there were few costs, and practically no political costs, to it. In the post-Snowden world, NSA collection programs are very costly along many dimensions, and the US government faces many tradeoffs and conflicting interests.[23]

Under conditions of unprecedented visibility, political blame was assigned to the White House for perceived intelligence excesses, and the president was compelled to assume greater control of the issues. The particular causal mechanisms that prompted presidential intelligence to take hold are inevitably numerous and overlapping.

---

out substantial NSA compliance issues with FISC orders governing its metadata program, and the president's decision to proceed with the program when Judge Walton on the FISC was threatening to shut it down); Press Release, Office of the Press Sec'y, Remarks by the President on Review of Signals Intelligence (Jan. 17, 2014) [hereinafter Presidential Remarks on Signals Intelligence] https://www.whitehouse.gov/the-press-office/2014/01/17/remarks-president-review-signals-intelligence ("I maintained a healthy skepticism toward our surveillance programs after I became President. I ordered that our programs be reviewed by my national security team and our lawyers, and in some cases I ordered changes in how we did business.").

[22] HARRY HOWE RANSOM, THE INTELLIGENCE ESTABLISHMENT 247 (1970). See also Kenneth deGraffenreid, Intelligence and the Oval Office, in INTELLIGENCE REQUIREMENTS FOR THE 1980S: INTELLIGENCE AND POLICY 9, 16 (Roy Godson ed., 1986) ("If a president is interested in having a closer look at one issue than another, he ought to, even if it means a reordering or restructuring of the intelligence community's collection and analytic efforts.").

[23] See Jack Goldsmith, A Partial Defense of the Front-Page Rule, HOOVER INSTITUTION: THE BRIEFING (Jan. 29, 2014), http://www.hoover.org/research/partial-defense-front-page-rule.

Structurally speaking, the Snowden leaks themselves (which came on the heels of Julian Assange's revelations and have already been followed by others), as well as the White House attention they generated, can be seen as a predictable response to the exponential growth that the intelligence bureaucracy has undergone since 9/11. Massive growth has increased the risk surface for leaks, both in the sense that it is that much harder to ensure the impenetrability of a greatly enlarged and complex workforce[24] (Snowden was working as a contractor) and because the expanded ambitions of post-9/11 intelligence have created more potential points of friction that could, in turn, galvanize insiders to expose what they perceive as official excess. Indeed, thinking even more macroscopically about the nature of technology itself, it has both greatly expanded the capacities of intelligence agencies to collect information and significantly increased vulnerability, for example by empowering individuals within the intelligence apparatus to undermine secrecy by exposing official practices on a heretofore unimaginable scale. Peter Swire has convincingly argued that secrets have a "declining half-life," and that intelligence agencies fail to internalize this reality at their own peril.[25] Swire's view appears to have shaped one of the recommendations of the President's Review Group on which he served: "[W]e should not engage in any secret, covert, or clandestine activity if we could not persuade the American people of the necessity and wisdom of such activities were they to learn of them as the result of a leak or other disclosure."[26]

Since 9/11, there has certainly been interest group contestation in national security, with civil libertarian groups tending to oppose a range of government policies for privileging security over core constitutional rights of expression, liberty, due process, and privacy.[27] But what is distinctive about the post-Snowden developments is that other, arguably more powerful, groups have united with privacy activists to challenge official surveillance policy.[28] The technology firms and foreign governments who have now added their voices to the discussion bring considerable economic and diplomatic clout to the table, as well as sophistication about intelligence.[29] It had been previously been written of intelligence that "[f]ew interest groups

---

[24] *See, e.g.*, Sir David Omand, *Ethical Guidelines in Using Secret Intelligence for Public Security*, 19 CAMBRIDGE REV. INT'L AFFS. 613, 616 (2006) ("The British Security Service will, for example, by 2008 be double the size it was before 9/11."). *See also* Charles Stross, Argument, *Spy Kids*, FOREIGN POL'Y, Aug. 29, 2013, http://foreignpolicy.com/2013/08/29/spy-kids/ (emphasizing the mobility of labor among the next generation of technology experts and its likely effects on the NSA workforce and its ethos).

[25] *See* Swire, *supra* note 11.

[26] *See* PRG, *supra* note 18, at 170 (2014). *See also* Goldsmith, *supra* note 23 ("[S]ecret intelligence actions—especially the ones that would most likely engender outrage, surprise, debate, or legal controversy—are increasingly difficult to keep secret.").

[27] *See, e.g., NSA Surveillance*, ACLU, http://www.aclu.org/issues/national-security/privacyand-surveillance/nsa-surveillance (last visited Jan. 16, 2015) (detailing the organization's challenges to intelligence programs and practices); NSA Spying on Americans, ELECTRONIC FRONTIER FOUND., http://www.eff.org/nsa-spying (last visited Jan. 16, 2015) (same).

[28] *See, e.g.*, Sam Gustin, *Apple, Google, Facebook Join Civil Liberties Groups for NSA Transparency Push*, TIME (July 18, 2013), http://business.time.com/2013/07/18/apple-google-facebook-join-civil-liberties-groups-for-nsa-transparency-push/.

[29] My argument does not depend on the motivations driving the firms and allies. It rests solely on their power and their ability to lean on the White House to achieve reforms. As a descriptive matter, the fact of interest group pressure on the president concerning intelligence practices bears out the accuracy of the observation that the White House is itself a site of interest group contestation.

exist in this policy domain."[30] But the Snowden revelations helped to usher in a change on this front.[31] Under pressure from this new constellation of actors, the White House has been forced to recalibrate its own outmoded assessment of the relative costs and benefits of disengagement from the governance of intelligence collection.[32] As Julian Sanchez has put it, "perhaps the most significant change wrought by the Snowden disclosures to date has not been the policy proposals it has inspired—which, however vital, tend to focus on rules rather than architectures—but in the way it has transformed the incentives of the technology companies that maintain those architectures."[33]

The technology firms have certainly been outspoken on these matters. The companies are also beginning to engage in forms of commercial "self-help," employing default encryption technologies on mobile devices and explicitly marketing them as being impervious to government snooping.[34] The message is clear: the global marketplace demands consumer technology (or cloud-based services) that defeats surveillance, and if the Apples of the world are not poised to provide it, some other company will. In yet another unmistakable nod to the imperatives of global competitiveness, Google's top lawyer has recently argued for

---

[30] *See* Loch K. Johnson, *Congressional Supervision of America's Secret Agencies: The Experience and Legacy of the Church Committee, in* INTELLIGENCE: THE SECRET WORLD OF SPIES, AN ANTHOLOGY, *supra* note 10 at 393, 394. Of course, it is not correct that major technology and telecommunications firms have been strangers to national security policymaking or politics until very recently. To take a striking example, the telecommunications firms fought hard to have immunity from civil liability made part of the FISA Amendments Act of 2008. *See* ERIC C. LIU, CONG. RESEARCH SERV., RL34600, RETROACTIVE IMMUNITY PROVIDED BY THE FISA AMENDMENTS ACT OF 2008 (2008). And some aspects of the current political economy remind thoughtful observers of a prior generation's so-called crypto wars. *See* Joris V.J. van Hoboken & Ira S. Rubinstein, *Privacy and Security in the Cloud: Some Realism about Technical Solutions to Transnational Surveillance in the Post-Snowden Era*, 48 MAINE L. REV. 487, 500–03 (2014) (describing a standoff between the tech industry and the national security state during the Clinton administration over commercial uses of encryption technology).

[31] The story of the emergence of presidential intelligence could itself be recast as a successful capture story, with the tech firms and foreign allies doing the capturing. *See, e.g.*, Michael A. Livermore & Richard L. Revesz, *Regulatory Review, Capture, and Agency Inaction*, 101 GEO. L. REV. 1337, 1340 (2013) ("Capture describes situations where organized interest groups successfully act to vindicate their goals through government policy at the expense of the public interest."). That is certainly how many intelligence insiders who oppose the influence that tech firms currently wield see it.

[32] It is of course the case that interest groups have also undertaken concerted lobbying efforts on Capitol Hill. For example, technology firms backed certain reform legislation in early 2014, but ultimately walked away from a Senate bill that would have embodied too many compromises on the privacy protections they sought.

[33] Julian Sanchez, *Snowden Showed Us Just How Big the Panopticon Really Was. Now It's Up to Us*, THE GUARDIAN (June 5, 2014), http://www.theguardian.com/commentisfree/2014/jun/05/edward-snowden-one-year-surveillance-debate-begins-future-privacy.

[34] *See, e.g.*, *Government Information Requests*, APPLE.COM, http://www.apple.com/privacy/government-information-requests/ (last visited Aug. 26, 2015) ("For all devices running iOS 8.0 and later versions, Apple will not perform iOS data extractions in response to government search warrants because the files to be extracted are protected by an encryption key that is tied to the user's passcode, which Apple does not possess."); *Our Approach to Privacy*, APPLE, http://www.apple.com/privacy/approach-to-privacy ("[W]e wouldn't be able to comply with a wiretap order even if we wanted to."); *see also* David E. Sanger & Brian X. Chen, *Signaling Post-Snowden Era, New iPhone Locks Out N.S.A.*, N.Y. TIMES (Sept. 26, 2014), http://www.nytimes.com/2014/09/27/technology/iphone-locks-out-the-nsa-signaling-a-post-snowden-era-.html.

the extension of American privacy protections to EU citizens.[35] In sum, a major American industry has now taken a stance against "overregulation" by the intelligence state—possibly the first time in the annals of post–World War II American national security that a set of powerful economic actors was so misaligned with national power and so vocal about it. Of late, some national security officials have begun to push back. FBI director Jim Comey has publicly argued that the pendulum has now swung too far in the direction of privacy,[36] specifically decrying the recent push toward encryption, and warning that "Apple and Google have the power to upend the rule of law."[37]

The president has also had to absorb pushback from allies.[38] U.S. envoys were summoned by the French,[39] German,[40] and Brazilian[41] authorities, among others, to explain U.S. surveillance practices, including surveillance of heads of state. No case was more inflammatory than the revelation that the United States had carried out surveillance of German chancellor Angela Merkel's cell phone.[42] As Henry Farrell and Abraham Newman have argued, Angela Merkel was already downplaying the impact of broad counterterrorism-motivated NSA surveillance when further Snowden revelations exposed widespread spying on European leaders.[43] It was at that point that Chancellor Merkel told the president that "she unmistakably

---

[35] David Drummond, *It's Time to Extend the US Privacy Act to EU Citizens*, Google Pub. Pol'y Blog (Nov. 12, 2014), http://googlepublicpolicy.blogspot.com/2014/11/its-time-to-extend-us-privacy-act-to-eu.html.

[36] *See* James B. Comey, Dir., FBI, Remarks at the Brookings Institution: Going Dark: Are Technology, Privacy, and Public Safety on a Collision Course? (Oct. 16, 2014).

[37] *60 Minutes: FBI Director on Privacy, Electronic Surveillance* (CBS television broadcast Oct. 12, 2014), *available at* http://www.cbsnews.com/news/fbi-director-james-comey-on-privacy-and-surveillance/.

[38] Sometimes pressure from allies has merged with pressure from tech firms, as when Google chairman Eric Schmidt spoke about his meeting with Angela Merkel and her sense of outrage at surveillance practices that evoked, for her, her childhood experience in an East German surveillance state. *See* Nancy Scola, *Google's Schmidt: Surveillance Fears Are "Going to End up Breaking the Internet*," Wash. Post (Oct. 8, 2014) http://www.washingtonpost.com/blogs/the-switch/wp/2014/10/08/googles-schmidt-surveillance-fears-are-going-to-end-up-breaking-the-internet/.

[39] Adrian Croft & Arshad Mohammed, *France Summons U.S. Ambassador over Spying Report*, Reuters (Oct. 21, 2013) http://www.reuters.com/article/2013/10/21/us-france-nsa-idUSBRE99K04920131021.

[40] *German Foreign Minister Summons US Ambassador over Merkel Spying Allegations*, Deutsche Welle (Oct. 24, 2013), http://www.dw.de/german-foreign-minister-summons-us-ambassador-over-merkel-spying-allegations/a-17180294. Merkel commented on the allegations by saying that "trust needs to be re-established" with Washington. *Id.* German defense minister Thomas de Maiziere said it would be "really bad" if the allegations turned out to be true: "We can't simply return to business as usual . . . [but] the relations between our countries are stable and important for our future; they will remain that way." *Id.*

[41] Simon Romero & Randal C. Archibold, *Brazil Angered over Report N.S.A. Spied on President*, N.Y. Times (Sept. 2, 2013), http://www.nytimes.com/2013/09/03/world/americas/brazil-angered-over-report-nsa-spied-on-president.html?_r=1&. Brazil's justice minister commented "this would be an unacceptable violation to our sovereignty, involving our head of state." *Id.*

[42] *See* Melissa Eddy, *File Said to Confirm N.S.A. Spied on Merkel*, N.Y. Times (July 1, 2015), http://www.nytimes.com/2015/07/02/world/europe/file-is-said-to-confirm-nsa-spied-on-merkel.html.

[43] *See* Henry Farrell & Abraham Newman, *Senseless Spying: The National Security Agency's Self-Defeating Espionage against the EU*, Foreign Aff. (July 9, 2013), http://www.foreignaffairs.com/articles/139567/henry-farrell-and-abraham-newman/senseless-spying.

disapproves of and views as completely unacceptable such practices," and that "[s]uch practices have to be halted immediately."[44]

In sum, the Snowden leaks have galvanized tech firms and allies to join long-standing skeptics of the surveillance state, such as privacy groups, to put pressure on the White House to resist the agenda of the intelligence bureaucracy. To be certain, the market- and strategy-based incentives that motivate these actors are morally shallower, and for that reason potentially more malleable, than the stances taken by the NGO critics of surveillance. But their impact has nevertheless been significant. Faced with mounting pressure from these influential groups, the president, perhaps for the first time, has something to gain—and a lot to lose—in the oversight of intelligence collection.[45]

IV. THE SHAPE OF PRESIDENTIAL INTELLIGENCE

In response to the Snowden leaks—and their catalytic effect on powerful interest groups—the president has looked to curtail the political damage and to respond to interest group pressures by intervening in the area of surveillance policy. The turn to presidential control can be seen across a number of distinct domains. First, there is the straightforward but noticeable phenomenon of the president becoming seized of the issue. In the aftermath of the Snowden leaks, President Obama convened various ad hoc groups—including one staffed by a number of academics and former officials called the President's Review Group on Intelligence and Communications Technologies, and another headed by the White House chief of staff that leveraged the expertise of Silicon Valley firms[46]—as well as the nascent Privacy and Civil Liberties Oversight Board,[47] and senior White House officials and leaders in the spy agencies themselves. With their input, and with the benefit of numerous direct meetings with the leadership of privacy groups, technology firms, and allied governments,[48] the president considered, in a newly systematic fashion, the yawning gaps that had emerged in intelligence governance.

The next—and arguably most significant—aspect of the assertion of President Obama's control in this area was the issuance of a presidential directive[49]—one of the classic vehicles

---

[44] Ian Traynor, Philip Oltermann & Paul Lewis, *Angela Merkel's Call to Obama: Are You Bugging My Mobile Phone?*, THE GUARDIAN (Oct. 23, 2013), http://www.theguardian.com/world/2013/oct/23/us-monitored-angela-merkel-german.

[45] *See* Terry M. Moe, *The Politicized Presidency, in* THE MANAGERIAL PRESIDENCY 144 (James P. Pfiffner ed., 2d ed. 1999).

[46] *See* JOHN PODESTA ET AL., EXEC. OFFICE OF THE PRESIDENT, BIG DATA: SEIZING OPPORTUNITIES, PRESERVING VALUES (2014), *available at* http://www.whitehouse.gov/sites/default/files/docs/big_data_privacy_report_5.1.14_final_print.pdf.

[47] GARRETT HATCH, CONG. RESEARCH SERV., RL34385, PRIVACY AND CIVIL LIBERTIES OVERSIGHT BOARD: NEW INDEPENDENT AGENCY STATUS 1 (2012), *available at* http://fas.org/sgp/crs/misc/RL34385.pdf.

[48] *See* Tony Romm, *Mark Zuckerberg, Tech Execs Meet Obama*, POLITICO (Mar. 21, 2014), http://www.politico.com/story/2014/03/mark-zuckerberg-barack-obama-tech-ceos-nsa-104907.html ("The meeting marked the second time in about four months that the White House has invited major technology CEOs to Washington to talk about the issue.").

[49] Press Release, The White House Office of the Press Sec'y, Presidential Policy Directive-Signals Intelligence Activities (Jan. 17, 2014) [hereinafter PPD-28], *available at* http://www.whitehouse.gov/the-press-office/2014/01/17/presidential-policy-directive-signals-intelligence-activities.

of presidential administration.[50] On January 17, 2014, President Obama issued Presidential Policy Directive-28 (PPD-28), articulating "principles to guide why, whether, when, and how the United States conducts signals intelligence activities for authorized foreign intelligence and counterintelligence purposes."[51] PPD-28 is divided into four sections: [52] (1) "principles governing" signals intelligence (SIGINT) collection, (2) "limitations" on bulk SIGINT collection, (3) alterations to the "process" for SIGINT collection, and (4) requirements and techniques for "safeguarding personal information" in the SIGINT collection process and reporting requirements[53] for the IC.[54] It is the directive's third section that speaks most straightforwardly to the formation of a new, White House-driven approach to intelligence oversight. Characterizing that change in his address, the president called for "strengthen[ing] executive branch oversight of our intelligence activities" inter alia by ensuring that the White House "will review decisions about intelligence priorities and sensitive targets on an annual basis so that our actions are regularly scrutinized by [the president's] senior national security team."[55]

The key move here is to define the potential risks associated with intelligence practices (and their possible revelation) broadly. As the president went on to explain, the oversight will take into "account our security requirements, but also our alliances, our trade and

---

[50] *See* Kagan, *supra* note 7.

[51] *See* PPD-28. *See also* Press Release, The White House Office of the Press Sec'y, FACT SHEET: The Administration's Proposal for Ending the Section 215 Bulk Telephony Metadata Program (Mar. 27, 2014), *available at* http://www.whitehouse.gov/the-press-office/2014/03/27/fact-sheet-administration-s-proposal-ending-section-215-bulk-telephony-m (detailing the president's proposed changes and the future steps to be taken by Congress in order to enact them).

[52] PPD-28. Among the significant policy changes ushered in by the directive and the accompanying speech are (1) imposing a two-hop (rather than three) standard on querying metadata; (2) recommending that the FISC, rather than the NSA, make findings about reasonable articulable suspicion (it is unclear what authority the president employed to make this change, but the FISC seems to have assumed the responsibility notwithstanding the public letter by Judge Bates suggesting the court was overburdened); and (3) extending certain heightened privacy protections to foreign nationals. This last point makes sense as a direct response to the global pressures that have been brought to bear on the White House, both by allied governments and by tech firms with global customers. *See id.*

[53] PPD-28 mandated several reports, by the PCLOB, the PIAB, as well as the DNI, who was required to prepare a report within 180 days "evaluating possible additional dissemination and retention safeguards for personal information collected through" SIGINT, "consistent with technical capabilities and operational needs." *Id.* The DNI report, issued in July 2014 but not released publicly until October 17, describes how the IC has begun to implement the requirements of the PPD, and plans to "afford protections that go beyond those explicitly outlined in PPD-28." Robert S. Litt & Alexander W. Joel, Office of the Dir. of Nat'l Intelligence, INTERIM PROGRESS REPORT ON IMPLEMENTING PPD-28, at 2 (2014), *available at* http://www.dni.gov/index.php/newsroom/reports-and-publications/204-reports-publications-2014/1126-interim-progress-report-on-implementing-ppd-28.

[54] PPD-28, *supra* note 49; Laura K. Donohue, *FISA Reform*, 10 I/S: J.L. & POL'Y INFO. SOC'Y 1, 11 (2014) ("PDD-28 . . . lay[s] out the current principles guiding SIGINT, such as the integration of privacy and civil liberties considerations in the collection of intelligence, limits on the collection of commercial information and trade secrets, and the tailoring of SIGINT to areas where the information is not otherwise available. The document restricts the use of bulk SIGINT data. It draws attention to . . . minimization [procedures], data security and access, data quality, and oversight.").

[55] Presidential Remarks on Signals Intelligence, *supra* note 21.

investment relationships, including the concerns of American companies, and our commitment to privacy and basic liberties."[56] This echoes a recognition in PPD-28 that intelligence
practices—especially insofar as they become public—potentially entail risk to

> our relationships with other nations, including the cooperation we receive from other
> nations on law enforcement, counterterrorism, and other issues; our commercial,
> economic, and financial interests, including a potential loss of international trust in
> U.S. firms and the decreased willingness of other nations to participate in international
> data sharing, privacy, and regulatory regimes.[57]

Institutionally, the National Security Council—what Terry Moe and Scott Wilson rightly
refer to as "the major centralizing institution" in foreign affairs[58]—is the place within the
White House where many of these competing equities are put on the table and discussed in
comprehensive fashion.

V. ASSESSING PRESIDENTIAL INTELLIGENCE

Of all the strengths that presidential intelligence entails, none is more significant than its
capacity to promote strategically sound intelligence. Presidential intelligence entails a centralized mechanism for reviewing intelligence practices in light of their overall consequences,
a job that requires the inputs of policymakers, and so cannot be performed within the intelligence bureaucracy itself. The motivating ideas here are as simple as they are attractive.
Intelligence collection practices ought to be assessed for their efficacy and employed only to
the extent that their overall benefits exceed their costs. Making those determinations entails
calling forth a wide range of perspectives and expertise to determine the appropriate scope
of intelligence gathering, a task to which the White House is well-suited. The idea that the
National Security Council is able to convene an interagency process through which to arrive
at better-calibrated intelligence collection resonates powerfully with a body of academic literature that assesses the role of Office of Information and Regulatory Affairs in performing
centralized review of regulatory decision-making.

    A second potential upside is presidential intelligence's capacity to promote heightened
democratic accountability. In one sense, the logic here verges on the tautological. By substituting presidential intelligence for a system that historically empowered the permanent
intelligence bureaucracy to self-regulate, responsiveness to the elected representative of the
people is promoted.[59] As one intelligence scholar has explained, "what some may perceive as

---

[56] *Id.*

[57] PPD-28, *supra* note 49.

[58] *See* Terry M. Moe & Scott A. Wilson, *Presidents and the Politics of Structure*, 57 L. & Contemp. Probs.
1, 19 (1994) ("The president clearly has strong reasons for not wanting the State Department, the Defense
Department, and other agencies to make their own foreign policy decisions.").

[59] *See* Jerry L. Mashaw, *Accountability and Institutional Design: Some Thoughts on a Grammar of Governance*,
in Public Accountability: Designs, Dilemmas and Experiences 115, 121 (Michael W. Dowdle ed.,
2006) (setting out various types of public accountability and describing political accountability as a system in

a president's 'preconceptions' and 'biases' may well be the entirely proper policy orientation that a president was elected to pursue."[60] But upon closer inspection, more nuanced judgments can be teased out, and two distinct concepts of accountability come into view. First, there is the way in which presidential intelligence underwrites (and is underwritten by) what might be thought of as a pluralist account of accountability. As noted above, the president has repeatedly interacted with emergent interest groups in the intelligence domain, including foreign heads of state, diplomats, and tech and telecom executives. Precisely because these conversations are relatively intimate and entail discussions with knowledgeable intelligence insiders (and efforts by American officials to mollify actors they need to keep on board), they are likely to involve candid talk about intelligence practices. In turn, these candid exchanges can be said to supply a measure of accountability with the interest groups standing in for (at least some portion of) the general public.

Second, presidential intelligence has inched toward a more straightforwardly democratic vision of accountability, a turn that is itself dependent on the heightened visibility of the intelligence apparatus. The allied presidential administration literature views its public-facing aspects as a core feature of the project.[61] The president and his senior advisors have spoken publicly and extensively about the changes at hand. For example, in a major speech that he delivered to accompany the issuance of PPD-28,[62] the president sought to reassure a skittish public that the United States grapples meaningfully with the political, ethical, and legal dilemmas posed by contemporary surveillance. As the president put it, "we will reform programs and procedures in place to provide greater transparency to our surveillance activities...."[63]

Finally, presidential intelligence may well mean more privacy-oriented intelligence, as compared with the baseline. This is true at the conceptual level. Intelligence collection that is better aligned with strategic judgment is more likely to pass muster under the Fourth Amendment, according to which reasonableness is a touchstone for establishing legality.[64] But it is also true

---

which "[t]op-level bureaucrats . . . are responsible or accountable to an elected official . . . for carrying out their discretionary functions in accordance with their political superiors' policies or ideological commitments.").

[60] Kenneth deGraffenreid, *Intelligence and the Oval Office, supra* note 22, at 16.

[61] Kagan, *supra* note 7, at 2301 ("Some of this activity no doubt related more to strategies of public relations than of administrative governance. All methods of 'going public,' in the sense that political scientists use the term, aim to cultivate public support, and Clinton focused on this goal with equal or greater intensity than any of his predecessors.").

[62] Presidential Remarks on Signals Intelligence, *supra* note 21. Speeches by the president and his senior staff have become an especially important means of shaping national security law and policy in the Obama administration. *See* Kenneth Anderson & Benjamin Wittes, Speaking the Law: The Obama Administration's Addresses on National Security Law (2013); *cf.* Richard E. Neustadt, Presidential Power 10 (1960) ("Presidential power is the power to persuade.").

[63] Presidential Remarks on Signals Intelligence, *supra* note 21.

[64] *See* U.S. Const. amend. IV ("The right of the people to be secure in their persons, houses, papers, and effects, against unreasonable searches and seizures, shall not be violated....."); MacWade v. Kelly, 460 F.3d 260, 269 (2d Cir. 2006) (holding that the reasonableness of a search in the "special needs" context turns on the "efficacy of the search in advancing the government interest," among other factors); Brief of Plaintiffs-Appellants at 2, 23, 28, ACLU v. Clapper, 785 F.3d 787 (2d Cir. 2015) (No. 14-42) (resting their claim that the bulk collection of telephone records, under Section 215 of the PATRIOT Act, violates the Fourth Amendment, partially upon the fact that the PRG and the PCLOB have questioned the effectiveness of the program).

in a more operational sense.[65] Greater political control from a White House under economic and strategic pressure from tech firms and allies may also yield more privacy-oriented intelligence. For example, as noted above, PPD-28 embodies a commitment to extend certain privacy protections to non-U.S. persons. This ratcheting up of privacy protections beyond the dictates of any statute or the Fourth Amendment—"an unprecedented change in U.S. intelligence policy, at least at the rhetorical level"[66]—dovetails with the interests of allies and global firms seeking to reassure skittish citizens and customers.[67] In PPD-28's demands that signals intelligence "be as tailored as possible" and that bulk data not be used for affirmative foreign intelligence gathering, the pressure from tech firms and allies is also detectable. ACLU lawyer Ben Wizner's observation that "one of the great contributions that Snowden has made is to make some very powerful tech companies adverse to governments"[68] captures something true about the emerging dynamic.

At the same time, presidential intelligence entails certain risks. Three are particularly noteworthy: interfering with expertise, fanning the flames of partisanship, and threatening abuse. I regard the first two concerns as essentially surmountable, or at least no more damaging to the case for presidential intelligence than comparable worries that surface in connection with presidential administration. The third concern is unique to the intelligence environment and necessitates thinking that is attuned to the dispiriting history at hand and alert to potential ways to prevent it from being repeated.

Striking the balance between political control and agency expertise is a core tension that runs throughout the administrative state.[69] Agencies in a sense owe their existence to a claim of technical know-how that they are able to deploy in the service of sound policymaking. But that commitment to expertise trades off against competing aspirations to democratic accountability rooted in the close ties between the agencies and their political overseers. The

---

[65] Another approach to thinking about presidential intelligence as a vector for rights protection emphasizes the tendency on the part of centralized reviewers to be less zealous in their regulatory outlook than officials serving in agencies. If we imagine that the average intelligence officer pays less heed to the costs of her zealousness, including costs measured in harm to privacy, than the White House overseer, then a system of presidential intelligence ought to yield greater rights protection as compared with the prior baseline of greater agency autonomy. *See generally* Ryan Bubb & Patrick L. Warren, *Optimal Agency Bias and Regulatory Review*, 43 J. LEGAL STUD. 95 (2014).

[66] *See* David S. Kris, *On the Bulk Collection of Tangible Things*, 7 J. NAT'L SECURITY L. & POL'Y 209, 289 (2014). Kris went on to caution that "[t]he degree of substantive change that will follow from PPD-28 is less certain." *Id.*

[67] Ashley Deeks has written of the capacity of foreign leaders, citizens, corporations, and intelligence services to serve as checks on American intelligence, both directly and indirectly (by stimulating American actors to play a checking role). *See* Ashley Deeks, *Checks and Balances from Abroad*, U. CHI. L. REV (forthcoming 2016) (manuscript at 1).

[68] As Wizner went on to say, "these tech companies, which are amassing some of the biggest fortunes in the history of the world, are among the few entities that have the power and the clout and the standing to really take on the security state." Henry Peck, *Pull Back to Reveal: Henry Peck Interviews Ben Wizner*, GUERNICA (Oct. 1, 2014), https://www.guernicamag.com/interviews/pull-back-to-reveal/.

[69] *See, e.g.*, Jody Freeman & Adrian Vermeule, Massachusetts v. EPA: *From Politics to Expertise*, 2007 SUP. CT. REV. 51, 87 ("This approach hearkens back to an older, pre-*Chevron* vision of administrative law in which independence and expertise are seen as opposed to, rather than defined by, political accountability, and in which political influence over agencies by the White House is seen as a problem rather than a solution."); Note, *Limits on Agency Discretion*, 121 HARV. L. REV. 415, 420 (2007).

presidential administration literature is attuned to this dilemma. In her 2001 article, Kagan allowed that "an important place for substantive expertise remains in generating sound regulatory decisions," and that "to the extent that presidential administration displaces this feature of agency decisionmaking in areas where it legitimately should operate, this substitution effect must weigh against the practice."[70] But cordoning off science from politics is famously knotty even in the abstract.[71] And the problems do not get easier when political actors and institutions are engaged. Indeed, the very worry about politicization is "a U.S. invention, one stemming from the specific structure and role of the US Intelligence Community in the recurring struggles over strategic issues in defense and foreign policy in the Cold War."[72] The debate pits those who subscribe to the classic, Sherman Kent scientistic view that intelligence and policy must remain separate and distinct[73] against those who subscribe to what is sometimes referred to as the Bob Gates view (although there were critics of Kent well before the 1990s[74]) and who insist that too much separation impedes the fulfillment of the purpose behind intelligence, which is to generate useful and relevant insights for policymakers.[75]

Regardless of how the balance is struck in shaping substantive intelligence judgments,[76] the issue of politicization takes on a somewhat different cast when it comes to heightened presidential oversight of intelligence collection. It makes sense to quarantine from politics the factual inquiry into whether Saddam Hussein possessed WMD, or how far along the Iranian government is in acquiring weapons-grade nuclear material.[77] But it is not comparably intuitive—and in fact, makes little sense—to bar the White House from expressing a view about the desirability of spying on this or that ally, say, or from weighing in on whether to forgo controversial programs such as metadata collection under Section 215 because their benefits may be negligible while their costs, including to the bottom lines of large American businesses, are potentially considerable. The intelligence agencies have no claim to comparative advantage here. Indeed, concerning the overall assessment of the value of intelligence programs in relation to overarching goals of strategic and economic statecraft, the spy

---

[70] Kagan, *supra* note 7, at 2353–54.

[71] *Id.* at 2341; *see also* David J. Barron, *From Takeover to Merger: Reforming Administrative Law in an Age of Agency Politicization*, 76 GEO. WASH. L. REV. 1095, 1135 (2008) ("There is a great deal of science on the issue of global warming, obviously. But the fact that there is a scientific consensus on the role that human activity plays in causing climate change hardly answers the policy question of what should be done in response. Thus, an embrace of scientific expertise alone cannot resolve the hardest policy questions in this area any more than is usually the case.").

[72] *See* WILHELM AGRELL & GREGORY F. TREVERTON, NATIONAL INTELLIGENCE AND SCIENCE: BEYOND THE GREAT DIVIDE IN ANALYSIS AND POLICY 162 (2015).

[73] SHERMAN KENT, STRATEGIC INTELLIGENCE FOR AMERICAN WORLD POLICY (1949).

[74] *See* Willmoore Kendall, *The Function of Intelligence*, 1 WORLD POLITICS 542 (reviewing KENT, *supra* note 73). (1949).

[75] *See* Richard L. Russell, *Achieving All-Source Fusion in the Intelligence Community*, in HANDBOOK OF INTELLIGENCE STUDIES 189, 195 (Loch K. Johnson ed., 2009).

[76] As Michael Hayden once put it, "[i]f it were a fact, it wouldn't be intelligence." BOB WOODWARD, PLAN OF ATTACK 219 (2004).

[77] *See* Gregory F. Treverton, *Estimating beyond the Cold War*, DEF. INTELLIGENCE J., FALL 1994, at 5; Greg Bruno & Sharon Otterman, *National Intelligence Estimates*, COUNCIL ON FOREIGN REL. (May 14, 2008), http://www.cfr.org/iraq/national-intelligence-estimates/p7758.

agencies are likely to be less informed (even cumulatively) than the White House, which, as discussed above, can summon the perspectives of multiple "customer" agencies to develop a comprehensive picture. Furthermore, traversing the fact-value divide, as these sorts of judgments inevitably do, makes them appropriate for White House decision-making. As Kagan put it, "[a]gencies . . . often must confront the question, which science alone cannot answer, of how to make determinate judgments regarding the protection of health and safety in the face both of scientific uncertainty and competing public interests. With respect to these matters, a strong presidential role is appropriate."[78]

A different concern focuses on the perils of heightening presidential power at the expense of Congress—and, more generally, of endorsing political controls in an age in which norms of hyper-partisanship have become pervasive across government, up to and including the national security state. Here, too, the normative debates sparked and informed by the presidential administration literature are suggestive. As to both accountability and effectiveness, that literature claims certain advantages rooted in the president's status as the nationally elected leader,[79] as well as the relative shortcomings of Congress, including its limited institutional attention span, the non-representative nature of committees,[80] their state of being captured and their stovepiped regulatory purviews, and the legislature's resource and expertise gaps—all of which get to the heart of why Congress chooses to delegate policymaking to agencies in the first instance.[81] Furthermore, unlike the president who (in Moe and Wilson's account[82]) is incentivized to take ownership of issues because he is held accountable for them regardless, no such political logic operates on Capitol Hill.[83]

---

[78] See Kagan, *supra* note 7, at 2356–57. *Cf.* Lisa Schultz Bressman & Robert B. Thompson, *The Future of Agency Independence*, 63 VAND. L. REV. 599, 634–35 (2010) ("[Bernanke] recognize[d] that for decisions so profoundly national in scope, the combination of politics and expertise is more powerful than expertise alone. All else equal, the President is likely to have information that is relevant to generating sound policy on market stability and to mobilizing the necessary political will to achieve the results.").

[79] Kagan, *supra* note 7, at 2347 ("Congress, of course, always faces disincentives and constraints in its oversight capacity. . . . Because Congress rarely is held accountable for agency decisions, its interest in overseeing much administrative action is uncertain; and because Congress's most potent tools of oversight require collective action (and presidential agreement), its capacity to control agency discretion is restricted."). *But see* Jide Nzelibe, *The Fable of the Nationalist President and the Parochial Congress*, 53 UCLA L. REV. 1217 (2006).

[80] See David J. Arkush, *Direct Republicanism in the Administrative Process*, 81 GEO. WASH. L. REV. 1458, 1478–79 (2013) ("[T]he notion of 'congressional' oversight, in the sense of the whole Congress watching over regulators, is rarely more than a metaphor. Legislative supervision typically takes the form of oversight by a small number of individuals in Congress, usually the heads of relevant committees or, more specifically, their staffs, some of whom may be as removed from electoral accountability as agency officials.").

[81] See id. at 1479 ("[C]riticisms point to a circularity in aspirations for congressional oversight: Congress delegates broad authority to administrative agencies because it is unwilling or unfit to make all of the decisions required in various policy areas. If Congress were willing and able to evaluate agency performance on the relevant matters, then it need not have delegated the authority in the first place.").

[82] See Terry M. Moe & Scott A. Wilson, *Presidents and the Politics of Structure*, L. & CONTEMP. PROBS., Spring 1994, at 1, 19.

[83] See Brian D. Feinstein, *Congressional Government Rebooted: Randomized Committee Assignments and Legislative Capacity*, 7 HARV. L. & POL'Y REV. 139, 160 (2013) ("Despite the theoretical importance and demonstrated efficacy of oversight, Congress appears relatively uninterested in performing its oversight function. Oversight-focused subcommittees tend to be disproportionately populated by less powerful legislators, with senior legislators, party leaders, and full committee chairs and ranking members rarely serving

Supporters of congressional oversight meanwhile resist these assumptions. They point to Congress's unmistakable power to control agencies through appropriations and, of course, through substantive legislation.[84] For example, Thomas Sargentich has cautioned that skepticism of the capacity of congressional committees to underwrite democratic accountability should not "defeat the claim that when Congress acts as a whole, with majorities of both the House of Representatives and the Senate in agreement, it represents a broad range of interests, geographical areas, and political orientations."[85]

Although the academic literature on presidential control of intelligence collection is relatively scant, a rich body of commentary diagnoses the limitations of congressional oversight. In its earlier days, there was a hopeful air about the project. No less than Bob Gates, himself a former Director of Central Intelligence, went so far as to suggest that, starting in 1975, the "CIA would move from its exclusive relationship with the President to a position roughly equidistant between the Congress and the President." [86] Furthermore, congressional oversight—especially of covert action—paid dividends early on, including helping to avoid operations that would have produced more harm than good. Gates has observed that "some awfully crazy schemes might well have been approved had everyone present not known and expected hard questions, debate, and criticism from the Hill."[87]

But over time the limits of congressional oversight came to the fore. For a host of reasons, congressional oversight began to decline, or at least so the familiar story goes. Public choice dynamics are frequently blamed; in the absence of the ability to take public credit for oversight work, legislators were disincentivized to invest time and effort.[88] The problem was only compounded by the difficulty of sharing highly classified information with committee members, or even with top congressional staff.[89] Add to that the fragmentation of oversight responsibilities among multiple committees, [90] the lack of meaningful budgeting authority

---

on subcommittees devoted to oversight and investigatory work."); Douglas Kriner, *Can Enhanced Oversight Repair "The Broken Branch"?*, 89 B.U. L. REV. 765, 792 (2009) ("[R]eforms do little to address the underlying problem of variable congressional motivation to oversee the executive in the first place.").

[84] *See* Peter L. Strauss, *Overseer, or "The Decider"? The President in Administrative Law*, 75 GEO. WASH. L. REV. 696, 759–60 (2007) ("Congress can, to be sure, give the President decisional authority, and it has sometimes done so. In limited contexts—foreign relations, military affairs, coordination of arguably conflicting mandates—the argument for inherent presidential decisional authority is stronger. But in the ordinary world of domestic administration, where Congress has delegated responsibilities to a particular governmental actor it has created, that delegation is a part of the law whose faithful execution the President is to assure. Oversight, and not decision, is his responsibility.").

[85] *See* Sargentich, *supra* note 14, 35–36 (2007).

[86] *See* ROBERT M. GATES, FROM THE SHADOWS: THE ULTIMATE INSIDER'S STORY OF FIVE PRESIDENTS AND HOW THEY WON THE COLD WAR 61 (1996).

[87] *Id.* at 559.

[88] *See* AMY B. ZEGART, EYES ON SPIES: CONGRESS AND THE UNITED STATES INTELLIGENCE COMMUNITY 74–75 (2011).

[89] Timothy B. Lee, *Obama Says the NSA Has Had Plenty of Oversight. Here's Why He's Wrong*, WASH. POST: WONKBLOG (June 7, 2013), http://www.washingtonpost.com/blogs/wonkblog/wp/2013/06/07/obama-says-the-nsa-has-had-plenty-of-oversight-heres-why-hes-wrong/. *See* Patrick Radden Keefe, *Listening In and Naming Names*, SLATE (Dec. 20, 2005), http://www.slate.com/articles/news_and_politics/politics/2005/12/listening_in_and_naming_names.html.

[90] *See* Anne Joseph O'Connell, *The Architecture of Smart Intelligence: Structuring and Overseeing Agencies in the Post-9/11 World*, 94 CALIF. L. REV. 1655, 1671 (2006) ("While Congress and the Administration have made at

on the part of congressional intelligence overseers,[91] and the inability to deploy police-patrol type oversight, and the limits of congressional oversight come into sharp relief.[92] As Representative Norman Mineta, who served on the House Intelligence Committee in the Reagan years, caustically observed, "We are like mushrooms. They keep us in the dark and feed us a lot of manure."[93] Intelligence scholar Amy Zegart quotes a frustrated congressional staffer to the effect that "the silver lining with the FBI is that at least they're nonpartisan in their non-cooperation with Congress."[94] Nor have things improved in the years since Zegart undertook her study. If anything, "[r]elations between the CIA and Congress" have recently been described as "more fraught than at any time in the past decade."[95]

And yet this (by now familiar) narrative is resisted by other commentators. Intelligence scholar Britt Snider has offered the view that whatever the shortcomings of the current system, "compared with the level of congressional awareness that existed in 1975, the difference is like night and day."[96] Furthermore, and not trivially, although Congress initially regulated the IC with an exceedingly light touch—the CIA's organic law is breathtakingly short on detail, while the FBI lacks a basic legislative charter altogether—the last decades have witnessed greater congressional regulation. The initial FISA law of 1978, the PATRIOT Act, the Intelligence Reform Act of 2004, the FISA Amendments Act of 2008, and the recently passed USA FREEDOM Act of 2015 attest to this evolution.

Against this backdrop, it is difficult to offer a confident assessment of how heightened presidential intelligence might interact with congressional controls. On one level, there are some reasons to be hopeful that the combination of presidential and congressional involvement might lead to better overall oversight. For example, a presidential "finding" on sensitive collection programs could then be briefed on the Hill (much as happens in the parallel case of covert action), teeing up and focusing congressional oversight of intelligence gathering. It is suggestive in this regard that the Senate Intelligence Committee has recently evinced an appetite for an enlarged role in overseeing intelligence collection under Executive Order

---

least some serious efforts to reorganize the intelligence community, Congress has made little effort to reorganize its overlapping committee oversight of the intelligence community.").

[91] See, e.g., NAT'L COMM'N ON TERRORIST ATTACKS UPON THE U.S., THE 9/11 COMMISSION REPORT 103 (2004), available at http://www.9-11commission.gov/report/911Report.pdf (discussing fragmented nature of congressional appropriations and oversight of intelligence organizations); see also id. at 419–21 (calling congressional oversight of the IC "dysfunctional" and recommending that each house of Congress create a single committee responsible for intelligence oversight).

[92] See generally Loch K. Johnson, supra note 30.

[93] Edward Luce, The Shifts in US National Security Policy Since 9/11, FIN. TIMES (Nov. 7, 2014), http://www.ft.com/intl/cms/s/0/21b69fca-6428-11e4-8ade-00144feabdc0.html#axzz3P2OkISia (quoting Representative Mineta).

[94] See Amy B. Zegart, Agency Design and Evolution, in THE OXFORD HANDBOOK OF AMERICAN BUREAUCRACY 207, 215 (Robert F. Durant ed., 2010).

[95] See Siobahn Gorman, CIA and Congress Clash over Classified Report on Interrogation Program, WALL ST. J. (July 2, 2014), http://online.wsj.com/articles/cia-and-congress-clash-over-classified-report-on-interrogation-program-1404316923?mod=europe_home.

[96] L. Britt Snider, Congressional Oversight of Intelligence: Some Reflections on the Last 25 Years 10, https://web.law.duke.edu/lens/downloads/snider.pdf ("For all of the situations in which the oversight committees—even today—might find themselves in the dark, they are, for the most part, aware of what the intelligence agencies are doing, however sensitive those activities might be.").

12,333—including an unprecedented step by that body to catalog and account for the full spectrum of American intelligence gathering.[97] Furthermore, an expanded list of intelligence posts that required Senate confirmation would increase the opportunities for congressional buy-in. Thinking more structurally, the same interest group pressures that have catalyzed and shaped the exercise of presidential controls are also in play on Capitol Hill, at least as far as privacy activists and technology firms are concerned (the lobbying efforts of allies are less visible in Congress). The recent passage of the USA FREEDOM Act may imply more sustained congressional attention to issues of surveillance in a way that is likely to be mutually compatible with presidential controls. In sum, it is not at all clear that presidential intelligence will have the effect of "crowding out" or (further) marginalizing congressional intelligence oversight; it is even possible that the emergence of presidential intelligence will promote better congressional oversight.

Finally, there is a worry that fusing presidential power with intelligence capabilities might enable the sorts of abusive practices that occasioned the significant intelligence reforms of the 1970s. Given the "very extensive history of intelligence activities infringing on the rights of Americans,"[98] this concern is undoubtedly serious. The case of the PSP is instructive. Through the PSP, the White House sought to authorize certain kinds of bulk collection that would otherwise have required permission from the FISC.[99] As former congresswoman Jane Harman recently revealed, as a member of the "Gang of Eight"[100] legislators initially briefed by the White House about the PSP, she was advised that the program was in full compliance with the law.[101] What she did not know at the time, and only learned when the *New York Times* exposed the program years later, is that the White House's claim to legality rested on a theory that the president is empowered to override statutory law in the area of national security.[102]

But this concern need not overwhelm the project of presidential intelligence. First, as noted above, presidential intelligence presupposes and entails greater visibility of the intelligence apparatus than has ever been the case. To be certain, visibility is not the same as transparency. But outright abuse is less likely to go unnoticed under conditions of greater visibility, including within the government. Jack Goldsmith's insight into the "synoptic" presidency— the president's state of being pervasively monitored by a vigilant press and civil-liberties bar,

---

[97] *See* Eli Lake, *Congress Scouring Every U.S. Spy Program*, THE DAILY BEAST (Oct.10, 2014), http://www.thedailybeast.com/articles/2014/10/10/congress-scouring-every-u-s-spy-program.html (quoting a source on the investigation's unprecedented scope encompassing "[a]ll the programs through which the intelligence community collects intelligence. Human intelligence, signal intelligence, open source. It is all subject to the review.").

[98] DAVID S. KRIS & J. DOUGLAS WILSON, 1 NATIONAL SECURITY INVESTIGATIONS AND PROSECUTIONS 38 (2d ed. 2012).

[99] John Yoo, Essay, *The Terrorist Surveillance Program and the Constitution*, 14 GEO. MASON L. REV 565, 565 (2007).

[100] This select group of elected officials, consisting of the chairmen and ranking minority members of the congressional intelligence committees, the speaker and minority leader of the House, and the majority and minority leaders of the Senate, have privileged access to certain high-level intelligence matters.

[101] *See* Jane Harman, *What the CIA Hid from Congress*, L.A. TIMES (July 25, 2009), http://articles.latimes.com/2009/jul/25/opinion/oe-harman25.

[102] *Id.*

as well as by internal watchdogs[103]—marks a significant difference between now and the era of abuses that led up to the Church Committee's damning inquest (and even between now and the period immediately after 9/11, when the PSP was debuted). Second, and related, as presidential intelligence becomes a matter of institutional habit within the White House, it will become increasingly difficult to operate outside of the internal processes that define it. Third, the sheer scale of the contemporary intelligence state (including the number of private actors who are part of its workforce), coupled with the interest group politics that have coalesced around these issues, also contributes to the unlikelihood that presidential intelligence could bring about a situation in which the intelligence arm ran amok. After Snowden, no president will reasonably assume that he can count on the obeisance of the intelligence bureaucracy—which includes legions of young techies who may well be inclined to leak what might be deemed evidence of abusive behavior. Fourth and finally, presidential intelligence need not translate readily to abuse in view of the growing availability of judicial review of intelligence programs.[104] This trend toward increasingly robust judicial checks on intelligence may help to deter and curtail certain potential excesses latent in a cozier relationship between the White House and the spy agencies.[105] It is suggestive that other countries, such as Israel, conjoin strong centralized control of the national security state (including the intelligence apparatus) with extensive avenues for judicial review of that power.[106]

VI. CONCLUSION

Almost 50 years ago, Aaron Wildavsky offered that "[t]he United States has one president but it has two presidencies; one presidency is for domestic affairs, and the other is concerned with defense and foreign policy."[107] For some time that claim has been off target concerning large swaths of the national security state, which have been on a convergence course with the ordinary regulatory state.[108] But, until very recently, Wildavsky's observation retained some of its descriptive accuracy with respect to the IC—specifically, as to the ways that spy agencies gather intelligence. Even as the president came to loom large in just about every other major area of policymaking, presidential involvement in the domain of intelligence

---

[103] *See* JACK GOLDSMITH, POWER AND CONSTRAINT: THE ACCOUNTABLE PRESIDENCY AFTER 9/11 205-07 (2012).

[104] This explanation is predicated on the classic Madisonian conception that, as Congress put it in the counterterrorism context, "a shift of power and authority to the Government calls for an enhanced system of checks and balances ...." 42 U.S.C. 2000ee(b)(2) (2012).

[105] *See* Samuel Issacharoff, *Political Safeguards in Democracies at War*, 29 OXFORD J. LEGAL STUD., 189, 206 (2009) ("However much the burdens of wartime democracy must rest on the political branches, there remains the need for a fuller rendition of the role of the judiciary.").

[106] *Cf.* Rick Pildes, *Does Judicial Review of National-Security Policies Constrain or Enable the Government?*, LAWFARE (Aug. 5, 2013, 1:48 PM), http://www.lawfareblog.com/2013/08/does-judicial-review-of-national-security-policies-constrain-or-enable-the-government/.

[107] Aaron Wildavsky, *The Two Presidencies*, 4 TRANS-ACTION Dec. 1966 at 7, 7.

[108] *Cf.* Robert Chesney & Jack Goldsmith, *Terrorism and the Convergence of Criminal and Military Detention Models*, 60 STAN. L. REV. 1079 (2008) (describing the convergence of civilian and military detention policies since the September 11 terrorist attacks).

collection remained episodic and muted. That, too, is now changing. Although the CIA, NSA, and FBI (and every other spy agency) each carries out a particular mission and maintains a distinctive organizational look-and-feel, the IC collectively is more than ever of a piece with the balance of government, in terms of the political and economic forces that affect it and the oversight methodologies and institutions that constrain it.

With intelligence having rejoined the regulatory mainstream after an extended hiatus, there is a lot of catching up that needs to be done. This chapter has emphasized the ways in which concepts and scholarly insights generated in administrative law are ripe for export to the intelligence bureaucracy. In particular, I have described a set of processes by which the IC has been presidentialized, and have expressed qualified optimism that the trend will promote more effective, accountable, and rights-protective intelligence collection practices. Under conditions of robustly implemented presidential intelligence, the indiscriminate collection of American metadata premised on a secret, dubious statutory interpretation, and the gratuitous eavesdropping on friendly foreign leaders' cell phone conversations will be less likely to come to pass. At a minimum, serious thought will have to be devoted to the upsides of these otherwise exceedingly costly efforts before officials embark on them.

10

Intelligence Oversight—Made in Germany

*Russell A. Miller**

I. INTRODUCTION

The outrage ignited in Germany by Edward Snowden's revelations of the United States' extensive intelligence activities has burned hot. Snowden's spark hit the dry tinder of a persistent, wide-spread, but mostly low-grade anti-Americanism in Germany.[1] Any American who has had meaningful contacts in Germany can confirm that many Germans have earnest doubts about America and American power. The Snowden disclosures about the United States National Security Agency (NSA) added new and particularly meaningful fuel to that fire. Considering Germans' privacy fetish,[2] it is no surprise that news of America's sweeping intelligence activities—including programs that seek to collect the content of European Internet communications—have plunged German-American relations to their nadir. In

---

* Professor of Law, Washington & Lee University School of Law. Editor of PRIVACY AND POWER: A TRANSATLANTIC DIALOGUE IN THE SHADOW OF THE NSA-AFFAIR (Russell Miller ed., forthcoming 2016) and U.S. NATIONAL SECURITY, INTELLIGENCE, AND DEMOCRACY (Russell A. Miller ed., 2009). 2013–2015 Senior Research Fellow—Center for Security and Society (University of Freiburg). Editor-in-Chief, *German Law Journal* (http:www.germanlawjournal.com). All translations of cited German language sources, unless otherwise noted, are those of the author.

[1] *See, e.g.*, Andrei S. Markovits & Lars Rensmann, *Anti-Americanism in Germany, in* ANTI-AMERICANISM: COMPARATIVE PERSPECTIVES 155 (Brendon O'Connor ed., 2007); *Germany and America: Ami Go Home*, ECONOMIST (Feb. 7, 2015), at 51, *available at* http://www.economist.com/news/europe/21642211-anti-americanism-always-strong-german-left-growing-right-ami-go-home.

[2] *See, e.g.*, James B. Rule, *Introduction, in* GLOBAL PRIVACY PROTECTION: THE FIRST GENERATION 1, 11 (James B. Rule & Graham Greenleaf eds., 2008) ("[P]rivacy sentiments [in Germany] have generated more substantial resistance to state monitoring there than in many other countries."); *see also* James Q. Whitman, *The Two Western Cultures of Privacy: Dignity versus Liberty*, 113 YALE L. J. 1151, 1186–87, 1189 (2004).

April, 2014, German politician Philipp Missfelder concluded that "[t]he current situation in transatlantic relations is worse than it was at the low-point in 2003 during the Iraq War."[3] He might be considered a reliable observer of such trends. At the time he offered this remark, he was the German government's Coordinator for Transatlantic Cooperation.

Of all the diverse facets of the NSA controversy upon which Germans might have fixed their rancor, the United States Foreign Intelligence Surveillance Court has been singled out for particular contempt. One report from the center-left newsmagazine *Der Spiegel* exemplifies the German stance:

> *Surveillance in the USA: The Shadow Court*
> No address. No transparency. No public. The Foreign Intelligence Surveillance Court, which is charged with monitoring the NSA's surveillance and data-collection activities, meets under the strictest secrecy. The Court approves most of the government's requests without any commentary.... Everything at the FISA Court is top secret: what it decides, how it decides, why it decides.[4]

I mention Germans' alarm over the FISA Court to open this examination of Germany's intelligence oversight regime because it offers a rare chance for me to unreservedly shrug off German criticism with a short, sharp truth: Germany does no better than the United States on this issue.[5] Germany, for all its concern about privacy, does not demand greater transparency or rigor from the institutions it has tasked with watching the watchers.[6]

Despite the great urge to substantiate the charge of German hypocrisy on this point,[7] I do not intend to offer a systematic comparison of the German and American intelligence oversight infrastructure in this contribution. Others have started that discussion for me.[8] Instead, I have two aims that draw exclusively on German law and policy.

---

[3] Andy Eckardt, *U.S.-Germany Relations Hit New Low amid NSA Spying Scandal, Official Says*, NBC News (Jan. 17, 2014), http://worldnews.nbcnews.com/_news/2014/01/17/22338261-us-germany-relations-hit-new-low-amid-nsa-spying-scandal-official-says.

[4] Marc Pitzke, *Überwachung in den USA: Das Schattengericht*, Spiegel Online (June 21, 2013), http://www.spiegel.de/netzwelt/netzpolitik/geheimes-fisa-gericht-segnet-nsa-ueberwachung-ab-a-907036.html (trans. Russell Miller). The center-right press in Germany has also focused on the FISA Court in its incredulous coverage of the NSA story. *See, e.g.*, Matthias Rüb, *Überwachung leicht gemacht*, Frankfurter Allgemeine (July 13, 2013), http://www.faz.net/aktuell/politik/ausland/nsa-affaere-ueberwachung-leicht-gemacht-12280603.html.

[5] Some German critics of the German intelligence community recognize this. *See, e.g.*, Kai Biermann, *Der BND ist nicht viel besser als die NSA*, Zeit Online (Oct. 1, 2013), http://www.zeit.de/digital/datenschutz/2013-09/nsa-gchq-bnd-gesetze.

[6] Before the NSA hysteria loosed in Germany by Edward Snowden's revelations, the similarities between the German and American intelligence oversight regimes were discussed by Claus Arndt, a long-serving member of the G10 Commission. *See* Claus Arndt, *25 Jahre Post- und Telefonkontrolle—Die G 10-Kommission des Deutschen Bundestages*, 24 Zeitschrift für Parlamentsfragen 621, 631–32 (1993); *see also* Gestorben (obituary), *Claus Arndt*, Der Spiegel (Feb. 17, 2014), *available at* http://www.spiegel.de/spiegel/print/d-125080852.html; Klaus Wiegrefe, *Sie sind der Hegemon hier*, Der Spiegel (July 8, 2013), *available at* http://www.spiegel.de/spiegel/print/d-102241615.html.

[7] *See* Maximilian Steinbeis, *Ein geisses Maß an Heuchelei in der deutschen Sorge*, Verfassungsblog (Oct. 30, 2013), http://www.verfassungsblog.de/gewisses-mass-an-heuchelei-in-der-deutschen-sorge/.

[8] *See* Stefan Heumann & Ben Scott, Law and Policy in Internet Surveillance Programs: United States, Great Britain and Germany, Impulse 25/13 (Sept. 2013), *available at* http://www.stiftung-nv.de/

First, I will introduce Germany's intelligence oversight regime, focusing in particular on the G10 Commission, which must approve all of the German intelligence community's telecommunications surveillance measures. The Commission serves a function not unlike (but by no means identical to) America's FISA Court.[9] But it is not a *parliamentary*, a *judicial*, or an *international* oversight institution. It is not a parliamentary committee, even if it is based at, funded by, and staffed with former members of the *Bundestag* (Federal Parliament). It is not a court, even if its members usually are trained jurists and it performs a distinctly judicial function. And, as will become clear, it also is not institutionally robust. This survey will reveal a shadowy and inadequately staffed entity that authorizes virtually all the surveillance the German intelligence community desires.[10]

Second, I suggest that the G10 Commission is at odds with German law. The German Federal Constitutional Court's 1970 judgment that confirmed the constitutionality of the G10 Commission was not persuasive at the time it was decided. Moreover, changes in technology and the law of privacy in the intervening years suggest that the Court should reconsider its decision and find that the G10 Commission violates the German Basic Law.

II. THE G10 COMMISSION—SUI GENERIS INTELLIGENCE OVERSIGHT
A. Overview of the German Intelligence Infrastructure

Germany's intelligence community should not be confused (or conflated) with the country's federal and state law enforcement authorities, whose surveillance activities are subject to a distinct oversight regime.[11] The German intelligence community consists of three organizations

---

sites/default/files/impulse.pdf; *see also* Benjamin Wittes, *Privacy, Hypocrisy, and a Defense of Surveillance,* in PRIVACY AND POWER: A TRANSATLANTIC DIALOGUE IN THE SHADOW OF THE NSA-AFFAIR (Russell Miller ed., forthcoming 2016); Andrew Borene, *"We're in This Together": Reframing EU Responses to Unauthorized Disclosures of US Intelligence Activities,* in PRIVACY AND POWER: A TRANSATLANTIC DIALOGUE IN THE SHADOW OF THE NSA-AFFAIR (Russell Miller ed., forthcoming 2016). The German intelligence services have also come under increasing scrutiny for their questionable conduct. *See, e.g.,* Maik Baumgärtner et al., *Überwachung: Neue Spionageaffäre erschüttert BND,* SPIEGEL ONLINE (Apr. 23, 2015), *available at* http://www.spiegel.de/politik/deutschland/ueberwachung-neue-spionageaffaere-erschuettert-bnd-a-1030191.html; Eckart Lohse, *BND-Spionage-Vorwürfe: Spionieren und spionieren lassen,* FRANKFURTER ALLGEMEINE (Apr. 26, 2015), *available at* http://www.faz.net/aktuell/politik/inland/berlin-wird-von-den-vorwuerfen-an-den-bnd-erschuettert-13557538.html.

9 The G10 Commission has no other oversight authority, beyond the review and approval of ministerial orders authorizing telecommunications surveillance. For example, it does not vet or supervise the German intelligence services' human intelligence activities.

10 *See infra,* note 103.

11 German law enforcement authorities gather evidence for the purpose of interdicting and prosecuting crimes. The legal framework for doing so is outlined in the Federal Code of Criminal Procedure and in the states' police law. Constitutional law (state constitutions and the Federal *Grundgesetz* [Basic Law]) secures individual liberty in the face of these often-intrusive practices, which can involve searches, seizures, and surveillance. The administrative, criminal, and constitutional courts play an active role in maintaining the integrity of this *rechtstaatlich* (rule of law) framework. In the first instance, for example, the Federal Code of Criminal Procedure requires a court order for the interception of telecommunication exchanges. STRAFPROZESSORDNUNG [StPO] [Code of Criminal Procedure], Apr. 7, 1987, BUNDESGESETZBLATT [BGBL. I] 1074, 1319, as amended, §§ 100(a)–(b), *available at* www.gesetze-im-internet.de [hereinafter StPO]. In the last instance, the Federal Constitutional

with authority to collect intelligence in three separate spheres.[12] The *Bundesnachrichtendienst* (BND or Federal Intelligence Service) is analogous to America's Central Intelligence Agency (CIA).[13] The BND's mandate is to "collect and analyze information required for obtaining foreign intelligence, which is of importance for the foreign and security policy of the Federal Republic of Germany."[14] Alongside other forms of intelligence gathering, the BND collects signals intelligence (SIGINT) and is not dependent on a separate agency (as the CIA relies on the NSA) for this vital source of national security information. For two reasons, I will concentrate on the authority for, limits on, and oversight of the BND's strategic SIGINT activities. First, to do more would swell this survey beyond the size and scope intended for this volume. Second, the BND's strategic SIGINT activities are likely of greatest comparative interest to non-German scholars of intelligence oversight because they can include foreign surveillance and most closely approximate the NSA programs that have stirred so much controversy in the last few years. The G10 Commission is central in regard to the BND's SIGINT operations.

Court has not hesitated to review, and reject as unconstitutional, wiretap orders issued by the ordinary courts. *See, e.g.*, Bundesverfassungsgericht [BVerfG] [Federal Constitutional Court], Apr. 18, 2007, 2 BvR 2094/05. Law enforcement activities, including the collection of evidence, are also subject to disciplinary proceedings. Whether initiated by the law enforcement authorities themselves or on the basis of a public complaint, disciplinary proceedings are conducted internally by the police, and then by ascending levels of the administration, ending with the state or federal interior ministries. Should it come to it, criminal proceedings against law enforcement authorities are handled by Germany's proudly independent and professional public prosecutors in the same manner as any other alleged crime. Civil society organizations and the media also closely watch and report on the conduct of law enforcement authorities.

[12] As a consequence of postwar Germany's unique history, the German intelligence community was not given a formal statutory-basis until 1990, when the newly reunified Parliament enacted enabling laws on December 20, 1990. *See* Bundesnachrichtendienstgesetz [BNDG] [Law on the Federal Intelligence Service], Dec. 20, 1990, Bundesgesetzblatt [BGBl I] at 2954, 2979, as amended, *available at* www.gesetze-im-internet.de [hereinafter BND Act]. Prior to reunification, the point at which Germany reacquired its full sovereignty, the West German intelligence services had operated at the pleasure of and with deep involvement from the Western Allies. *See* Wolfgang Krieger, *The German Bundesnachrichtendienst (BND): Evolution and Current Policy Issues, in* The Oxford Handbook of National Security Intelligence 790, 791–92 (Loch K. Johnson ed., 2010).

[13] The remaining components of the German intelligence community are the *Verfassungsschutzämter* (state and federal offices for the protection of the Constitution) and the *Militärische Abschirmdienst* (MAD or Military Intelligence Service). The former develops and analyzes domestic intelligence. *See* Bundesverfassungsschutzgesetz [BVerfSchG] [Federal Act for the Protection of the Constitution], Dec. 20, 1990, Bundesgesetzblatt [BGBl. I] at 2954, 2979, as amended, *available at* http://www.gesetze-im-internet.de/ [hereinafter Constitutional Protection Act]. The latter develops and analyzes military counterintelligence. *See* Gesetz über den militärischen Abschirmdienst [MADG] [Law on the Military Counterintelligence Service], Dec. 20, 1990, Bundesgesetzblatt [BGBl I] at 2954, 2977, as amended, *available at* http://www.gesetze-im-internet.de/ [hereinafter Military Intelligence Act]. Both institutions are also authorized to monitor and collect telecommunications information under the same legal regime as the BND, albeit with some variation in the standards, that governs the BND's SIGINT activities. *See* Thorsten Kornblum, Rechtsschutz gegen geheimdienstliche Aktivitäten (2011).

[14] BND Act, *supra* note 12, § 1(2).

The BND has roots in the *Wehrmacht's* wartime intelligence operations.[15] These capacities (including personnel, technology, and expertise) were salvaged and revived after the Second World War by the Western Allies—specifically the United States—in the hopes of putting them to use in the ever-hotter Cold War.[16] Germany's modern intelligence service began as a division of the United States Department of Defense, and later transformed into a modest and autonomous unit of the CIA.[17] In this nascent role German intelligence primarily contributed to *Ostaufklärung*—gathering information about the Soviet Union and the emerging *Ostblock*. Former *Wehrmacht* Major General Reinhard Gehlen directed these initiatives throughout the immediate postwar years, leading to the sobriquet "Organisation Gehlen."[18] He continued as the first president of the BND after the Federal Republic took control of the agency through an executive act of the Federal Cabinet in 1955.[19] Gehlen dominated the BND and West German intelligence activities with the kind of control, intrigue, and longevity that J. Edgar Hoover would have admired.

Throughout this time the BND operated as part of the Federal Government, securing its authority from "organizational decisions" or "service instructions."[20] Gehlen retired from the presidency of the BND in 1968,[21] the year that the West German Basic Law was amended to include bitterly contested "emergency" provisions. The emergency laws harkened back to a troubling framework in Germany's inter-war Weimar Constitution, which granted the Imperial President the authority to suspend constitutional rights and domestically deploy the armed forces if the "public safety is seriously threatened or disturbed."[22] Hitler made perverse use of these measures.[23] But it was argued in 1968 that the Western Allies would surrender their reserved rights of authority over the still-occupied Federal Republic only if emergency laws were in place.[24] The emergency laws, so the argument went, would reassure the Allies that legal formalities would neither endanger their troops stationed in West Germany nor prevent the West German government from acting to put down anti-democratic threats to the state.[25] The riotous and sometimes bloody student uprising in the spring of 1968 (in

---

[15] *See* Krieger, *supra* note 12; *see also* DIE GESCHICHTE DER ORGANISATION GEHLEN UND DES BND 1945–1968: UMRISSE UND EINBLICKE (Jost Dülffer et al. eds., 2013); PETER F. MÜLLER ET AL., GEGEN FREUND UND FEIND. DIE GESCHICHTE DES BND (Rowohlt 2002).

[16] MÜLLER ET AL., *supra* note 15.

[17] *See* JENS WEGENER, DIE ORGANISATION GEHLEN UND DIE USA: DEUTSCH-AMERIKANISCHE GEHEIMDIENSTBEZIEHUNGEN, 1945–1949 (Lit Verlag 2008).

[18] JAMES H. CRITCHFIELD, AUFTRAG PULLACH: DIE ORGANISATION GEHLEN 1948–1956 (Mittler 2005).

[19] *See* Krieger, *supra* note 12.

[20] *Id.*

[21] MÜLLER ET AL., *supra* note 15.

[22] WEIMARER REICHSVERFASSUNG of 14 Aug. 1919 [WRV] [Weimar Imperial Constitution] art. 48.

[23] *See* Verordnung des Reichspriisidenten zum Schutz von Volk und Staat [Order of the Reich President for the Protection of People and State], Feb. 28, 1933, RGBl. I, at 83.

[24] *See* Gesetz zur Änderung des Grundgesetzes [Law Amending Basic Law], June 24, 1968, BGBl. I at 701; Wolfgang Durner, *Art. 10, in* MAUNZ/DÜRIG, GRUNDGESETZ KOMMENTAR margin nos. 20–21 (Roman Herzog et al. eds., 68th ed., 2010).

[25] *See* Treaty over the Relations between the Federal Republic of Germany and the Three-Powers (Germany Treaty) art. 5(2)(1), May 26, 1952, 6 U.S.T. 4251, T.I.A.S. 3425, 331 U.N.T.S. 327; Declaration of the Three-Powers from 27 June 1968 with Respect to the Dissolution of the Allies' Conditional Rights based in Art.

Germany as well as elsewhere in Western Europe and America) provided a contemporary example of the kind of social upheaval that just might necessitate emergency laws.[26] With that nudge, and despite the questionable pedigree, the Basic Law was amended to include the provisions of a *Notstandsverfassung* (emergency constitution). Among other things, the 1968 constitutional amendments altered Article 10 of the Basic Law to permit statutorily authorized secret telecommunications surveillance.[27] The resulting law, known as the G10 Act (*Gesetz zur Beschränkung des Brief-, Post- und Fernmeldegeheimnisses*), contained the first statutory reference to the BND, which was at last given formal authority to request orders to carry out telecommunications surveillance.[28]

It was not until 1990, following reunification and the full restoration of German sovereignty, that the BND was formally enabled by an act of the *Bundestag*.[29] It is a cursory statute, consisting of only 12 paragraphs that establish the agency's organization, purposes, and powers. The BND Act provides that the BND may gather intelligence "about events abroad that are important for the foreign and security policy of the Federal Republic of Germany, if such information can be obtained only in this way and no other authority is responsible for its collection."[30] The BND Act also imposes a number of limits on the agency's collection, use, and storage of personally identifying data. The BND does not possess law enforcement powers.[31] The agency is obliged to use the least intrusive means in pursuit of its mandate[32] and must observe strict limits when acquiring information from or distributing information to other institutions.[33] It must report on its activities to designated government officials.[34]

The BND operates parallel to and with many of the same parameters as the *Verfassungsschutzämter* (the federal and state offices for the protection of the constitution,

---

5(2) of the Germany Treaty in the version published on 18 June (Federal Law Gazette [*Bundesgesetzblatt*] Part I p. 714).

[26] *See, e.g.,* Boris Spernol, Notstand der Demokratie: der Protest gegen die Notstandsgesetze und die Frage der NS-Vergangenheit (2008); Mark Kurlansky, 1968: The Year That Rocked the World (2010); 1968 in Europe: A History of Protest and Activism, 1956–1977 (Martin Klimke & Joachim Scharloth eds., 2008).

[27] *See* Grundgesetz füre die Bundesrepublik Deutschland [Grundgesetz] [GG] [Basic Law], May 23, 1949, BGBl. I art. 10, *available at* http://www.gesetze-im-internet.de (original version) [hereinafter Basic Law]. ("(1) The privacy of correspondence, posts and telecommunications shall be inviolable. Restrictions may be ordered only pursuant to a law."); Art. 10, Basic Law (amended version) ("(1) The privacy of correspondence, posts and telecommunications shall be inviolable. (2) Restrictions may be ordered only pursuant to a law. If the restriction serves to protect the free democratic basic order or the existence or security of the Federation or of a country, the law may provide that the person affected shall not be informed of the restriction and that recourse to the courts shall be replaced by a review of the case by agencies and auxiliary agencies appointed by the legislature.").

[28] Gesetz zur Beschränkung des Brief-, Post- und Fernmeldegeheimnisses [G-10 Act], Aug. 13, 1968 Bundesgesetzblatt [BGBl I] at 949, § 1, *available at* http://www.gesetze-im-internet.de [hereinafter G10 Act].

[29] *See* BND Act, *supra* note 12.

[30] *Id.* § 2.

[31] *Id.* § 1(1).

[32] *Id.* § 2.

[33] *Id.* §§ 2–12.

[34] *Id.* § 12.

which are essentially domestic political espionage agencies) when it pursues targeted intelligence gathering (specific to a person or region). The two agencies diverge, however, where the BND is authorized to collect strategic foreign intelligence. Until 1994, this competence was justifiable only in relation to serious threats to state security and the free democratic order. The list of justifications for the BND's strategic foreign intelligence initiatives has grown since 1994 to include international criminal threats such as organized crime, money laundering, currency counterfeiting, weapons trafficking, and terrorism.[35] With the exception of some procedural elements, the Federal Constitutional Court upheld this expansion in a major decision in 1999.[36] The BND Act has been amended in recent years to account for technological change (extending the agency's surveillance authority to "bundled" communications) and adding smuggling to the list of activities justifying strategic foreign intelligence gathering.[37]

Today, the BND is a large federal bureaucracy that will soon take up residence at a new, state-of-the-art campus in Berlin.[38] The agency and its half-billion Euro budget are under the authority of the Chief of the Federal Chancellery,[39] currently Christian Democratic Union (CDU) politician Peter Altmaier. The Chief, who is assisted in his management of the BND by a *Staatssekretär* (State Secretary), can conveniently provide political cover for the chancellor because he bears direct political responsibility for the BND while at the same time enjoying direct access to the chancellor.[40] The BND's informational brochure explains that its 6,500 employees—under the leadership of President Gerhard Schindler—are charged with "meeting the information needs of Germany's political decision-makers."[41] This includes the work of the *Technische Aufklärung* Unit, which:

[O]btains information with technical means (SIGINT). Foreign information with an intelligence value is obtained through targeted filtering of international

---

35 *See* G10 Act, *supra* note 28, § 5.

36 Bundesverfassungsgericht [BVerfG] [Federal Constitutional Court] July 14, 1999, 100 Entscheidungen des Bundesverfassungsgerichts [BVerfGE] 313 (Telecommunications Surveillance Act Case).

37 *See* Bertold Huber, *Die Reform der parlamentarischen Kontrolle der Nachrichtendienste und des Gesetzes nach Art. 10 GG*, 28 Neue Zeitschrift für Verwaltungsrecht 1321 (2009).

38 *See* Ulrich Paul, *Die Spione kommen—und mit ihnen die Luxuswohnungen*, Berliner Zeitung (Jan. 13, 2015), http://www.berliner-zeitung.de/berlin/neue-bnd-zentrale-in-berlin-mitte-die-spione-kommen---und-mit-ihnen-die-luxuswohnungen,10809148,29425002.html; Florian Flade, *Großumzug für Deutschlands Agenten*, Die Welt (Mar. 23, 2014), http://www.welt.de/politik/deutschland/article126097610/Grossumzug-fuer-Deutschlands-Agenten.html.

39 BND Act, *supra* note 12, § 1.

40 *See* Geschäftsordnung der Bundesregierung [Rules of Procedure for the Federal Government], May 11, 1951, last amended by Änderungsbekanntmachung, Nov. 21, 2002, GMBI at 848, § 7(1). The Federal Chancellor has political responsibility but the BND is under the control of the Chief of the Federal Chancellery. *See* Volker Busse, *Para. 7, in* Geschäftsordnung Bundesregierung—Kommentar margin no. 2 (2013); Patrick Spitzer, Die Nachrichtendienste Deutschlands und die Geheimdienste Russlands: Ein Vergleich 68 (2011).

41 Bundesnachrichtendienst, Der Auslandsnachrichtendienst Deutschlands 12 (2014), *available at* http://www.bnd.bund.de/EN/Service/Downloads/BND_Broschuere.pdf?__blob=publicationFile&v=1.

telecommunications .... This is a complex intelligence gathering process under permanent judicial oversight.[42]

The brochure's reference to "judicial oversight" must refer to the G10 Commission. Yet, as the following section reveals, this is an inaccurate portrayal of the nature and function of that distinct intelligence oversight body, which is neither fully parliamentary nor fully judicial in character.

B. The G10 Commission—Law and Practice

The BND operates within a general framework of external oversight and accountability that includes:

- Ministerial supervision (Minister of the Chancellery);
- Standing parliamentary oversight (particularly the Parliamentary Control Committee but also potentially the *Bundestag's* Interior Committee and Defense Committee);
- Case-specific parliamentary inquiries (for example, the present NSA Investigative Committee, but also proceedings undertaken by the *Bundestag's* Committee on Petitions or a *Bundestag* member's right to information);
- Budget-specific review (from the Confidential Sub-Committee of the parliamentary Budget Committee and the Federal Auditor);
- Data-protection accountability (the Federal Commissioner for Data-Protection and Information);
- Potential scrutiny from the administrative courts and, eventually, the Constitutional Court; and
- Scrutiny from the media, press, and civil society.

Alongside these general oversight mechanisms, if the BND's SIGINT activities involve intrusions upon constitutionally protected telecommunications privacy, then very particular legal conditions are triggered, including the operational oversight provided by the G10 Commission. It is called the "G10 Commission" because it is established by the G10 Act, which authorizes and constrains the state's interference with the telecommunications privacy that Article 10 of the Basic Law is otherwise meant to guarantee.

Article 10 provides that "the privacy of correspondence, posts and telecommunications shall be inviolable."[43] Still, the Constitution anticipates that the law may restrict the right to telecommunications privacy. In the national security context the Constitution grants the government two additional privileges. First, it need not inform individuals that they have

---

[42] *Id.* at 26.

[43] BASIC LAW, *supra* note 27, art. 10(1). *See* Hans Jarass, *Art. 10*, *in* GRUNDGESETZ FÜR DIE BUNDESREPUBLIK DEUTSCHLAND—KOMMENTAR 296, 297 (Hans Jarass & Bodo Pieroth eds., 10th ed. 2009) ("As regards the technology in specific cases, the following would be covered: Telephone, Telefax, Telegram, and Telex. Computer Networks would also be covered, including the Internet, and thereby E-mail and SMS.") (trans. Rusell Miller).

been the subject of telecommunications surveillance.[44] Second, review of surveillance measures need not be conducted by the judiciary, but can instead be carried out by "agencies and auxiliary agencies appointed by the legislature."[45]

The state's authority to conduct telecommunications surveillance without traditional judicial approval and without notifying the subjects of the surveillance was secured as part of the controversial *Notstandsverfassung* amendments that were discussed above. The *Bundestag* simultaneously enacted the *Gesetz zur Beschränkung des Brief-, Post- und Fernmeldegeheimnisses*—also known as the "G10 Act"—to allow the German state to capitalize on those privileges.[46] In its current form, the G10 Act provides a comprehensive framework for the German intelligence community's efforts to collect telecommunications information. The G10 Act gives the BND, the *Verfassungsschutzämter*, and the Military Counterintelligence Service (MAD) the authority to engage in targeted telecommunications monitoring.[47] The monitoring must be limited to measures aimed at protecting against "dangers that threaten the free democratic basic order, or the security of the federation or of the states, or the security of non-German NATO troops stationed in Germany."[48] In order to fulfill its duty to "collect and analyze information required for obtaining foreign intelligence, which is of importance for the foreign and security policy of the Federal Republic of Germany," the BND is also authorized to engage in strategic foreign telecommunications monitoring.[49]

Paragraph 1 of the G10 Act concludes by assigning oversight and control of the BND's telecommunications surveillance to the Parliamentary Control Committee and "a special commission (G10 Commission)."[50] The former is a standing committee of the *Bundestag* to which the responsible Federal Ministers must report every six months regarding their requests to monitor telecommunications.[51] The latter—the G10 Commission—is the primary focus of this chapter.

Paragraph 15 of the G10 Act establishes the G10 Commission and gives it direct operational authority to decide on the "permissibility and necessity of telecommunications monitoring activities."[52] The G10 Commission's control extends to every aspect of the BND's intrusion upon constitutionally protected telecommunications privacy, including the collection, analysis, use, and transfer (to German and non-German entities) of personally-identifying telecommunications data.[53] It also has authority to decide when an individual who has been the subject of telecommunications monitoring must be given notice of the surveillance measures.[54] The G10 Commission exercises its control—sua sponte or on the

[44] *See* BASIC LAW, *supra* note 27, art. 10(2).
[45] *Id.*
[46] *See* G10 Act, *supra* note 28.
[47] *Id.* § 1.
[48] *Id.*
[49] BND Act, *supra* note 12, §1(2); G10 Act, *supra* note 28, § 5.
[50] G10 Act, *supra* note 28, § 1.
[51] *Id.* § 14.
[52] *Id.* § 15.
[53] *Id.* § 15(5).
[54] *Id.*

basis of a complaint—at the required monthly meetings during which the responsible federal ministers are obliged to report on planned telecommunications monitoring measures before they are implemented.[55]

The G10 Commission is an "auxiliary agency" appointed by the *Bundestag*. It meets across the hall from the *Bundestag's* basement cafeteria, in a room curiously labeled "*Bundestag* Administration" and secured by thick steel doors.[56] Its resources are provided by a modest line in the federal budget's appropriation for the *Bundestag*.[57] But membership is not limited to representatives serving in the Parliament, even if the commissioners almost always are former parliamentarians (two of the current commissioners happen to be sitting members of the *Bundestag*).[58] In fact, the G10 Act mandates the commissioners' independence and autonomy: "they are not under instructions."[59] Despite its parliamentary *locus* and orientation, the G10 Commission is not a committee of elected parliamentarians.

The G10 Commission also is not a judicial organ, even if it substitutes for, in some sense, ordinary judicial processes.[60] It is true that the G10 Commission's review of the German intelligence community's telecommunications surveillance operations occurs prior to implementation in much the same way as German judges must consider and approve (by issuing a warrant) law enforcement requests for surveillance measures.[61] It is also true that the G10 Commission's chairperson must be qualified to serve as a judge, and that one of the current commissioners recently was a sitting judge.[62] But the commissioners do not have to be active members of the Germany judiciary. And the Commission's proceedings lack nearly all of the formalities of a typical judicial process. To settle any doubts about the G10 Commission's status as something other than a judicial organ, the G10 Act declares: "Judicial review of an order authorizing telecommunications monitoring pursuant to paras. 3 and 5, and any actions taken to implement such an order, is prohibited until such time as the subject has been notified of the surveillance."[63] Despite the quasi-judicial function it seems to serve, the G10 Commission is not a court.

The Parliamentary Control Committee appoints the G10 Commission's chairperson and the three co-commissioners (as well as the four alternate commissioners) at the start of each

---

[55] *Id.* §§ 15(5)–(6). The intelligence service may implement a ministerial order for telecommunications surveillance prior to the G10 Commission's approval in the exceptional circumstance that harm may result from the delay. *Id.* § 15(6).

[56] Hannes Koch, *Eine Frage des Glaubens*, DER FREITAG (Oct. 20, 2011), https://www.freitag.de/autoren/der-freitag/eine-frage-des-glaubens.

[57] Bundeshaushaltsplan 2015: Einzelplan 02, Deutscher Bundestag, Haushaltstelle F52605/011 (€182,000), *available at* http://www.bundeshaushalt-info.de/fileadmin/de.bundeshaushalt/content_de/dokumente/2015/soll/Haushaltsplan-2015.pdf.

[58] Deutscher Bundestag, *Complete List of Members*, http://www.bundestag.de/htdocs_e/bundestag/members18/complete (last visited Jan. 11, 2016).

[59] G10 Act, *supra* note 28, § 15(1).

[60] Bundesverfassungsgericht [BVerfG] [Federal Constitutional Court] Dec. 15, 1970, 30 Entscheidungen des Bundesverfassungsgerichts [BVerfGE] 1, 23 (G10 Surveillance Case).

[61] StPO, *supra* note 11, §§ 101(a)–(b).

[62] G10 Act, *supra* note 28, § 15(1). *See* Bundestag, *supra* note 58.

[63] G10 Act, *supra* note 28, § 13 (trans. Russell Miller).

four-year parliamentary session.[64] This dependence on the *Bundestag* is meant to give the Commission its democratic legitimacy.[65] The commissioners' unsalaried tenure lasts for the duration of the four-year parliamentary session.[66]

The proceedings of the G10 Commission are highly secretive.[67] The G10 Commission has suffered nothing like the sensational leaks that have bedeviled the American Intelligence Community.[68] Even the Parliamentary Control Committee is less successful at maintaining the confidentiality of its work.[69] Still, it is possible to draw a sketch of the G10 Commission's process and procedure by referring to the provisions of the G10 Act, government documents, and the limited coverage scholars and the media have given the G10 Commission.

The German intelligence services present their requests to pursue telecommunications monitoring to the relevant ministries, which independently assess them for suitability, necessity, and proportionality.[70] For example, the BND's requests for monitoring measures (targeted and strategic) are presented to the Federal Minister of the Interior, who may issue an order authorizing telecommunications surveillance or data collection.[71] There are a number of general requirements for the minister's order that are applicable in all cases. For each authorized telecommunications surveillance operation, the ministerial order must list the search terms/markers that are to be used.[72] The order has to be approved by the minister in consultation with the Parliamentary Control Committee.[73] The order also must identify the region from which information will be gathered and the telecommunications sources/channels that will be accessed.[74] The order must ensure that not more than 20 percent of the designated telecommunications sources/channels will be accessed.[75] Finally, the order must

---

[64] *Id* § 15(1). At the time of this writing, the commissioners are: Chairman Andreas Schmidt (lawyer) (CDU member of parliament 1990–2009); Frank Hoffman (management degrees and service in the administration of Germany's Federal Criminal Police) (SPD member of parliament 1975–2013); Dr. Bertold Huber (former judge—Administrative Court, Frankfurt am Main); Ulrich Maurer (lawyer) (Die Linke member of parliament 2005–2013). The alternate commissioners are: Dr. Wolfgang Götzer (lawyer) (CSU member of parliament 1984–2013); Burkhard Lischka (lawyer) (SPD member of parliament 2009–present, active member of the Parliamentary Control Committee); Halina Wawzyniak (lawyer) (Die Linke member of parliament 2009–present); Wolfgang Wieland (lawyer) (Bündnis 90/Die Grünen member of parliament 2005–2013). *See* Deutscher Bundestag, *Mitglieder der G10-Kommission, available at* https://www.bundestag.de/bundestag/gremien18/g10/mitglieder/281886 (last visited Jan. 11, 2016).

[65] *See* Fredrik Roggan, *§ 15 G-10-Kommission, in* G-10-Gesetz Kommentar margin no. 4 (2012).

[66] G10 Act, *supra* note 28, § 15(1).

[67] *See* G10 Act, *supra* note 28, § 15(2). *See* Koch, *supra* note 56.

[68] *See* Koch, *supra* note 56.

[69] *Id.* ("Actually, secret information has not yet leaked out of the Commission . . . which has not always been the case for the Parliamentary Control Committee.") (quoting Volker Neumann) (trans. Russell Miller).

[70] *See* G10 Act, *supra* note 28, §§ 9–10.

[71] *Id.* § 10.

[72] *Id.*

[73] *Id.* § 5(1)[2].

[74] *Id.*

[75] *Id.* There are criticisms of this limit, which is dependent on the scope of the search. If, for example, the channels/sources designated include the entire Internet, then all email traffic within that broad target range might account for less than 20 percent of the targeted channels/sources. *See* Matthias Bäcker, *Strategische Telekommunikationsüberwachung auf dem Prüfstand,* 16 Kommunikation und Recht 556, 558 (2014).

restrict the monitoring to no more than three months.[76] In the case of the BND's strategic intelligence initiatives, there are additional, more specific parameters. The monitoring must be aimed at collecting information that is necessary for the timely recognition of a danger from, inter alia, an armed attack on the Federal Republic of Germany, preparation for an international terrorist attack with direct consequences for the Federal Republic of Germany, and arms trafficking.[77] Furthermore, the search terms/markers may not reveal any personally identifying information that could lead to the targeted recognition of a specific telecommunications connection.[78] Finally, strategic monitoring measures may not intrude upon the core of a person's private sphere as that interest is defined by the G10 Act.[79]

These are the ministerial orders that the G10 Commission is empowered to confirm or deny in its quasi-judicial role supervising the German intelligence community's intrusions on constitutionally enshrined telecommunications privacy. The Commission assesses the "admissibility" and "necessity" of the requested surveillance measures.[80] "Necessity" is understood to play the same role here as the concept plays in the deeply entrenched proportionality principle in German law.[81] A measure is "necessary" only if there are no other means for obtaining the hoped-for results that would be less harmful to the constitutionally protected interest. When reviewing the orders seeking to implement telecommunications surveillance the Commission "acts as the representative of German citizens but is, at the same time, utterly isolated. ... [I]t has no support, neither political nor in the media nor from civil society."[82] It is isolated, but the Commission has great power. As Hans de With, the Commission's former chairman, put it: "Stated simply: If the Commission says 'yes' to requested measures, they can be implemented; if the Commission says 'no,' then the requested measures cannot be implemented."[83]

I have doubts about the intensity with which the G10 Commission pursues its mandate. The latest information about the Commission's work, published as part of the Parliamentary Control Committee's reporting duties,[84] comes from 2013.[85] That year, the G10 Commission considered a total of 25,526 monitoring measures (including all facets of its authority over targeted and strategic monitoring).[86] That is a staggering average of 2,127 monitoring requests to be considered at

---

[76] See G10 Act, *supra* note 28, § 10(5).

[77] *Id.* § 5(1).

[78] *Id.* § 5(2). Search terms/markers—what the Germans refer to as "Selektoren"—might include a calling number, other telecommunications connections identifiers, or an identifier for the receiving device. *See id.* § 10(3).

[79] *Id.*

[80] *Id.* § 15(5).

[81] Roggan, *supra* note 65, at margin no. 10. See ALEC STONE SWEET & JUD MATHEWS, HOW JUDICIAL GOVERNANCE WORKS: PROPORTIONALITY BALANCING AND GLOBAL CONSTITUTIONALISM (forthcoming 2016).

[82] Koch, *supra* note 56.

[83] *Id.*

[84] See G10 Act, *supra* note 28, § 14(1).

[85] Deutscher Bundestag, UNTERRICHTUNG DURCH DAS PARLAMENTARISCHE KONTROLLGREMIUM—BERICHT ZU DEN MASSNAHMEN NACH DEM TERRORISMUSBEKÄMPFUNGSGESETZ FÜR DAS JAHR 2013, Bundestag Drucksache 18/3708 (2015), *available at* http://dip21.bundestag.de/dip21/btd/18/037/1803708.pdf.

[86] *Id.*

each of its monthly sessions. Of course, many of these requests are grouped as part a single ministerial order. In a four- or five-hour session the Commission can work through as many as 70 of
these orders.[87] One media report estimated that, at most, the Commission devoted five minutes
to each order.[88] Former chairman de With has remarked that, faced with a swelling workload, the
Commission was considering whether it should meet more often.[89] There is no evidence that it has
begun to do this. Former chairman de With defended the Commission's hurried pace by explaining that new orders require more attention than requests to add new search terms/markers to, or
renew for another three months, previously approved telecommunications monitoring orders.[90]

The Commission's practice of summarily renewing or expanding existing surveillance
orders has been confirmed by another former Commissioner.[91] The less stringent review the
Commission applies to monitoring measures that have already been approved forms part of
the criticism raised by the left-wing human rights NGO "Libertad!" As part of a legal challenge the German group has filed, it claims to have obtained orders approved by the G10
Commission that authorized monitoring measures against several of the NGO's members.[92]
In its online commentary the group claims that every three months, over the course of a
decade, the G10 Commission was presented with nearly identical orders, sometimes as many
as 30 times.[93] The group insinuates that the G10 Commission did not read these requests,
let alone express any concern about the German intelligence community's practice of seeking
almost perpetual renewal of long-ago authorized monitoring measures.[94]

The Commission's proceedings are not adversarial.[95] They are conducted in total secrecy
and involve surveillance measures about which the subjects are supposed to be kept in the
dark until they have been discontinued. The representatives of the intelligence community
and ministries remain in the room while the Commission deliberates so that they can answer
the commissioners' questions.[96] According to former chairman de With, the commissioners
almost always act unanimously.[97]

---

[87] Koch, *supra* note 56.

[88] *Id.*

[89] *See* Christian Rath, *Hans de With über Überwachung—"Nicht mit uns!"*, TAZ.DE (Aug. 2, 2013), http://www.
taz.de/!121082/.

[90] *Id.* "Of course, new applications require more time when compared with the review needed to approve the addition of a new telephone number to ongoing surveillance measures that have already been approved or to approve
the extension of surveillance measures at the end of the permitted three-month period." (trans. Russell Miller).

[91] Koch, *supra* note 56 ("Five minutes is enough for each case. When reviewing new surveillance initiatives, however, we debate the case for as much as a half-hour before we reach a decision." (quoting Volker Neumann)
(trans. Russell Miller).

[92] *See* Verwaltungsgericht Berlin, Pressemitteilung Nr. 9/2012 from March 1, 2012—Abhörmaßnahmen durch
Verfassungsschutz waren rechtswidrig, *available at* https://www.berlin.de/sen/justiz/gerichte/vg/presse/
archiv/20120301.1700.366871.html. *See also* Andreas Förster, *Gericht rügt Geheimdienst—Überwachung von
Linken in Berlin war rechtswidrig*, BERLINER ZEITUNG (Mar. 2, 2012), at 6.

[93] *Staatliche Kontrolle der Geheimdienste?*, LIBERTAD! ONLINE (Jan. 6, 2015), http://www.info.libertad.de/
blogs/7/623.

[94] *Id.*

[95] *See* Claus Arndt, *25 Jahre Post- und Telefonkontrolle—Die G 10-Kommission des Deutschen Bundestages*, 24
ZEITSCHRIFT FÜR PARLAMENTSFRAGEN 621, 631–32 (1993).

[96] Rath, *supra* note 89.

[97] *Id.*

The integrity of the G10 Commission's scrutiny may be undermined by the limits on the resources at its disposal.

This concern has a quantitative dimension. The G10 Act ensures that the Commission has full, unhindered access to the work of the German intelligence services.[98] The Act also grants the Commission the resources, in personnel and expertise, that it needs.[99] But the G10 Commission seems to have a very small staff. In an interview in 2011, former commissioner Volker Neumann explained that the G10 Commission's monthly meetings are usually attended by 20 to 30 people.[100] Accounting for the 8 commissioners and perhaps as many as 18 representatives from the relevant ministries and 3 intelligence services (3 participants each), the G10 Commission might have as many as 4 staff assistants on hand at its monthly sessions. Even this modest figure seems high. In 2015, the Commission had a budget of €182,000.[101] One-third of the budget (€66,000) is dedicated to reimbursing the commissioners' travel costs (€8,250 per commissioner each year).[102] The remaining €116,000 hardly seems adequate to support four full-time staff assistants.

The concern about the resources available to the G10 Commission also has a qualitative dimension. Thorsten Kornblum and Kai Biermann have concluded that the Commission's personnel have adequate training in the law (all but one of the current commissioners and alternate commissioners are legally trained) but lack the technical competence to understand the complex technology involved in the intelligence initiatives they are reviewing.[103] To illustrate his argument, Biermann reported that, on one occasion, the G10 Commission "examined" the BND's filtering technology.[104] But this merely involved a number of presentations from the BND's staff.[105] Biermann explained that "the Commission does not have the technology experts it needs to confirm the accuracy of everything they are told."[106]

The practical effect of the constraints on the G10 Commission's review is that the Commission simply "waves through everything the intelligence community wants."[107] Former chairman de With has offered only a modest correction of this critique. The Commission does not approve *all* the orders it reviews. But former chairman de With guessed that it disallows fewer than 10 percent of them. "Ordinarily, orders that are not fit for approval are not presented," he explained. "The intelligence services do not want to get their noses bloodied by the Commission."[108] Even this nominal rejection rate is less reassuring than de

---

[98] *See* G10 Act, *supra* note 28, § 15(5).

[99] *Id.* § 15(3).

[100] Koch, *supra* note 56.

[101] *See* Gesetz über die Feststellung des Bundeshaushaltsplans für das Haushaltsjahr 2015 [Act for the Establishment of the Federal Budget Plan for the Budget Year 2015], Dec. 23, 2014, BGBL. I at 2442 [hereinafter 2015 Budget Act].

[102] *Id.*

[103] *See* KORNBLUM, *supra* note 13, at 187; Kai Biermann, *BND-Kontrolleure verstehen nichts von Überwachungstechnik*, ZEIT ONLINE, Oct. 7, 2013), http://www.zeit.de/digital/datenschutz/2013-10/bnd-internet-ueberwachung-provider.

[104] Biermann, *supra* note 103.

[105] *Id.*

[106] *Id.* (trans. Russell Miller).

[107] *Id.* (trans. Russell Miller).

[108] Rath, *supra* note 89.

With may have intended it to be. In the few cases in which the Commission does not get adequate answers to its questions, former chairman de With explained that the Commission merely urges the BND to "come back next month," presumably with the information needed to permit the Commission to authorize the order.[109] Fredrik Roggan expressed similar concerns about the rigor of the G10 Commission's review in his Commentary to the G10 Act. He attributed the "summary" nature of the Commission's review to its "limited staffing, technical and factual capacities."[110] Roggan concluded that the review provided by the G10 Commission is structurally inadequate.[111]

Perhaps the strongest indictment of the G10 Commission's efficacy emerges from its record. The G10 Commission's review did little to impede the BND's alleged surveillance of German and other European targets, including industrial interests, in the BND's intensely disputed cooperation with America's NSA.[112] As that chapter in the ongoing NSA-Affair was unfolding in the spring of 2015, criticism was focused on the BND President, the Interior Minister, the Minister of the Chancellery, Chancellor Merkel, and the Parliamentary Control Committee. But there was no handwringing over the fact that the G10 Commission must have approved the surveillance measures that targeted German-based telecommunications activities or sources.

The following statistics from the Parliamentary Control Committee's annual reports confirm that the German intelligence community is no wallflower, and that the G10 Commission is no insuperable barrier to its vigorous work on behalf of German security. These statistics refer to the strategic telecommunications monitoring measures (in only two classes of threats) that the G10 Commission authorized the BND to implement in 2012 and 2013.[113]

When asked about the rather modest results of the BND's telecommunications surveillance programs (only 244 and 105 relevant strategic intercepts in 2012 and 2013 in these two threat areas), former chairman de With deflected the question toward the political institutions involved in intelligence oversight, such as the Parliamentary Control Committee: "The G10 Commission," he insisted, "is only responsible for ensuring that the law is respected."[114]

---

[109] *Id.*

[110] Roggan, *supra* note 65, at margin no. 11.

[111] *Id.*

[112] *See* Maik Baumgärtner et al., *Spying Close to Home: German Intelligence under Fire for NSA Cooperation*, Der Spiegel (Apr. 25, 2015), *available at* http://www.spiegel.de/international/germany/german-intelligence-agency-bnd-under-fire-for-nsa-cooperation-a-1030593.html.

[113] *See* Unterrichtung durch das Parlamentarische Kontrollgremium—Bericht zu den Maßnahmen nach dem Terrorismusbekämpfungsgesetz für das Jahr 2013 [Information Delivered to the Parliamentary Control Committee—Report on the Measures Taken Pursuant to the Anti-Terror Act for the Year 2013], BTDrucks 18/3708 (2015), *available at* http://dip21.bundestag.de/dip21/btd/18/037/1803708.pdf; Unterrichtung durch das Parlamentarische Kontrollgremium—Bericht zu den Maßnahmen nach dem Terrorismusbekämpfungsgesetz für das Jahr 2012 [Information Delivered to the Parliamentary Control Committee—Report on the Measures Taken Pursuant to the Anti-Terror Act for the Year 2012], BTDrucks 18/216 (2013), *available at* http://dip21.bundestag.de/dip21/btd/18/002/1800216.pdf.

[114] Rath, *supra* note 89.

STRATEGIC MONITORING—§5 OF THE G10 ACT[115]

	2012	2013
International Terrorism	2,229 discrete search terms/markers	1,643 discrete search terms/markers
	1,804 telecommunication sources/channels implicated	906 telecommunications sources/channels implicated
	595 emails	1 email
	290 faxes	20 faxes
	9 telexes	11 telexes
	58 voice communications	175 voice communications
	816 metadata links	639 metadata links
	36 SMS messages	60 SMS messages
	137 relevant intercepts	73 relevant intercepts
Arms Trafficking	24,775 discrete search terms/markers	23,400 discrete search terms/markers
	849,497 telecommunication sources/channels implicated	14,411 telecommunication sources/channels implicated
	107 relevant intercepts	32 relevant intercepts

Whatever the shortcomings of the process and standards the G10 Commission implements pursuant to the G10 Act, the regime extends some (perhaps purely ritualistic) protection to Germans' telecommunications privacy. That is more than can be said for the privacy of telecommunications interceptions conducted outside Germany and involving non-Germans. The BND, with the blessing of the Federal Government, has concluded that the G10 Act does not apply to the surveillance of telecommunications that take place outside Germany and do not involve Germans as one of the parties.[116] The Federal Government confirmed this fact in its presentation of facts in the *G10 Case* that was decided by the Federal Constitutional Court in 1999. The Federal Minister of the Interior explained that, of the approximately 15,000 telecommunications sources/channels the BND screened each day, only approximately 700 fell "under the authority of the G10 Act,"[117] which establishes and provides for the G10 Commission's role.

The Federal Government more recently confirmed the BND's pursuit of unregulated surveillance outside Germany in the answers it provided to a set of formal parliamentary

---

[115] The chart, drawing on the data presented by the intelligence services to the Parliament and then packaged for public use in the Parliament's annual report, documents the following: (1) the number of search terms for which surveillance was orderd; (2) the declared number of sources/channels to which the surveillance was applied (never exceeding 20 percent of the proposed source/channel); and (3) the total number of relevant intercepts culled from the collected telecommunications information.

[116] Bäcker, *supra* note 75, at 559.

[117] Bundesverfassungsgericht [BVerfG] [Federal Constitutional Court] July 14, 1999, 100 Entscheidungen des Bundesverfassungsgerichts [BVerfGE] 313, 337 (Telecommunications Surveillance Act Case) (trans. Russell Miller).

questions presented to it by *Die Linke* (the Left Party).[118] The Federal Government explained that, in those circumstances, the BND pursues strategic telecommunications surveillance under the exclusive authority of Paragraph 1(2) of the BND Act, which establishes the BND for the generic purpose of "collecting and analyzing foreign intelligence information which is of importance for the foreign and security policy of the Federal Republic of Germany."[119] The Federal Government has not offered a full justification for its conclusion that the protections of the G10 Act do not apply outside Germany. In its answers to the Left Party's formal parliamentary questions about this practice the Federal Government insisted that "in the fulfillment of its responsibilities the BND acts in conformity with the prevailing constitutional and statutory norms."[120] On these terms the BND can monitor and collect the telecommunications traffic of whole states or world-regions without constitutional or statutory limits so long as the German territory or a German citizen is not implicated.[121]

A growing chorus of scholars and commentators thinks the Federal Government's position on foreign telecommunications surveillance violates German constitutional law.[122] They argue that the telecommunications privacy secured by Article 10 of the Basic Law must apply outside the German territory, including the G10 Act's implementation of those constitutional protections. That, in turn, would require the G10 Commission to review and approve the BND's exclusively foreign strategic telecommunications surveillance activities. First, these critics wonder if the technology involved in the contemporary telecommunications infrastructure has rendered territorial distinctions of this kind obsolete. The Federal Government's stance, the critics argue, does not adequately account for the fact that a significant share of German telecommunications contacts—involving the German territory or at least one German—will be routed through international telecommunication and Internet infrastructure that is based wholly outside Germany. Unregulated and unlimited surveillance of those extraterritorial sources/channels are very likely to involve German telecommunications contacts, which are undoubtedly owed the protection of the G10 Act.

---

[118] Kleine Anfrage der Abgeordneten Jan Korte, et al. [Limited Inquiry of the Parliamentarian Jan Korte et al.], BTDrucks 18/1986 (2014), *available at* http://dip21.bundestag.de/dip21/btd/18/019/1801986.pdf.

[119] BND Act, *supra* note 12, § 1.

[120] Antwort der Bundesregierung auf die Kleine Anfrage der Abgeordneten Jan Korte, et al. [Answer of the Federal Government on the Limited Inquiry of the Parliamentarian Jan Korte et al.], BTDRucks 18/2128 (2014, *available at* http://dip21.bundestag.de/dip21/btd/18/021/1802128.pdf.

[121] Bäcker, *supra* note 75, at 559.

[122] *See id. See also* Bertold Huber, *Die Strategische Rasterfahndung des Bundesnachrichtendienstes—Eingriffsbefugnisse und Regelungsdefizite*, 66 Neue Juristische Wochenschrift 2573 (2013); Stefan Heumann & Thorsten Wetzling, *Strategische Auslandsüberwachung: Technische Möglichkeiten, rechtlicher Rahmen und parlamentarische Kontrolle*, Policy Brief—Stiftung Neue Verantwortung (May 2014), *available at* http://www.stiftung-nv.de/sites/default/files/052014_snv_policy_brief_strategische_auslandsuberwachung.pdf; Wolfgang Hoffmann-Riem, *Stellungnahme zur Anhörung des NSA Untersuchungsausschusses* (May 22, 2014), *available at* https://www.bundestag.de/blob/280846/04f34c512c86876b06f7c162e673f2db/mat_a_sv-2-1neu--pdf-data.pdf; Hans-Jürgen Papier, Gutachtliche Stellungnahme Beweissbeschluss SV-2 des ersten Untersuchungsausschusses des Deutschen Bundestages der 18. Wahlperiode (May 16, 2014), *available at* https://www.bundestag.de/blob/280842/9f755b0c-53866c7a95c38428e262ae98/mat_a_sv-2-2-pdf-data.pdf; Klaus F. Gärditz, *Legal Restraints on the Activities of Germany's Intelligence Services When Acting Abroad*, in Privacy and Power: A Transatlantic Dialogue in the Shadow of the NSA-Affair (Russell Miller ed., forthcoming 2016).

Second, the critics argue that the Federal Government's stance involves a troubling misreading of the Basic Law, which they say does not recognize territorial parameters on the limits it imposes on German state power. Instead, these commentators argue that all German state authority, regardless of where in the world it is exercised, must show respect for the rights secured by the Basic Law.[123]

Judge Bertold Huber of the Frankfurt Administrative Law Court offered a particularly important objection on these grounds. In an article published in the summer of 2013 in Germany's most widely read law journal, the *Neue Juristische Wochenschrift*,[124] Judge Huber insisted that Article 10 of the Basic Law, in addition to applying to Germans, also inevitably "includes non-Germans in the scope of its protection, indeed, regardless whether non-Germans are present in, or are outside, the German territory."[125] As with the other commentators who have raised this critique, Judge Huber concluded that, as a foundational matter, Article 1(3) of the Basic Law binds all exercises of German state power no matter where they occur.[126] Judge Huber's arguments are important because, at the time he wrote the article, he was an alternate member of the G10 Commission. After retiring from his judgeship Huber was appointed by the Parliamentary Control Committee to serve as a G10 Commissioner after the federal elections that took place only a month after his article appeared in the *Neue Juristische Wochenschrift*.

The German constitutional and international law experts subpoenaed to appear before the *Bundestag's* committee investigating the NSA-Affair shared Judge Huber's conclusions on this point.[127] In a chapter he is contributing to a forthcoming book that will examine German and American relations in the shadow of the *NSA-Affäre*, Klaus Gärditz was unequivocal on this point:

> From a constitutional perspective this is indefensible. Articles 1(3) and 20(3) of the Basic Law stipulate that the executive must conform to the basic rights and is bound by law and justice. The rule of law applies without exception and independent of the locality where an administrative agent is acting. There is neither an extraterritorial nor a security exception; and the rule of law stays unimpaired, even in the case of a national emergency. It is beyond doubt that the BND must comply with applicable German law, even if acting abroad.[128]

---

[123] *See* BASIC LAW, *supra* note 27, art. 1(3). ("The following basic rights shall bind the legislatures, the executive and the judiciary as directly applicable law."). Matthias Bäcker's views are representative of this position. He asserted that "according to Art. 1(3) of the Basic Law the basic rights comprehensively bind German public authority. A territorial exception for extraterritorial exercises of public authority is not supported by the text or the aims of this provision." Bäcker, *supra* note 75, at 560 (trans. Russell Miller).

[124] Huber, *supra* note 122.

[125] *Id.* at 2574.

[126] *Id.* at 2575.

[127] *See* Hoffmann Riem, *supra* note 122; Papier, *supra* note 122. *See also* Yasin Musharbash, *Bundestagskommission zweifelt an Rechtmäßigkeit der BND-Überwachung*, ZEIT ONLINE (May 23, 2014), http://www.zeit.de/politik/2014-05/G-10-Kontrollkommission-bundesnachrichtendienst-kritik.

[128] *See* Gärditz, *supra* note 122.

C. Conclusion

The G10 Commission is the principal organ for monitoring and limiting the BND's tele-communications surveillance initiatives. By design, it is neither a fully-judicial nor a fully-parliamentary body. The G10 Act that establishes the G10 Commission characterizes the body as an "auxiliary agency appointed by the legislature." It would be better to acknowledge that the G10 Commission merely provides cover for the German executive and legislative branches, crudely legitimizing the often unseemly work of collecting intelligence. In practice the understaffed and inexpert commissioners impose almost no restraint on the German state's clamor for the intelligence that can be obtained from intrusions upon our increasingly pervasive and encompassing telecommunications activities. In cases involving non-German telecommunications connections, the G10 Commission plays no role at all. The state gains much from this arrangement. On one hand, it is free to pursue nearly all the telecommu-nications surveillance it wants. On the other hand, those efforts benefit from a veneer of *Rechtsstaatlichkeit* (being bound by the rule of law) and democratic legitimacy.

III. CONSTITUTIONAL OBJECTIONS TO THE G10 COMMISSION

The G10 Commission does little to protect telecommunications privacy. It also may be unconstitutional. First, the G10 Commission's constitutionality was only dubiously settled by the Federal Constitutional Court's 1970 ruling on the matter.[129] That decision was reached by a thin majority relying on unpersuasive reasoning. The majority did not show the required respect for two cherished constitutional commitments that form the core of the principle of the rule of law: the separation of powers and the right to be heard by a lawful judge. The majority's neglect of these principles paved the way for the Court's conclusion that the 1968 constitutional amendments (envisioning the G10 Act and the G10 Commission) could stand, despite the prohibition in Article 79(3) against constitutional amendments that com-promise fundamental principles in the Basic Law.[130]

Second, changes in the law and technology in the years since 1970 have significantly eroded the G10 Commission's already flimsy constitutional footing. Recognizing the far-reaching and personally revealing role of telecommunications technology in today's society, the German Constitutional Court has been increasingly concerned with the privacy impli-cations of the state's collection and use of the data created by modern telecommunications activities.[131] That jurisprudence now demands that the Constitutional Court's 1970 decision crediting the G10 Commission's constitutionality be re-examined and overturned.

---

[129] Bundesverfassungsgericht [BVerfG] [Federal Constitutional Court] Dec. 15, 1970, 30 Entscheidungen des Bundesverfassungsgerichts [BVerfGE] 1, 23 (G10 Surveillance Case).

[130] BASIC LAW, *supra* note 27, art. 79(3).

[131] *See* Bundesverfassungsgericht [BVerfG] [Federal Constitutional Court] Mar. 3, 2004, 109 Entscheidungen des Bundesverfassungsgerichts [BVerfGE] 279 (Acoustical Surveillance Act Case); Bundesverfassungsgericht [BVerfG] [Federal Constitutional Court] Apr. 12, 2005, 112 Entscheidungen des Bundesverfassungsgerichts [BVerfGE] 304 (Global Positioning System Case); Bundesverfassungsgericht [BVerfG] [Federal Constitutional Court] Apr. 4, 2006, 115 Entscheidungen des Bundesverfassungsgerichts [BVerfGE] 320 (Data Mining Case); Bundesverfassungsgericht [BVerfG] [Federal Constitutional Court] Feb. 27, 2008, 120 Entscheidungen des Bundesverfassungsgerichts [BVerfGE] 274 (Online Computer Surveillance Case); Bundesverfassungsgericht

A. *The Constitutional Court's Ill-Conceived Assessment of the G10 Act*

The G10 Act, and the G10 Commission it created, were legal developments made possible in the first instance by the controversial 1968 amendments to the Basic Law. In most constitutional systems a constitutional amendment authorizing the exercise of a discrete form of state power might be the end of any discussion about the constitutionality of the competence in question.[132] But the Nazis' manipulation and eventual debasement of the Weimar Constitution haunted the drafters of what was to be the new, postwar West German Constitution.[133] To prevent this from happening again the Basic Law provides a list of the values that are to animate and define the new West German state.[134] Moreover, in Article 79(3), the Basic Law prohibits any amendments to those core principles.[135] This provision is sometimes referred to as the "eternity clause" because it aims to secure a fundamental set of social and political commitments, even from change by an amending supermajority, for as long as the Basic Law serves as Germany's constitution.[136] In practice this means that the Constitutional Court can be called on to assess the permissibility of constitutional amendments by testing their conformity to the Basic Law's fundamental principles. After more than 60 years (and counting) of effective constitutional governance, Article 79(3) still stands as a sentinel, ensuring the security of the central aims of the Basic Law, giving them enduring—if not eternal—effect and meaning.[137]

The principles secured by Article 79(3) include Germany's federalist structure, the supreme value of human dignity, representative democracy, a commitment to social welfare,

---

[BVerfG] [Federal Constitutional Court] Mar. 2, 2010, 125 Entscheidungen des Bundesverfassungsgerichts [BVerfGE] 260 (Data Stockpiling Case). *See also* DONALD P. KOMMERS & RUSSELL A. MILLER, THE CONSTITUTIONAL JURISPRUDENCE OF THE FEDERAL REPUBLIC OF GERMANY 415–18 (3d ed. 2012).

[132] *See* Rosalind Dixon, *Constitutional Amendment Rules: A Comparative Perspective, in* COMPARATIVE CONSTITUTIONAL LAW 96 (Tom Ginsburg & Rosalind Dixon eds., 2011); Richard Albert, *Amending Constitutional Amendment Rules*, 13 INT'L J. CONST. L. 655 (2015). *But see* Richard Albert, *Constitutional Amendment by Stealth*, 60 MCGILL L.J. 673 (2015).

[133] *See* Matthias Herdegen, *Art. 79, in* MAUNZ/DÜRIG GRUNDGESETZ KOMMENTAR margin no. 64 (Roman Herzog et al. eds., 68th ed. 2010) (referring to the "trauma of Weimar") (trans. Russell Miller).

[134] *See* BASIC LAW, *supra* note 27, art. 20(1).

[135] *Id.* art. 79(3).

[136] *See, e.g.,* Bundesverfassungsgericht [BVerfG] [Federal Constitutional Court] June 30, 2009, 123 Entscheidungen des Bundesverfassungsgerichts [BVerfGE] 267, 343 (Lisbon Treaty Case) ("The so-called eternity guarantee even prevents a constitution-amending legislature from disposing of the identity of the free constitutional order. The Basic Law thus not only presumes sovereign statehood for Germany but guarantees it.").

[137] *See* Michael Brenner, *Möglichkeiten und Grenzen grundrechtsbezogener Verfassungsänderungen*, 32 DER STAAT 493 (1993); Günter Dürig, *Zur Bedeutung und Tragweite des Art. 79 Abs. 3 des Grundgesetzes, in* FESTGABE FÜR THEODOR MAUNZ 41 (Hans Spanner et al. eds., 1971); Hans-Uwe Erichsen, *Zu den Grenzen von Verfassungsänderungen nach dem Grundgesetz*, 62 DAS VERWALTUNGSARCHIV 291 (1971); Dieter Grimm, *Das Grundgesetz als Riegel vor einer Verstaatlichung der Europäischen Union*, 48 DER STAAT 475 (2009); Paul Kirchhof, *Die Identität der Verfassung in ihren unabänderlichen Gehalten, in* II HANDBUCH DES STAATSRECHTS DER BUNDESREPUBLIK DEUTSCHLAND Sec. 21 (Josef Isensee & Paul Kirchhof eds., 3d ed. 2004); Klaus Stern, *Die Bedeutung der Unantastbarkeitsgarantie des Art. 79 Abs. 3 GG für die Grundrechte*, 25 DIE JURISTISCHE SCHULUNG 329 (1985); HANS HUGO WEBER, DIE MATERIELLEN SCHRANKEN FÜR DIE ÄNDERUNG DES BONNER GRUNDGESETZES UND ART. 79 ABS. 3 (1954).

and the rule of law.[138] These unamendable commitments are so fundamental to the nature and character of the German state under the Basic Law that, together, they are sometimes referred to as Germany's "constitutional identity" and at other times as the core components of Germany's "free democratic basic order."[139] The rule of law, as just one of the eternal elements of the German constitutional identity, itself has several facets. The first is the separation of state authority into three discrete functions: the legislative power, the executive power, and the judicial power.[140] The second facet is that the exercise of German state power must conform to the basic rights secured by the Basic Law.[141] The third facet is that the "legislature is bound by the constitutional order, the executive and judiciary by law and justice."[142] For the purposes of my critique I want to focus on one basic right that is clearly implicated by the decision to displace the ordinary courts' review of the state's surveillance activities for the review of the nonjudicial G10 Commission. Article 19(4) of the Basic Law commands: "Should any person's rights be violated by public authority, he may have recourse to the courts."[143]

The G10 Commission brazenly crashes through each of these constitutional mandates. By assigning the judicial function of reviewing the state's telecommunications surveillance to a quasi-legislative body, the principle of the separation of powers is fouled. At the same time, excluding the judiciary from reviewing these intrusions upon telecommunications privacy denies Germans their constitutional right to recourse to the courts. These affronts to the rule of law, made possible by the 1968 emergency constitutional amendments, would seem to be precisely the kind of distortion of Germany's constitutional identity that Article 79(3) was designed to prevent.

A number of constitutional complaints and a demand for abstract judicial review were filed against the 1968 constitutional amendments, citing, among other constitutional objections, the elimination of the courts' jurisdiction over telecommunications surveillance in lieu of the G10 Commission.[144] The complaints pointed to the unamendable significance of the rule of law.[145] The complainants also argued that the G10 Commission constituted a violation of a troubling number of basic rights, including: the protection of human dignity, telecommunications privacy, the right to occupational freedom, the right to have recourse to the courts, the guarantee of the essential integrity of the basic rights, the ban on extraordinary

---

[138] *See* BASIC LAW, *supra* note 27, arts. 1 and 20; *see also* Hans Jarass & Bodo Pieroth, *Art. 20, in* GG—GRUNDGESETZ FÜR DIE BUNDESREPUBLIK DEUTSCHLAND—KOMMENTAR 497 (Übersicht and margin no. 1) (13th ed. 2014).

[139] *See, e.g.,* Bundesverfassungsgericht [BVerfG] [Federal Constitutional Court] June 30, 2009, 123 Entscheidungen des Bundesverfassungsgerichts [BVerfGE] 267, 340 (Lisbon Treaty Case) (remarking that the principles that are codified in Article 79(3) of the Basic Law are the "identity of the constitution.").

[140] *See* BASIC LAW, *supra* note 27, art. 20(2); Helmuth Schulze-Fielitz, *Art. 20, in* II GRUNDGESETZ-KOMMENTAR margin no. 67 (Horst Dreier ed., 2d ed. 2006).

[141] *See* BASIC LAW, *supra* note 27, art. 1(3) and 20(3). *See* Schulze-Fielitz, *supra* note 140, at margin no. 81.

[142] BASIC LAW, *supra* note 27, art. 20(3).

[143] *Id.* art. 19(4).

[144] *See* Bundesverfassungsgericht [BVerfG] [Federal Constitutional Court] Dec. 15, 1970, 30 Entscheidungen des Bundesverfassungsgerichts [BVerfGE] 1, 11–15 (G10 Surveillance Case).

[145] *Id.*

courts, and the right to a fair trial.[146] The complaints did not raise concerns about the violation of the Basic Law's general—and wide-ranging—protection of personal privacy. This is
because Article 10, as the *lex specialis*, is given priority with regard to telecommunications
privacy.

In a divided judgment that attracted the first dissenting opinions in its history, the Court
rejected the complaints.[147] The majority of the Court focused exclusively on the complain-
ant's argument that the 1968 amendments—and the G10 Commission as their practical
consequence—violated the Basic Law's eternal commitment to the rule of law. The Court
did not need to resolve the basic rights concerns raised by the complainants, the majority
reasoned, because the Basic Law did not establish a regime of absolute rights protection.[148]
The majority noted that this was particularly true of the protection of telecommunications
privacy. The original version of Article 10 allowed the government to intrude upon telecommunications privacy if authorized to do so by law.[149]

The majority's reasoning with respect to the rule-of-law issue is unpersuasive.

One reason that the majority fails to convince is that it resorted to an embarrassingly pragmatic tautology in justifying its decision. If the German government must gather secret intelligence, the majority reasoned, then it cannot be expected to do so under the very public and
revelatory glare of the judiciary.[150] Only the exclusion of the courts, the majority explained,
would make Germany's secret intelligence gathering effective and sensible.[151] This, of course,
begs the question: Must the German government be in the business of gathering secret
intelligence? It is true that the Basic Law anticipates a number of government activities that
would be aided by intelligence gathering.[152] Additionally, the Basic Law assigns the legislative competence for the "protection of the free democratic basic order" to the Federation.[153]

Nevertheless, the choice to seize upon these competences to establish the *Verfassungsschutz*
regime (federal office for the protection of the Constitution), which pursues domestic intelligence gathering, remains a policy choice settled by the legislative majority in the Parliament
(taking the form of the Federal Constitutional Protection Act). Nothing at all in the Basic
Law *mandates* the creation of this intrusive and problematic institution. The same can be
said of the BND (the establishment of which is also a policy choice achieved by the BND
Act). Granting the state the power to act is not the same thing as imposing a constitutional
duty on the state to act.[154] But the Court's majority assumed that the grant of these powers
obliges the German state to implement them.[155]

---

[146] *Id.*
[147] *Id.*
[148] *Id.* at 17.
[149] *Id.* at 18.
[150] *Id.* at 19.
[151] *Id.*
[152] *See, e.g.*, BASIC LAW, *supra* note 27, arts. 9, 18, and 21.
[153] *Id.* art. 73(10).
[154] *See* Rupert Stettner, *Art. 70, in* II GRUNDGESETZ-KOMMENTAR margin no. 23 (Horst Drier ed., 2d ed. 2006);
    Michael Bothe, *Art. 70, in* KOMMENTAR ZUM GRUNDGESETZ FÜR DIE BUNDESREPUBLIK DEUTSCHLAND
    (AK-GG) margin no. 25 (Ekkehart Stein et al. eds., 3d ed. 2002).
[155] Bundesverfassungsgericht [BVerfG] [Federal Constitutional Court] Dec. 15, 1970, 30 Entscheidungen
    des Bundesverfassungsgerichts [BVerfGE] 1, 11-15 (G10 Surveillance Case) ("It cannot be the case that the

This is not the correct approach under the Basic Law. On the one hand, the Constitutional Court has consistently refused to find that the Basic Law grants the Federation the general and implied powers needed to fulfill its competences.[156] The Court has jealously sought to keep German state authority strictly within its constitutionally ordained boundaries. On the other hand, it turns the Constitution on its head to say that (non-excluded) policy choices taken by the majority in Parliament provide the justification for the departure from one of the Basic Law's fundamental principles. The Constitutional Court has insisted, for example, that the essential content of the Basic Law's protections cannot be made dependent on the pursuit of a related parliamentary competence.[157] In these cases the Court correctly concluded that this would impermissibly make the Constitution subservient to the will of the legislative majority. It simply thwarts the very purpose of constitutional supremacy to accept that a legislative majority might be able to reach a policy decision (such as the G10 Act and the G10 Commission) that countenances a restriction of basic rights or fundamental constitutional principles. Article 20(3) of the Basic Law—and constitutional theory generally—preclude this by binding the legislature to the constitutional order.[158]

In any case, the majority's objection that judicial review of intelligence gathering measures would necessarily involve disruptive public processes is patently results-oriented. Germany's law enforcement authorities are required to present their requests for surveillance to the ordinary courts,[159] which have developed sophisticated and effective procedures for judicial review that do not have the effect of rendering law enforcement's efforts impotent and dysfunctional.[160] In fact, the ordinary courts effectively review and supervise several hundred thousand more surveillance requests each year than the G10 Commission manages, without plunging Germany's law enforcement institutions into irrelevance and leaving the country dangerously in the grip of criminal elements.[161] These measures are specific to the criminal

---

constitution gives the higher constitutional organs of the state a responsibility to fulfill and envision a special office for the fulfillment of that responsibility, and nevertheless deny the constitutional organs and the anticipated office the means they need to fulfill their constitutional duty.") (trans. Russell Miller).

[156] *See, e.g.,* Bundesverfassungsgericht [BVerfG] [Federal Constitutional Court] Jan. 14, 2015, 1 BvR 931/12 (Saturday Work Case), *available at* http://www.bundesverfassungsgericht.de/EN/Homepage/home_node. html.

[157] The Constitutional Court has insisted on this point in several contexts. Perhaps most famously, in the *Lüth Case* the Court explained that "it would be inconsistent to allow the substance of [a] basic right to be limited by an ordinary law." Bundesverfassungsgericht [BVerfG] [Federal Constitutional Court] Jan. 15, 1958, 7 Entscheidungen des Bundesverfassungsgerichts [BVerfGE] 198, 208–09 (Lüth Case), *available at* http://www. bundesverfassungsgericht.de/EN/Homepage/home_node.html. (trans. Donald Kommers/Russell Miller). *See also* Bundesverfassungsgericht [BVerfG] [Federal Constitutional Court] Dec. 18, 1968, 24 Entscheidungen des Bundesverfassungsgerichts [BVerfGE] 367, 389–90 (Hamburg Flood Control Case) ("Property could not be effectively secured if lawmakers were empowered to replace private property with something no longer deserving the label 'ownership.'") (trans. Donald Kommers/Russell Miller).

[158] BASIC LAW, *supra* note 27, art. 20(3).

[159] StPO, *supra* note 11, §§ 100(a)–(b).

[160] Judicial approval/warrant measures are prevalent throughout the Code of Criminal Procedure. *See id.* §§ 81(a) (2), 81(f)(1), 81(g)(3), 98, 100, 105.

[161] *See* Bundesamt für Justiz, Übersicht Telekommunikationsüberwachung (Maßnahmen nach § 100a StPO für 2013), Stand 28.07.2014, *available at* https://www.bundesjustizamt.de/DE/SharedDocs/Publikationen/ Justizstatistik/Uebersicht_TKUE_2013.pdf?__blob=publicationFile&v=3; Bundesamt für Justiz, Übersicht

law processes in Germany, but they provide a workable model for judicial review of the intelligence community's surveillance needs. More general measures and rules also anticipate secret or ex parte proceedings before the ordinary courts, especially where national security issues are involved.[162]

A second reason that the majority's decision stumbles is that it asserts that the exclusion of the judiciary from the realm of intelligence gathering—and the denial of all the liberty interests this involves—was part of the Basic Law's general tolerance for a limited and discrete set of illiberal measures that are meant to protect German democracy from the risk that undemocratic movements might take advantage of the Constitution's democratic rights to acquire the power needed to fatally undermine or abolish German democracy.[163] This is the Basic Law's "militant democracy," which is justified by the Nazis' cynical use of the Weimar era's democratic framework to seize power with the singular intention of bringing that democracy to an end.[164]

It is not obvious that this commitment must involve a departure from the rule of law of the kind achieved by the G10 Act's creation of the G10 Commission. Intrusion on telecommunications privacy without judicial supervision was not one of the measures the scholar Karl Loewenstein proposed in his seminal work that first theorized a militant democracy.[165] More important, Loewenstein—and the Basic Law—focus these exceptional measures on internal or domestic threats to the free democratic basic order, in particular, the fascist threat posed by the National Socialists.[166] This, after all, was the Nazi model to which they respond. Militant democracy says nothing about the state's authority to engage in international intelligence gathering as the BND does. The BND simply lacks the resonant—even if only implied—constitutional grounding enjoyed by Germany's *Verfassungsschutz* system. But it is precisely the BND's international telecommunications surveillance that has been the focus of this survey because it is conduct of that sort (when carried out by the NSA) that has stirred the greatest consternation in Germany. Even if the Basic Law's commitment to militant democracy could be read to include the elimination of judicial review from domestic

---

Telekommunikationsüberwachung (Maßnahmen nach § 100g StPO für 2013), Stand 28.07.2014, *available at* https://www.bundesjustizamt.de/DE/SharedDocs/Publikationen/Justizstatistik/Uebersicht_Verkehrsdaten_2013.pdf?__blob=publicationFile&v=3.

[162] *See* Gerichtsverfassungsgesetz [GVG] [Courts Constitution Act], May 9, 1972, BGBL. I at 1077, § 172, as amended (providing for the exclusion of the public from court proceedings, especially in the interest of state security). Norbert Juretzko, a former member of the BND staff, was convicted and sentenced to 11 months of probation in 2003 by the Munich Regional Court following a process that was closed to the public. *See* Andreas Förster, *Verratene und Verräter*, BERLINER ZEITUNG, Sept. 10, 2004, http://www.berliner-zeitung.de/archiv/norbert-juretzko-hat-fuenfzehn-jahre-lang-fuer-den-bnd-gearbeitet--nun-hat-er-ein-buch-geschrieben--es-soll-eine-abrechnung-sein-verratene-und-verraeter,10810590,10211582.html.

[163] Bundesverfassungsgericht [BVerfG] [Federal Constitutional Court] Dec. 15, 1970, 30 Entscheidungen des Bundesverfassungsgerichts [BVerfGE] 1, 19-20 (G10 Surveillance Case).

[164] *See* BASIC LAW, *supra* note 27, arts. 9(2), 18, and 21(2); *see also* Karl Loewenstein, *Militant Democracy and Fundamental Rights II*, 31 AM. POL. SCI. REV. 638 (1937); Karl Loewenstein, *Militant Democracy and Fundamental Rights I*, 31 AM. POL. SCI. REV. 417, 426-27 (1937).

[165] *See* Loewenstein, *supra* note 164.

[166] *See id.*; Bundesverfassungsgericht [BVerfG] [Federal Constitutional Court] Oct. 23, 1952, 2 Entscheidungen des Bundesverfassungsgerichts [BVerfGE] 1 (Socialist Reich Party Case).

intelligence gathering, it is not at all obvious that the concept of militant democracy extends to a state's foreign intelligence-gathering activities.

A final shortcoming in the majority's reasoning is the conclusion that the Basic Law's unamendable commitment to the rule of law had not been compromised by the 1968 amendments and the resulting statutory regime, including the G10 Commission's exclusive review of the BND's telecommunications surveillance.[167] The majority offered two reasons for this finding. First, the G10 Commission had the character of a court. Second, the G10 Commission's exercise of the judicial function as an "auxiliary agency of the parliament" was not a violation of the separation of powers.

The majority found that the G10 Commission constituted an adequate substitute process for the consideration of the legal implications of the intelligence community's telecommunications surveillance.[168] The majority explained that the Basic Law's fundamental commitment to the rule of law and the separation of powers merely required a form of review "that is, as a matter of substance and procedure, the equivalent of—and just as effective as—judicial review."[169] The majority found that the G10 Commission satisfied this standard because, in the same way as ordinary judges, the G10 Act made the commissioners "independent," and ensured that they were "not under instructions."[170] If this had been so reassuringly the case at the time of the Court's decision in 1970, then it is curious that the Parliament would have thought it necessary to explicitly add these precise guarantees to the G10 Act in a subsequent overhaul of the law.

In any case, the majority found that, in a number of other important ways, the G10 Commission provided a process that was equivalent—in the necessary ways—to the review provided by an ordinary court. The majority of the Court identified seven such necessary "judicial" elements: (1) the Commission would possess the necessary factual and legal bases and expertise to adequately review surveillance requests; (2) the commissioners were independent and not under instructions; (3) the commissioners' independence was partly secured by their fixed-term appointments; (4) the Commission had been given the full jurisdiction needed to review and supervise the conduct of all the institutions involved in telecommunications surveillance; (5) the Commission had a running, uninterrupted mandate; (6) the Commission was given access to all the materials produced by the intelligence community that might be relevant to its review; and (7) the Commission had been charged with conducting its review on the basis of legal standards and not political or policy interests.[171] The majority of the Court was satisfied that, with a view to these judicial qualities, the G10 Commission was of a "different form but had the equal effect" of a court.[172]

The majority also found that the G10 Commission's exercise of these judicial competences, despite its close nexus with the Parliament, was not an unacceptable departure from the constitutional mandate for the separation of powers. The majority explained that the separation of

---

[167] Bundesverfassungsgericht [BVerfG] [Federal Constitutional Court] Dec. 15, 1970, 30 Entscheidungen des Bundesverfassungsgerichts [BVerfGE] 1, 23, 27–28 (G10 Surveillance Case).

[168] *Id.* at 30–32.

[169] *Id.* at 23.

[170] *Id.*

[171] *Id.* at 23–24.

[172] *Id.* at 27.

powers was not meant to be strictly enforced.[173] Instead, the separation of powers allowed—in exceptional cases—the executive or legislative implementation of judicial powers.[174] In these exceptional cases, the majority reasoned, it is only necessary that the overall balance between separate branches—and the mutual limiting effect this balance creates—is not undermined.[175] The majority was satisfied that this was the case with respect to the G10 Commission because it could not exercise arbitrary and unchecked judicial power on behalf of the legislature. Instead, the G10 Commission had been given clear standards for the exercise of limited judicial authority in discrete circumstances justified by a clear and convincing need.[176] It is only important in these exceptional cases, the majority explained, that the legislature's exercise of judicial power not interfere with the judiciary's reserved core competence.[177]

I have already remarked that the majority decision in this case prompted the first dissenting opinions in the Court's history. This fact alone is a strong indication of the questionable character of the majority's reasoning.[178] The dissenting justices raised three critiques. First, relying on legislative history, they challenged the majority's characterization of the G10 Commission as a substitute judicial process. Second, the dissenters argued for a more robust vision of the rule of law than the one that was applied by the majority. Third, they rejected altogether the majority's reliance on the Basic Law's militant democracy as a justification of the G10 Commission.

The dissenting justices agreed with the majority that, should a state engage in secret intelligence gathering, it makes sense to exclude a role for the judiciary in the review of that conduct. It would not remain secret intelligence gathering, the dissenters acknowledged, if the courts' public processes were involved.[179] But, unlike the majority of the Court, the dissenting justices fully embraced the logic of this banal insight. The dissenting justices reasoned that, if judicial involvement would be perilously disruptive of intelligence-gathering activities, then the choice to have an auxiliary organ of the Parliament review the BND's telecommunications surveillance activities only makes sense if it *is not a court*. "If the provisions of the 1968 amendments are to make any sense at all," the dissenting justices reasoned, "then the so-called 'substitute system of review' must deviate significantly from the normal judicial function."[180]

---

[173] *Id.* at 27–28.

[174] *Id.*

[175] *Id.*

[176] *Id.*

[177] *Id.*

[178] There is a very strong culture of unanimous decision-making at the German Constitutional Court. And when the strong pressure for consensus breaks down, it is even rarer for the dissenting justices to express their doubts in published dissenting opinions. *See* KOMMERS & MILLER, *supra* note 131, at 28–29. The Court has published 2,137 Senate judgements since 1970, when the opportunity to offer dissenting opinions was first extended to the justices. Including the G10 Surveillance Act Case, in the 45 years since, there have been only 154 dissents. *See Entscheidungen mit oder ohne Sondervotum in der amtlichen Sammlung (BVerfGE)—Bände 30—134 (1971–2014)*, BUNDESVERFASSUNGSGERICHT http://www.bundesverfassungsgericht.de/DE/Verfahren/Jahresstatistiken/2014/gb2014/A-I-7.html.

[179] Bundesverfassungsgericht [BVerfG] [Federal Constitutional Court] Dec. 15, 1970, 30 Entscheidungen des Bundesverfassungsgerichts [BVerfGE] 1, 36 (Geller, J., dissenting) (G10 Surveillance Case).

[180] *Id.* at 34.

The dissenting justices argued that the drafting history of the 1968 amendments confirmed that the G10 Commission was not meant to be seen as a court. For example, judicial review of intelligence gathering had been included in earlier drafts of the amendments and related statutes.[181] It was dropped from the subsequent draft that would ultimately be enacted because the drafters feared that the scope and character of the aims of intelligence gathering would require decision-making that is not at all in line with the judicial function, which is oriented to testing facts against legal standards.[182] In their reading of the legislative history the dissenting justices found evidence that the drafters never meant for the G10 Commission to have judicial character. Instead, they quoted a member of the Parliament who called the proposed G10 Commission a "political solution," which involved the supervision of the responsible minister and replaced the judiciary with the review of the envisioned political bodies.[183] The parliamentarian concluded, "this is about a political and not a judicial decision."[184] The dissenting justices complained that the judicial mantle the majority bestowed on the G10 Commission was an act of judicial activism that served to rewrite the law as intended by the Parliament.[185]

The majority's conclusion that the G10 Commission constituted an adequate substitute for proper judicial review played fast and loose with the cherished constitutional guarantee that individuals, whose rights have been violated by an exercise of public authority, must have "recourse to the courts." This protection, specifically concerned with public authority, is secured by Article 19(4) of the Basic Law.[186] But it is a precise—and fundamental—expression of the more general constitutional assurance of the judiciary's integrity.[187] It is also an obvious and important facet of the rule of law and the separation of powers.[188] This means that the right to recourse to the courts is a central constitutional concern that has been described as the crown jewel of the rule of law.[189] The Constitutional Court has recognized it as such. Much of the Court's jurisprudence is concerned with defining the scope and limits of the protection; there are few examples of the outright exclusion of the judiciary as achieved by the G10 Act.[190] This is reproachful evidence of the truly exceptional character of the G10 Commission, which supplants the judiciary altogether.

---

[181] *Id.* at 35.

[182] *Id.* at 35–36.

[183] *Id.* at 37.

[184] *Id.*

[185] *Id.*

[186] BASIC LAW, *supra* note 27, art. 19(4). It is no defense to point out that Article 19(4) was amended to provide that "the second sentence of paragraph (2) of Article 10 shall not be affected by this paragraph." This clause—as part of the extended complex of constitutional provisions that facilitated the establishment of the G10 Commission—is doubtful under Article 79(3) for all the same reasons the amendments to Article 10 are impermissible.

[187] *See id.* art. 92.

[188] Helmuth Schulze-Fielitz, *Art. 19(4)*, *in* I GRUNDGESETZ-KOMMENTAR margin no. 35 (Horst Dreier ed., 3d ed. 2013); Eberhard Schmidt-Aßmann, *Art. 19(4)*, *in* MAUNZ/DÜRIG GRUNDGESETZ KOMMENTAR margin nos. 10, 15 (Roman Herzog et al. eds., 68th ed. 2010).

[189] "Art. 19(4) is a foundation stone of the *Rechtsstaat*." Schmidt-Aßmann, *supra* note 188, at margin no. 16 (quoting Richard Thoma) (trans. Russell Miller).

[190] *See* Schulze-Fielitz, *supra* note 188, at margin no. 53. *See also* Bundesverfassungsgericht [BVerfG] [Federal Constitutional Court] Feb. 20, 2001, 103 Entscheidungen des Bundesverfassungsgerichts [BVerfGE] 142

B. Contemporary Constitutional Privacy Protections

Ultimately the majority's position in the 1970 case depended on a pragmatic conclusion that conditioned all of its unconvincing reasoning. The majority was persuaded that the small intrusion on privacy that would result from the G10 Commission's enforcement of individuals' privacy interests in this context (as opposed to proper courts playing that role) amounted to only a minor sacrifice of liberty in exchange for the broad security benefits these measures would provide to everyone.[191] In this respect, the Court was following its well-established practice of resolving constitutional dilemmas with a carefully calibrated proportionality analysis.[192]

The majority's cost-benefit assessment, however, no longer holds up.

First, the majority significantly understated the harm done to individuals' telecommunications privacy interests by trusting surveillance oversight to the G10 Commission. The majority was satisfied that the G10 Commission, although not a court in the traditional sense, would provide the same level of scrutiny (and attending privacy protection) as a court.[193] But we now know that this is simply not the case. The G10 Commission does almost nothing to protect individuals' telecommunications privacy against intrusions by Germany's intelligence services. And the Commission literally does nothing at all when non-German telecommunications activities are involved. It turns out that the intrusion on telecommunications privacy taking place with the G10 Commission's approval is of a quantity that the Court's majority either cynically or naively refused to acknowledge.

Second, the majority's assessment of the harm done to individuals' telecommunications privacy interests by trusting surveillance oversight to the G10 Commission is no longer apposite because, in the intervening years, the role of telecommunications in our lives has changed dramatically. Especially in the age of ubiquitous computing and the so-called "Internet of things," telecommunications activities have become so omnipresent that they now touch nearly every part of life in a deeply revealing way. With access to telecommunications data (even if limited to metadata and not telecommunications content)—including our Internet usage, mobile phone calls, SMS communications, and emails—intelligence services are able to paint a profoundly intimate portrait of each of us. Whatever analog telecommunications privacy interests the majority had in mind when it ruled on the amendments to Article 10 of the Basic Law, they are nothing like the privacy interests at stake in the digital-wireless era of pervasive telecommunication. The intrusion on privacy now taking place with the G10 Commission's approval is of a quality that the Court's majority in 1970 likely could not have imagined.

(Apartment Search Case); Bundesverfassungsgericht [BVerfG] [Federal Constitutional Court] May 23, 2006, 116 Entscheidungen des Bundesverfassungsgerichts [BVerfGE] 1 (Bankruptcy Administrator Case).

[191] When discussing the need to balance the interests involved, the majority of the Court referred to the balancing necessitated by the proportionality principle. See Bundesverfassungsgericht [BVerfG] [Federal Constitutional Court] Dec. 15, 1970, 30 Entscheidungen des Bundesverfassungsgerichts [BVerfGE] 1, 20–21 (G10 Surveillance Case).

[192] See KOMMERS & MILLER, supra note 131, at 67.

[193] See Bundesverfassungsgericht [BVerfG] [Federal Constitutional Court] Dec. 15, 1970, 30 Entscheidungen des Bundesverfassungsgerichts [BVerfGE] 1 (G10 Surveillance Case).

The German Constitutional Court has been a pioneer in recognizing, and protecting against, the significant privacy risks posed by the ascendance of digital computing and communications. This awareness led the Court to recognize a right to "informational self-determination" in the 1983 *Census Act Case*.[194] The Court offered qualified approval of public authorities' collection of revealing census data. But with remarkable foresight the Court nevertheless expressed grave concern. The Court concluded that:

> [t]he individual's decisional authority [regarding personal information] needs special protection in view of the present and prospective conditions of automatic data processing [because] ... the technical means of storing highly personal information about particular persons today are practically unlimited, and information can be retrieved in a matter of seconds with the aid of automatic data processing, irrespective of distance. Furthermore, such information can be joined to other data collections—to produce a partial or virtually complete personality profile, with the person concerned having insufficient means of controlling either its veracity or its use. The possibilities of acquiring information and exerting influence have increased to a degree hitherto unknown ....[195]

The Court has deepened this jurisprudence as computer and telecommunications usage have become ever-more prevalent and revealing. The Court has especially advanced this distinct privacy protection against German security and counter-terrorism initiatives. In 2006, citing the right to informational self-determination, the Constitutional Court invalidated a state data-mining initiative that permitted the local police to filter information out of various electronic sources, both public and private, in an effort to identify suspected terrorists.[196] The Court found that collection of the most basic personal information (name, address, date and place of birth) constituted an intrusion upon protected privacy, especially if that information could be combined with other forms of data, including religious practices, nationality, family status, and program of study at one's university.[197] All of this, the Court worried, could be detrimental to personal privacy.[198]

The *Online Computer Surveillance Case*, decided in 2008, extended this privacy protection to include a "right to the confidentiality and integrity of information-technology systems."[199] The Court found a state law authorizing covert computer infiltration to be a constitutional violation because "[t]oday's personal computers can be used for a wide variety of purposes, some for the comprehensive collection and storage of highly personal information ... corresponding to the enormous rise in the importance of personal computers for the development

---

[194] Bundesverfassungsgericht [BVerfG] [Federal Constitutional Court] Dec. 15, 1983, 65 Entscheidungen des Bundesverfassungsgerichts [BVerfGE] 1 (Census Act Case).

[195] *Id.* at 41–42.

[196] Bundesverfassungsgericht [BVerfG] [Federal Constitutional Court] Apr. 4, 2006, 115 Entscheidungen des Bundesverfassungsgerichts [BVerfGE] 320 (Data Mining Case).

[197] *Id.* at 349.

[198] *Id.*

[199] Bundesverfassungsgericht [BVerfG] [Federal Constitutional Court] Feb. 27, 2008, 120 Entscheidungen des Bundesverfassungsgerichts [BVerfGE] 274 (Online Computer Surveillance Case).

of the human personality."[200] Access to that information, the Court explained, "facilitates insight into significant parts of the life of a person or indeed provides a revealing picture of his or her personality."[201] Similar concerns led the Court, in 2010, to find Germany's law implementing the European Data Retention Directive to be constitutionally invalid.[202] The Court worried that the telecommunications metadata that the law ordered companies to retain—including phone numbers, dates, times, and locations—could be used to sketch a deeply personal and revealing portrait of an individual's political associations, personal preferences, inclinations, and weaknesses.[203]

The Constitutional Court has recognized that telecommunications activities now have qualitatively different and utterly more meaningful privacy implications than they did in 1970 when the Court upheld the G10 Commission's non-judicial oversight of the intelligence community's telecommunications surveillance. Now, after decades of practice, we have clear evidence of the G10 Commission's permissive posture toward surveillance that the Court lacked—and did not dare to anticipate—when it considered the challenges to the 1968 constitutional amendments and the resulting G10 Act. These developments and insights ought to compel the Court to reconsider the balancing analysis it undertook when ruling on the G10 Commission's constitutionality. It is difficult to see how the Court could reach the same deferential result today.

C. Conclusion

Wrong when it was decided, the German Constitutional Court's 1970 decision is dangerously misaligned with the present-day German intelligence community's voracious appetite for surveillance and, more generally, the radically evolved nature of telecommunications privacy. The Court should reconsider the issue and conclude that substituting the G10 Commission's oversight of telecommunications surveillance for the review of the ordinary courts amounts to a violation of the Basic Law's enduring commitment to the rule of law, including the separation of powers and the right to recourse to the courts. The 1968 emergency constitutional amendments are unconstitutional and should be found to be violations of Article 79(3) of the Basic Law.

IV. RESUMÉ

Germany's flawed homegrown regime for intelligence oversight, with the G10 Commission at its center, does not square with persistent German demands that America's NSA should be placed under stricter scrutiny. The G10 Commission is no more effective than the United States' Foreign Intelligence Surveillance Court at protecting telecommunications privacy. Operating in the interstices between these traditional frameworks for accountability and

---

[200] *Id.* at 311.

[201] *Id.* at 314.

[202] Bundesverfassungsgericht [BVerfG] [Federal Constitutional Court] Mar. 2, 2010, 125 Entscheidungen des Bundesverfassungsgerichts [BVerfGE] 260 (Data Stockpiling Case).

[203] *Id.* at 317–19.

legitimacy, and hobbled by structural deficiencies, the G10 Commission has been free to authorize virtually all the surveillance the German intelligence community desires. Worse, the G10 Commission has a less stable constitutional basis than the American oversight regime. Especially in light of the dramatic changes in technology and the law of privacy, the German Constitutional Court should revisit its outdated conclusion that the G10 Commission is constitutional.

11

Intelligence Powers and Accountability in the U.K.

Jon Moran and Clive Walker

I. INTRODUCTION

The issue of intelligence accountability is crucial for democracy. Recent revelations in both the U.K. and United States have shown that surveillance programs have become widespread, and, according to critics, out of control. One of the key principles of a free civil society at the individual and group level is freedom from unjustifiable monitoring. If state agencies can intrude into the lives of people and organizations in constant and disproportionate ways, then democracy is undermined. On the other hand, surveillance is crucial to successful law enforcement in late modern societies. The range of technologies that can be used by offenders to plan, commit, and then conceal offenses is evident. These points apply to the problem of terrorism in a particularly acute way.

One "solution" to the tension between civil liberty and surveillance in theory rests on proper accountability mechanisms. This chapter examines intelligence accountability in the U.K., concentrating on surveillance accountability in the main jurisdiction, England and Wales.[1] We concentrate on surveillance as this is the key area for accountability in the U.K. context because intelligence agencies in the U.K. do not have formal powers of investigation, of detention, or of covert action (for example, in the form of targeted assassination), that other intelligence agencies covered in this volume have. Inappropriate surveillance is at the core of most of the debates about the nature of legal accountability in the U.K. Until the

---

[1] Scotland and Northern Ireland are separate legal jurisdictions, although they share many of the same laws. *See* Police and Criminal Evidence (Northern Ireland) Order 1989, S.I. 1989/1341; Regulation of Investigatory Powers (Scotland) Act, 2000, (A.S.P. 11).

late twentieth century, extraordinarily, the establishment and objectives of the intelligence agencies and many surveillance techniques were not even established or defined in law.

Therefore, the first section of this chapter examines the historical context of surveillance and the law, because this has conditioned the debates in the U.K. today. Second, now that surveillance techniques have been enshrined in law, the chapter asks whether the law is merely a rubber stamp, which confirms the legality of disproportionate state powers, or whether instead it imposes effective restraints. Third, the chapter assesses how the law has developed as surveillance techniques have themselves developed. We claim that in the U.K., as compared to the United States, accountability has been limited and "bureaucratic" in the sense that an impoverished application of legal formality rather than more substantive and principled oversight has been the extent of the concession to legal accountability to date. Although important advances have been made in surveillance accountability, they have created an organizational system that which is inflexible and partial, and lacks dynamism. The result is that campaigns against surveillance became prominent, sparked not just by counterterrorism measures but also by more prevalent techniques, such as CCTV and DNA sampling.[2] Indeed, surveillance had become so contentious that the Coalition government elected in 2010 promoted the Protection of Freedoms Act 2012, so as to reduce and better control some of the surveillance powers of the state.

II. SURVEILLANCE AND ACCOUNTABILITY: THE HISTORICAL CONTEXT

The British state has long practiced surveillance. Spies and informers had an important role in protecting the state in England in the sixteenth century. The regime of Queen Elizabeth the First engaged in a struggle for national security against the external threat from Spain, and the internal threat from Catholic rebels; effective use of spying was an integral part of its success. Sir Francis Walsingham, secretary to Queen Elizabeth, presided over a network of spies and covert agents pretending to be Catholic agitators.[3] Intelligence was gained through blackmail, torture, and entrapment, but also through the opening of letters, which took place throughout Europe under the remit of vague prerogative powers.[4]

The "Glorious Revolution" of 1688, followed by the Bill of Rights 1689 that curtailed prerogative powers, accompanied by ideas of liberty and later Enlightenment, placed a limit

---

[2] See generally INFORMATION COMMISSIONER, A REPORT ON THE SURVEILLANCE SOCIETY (2006); HOUSE OF COMMONS HOME AFFAIRS COMMITTEE, A SURVEILLANCE SOCIETY?, 2007–2008, H.C. 58, and GOVERNMENT REPLY, 2008, Cm. 7449; HOUSE OF LORDS SELECT COMMITTEE ON THE CONSTITUTION, SURVEILLANCE: CITIZENS AND THE STATE, 2008–2009, H.L. 18, and GOVERNMENT RESPONSE, 2009, Cm. 7616.

[3] "Spies" refer to state officers, whereas "covert agents" were nonstate agents who infiltrated suspect groups. This terminology departs from that used elsewhere in the book mainly in connection with U.S. practices whereby "clandestine" means activities conducted in secret, and "covert" means activities meant to be both secret and deniable. The term "covert" continues in contemporary U.K. practice to refer (primarily but not exclusively) to nonstate agents (see below).

[4] See, e.g., ALAN HAYNES, INTRODUCTION THE ELIZABETHAN SECRET SERVICES (2009); STEPHEN ALFORD, THE WATCHERS: A SECRET HISTORY OF THE REIGN OF ELIZABETH I 19, 145 (2012); Safety of the Queen, etc. Act 1584, 27 Eliz. 1, c. 1 (Eng.).

on the emergence of a security state and instilled a supposed mistrust of the power of state security. England set itself apart from Europe, in particular after the French Revolution, and expressed distaste not only for spies but for any sort of regular police force with statutory powers: "In England the idea of a uniformed body of policemen patrolling the streets to prevent crime and disorder was anathema. Such a force smacked of the absolutism of continental states."[5]

Instead of secret surveillance and secret police, the English state was said to rely on a strict penal code.[6] However, this often standard narrative of English liberty and security hides some tensions. Following the French Revolution, Prime Minister William Pitt (the Younger), in the name of countering subversion, deployed militia regiments and, using surveillance by government agents and widely framed laws of sedition, crushed domestic agitators for parliamentary reform (such as Thomas Paine), a period known as the "terror."[7] As Vic Gattrell tells us, "[i]n inflammatory times juries were packed, spies employed, show trials arranged, aged radicals pilloried, men and women easily hanged, traitors decapitated . . . liberties, rule of law, and public opinion notwithstanding."[8] Networks of spies were also important abroad, especially during the existential struggle against Napoleon's Revolutionary forces.[9]

Domestic political dissent returned to England in the period after Napoleon had been defeated: "[D]uring the thirty or so years following the victory of Waterloo and the end of the [Napoleonic] wars . . . popular politics meant radicals organising mass meetings, mass demonstrations and petitions, seriously threatening open constitutional confrontation."[10] However violence did not often result. Emsley says this was due to the culture of moderation in England,[11] though some bursts of state violence and the effective employment of informers also played a role. In combating the Luddites and Chartist movements in the first half of the nineteenth century, local authorities in England used the surveillance services of informers and agent provocateurs. Their evidence was used in courtrooms in which the rules of evidence and procedures were then further warped to secure convictions.[12]

Already we have a flavor of some of the controversy about surveillance and the laws set out here, even before the advance of technology: whether there should be surveillance at all by state authorities, whether state authorities should use informers, and whether surveillance should extend to controversial uses of the law (such as entrapment). Indeed, concerns about the threat

---

[5] CLIVE EMSLEY, CRIME AND SOCIETY IN ENGLAND 1750–1900, at 227 (2010). This distaste did not extend to policing in Ireland, even in more modern times. *See* Clive Walker, *Police and Community in Northern Ireland*, 41 N. IR. LEGAL Q. 105 (1999).

[6] *See generally* EDWARD P. THOMPSON, WHIGS AND HUNTERS (1975); DOUGLAS HAY ET AL., ALBION'S FATAL TREE: CRIME AND SOCIETY IN EIGHTEENTH-CENTURY ENGLAND 18, 24 (1976).

[7] *See generally* EDWARD ROYLE, REVOLUTIONARY BRITANNIA? (2000); JOHN BARRELL, THE SPIRIT OF DESPOTISM: INVASIONS OF PRIVACY IN THE 1790S 4 (2006); BOYD HILTON, A MAD, BAD AND DANGEROUS PEOPLE? 65 (2007).

[8] VIC GATTRELL, THE HANGING TREE: EXECUTION AND THE ENGLISH PEOPLE, 1770–1868 531 (1996).

[9] For factual accounts, *see* ELIZABETH SPARROW, SECRET SERVICE: BRITISH AGENTS IN FRANCE, 1792–1815 (1999); MARK URBAN, THE MAN WHO BROKE NAPOLEON'S CODES (2001).

[10] CLIVE EMSLEY, THE ENGLISH AND VIOLENCE SINCE 1750 121 (2005).

[11] *Id.* at 122.

[12] Catherine Lewis, *Samuel Holbery: Chartist Conspirator or Victim of a State Conspiracy?*, in CRIMES AND MISDEMEANOURS 3/1109 (2009). *See also* the Peace Preservation Act, 1814, 54, Geo. 3, c. 131 (U.K.).

to liberty, along with a complex political context, meant that even after the formation of the uniformed Metropolitan Police in 1829 there remained a reluctance to employ plainclothes detectives as this raised the specter of "Continental" undercover spies, "and the recollection of the spies and secret agents employed against English Jacobins and Regency Radicals remained painful."[13]

It took until the latter nineteenth/early twentieth century for a permanent architecture of surveillance to be erected by the British state. The violent activities of Irish nationalists met a response in 1883 with the development of a "surveillance police," the Irish Special Branch of the Metropolitan Police, which later focused on the rise of anarchism, reflected in 1888 in its broader title of "Special Branch."[14] Their main success was in recruiting informants, which fueled paranoia in anarchist networks. Indeed, "a large proportion of the most incendiary figures in the anarchist movement" were in fact Branch informants, leading one Chief Inspector to argue that the informer "is very apt to drift into an agent provocateur in his anxiety to secure a conviction."[15] In the (in)famous Walsall case, members of an anarchist bomb-making network were convicted under the Explosives Act 1883. That group had been encouraged into bomb-making by Auguste Coulon, a Special Branch informer; in addition, Inspector William Melville, the Special Branch officer in charge of the case who had a close relationship with Coulon, was excused by the judge from having to answer defense questions on this relationship.[16]

The specter of German spies in the early twentieth century prompted further momentous institutional formations. In 1909 the Secret Service Bureau was established to gain intelligence on German espionage activity in the U.K.[17] It was at this time a tiny organization and would not develop into the major organizations, the Security Service (MI5) and the Secret Intelligence Service (MI6), until the 1920s and 1930s. Following the 1917 Russian Revolution, both Special Branch and MI5 focused on communism. MI5 mounted close surveillance of the Communist Party of Great Britain's leadership,[18] but "[t]he remarkable feature of the state response to communism was its relative informality so far as the student of law is concerned."[19] This absence of legal coverage for surveillance activities and the use of paid informants did not prevent prosecutions of communists for sedition or other offenses.[20]

---

[13] EMSLEY, *supra* note 5, at 248.
[14] *See generally* TONY BUNYAN, THE HISTORY AND PRACTICE OF THE POLITICAL POLICE IN BRITAIN (1977); BERNARD PORTER, THE ORIGINS OF THE VIGILANT STATE (1991); RUPERT ALLASON, THE BRANCH: A HISTORY OF THE METROPOLITAN POLICE SPECIAL BRANCH 1883–1983 (1983); PAUL McMAHON, BRITISH SPIES AND IRISH REBELS: BRITISH INTELLIGENCE AND IRELAND, 1916–1945 7 (2008).
[15] ALEX BUTTERWORTH, THE WORLD THAT NEVER WAS: A TRUE STORY OF DREAMERS, SCHEMERS, ANARCHISTS AND SECRET AGENTS 320 (2011); JOHN LITTLECHILD, THE REMINISCENCES OF CHIEF INSPECTOR LITTLECHILD 96 (1894).
[16] BUTTERWORTH, *supra* note 15, at 292–99. *See further* http://cms.walsall.gov.uk/the_walsall_anarchist_bomb_plot.pdf (last visited July 31, 2015).
[17] *See generally* CHRISTOPHER ANDREW, DEFEND THE REALM: THE AUTHORIZED HISTORY OF MI5 3 (2009); KEITH JEFFERY, MI6: THE HISTORY OF THE SECRET INTELLIGENCE SERVICE 1909–1949 3 (2010).
[18] John Callahan & Mark Phythian, *State Surveillance of the CPGB Leadership: 1920s–1950s,* 69 LABOUR HIST. REV. 19 (2004).
[19] KEITH EWING & CONOR GEARTY, THE STRUGGLE FOR CIVIL LIBERTIES: POLITICAL FREEDOM AND THE RULE OF LAW IN BRITAIN 1914–1945 94 (2000).
[20] *Id.* at 94–95, 105–06, 112–18.

Subsequently, the Second World War fueled the expansion of both civilian and military intelligence, with the latter spawning what would become the Government Communications Headquarters (GCHQ) to handle the technological innovations of signals and communications surveillance in the post-1945 period.[21]

The legal foundations for these new organizations were much sparser. State intelligence gathering became important both within the U.K. and in imperial possessions,[22] but statutory law pertaining to security was almost entirely absent, apart from that passed during wartime emergencies. For example, it took until after World War I for the Official Secrets Act of 1920 to be enacted which, for example, permitted the government to inspect all overseas cables and telegrams.[23] It was also believed that there was legislation that implicitly allowed the interception of mail from as early as 1710, and of telegraph via the Telegraph Acts of 1863 and later.[24] But Winston Churchill, as Home Secretary before the First World War, was advised that the legislation required a separate warrant for each item of mail; he then introduced *general* warrants allowing the opening of all of a person's mail but without any parliamentary scrutiny.[25] With regard to telephone tapping, "since no offence of interference with telephone messages existed before 1985, it was conducted up to 1937 without even the authorization of a warrant," and tapping was only officially acknowledged in 1952.[26] Similarly, the surveillance of both domestic and foreign communications was implemented up to the 1970s without any debate or statutory authorization.[27]

By the end of the Second World War, Prime Minister Winston Churchill had become concerned over the wartime expansion of security powers, and instituted a panel (meeting *in camera*) that would review the blacklisting of communists and others, but MI5 refused to bring any cases before the panel and the system continued as before.[28] In 1951, the Cabinet Secretary recommended that the prime minister's role in overseeing MI5 should be reduced, and the head of MI5 made responsible to the Home Secretary, who then should not require full detail of MI5's operations.[29] Although this change was politically expedient as it allowed

---

[21] *See generally* RICHARD ALDRICH, GCHQ: THE UNCENSORED STORY OF BRITAIN'S MOST SECRET INTELLIGENCE AGENCY (2010).

[22] *See generally* CALDER WALTON, EMPIRE OF SECRETS: BRITISH INTELLIGENCE, THE COLD WAR AND THE TWILIGHT OF EMPIRE (2013); MARTIN THOMAS, EMPIRES OF INTELLIGENCE: SECURITY SERVICES AND COLONIAL DISORDER AFTER 1914 (2007).

[23] LAURENCE LUSTGARTEN & IAN LEIGH, IN FROM THE COLD: NATIONAL SECURITY AND PARLIAMENTARY DEMOCRACY 65 (1994). *See previously* Defence of the Realm Consolidated Regulations 1914, rr.22b, 54, which were described as powers lost at the Armistice that had been "of the greatest possible value and importance": 135 PARL. DEB., H.C. (5th ser.) (1920) 1539 per Sir Gordon Hewart.

[24] *See, e.g.,* REPORT OF THE COMMITTEE OF PRIVY COUNCILLORS APPOINTED TO INQUIRE INTO THE INTERCEPTION OF COMMUNICATIONS, 1957, Cm. 283; Malone v. United Kingdom, App. No. 8691/79, Ser A 82 24 et seq. (1984).

[25] DAVID STAFFORD, CHURCHILL AND SECRET SERVICE 7 (1997).

[26] LUSTGARTEN & LEIGH, *supra* note 23, at 53.

[27] ALDRICH, *supra* note 21, at 343–44.

[28] STAFFORD *supra* note 25, at 257–58.

[29] LUSTGARTEN & LEIGH, *supra* note 23, at 375; *See also* Daniel Lomas, "... *the Defence of the Realm and Nothing Else": Sir Findlater Stewart, Labour Ministers and the Security Service, in* 30 INTELLIGENCE & NAT'L SEC. 793 (2015).

greater deniability, it equally gave MI5 an even wider degree of unaccountability, especially as the organization was not then recognized in law. Thus, the development of MI5 and MI6 (1909) and the Government Code and Cipher School (1919) had taken place without any law setting out the surveillance powers of the agencies. The activities of GCCS and its successor GCHQ were not even revealed to the public until the 1970s.[30] MI5's existence was not legally acknowledged until the Security Service Act of 1989, with MI6 and GCHQ being formally constituted by the Intelligence Services Act 1994.

The limited oversight and accountability of intelligence and surveillance are exemplified by the revelation that the domestic security service, MI5, had placed listening devices in the Prime Minister's offices during the period 1963–1977, with the exception of a few months after Harold Macmillan left office in 1963, probably without authorization but without resulting in any public announcement or inquiry.[31] "In all, the equipment monitored the most sensitive areas of Downing Street for around 15 years. It was finally removed on the orders of James Callaghan in 1977, the year after he took office."[32] Christopher Andrew, the official historian of MI5, wished to have this revealed in his authorized history but was blocked.[33] Another example of sensitive, unregulated surveillance concerned the interception of the communications of members of Parliament, which for many years was handled under the aegis of a Prime Ministerial edict.[34]

The use of informants also remained largely unregulated. Any regulatory development took place "on the ground," and as Sir Desmond de Silva QC's report into the murder of Northern Irish solicitor Patrick Finucane made clear, "there was a wilful and abject failure by successive governments to provide the clear policy and legal framework necessary for agent-handling operations to take place effectively and within the law."[35]

In sum, before the last decade or so, the surveillance powers of the state had rarely been enshrined in law. Accountability was, if anything, even less developed. The prevailing practices rested on the idea that the best measure for accountability came via control from elected politicians, as they had access to a full range of information, were attuned to political sensitivities, and were accountable to judges. These arguments are highly contestable,[36] and have now been challenged in the report of David Anderson, the U.K.'s Independent Reviewer of Terrorism Legislation, on investigatory powers.[37] Certainly, the U.K. experienced no

---

[30] ALDRICH, *supra* note 21, at 354.

[31] *See* Jon Moran, *Conspiracy and Contemporary History: Revisiting MI5 and the Wilson Plot[s]*, 13 J. INTELLIGENCE HIST. 161, 169 (2014).

[32] Jason Lewis & Tom Harper, *Revealed: How MI5 Bugged 10 Downing Street, the Cabinet and at Least Five Prime Ministers for 15 YEARS*, DAILY MAIL (Apr. 18, 2010, 9:11 EST), http://www.dailymail.co.uk/news/article-1266837/Revealed-How-MI5-bugged-10-Downing-Street-Cabinet-Prime-Ministers-15-YEARS.html.

[33] *Id.*

[34] *See* Andrew Defty et al., *Tapping the Telephones of Members of Parliament: The "Wilson Doctrine" and Parliamentary Privilege*, in 29 INTELLIGENCE & NAT'L SEC. 675 (2014).

[35] Rt Hon Sir Desmond de Silva, *The Report of the Patrick Finucane Review*, 2012, H.C. 802-I, at 7. *See generally* Kingsley Hyland & Clive Walker, *Undercover Policing and Underwhelming Laws*, 2014 CRIM. L. REV. 555.

[36] *See* Clive Walker, *The Threat of Terrorism and the Fate of Control Orders*, PUB. L. 4 (2010) and *The Judicialisation of Intelligence in Legal Process*, PUB. L. 4, 13–17 (2010).

[37] *See* DAVID ANDERSON, A QUESTION OF TRUST (2015).

intelligence scandals akin to the U.S. COINTELPRO scandal or the use by the Nixon White House of intelligence operatives to bug opponents.[38] But this was not due to the effectiveness of accountability. Rather it was because of the political classes' acceptance of its limited accountability, lower tolerance of investigative journalism and whistle-blowers,[39] and perhaps a stronger tradition of trust in governmental power and the worthiness of public officials.

It was not until the 1980s and 1990s that the use of general and intrusive surveillance techniques began to be covered by a formal legal framework via the agency legislation mentioned above, as well as the Interception of Communications Act 1985, the Police Act 1997, and the Regulation of Investigatory Powers Act 2000.[40] However, these changes were driven more by the deficiencies in legality than those in accountability, and so did not seek to alter contemporary practices. The shortcomings had been pointed out in adverse decisions before the European Court of Human Rights, whereby it was often a lack of "accordance with the law" that was the stumbling block rather than any substantive failure to accord sufficient respect for rights such as privacy.[41] Anticipation of a stream of further challenges before the U.K. courts, as enabled by the Human Rights Act 1998, was a major reason for the passage of the most comprehensive statutory reform, the Regulation of Investigatory Powers Act 2000.[42]

The next sections analyze the current structures for surveillance accountability in the U.K. The development of these structures is not only recent but still controversial, especially because of counterterrorism policies. In reflecting on these developments, it is accepted that "[the] trend towards legalism in the intelligence field is desirable: law is a necessary condition for constitutionalism."[43] However, there are risks inherent in simplistically merging intelligence and evidence.[44] The safeguards of oversight and accountability should be carefully applied to ensure fairness and continued effectiveness. Subsequently, this chapter sets

---

[38] *See* FINAL REPORT OF THE SELECT COMMITTEE TO STUDY GOVERNMENTAL OPERATIONS WITH RESPECT TO INTELLIGENCE ACTIVITIES, S. REP. NO. 94-755 (1976); FRED EMERY, WATERGATE (1994).

[39] The fate of Peter Wright (author of SPYCATCHER [1987]) contrasts with those of Carl Bernstein and Bob Woodward, ALL THE PRESIDENT'S MEN (1974), or even Daniel Ellsberg and Anthony Russo. *See* New York Times Co. v. United States, 403 U.S. 713 (1971). *See further* Clive Walker, *Investigative Journalism and Counter-Terrorism Laws Post-9/11*, NOTRE DAME JOURNAL OF LAW, ETHICS & PUBLIC POLICY (forthcoming).

[40] *See* Ian Leigh, *Accountability of Security and Intelligence in the United Kingdom, in* WHO'S WATCHING THE SPIES? ESTABLISHING INTELLIGENCE SERVICE ACCOUNTABILITY (Hans Born et al. eds., 2005).

[41] Malone, *supra* note 24, ¶ 8; *see also* Iain Cameron, *Beyond the Nation State; The Influence of the European Court of Human Rights on Intelligence Accountability in the United States, in* WHO'S WATCHING THE SPIES, *supra* note 40.

[42] Karen Bullock & Paul Johnson, *The Impact of the Human Rights Act 1998 on Policing in England and Wales*, 52 BRIT. J. CRIMINOLOGY 630, 634–35 (2012); Yaman Akdeniz et al., *Regulation of Investigatory Powers Act 2000 (1): BigBrother.gov.uk: State Surveillance in the Age of Information and Rights*, CRIM. L. REV. 73, 74 (2001).

[43] Clive Walker, *Keeping Control of Terrorists without Losing Control of Constitutionalism*, 59 STAN L. REV. 1395, 1456 (2007).

[44] *See generally* Clive Walker, *Intelligence and Anti-terrorism Legislation*, 44 CRIME, L. & SOC. CHANGE 390 (2005); Clive Walker, *Neighbor Terrorism and the All-Risks Policing of Terrorism*, 3 J. NAT'L SEC. L. & POL'Y 121, 130 (2009).

out the existing intelligence and surveillance powers of the British state, before proceeding to an analysis of accountability and oversight issues.

III. THE CONSTITUTION OF THE INTELLIGENCE AGENCIES

The Regulation of Investigatory Powers Act 2000 (RIPA 2000) deals with the authorization and oversight of the dynamic activities of agencies that engage in surveillance. Other legislation covers the constitution of such agencies, and some of it incidentally grants further surveillance powers.

The Security Services Act 1989, section 1, sets out the duties of MI5, which are stated to comprise:

> (2) . . . the protection of national security and, in particular, its protection against threats from espionage, terrorism and sabotage, from the activities of agents of foreign powers and from actions intended to overthrow or undermine parliamentary democracy by political, industrial or violent means. (3) It shall also be the function of the Service to safeguard the economic well-being of the United Kingdom against threats posed by the actions or intentions of persons outside the British Islands. (4) It shall also be the function of the Service to act in support of the activities of police forces and other law enforcement agencies in the prevention and detection of serious crime.[45]

The duties of MI6 under the Intelligence Services Act 1994, section 1, are:

> [T]o obtain and provide information relating to the actions or intentions of persons outside the British Islands; and to perform other tasks relating to the actions or intentions of such persons. The functions of the Intelligence Service shall be exercisable only in the interests of national security, with particular reference to the defence and foreign policies of Her Majesty's Government in the United Kingdom; or in the interests of the economic well-being of the United Kingdom; or in support of the prevention or detection of serious crime.

Under section 3 of the same Act, the functions of GCHQ are:

> [T]o monitor or interfere with electromagnetic, acoustic and other emissions and any equipment producing such emissions and to obtain and provide information derived from or related to such emissions or equipment and from encrypted material, but only in the interests of national security, with particular reference to the United Kingdom Government's defence and foreign policies, or in the interests of the UK's economic

---

[45] A precise definition of economic well-being is resisted. *See* INTELLIGENCE AND SECURITY COMMITTEE, ANNUAL REPORT, 2005–2006, Cm. 6864, ¶ 97. But the meaning is affected by Directive 97/66/EC, which requires a link to national security if personal data is affected.

well-being in relation to the actions or intentions of persons outside the British Islands, or in support of the prevention or detection of serious crime; and . . . to provide advice and assistance about languages (including technical terminology) and cryptography (and other such matters) to the armed services, the government and other organisations as required.

IV. CONTEMPORARY SURVEILLANCE LAWS
A. Surveillance Powers in Action

The current legal framework for surveillance, which primarily applies to domestic activities but also contains some measures for overseas work, is set out primarily in the Police Act 1997 and the RIPA 2000. There are at least five types of surveillance that state agents are permitted to employ. The use of these five techniques is governed by tests along the following lines: (1) is the authorization necessary in the interests of national security; for the purpose of preventing or detecting crime or of preventing disorder; in the interests of the economic well-being of the United Kingdom, in the interests of public safety, or for the purpose of protecting public health; (2) can the information be gathered another, less intrusive way; (3) is the authorization proportionate to the aim?[46]

1. Directed Surveillance

Surveillance in a public place (within the U.K.) for the purposes of a specific investigation is "directed surveillance" under RIPA 2000, section 26. The conditions are as follows: it is "covert" (meaning that it is carried out in a way that is calculated to ensure that the subject is unaware),[47] but not intrusive (defined below), surveillance; it is conducted for the purposes of a specific investigation or operation; it is likely to result in the obtaining of private information about a person (whether or not one specifically identified for the purposes of the investigation or operation); it is conducted otherwise than by way of an immediate response to events or in circumstances the nature of which is such that it would not be reasonably practicable to engage in less intrusive surveillance activity. Authorization is by a "designated person" within the authorities set out in section 28 and Schedule 1 of RIPA 2000 (most likely a police inspector or General Duties 3 level security officer).[48]

2. Intrusive Surveillance

Surveillance becomes "intrusive" under RIPA 2000, section 26, if conducted in relation to activities in residential premises or a private vehicle within the U.K. Authorization under section 32 for this more serious interference with privacy requires either the assent of a police Chief Constable or the Secretary of State (for the security agencies),

---

[46] For a detailed discussion, *see* SIMON MCKAY, COVERT POLICING: LAW AND PRACTICE 5 (2014).

[47] Regulation of Investigatory Powers § 26(9).

[48] *See* Regulation of Investigatory Powers (Prescription of Offices, Ranks and Positions) Order 2000, S.I. 2000/2417 (as amended).

and any police authorization must be also notified under section 35 to a Surveillance Commissioner (see below) who must also give approval. If it involves the entry into private premises or a vehicle, this is covered by the Police Act 1997, Part III (for the police), and the Intelligence Services Act 1994 (for the security and intelligence services) and requires the further approval of the Secretary of State (Home Office, Foreign Office, or Minister of Defence).

3. Undercover Informants

When either plainclothes police or security officers or private individuals tasked by the police or security services use a relationship with a private person to obtain information, these are known under RIPA 2000, section 26(8) as "Covert Human Intelligence Sources" (CHIS). An individual is a CHIS if (1) he or she establishes or maintains a personal or other relationship with a person for the covert purpose of facilitating the actions specified in (2) or (3); namely, (2) he or she covertly uses such a relationship to obtain information or to provide access to any information to another person; or (3) he or she covertly discloses information obtained by the use of such a relationship or as a consequence of the existence of such a relationship. The use of any CHIS must be authorized under RIPA 2000, section 29 by a senior officer in the police, armed services, or intelligence services or a senior local government officer. The High Court has concluded that interferences by a CHIS with the right to privacy, even to the extent of sexual intercourse, can be authorized but not to the extent that they amount to degrading treatment.[49] Long-term infiltrations (roughly 12 months) must be thereafter approved by a Surveillance Commissioner.[50]

4. Collection of Communications Data

The data about the identity of callers, websites visited, email addresses, and other traffic data, but not the content of communications[51] can be acquired and disclosed under RIPA 2000, sections 21 and 22. To aid the capture of data, communications service providers are required to retain it for a period specified up to 12 months under the Data Retention and Investigatory Powers Act 2014.[52] The collection requires the authorization (or issuance of a notice to a postal or telecommunications operator) from a designated senior official who may be a senior police officer, a senior official in an intelligence service or the armed forces, or a senior official in a local government unit or public authority (for example the Post Office).[53]

---

[49] See AKJ v. Commissioner of Police of the Metropolis, [2013] EWHC 32 (QB); Hyland & Walker, *supra* note 35; McKay, *supra* note 46, at 223.

[50] Regulation of Investigatory Powers (Covert Human Intelligence Sources: Relevant Sources) Order 2013, S.I. 2013/2788.

[51] For details, *see* McKay, *supra* note 46, at 126.

[52] See ANDERSON, *supra* note 37.

[53] See Regulation of Investigatory Powers (Communications Data) Order 2010, S.I. 2010/480. Note also the involvement of the single point of contact and the senior responsible officer. See HOME OFFICE, ACQUISITION AND DISCLOSURE OF COMMUNICATIONS DATA CODE OF PRACTICE §§ 3.19–3.42 (2015).

5. Interception of Communications

Interception of transmissions by means of a postal service or telecommunication system is much less common than communications data acquisition, but it is much more intrusive because it captures the content of the communication. RIPA 2000, section 5, requires the authorization of the Secretary of State (the Home Secretary or the Foreign Secretary) by warrant on the following grounds:

(2) The Secretary of State shall not issue an interception warrant unless he believes
    (a) that the warrant is necessary on grounds falling within subsection (3); and
    (b) that the conduct authorised by the warrant is proportionate to what is sought to be achieved by that conduct.
(3) Subject to the following provisions of this section, a warrant is necessary on grounds falling within this subsection if it is necessary
    (a) in the interests of national security;
    (b) for the purpose of preventing or detecting serious crime;
    (c) for the purpose of safeguarding the economic well-being of the United Kingdom; or
    (d) for the purpose, in circumstances appearing to the Secretary of State to be equivalent to those in which he would issue a warrant by virtue of paragraph (b), of giving effect to the provisions of any international mutual assistance agreement.
(4) The matters to be taken into account in considering whether the requirements of subsection (2) are satisfied in the case of any warrant shall include whether the information which it is thought necessary to obtain under the warrant could reasonably be obtained by other means.

Because MI6 and GCHQ are outward-facing in their activities, extra powers are granted to cover such activities. For MI6, section 7 of the 1994 Act provides for an authorization to be given by the Secretary of State for acts committed outside the U.K. where the person would otherwise be liable in the U.K. under the criminal or civil law of any part of the U.K. (including the general liability of Crown servants under section 31 of the Criminal Justice Act 1948). As a result, agents involved in bugging, burglary, or bribery may be excused from any legal consequences under U.K. law if duly authorized. Such activities may remain illegal both under the laws of the country of commission and under international law (such as interference with diplomatic property). However, international law—as further implemented in domestic law by the Human Rights Act 1998—may rule out some further activities even if committed abroad;[54] in this way, section 7 could still provide a "license to kill" but probably not a license to torture.

As for GCHQ, the requirement to name a single person or premises for a warrant to be issued under section 5 of RIPA 2000 is disapplied by section 8(4) to the interception of "external communications." In *Liberty v. GCHQ*,[55] the Investigatory Powers Tribunal (described

[54] *See further* Extra-Territorial Jurisdiction of States Parties to the European Convention on Human Rights (Press Unit Council of Europe, 2014).
[55] [2014] UKIPTrib 13_77-H. *See further* Interception Commissioner, Annual Report, 2013-14 H.C. 1184, ¶ 6.5.27 et seq.; McKay, *supra* note 46, at 97; Robin Simcox, Surveillance after Snowden (2015).

below) rejected the challenges based on the Snowden allegations in relation to the PRISM, UPSTREAM, and TEMPORA programs. There was sufficient oversight and detail in the legislative schemes (including RIPA 2000) to avoid breaches of privacy. The further possibility that overseas assistance would allegedly be used to evade the necessary controls was accepted as a theoretical possibility in *Liberty v. Secretary of State for the Foreign & Commonwealth Office*, but the Tribunal accepted that this issue had since been addressed administratively.[56]

V. OVERSIGHT AND ACCOUNTABILITY: OVERALL PICTURE

The next sections examine the legal mechanisms of oversight and accountability for the state agencies in the field of surveillance. Two features emerge.

The first is the complexity of the range of oversight bodies that are discussed below. Though U.K. surveillance laws mainly grew in the decade from the mid-1990s, no attempt has been made to consolidate or clarify this broad range of measures that can confusingly overlap at various points. It follows that there are now proposals for wholesale revision.[57]

The second point is that the multiple bodies tend to stress oversight rather than account-ability. Their approach is bureaucratic in that they seek overall compliance by way of sampling the processes rather than assertive verification in advance of proposed action, or reporting or correction once a given action has been taken. There are a few bodies that deal with more spe-cific cases, such as the Investigatory Powers Tribunal, but these are also quite constrained in their approach. In terms of both types of organization, most (if not all) of the controversies they have ruled on in the past decade have arisen not from their proactive interventions (as one might expect from the nature of litigation though less so in regard to appointed oversight com-missioners), but from journalistic investigations and/or the work of civil liberties campaigners.

VI. DETAILED SURVEILLANCE POWERS: OVERSIGHT AND ACCOUNTABILITY
A. Police Intelligence

Police specialist units that engage in surveillance intelligence have had little internal, let alone external, scrutiny. The Police Special Branch units in each Constabulary of the 43 areas in England and Wales have traditionally concentrated on extremism, terrorism, and security from external threats, especially at ports and airports.

Much of their work has shifted to more specialist policing bodies.[58] For terrorism, there appeared in 1970 a separate Metropolitan Police Bomb Squad with a focus going beyond

---

[56] [2015] UKIP Trib 13-77-H, ¶¶ 21, 30, 31. A challenge is pending in Big Brother Watch v. United Kingdom, App. No. 58170/13.

[57] *See* INTELLIGENCE AND SECURITY COMMITTEE, PRIVACY AND SECURITY: A MODERN AND TRANSPARENT LEGAL FRAMEWORK, 2013–2014, H.C. 1075; ANDERSON, *supra* note 37.

[58] *See further* Clive Walker & Andrew Staniforth, *The Amplification and Melding of Counter-Terrorism Agencies: From Security Services to Police and Back Again, in* COUNTER-TERRORISM, HUMAN RIGHTS AND THE RULE OF LAW: CROSSING LEGAL BOUNDARIES IN DEFENCE OF THE STATE (Aniceto Masferrer & Clive Walker eds., 2013).

covert intelligence, disruption activities, and responding to more defined operational threats and incidents. It was reconstituted as the Anti-Terrorist Squad (SO13) in 1976, with national coverage later conferred.[59] In 2006, the Counter-Terrorism Command in the Metropolitan Police Service combined the local Special Branch and Anti-Terrorist Squad.[60] There are now four regional Counter Terrorism Units (situated in the North West, North East, Midlands, and South East of England) and a further five regional Counter Terrorism Intelligence Units (South West and Eastern England, plus Scotland, Wales, and Northern Ireland).[61]

To deal with more overt extremism, such as at public demonstrations, the National Public Order Intelligence Unit (NPOIU) was established in 1999 in succession to a range of units existing since 1968, and located within the Association of Chief Police Officers (ACPO) and funded by the Home Office. The unit was deployed to gather coordinated intelligence, rather than evidence that could be used to support criminal prosecutions. In 2011, the NPOIU was subsumed within the National Domestic Extremism Unit (NDEU), and became part of the Metropolitan Police Service. In 2013, "its remit was confirmed as the National Domestic Extremism and Disorder Intelligence Unit (NDEDIU) and it forms part of the Counter Terrorism Command."[62] The concept of "domestic extremism" was used as the term to cover a wide range of groups protesting on environmental, antiglobalization, anti-GM crops, anti-tax evasion, anti-airport expansion, antiracism, and anti-arms trade issues. This wide definition, which was devised by ACPO but lacks any legal basis,[63] resulted in the compilation of a database to cover protestors with no criminal record, including peaceful protesters. The intelligence gained therefore seemed to have little quality control and did not conform to the police's own National Intelligence Model,[64] which is a self-governing internal check on procedures and standards rather than a check based on external legal principle.

Not surprisingly, the broad and untrammeled powers of police surveillance, especially in relation to "domestic extremism," have been the subject of legal challenges. One protestor who was placed on the NPOIU database, John Catt, succeeded in his case at the Court of Appeal on grounds of a breach of privacy rights. The Court stated that "[t]he systematic collection, processing and retention on a searchable database of personal information, even of a relatively routine kind, involves a significant interference with the right to respect for private life."[65] The Court argued that such details should not be held indefinitely, particularly in a

---

[59] 187 PARL. DEB., H.C. (6th ser.) (1991) 27.

[60] *Counter Terrorism Command*, METROPOLITAN POLICE, http://content.met.police.uk/Article/Counter-Terrorism-Command/1400006569170/1400006569170 (last visited July 19, 2015).

[61] *See* HOME OFFICE, PURSUE, PREVENT, PROTECT, PREPARE, 2009, Cm. 7547, § 8.10; ANDREW STANIFORTH, BLACKSTONE'S COUNTER-TERRORISM HANDBOOK 76–100 (2009).

[62] *See* Hyland & Walker, *supra* note 35, at 566.

[63] HM INSPECTORATE OF CONSTABULARY, A REVIEW OF NATIONAL POLICE UNITS WHICH PROVIDE INTELLIGENCE ON CRIMINALITY ASSOCIATED WITH PROTEST 11 (2012). The definition states: "[d]omestic extremism and extremists are the terms used for activity, individuals or campaign groups that carry out criminal acts of direct action in furtherance of what is typically a single issue campaign. They usually seek to prevent something from happening or to change legislation or domestic policy, but attempt to do so outside the normal democratic process."

[64] NATIONAL CRIMINAL INTELLIGENCE SERVICE, NATIONAL INTELLIGENCE MODEL (2000).

[65] R (Catt) v. Association of Chief Police Officers, [2013] EWCA Civ 192, [44].

centralized searchable database and particularly of someone not convicted of any offense. The police appealed to the Supreme Court, which in 2015 ruled against Catt, supporting the police in their claim that the previous judgment gave individual rights to privacy too wide a scope.[66] As a result, the English courts have yet to set out a clear position on where intelligence collection begins to chill the right to protest.[67]

B. Police Undercover (CHIS) Surveillance

Another example of the limited reach of surveillance accountability is police undercover surveillance. For example, the Special Demonstration Squad (SDS), a police intelligence unit that operated from 1968 to 2008 as a forerunner to the NPOIU, employed 147 officers, and 106 covert identities were used over the period. "Until the later years of the SDS's existence, very few people outside of the MPS Special Branch knew about it,"[68] so it was not challenged during its lifetime. Later, the NPOIU subsumed the SDS, and NPOIU officers did begin to bring protestors to court, but the first major contested case collapsed as officers were found to have clearly acted as (undisclosed) agents provocateurs.[69] That these units had little supervision was perhaps best represented by the cases of a number of undercover SDS and NPOIU officers (such as Bob Lambert and Mark Kennedy) who had long-term sexual relationships with protestors, and in a number of cases fathered children with the women before "disappearing."[70] One source at the Metropolitan Police (within which the SDS was based) stated, "[q]uite simply, they lost their moral compass and as a result nothing was out of bounds. A quite shocking vacuum of any supervision and leadership allowed this to happen."[71] Similar concerns were expressed over the NPOIU in a report by the Home Affairs Parliamentary Select Committee: "Oversight for surveillance under the Regulation of Investigatory Powers Act 2000 is provided by the Office of Surveillance Commissioners, but HMIC [Her Majesty's Inspector of Constabulary] found that this oversight was weak in the case of the NPOIU because there was no expectation that evidence would need to stand up in court. HMIC found differences in the training, tactics, review and integration of different units, rather than a unified set of standards to govern all

---

[66] R (Catt) v. Metropolitan Police Commissioner, [2015] UKSC 9.

[67] See European Convention on Human Rights, 213 U.N.T.S. 221, E.T.S. 5, Article 11. The ECHR is given force in domestic law by the Human Rights Act 1998.

[68] MICK CREEDON, OPERATION HERNE: REPORT ONE, USE OF COVERT IDENTITIES ¶ 1.6 (2013).

[69] Mark Kennedy, an NPOIU operative, had assisted climate change protestors to plan an invasion of a power station. Some of the protestors were subsequently charged with public order offenses, but the prosecution in 2011 at Nottingham Crown Court collapsed when it was revealed that Kennedy was an undercover officer. See R v. Barkshire, [2011] EWCA Crim 1885; INDEPENDENT POLICE COMPLAINTS COMMISSION, RATCLIFFE-ON-SOAR POWER STATION (OPERATION AEROSCOPE) DISCLOSURE NOTTINGHAMSHIRE POLICE (2012); SIR CHRISTOPHER ROSE, RATCLIFFE-ON--SOAR POWER STATION PROTEST: INQUIRY INTO DISCLOSURE (2011); ROB EVANS & PAUL LEWIS, UNDERCOVER: THE TRUE STORY OF BRITAIN'S SECRET POLICE 314 (2013).

[70] See AKJ v. Commissioner of Police of the Metropolis, [2013] EWCA Civ 1342.

[71] Vikram Dodd & Rob Evans, Police Chiefs Were Aware Six Years Ago That Undercover Unit Had Lost Moral Compass, THE GUARDIAN (July 24, 2014, 16:55 EDT), http://www.theguardian.com/uk-news/2014/jul/24/undercover-police-unit-collected-information-family-campaigners.

undercover operations."[72] Further, the Committee found that "[d]espite this strong framework of statutory regulation, supplemented by guidance from ACPO, the Surveillance Commissioners and others, there is an alarming degree of inconsistency in the views of Ministers and senior police officers about the limits of what may and may not be lawfully authorised."[73] The Committee as a result recommended "that there is a compelling case for a fundamental review of the legislative framework governing undercover policing, including the Regulation of Investigatory Powers Act 2000, in the light of the lessons learned from these cases."[74]

So many abuses and miscarriages of justice as allegedly perpetrated by these specialist police intelligence units have now come to light that the government ordered a wide-ranging judicial inquiry in 2015.[75]

C. Undercover Surveillance by Other Public Bodies

A total of 653 public bodies in the U.K. were permitted under RIPA 2000 to access phone, email, and web-search communications data with only the authorization of an in-house senior official required.[76] Local government was also given powers of covert surveillance, and were accused of using these powers widely and disproportionately after several cases were made public (see below).[77] Therefore, further doubts have arisen about the legal oversight and accountability for these surveillance powers, with which the next sections deal.

D. Oversight for Public Authority Surveillance (including the Police): The Office of the Surveillance Commissioners

The Office of the Surveillance Commissioners (OSC) provides accountability for public agencies' use of surveillance, primarily the police and other law enforcement agencies. The OSC does not, however, cover the intelligence or security services. The OSC commissioners grant authority for the use of some surveillance measures (as described above), and OSC inspectors conduct inspections of agencies that use such measures.

---

[72] House of Commons Home Affairs Committee, Undercover Policing: Interim Report, 2012–2013, H.C. 857, ¶ 17.

[73] *Id.* ¶ 11.

[74] *Id.* ¶ 15.

[75] *See* Mick Creedon, Operation Herne: Part One, Use of Covert Identities (2013); and Mick Creedon, Operation Herne: Part 2, Allegations of Peter Francis (2014); Mark Ellison, The Stephen Lawrence Independent Review (2013–2014 HC 1094); Stephen Taylor, Investigation into Links between Special Demonstration Squad and Home Office (2015); Mark Ellison & Alison Morgan, Review of Possible Miscarriages of Justice (2015–2016 HC 291), https://www.gov.uk/government/news/home-secretary-announces-statutory-inquiry-into-undercover-policing (last visited July 31, 2015).

[76] *See* Richard Edwards, *Every Phone Call, Email and Internet Click Stored by State Spying' Databases,'* Daily Telegraph (Nov. 9, 2009, 9:00 PM), http://www.telegraph.co.uk/news/uknews/law-and-order/6533107/Every-phone-call-email-and-internet-click-stored-by-state-spying-databases.html.

[77] *Restraining RIPA,* Local Government Lawyer (Feb. 3, 2011, 8:23 PM), http://localgovernmentlawyer.co.uk/index.php?option=com_content&view=article&id=5770:restraining-ripa&catid=55:community-safety-articles&q=.

Directed surveillance by law enforcement stood at approximately 20,000 cases in 2006–2007; likewise, directed surveillance by other public authorities was at its height in 2006–2007 at over 12,000, reflecting the climate of counterterrorism after the 7/7 attacks. Directed surveillance by law enforcement reduced to just under 10,000 cases in 2013–2014, and for public authorities in the same period, the figure reduced to just over 4,000.[78]

Intrusive surveillance remains limited and generally focused on areas other than terrorism. For example, in the last three years, authorization for the security agencies to enter property and plant surveillance devices was granted in 2,447 cases. Of these, 1,344 involved suspected drugs trafficking, 235 robbery, 152 kidnap/extortion, 148 murder, 106 money laundering, and just 17 terrorism.[79]

The overall picture reveals that this type of surveillance is being limited in numerical terms and is properly approved, though with continued indulgence for the intelligence agencies.

Beyond these annual reports, "[t]he Office of Surveillance Commissioners is not subject to the Freedom of Information Act 2000 and does not make public its findings from the inspection process."[80] Furthermore, a former head of the OSC (an ex-military intelligence officer) stated that the OSC, in making surveillance accountable, relied on cooperation from the services it was overseeing, stating that he and his inspectors examined just 10 percent of all authorizations and that "[w]e had no power to dictate . . . persuasion was the only tool in the box." [81] He further pointed out that the culture was legalistic so that scrutiny centered on whether actions were lawful rather than ethical.[82]

E. Oversight for Police and Security Surveillance: Interception of Communications Commissioner (IOCC)

The IOCC reports under RIPA 2000, section 57, on the harvesting of communications data (information, not content) and the interception of communications, whether by the police or the security agencies.[83] It has engaged in an important recent case, wherein complainants argued that the police were disproportionately using RIPA 2000 to access the details of journalists. Nineteen police services lodged 608 applications in 34 investigations to see communications data on links between journalists and public officials. A large percentage of these requests were part of the police investigation (Operation Elveden) into possible criminal offences of police and other public officials leaking information to journalists. This resulted from the "phone hacking" scandal exposed by *The Guardian* newspaper, which

---

[78] Annual Report of the Chief Surveillance Commissioner to the Prime Minister and to the Scottish Ministers for 2013–2014, H.C. 343, ¶¶ 4.7–4.9.

[79] *Id.* at Appendix B.

[80] *Inspection Reports*, Office of Surveillance Commissioners, https://osc.independent.gov.uk/inspection-reports/ (last visited July 19, 2015).

[81] Vikram Dodd, *Government's Defence of Surveillance Unconvincing, Says Ex-watchdog*, The Guardian (June 18, 2014, 2:06 PM EDT), http://www.theguardian.com/world/2014/jun/18/government-surveillance-watchdog-loopholes.

[82] *Id.*

[83] *The Commissioner and Regulation of Investigatory Powers Act (RIPA)*, Interception of Communications Commissioner's Office, http://iocco-uk.info/sections.asp?sectionID=2&type=top, (last visited July 19, 2015).

alleged that newspapers were illegally accessing private information about individuals—such as celebrities—often via leaks from the police or other public officials. These requests were authorized by senior officers within the police, as specified by RIPA 2000 (in other words, were self-authorized by that organization).[84] However, the IOCC argued that these requests, despite being part of a criminal investigation, did not give the question of necessity, proportionality, and collateral intrusion sufficient consideration.[85] They focused on privacy considerations—Article 8 of the European Convention on Human Rights (ECHR)—and did not give due consideration to freedom of speech (Article 10).[86] The Report advised that in the future authorization to access communications data between journalists and others should require external authorization from a judge.[87] This shows that bureaucratic oversight can achieve gains, even in the relatively reactive context in which it operates in the U.K.

F. *Specific Accountability for Public Authority Surveillance: The Investigatory Powers Tribunal*

The Investigatory Powers Tribunal (IPT) is the arena in which specific complaints about surveillance are made. It has become slightly more assertive recently (as shown below), which may be due to the growing journalistic coverage of the misuse of surveillance powers.

The IPT was established under RIPA 2000 to provide accountability for surveillance by public authorities (including the police and security agencies). During 2001–2014, the IPT investigated 1,500 complaints and upheld 10, 5 relating to members of one family; in more detail, from 2010 to 2013, it dealt with 756 complaints and upheld 6, while 283 were ruled no determination, and 336 were ruled to be frivolous and vexatious.[88] The meager number of positive findings highlights the frequent criticism made of the IPT—that it is too conservative. Its recent judgment on the Snowden-related case, *Liberty v. Secretary of State for the Foreign and Commonwealth Office*,[89] created a media stir for finding even a small fault. Before that, to give a flavor of excessive surveillance, the complainants in one case (all members of the same family) were placed under directed surveillance after the local authority suspected that they did not live in the area that they claimed to live in and so were making a false claim in relation to school place allocation for their child. The IPT found that although local authorities faced a growing problem of parents providing fraudulent addresses to get their children into the best schools, the surveillance was disproportionate when considered in light of the aims of RIPA 2000, and it was particularly disproportionate as it involved officials engaging in

---

[84] *See* Lord Justice Leveson, Inquiry into the Culture, Practices and Ethics of the Press: Report, 2012–2013, H.C. 1213.

[85] Interception of Communications Commissioner's Office, IOCCO Inquiry into the Use of Chapter 2 of Part 1 of the Regulation of Investigatory Powers Act (RIPA) to Identify Journalistic Sources ¶ 8.6 (2015).

[86] *Id.*

[87] *Id.* ¶ 8.9(1).

[88] *Annual Case Statistics*, Investigatory Powers Tribunal, http://www.ipt-uk.com/section.aspx?pageid=5 (last visited July 19, 2015). *See further* Ian Cobain & Leila Haddou, *"Independent" Court Scrutinising MI5 Is Located inside Home Office*, The Guardian (Mar. 5, 2014, 4:27 PM EST), http://www.theguardian.com/politics/2014/mar/05/independence-ipt-court-mi5-mi6-home-office-secrecy-clegg-miliband.

[89] [2015] UKIPTrib 13_77-H.

directed surveillance of children.[90] The IPT found in 2010 that RIPA 2000 had been misused only occasionally by local authorities;[91] by contrast, following the change of government in the U.K. in 2010, the Protection of Freedoms Act 2012 was passed, which restricted the ability of local authorities and similar lower level public bodies to either self-authorize surveillance or carry it out. As a result, according to the Chief Surveillance Commissioner:

> The changes brought about for local authorities by The Protection of Freedoms Act 2012 have now had time to bed in. My Surveillance Inspectors and Assistant Surveillance Commissioners have identified a downward trend in the number of applications made and authorisations granted, which may or may not be attributable to this enactment. A number of local authorities have decided not to engage in covert activity as a matter of policy, but the reasons for that decision vary and are not always expressed.[92]

As mentioned above, in 2014 and early 2015, the IPT made perhaps its most high profile judgments, over the cooperation of the U.K.'s technical surveillance organization GCHQ with the NSA in the United States in the PRISM, UPSTREAM, and TEMPORA programs. According to the material disclosed by Edward Snowden, the NSA has been accessing live and stored communications data from the following organizations: Microsoft (from 2007); Yahoo (2008); Google, Facebook and PalTalk (2009); YouTube (2010); Skype and AOL (2011); and Apple (2012).[93] The IPT accepted that RIPA 2000, section 8, along with the Security Services Act 1989, the Intelligence Services Act 1994 and the Counter Terrorism Act 2008, provided a lawful framework for the U.K. to share data with foreign agencies including the NSA, and that the data collection, analysis, and sharing had proper oversight (via the Intelligence Services Commissioner—see below). Though it also raised privacy issues that should be made perhaps more open to public scrutiny, the IPT seemed keen to give public reassurance:

> Technology in the surveillance field appears to be advancing at break-neck speed. This has given rise to submissions that the UK legislation has failed to keep abreast of the consequences of these advances, and is ill fitted to do so; and that in any event Parliament has failed to provide safeguards adequate to meet these developments. All this inevitably creates considerable tension between the competing interests, and the "Snowden revelations" in particular have led to the impression voiced in some quarters that the law in some way permits the Intelligence Services *carte blanche* to do what they will. We are satisfied that this is not the case.[94]

---

[90] Paton v. Poole Borough Council, [2010] IPT/09/01 [62]–[75].

[91] INVESTIGATORY POWERS TRIBUNAL, ANNUAL REPORT, 4 (2010).

[92] ANNUAL REPORT OF THE CHIEF SURVEILLANCE COMMISSIONER TO THE PRIME MINISTER AND TO THE SCOTTISH MINISTERS FOR 2013–2014, H.C. 343, ¶ 3.9.

[93] *See* GLENN GREENWALD, NO PLACE TO HIDE: EDWARD SNOWDEN, THE NSA, AND THE US SURVEILLANCE STATE 21 (2014).

[94] Liberty & Others v. Security Service, SIS, GCHQ, [2014] IPT/13/77/H, [158].

Its later judgment did call into question the legality of the PRISM scheme with regard to a specific period of time (2007–2014) when it appeared that surveillance was not properly authorized: "[T]he regime governing the soliciting, receiving, storing and transmitting by UK authorities of private communications of individuals located in the UK, which have been obtained by US authorities . . . contravened Articles 8 or 10 [of the ECHR]."[95]

It should be noted that the IPT only investigates cases of surveillance authorized by warrant. Unlawful surveillance is left to the police to investigate under the relevant criminal legislation.[96] Therefore, there is almost no information available on any "dark figure" of state surveillance activity (let alone private sector surveillance), aside from some recent cases of police officers who have sold data to journalists, which has ironically produced much more public attention to journalistic standards than to police standards.[97] Nevertheless, reforms to the wide scope of state bodies for surveillance were made as a result of press and civil society criticisms, arising from local authority and NPOIU excesses. The OSC and the IPT have played only minor roles in challenging the powers, and have given the impression of being overly cautious.

This chapter has concentrated on surveillance because that is the core of the powers of the intelligence agencies in the U.K. However the final section deals with accountability generally, and raises similar points to those already made about the bureaucratic nature of oversight in the U.K. context.

VII. FURTHER OVERSIGHT OF THE INTELLIGENCE AND SECURITY SERVICES
A. Intelligence Services Commissioner

Under the RIPA 2000, section 59, the Intelligence Services Commissioner (ISCom) keeps under review: the exercise by the Secretaries of State of their powers to issue warrants and authorizations to enable the intelligence and security services to carry out their functions; the performance of the powers and duties imposed on the intelligence services and MOD/Armed Forces personnel in relation to surveillance and covert activities, which are the subject of RIPA 2000; and the carrying out of any aspect of the functions of the Intelligence Services as might be directed by the prime minister. The ISCom also works with the IPT where necessary to examine complaints. However, the role of the ISCom is not of an

---

[95] Liberty & Others v Secretary of State for Foreign and Commonwealth Affairs & Others [2015] UKIPTrib 13_77-H, 23.

[96] *See* Gareth Crossman et al., Overlooked: Surveillance and Personal Privacy in Modern Britain 26 (2007).

[97] *See* Information Commissioner's Office, What Price Privacy? The Unlawful Trade in Confidential Personal Information (2006); Information Commissioner's Office, What Price Privacy Now? The First Six Months Progress in Halting the Unlawful Trade in Confidential Personal Information (2006); Leveson Inquiry, *supra* note 84. *See generally* House of Commons Culture, Media and Sport Committee, News International and Phone Hacking, 2010–2012, H.C. 903; House of Commons Home Affairs Committee, Unauthorised Tapping into or Hacking Of Mobile Communications, 2010–2012, H.C. 907 and Government Response, 2011, Cm. 8182.

independent and critical scrutineer. He checks that warrants are issued correctly and have been authorized correctly. He does not examine the reasoning behind such issuances, nor does he see a substantial proportion of the issued warrants: "The total number of warrants and authorisations approved across the intelligence services and the MOD in 2013 was 1887. Provided with details of all warrants, I scrutinised 318 warrants extant and paperwork during 2013, 16.8% of the total."[98]

B. Intelligence and Security Committee (ISC)

The ISC, established by the Intelligence Services Act 1994, section 10, is the main mechanism for legislature accountability for the security and intelligence services. However, its role as a force for surveillance accountability has long been subject to doubt.[99] The ISC was therefore overhauled by the Justice and Security Act 2013, Part I, which included a provision for making it a committee of Parliament rather than being entirely beholden to the Prime Minister, and expanding its terms of reference so as to include oversight of operational activity and the wider intelligence and security activities of government.[100] The ISC has also vaunted its new powers to demand information and call witnesses under Schedule 1 of the 2013 Act, but such powers it may have to review operational matters are still for all practical purposes subject to the consent of the intelligence agencies to release information.[101] Insofar as the powers relate to nonoperational matters, they are subject to a veto if they are sensitive or they may touch on issues of national security.[102] The absence of independent advisers and other resources has also been a major problem for the effectiveness of the ISC.

The performance of the ISC has been criticized as weak on several occasions,[103] including in response to the revelations of mass data collection programs by Edward Snowden. The ISC briefly investigated and peremptorily opined:

Although we have concluded that GCHQ has not circumvented or attempted to circumvent UK law, it is proper to consider further whether the current statutory framework governing access to private communications remains adequate . . . In some areas

---

[98] Sir Mark Waller, Report of the Intelligence Services Commissioner for 2013, 2013–2014, H.C. 304, at 35.

[99] See, e.g., Mark Phythian, The British Experience with Intelligence Accountability, 22 Intelligence & Nat'l Sec. 75 (2007); Andrew Defty, Educating Parliamentarians about Intelligence: The Role of the British Intelligence and Security Committee, 61 Parl. Aff. 621, 638 (2008); Hugh Bochel et al., "New Mechanisms of Independent Accountability": Select Committees and Parliamentary Scrutiny of the Intelligence Services, 68 Parl. Aff. 314, 315 (2015).

[100] See Justice and Security Act, 2013, c. 18, § 1; Ian Leigh, Rebalancing Rights and National Security: Reforming UK Intelligence Oversight a Decade after 9/11 27 Intelligence & Nat'l Sec. 722, 726 (2012).

[101] Justice and Security Act, 2013, c. 18, § 2(3)(c).

[102] Justice and Security Act, 2013, c. 18, § 4(4)(a)(i), sch. 1 ¶ 4.

[103] The performance of the ISC was even criticized by the Parliamentary Joint Committee on Human Rights. See, e.g., Allegations of UK Complicity in Torture, Twenty-Third Report of Session 2008–2009, H.L. 152, H.C. 230; Counter-Terrorism Policy and Human Rights (Seventeenth Report): Bringing Human Rights Back In, Sixteenth Report of Session 2009–2010, H.L. 86, H.C. 111.

the legislation is expressed in general terms and more detailed policies and procedures have, rightly, been put in place around this work by GCHQ in order to ensure compliance with their statutory obligations under the Human Rights Act 1998. We are therefore examining the complex interaction between the Intelligence Services Act, the Human Rights Act and the Regulation of Investigatory Powers Act, and the policies and procedures that underpin them, further. We note that the Interception of Communications Commissioner is also considering this issue.[104]

There is perhaps more at stake here than unraveling the undoubted complexity of the application of RIPA 2000. A more critical approach would suspect that the security services, particularly GCHQ, used an absence of legal clarity to develop their own framework for linking with the NSA. Despite the ISC's initial pronouncements, and despite the fact that the ISC chair, Sir Malcolm Rifkind, had to resign in February 2015 after the *Daily Telegraph* and Channel 4's *Dispatches* asserted that he had offered to utilize his position as a senior politician on behalf of a fictitious Chinese company (an obvious potential security risk) in return for substantial financial payments, the ISC eventually called for wholesale reform of RIPA 2000 in its report, *Privacy and Security: A Modern and Transparent Legal Framework.*[105] Compared to previous ISC work, it bore some promising signs of greater transparency, as evidenced by the substantial list of external witnesses invited to make submissions to the inquiry arising from the Snowden revelations. In substance, this Report reveals that a small number of security staff had been disciplined for misusing their surveillance powers, and it further reassures that mass surveillance is not being conducted. However, the ISC found that the existing legal powers under RIPA 2000 could be construed as providing the agencies with a " 'blank cheque' to carry out whatever activities they deem necessary,"[106] a belated discovery for a review body that was established under the same legislation. The relatively brief document calls for wide-scale but largely amorphous legislative reforms. Since the Report was published in March 2015, its impact, if any, is as yet too early to judge; however it already seems to have been overtaken in part by the much fuller and specific remedies in the report *A Question of Trust,* of the Independent Reviewer of Terrorism Legislation, David Anderson, which has been justly praised (and is detailed later in this chapter).[107]

VIII. GENERAL OVERSIGHT AND ACCOUNTABILITY
A. CCTV

The growth of CCTV in the U.K. has not been accompanied by any strong regulatory framework, which is one reason it expanded so markedly in the 1990s[108] in response to fears of

---

[104] Intelligence and Security Committee, Statement on GCHQ's Alleged Interception of Communications under the US PRISM Programme (2013).

[105] Intelligence and Security Committee, *supra* note 57.

[106] *Id.* at 117.

[107] Anderson, *supra* note 37.

[108] Clive Norris & Gary Armstrong, The Maximum Surveillance Society: The Rise of CCTV 26–27 (1999).

IRA terrorism[109] and also to faith in situational crime prevention. As a result, breaches of privacy have sometimes been sustained[110] during the development of what is often termed "routine surveillance"—the constant monitoring by CCTV of public and private spaces on a significant scale. CCTV is not covered by RIPA 2000 unless it is used as part of a directed surveillance operation.[111] The Data Protection Act 1998 has been the underlying legal tool covering CCTV use, but it is essentially concerned with the use of recorded data rather than the use of surveillance. It also does not cover cameras that observe but do not record.[112] The Protection of Freedoms Act 2012, section 29, subjects CCTV—and also Automatic Number Plate Recognition (ANPR)—to a Surveillance Camera Code of Practice, which is overseen by the office of Surveillance Camera Commissioner under section 34. However, this role covers only the estimated 100,000 public CCTV cameras in the U.K., leaving aside the 6 million privately owned cameras in fixed points that record movements of the public, and the Commissioner has only limited enforcement powers.[113] In pursuance of the 2012 Act, the Home Office has also published National Standards for ANPR (2013), though they relate more to the quality standards of cameras and the data recorded rather than regulating police operational decisions to deploy ANPR in the first place.[114]

B. Information Commissioner's Office (ICO)

The exception to the narrow focus that has generally prevailed in the mechanisms discussed in this chapter is the ICO, which takes a proactive line to issues of surveillance and civil liberty. The ICO has a more wide-ranging brief to protect citizens' data, including data held by the security services, though subject to express limitations.[115] The ICO monitors the use of personal data according to the Data Protection Act 1998 and ensures that Freedom of Information Act 2000 requests are dealt with. In serious cases after breaches are reported, the ICO can fine the individual or organization concerned or can facilitate a prosecution.[116]

The ICO head has taken a proactive role with regards to publicizing the threat of surveillance. Richard Thomas, the then Commissioner, commissioned research into whether the

---

[109] Clive Walker, *Political Violence and Commercial Risk*, 56 Current L. Probs. 531, 562–63 (2004) (noting the employment of CCTV as a part of the City of London's response to IRA bombing campaigns during the 1990s).

[110] Peck v. United Kingdom, App. No. 44647/98 (2003-I).

[111] *See* R v. Rosenberg, [2006] EWCA Crim 6 (Eng. and Wales).

[112] House of Lords Constitution Committee, *supra* note 2, ¶ 213.

[113] *See* Matthew Weaver, *UK Public Must Wake Up to Risks of CCTV, Says Surveillance Commissioner*, The Guardian, (Jan. 6, 2015, 10:10 EST); *The Surveillance Camera Commissioner homepage*, UK.gov, https://www.gov.uk/government/organisations/surveillance-camera-commissioner/about (last visited July 19, 2015) ("The Commissioner has no enforcement or inspection powers...").

[114] *See* Home Office, National ANPR Standards for Policing: Part 1—Data Standards, (2013); Home Office, National ANPR Standards for Policing: Part 2—ANPR Infrastructure Standards (2013).

[115] *See* Data Protection Act 1998, § 28 (allowing exemption from data protection principles where "required for the purpose of safeguarding national security").

[116] *Taking Action—Data Protection*, Information Commissioner's Office, https://ico.org.uk/about-the-ico/what-we-do/taking-action-data-protection/ (last visited July 19, 2015).

U.K. was becoming a "surveillance society." Two of the many faults identified by the ensuing report included that:

> Regulation has tended to be reactive: that is, response had been made to technological development, implementation and practice after the fact. Regulation has had a largely technical and managerial focus, based on codes of practice, the fulfilment of standard legal requirements, and the application of privacy-protective technologies, leaving little room for anticipation.[117]

The ICO has therefore been one of the few formal public offices in the U.K. that has taken the initiative in examining the wide range of surveillance issues. However, it has only a small staff and limited investigatory capacity.

C. Court Procedures

If a case involving surveillance reaches trial and unfair techniques of criminal investigation and evidence gathering have been employed, they can be excluded under section 78 of the Police and Criminal Evidence Act 1984 if they "would have such an adverse effect on the fairness of the proceedings that the court ought not to admit it." However, English courts take a perhaps less robust attitude than U.S. courts to the actions of agents provocateurs. While use of agents provocateurs may be a factor in excluding evidence, such exclusion is not automatic.[118]

The case of undercover police officer Mark Kennedy (mentioned previously) was such an egregious example that the court did see it as unfair. But a defendant may not know of the use of surveillance against him or her, if a Public Interest Immunity (PII) certificate is successfully applied for by the state and agreed to by the trial judge on the grounds that the product from surveillance is not to be viewed as material evidence.[119] A PII may be issued to protect certain intelligence-gathering techniques, the provision of surveillance or intercept product from a foreign state, and the identity of a CHIS (as applied in the Mark Kennedy cases).

A further important limitation on court inquiry into surveillance is the application of Closed Material Procedures (CMP).[120] In the light of the growing use of the courts to challenge security activities, and the growing willingness of judges to entertain such plaints,[121] a CMP was allowed for all forms of civil process (but not criminal process) by the Justice and Security Act 2013, Part II. Safeguards include the fact that a more active judicial role is

---

[117] INFORMATION COMMISSIONER, *supra* note 2, at 77.

[118] *See* Hyland & Walker, *supra* note 35.

[119] For a detailed discussion, *see* MCKAY, *supra* note 46.

[120] The IPT can operate with private hearings, which go further than CMP. *See* Investigatory Powers Tribunal Rules, 2000, S.I. 2000/2665.

[121] The most notable decision adverse to the government's request to suppress evidence was R (Binyam Mohamed) v. Secretary of State for the Foreign & Commonwealth Office, [2008] EWHC 2048, 2100, 2519, 2549, 2973 (Admin), [2009] EWHC 152 (Admin), [2010] EWCA Civ 65. Other similar cases were reported in GOVERNMENT RESPONSE TO THE HOUSE OF LORDS SELECT COMMITTEE ON THE CONSTITUTION, JUSTICE AND SECURITY BILL, 4TH REPORT OF SESSION 2010–2012 (2012).

evident in the decision to enact a CMP, and the judge may end CMP proceedings if he or she assesses that they are making the process unfair.[122] However, a number of legal commentators and senior judges have said that this statutory CMP procedure tilts the balance of court proceedings in favor of the state.[123]

IX. CONCLUSION

Oversight and accountability for intelligence and surveillance in the U.K. is of remarkably recent origin. The regulatory systems that are now in operation date largely from the last 20 years, especially via the RIPA Act 2000. This produced a complex and bureaucratic landscape, perhaps reflecting British tradition for ad hoc solutions and organizational outgrowth. It might be uncharitably argued that the British approach seems to rest on the ideology of "gentlemanly critique," based on peer review by ex- or serving legal and security professionals. In addition, although a human rights culture is embedded in the U.K. under the Human Rights Act 1998, a marked change from the period of the 1970s, this factor has also gone hand in hand with an expansion of the surveillance activities of the U.K. state.

Overall, counterterrorism in the U.K. has been largely compatible with the ECHR. It is claimed that the courts have been an "irritant" rather than obstacle,[124] but that observation underplays the development of judicial scrutiny and also the extent to which there have been some genuine attempts to adapt legislation and professional cultures to the rights environment. In addition, much opposition to the expansion of surveillance has been *political*. By the end of 2007, the Labour government faced criticism from across many different sectors of society.[125] Indeed, by that stage, even the former head of MI5 and the government's own senior law officer were criticizing the disproportionate approach of the government.[126] It is this political shift that allowed the Coalition government to endorse this criticism after 2010.[127] As a result, the Protection of Freedoms Act 2012, as well as the reforming of key

---

[122] Tom Hickman, *Turning Out the Lights? The Justice and Security Act 2013*, UK CONST. L. BLOG (June 11, 2013), http://ukconstitutionallaw.org/2013/06/11/tom-hickman-turning-out-the-lights-the-justice-and-security-act-2013/ (last visited July 19, 2015).

[123] *See* Adam Tomkins, *Justice and Security in the United Kingdom*, 47 ISRAEL L. REV. 305 328–29 (2014); Clive Walker, *Living with National Security Disputes in Court Processes in England and Wales, in* SECRECY, LAW AND SOCIETY 25, 32 (Greg Martin et al. eds., 2015).

[124] Keith Ewing & Joo-Cheong Tham, *The Continuing Futility of the Human Rights Act*, PUB. L. 668 (2008).

[125] *See, e.g.*, PETER HITCHENS, THE ABOLITION OF LIBERTY (2004); PETER OBORNE, THE USE AND ABUSE OF TERROR: THE CONSTRUCTION OF A FALSE NARRATIVE ON THE DOMESTIC TERROR THREAT (2006); Henry Porter, http://www.henry-porter.com/. (last visited Jan. 3, 2016).

[126] Kim Sengupta, *Terrorist Threat "Exploited to Curb Civil Liberties,"* THE INDEPENDENT (Feb. 17, 2009), http://www.independent.co.uk/news/uk/politics/terrorist-threat-exploited-to-curb-civil-liberties-1623795.html (last visited July 19, 2015). The former Director of Public Prosecutions Ken Macdonald was also highly critical. *See Centuries of British Freedoms Being "Broken" by Security State, Says Sir Ken Macdonald*, DAILY TELEGRAPH (Oct. 20, 2008, 7:07 PM), http://www.telegraph.co.uk/news/uknews/law-and-order/3230452/Centuries-of-British-freedoms-being-broken-by-security-state-says-Sir-Ken-Macdonald.html.

[127] *See* LORD MACDONALD, REVIEW OF COUNTER TERRORISM AND SECURITY POWERS, 2011, Cm. 8003; HOME OFFICE, REVIEW OF COUNTER-TERRORISM AND SECURITY POWERS: REVIEW FINDINGS AND RECOMMENDATIONS, 2011, Cm. 8004.

antiterrorism laws,[128] restricted local authority surveillance powers, and introduced the role of the CCTV Commissioner. Further, a number of recent parliamentary investigations and police examinations of covert policing have argued that surveillance law and practice should be clarified and changed.

Yet, the system of accountability remains bureaucratized and fragmented. A plethora of organizations are involved. Beyond the half dozen set out in RIPA 2000, (which doubtless perform their roles to a high standard of professionalism and integrity), the dynamic of accountability, in the senses of fundamentally questioning of roles and responsibilities, highlighting potential abuses, and sparking public debate, has come from civil society, the media, campaigning organizations, and sporadic litigation. This is to be welcomed but not relied on as a regular or consistent mode of oversight and accountability, or one that can replace the precision and power of review bodies or the legislature.

This chapter recommends a more unified and robust system be instituted along the lines advocated by the report of David Anderson.[129] His recommendations would entail a new comprehensive and transparent legal framework. As for the initiation of surveillance powers, the new framework would impose a new requirement of judicial authorization (by Judicial Commissioners) of all warrants for interception. Accordingly, the role of the Secretary of State would be limited to certifying that certain warrants are required in the interests of national security relating to the defense or foreign policy of the U.K. Measures would also be required to reinforce the independence of those authorizing requests for communications data, particularly within the security and intelligence agencies, and there should be a statutory requirement of judicial authorization of novel and contentious requests for communications data, and of requests for privileged and confidential communications such as involving journalists and lawyers. The Anderson Report also advocates the replacement of the three existing Commissioners' offices by a new Independent Surveillance and Intelligence Commission, which would comprise an intelligence and surveillance auditor and regulator whose judicial commissioners would take over responsibility for issuing warrants; for authorizing novel, contentious, and sensitive requests for communications data; and for issuing guidance. There should also be expanded jurisdiction for the Investigatory Powers Tribunal, and a right to apply for permission to appeal its rulings. This more independent, judicialized, and proactive form of accountability and oversight would promote fairness and efficiency in the ICs in ways that better meet domestic and international expectations as to the observation of the rule of law[130] even in this most challenging of state functions.

In response, the Government's Draft Investigatory Powers Bill 2015[131] does not wholly live up to these expectations. On the one hand, transparency is significantly advanced by the full explication of 'bulk' surveillance powers and also of some powers of interference (such as with equipment and personal data sets) which were never acknowledged until the debates

---

[128] *See* CLIVE WALKER, THE ANTI-TERRORISM LEGISLATION (3rd ed. 2014).

[129] ANDERSON, *supra* note 37.

[130] *See* VENICE COMMISSION, UPDATE OF THE 2007 REPORT ON THE DEMOCRATIC OVERSIGHT OF THE SECURITY SERVICES AND REPORT ON THE DEMOCRATIC OVERSIGHT OF SIGNALS INTELLIGENCE AGENCIES, 2015, Study No. 719/2013, CDL-AD(2015)006.

[131] 2015, Cm. 9152. See also JUDITH DAWSON, *DRAFT INVESTIGATORY POWERS BILL*, 2015, CBP-7371, House of Commons Library.

leading up to the Bill. On the other hand, the Bill is far from comprehensive. It concentrates on the interception powers of RIPA 2000, and so only Part I and the Data Retention and Investigatory Powers Act 2014 are replaced wholesale. Conversely, the Bill is almost entirely silent on subjects such as CHIS and encryption. Furthermore, the oversight of the powers is not as strong as many critics would wish. The more intrusive powers in the Bill (warrants for interception, equipment interference by the security and intelligence agencies, and powers in bulk) will be overseen by independent Judicial Commissioners who will consider the justification for executive warrants on judicial review principles. At the same time, full judicial pre-authorisation is not advanced by the Bill, which leaves most authorisations being issued by the Secretary of State. The justification is that the importance of executive authorization in overseeing the use of intrusive powers and ensuring accountability to Parliament must remain predominant. This empowerment of the executive is based on dubious assertions about the skills of ministers[132] and their willingness to discuss in public security decisions.[133] In conclusion, while battles remain as to the future shape of intelligence powers and accountability in the UK, one might predict that the allure and convenience of executive control over security matters will not be wrested easily from the firm grasp of Ministers of the Crown.

---

[132] See Walker, C., 'Terrorism prosecutions and the right to a fair trial' in RESEARCH HANDBOOK ON INTERNATIONAL LAW AND TERRORISM (Saul, B., ed.) (Edward Elgar, Cheltenham, 2014).

[133] For multiple examples of refusals to respond to Parliamentary questions, see House of Commons Public Administration Select Committee, *Ministerial Accountability and Parliamentary Questions* (2004-05 HC 449) vol.II.

12

Executive Oversight of Intelligence Agencies in Australia

Keiran Hardy* and George Williams**

I. INTRODUCTION

When it comes to government accountability, intelligence agencies present a special case. Ordinarily, government departments are subject to robust scrutiny from a variety of sources. The media constantly inspects, evaluates, and critiques the conduct of government and its policies. This fuels further discussion by the general public through print, radio, and social media. Courts assess whether government officials have used their statutory powers in accordance with the law and whether the legislation that provides those powers is constitutional. Parliament examines the expenditure, administration, and operation of government agencies through estimates hearings and committee inquiries and by inspecting their annual reports. Tribunals assess whether government officials made their decisions correctly,[1] and ombudsmen investigate whether those decisions were unjust, oppressive, or discriminatory.[2] This combination of public, judicial, legislative, and executive scrutiny is a comprehensive system for maintaining the accountability of government.

Many of these avenues are ineffective or problematic when applied to intelligence agencies due to the inherent secrecy of their work. The classification of national security information and exemptions from freedom of information (FOI) legislation mean that media and public

* Lecturer, School of Criminology and Criminal Justice, Griffith University.

** Anthony Mason Professor, Scientia Professor and Foundation Director, Gilbert + Tobin Centre of Public Law, Faculty of Law, University of New South Wales; Australian Research Council Laureate Fellow; Barrister, New South Wales Bar.

[1] *Drake v. Minister for Immigration and Ethnic Affairs* (1979) 24 ALR 577, 591.

[2] *Ombudsman Act 1976* (Cth) § 15(1)(a)(ii).

scrutiny of intelligence agencies can be superficial at best.[3] Indeed, some laws are specifically designed to outlaw public discussion of intelligence operations. For example, in October 2014, the conservative Liberal-National Coalition government led by Australian prime minister Tony Abbott enacted a Special Intelligence Operations (SIO) regime.[4] This regime grants officers of the Australian Security Intelligence Organisation (ASIO) immunity for unlawful acts done in the course of specially approved undercover operations.[5] Attached to this regime is a criminal offense punishable by five years imprisonment that applies to anyone who discloses information relating to an SIO.[6] This offense prohibits any public discussion of SIOs—even if, for example, a journalist revealed that ASIO officers had mishandled an operation, caused death or serious injury to a suspect, or been involved in an illegal activity.

The possibilities for holding intelligence agencies accountable in the courts are also limited. Judges may defer to the executive branch when a case involves national security concerns,[7] and the use of secret evidence can make it difficult for individuals to challenge the conduct of intelligence officers or decisions by intelligence officials.[8] In Australia, the possibilities for judicial review are further limited because intelligence agencies are exempt from the Administrative Decisions (Judicial Review) Act 1977 (Cth), which provides for statutory judicial review of administrative action.[9] Australia also lacks a national, judicially enforceable Bill of Rights, which further limits opportunities for individuals to challenge the lawfulness of statutory powers granted to intelligence agencies. Individuals cannot, for example, challenge such legislation on the grounds that it infringes a general right to freedom of speech or association. To give rise to constitutional concerns, the legislation must, for example, infringe the separation of powers or one of a few implied rights in the Australian Constitution.[10] No such constitutional limits have ever proven to be of use in challenging the statutory powers of Australian intelligence agencies.

---

[3] *Freedom of Information Act 1982* sch 3.

[4] *Australian Security Intelligence Organisation Act 1979* (Cth) pt III div 4, which was enacted pursuant to *National Security Legislation Amendment Act (No. 1) 2014* (Cth) sch 3.

[5] *Australian Security Intelligence Organisation Act 1979* (Cth) § 35K.

[6] *Id.* § 35P.

[7] *See generally*, Ashley S. Deeks, *The Observer Effect: National Security Litigation, Executive Policy Changes, and Judicial Deference*, 82 FORDHAM L. REV. 827 (2013); Robert M. Chesney, *National Security Fact Deference*, 95 VA. L. REV. 1361 (2009); Kim Lane Scheppele, *The New Judicial Deference*, 92 B.U. L. REV 89 (2012). In Australia, judicial deference to the executive branch is particularly apparent when policy or administrative decisions combine immigration and national security concerns. *See* Brian Galligan & Emma Larking, School of Political Sciences, Criminology & Sociology, The University of Melbourne, Paper presented at Australasian Political Science Association Conference, University of Queensland: *The Separation of Judicial and Executive Powers in Australia: Detention Decisions and the Haneef Case* (July 9, 2008), at 15–16. For example, in *Leghaei v. Director-General of Security* [2005] FCA 1576, the Federal Court held (at ¶ 88) that procedural fairness requirements applied to adverse security assessments issued by ASIO, but due to national security considerations these requirements were, in practical terms, reduced to "nothingness." On ASIO's power to issue adverse security assessments, see discussion below in Section III(B).

[8] *See, e.g.*, Nicola McGarrity & Edward Santow, "Anti-Terrorism Laws; Balancing National Security and a Fair Hearing" *in* GLOBAL ANTI-TERRORISM LAW AND POLICY (Victor V Ramraj et al. eds., 2d ed, 2012); Keiran Hardy, *ASIO, Adverse Security Assessments and a Denial of Procedural Fairness*, 17 AUSTL. J. ADMIN. L. 39, 44–45 (2009); Rebecca Scott Bray & Greg Martin, *Closing Down Open Justice in the United Kingdom*, 37 ALTERNATIVE L.J. 126 (2012).

[9] *Administrative Decisions (Judicial Review) Act 1977* (Cth) sch 1 § 3 item 3.

[10] For example, the Australian High Court has read into the Constitution an implied freedom of political communication and an implied right to vote. *Lange v. Australian Broadcasting Corporation* (1997) 189 CLR 520;

Parliamentary scrutiny of intelligence agencies is also limited. Only one of the six intelligence agencies in Australia is required to produce an annual report to Parliament,[11] and any operationally sensitive parts of that report are redacted.[12] Even if the intelligence agencies were required to provide more information to Parliament, parliamentarians do not typically have the knowledge and experience required to assess the appropriateness of intelligence-gathering priorities or operations.[13]

Specialized parliamentary committees are playing an increasingly important role to fill this gap,[14] but their effectiveness can also be limited due to political interests, tightly defined statutory powers, and the protection of classified information. Australia's Parliamentary Joint Committee on Intelligence and Security (PJCIS) examines new counterterrorism laws introduced by the government,[15] but is required to have a majority of government members,[16] and so its findings usually align with the political and policy priorities of the government of the day. As a result, the Committee may not recommend substantive changes to otherwise extraordinary counterterrorism measures.[17] The PJCIS also reviews the expenditure and administration of Australia's six intelligence agencies,[18] but it is not permitted to review intelligence-gathering priorities or operations, and it has no power to launch inquiries of its own choosing.[19] Much of the Committee's work is also conducted behind closed

---

Roach v Electoral Commission (2007) 233 CLR 162. *See generally* DAVID HUME & GEORGE WILLIAMS, HUMAN RIGHTS UNDER THE AUSTRALIAN CONSTITUTION (2d ed. 2013).

[11] *Australian Security Intelligence Organisation Act 1979* (Cth) § 94. The Director-General of the Australian Secret Intelligence Service is also required to produce an annual report, but this is given only to the Minister for Foreign Affairs, and is not required to be submitted to Parliament. *Intelligence Services Act 2001* (Cth) § 42.

[12] *Australian Security Intelligence Organisation Act 1979* (Cth) § 94(5).

[13] HUGH BOCHEL ET AL., WATCHING THE WATCHERS: PARLIAMENT AND THE INTELLIGENCE SERVICES 5–6 (2014).

[14] *See id.* at 75–102; Andrew Defty, *Educating Parliamentarians about Intelligence: The Role of the British Intelligence and Security Committee*, 61(4) PARLIAMENTARY AFFAIRS 621 (2008); Peter Gill, *Evaluating Intelligence Oversight Committees: The UK Intelligence and Security Committee and the "War on Terror,"* 22(1) INTELLIGENCE & NAT'L SECURITY 14 (2007); Jennifer Kibbe, *Congressional Oversight of Intelligence: Is the Solution Part of the Problem?*, 25(1) INTELLIGENCE & NAT'L SECURITY 24 (2010).

[15] *See. e.g.,* PARLIAMENTARY JOINT COMMITTEE ON INTELLIGENCE AND SECURITY, PARLIAMENT OF AUSTRALIA, ADVISORY REPORT ON THE COUNTER-TERRORISM LEGISLATION AMENDMENT (FOREIGN FIGHTERS) BILL 2014 (2014) [hereinafter PJCIS Report]; PARLIAMENTARY JOINT COMMITTEE ON INTELLIGENCE AND SECURITY, PARLIAMENT OF AUSTRALIA, ADVISORY REPORT ON THE NATIONAL SECURITY LEGISLATION AMENDMENT BILL (NO. 1) 2014 (2014).

[16] *Intelligence Services Act 2001* (Cth) § 28(3).

[17] For example, in September 2014 the Abbott government introduced a range of controversial new measures in response to the threat of foreign fighters returning from Syria and Iraq. These new laws included an offense punishable by 10 years imprisonment for entering or remaining in a "declared area." An area of a foreign country may be designated as a "declared area" where the Minister for Foreign Affairs is satisfied that a terrorist organization is engaged in hostile activity in that area. The person need only travel to the area, and need not have any malicious intent. The PJCIS recommended some improvements to the legislation, such as removing the power to declare a whole country as a "declared area" and providing for Committee oversight of the minister's declarations, but it recommended no substantive changes to this otherwise extraordinary offense. *See Criminal Code Act 1995* (Cth) § 119.2; PJCIS Report, *supra* note 15, at 103–08.

[18] *Intelligence Services Act 2001* (Cth) § 29(1)(a).

[19] *Id.* at § 29(3). Inquiries must be referred to the PJCIS either by the responsible minister or by a resolution of either House of Parliament: *Intelligence Services Act 2001* (Cth) § 29(1)(b). The Committee may, by resolution,

doors, as it frequently relies on classified submissions, and its reports may be redacted by the responsible minister on the advice of the intelligence agencies.[20] This means that the public must often trust that the PJCIS is using its limited powers to hold the intelligence agencies to account, rather than knowing this to be the case.

The fact that public, judicial, and parliamentary scrutiny of Australia's intelligence agencies is severely constrained means that the executive branch takes on a particularly important role in holding these agencies to account. Specially appointed office holders and inquiries are trusted, where others are not, to access classified information and assess the appropriateness of intelligence agencies' powers and operations. This is not to suggest that the other mechanisms considered above are not also important or complementary, where they are available. However, it is clear that these other mechanisms are less robust and effective when applied to intelligence agencies as compared to other aspects of government.

The key conceptual and practical problem with executive oversight of intelligence agencies is that the relevant accountability mechanisms—including statutory officeholders, royal commissions, and administrative tribunals—are part of the same arm of government to which the intelligence agencies belong. This undermines the notion of "horizontal" accountability, being that the different arms of government—legislature, judiciary, executive—should keep each other in check.[21] There is an increasing amount of scholarship on executive oversight mechanisms as an "integrity branch" of government,[22] but these integrity mechanisms are not yet sufficiently independent from the rest of government to compare their accountability function to the traditional separation of powers.

Executive oversight mechanisms therefore play an important but also potentially problematic role in keeping intelligence agencies accountable. Given this, the aim of this chapter is to assess whether executive oversight of the Australian intelligence agencies is robust, stringent, and effective. It considers whether there are any gaps or vulnerabilities in this system of executive accountability, and whether stronger powers or other improvements are needed to further counterbalance the limited public, judicial, and parliamentary scrutiny of intelligence agencies.

In Section II, we set out the six Australian intelligence agencies and their functions. In Section III, we set out the executive bodies that oversee those agencies, including their responsible ministers, the Inspector-General of Intelligence and Security, the Independent National Security Legislation Monitor, and other various forms of oversight and inquiry. We categorize these mechanisms according to the function they perform (such as authorizing the use of covert powers, or reviewing legislation) and explain their jurisdiction and investigative powers. In line with the other contributions to this collection,[23] we also consider a range of *governance* mechanisms: those that oversee the intelligence agencies by developing intelligence policy and setting their collection priorities—rather than simply ensuring their compliance with the law.

---

ask the minister to refer something for its consideration, but a referral is not guaranteed. *See Intelligence Services Act 2001* (Cth) § 29(2).

[20] *Intelligence Services Act 2001* (Cth) sch 1 cl 7.

[21] BOCHEL ET AL., *supra* note 13, at 4.

[22] *See, e.g.*, Lisa Burton & George Williams, *The Integrity Function and ASIO's Extraordinary Questioning and Detention Powers*, 38(3) MONASH U. L. REV. 1 (2012).

[23] *See, e.g.*, the contributions of Zachary Goldman, Jane Harman, Jon Moran and Clive Walker, and Kent Roach to this volume.

In Section IV, we evaluate the strengths and weaknesses of this executive accountability system. To this end, we consider a range of important questions. Do executive oversight bodies sufficiently cover the activities and administration of Australia's intelligence agencies, or are there significant gaps in jurisdiction? Are the investigative powers of these bodies sufficiently strong to undertake robust inquiries? Do these bodies have appropriate powers to remedy instances of misconduct or wrongdoing? Have executive oversight mechanisms proved effective in keeping the Australian intelligence agencies accountable? The conclusion returns to these questions and draws some broader lessons about the role that the executive branch plays in holding secret intelligence organizations to account. In particular, our analysis suggests that executive accountability mechanisms are weak to the extent that they possess only recommendatory powers, and their effectiveness depends on whether the government of the day is willing to accept recommendations for change. Our analysis also suggests there are limits to what executive oversight can achieve when the government of the day grants intelligence agencies statutory powers of extraordinary reach. These conclusions emerge from the Australian experience, but they are also of more general application in identifying broader themes and concerns that relate to the operation of intelligence organizations in a range of nations.

II. AUSTRALIAN INTELLIGENCE AGENCIES

Australia has six intelligence agencies, which are collectively known as the Australian Intelligence Community (AIC). Two of these agencies are responsible for collecting intelligence from human sources (HUMINT): a foreign intelligence collection agency and a domestic security service, the latter being also responsible for intelligence assessment. There are three intelligence agencies situated within the Department of Defence, one of which is an assessment (as opposed to collection) agency. Finally, another assessment agency is responsible to the Prime Minister.

A. Human Intelligence

1. Australian Secret Intelligence Service

The Australian Secret Intelligence Service (ASIS) is Australia's foreign intelligence collection agency. Like the other foreign intelligence collection agencies set out below, ASIS is governed by the Intelligence Services Act 2001 (Cth) (ISA 2001). Its main functions under the ISA 2001 are "to obtain . . . intelligence about the capabilities, intentions or activities of people or organizations outside Australia,"[24] and to communicate that intelligence to government as required.[25] ASIS also conducts counterintelligence activities and provides assistance to the Australian Defence Force (ADF) in its overseas military operations.[26] In these respects, ASIS is the Australian equivalent of MI6, the British Secret Intelligence Service.[27]

---

[24] *Intelligence Services Act 2001* (Cth) § 6(1)(a).

[25] *Id.* § 6(1)(b).

[26] *Id.* § 6(1)(ba)–(c).

[27] *Intelligence Services Act 1994* (UK) c 13, § 1.

In contrast to the U.S. Central Intelligence Agency (CIA), ASIS officers are not permitted to undertake paramilitary activities, nor to proactively engage in the use of violence.[28] Like all the other Australian intelligence agencies, ASIS is also prohibited from carrying out police functions (such as arresting and charging individuals for criminal offenses) or enforcing the law in any other way.[29] ASIS officers employed overseas are, however, trained in the use of some weapons—including handguns, batons, and capsicum spray—for the purposes of self-defense.[30]

2. Australian Security Intelligence Organisation

The Australian Security Intelligence Organisation is Australia's domestic security service. Its main role is to "gather information and produce intelligence that will enable it to warn the government about activities or situations that might endanger Australia's national security."[31] In the post-9/11 era, this means that much of ASIO's work involves collecting and assessing intelligence on potential terrorist threats within Australia's borders. In this respect, ASIO is the Australian equivalent of MI5, the British security service. ASIO also undertakes security assessments of foreign nationals applying for refugee status in Australia.[32]

ASIO is governed by the Australian Security Intelligence Organisation Act 1979 (Cth) (ASIO Act).[33] The organization's main function under the ASIO Act is to "obtain, correlate and evaluate intelligence relevant to security."[34] Under section 4 of the ASIO Act, "security" is defined broadly as the protection of the Australian government and its people from espionage, sabotage, politically motivated violence, the promotion of communal violence, attacks on Australia's defense system, acts of foreign interference, and serious threats to border security.[35] Like ASIS, ASIO is not permitted to perform police functions such as arrest.[36] However, ASIO officers exercise a range of clandestine powers similar to those used by law enforcement, such as searching private premises and installing telephone intercept devices.[37]

B. Defense Intelligence Agencies

1. Australian Signals Directorate

The Australian Signals Directorate (ASD), formerly the Defence Signals Directorate (DSD), is Australia's signals intelligence agency. It is the equivalent of Britain's Government

---

[28] *Intelligence Services Act 2001* (Cth) § 6(4).

[29] *Id.* § 11(2). It may however communicate that intelligence to law enforcement where necessary. *See Intelligence Services Act 2001* (Cth) § 11(2)(c).

[30] *See id.* at sch 2.

[31] AUSTRALIAN SECURITY INTELLIGENCE ORGANISATION, *available at* http://www.asio.gov.au (last visited June 15, 2015).

[32] *Australian Security Intelligence Organisation Act 1979* (Cth) pt 4.

[33] Prior to this Act, the relevant legislation was the *Australian Security Intelligence Organisation Act 1956* (Cth).

[34] *Id.* § 17(1)(a).

[35] *Id.* § 4.

[36] *Id.* § 17(2).

[37] *See id.* at pts 2, 3.

Communication Headquarters (GCHQ) or the U.S. National Security Agency, although ASD is more specifically focused on military activities than its American and British counterparts. Like ASIS, ASD is governed by the ISA 2001. Under the ISA 2001, ASD's primary functions are to collect foreign signals intelligence and communicate that intelligence to the Australian government and the ADF in support of its military operations.[38] ASD also plays an important role in information and cyber security—such as advising government departments how to protect their computer networks, coordinating responses to cyber attacks, and providing services in codebreaking and encryption.[39]

2. Australian Geospatial-Intelligence Organisation

The Australian Geospatial-Intelligence Organisation (AGO) is Australia's geospatial intelligence agency. Geospatial intelligence is intelligence gained from imagery and geospatial data—such as topographical maps and images from aircraft and satellites. Like ASIS and ASD, AGO is a foreign intelligence collection agency governed by the ISA 2001; its main function is to collection intelligence "about the capabilities, intentions or activities of people or organisations outside Australia."[40] AGO communicates that intelligence to the Australian government and the ADF, and assists Commonwealth and state bodies in responding to security threats and natural disasters.[41]

3. Defence Intelligence Organisation

The Defence Intelligence Organisation (DIO) is a strategic, all-source assessment agency. This means that DIO does not collect intelligence, but rather relies on intelligence collected by the foreign collection agencies (i.e., ASIS, ASD, and AGO), as well as open source material such as media and policy documents, to produce strategic policy advice to the Australian government and the ADF. DIO assessments are used to support ADF operations as well as government planning on defense and national security issues.[42] For example, an assessment produced by DIO might include information about the military capabilities, weapons systems, and cyber-warfare capabilities of countries relevant to Australia's security environment.[43] Whereas the functions of ASIS, ASD, and AGO are each set out in the ISA 2001,[44] DIO has no explicit statutory function.[45]

---

[38] *Intelligence Services Act 2001* (Cth) § 7.

[39] *See* AUSTRALIAN SIGNALS DIRECTORATE, INFORMATION SECURITY, *available at* http://www.asd.gov.au/infosec/index.htm (last visited July 9, 2015).

[40] *Intelligence Services Act 2001* (Cth) § 6B(a).

[41] *Id.* §§ 6B(d), (e)(iii).

[42] DEFENCE INTELLIGENCE ORGANISATION, ABOUT US, *available at* http://www.defence.gov.au/dio/about-us.shtml (last visited July 9, 2015).

[43] *Id.*

[44] *Intelligence Services Act 2001* (Cth) §§ 6, 6B, 7.

[45] *See* AUSTRALIAN GOVERNMENT, THE AUSTRALIAN INTELLIGENCE COMMUNITY: AGENCIES, FUNCTIONS, ACCOUNTABILITY AND OVERSIGHT 5 (2006). However, the ISA 2001 does include some relevant provisions, including offenses where a DIO employee discloses or unlawfully records classified information. *Intelligence Services Act 2001* (Cth), §§ 40B, 40M.

C. Intelligence Assessment

1. Office of National Assessments

The Office of National Assessments (ONA) is an all-source assessment agency that produces reports for the prime minister and the Australian government on international matters of political, strategic, and economic importance.[46] Like DIO, ONA relies on intelligence collected by the other intelligence agencies and open source material, as well as information from other government departments. ONA also helps to coordinate and evaluate Australia's foreign intelligence activities, such as by providing advice to the government as to whether the intelligence agencies have sufficient resources.[47] ONA is an independent body established under section 4(1) of the Office of National Assessments Act 1977 (Cth).

III. EXECUTIVE OVERSIGHT

In this section, we set out the key executive bodies that oversee Australia's six intelligence agencies. We categorize these bodies according to the function they perform, such as authorizing clandestine powers and reviewing intelligence operations. These oversight bodies supplement the role of the PJCIS, which reviews new counterterrorism laws and oversees the administration and expenditure of the intelligence agencies.[48] However, as explained in the introduction, the PJCIS has a tendency to align with government policy, and its statutory powers are tightly defined.[49] Many of the mechanisms outlined below have a wider remit, such as by being able to launch their own inquiries and review intelligence operations.

A. Ministerial Authorization of Powers

Each of Australia's intelligence agencies is responsible to a cabinet minister in the federal government. ASIS is responsible to the Minister for Foreign Affairs, ASIO to the Attorney-General, the three defense intelligence agencies to the Minister for Defence, and ONA to the prime minister. Unlike in the United States, these senior members of the executive branch are required to sit in Parliament.[50] In theory, this means that the responsible ministers are accountable via Parliament to the Australian people for any misconduct or maladministration by the intelligence agencies. This is one of the core characteristics of the system of responsible government adopted as part of the Westminster system by Australia, the U.K., and other like nations.

Responsible government in this case is undermined by the inherent secrecy of intelligence operations. As explained above, only one of the six intelligence agencies (ASIO) is required to table an annual report in Parliament,[51] and any operationally sensitive information in that report is redacted.[52] This makes it virtually impossible to identify from the report whether

---

[46] Office of National Assessments Act 1977 (Cth) § 5(1)(a).

[47] Id. § 5(1B)(b).

[48] Intelligence Services Act 2001 (Cth) § 29.

[49] Id.

[50] AUSTRALIAN CONSTITUTION § 64.

[51] Australian Security Intelligence Organisation Act 1979 (Cth) § 94.

[52] Id. § 94(5).

ASIO has misused its powers, or to make that determination unless such information is forthcoming from other sources.[53]

The more significant accountability function performed by the responsible ministers is to authorize the use of clandestine powers by intelligence officers. For example, the Director-General of Security (the head of ASIO) may request the Attorney-General to issue a warrant allowing ASIO officers to search private premises.[54] The Attorney-General may do so where he or she is satisfied on reasonable grounds that ASIO officers accessing records or things on those premises would "substantially assist the collection of intelligence . . . that is important in relation to security."[55] Similar examples include ministerial warrants that allow ASIO officers to intercept telephone calls, install surveillance devices, inspect postal articles, and access data held on computers.[56]

Ministerial authorization is also required before the foreign intelligence collection agencies are able to collect any intelligence on Australian citizens.[57] These agencies are prohibited from collecting intelligence on Australian citizens unless the relevant minister is satisfied that the person is likely to be involved in one of a range of serious activities—including those that pose a significant risk to safety, are likely to be a threat to security, or are related to the proliferation of weapons of mass destruction.[58] These ministerial authorizations may also be issued in relation to a "class of Australian persons" where one of the intelligence agencies is assisting the ADF in its overseas military operations.[59] What constitutes a "class of Australian persons" is not defined or otherwise set out in the Act.

Stronger protections apply to ASIO's questioning and detention warrants.[60] These are one of the most controversial counterterrorism powers available to ASIO. They allow, pursuant to a warrant, any person to be questioned for up to 24 hours, and detained for up to one week for that purpose, without being suspected of any involvement in terrorism.[61] A person must

---

[53] For example, ASIO's most recent annual report includes the findings of the Independent Reviewer of Adverse Security Assessments, who concluded that one adverse security assessment issued by ASIO was not appropriate, and that ASIO had updated that assessment as a result. *See* AUSTRALIAN SECURITY INTELLIGENCE ORGANISATION, ASIO REPORT TO PARLIAMENT: 2013–2014, at 48 (2014) [hereinafter ASIO Annual Report 2014].

[54] *Australian Security Intelligence Organisation Act 1979* (Cth) § 25(1).

[55] *Id.* § 25(2).

[56] *Id.* §§ 25A, 26, 27; *Telecommunications (Interception and Access) Act 1979* (Cth) § 9.

[57] By contrast, ASIO is charged with collecting and analyzing intelligence relevant to "security," which is defined as a range of threats to Australia's national interests, including espionage, sabotage, and politically motivated violence. *See Australian Security Intelligence Organisation Act 1979* (Cth) §§ 4, 17. This ensures a division of responsibilities, similar to that between the FBI and CIA, by which ASIO is responsible for collecting intelligence on Australian citizens and foreign nationals within Australia's borders, and the foreign collection agencies are responsible for collecting intelligence overseas, including intelligence on Australian citizens. The agencies can, however, cooperate in the performance of their functions, provided that they do so subject to any arrangements or directions by the responsible minister. *See Australian Security Intelligence Organisation Act 1979* (Cth) §§ 17(1)(f), 19A; *Intelligence Services Act 2001* (Cth) § 13A.

[58] *Intelligence Services Act 2001* (Cth) § 9(1A).

[59] *Id.* § 8(1)(a)(ia)–(ib).

[60] *Australian Security Intelligence Organisation Act 1979* (Cth) pt 3 div 3.

[61] *Id.* §§ 34G, 34R, 34S.

answer a question put to him or her by ASIO, or face imprisonment for up to five years.[62] To apply for one of these warrants, the Director-General of Security must first obtain the Attorney-General's consent to apply to an "issuing authority" (who must be a serving judge, and has the same protection and immunity as a Justice of the High Court of Australia).[63] The Attorney-General may grant consent only where he or she is satisfied about a range of conditions, including that the warrant would substantially assist in the collection of intelligence and that other means of collecting the intelligence would be ineffective.[64] The issuing authority provides an added layer of executive oversight,[65] and is permitted to issue the warrant only if he or she agrees that the person's detention would substantially assist in the collection of intelligence that is relevant to security.[66] The Director-General of Security must also provide details on the use of questioning and detention warrants in ASIO's annual report, including the number of requests made, the number of warrants issued, and the number of hours each person spent under questioning and in detention.[67]

B. Review of Operations

When an intelligence agency seeks to rely upon special powers such as clandestine searches and surveillance, it is important not only that those powers are independently authorized before their use, but that they are also subject to rigorous post-hoc review to assess whether they have been misused or used unlawfully. In Australia, primary responsibility for this lies with the Inspector-General of Intelligence and Security (IGIS), an independent statutory office established by the Inspector-General of Intelligence and Security Act 1986 (Cth). The office was created in response to concerns that Australia's intelligence agencies "were not sufficiently under ministerial control, nor subject to enough scrutiny."[68] The position is currently held by Dr. Vivienne Thom, a former Deputy Ombudsman.

The IGIS supervises the six intelligence agencies by assessing whether they have acted in accordance with laws, directions, and guidelines, and whether their activities are consistent with human rights.[69] The IGIS also assesses the "propriety" of their activities, although the precise meaning of this term remains unclear.[70] To assess the intelligence agencies' activities against these criteria, the IGIS conducts two forms of review: inquiries and formal inspections.[71] Inspections involve regular scrutiny of intelligence agencies' records and oversight of

---

[62] Id. § 34L(2).

[63] Id. §§ 34AB, 34F, 34ZM.

[64] Id. § 34F(4).

[65] In Australia, judges can perform executive or administrative functions such as issuing warrants if Parliament confers a function on the judge in his or her personal capacity, the judge consents to performing that function, and the function is not incompatible with the holding of judicial office. See Hilton v. Wells (1985) 157 CLR 57; Grollo v. Palmer (1995) 184 CLR 348; Wilson and Ors v. Minister for Aboriginal and Torres Strait Islander Affairs and Anor (1996) 189 CLR 1.

[66] Australian Security Intelligence Organisation Act 1979 (Cth) § 34G(1)(b).

[67] Id. § 94(1).

[68] Vivienne Thom, Inspector-General of Intelligence and Security, Speech at the Supreme and Federal Court Judges' Conference: Address to Supreme and Federal Court Judges' Conference (Jan. 26, 2009), at 2.

[69] Inspector-General of Intelligence and Security Act 1986 (Cth) §§ 8(1)(a)(i)–(ii), (v).

[70] Id. § 8(1)(a)(iii). See Burton & Williams, supra note 22, at 12.

[71] Inspector-General of Intelligence and Security Act 1986 (Cth) §§ 8, 9A.

some statutory powers.[72] For example, when the head of ASIO requests a questioning and detention warrant, the IGIS must be informed and may be present during the questioning or enter any place of detention.[73]

The IGIS has conducted several inquiries into alleged misconduct by the Australian intelligence agencies, including one relating to the detention and torture overseas of Mamdouh Habib, a dual Australian-Egyptian citizen.[74] These inquiries may be conducted at the request of a responsible minister, at the request of the prime minister, after a complaint to the IGIS, or on the IGIS's own motion.[75] To conduct these inquiries, the IGIS is bestowed with strong investigative powers akin to those held by royal commissions—including powers to summon witnesses, compel documents, and enter the intelligence agencies' premises at any reasonable time.[76]

The IGIS also conducts an inquiry if an intelligence employee seeks protection for disclosing information under the Public Interest Disclosure Act 2013 (Cth) (PID Act).[77] The PID Act is a new federal whistle-blower scheme; it provides immunity from civil, criminal, and administrative liability for public officials who according to a specified procedure disclose wrongdoing by government departments.[78] Generally, the opportunities for intelligence officers to seek protection under the scheme are very limited.[79] However, they may disclose information to the IGIS where they believe on reasonable grounds that it would be appropriate for one or more instances of misconduct to be investigated by the office.[80]

The other major post-hoc review of ASIO's activities is undertaken by the Security Appeals Division of the Administrative Appeals Tribunal (AAT). Merits review of decisions by intelligence agencies is generally prohibited, although the Security Appeals Division has jurisdiction to review adverse security assessments issued by ASIO.[81] An adverse security assessment is a security assessment made by ASIO that recommends that certain administrative action

---

[72] *Id.* § 9A. *See* Thom, *supra* note 68, at 1–2.

[73] *Australian Security Intelligence Organisation Act 1979* (Cth) §§ 34ZI, 34P, 34Q; *Inspector-General of Intelligence and Security Act 1986* (Cth) §§ 9B, 19A. Most recently, the inspection functions of the IGIS were expanded to include oversight of ASIO's Special Intelligence Operations (SIO) regime: *Australian Security Intelligence Organisation Act 1979* (Cth) s 35PA.

[74] Inspector-General of Intelligence and Security, Inquiry into the Actions of Australian Government Agencies in relation to the Arrest and Detention Overseas of Mr Mamdouh Habib from 2001 to 2005 (2011). Habib was suspected of having prior knowledge of the September 11 attacks; he was arrested in Pakistan, then sent to Egypt under the CIA's rendition program, and then detained as an enemy combatant for approximately three years in Guantanamo Bay.

[75] *Inspector-General of Intelligence and Security Act 1986* (Cth) § 8.

[76] In line with royal commission powers, the IGIS can compel a person to answer a question or produce a document that would incriminate him- or herself. *See Inspector-General of Intelligence and Security Act 1986* (Cth) § 18(6). However, the information or document cannot be used in evidence except in a prosecution for refusing to provide information or documents to the IGIS, or for providing false or misleading information: *id.*

[77] *Inspector-General of Intelligence and Security Act 1986* (Cth) § 8A.

[78] *Public Interest Disclosure Act 2013* (Cth) §§ 10(1), 26.

[79] Due to exemptions for intelligence information. *Public Interest Disclosure Act 2013* (Cth) §§ 26(1)(c). *See* Keiran Hardy & George Williams, *Terrorist, Traitor or Whistleblower? Offences and Protections in Australia for Disclosing National Security Information*, 37(2) U. New South Wales L.J. 784, 814–15 (2014).

[80] *See id.* at 814; *Public Interest Disclosure Act 2013* (Cth) § 34(1).

[81] *Australian Security Intelligence Organisation Act 1979* (Cth) § 54.

be taken against the interests of an individual (such as cancelling a passport or denying employment at an airport).[82] Australian citizens can apply to the Security Appeals Division to have these decisions reviewed on their merits.[83]

A significant number of adverse security assessments are issued in relation to noncitizens applying for refugee status in Australia.[84] A noncitizen who is denied refugee status due to an adverse security assessment cannot seek merits review of that decision in the AAT.[85] However, the person can apply to the Independent Reviewer of Adverse Security Assessments (Independent Reviewer of ASAs), an office that was established in December 2012 and extended in 2014 for a further two-year term.[86] The Independent Reviewer of ASAs conducts independent advisory reviews and 12-month periodic reviews of adverse security assessments issued in relation to noncitizens seeking refugee status.[87] The position is currently held by the Honorable Margaret Stone, a former federal court judge.

Occasionally, review of the intelligence agencies' activities is conducted by royal commissions and other ad hoc inquiries. Early in ASIO's history, the Menzies government appointed a royal commission into Soviet espionage in Australia after a KGB agent posing as a senior member of the Soviet Embassy defected.[88] Two further royal commissions in the 1970s and 1980s, led by New South Wales Supreme Court Judge Robert Hope, examined the structure, functions, and accountability of the intelligence agencies.[89] The Hope Royal Commissions resulted in significant changes to the administrative structure and accountability mechanisms applying to Australia's intelligence agencies, including the division of intelligence-gathering functions between ASIO and the foreign collection agencies, the creation of ONA as an independent statutory agency, and the creation of the IGIS and PJCIS.[90]

---

[82] *Id.* § 35.

[83] *Id.* § 54.

[84] In 2013/14, ASIO issued 27,149 security assessments in relation to visa applications by noncitizens. *See ASIO Annual Report 2014, supra* note 53, at xiii.

[85] *Australian Security Intelligence Organisation Act 1979* (Cth) § 36.

[86] Attorney-General, Continuation of the Office of the Independent Reviewer of Adverse Security Assessments (Dec. 11, 2014), *available at* http://www.attorneygeneral.gov.au/ Mediareleases/Pages/2014/FourthQuarter/11December2014-ContinuationoftheOfficeofthe IndependentReviewerofAdverseSecurityAssessments.aspx.

[87] Nicola Roxon, Independent Reviewer of Adverse Security Assessments: Independent Review Function—Terms of Reference (Oct. 16, 2012), *available at* http://www.cla.asn.au/ Submissions/2012/Independent%20Reviewer%20for%20Adverse%20Security%20Assessments.pdf.

[88] *See* John Faulkner, *Surveillance, Intelligence and Accountability: An Australian Story,* Australian Fin. Rev., Oct. 24, 2014, at 21 (full essay *available at* http://www.afr.com/rw/2009-2014/AFR/2014/10/23/Photos/ cad23366-5a65-11e4-a5ea-c145dc509150_Surveillance,%20Intelligence%20and%20Accountability%20by%20 senator%20John%20Faulkner.pdf); Museum of Australian Democracy, *The Petrov Affair: Royal Commission, available at* http://moadoph.gov.au/exhibitions/online/petrov/royal-commission.html (last visited, Jan. 7, 2016)).

[89] *See* Faulkner, *supra* note 88, at 21–22.

[90] *See* Office of National Assessments, History of the Australian Intelligence Community (2010), *available at* http://www.ona.gov.au/history/australian-intelligence-community.html (last visited June 15, 2015). *See also* Faulkner, *supra* note 88, at 14–18. Although Justice Hope recommended against creating a parliamentary oversight committee, the Labor government nonetheless created the Parliamentary Joint Committee on the Australian Security Intelligence Organisation (later expanded into the PJCIS). Parliamentary Debates, House of Representatives, 22 May 1985 (Robert Hawke, Prime Minister) (Austl.), *available at*

More recent inquiries have investigated specific instances of wrongdoing. For example, in 2008, the then Attorney-General Robert McClelland appointed the Honorable John Clarke QC to report on the arrest and detention of Mohamed Haneef.[91] Haneef was an Indian doctor working in Australia who was mistakenly linked to the bombing attempt on Glasgow airport.

Ordinarily, the Commonwealth Ombudsman would play a key role in reviewing the administrative decisions of government departments,[92] but that office does not have jurisdiction over the intelligence agencies.[93] The Commonwealth Ombudsman does play a limited role in overseeing ASIO's questioning and detention warrant regime, as a person being detained must be informed of his or her right to make a complaint to the office.[94] However, such complaints may only be made in relation to the conduct of Australian Federal Police (AFP) officers in taking the person into custody.[95]

C. Law Reform

In addition to the authorization and post-hoc review of intelligence agencies' powers, it is important to assess whether the legislation that provides those powers is appropriate and does not unduly infringe rights. In Australia, the key executive body responsible for this is the Independent National Security Legislation Monitor (INSLM).[96] Although many individuals and organizations contribute to law reform debates, such as by making submissions to parliamentary inquiries, the INSLM plays a unique role as the office has access to classified information and strong investigative powers.

The INSLM is an independent statutory office, which is loosely modeled on the U.K.'s Independent Reviewer of Terrorism Legislation.[97] The position was held from 2011 to 2014 by Bret Walker SC, a prominent Sydney barrister. After Walker had completed his three-year term, the Abbott government introduced legislation to abolish the office,[98] but then decided against this and appointed former judge Roger Gyles AO QC to the position.[99] In March 2015, the new INSLM began an inquiry into section 35P of the ASIO Act, mentioned in the introduction, which prohibits the disclosure of any information relating to specially approved undercover operations.[100]

---

http://parlinfo.aph.gov.au/parlInfo/search/display/display.w3p;query=%28Dataset%3Aweblas tweek,hansardr,noticer,webthisweek,dailyp,votes,journals,orderofbusiness,hansards,notices,web sds%29%20ParliamentNumber%3A%2234%22%20Government_Phrase%3A%22yes%22%20Context_ Phrase%3A%22ministerial%20statement%22%20Speaker_Phrase%3A%22mr%20hawke%22;rec=13.

[91] JOHN CLARKE QC, REPORT OF THE CLARKE INQUIRY INTO THE CASE OF DR MOHAMED HANEEF (2008).

[92] *Ombudsman Act 1976* (Cth) §§ 5, 15.

[93] *Ombudsman Regulations 1977* (Cth) sch 1 reg 4.

[94] *Australian Security Intelligence Organisation Act 1979* (Cth) §§ 34J, 34K.

[95] *Id.* § 34J(1)(e)(ii).

[96] *Independent National Security Legislation Monitor Act 2010* (Cth).

[97] *See* INDEPENDENT REVIEWER OF TERRORISM LEGISLATION, THE REVIEWER'S ROLE (2015), *available at* https://terrorismlegislationreviewer.independent.gov.uk/about-me/ (last visited July 9, 2015).

[98] *Independent National Security Legislation Monitor Repeal Bill 2014* (Cth).

[99] PRIME MINISTER OF AUSTRALIA, APPOINTMENT OF INDEPENDENT NATIONAL SECURITY LEGISLATION MONITOR (Dec. 7, 2014), *available at* https://www.pm.gov.au/media/2014-12-07/appointment-independent-national-security-legislation-monitor (last visited July 9, 2015).

[100] *Australian Security Intelligence Organisation Act 1979* (Cth), § 35P. *See* DEPARTMENT OF THE PRIME MINISTER AND CABINET, INDEPENDENT NATIONAL SECURITY LEGISLATION MONITOR (2015),

The INSLM has two main functions. The first is to review the operation and effectiveness of Australia's counterterrorism laws.[101] The second is to assess whether Australia's counterterrorism laws remain proportionate and necessary, and contain appropriate safeguards to protect the rights of individuals.[102] These reviews can be undertaken on the INSLM's own motion or a matter may be referred to the INSLM by the prime minister or the PJCIS.[103] To conduct these reviews, the INSLM has strong investigative powers similar to those of the IGIS and royal commissions—including the power to hold hearings, summon witnesses, and compel documents.[104]

Ad hoc and statutory inquiries also play an important role in reviewing and reporting on the legislation that grants intelligence agencies their powers. The Security Legislation Review Committee (Sheller Committee), for example, was established in accordance with section 4 of the Security Legislation Amendment (Terrorism) Act 2002 (Cth) (SLAT Act).[105] Its members included the IGIS, the Commonwealth Ombudsman, and the Human Rights and Privacy Commissioners. In 2006, the Sheller Committee published a detailed report on the operation and effectiveness of Australia's counterterrorism laws, including their impact on human rights and Muslim communities.[106]

Beginning in August 2012, another comprehensive review of Australia's counterterrorism laws was undertaken by the Council of Australian Governments Review of Counter-Terrorism Legislation (COAG Review).[107] The COAG Review received a wide range of submissions from individuals and organizations, and it held public hearings in major cities around Australia.[108] It had a similar mandate to the INSLM in that its role was to assess the operation and effectiveness of Australia's counterterrorism laws and whether those laws contained appropriate safeguards.[109]

A more limited ongoing role is played by the Australian Law Reform Commission (ALRC). The ALRC is an independent statutory body established under section 5 of the Australian Law Reform Commission Act 1996 (Cth). It reviews Commonwealth (federal) laws for the purpose of "removing defects" in those laws and "providing improved access to justice."[110] It has conducted some important reviews into Australia's counterterrorism and

---

[101] *Independent National Security Legislation Monitor Act 2010* (Cth) § 6(1)(a).

[102] *Id.* § 6(1)(b).

[103] *Id.* §§ 6(1), 7, 7A.

[104] *See id.* pt 3. In contrast to the IGIS, the INSLM does not have the power to compel answers that would incriminate a person. *See Independent National Security Legislation Monitor Act 2010* (Cth) § 25(6). The INSLM may also conduct public hearings, whereas IGIS inquiries are conducted in private: *Independent National Security Legislation Monitor Act 2010* (Cth) § 21(1); *Inspector-General of Intelligence and Security Act 1986* (Cth) § 17(1).

[105] *Security Legislation Amendment (Terrorism) Act 2002* (Cth) § 4, as amended by the *Criminal Code Amendment (Terrorism) Act 2003* (Cth).

[106] Security Legislation Review Committee, Report of the Security Legislation Review Committee (2006) [hereinafter *Sheller Committee Report*].

[107] Australian Government, Council of Australian Governments Review of Counter-Terrorism Legislation (2013) [hereinafter COAG Review].

[108] *See id.* at 2–3.

[109] *See id.* at 3.

[110] *Australian Law Reform Commission Act 1996* (Cth) § 21.

national security legislation, including sedition offenses and secrecy laws.[111] However, these reports have covered only a limited range of topics as the ALRC cannot initiate investigations on its own; it can only inquire into matters that are referred by the Attorney-General.[112]

The role of the Australian Human Rights Commission (AHRC) is also limited in relation to national security matters. Ordinarily, the AHRC plays a key role in investigating breaches of human rights by government departments,[113] but its mandate does not extend to examining the conduct of the intelligence agencies.[114] Its role in this context is therefore limited to advocacy and law reform, such as contributing to PJCIS inquiries on counterterrorism laws.[115] Where the AHRC receives a complaint about the intelligence agencies, this must be referred to the IGIS for investigation.[116]

D. *Review of Finances and Administration*

One of the few accountability measures that applies equally to intelligence agencies as other government departments is the independent auditing of their finances and expenditure. The Commonwealth Auditor-General is an independent office that conducts annual performance and financial statement audits of all Commonwealth entities.[117] Agencies must submit financial reports to the office,[118] and the audits are conducted with the support of the Australian National Audit Office (ANAO).

Australia's intelligence agencies also have a range of internal mechanisms for ensuring compliance with financial obligations—including employee guidelines, training programs, and software to monitor compliance.[119] For example, ASIO has an Internal Audit directorate, and it has developed Fraud Management Guidelines that provide staff with specific guidance on the fraud control framework.[120] ASIO also conducts fraud awareness training for all new employees and contractors.[121]

E. *Governance*

A key theme across the chapters in this book is that intelligence agencies are subject not only to accountability mechanisms that ensure their compliance with the law, but also governance mechanisms that set their policy and intelligence collection priorities. In Australia,

---

[111] Australian Law Reform Commission, Fighting Words: A Review of Sedition Laws in Australia (2006); Australian Law Reform Commission, Secrecy Laws and Open Government in Australia (Report No. 112, 2009).

[112] *Australian Law Reform Commission Act 1996* (Cth) § 21(1).

[113] *Australian Human Rights Commission Act 1986* (Cth) § 11(1)(f).

[114] *Id.* § 11(3).

[115] *See, e.g.,* Australian Human Rights Commission, Submission No 7 to Parliamentary Joint Committee on Intelligence and Security: Inquiry into Counter-Terrorism Legislation Amendment (Foreign Fighters) Bill 2014, Oct. 2, 2014.

[116] *Australian Human Rights Commission Act 1986* (Cth) § 11(3).

[117] *Auditor-General Act 1997* (Cth) pt 4.

[118] *Public Governance, Performance and Accountability Act 2013* (Cth) § 42.

[119] *See* Faulkner, *supra* note 88, at 25.

[120] *ASIO Annual Report 2014, supra* note 53, at 56.

[121] *Id.*

a range of executive bodies perform this function. The key example is the National Security Committee of Cabinet (NSC), which comprises the prime minister and senior cabinet ministers (the Deputy Prime Minister, Attorney-General, Foreign Minister, Defence Minister, Immigration Minister, and Treasurer). The NSC is the "primary decision-making body on national security, including intelligence matters."[122] It sets the priorities of the intelligence agencies (generally once per year), and it supports the Attorney-General in coordinating responses to national security matters.[123] For example, when a gunman held 17 hostages in a central Sydney café in December 2014, the NSC was immediately convened to discuss responses to the crisis.[124]

The National Security Adviser (NSA), a position established by the Rudd government in 2008, supplements the NSC in developing national security policy and crisis responses.[125] In the event of a terrorist act, the NSA or Deputy NSA would chair the National Crisis Committee (NCC) to coordinate the exchange of information between the Commonwealth and state governments.[126] Formally, the Deputy NSA also co-chairs the National Counter-Terrorism Committee (NCTC), which includes senior representatives from the intelligence agencies and law enforcement, and further seeks to "coordinate an effective nation-wide counter-terrorism capability."[127] Reports from government insiders, however, suggest that the Abbott government has sidelined the NSA and Deputy NSA with a view to abolishing those offices.[128]

The Council of Australian Governments (COAG), Australia's peak intergovernmental forum, also helps to develop government policy and strategy on counterterrorism matters, particularly with regard to cooperation between the federal and state governments.[129]

Finally, the ministers responsible for the intelligence agencies govern the conduct of those agencies by developing and introducing new legislation that defines the scope of their powers,[130] and by making regulations under that legislation. For example, under section 8A of the ASIO Act, the Attorney-General is empowered to make guidelines to be observed by ASIO

[122] AUSTRALIAN GOVERNMENT, THE AUSTRALIAN INTELLIGENCE COMMUNITY, *supra* note 45, at 13–14. *See also* NATIONAL COUNTER-TERRORISM COMMITTEE, PLAN 6 (3d ed. 2012) [hereinafter *National Counter-Terrorism Plan*].

[123] *See* Faulkner, *supra* note 88, at 23; *National Counter-Terrorism Plan, supra* note 122, at 6.

[124] *See* David Wroe & Lisa Cox, *Martin Place Siege: Tony Abbott Convenes National Security Committee*, SYDNEY MORNING HERALD (Dec. 15, 2014), *available at* http://www.smh.com.au/federal-politics/political-news/martin-place-siege-tony-abbott-convenes-national-security-committee-20141215-127brq.html.

[125] *National Counter-Terrorism Plan, supra* note 122, at 6.

[126] *Id.*

[127] *Id.* at 5.

[128] *See* Jason Koutsoukis, *Tony Abbott Dismantles Role of National Security Adviser by Stealth, Insiders Say*, SYDNEY MORNING HERALD (Oct. 25, 2013), *available at* http://www.smh.com.au/federal-politics/political-news/tony-abbott-dismantles-role-of-national-security-adviser-by-stealth-insiders-say-20131024-2w4do.html.

[129] *See, e.g.*, AUSTRALIAN GOVERNMENT, COUNCIL OF AUSTRALIAN GOVERNMENTS' COMMUNIQUÉ, SPECIAL MEETING ON COUNTER-TERRORISM (Sept. 27, 2005), *available at* http://archive.coag.gov.au/coag_meeting_outcomes/2005-09-27/docs/coag270905.pdf.

[130] For example, Attorney-General George Brandis recently played the lead role in introducing legislation to expand ASIO's powers in response to the threat of returning foreign fighters. *See* ATTORNEY-GENERAL, NEW COUNTER-TERRORISM MEASURES FOR A SAFER AUSTRALIA (Aug. 5, 2014).

officers in the performance of their functions.[131] Those guidelines set out advice on a range of matters, such as how ASIO should collect and use personal information, and when it should investigate politically motivated violence.[132]

IV. IS EXECUTIVE OVERSIGHT OF INTELLIGENCE AGENCIES ROBUST AND EFFECTIVE?

In this section, we evaluate the strengths and weaknesses of the executive accountability measures outlined above. Do these accountability measures provide sufficient jurisdiction to cover the range of activities undertaken by Australia's intelligence agencies? Are their investigative powers sufficiently strong to allow robust inquiries to be undertaken? Do they have the capacity to allow instances of misconduct and wrongdoing to be remedied? Have they proved effective in keeping the intelligence agencies accountable? And what about vulnerabilities and weaknesses in the system? Below we answer these questions by identifying a range of themes, including the difficulties in holding governments to account with recommendatory powers, and in holding intelligence agencies accountable for the use of broadly defined statutory powers.

A. Strengths

The first thing that becomes apparent from the previous section is that a wide range of executive accountability measures are used to oversee Australia's six intelligence agencies. The intelligence agencies are each responsible to senior government ministers, who authorize the use of their clandestine powers. Their activities are subject to inspections and inquiries by the IGIS. ASIO's security assessments in regard to Australian citizens are subject to merits review by the Security Appeals Division of the AAT, and this process is supplemented by the Independent Reviewer of ASAs for assessments in regard to noncitizens. The INSLM reviews the legislation that provides intelligence agencies with their powers. The Auditor-General reviews each intelligence agency's resources and finances. Ad hoc and statutory inquiries supplement these forms of accountability, and advisory panels and senior ministers oversee intelligence policy and collection priorities.

The quantity and broad jurisdiction of these accountability measures is crucial given the difficulties posed by public, judicial, and parliamentary scrutiny of the intelligence agencies. These accountability measures allow oversight not only of the use of clandestine powers by the intelligence agencies, but also their finances, legislation, and policy direction. This lends support to the views of the previous IGIS, who believed that the intelligence agencies were subject to a "multi-faceted set of accountability arrangements," and that those arrangements should provide "considerable reassurance to the community that the day-to-day activities of the agencies are subject to substantial scrutiny."[133]

---

[131] *Australian Security Intelligence Organisation Act 1979* (Cth) § 8A.
[132] AUSTRALIAN SECURITY INTELLIGENCE ORGANISATION, THE ATTORNEY-GENERAL'S GUIDELINES (2015) *available at* http://www.asio.gov.au/About-ASIO/Oversight-and-Accountability/Attorney-General-Guidelines.html.
[133] Ian Carnell, Accountable Intelligence Agencies: Not an Oxymoron. Address at the National Security and Counter-Terrorism Summit (Oct. 24, 2006), at 3, 6.

Another obvious strength of the system is that the independent officeholders possess strong investigative powers. Both the IGIS and the INSLM are empowered to compel witnesses for questioning,[134] to examine those witnesses on oath or affirmation,[135] and to compel the production of documents.[136] These powers are backed by the force of the criminal law, as it is an offense punishable by six months imprisonment to fail to comply with any of these demands.[137] The IGIS may also enter an intelligence agency's premises, or any place where a person is being detained by ASIO, at any reasonable time.[138] Importantly, the IGIS and INSLM, as well as the Auditor-General and Independent Reviewer of ASAs, all have access to classified information held by the intelligence agencies.[139] This puts the offices in a unique position to assess the appropriateness of intelligence agencies' powers and conduct and, where relevant, to uncover instances of misconduct and maladministration.

The independence of these officeholders is ensured by their statutory tenure and protection from liability. The IGIS is appointed for a period of five years, and the INSLM for a period of three years.[140] These appointments may only be terminated by reason of misbehaviour, or physical or mental incapacity,[141] which is equivalent to judicial tenure.[142] Both offices are protected from civil liability for any act or omission done in good faith in the performance of the office's functions or the exercise of its powers.[143]

The inquiries undertaken by the INSLM in particular have been detailed and rigorous. In his three years in office, Walker produced four reports, which examined a range of controversial powers held by the intelligence agencies and law enforcement.[144] He was highly

[134] *Inspector-General of Intelligence and Security Act 1986* (Cth) § 18(3); *Independent National Security Legislation Monitor Act 2010* (Cth) § 22.

[135] *Inspector-General of Intelligence and Security Act 1986* (Cth) § 18(4); *Independent National Security Legislation Monitor Act 2010* (Cth) § 23.

[136] *Inspector-General of Intelligence and Security Act 1986* (Cth) § 18; *Independent National Security Legislation Monitor Act 2010* (Cth) § 24.

[137] *Inspector-General of Intelligence and Security Act 1986* (Cth) § 18(7); *Independent National Security Legislation Monitor Act 2010* (Cth) § 25. It is also an offense to fail to attend a public hearing when served with a notice by the INSLM to do so. *See Independent National Security Legislation Monitor Act 2010* (Cth) § 25(2). Similar powers are held by the Auditor-General, although failure to comply with the orders of that office will amount to a fine and not a criminal offense. *See Auditor-General Act 1997* (Cth) § 32.

[138] *Inspector-General of Intelligence and Security Act 1986* (Cth) §§ 9B, 19, 19A. The Auditor-General also has a power to enter a government department's premises at any reasonable time. *See Auditor-General Act 1997* (Cth) § 33.

[139] *See Inspector-General of Intelligence and Security Act 1986* (Cth) § 20; *Independent National Security Legislation Monitor Act 2010* (Cth) § 28; *Auditor-General Act 1997* (Cth) § 26; ROXON, *supra* note 87.

[140] *Inspector-General of Intelligence and Security Act 1986* (Cth) § 26; *Independent National Security Legislation Monitor Act 2010* (Cth) § 12. The Auditor-General is appointed for a period of 10 years. *See Auditor-General Act 1997* (Cth) sch 1 item 1(1).

[141] *Inspector-General of Intelligence and Security Act 1986* (Cth) § 30; *Independent National Security Legislation Monitor Act 2010* (Cth) § 19.

[142] *Australian Constitution* § 72(ii).

[143] *Inspector-General of Intelligence and Security Act 1986* (Cth) § 33; *Independent National Security Legislation Monitor Act 2010* (Cth) § 31.

[144] BRET WALKER SC, ANNUAL REPORT: 16 DECEMBER 2011 (2012) [hereinafter *INSLM 2011 Report*]; BRET WALKER SC, DECLASSIFIED ANNUAL REPORT: 20TH DECEMBER 2012 (2013) [hereinafter *INSLM 2012*

critical of some of these laws,[145] but supportive of others,[146] which suggests that he was sufficiently independent from government and adopted a fair and balanced approach rather than simply criticizing the government or echoing its policies. On this basis Walker has been praised in comparison to Lord Carlile, the U.K.'s former Independent Reviewer of Terrorism Legislation, as Carlile repeatedly advocated the U.K. government's position and failed to recommend changes to problematic laws.[147] This distinction was partly the result of how the two offices were designed, as the INSLM is tasked with assessing both the operation of the laws and whether they include sufficient protections for rights, whereas the U.K.'s Independent Reviewer only assesses the operation of the laws.[148]

Other inquiries into Australia's counterterrorism laws, including those by the Sheller Committee and the COAG Review,[149] have been conducted in a similarly thorough fashion. They have involved submission processes, public hearings, and detailed analysis of complex legislation. As discussed below, government responses to these reports have frequently been inadequate, but there is no question that the inquiries have been thorough, balanced, and conducted in a professional manner.

The Clarke Inquiry into the Haneef affair is a good example of how executive branch oversight of the intelligence agencies can lead to substantive change. Haneef was detained and questioned without charge for 12 days in 2007 after being mistakenly linked to the bombing attempt on Glasgow airport. After examining the roles of ASIO, the AFP, and other authorities in detaining Haneef, Clarke made a number of recommendations, including that the office of the INSLM should be created and that limits should be placed on the time allowed for pre-charge detention of terrorist suspects.[150] Both of these recommendations were put into law in 2010.[151] This demonstrates that executive branch oversight mechanisms can be taken seriously by government and act as a catalyst for substantive change in how the intelligence and law enforcement agencies operate.

The reports produced by the IGIS have also been rigorous, and there is no doubt that those appointed to the position have taken their job seriously in inspecting the activities of the intelligence agencies and investigating allegations of misconduct. However, the

---

Report]; Bret Walker SC, Annual Report: 7th November 2013 (2013); Bret Walker SC, Annual Report: 28th March 2014 (2014) [hereinafter *INSLM 2014 Report*].

[145] For example, Walker recommended the repeal of control orders, preventative detention orders, and ASIO's power to detain people for the purposes of questioning. *See INSLM 2012 Report, supra* note 144, at 44, 67, 106.

[146] For example, Walker recommended that ASIO retain its coercive questioning powers, and that it be granted a power to temporarily suspend passports while further security checks are conducted. *See INSLM 2012 Report, supra* note 144, at 70; *INSLM 2014 Report, supra* note 144, at 48–49.

[147] *See* Jessie Blackbourn, *Who's Watching Counter-Terrorism Laws in Australia*, The Conversation, Apr. 3, 2012; Jessie Blackbourn and Nicola McGarrity, *National Security Monitor: Off to a Good Start*, The Drum (ABC) (Mar. 30, 2012), *available at* http://www.abc.net.au/news/2012-03-30/blackbournmcgarrity-national-security-monitor-good-start/3920962.

[148] *Independent National Security Legislation Monitor Act 2010* (Cth) § 6(1); *Terrorism Act 2006* (UK) c 11, § 36(1).

[149] *Sheller Committee Report, supra* note 106; *COAG Review, supra* note 107.

[150] Clarke, *supra* note 91, at xii, 246, 255–56.

[151] *Independent National Security Legislation Monitor Act 2010* (Cth); *National Security Legislation Amendment Act 2010* (Cth) sch 3.

effectiveness of the office and its independence from the intelligence agencies is difficult to gauge due to protections for classified information. Many IGIS reports contain valuable recommendations, such as how the intelligence agencies can improve their procedures in line with legislative requirements,[152] and most of these seem to have been adopted by the relevant agencies.[153] However, many other recommendations are classified,[154] so it is often difficult to know the extent to which the office is holding the agencies to account.

B. Weaknesses

Although there are clearly a number of strengths to this system of executive accountability, there are also a number of key weaknesses and vulnerabilities. An initial point is that breadth should not be mistaken for depth. Although the number and broad coverage of the executive branch oversight mechanisms outlined above is commendable, this does not mean that the framework operates effectively or is sufficient to hold the intelligence agencies to account, even where the exercise of one power might be subject to multiple forms of oversight. The INSLM, for example, described the safeguards applying to ASIO's questioning and detention powers as having "a degree of commendable redundancy."[155] However, having several bodies overseeing the same agencies or powers does not lead to greater accountability if the functions of those bodies overlap, or if they do not delve any deeper into an agency's activities.

One major weakness is that ministerial accountability of the intelligence agencies is not—or at least is not perceived to be—as robust as it might be. Today, ministers tend to have a close relationship with Australia's intelligence agencies, and indeed tend to highlight this for political benefit. Since the events of 9/11, Australian ministers have frequently championed the expansion of the powers of intelligence agencies, without at the same time emphasizing the need for those powers to be tightly constrained to their purpose, or subjected to stringent oversight.

In 2014, for example, Attorney-General George Brandis played the lead role in developing and introducing legislation to dramatically expand ASIO's powers. This included the enactment of a Special Intelligence Operations (SIO) regime, mentioned in the introduction, which provides immunity from civil and criminal liability for ASIO officers involved in specially approved undercover operations.[156] Attached to this regime is a criminal offense that prohibits the public discussion of any information relating to SIOs.[157] The Attorney-General must authorize SIOs in advance and consent to any prosecutions under that offense,[158] but

---

[152] *See, e.g.,* INSPECTOR-GENERAL OF INTELLIGENCE AND SECURITY, INQUIRY INTO THE ATTENDANCE OF LEGAL REPRESENTATIVES AT ASIO INTERVIEWS, AND RELATED MATTERS 4 (2014).

[153] *See id.; ASIO Annual Report 2014, supra* note 53.

[154] INSPECTOR-GENERAL OF INTELLIGENCE AND SECURITY, INQUIRY INTO THE ATTENDANCE OF LEGAL REPRESENTATIVES AT ASIO INTERVIEWS, *supra* note 152, at 4.

[155] *INSLM 2011 Report, supra* note 144, at 30.

[156] *Australian Security Intelligence Organisation Act 1979* (Cth) pt 3 div 4.

[157] *Id.* § 35P.

[158] *Id.* § 35B, 35C; ATTORNEY-GENERAL, PRESS CONFERENCE ANNOUNCING THE INTRODUCTION OF THE TELECOMMUNICATIONS (INTERCEPTION AND ACCESS) AMENDMENT (DATA RETENTION) BILL 2014 (Oct. 30, 2014), *available at* http://www. attorneygeneral.gov.au/transcripts/Pages/2014/

when Brandis was the key advocate arguing that ASIO needed those powers,[159] it must be questioned whether he, or his successors, will bring a skeptical critical approach to the exercise of those powers. Certainly it does not reflect the same level of independent accountability as if those powers were authorized by a judge or independent statutory office.

This close relationship between the Attorney-General and ASIO differs from that of some previous eras. In 1973, the then Attorney-General Lionel Murphy famously "raided" ASIO's headquarters after he accused the organization of withholding information on a terrorist group.[160] It is difficult to imagine an Attorney-General in the contemporary security environment taking such a radical step in holding the intelligence agencies to account. This may simply reflect the individual approaches of different Attorneys-General, but it also suggests a shift in how the role of the Attorney-General is perceived. The more traditional view, inherited from the U.K., is that the Attorney-General is the first law officer who provides legal advice to the government, oversees the drafting of legislation, and represents the public interest by protecting public rights and upholding the rule of law.[161] In contemporary Australia, the Attorney-General is more frequently viewed as a politician who is more likely to advocate the expansion of executive power than to protect individual rights.

Another key weakness in the system is that independent officeholders such as the IGIS and INSLM have strong investigative powers but no remedial powers. The role of the IGIS, INSLM and Independent Reviewer of ASAs is limited to providing recommendations, and whether these recommendations are adopted depends on whether the government of the day is willing to accept and implement them. Certainly, the record to date demonstrates that Australian governments (on both sides of politics) are very reluctant to accept recommendations for change from executive bodies, and particularly from the INSLM. The government has employed obvious political tactics (such as introducing the INSLM's reports into Parliament on budget day) so that valuable recommendations have been overshadowed by other events.[162] Indeed, the government has not only ignored the INSLM's recommendations to reduce the scope of Australia's counterterrorism laws, but also to expand them. As the INSLM repeated in his final report:

> When there is no apparent response to recommendations that would increase powers and authority to counter terrorism, some skepticism may start to take root about the political imperative to have the most effective and appropriate counter-terrorism laws.[163]

It was significant that this was not the first but the second time he had made this criticism. On neither occasion did even this very pointed observation elicit a government response.

FourthQuarter2014/30October2014-PressConferenceAnnouncingIntroduction OfTelecommunicationsInterceptionAndAccessAmendmentDataRetentionBill.aspx.

[159] *See* ATTORNEY-GENERAL, NEW COUNTER-TERRORISM MEASURES FOR A SAFER AUSTRALIA, *supra* note 130.

[160] *See generally* JENNY HOCKING, LIONEL MURPHY: A POLITICAL BIOGRAPHY 163–66 (1997).

[161] *See* Ross Ray, The Role of the Attorney-General: An Australian Perspective. Address at the International Bar Association Conference (Oct. 13, 2008), at 3–5.

[162] Jessie Blackbourn, *Non-response Reduces Security Monitor's Role to Window Dressing*, THE CONVERSATION, Dec. 19, 2013.

[163] *INSLM 2014 Report, supra* note 144, at 2.

Indeed, the current prime minister Tony Abbott recognized that "the former government ignored all the Monitor's recommendations,"[164] but then used this as a reason to try to abolish the office rather than to change that record.[165]

The government's reluctance to accept the advice of executive oversight bodies can be seen over time in the lack of response to reviews of Australia's counterterrorism laws. This is especially the case where different committees and inquiries reach different conclusions, as the government can adopt a "lowest common denominator" approach or choose to do nothing by claiming that there is no consensus for change.[166] As one of us has written:

> [W]here effective reviews have been conducted, the level of political commitment to implementing their recommendations has been low. Findings even of high-level, expert panels have been ignored or only implemented some years after a change of government. The common thread of Australia's anti-terror laws is thus that such laws have often been enacted in undue haste and reviewed and repaired sometimes at leisure, or often not at all.[167]

One positive counterexample, as detailed above, is the Clarke inquiry into the Haneef affair.[168] That inquiry led to some substantive improvements in the laws relating to pre-charge detention for terrorist suspects.[169] However, those changes were accompanied by an expansion of police power (to conduct warrantless searches of private premises),[170] so the impact of that inquiry in promoting appropriate limits to counterterrorism operations should not be overstated.

Intelligence agencies appear to have accepted the majority of recommendations from the IGIS,[171] although there are some anomalies in the IGIS reports that raise questions about the effectiveness of the office. For example, in 2013, the IGIS began an inquiry into weapons training by ASIS officers. One of the concerns raised by the inquiry related to the requirement that ASIS officers must not handle firearms if their blood alcohol content is above 0.00.[172] In her 2013 report, the IGIS noted that there was "some misconception by staff in relation to this matter," and that "ASIS did not have adequate controls in place," but she

---

[164] Prime Minister, Ministerial Statement on Deregulation (Mar. 19, 2014).

[165] *Independent National Security Legislation Monitor Repeal Bill 2014* (Cth).

[166] Andrew Lynch, *The Impact of Post-Enactment Review on Anti-Terrorism Laws: Four Jurisdictions Compared*, 18(1) J. Leg. Stud. 63, 66 (2012).

[167] George Williams, *A Decade of Australian Anti-Terror Laws*, 35 Melbourne U. L. Rev.1136, 1168 (2011).

[168] Clarke, *supra* note 91.

[169] *National Security Legislation Amendment Act 2010* (Cth) sch 3.

[170] *Id.* at sch 4.

[171] *See, e.g.*, Inspector-General of Intelligence and Security, Inquiry into the Attendance of Legal Representatives at ASIO Interviews, *supra* note 152, at 4; *ASIO Annual Report, supra* note 53, at 44.

[172] Inspector-General of Intelligence and Security, Executive Summary to the Inquiry into the Provision of Weapons and the Training in and Use of Weapons and Self-Defence Techniques in the Australian Secret Intelligence Service 2 (Nov. 2013).

otherwise concluded that there was "no direct evidence that any ASIS staff member had retrieved a weapon with a blood alcohol level greater than 0.00."[173]

In her 2014 annual report, however, the IGIS revealed that an incident involving alcohol and a firearm occurred overseas that "had the potential to cause serious injury."[174] She also revealed that there were "substantial discrepancies" in the information provided to her by ASIS officers in the original inquiry.[175] This admission raises questions about just how effective IGIS is in its oversight in this area, in part because of an apparent lack of willingness on behalf of the intelligence agencies to comply with its inquiries. It is an offense to fail to swear an oath or to refuse to answer a question asked by the IGIS,[176] but in this case the intelligence officers did not face any formal consequences for misleading the IGIS in her inquiries.[177]

The inquiry into the questioning of Izhar Ul-Haque also raises questions about the role of the IGIS, and its independence from the intelligence agencies. Ul-Haque was a young medical student who was suspected of involvement in terrorism and associating with other known terrorists. He was confronted by ASIO officers at a train station and then taken in their car to a nearby park, where he was told there would be serious consequences if he did not cooperate and answer the officers' questions.[178] The IGIS found no evidence to make out a case of trespass, false imprisonment, or unlawful detention.[179] In reaching this conclusion, she seemed to place significant weight on the views of the intelligence agencies as to the threat of terrorism at that time,[180] as well as the testimony of the ASIO officers involved, who "denied that their tone . . . had been threatening or coercive."[181]

By contrast, Justice Adams in the New South Wales Supreme Court delivered a scathing judgment that led the Crown to abandon its case against Ul-Haque. Justice Adams found that the ASIO officers were guilty of trespass, false imprisonment, kidnapping, and unlawful detention.[182] He concluded that their conduct was "grossly improper and constituted an unjustified and unlawful interference with the personal liberty of the accused."[183] On one view, it would be possible to conclude that the IGIS reached a different and more accurate conclusion because she was privy to classified information that the court was not. At the same time, the serious discrepancy between the IGIS report and Supreme Court judgment gives rise to questions about the degree of closeness and common ground between the IGIS and the intelligence agencies, and whether this may hamper the ability of the office to act as a strong accountability mechanism.

---

[173] *Id.*

[174] INSPECTOR-GENERAL OF INTELLIGENCE AND SECURITY, *Annual Report: 2013–2014* , at 11 (2014).

[175] *Id.*

[176] *Inspector-General of Intelligence and Security Act 1986* (Cth) § 18(7).

[177] It is however an offense to provide false or misleading information to a person exercising powers or performing functions under a law of the Commonwealth: *Criminal Code Act 1995* (Cth), § 137.1.

[178] *See R v Ul-Haque* [2007] NSWSC 1251, ¶¶ 15–25.

[179] INSPECTOR-GENERAL OF INTELLIGENCE AND SECURITY, REPORT OF INQUIRY INTO THE ACTIONS TAKEN BY ASIO IN 2003 IN RESPECT OF MR IZHAR UL-HAQUE AND RELATED MATTERS 37, 39, 41 (2008).

[180] *Id.* at 7–8.

[181] *Id.* at 33, 35.

[182] *R v Ul-Haque* [2007] NSWSC 1251, ¶ 62, ¶ 95.

[183] *Id.* ¶ 62.

Oversight of the intelligence agencies by other executive bodies is also limited in key respects. The Commonwealth Ombudsman and the AHRC would both ordinarily play an important role in investigating the conduct of government departments, but neither has jurisdiction over the intelligence agencies.[184] The ALRC plays a limited role in the national security context given that it has no capacity to self-initiate investigations, and is restricted to assessing legislation on its face (rather than by accessing classified information to assess how that legislation has been used).[185] Even the INSLM, for all the strengths of that office, is only a part-time position with limited resources.[186]

Merits review of the intelligence agencies is particularly weak. It is only available in the Security Appeals Division of the AAT in relation to ASIO's adverse security assessments,[187] and then only to citizens affected by those assessments.[188] The more significant concern with adverse security assessments relates to their use in applications for refugee status,[189] but merits review in the Security Appeals Division is not available to noncitizens.[190] Even where citizens apply to the Security Appeals Division to challenge an assessment, this is incredibly difficult due to the issuing of public interest certificates by the Attorney-General.[191] Those certificates allow the tribunal to rely on classified information without revealing it to the applicant.

The difficulties that noncitizens face in challenging adverse security assessments were eased somewhat after the first Independent Reviewer of ASAs was appointed in 2012. However, that position only exists by virtue of terms of reference issued by the Attorney-General: in contrast to the IGIS and INSLM,[192] the office has no legislative backing and therefore no statutory tenure or questioning powers. This means that the Independent Reviewer of ASAs is less independent from government compared to the IGIS and INSLM, and also in a much weaker position to conduct robust inquiries. The terms of reference permit the Independent Reviewer of ASAs to access all information held by ASIO in issuing its adverse security assessments,[193] but the office cannot, for example, compel intelligence officers to appear for questioning.

The initial reports of the Independent Reviewer of ASAs largely confirm that ASIO has acted appropriately in declaring certain noncitizens to be a security risk,[194] but this is curious

---

[184] *Ombudsman Regulations 1977* (Cth) sch 1 reg 4; *Australian Human Rights Commission Act 1986* (Cth) § 11(3).

[185] *Australian Law Reform Commission Act 1996* (Cth) § 21(1).

[186] *Independent National Security Legislation Monitor Act 2010* (Cth) § 11(1).

[187] *Australian Security Intelligence Organisation Act 1979* (Cth) § 54.

[188] *Id.* § 36.

[189] *See generally* Ben Saul, *Dark Justice: Australia's Indefinite Detention of Refugees on Security Grounds under International Human Rights Law*, 13 MELBOURNE J. INT'L L. 685 (2012); Ben Saul, *"Fair Shake of the Sauce Bottle": Fairer ASIO Security Assessment of Refugees*, 37(4) ALTERNATIVE L.J. 221 (2012); Ben Saul, *The Kafka-esque Case of Sheikh Mansour Leghaei: The Denial of the International Human Right to a Fair Hearing in National Security Assessments and Migration Proceedings in Australia*, 33(3) U. NEW SOUTH WALES L.J. 629 (2010).

[190] *Australian Security Intelligence Organisation Act 1979* (Cth) § 36.

[191] *Id.* § 38(2); *Administrative Appeals Tribunal Act 1975* (Cth), § 36. *See* Hardy, *supra* note 8, at 44–48.

[192] *Inspector-General of Intelligence and Security Act 1986* (Cth); *Independent National Security Legislation Monitor Act 2010* (Cth).

[193] *See* ROXON, *supra* note 87, at 1.

[194] *See ASIO Annual Report 2014, supra* note 53, at 47–49.

given the weight of other expert evidence suggesting that certain populations subject to adverse security assessments (particularly the Tamil community from Sri Lanka) pose no risk of terrorism.[195] This is not to suggest that the Independent Reviewer of ASAs does not take her review functions seriously, or is helping ASIO to cover up misconduct, but it does suggest a more general problem—which is that it is very difficult to gauge the effectiveness of an executive oversight body that relies on classified information. The IGIS, INSLM, and Independent Reviewer of ASAs, as well as other inquiries such as the COAG Review, all rely on classified submissions from the intelligence agencies and law enforcement to reach their conclusions and recommendations. The public must ultimately trust that these bodies are holding the intelligence agencies to account, rather than (for example) being able to access and inspect that information themselves through freedom of information requests.[196]

This degree of secrecy could be excused if there were greater confidence that serious misconduct would be uncovered if existing oversight mechanisms fail. This is where whistleblower protections play a crucial role, as they provide a "release valve" that allows employees of a government department to disclose wrongdoing that has not been uncovered by other means. However, in Australia, the broad exemptions for intelligence information in the PID Act mean that the scheme does not provide any greater accountability than the IGIS already provides.[197] If an intelligence officer sought to reveal one or more instances of misconduct by disclosing classified information, he or she would only receive whistle-blower protections if the information was disclosed internally to the officer's supervisors, to the IGIS, or to a lawyer.[198] It would be virtually impossible for the officer to receive protection for disclosing that information externally, such as to a respected journalist or member of Parliament.[199] Indeed, Parliament has recently enacted a range of stronger offenses to prevent whistle-blowing by intelligence officers.[200]

Perhaps the major vulnerability in executive oversight of the intelligence agencies is that it is extremely difficult to hold those agencies to account when the government has granted them such extraordinary statutory powers. For example, ASIO's questioning and detention warrant regime allows the organization to detain non-suspect citizens for up to a week for questioning.[201] When legislation empowers ASIO to do this, what can the IGIS or INSLM do if those powers are used correctly, other than suggest changes to the legislation, which the government is then free to ignore? Those powers may be exercised to the letter of the law, but they are still of concern for their impact on fundamental rights.

---

[195] *See* Andrew & Renata Kaldor Centre for International Refugee Law, *Factsheet: Refugees with an Adverse Security Assessment by ASIO* (Feb. 24, 2015), *available at* http://www.kaldorcentre.unsw.edu.au/sites/default/files/ASIO%20factsheet%20%2024%202%2015.pdf. For example, one Tamil refugee classified as a security risk was a mentally ill young man who was left brain-damaged after being beaten by the Sri Lankan military: Kerry Brewster, *Tamils Speak Out against ASIO Security Rulings*, LATELINE (ABC TV) (Aug. 13, 2012), *available at* http://www.abc.net.au/lateline/content/2012/s3567008.htm.

[196] Due to numerous exemptions: *see, e.g. Freedom of Information Act 1982* (Cth) sch 3.

[197] *Public Interest Disclosure Act 2013* (Cth) §§ 26(1)(c). *See* Hardy & Williams, *supra* note 79, at 814–15.

[198] *See* Hardy & Williams, *supra* note 79, at 814–15.

[199] *See id.*

[200] *National Security Legislation Amendment Act (No 1) 2014* (Cth) sch 6; *Intelligence Services Act 2001* (Cth) pt 6; *Australian Security Intelligence Organisation Act 1979* (Cth) §§ 18–18B, 35P.

[201] *Australian Security Intelligence Organisation Act 1979* (Cth) pt III div 3.

This suggests that the larger problem is not necessarily how the current system of executive accountability has been designed, or whether statutory officeholders have sufficient investigative powers. Rather, it is how executive accountability mechanisms can counterbalance the vast expansion of counterterrorism laws over more than a decade, from those introduced in the wake of the 9/11 attacks to those introduced in 2014 and 2015 in response to the threat of foreign fighters returning from Syria and Iraq.[202] An intelligence agency will seldom be held to account for exercising statutory powers that are difficult to exceed.

V. CONCLUSION

Executive oversight mechanisms play a crucial role in keeping intelligence agencies accountable because it is difficult to scrutinize those agencies' activities in the media, courts, and Parliament. In Australia, a broad range of executive oversight mechanisms allow oversight of the six intelligence agencies. These overseeing bodies include the IGIS, a statutory office that inspects and inquires into the intelligence agencies' activities; the INSLM, an independent monitor of Australia's counterterrorism laws; the Security Appeals Division of the AAT and the Independent Reviewer of ASAs, both of which review the merits of adverse security assessments issued by ASIO; the Auditor-General and the Australian National Audit Office, which conduct performance and financial audits of the intelligence agencies; and several committees comprising senior members of the executive branch, which govern intelligence policy and collection priorities.

This system of executive accountability has several strengths. The number and broad coverage of oversight mechanisms is evidence of a commitment to maintaining the accountability of intelligence agencies, despite their secret activities. The IGIS and the INSLM in particular have statutory tenure and strong investigative powers,[203] which preserves their independence from government and allows the officeholders to conduct thorough inspections, inquiries, and reviews. Other statutory and ad hoc inquiry bodies, such as the COAG Review of Counter-Terrorism Legislation, have conducted rigorous inquiries involving written submissions and oral evidence from a wide range of interested individuals and organizations. These inquiries have produced detailed reports on complex areas of Australia's counterterrorism laws.[204]

At the same time, there are a number of weaknesses and vulnerabilities in the system that suggest room for improvement. The relationship between the intelligence agencies and their responsible ministers is perceived as being very close, rather than an effective check on the misuse of statutory powers. The most that executive oversight mechanisms can do to remedy wrongdoing or problematic legislation is to recommend change, which is rarely forthcoming from the government. Some bodies that play an important role in holding other government departments accountable—namely the Commonwealth Ombudsman, Australian Law

---

[202] *Security Legislation Amendment (Terrorism) Act 2002* (Cth); *National Security Legislation Amendment Act (No 1) 2014* (Cth); *Counter-Terrorism Legislation Amendment (Foreign Fighters) Act 2014* (Cth).

[203] *Inspector-General of Intelligence and Security Act 1986* (Cth) §§ 18, 30; *Independent National Security Legislation Monitor Act 2010* (Cth) § 19, pt 3.

[204] *See, e.g., Sheller Committee Report, supra* note 106; *COAG Review, supra* note 107.

Reform Commission, and Australian Human Rights Commission—are limited to advocacy and law reform work with regard to national security matters. Merits review of the intelligence agencies is particularly weak, as the Security Appeals Division of the AAT only has jurisdiction to review adverse security assessments issued by ASIO in relation to Australian citizens.

Although the details of these accountability mechanisms are specific to the Australian context, they raise a number of themes or lessons relating to executive oversight of intelligence agencies generally and how this oversight might be improved. These may have some resonance beyond Australia. The first is that recommendatory powers can have only limited impact in holding intelligence agencies to account. This is because governments are free to accept or ignore the recommendations of executive bodies as they see fit. It is difficult to conceive of how independent officeholders or other inquiry bodies could have stronger remedial powers along the lines of those possessed by a court, and indeed this is a weakness inherent in any form of executive oversight. Nevertheless, small changes to strengthen their existing recommendatory powers could be a notable improvement. For example, the government and the intelligence agencies could be required to consider the recommendations of independent officeholders and to provide reasons (so far as possible while protecting classified information) within a set period of time as to why any recommendations have not been followed.[205] This would prevent government from ignoring important reports or burying them with political tactics.

A second point is that the success and effectiveness of executive oversight mechanisms is difficult to gauge as they rely heavily on classified information. The need to protect classified information is the reason special statutory offices and inquiries are needed to review the activities of the intelligence agencies. However, those offices and inquiries are, understandably, subject to the same protections as the agencies themselves,[206] so the public must often trust that they are holding the intelligence agencies to account rather than knowing this to be the case. Trust in this process can be maximized if governments appoint experienced and well-respected individuals to positions such as the IGIS and INSLM, if the independence and tenure of those offices is guaranteed by statute, and if the offices possess strong statutory powers to undertake their reviews and inquiries.

Third, given this need for secrecy, whistle-blower legislation will provide a crucial "release valve" in circumstances where misconduct or maladministration by the intelligence agencies is not uncovered by other means. Striking the right balance in whistle-blower legislation between protecting classified information and promoting accountability will be difficult, but it is an important task that requires ongoing attention. On the one hand, any information leaked by intelligence officers must be kept to the minimum necessary to reveal wrongdoing, and that information must not endanger lives or expose intelligence sources or methods. On the other hand, public confidence in the accountability of intelligence agencies is undermined by blanket exemptions to whistle-blower legislation and strong anti-whistle-blower

---

[205] The IGIS may produce a report when a government response is inadequate, but there is no obligation on the government or an agency to respond to a report or provide reasons as to why any recommendations have not been adopted. See *Inspector-General of Intelligence and Security Act 1986* (Cth) § 24A.

[206] See *Inspector-General of Intelligence and Security Act 1986* (Cth) § 20; *Independent National Security Legislation Monitor Act 2010* (Cth) § 28; *Auditor-General Act 1997* (Cth) § 26; ROXON, *supra* note 87.

offences.[207] The Australian government's recent crackdown on intelligence whistle-blowing gives the impression that it is unwilling for misconduct or maladministration by the intelligence agencies to see the light of day.

If the Australian intelligence agencies are to be held to a sufficient standard of accountability, intelligence officers should have some capacity to responsibly disclose serious wrongdoing by their employers where other avenues, including the IGIS, have been exhausted. This could be achieved by amending the PID Act to allow an intelligence officer to disclose serious wrongdoing or unlawful conduct to specified persons or bodies outside the agency and executive branch (such as a judge, another member of Parliament, or the PJCIS) where he or she believes on reasonable grounds that all other inquiries into that wrongdoing have been inadequate.

Fourth, executive oversight of the intelligence agencies could be improved if tribunals equipped to handle classified information were granted a wider jurisdiction. In Australia, the Security Appeals Division of the AAT assesses the merits of adverse security assessments issued by ASIO, but this is only a small portion of one intelligence agency's activities. Given the difficulties in holding the intelligence agencies to account through other means, specialist tribunals could take on a larger share of the burden by scrutinizing a wider range of intelligence agencies' activities. Improved procedures for handling classified information, such as a program whereby applicants could rely on special advocates with security clearances,[208] would help to improve the fairness of merits review proceedings.

Last, counterterrorism laws that define the intelligence agencies' powers require ongoing attention and scrutiny. It is these powers, and not necessarily weaknesses in executive oversight, which pose the greatest threat to the accountability of intelligence agencies. Whichever form it takes, such oversight should be rigorous and recurring, and it must be taken seriously by the government. This is crucial given the extraordinary breadth of clandestine powers granted to intelligence agencies in response to the ongoing threat of terrorism. Unless the powers granted to intelligence agencies are themselves properly constrained in the first place, no form of executive oversight is likely to be effective.

---

[207] Hardy & Williams, *supra* note 79, at 814–15; *National Security Legislation Amendment Act (No. 1) 2014* (Cth) sch 6.

[208] *See generally* McGarrity & Santow, *supra* note 8; Bray & Martin, *supra* note 8; Aileen Kavanagh, *Special Advocates, Control Orders and the Right to a Fair Trial*, 73(5) MODERN L. REV. 836 (2010); John Ip, *The Rise and Spread of the Special Advocate*, PUBLIC L. 717 (2008).

Notes and tables are indicated by n and t following the page number.

Ben Ali, Zine El Abidine, 100
Biermann, Kai, 270
Big data analytics, 96, 113
Bin Laden, Osama, 9
Boko Haram, xv
Bolger, Jim, 62
Born, Hans, 199
Brandis, George, 330n130, 334, 335
Brazil
  Agência Brasileira de Inteligência (ABIN), 66n153
  Serviço Nacional de Informações (SNI), 66n153
Brennan, John, 110, 112, 221, 221n78, 238n16
Breyer, Stephen G., 91n100
Britain. *See* United Kingdom
Bruneau, Thomas C., 66, 70
BRUSA agreement (2010), 37
Bulgaria, 79–81, 84, 91, 91n99
Bundesverfassungsgericht. See Federal
  Constitutional Court
Bush, George W., 9
BVerfG. *See* Federal Constitutional Court

Cambodia, 105
Cambridge Five espionage ring, 53, 54n90
Camera surveillance, 88, 184, 310. *See also* CCTV
Cameron, David, 187
Canada. *See also specific courts*
  Access to Information Act 1983, 70n162
  accountability gaps in, 177–178, 180–183.
    See also Accountability
  Advisory Council on Security and Intelligence, 61
  Air India Commission, 177n8, 181, 182, 197–198,
    202, 203
  Anti-Terrorism Act 2001, 14
  Arar Commission, 18, 21, 21n111, 31, 31n166,
    177, 180–182, 188–189, 194, 196, 198–199
  Border Services Agency, 177, 194
  Canadian Forces Joint Imagery Centre, 44t
  Canadian Intelligence Forces Command, 44t
  Canadian Security Intelligence Service (CSIS),
    xxiii, 21, 34, 34n176, 43, 43n30, 44t, 47–48,
    61, 68–69, 176–184, 189–195, 198, 202–203
  Canadian Security Intelligence Service Act
    (1985), 45t
  Charter of Rights and Freedom, 178
  Civilian Review and Complaints
    Commission, 195
  Communications Security Establishment
    (CSE), 14, 44–45t, 47, 180–183, 191–196, 201

Conservative government, 176–178, 183, 185,
  190, 195, 197, 202
counterterrorism in, 198–201
CSE Commissioner, 180, 182–183, 189, 191,
  193, 194–196, 201
Evidence Act 1985, 70n162
executive oversight, 180–181
Five Eyes partnership and, 6, 37, 44–45t,
  191–192, 200–201
independent reviewers in, 180
Information Sharing Act, 177, 182, 195, 203
Integrated Threat Assessment Centre, 181
intelligence capabilities in, 7, 176–179
Joint Intelligence Committee proposal, 197–198
Joint Parliamentary Committee on Security
  and Intelligence, 61
judicial oversight in, xxiii, 189–194
legislative oversight in, 183–189
McDonald Commission, 48, 61, 182, 184, 186
Minister of Defence, 181
Minister of Public Safety, 180–181, 182,
  197, 202
National Defence Act, 196
National Research Council, 47
peer constraints and, 34
Prime Minister's National Security
  Advisor (PMNS Advisor), 177, 180–181,
  196–197
Privacy Commissioner, 182, 188, 195, 328
Protection of Canada from Terrorists Act
  2015, 178n12
Security Intelligence Review Committee
  (SIRC), 34, 47, 156, 171, 180, 182–185, 189,
  192, 194–196, 201–202
Security Intelligence Service Act, 61, 178–179,
  190, 191, 192–193, 203
Security of Canada Information Sharing Act
  (2015), 195
Security of Information Act, 182, 185
Standing Committee on Public Safety and
  National Security, 45t
UN 1267 Ombudsperson, 199–200
warrant requirements in, 193
Cao, Xun, 67
Carlile, Lord, 333
Casey, William, 238n16
CBC News, 11, 183, 185–186, 188, 190, 199
CCTV, 309–310. *See also* Camera surveillance
Center on Law and Security, 37, 235